EUROPE'S WONDERFUL LITTLE HOTELS & INNS, 1990

The Continent

EUROPE'S WONDERFUL LITTLE HOTELS & INNS, 1990

The Continent

Edited by Hilary Rubinstein

Managing Editor: Caroline Raphael

Continental Editor: John Ardagh

Contributing Editor: Susan Gillotti

Published in London as
THE GOOD HOTEL GUIDE, 1990

St. Martin's Press ● *New York*

Illustrations copyright © 1989 by Ray Evans
Maps copyright © 1989 Consumers' Association Ltd

Cover illustration Garnet Henderson

Editorial assistants: Katinka Ardagh, Pier Bryden, Philippa Carlile, Susan
Carlile, Hilary Hodgson

ISBN 0-312-03333-8

Library of Congress Catalog Number 89- 63225

Published in Great Britain as *The Good Hotel Guide, 1990* by Consumers'
Association and Hodder & Stoughton

First U.S. Edition
10 9 8 7 6 5 4 3 2 1

Contents

A note for new readers

This is an annual guide to hotels and inns on the continent of Europe (with Morocco now included as well as Turkey) that are of unusual character and quality. The entries are based on reports from readers who write to us when they come across an establishment which has given them out-of-the-ordinary satisfaction, and who also send us their comments, critical or appreciative, when they visit places already included in the guide. Our task is to collate these reports, check and verify them, making inspections where necessary, and select those which we consider make the grade. No cash changes hands at any point: contributors are not rewarded for writing to us; hotels do not pay for their entries; the editor and his staff accept no free hospitality.

We do not attempt to be comprehensive. There are many blank areas on our maps, including many major cities which lack a single entry. We see no point in lowering our standards in order to recommend an indifferent establishment as "the best available". But of course we are always particularly glad to receive nominations for hotels in a town or a region which is poorly represented.

The entries in the book cover a wide range. People want different things from a hotel according to whether they are making a single night stop or spending a whole holiday in one place, whether they have young children with them, whether they are visiting a city or staying in the remote countryside, and according to their age and means. We make no claims of universal compatibility, but we hope that our descriptions will help you to find hotels that suit your tastes, needs and purse. If an entry has misled you, we beg you to use one of the report forms at the back of the book and tell us, in order that we can do better next time; and we hope that you will also write to us if you have found the guide useful and a hotel has fulfilled your expectations: endorsement and criticism are both essential if the guide is to achieve its purpose. A hotel is dropped unless we get a positive feedback.

Introduction

Welcome to the 1990 edition of Europe's Wonderful Little Hotels and Inns. This is our thirteenth edition, but for the first time we have split the book in two to meet the needs of North American travelers, most of whom choose to take their European vacations in either the UK or the Continent – but usually not both. This edition covers most countries of Western Europe from Norway to Spain and from Portugal to the Eastern Mediterranean. Turkey (apart from Istanbul) isn't strictly in Europe, but we have a growing Turkish section as more and more visitors discover the relatively unspoiled pleasures of Turkish travel. We also have a short section on Morocco. We formerly had a Hungarian section, but have had to abandon it: there just aren't any wonderful hotels in Hungary yet – or our readers have failed to discover them. The companion volume covers Britain and Ireland and the offshore Channel Islands – opulent country-house hotels, seaside family hotels, sophisticated guest-houses and rural inns. If you prefer the two books together, you can still obtain the comprehensive one-volume work in the UK where it is published under the title of The Good Hotel Guide.

If you are a first-time buyer, you will find a formal note to new readers on the previous page. But it might be as well if we remind readers, both old and new, about the essentially personal nature of this work. We started the guide in the seventies because we wanted a book that would really tell us what to expect when we made a reservation. Brochures are an aid, but are often deceptive. It's not the fault of the copywriters that most of their products sound alike: they mostly *are* alike. Travel agents can sometimes be helpful if they specialise in particular localities, but they often only know at recent first-hand a fraction of the hotels on their books, and may be tempted to push a hotel or a chain that offers them a higher commission. Thus many hotels in this guide would never be recommended by agents as they don't offer commissions. *Michelin* is an invaluable touring companion to many parts of Western Europe, but all those conventional signs, useful though they are, can tell us almost nothing about the feel of a place. By far the most reliable way to choose a hotel is by word-of-mouth recommendation. One way to describe this guide is to say that it is the word of mouth in print.

This book is shamelessly idiosyncratic, and full of the Editor's personal prejudices and preferences. We loathe big anonymous hotels where you might as well be in Honolulu or Hong Kong as in Hamburg. We avoid, if we can, those boring establishments which lack any individuality in their decor or any warmth in their welcome. We decry pretentiousness in cooking. We cherish the dedicater hotelier who, like a monk, has taken a solemn vow of hospitality, and works from seven in the morning to one in the morning to cosset his guests.

Because the guide is concerned only to recommend hotels that meet the Editor's own criteria, it is far from comprehensive. There are large areas on the map where we have little or nothing to offer the traveler, including many great cities. Of course there are plenty of hotels to choose from in any industrial centre. But most large business-oriented city hotels are relatively indistinguishable one from another. They may differ in their architecture and facilities: some will have air-conditioning and double glazing, four-posters and mini-bars, more spacious public areas, more boutiques. And of course their management and service may be smart and spick and span or, alternatively, slack, snooty or sullen. *That* can make a difference. But however good a big corporation-owned city hotel may be of its kind, it will remain the hotel equivalent of fast food. And some of us want something else when we travel abroad.

This guide is – and intends to remain – committed to a more rewarding experience. But why are there so many major cities, especially business and industrial cities, that lack attractive small hotels? Plainly one reason is that the kind of individually owned hotel of character appeals more to tourists than to the business trade, but it is also unhappily the case that the bad – or at least the mediocre – drives out the good. When a major corporation acquires an old hotel, it will certainly improve its facilities, put in baths *en suite* and colour TV, and yet, again and again, its presence is a kind of kiss – not of death certainly – but of half life. And that is because it is in the business of catering more for customers en masse than for the individual.

We are witnessing a period of astonishing growth in the hotel and catering business. Tourism, it is reckoned, is likely to become the world's biggest single industry within the next decade and conference-ism isn't far behind. Every day we receive PR handouts for new custom-built hotels in cities and extravagant conversions of old country houses, recommending themselves as "the ideal venue for all your conference and banqueting needs." Nearly all the new country house hotel openings we have heard about this year have been of this ilk. And at the same time it is harder and harder for the new individual enterprise, without benefit of economies of scale and corporate promotion, to get adequate recognition of its quieter virtues and to survive its early years.

We give the last word on this subject to Dickens, writing 140 years ago in *The Uncommercial Traveller*, though his insights are every bit as true today as they were then:

> "We all know the great hotel belonging to the company of proprietors. . .in which we can get anything we want, after its kind, for money; but where nobody is glad to see us, or sorry to see us, or minds (our bill paid) whether we come or go, or how, or when, or why, or

cares about us. We all know this hotel, where we have no individuality, but put ourselves into the general post, as it were, and are sorted and disposed of according to our division. We all know that we can get on very well indeed at such a place, but still not perfectly well; and this may be because the place is largely wholesale, and there is a lingering personal retail interest within us that asks to be satisfied."

Are hotels staying tuned?

As we move into the nineties, it is useful to ask how far the hotel industry is adapting itself to the changing needs of its customers. They have certainly moved a long way from 1980 in embracing new appliances: remote control TV, direct-dial telephones, hair-dryers and trouser presses are now commonplace bedroom conveniences when once they were the rare exception. And more and more hotels now have fax and computerised accounts which in principle minimise mistakes and make them easier to spot.

But hoteliers have been deplorably slow, we believe, to recognise other less tangible consumer needs. Consider smoking. How few hotels have registered the extraordinary shift in the public's attitude to smoking in the last few years, especially among the main hotel-using classes. According to one recent opinion poll, 85% of the public agree that smoking is a health hazard and 91% think that all restaurants should provide non-smoking areas. Nobody has thought to ask what percentage of people believe hotels should earmark some of their rooms as smokeless zones, but presumably the hotel poll would be similar to the restaurant one. Few hotels yet provide such rooms, few offer smoke-free zones in their restaurant.

Hoteliers have been just as tardy to perceive other shifts in public demand. Many are still boasting of five-, six- or seven-course set menus – feasts for Gargantuas – ignoring the evidence that more and more of their customers are looking these days for lighter diets and dishes, and not just the older generation whose appetites diminish with age. At one time we were used to getting complaints about the modest portions of *nouvelle cuisine*. We hardly ever hear from the anti-*nouvelle* faction these days, but correspondents often tell us how they pine for a two or three-course option. We hear plenty these days about the risks of high cholesterol diets, but many hotels continue to boast of their chariots of rich desserts, the mere sight of which give those who know about such things the intimations of cardiac arrest. And how few hotels are putting themselves out to cater imaginatively for the ever-growing brigade who prefer (at least sometimes) not to eat meat or fish.

It is always difficult to predict future trends in eating, but as we become more health and hygiene conscious – and people all over the western world are taking responsibility for their health as never before – the demand for simpler meals, using fresh not frozen or packaged or vacuum-packed produce, will certainly grow. We believe that many of the smaller hotels would give greater satisfaction to their guests if they were to be less ambitious in their menus and try less hard to imitate (so often lamentably) the bravura performances of the culinary maestros.

Department of Complaints

Many grouses surface every year: the lack of sufficient shelves in bathrooms, for example, poor lighting or inadequate heating are hardy perennials which should be easy and not impossibly expensive to correct. We are also accustomed to getting complaints about beds: that they are either too soft or too hard. We reckon that these cancel each other out. People who feel strongly about their mattresses should make a point of mentioning their concern when they book.

Other problems are more intractable. We sympathise with the plight of the single person, constantly being fobbed off with inferior accommodation or else made to pay extra for a double room. But we doubt whether many hoteliers will find it worth their while wooing these voters except in towns where there is a constant demand for single rooms from business folk – and the latter often don't mind paying more for a double room if the extra cost isn't hitting their own pocket.

We have had a plethora of complaints this year about hotels not honouring guests' bookings despite – in many cases – confirmation by letter, telex or fax, and the payment of deposits. French hotels figure often in these charges, Parisian ones especially. Some hotels, we suspect, like some airlines, operate a deliberate policy of double-booking, hoping that it will work out on the night. Deposits may be returned, with or without an adequate apology, but the customer often loses out on the exchange rate. There is no instant remedy, but we urge readers to make a point of reporting all such incidents to the appropriate bodies – to any guide which lists the hotel and to the relevant tourist board – unless satisfactory amends are made. It's a boring, time-consuming exercise, but hotels ought not to be allowed to get away with over-booking any more than travellers should be permitted to book themselves into more than one hotel and flagrantly overlook the loss to the innkeeper of a "no show". Readers often criticise hotel for taking credit card numbers when they are making a reservation; it may seem unfriendly, but we sympathise with hoteliers who need that self-protection.

A message to our volunteer inspectors

Everyone who sends a report is helping to enrich or make more accurate the next edition. But we must urge correspondents never under any provocation to reveal that they are planning to write to us, which could be construed by the hotel as an attempt to obtain favours. Total discretion is of paramount importance.

There is also a danger that reporters in their enthusiasm may start to hunt for faults. Some people are incurable nit-pickers, and must be a curse to their hosts as well as not much pleasure to themselves or their companions. We enjoy reading (and printing)

Travellers' Tales, which record some of the terrible things they come across, but would urge our correspondents to do their best to travel hopefully and to be as eager to praise as to condemn. There is plenty wrong with hotels, even the best of them, but the owners do take a lot of flak, and not all of it is deserved. We sympathise with hoteliers who sometimes send us perfectly awful letters they have received from patronising ingrates. One inn-keeper this year was provoked into replying to such a complain-ant, who happened to be a clergyman: "With respect, Reverend, I hope you are not as uncharitable towards your parishioners."

While on the subject of reports, may we say that those of the gushing or bland variety that tell us "everything was simply marvellous, nothing was too much trouble for the staff, the meals were uniformly delicious, the furnishings all in the best of taste" etc, are, alas, of litle use to us. What we are looking for are detailed appraisals, reflecting the shade as well as the light.

HILARY RUBINSTEIN

Special hotels

City hotels with luxury and grandeur

Austria Schloss Fuschl, Hof bei Salzburg; Schloss Mönchstein, Salzburg, Sacher, Vienna
Denmark Angleterre, Copenhagen
France Cour des Loges, Lyon; Résidence du Bois, Paris; Opéra, Toulouse
Germany Vier Jahreszeiten, Hamburg
Norway Continental, Oslo
Spain San Marcos, León; Reyes Católicos, Santiago de Compostela
Switzerland L'Arbalète, Geneva

Town hotels of character and/or value

Austria Elefant, Salzburg; Amadeus, Vienna; König von Ungarn, Vienna
Belgium Swaene, Bruges; Ter Duinen, Bruges
Denmark 71 Nyhavn, Copenhagen; Weis Stue, Ribe
France d'Arlatan, Arles; Europe, Avignon; Lameloise, Chagny; Diderot, Chinon; Pullman Beauvau, Marseille; La Pérouse, Nice; L'Abbaye St-Germain, Paris; Vieux Puits, Pont Audemer; Pyrénées, St-Jean-Pied-de-Port; Colombe d'Or, St-Paul-de-Vence
Germany Mönchs Posthotel, Bad Herrenalb; Kleine Prinz, Baden-Baden; Böttingerhaus, Bamberg; Sankt Nepomuk, Bamberg; Westend, Frankfurt-am-Main; Roten Bären, Freiburg; Hanseatic, Hamburg; Bären, Meersburg
Italy Umbra, Assisi; Villa

Belvedere, Florence; Villa Mozart, Merano; Cesari, Rome; Gregoriana, Rome; Flora, Venice
The Netherlands Ambassade, Amsterdam; Pulitzer, Amsterdam
Norway Myklebust, Bergen
Portugal Quinta Penha da França, Funchal; Infante de Sagres, Oporto
Spain Parador, Carmona; Hostal América, Granada
Sweden Tidbloms, Gothenberg
Switzerland Florhof, Zürich
Turkey Çeşme Kervansaray, Çeşme; Yeşil Ev, Istanbul

Rural charm and character in the luxury class

Austria Schloss Dürnstein, Dürnstein
Belgium Moulin Hideux, Noirefontaine
Denmark Falsled Kro, Falsled
France Beaumanière, Les Baux; Moulin du Roc, Champagnac-de-Belair; Château de Divonne, Divonne-les-Bains; Prés d'Eugénie, Eugénie-les-Bains; Boyer "les Crayères", Reims; Moulin de la Gorce, La Roche-l'Abeille; Mas de Chastelas, St-Tropez; Cantemerle, Vence
Germany Klostergut Jakobsberg, Boppard; Pflaums, Pegnitz
Greece Argentikon, Chios
Italy Villa Cipriani, Asolo; Villa Corner, Cavasagra; Palumbo, Ravello; Certosa di Maggiano, Siena; Condulmer, Zerman
Spain Residencia, Deyá; Bobadilla, Loja; El Castell, La Seu d'Urgell
Sweden Grythyttans, Grythyttan
Yugoslavia Vila Bled, Bled

Rural charm and character at medium price

Austria Gams, Bezau
Belgium 't Convent, Renige
Denmark Steensgaard
Herregårdspension, Millinge
France Bérard, Cadière-d'Azur;
Benvengudo, Les-Baux-de-
Provence; Pescalerie, Cabrerets;
Marais St-Jean, Chonas
l'Amballan; Moulin de Vey,
Clécy; Poste, Corps-la-Salette;
Cro-Magnon, Les Eyzies-de-
Tayac; Relais de la Magdeleine,
Gémenos; Cagnard, Haut-de-
Cagnes; Bon Coin, Mimizan;
Trois Roses, La Petite Pierre;
Hospitaliers, Poët-Laval; Cheval
Blanc, Sept-Saulx
Germany Töpferhaus, Alt-
Duvenstedt; Erbguth's
Landhaus, Hagnau; Schönberg,
Oberwesel; Zum Ochsen,
Schönwald; Wehrle, Triberg
Italy Tenuta di Ricavo,
Castellina in Chianti; Saügo,
Cavalese; Castello, Gargonza;
Sant' Uffizio, Cioccaro;
Amorosa, Sinalunga
Norway Utne, Utne
Portugal Quinta das Torres,
Azeitão; Abrigo da Montanha,
Monchique; Santa Maria,
Marvão; Quinta dos Lobos and
Quinta da Capela, Sintra
Spain Es Molí, Deyá;
Monasterio de Piedra, Nuévalos;
L'Hermitage, Orient
Sweden Åkerblads, Tällberg
Switzerland Eden, Engelberg;
Rothorn, Schwanden; Soglina,
Soglio

Rural charm, simple style

France Relais de St-Jacques,
Collonges-la-Rouge; Vieux
Logis, Lestelle-Bétharram; Clos
Normand, Martin Église;
Équipe, Molines-en-Queyras;
Rostaing, Passenans; Pélissaria,
St-Cirq-Lapopie; Poids Public,
St-Félix-Lauragais; Midi, St-
Jean-du-Bruel; Hameau, St-Paul-
de-Vence; Vert, Wierre-Effroy
Germany Lipmann, Beilstein
Turkey Turbel Pansion,
Çavuşin

Hotels by the sea, luxury style

France Langoustier,
Porquerolles; Maquis, Porticcio;
Caribou, Porticciolo; Plage, Ste-
Anne-la-Palud
Greece Akti Myrina, Myrina
Italy Luna Convento, Amalfi;
Pellicano, Porto Ercole
Portugal Reid's, Madeira
Turkey Kismet, Kuşadasi

Hotels by the sea, medium-priced or simple

Denmark Sønderho Kro,
Sønderho
France Menez-Frost, Bénodet;
Chez Pierre, Raguenès-Plage;
Ty-Pont, St-Jean-du-Doigt; Ti al-
Lannec, Trebeurden
Greece Aliki, Simi
Italy Casa Albertina, Positano;
Nido di Fiascherino, Tellaro
Spain Aigua Blava, Bagur; Mar I
Vent, Bañalbufar; Parador,
Gomera

Skiing, walking or mountain hotels

Austria Senger, Heiligenblut;
Salome, Lech am Arlberg
France Albert Premier et de
Milan, Chamonix
Germany Unterstmatt,
Schwarzwald-Hochstrasse
Norway Mundal, Fjaerland;
Besså Touristhytta, Øvre
Eidfjord
Spain Sant Pere, Soldeu,
Andorra
Switzerland Flüela, Davos Dorf;
Chesa Grischuna, Klosters;
Metropol, Zermatt

Small hotels and inns with outstanding cuisine

Belgium Shamrock, Ronse
France Côte St-Jacques, Joigny;
Alain Chapel, Mionnay;
Bretagne, Questembert; Pic,
Valence; Espérance, Vézelay;
Georges Blanc, Vonnas
The Netherlands De Swaen,
Oisterwijk
Spain Ses Rotges, Cala Ratjada;
Posada, Gualchos
Switzerland Fischerzunft,
Schaffhausen

Friendly informality/hotel run like a private house

Austria Erike, Kitzbühel

France Parc des Maréchaux,
Auxerre; Châtenet, Brantôme;
Château de Roussan, St-Rémy-
de-Provence; Pontot, Vézelay
Greece Ganimede, Galaxidion
Portugal Villa Hostilina,
Lamego; Quinta São Thiago,
Sintra

Hotels which are welcoming to families with children

Austria Madrisa, Gargellen;
Erika, Kitzbühel
France Étrier Camarguais, Les
Stes-Maries-de-la-Mer
Switzerland Bellevue,
Braunwald

How to read the entries

As in previous editions, entries are in two parts – a citation, usually endorsed by one or several names, followed by relevant information about accommodation, amenities, location and tariffs.

We must emphasise once again that the length or brevity of an entry is not a reflection of the quality of a hotel. The size of an entry is determined in part by what we feel needs to be said to convey a hotel's special flavour and in part by the character and interest of the commendation. In general, country hotels get more space than city hotels because the atmosphere of the hotel matters more with the former and also because it is often helpful, when a hotel is in a relatively remote or little-known area, for the entry to say something about the location.

The names at the end of the citation are of those who have nominated that hotel or endorsed the entry that appeared in a previous edition. Some entries are entirely or largely quoted from one report; if several names follow such an entry, we have distinguished writers of quoted material by putting their names first. We do not give the names of those who have sent us adverse reports – though their contributions are every bit as important as the laudatory ones.

The factual material also varies in length. Some hotels provide a wide variety of facilities, others very little. But the paucity of information provided in some cases may derive from the fact that the hotel has failed to return our detailed questionnaire or send us a brochure even though we send out this form in five languages, and repeat the operation for any recalcitrants a month later. Around a quarter of the hotels in the book ignore our form or return it months later when the guide has gone to press. In these instances, we have to rely on the information available from national tourist offices. The fact that no lounge or bar is mentioned in an entry does not mean that a hotel lacks public rooms – only that we can't be sure. The same applies to availability of parking, which we aim to mention in the case of town and city hotels. As to tariffs, in those cases where we have had no communication with a hotel, or where it was unable to give next year's rates, we print the 1989 tariffs, making it clear that these are last year's terms.

Our italicised entries indicate hotels which we feel are worth considering, but which because of inadequate information or for lack of feedback do not at the moment justify a full entry. A hotel whose entry is in italics, with briefer information about its tariffs and facilities, need not be thought of as a half-good establishment, only as one about which we are eager to have more opinions. We hope that, with the help of such feedback, many will rate full entries next year.

There is a limit to the amount of "nuts and bolts" that can be given in any guide book, and we are against providing, as some other guide books do, a lot of condensed information in complicated, hard-to-decipher hieroglyphic form. Days and months are abbreviated, but virtually the only other shorthand we use is "B&B" for bed and breakfast and "alc" for à la carte; the "full alc" price is the hotel's estimate per person for a three-course meal and a half-bottle of modest wine, including service and taxes. We try to give as much information as possible (ground-floor rooms, lifts, etc) to enable disabled people to judge whether or not a hotel will be suitable for them. If a hotel tells us it has special facilities for the disabled we give details; if we know it is not suitable we say so. But we do sometimes lack precise information; disabled people should *always* check with the hotel.

Terms are difficult enough to cope with at the best of times. A few hotels have a standard rate for all rooms regardless of season and length of stay, but most operate a highly complicated system which varies from low season to high (and some have a medium-high season as well), according to length of stay, whether there is a bathroom *en suite*. When we can, we give a room rate rather than a rate per person and hope thereby to give a reliable idea of what people, especially those travelling on their own, can expect to pay. When figures are given without mention of single or double rooms they indicate the range of tariffs per person. Lowest rates are what you pay for the simplest room, or out of season, or both; highest rates are for the "best" rooms – and in high season if the hotel has one. Meal prices are per person. Tax and service are included unless we state otherwise.

There is one crucial point that must be emphasised with regard to the tariffs: their relative unreliability. We ask hotels when they complete our questionnaire in the spring of one year to make an informed guess at their tariffs the following year. There are many reasons why this is a difficult exercise. Please don't rely on the figures printed. *You should always check at the time of booking and not blame the hotel or the guide if the prices are different from those printed.*

We also strongly advise you to check whether a hotel is open before making a long detour. We try in all cases to give accurate information, but hotels, particularly small ones, do sometimes close at times when they have told us they expect to be open. And hotels on the Continent often have a weekly closing date, but sometimes fail to make this clear when returning our questionnaire. Finally, they do not always give reliable information about whether or not they take credit cards. If it is vital to you, please check.

xvi

We end with our customary exhortation: we implore readers to tell us of any errors of omission or commission in both the descriptive and informative parts of the entries. We make constant efforts to improve our information under "Location", especially with the more out-of-the-way places, but would be very grateful if readers would let us know of any cases where they have found our directions inadequate. We recognise what an imposition it is to be asking readers to write us letters or fill in report forms, but it is essential that people do let us know their views if the guide is to meet consumer needs as well as it can.

Austria

SINGER SPORTHOTEL, BERWANG

ALPBACH 6236 Tyrol   Map 9

Hotel Alpbacherhof   *Tel* (05336) 5237
                                                Fax (05336) 5016

The skiing is good and the air superbly clear at this very pretty village,
venue of the European Forum since the end of World War II. The
Alpbacherhof has an indoor pool, a terrace and a garden, and it serves
dinners by candle-light. Most rooms have balconies with views, but the
smaller and darker ones on the north side do not. "Very friendly, with
spacious rooms and good dinners", is a report this year. "You are
constantly waited on hand and foot – I have never known anything like
it. Beaming, helpful servants, charming receptionist." "Service is superb –
they will even look after an aged parent for you." One reader this year
found the food disappointing. (*Jill Haslett, CA Bratherton*)

Open 16 Dec–25 Mar, 13 May–30 Sept.
Rooms 2 suites, 48 double, 5 single – 50 with bath, 5 with shower, all with
telephone, radio and mini-bar; some with TV.

1

Facilities Lift. Bar, lounge, TV room, 2 restaurants; conference facilities; indoor heated swimming pool; terrace (where meals are served in fine weather). Garden.
Location Alpbach is in a valley S of Innsbruck–Kufstein main road. Hotel is central. Parking.
Restriction Not suitable for &.
Credit card Visa.
Terms [1989 rates] B&B 500–1,000 Sch. Dinner, B&B 600–1,200 Sch. Set lunch 200 Sch, dinner 250 Sch; full alc 500 Sch. Reduced rates for children sharing parents' room; special meals on request.

Hotel Böglerhof

Tel (05336) 5227
Telex 051160

A smart and attractive old inn, built in 1470 to house workers at the nearby silver and copper mines. Large lounge, 3 dining rooms, excellent food served by dignified waitresses. Nice bedrooms; splendid views from their balconies. Open Dec–Mar, mid-May–Sept. 48 rooms, all with bath or shower. B&B 550–1,100 Sch; half board 650–1,100 Sch [1989]. Endorsed briefly, but fuller reports welcome.

ANIF 5081 Salzburg   Map 9

Hotel Friesacher

Tel (06246) 2075
Telex 632943

Anif is an attractive village and all-season resort just south of Salzburg, amid woods and mountains. The *Friesacher*, again approved this year both for cooking and comfort, is a sizeable modern chalet-style hotel with large neo-rustic bedrooms and scenic balconies overlooking meadows and hills. "Good value and very peaceful. Waitresses in pretty national costume serve good basic food either in the rather airless restaurant or in the garden." "Friendly service, warm and cosy room with large bathroom." Besides the hotel restaurant, the Friesacher family own two cheaper ones next door which serve buffet-style meals. A recent visitor enjoyed eating outdoors listening to accordion music at one of these. Less attractive noises were complained of this year by one reader: traffic from the nearby main road, aircraft buzz from the airport. The hotel has just added a sauna, solarium and fitness-centre, as well 15 new bedrooms.

Open All year except 23 Dec – 15 Jan.
Rooms 3 suites, 44 double, 7 single – 49 with bath, 5 with shower, all with telephone, radio and TV; many with balcony. 18 in annexe. Some ground-floor rooms.
Facilities Lift. Lounge, bar, dining room; conference facilities. Sauna, solarium and fitness-room. Garden with children's play area and café.
Location 4 km S of Salzburg. Leave *Autobahn* at Salzburg, turn right at Anif (1 km) and turn ½ km on road to Hellbrunn. Parking.
Restriction Not suitable for &.
Credit cards Access, Diners, Visa.
Terms [1989 rates] B&B: single 580–780 Sch, double 880–1,060 Sch, suite 1,160 Sch. Set lunch 120 Sch, dinner 200 Sch; full alc 280 Sch. Reduced rates for children.

> When hotels have failed to return their questionnaire, we have quoted 1989 prices, with a note to that effect.

BERWANG 6622 Tyrol

Map 9

Singer Sporthotel

Tel (05674) 8181
Fax (05674) 8181-83
Telex 55544

Berwang is a busy summer and skiing resort a few miles west of the towering Zugspitze, just off the Innsbruck–Stuttgart main road; here the Singer family's chalet-hotel, sizeable and fairly smart, stands on a pine-studded hillside. Readers this year have again written approvingly of the owners' personal attention, of the efficient and courteous staff, the good food and the spacious rooms with balconies. "The facilities of bathing, sauna, massage, jacuzzi did not impinge on those looking merely to enjoy strolling in the countryside", said an earlier visitor. One reader, this year, visiting out of season, was dismayed to find an old people's bingo session in progress. But another, also a summer visitor, found it one of the best hotels of its kind he had ever stayed in – "hard to manufacture even the smallest complaint". (*RS McNeill*)

Open 17 Dec–10 Apr, 18 May–1 Oct.
Rooms 25 suites, 35 double, 10 single – 58 with bath and/or shower, telephone, radio; many with balcony; TV in suites.
Facilities Lift. Lounge, *Stube*, 2 bars, 2 restaurants; dancing, Tyrolean evenings; fitness/sports centre with whirlpool, sauna and massage. Small garden with terraces. **Location** 80 km NW of Innsbruck. Garages and open parking.
Credit cards Diners, Visa.
Terms [1989 rates] B&B: single 380–950 Sch, double 820–1,600 Sch, suite 1,000–2,100 Sch. Dinner, B&B double 980–1,800 Sch. Set lunch 95–220 Sch, dinner 130–350 Sch; full alc 210–450 Sch. Reduced rates and special meals for children.

BEZAU 6870 Vorarlberg

Map 9

Gasthof Gams

Tel (05514) 2220
Fax (05514 2220-24)
Telex 59144 VVWALD-GAMS

A quiet little town on the edge of the Bregenz forest. The road on one side winds down to the busy resorts of Lake Constance; on the other, it loops over the mountains to the ski-stations of Lech and St-Anton. *Gasthof Gams* is a sizeable 17th-century coaching inn, with modern additions such as jacuzzi (in the basement), heated outdoor swimming pool, and under-floor heating in the rooms. Public rooms are furnished in traditional Austrian style. A report this year: "The succession of small dining rooms adds to the charm, service is quick and friendly, the Austrian cooking is superb." Others have enjoyed the quiet and comfort in this genuinely personal family hotel. But rooms do vary in size. The hotel bus takes guests to and from the ski-slopes in season. (*Mr and Mrs RW Beacroft, Stephen Ruell, BJ Walter*)

Open All year except 1–18 Dec.
Rooms 6 suites, 24 double, 10 single – 15 with bath, 25 with shower, all with telephone; TV on request; some with balcony. Some ground-floor rooms.
Facilities Lift. Lounge, bar, dining rooms; conference/functions rooms; games room, sauna, solarium, hot whirlpool; terraces. Large garden with swimming pool (heated May–Oct) and 3 tennis courts.
Location 30 km SE of Bregenz, 37 km NW of Lech. Central. Parking.
Credit cards Access, Visa.

AUSTRIA

Terms B&B: single 390–540 Sch, double 740–1,080 Sch; dinner, B&B: single 550–700 Sch, double 1,060–1,400 Sch. Set lunch/dinner 160–350 Sch; full alc 320 Sch. Reduced rates and special meals for children.

DÜRNSTEIN 3601 Lower Austria   Map 9

Hotel Schloss Dürnstein

Tel (02711) 212
Fax (02711) 351
Telex 71147

"One of the world's most beautiful hotels"; "Herr Thiery runs the best hotel in Austria"; "excellent food on a spacious terrace overlooking the Danube" – three new tributes to this always-admired *Schloss*, which stands inside a lovely old village (Richard Cœur de Lion was imprisioned here in 1192). It is perched above the Danube, with spectacular views of the winding river from most bedrooms. Built in 1630, it was owned by the Princes Starhemberg for centuries, and was used as a refuge by the Emperor Leopold I when he was fleeing from the Turks. Some 50 years ago, it was reincarnated by the Thiery family, who still own and run it. Rather a formal place, it has beautiful antique furniture both in the public rooms and in the bedrooms. "Each year Herr Thiery improves his cuisine", says a reader this year; "breakfast on the terrace in the early dawn with the Danube, and the birds singing, is sheer perfection. Our comfortable room was both homely and grand." "Our room the size of a tennis court was filled with antiques. You live with the family as in a stately home, with no choice for dinner." "Breakfast arrived on two huge trays and was placed on a genuine 16th-century table in our room. Go there just for the history and romance." (*M and D Chambers, Ruth H and Robert D Todd, Peter Brown*)

Open 1 Apr–8 Nov.
Rooms 2 suites, 31 double, 4 single – all with bath and/or shower, telephone, radio and TV; baby-listening on request. Some ground-floor rooms.
Facilities Lift. Lounge, TV room, bar, restaurant, grill room with dance floor; private dining room. Courtyard with heated swimming pool. Terrace overlooking Danube; fishing and boating.
Location At end of main street in village. Parking.
Credit cards All major cards accepted.
Terms [1989 rates] Dinner, B&B 875–1,500 Sch. 10% reduction in low season. No charge for children under 6 sharing parents' room; special meals on request.

FILZMOOS 5532 Salzburg   Map 9

Hotel Hanneshof

Tel (06453) 275
Telex 67728

In a skiing and summer resort at the foot of the Dachstein, about an hour by road from Salzburg, the Mayr family run this very friendly and efficient chalet-style hotel, spruce and modern, next to their butcher's shop. Indoor swimming pool, good Austrian cooking, children welcomed. Closed November. 45 rooms, most with private facilities. B&B 350–450 Sch. Half board 500–750 Sch [1989]. New nomination. More reports welcome.

> Please write and confirm an entry when it is deserved. If you think that a hotel is not as good as we say, write and tell us.

FREISTADT 4240 Upper Austria

Map 9

Gasthof Deim zum Goldenen Hirschen
Böhmergasse 8

Tel (07942) 2258 and 2111

Set on a wild granite plateau between Linz and the Czech frontier, Freistadt is a handsome old town with towers, gateways and traces of ramparts. Within these walls is the *Deim*, a genuine old inn with a pretty garden. "Beautiful and charming, with flowers everywhere and the best goulash in Austria or Hungary." "It is still very good – from the individual character of the bedrooms to the excellence of the food (dining rooms get crowded at weekends). All the modern conveniences and luxuries combined with old-world charm." These are last year's tributes. Could we have some more recent travellers' tales please?

Open All year except 2 weeks in Jan.
Rooms 17 double, 6 single – 17 with bath, 2 with shower, all with telephone and radio; 4 with TV.
Facilities Lounge, TV room, 3 restaurants. Garden (meals can be taken outside).
Restriction Not suitable for &.
Location Central. Parking. Town is 40 km NE of Linz.
Credit card Diners.
Terms B&B: single 300 Sch, double 520 Sch; dinner, B&B: single 380 Sch, double 680 Sch. Set lunch/dinner 100–120 Sch; full alc 200 Sch. Reduced rates and special meals/portions for children.

FUSCHL-AM-SEE 5330 Salzburg

Map 9

Pension Rupertihof
Fuschl-am-See 106

Tel (06226) 447

A clean modern chalet-style *pension* with flower-decked balconies by the shore of the nearest of the Salzburg lakes to Salzburg. It is just outside the village, an easy walk to several hotels for dinner. Recent verdicts: "Excellent value, friendly family owners"; "Comfortable beds, many rooms with balcony; excellent varied breakfasts (muesli, eggs, cheese)." Fuller reports welcome.

Open All year.
Rooms 12 double – 3 with bath, 9 with shower; some with balcony.
Facilities Breakfast room, lounge with TV. Small garden. Lake Fuschl 50 metres (beach and safe bathing, sailing, etc). Walks arranged.
Location 22 km E of Salzburg on road to Bad Ischl. Hotel is first on right at entrance of village. Parking.
Restriction Not suitable for &.
Credit cards None accepted.
Terms B&B 170–210 Sch. Reduced rates for children. (No restaurant.)

GARGELLEN 6787 Vorarlberg

Map 9

Hotel Madrisa
Montafon

Tel (05557) 6331
Fax (05557) 6331-82
Telex 52269 MADRIS

"A great place for children" is a frequent comment on this friendly family-run ski hotel, traditional in style but well modernised, which stands next to nursery slopes in the lovely Montafon valley. "Simply wonderful", runs one report this year: "we had a large airy room in the new wing, with a balcony facing the village church and mountains beyond. The food was scrumptious, and the service very friendly, with the Rhomberg family, the owners, much involved." Earlier views: "The breakfasts were a wonderful array, and the evening meals were imaginative." "As well as for winter holidays, it's splendidly situated for spring and summer." "The Rhomberg family carried our bags and gave us extra bedding. The hotel exuded warmth, and mountains of food appeared regularly. The value for money makes me blink when I think of other ski resorts." The rooms in the older part have been called "ample, warm and rustic", but unlike the newer ones they do not have balconies. (*I Fishman, Ian and Anne Steel*) One reader regretted the limited choice on the half-board dinner, and felt that the hotel's popularity and increase in size was harming its personal touch.

Open 16 Dec–22 Apr, 22 Jun–26 Sept.
Rooms 5 suites, 48 double, 12 single – most with bath and/or shower, telephone and radio; TV on request.
Facilities Lift. Hall, lounge, reading room, games room, *Stüberl*, dining room; children's playroom (with children's films); disco; indoor swimming pool, sauna. Large grounds with terrace, lawn, ski lift.
Location 28 km S of Bludenz. In centre of Gargellen. Parking.
Credit cards Access, Amex, Diners (for extras only).
Terms Dinner, B&B 770–1,275 Sch in winter, 540–840 Sch in summer. Set meals 260 Sch; full alc 330 Sch. In skiing season bookings are normally for 1 week (Sat–Sat). Weekly and Christmas packages. Reductions for children sharing parents' room; special meals on request.

GRAZ 8010 Styria — Map 9

Schlossberg Hotel
Kaiser-Franz-Joseph-Kai

Tel (0316) 8070
Fax (0316) 8070-160
Telex 312672

A newly renovated 400-year-old inn, in a quiet but central side-street of Austria's second city. Beamed ceilings and rambling corridors but modern lift; large rooms with antiques. Roof garden with swimming pool. Private parking. Good breakfasts: no restaurant, but lots nearby. Open all year. 54 rooms, all with bath or shower. B&B double 1,400–1,700 Sch [1989]. Re-nominated this year. More reports welcome.

HALLSTATT 4830 Upper Austria — Map 9

Seehotel Grüner Baum

Tel (06134) 263

Hallstatt is a well-known picturesque village on a clear lake south-east of Salzburg, backed by steep wooded hills, with snowy mountains above. The *Seehotel* dates from 1670 and has been in the hands of the Lissbauer family for six generations. It has a terrace by the lake where meals and drinks can be taken; many bedrooms also face the lake and have balconies with geraniums, others overlook the pretty market square. "The quaint village has a lovely atmosphere. Our comfortable rooms in this homely hotel were furnished in typical Austrian style, and from our balcony we enjoyed the view of the lake and mountains. The food was good, though not memorable, and the staff were all helpful and amicable.''

Open May–Sept.
Rooms 24 double, 8 single – 13 with bath, 12 with shower, 16 with telephone; T V on request. Some with balcony.
Facilities Lounge, T V room, bar, restaurant; conference facilities. Garden on lake.
Location 50 km SE of Salzburg. Parking in market square.
Credit card Amex.
Terms B&B 230–420 Sch; half board 380–580 Sch; full board 450–670 Sch. Reduced rates and special meals for children.

HEILIGENBLUT 9844 Carinthia   Map 9

Hotel Haus Senger   *Tel* (04824) 2215
Grossglockner

Heiligenblut is a village just below the Grossglockner, in high, wild mountainous country, good for walking or skiing. "Friendly and personal staff, rooms beautifully kept, food delicious, varied and copious, including the world's best apfelstrudel.'' So runs a recent letter on this "very *gemütlich*'' family-run hotel, a typical old mountain chalet with a new extension. It has comfort and the kind of personal attention that makes everyone feel relaxed and good-humoured. Most rooms have a balcony. "The cook bakes Sachertorte and apfelstrudel almost every day and there is always the temptation to try them warm from the oven after a day out on the mountains.'' More reports welcome.

Open Christmas–Easter, mid-Jun–mid-Oct.
Rooms 8 suites, 6 double, 3 single – all with bath or shower, telephone, radio, T V and tea-making facilities.
Facilities Lift. Lounge with T V, restaurant with bar; games room, fitness room, sauna and turkish bath. Garden and terraces. Winter sports.
Location On the edge of Heiligenblut, which is on route 107, 40 km N of Lienz. Parking.
Credit cards All major cards accepted.
Terms B&B 390–560 Sch; half board 510–690 Sch. Set lunch/dinner 170–230 Sch; full alc 180–250 Sch. Special meals for children.

HOF BEI SALZBURG 5322 Salzburg   Map 9

Hotel Schloss Fuschl   *Tel* (06229) 22530
Telex 633454

The former hunting lodge of the prince-archbishops of Salzburg is today a most elegant and luxurious hotel – still distinctly regal, but now wholly secular. It overlooks Lake Fuschl with the mountains as backdrop, 20 kilometres from Salzburg: you can lunch or dine overlooking the lake, where the sunsets can be spectacular. Two reports this year: "A most sumptuous hotel, with very good food''; "A dream! Sparkling lake and lilac-lined gardens. Very good food, but tiny portions.'' Earlier accounts: "It retains much of its castle/hunting lodge atmosphere, despite addition of marble swimming pool and jacuzzi. *Nouvelle cuisine* very, very good, but also happy to serve us a lunch of pumpkin soup and smoked ham'' (the food has also been described as 'Austrian international'). "Beautifully situated, with an elegant and interesting interior. The staff were outstandingly welcoming and helpful." Rooms facing the roadway can be a bit noisy, owing to the influx of visitors: best are those facing the lake, or the chalets in the garden. Swimming both in an indoor pool and in the lake. (*Marie and Hans Haenlein, and others*)

Open All year.
Rooms 23 suites, 56 double, 5 single – all with bath and/or shower, telephone, radio and TV. 60 in buildings in the garden. Some ground-floor rooms.
Facilities Salons, bar, 2 restaurants, conservatory; conference facilities; beauty farm; indoor heated swimming pool. Large park with terrace for outdoor meals; private beach and swimming area on lake, fishing, boating, refreshments, tennis, 9-hole golf course.
Location 20 km E of Salzburg; take road 158 to St Gilden; turn left 1 m after village of Hof.
Restriction Not suitable for &.
Credit cards All major cards accepted.
Terms [1989 rates] B&B: single 1,200–1,800 Sch, double 1,900–3,200 Sch, suite 2,400–5,500 Sch. Set lunch 420 Sch, dinner 500 Sch; full alc 600 Sch. Children under 12 sharing parents' room free; special meals on request.

IGLS 6080 Tyrol   **Map 9**

Hotel Astoria   *Tel* (05222) 77481
Badhausstrasse 1   *Fax* (05222) 77481-44
                                                              Telex 534121

On the edge of a village above Innsbruck that featured in the 1964 Winter Olympics, a sizeable modern chalet-style hotel, family-run; rather heavily furnished, but with courteous staff and spacious rooms. Flowery balconies, indoor swimming pool, buffet breakfast. 42 rooms, all with bathroom. Half board 480–750 Sch. New nomination. More reports needed.

INNSBRUCK 6020 Tyrol   **Map 9**

Weinhaus Happ   *Tel* (05222) 582980
Herzog-Friedrich Strasse 14   *Telex* 533511

"Right in the centre of the action", a small *Weinhaus*-cum-hotel in an old street flanked with arcades, that leads directly to the 15th-century Goldenes Dächl (golden roof). Reports this year: "Not quaint or charming but clean and comfortable." "A narrow winding staircase leads up to the reception where Madame's welcome was warm; another two floors up, our large, rather bare room had a small balcony overlooking the street." Some rooms are larger and better furnished than others; the food has been found "very good and copious" by some (notably the game in autumn), only adequate by others, who suggest the *Weisses Kreuz* down the street as an alternative. (*Angela and David Stewart, A Smith and others*)

Open All year. Restaurant closed Sun.
Rooms 10 double, 5 single – 3 with bath, 5 with shower, all with telephone and radio; TV on request.
Facilities Lift. 3 restaurants; conference facilities. Garden.
Location Central, in pedestrian zone. Hotel garage 3 mins' walk.
Credit cards All major cards accepted.

Terms B&B 390–500 Sch; dinner, B&B 510–620 Sch. Reduced rates and special meals for children.

Gasthof Weisses Rössl   *Tel* (0512) 583057
Kiebachgasse 8

An attractive, unassuming little hotel in the old part of town, owned and run by the enterprising Plank family; commended for comfort, charm, good breakfasts and dinners (Tyrolean dishes), fair prices. 14 rooms all with bath and/or shower. B&B single 550–740 Sch, double 880-1020 Sch. Set menus 70–155 Sch. [1989 rates] *New nomination. More reports please.*

KITZBÜHEL 6370 Tyrol   **Map 9**

Hotel Erika   *Tel* (05356) 4885
                                                    Fax (05356) 467413
                                                    Telex 51264

"The hiking and adventure-hotel *Erika*" (as its brochure calls it), where there's never a dull moment and you all join in the fun, might not seem quite our sort of place. It's a large red mansion with a modern annexe, beside a busy road junction at the edge of Kitzbühel. Last year a reader who had just completed her *forty-fifth* holiday there told us, "Uschi and Benedikt Schorer work hard to please. One wet and cold day they produced paints and sheets of glass and we were all put to painting on glass. On other days, Mrs Schorer would take us up the mountains, or inflict an adventurous bicycle ride on us, or Mr Schorer would take guests for a day on the golf course. At the start of each walk or other fiendish activity, we would all join hands in a circle, announce our name, profession, where we came from. Drinks are served in the large garden, and light classical concerts are held in the swimming pool area. Food is ample and enjoyable." An informative orange leaflet, with the programme for the day, is handed out at breakfast – e.g. "Good morning, dear *Erika*-guest! This afternoon at 5 pm we will do some ARCHERY! Tomorrow we will organise a funny ERIKA–BICYCLE–TOUR!"

This year two visitors, admittedly Club Med freaks, also, to their surprise, succumbed to *Erika*'s charms: "The deft professionalism, and the expert exploitation of Austrian charm, simply disarm criticism. The Schorers (their family have owned and run the *Erika* since 1920) are totally dedicated and delightful. The hotel may be no beauty outside, but inside it's been modernised most sprucely with charming trelliswork decor ('we've tried to avoid the usual Tyrolean clichés'); bedrooms, most with balcony, are all comfy and homely. In summer, 80 per cent of guests are English. Rucksacks, Elastoplast and yellow *Erika*-umbrellas are provided free of charge. We were awestruck by the overall good humour and its incredible value." (*JA and KA*)

Open All year except Nov, 15 Apr–15 May.
Rooms 36 double – all with bath, shower, telephone, radio; TV on request.
Facilities Hall, sitting rooms, bar. Indoor swimming pool, sauna, solarium and steam-bath. Garden with children's playground.
Location 3 mins' walk from town centre. Parking.
Restriction Not suitable for &.

Credit cards Amex, Diners, Visa.
Terms Dinner, B&B: 530–600 Sch in summer, 750–990 Sch in winter. Reduced rates and special meals for children.

Hahnenhof   *Tel* (05356) 2582

A converted 17th-century farmhouse, ten minutes' walk up from the town, set in its own informal garden amid fields: it is a genuine Tyrolean hotel in local style, decorated with knick-knacks and antiques, and run with warmth by the Sauritz family. Substantial, if uninspired, cooking. Closed Apr, May, Oct, Nov. 15 rooms, all with private facilities. B&B 330–650 Sch; half board 420–740 Sch [1989]. Recent nomination. More reports welcome.

LANS 6072 Tyrol   **Map 9**

Gasthof Zur Traube   *Tel* (05222) 77261 and 77406
Lans, Nr Innsbruck

In a pretty village above Innsbruck, with fine mountain views, Zur Traube is a typical Tyrolean inn with flowered balconies, run by the friendly Raitmayr family for 15 generations. The welcome, comfort and cooking are all admired. Closed 20 Oct–10 Nov. 24 rooms, all with bath and/or shower. B&B double 740–800 Sch. Set menus 130–180 Sch. No recent reports. More welcome.

LECH AM ARLBERG 6764 Vorarlberg   **Map 9**

Hotel Alexandra   *Tel* (05583) 2848
                              Telex 52550 ALEXA

Slightly cheaper than our other Lech entries, a very friendly family-run chalet-hotel beside fields and hills, furnished in local style, with excellent food (notably the weekly buffet of roast sucking-pig). Owner is also a ski-instructor. Closed May, Oct, Nov. 19 rooms, all with bath and/or shower. Half board 350–1,050 Sch [1989]. New nomination. More reports welcome.

Hotel Post   *Tel* (05583) 22060
                         Fax (05583) 220623
                       Telex 52677 PHOT

Here in one of Europe's finest ski resorts is a sophisticated hotel for summer or winter, run by three generations of the Moosbrugger family. Recent visitors loved it: "Lots of atmosphere, friendly reception, antiques and fresh flowers everywhere, food very tasty and nicely presented, charming bedrooms with a small sitting room in each." Others have agreed: "We have been coming here for 25 years. Nowhere else in the world have we met this mixture of perfection and the casual charm of a *pension de famille*. It would be worth staying here for the hotel itself, but it is also in the middle of the most delightful village and the centre of wonderful mountain walking." "Combines efficiency with the friendliness of a family operation. First-class food." (*Berneil Odell, Tim Hart*) More reports welcome.

Open 1 Dec–24 Apr, 24 June–1 Oct.
Rooms 12 suites, 21 double, 8 single – 35 with bath, 6 with shower, all with telephone, radio and T V; baby-listening on request. 2 suites in a chalet opposite.
Facilities Lift. Hall, bar, T V room, dining room, restaurant; conference facilities; children's playroom; indoor heated swimming pool, sauna, massage. Large grounds with landscaped gardens, meadows, café.
Location Central. Garage and parking.
Credit cards Amex, Visa (but only in restaurant).
Terms B&B double 1,150–2,300 Sch; dinner B&B 1,520–2,670 Sch. Set meals 220–420 Sch. In winter only reservations for 1 week or more accepted; Christmas and touring packages. Reduced rates for children; special meals on request.

Hotel-Gasthof Salome   *Tel* (05583) 23060
Oberlech   *Fax* (05583) 230640
       Telex 52588 SALHO

A 600-year-old farmhouse, renovated in Alpine style with wooden ceilings and carved beams, now a fairly expensive ski hotel, quite stylish in its cosy Tyrolean way. It is perched on the mountainside at Oberlech with fine views all round and a nursery slope in front (in winter it is probably best approached in daytime, as you have to drive up a narrow winding snow-covered road). A recent verdict, "Constant courtesy and cosiness, style and immense comfort. Our room had a veranda with breathtaking views. Food is out of this world." Others have written: "Seven of us, including three children, had a happy and comfortable week, with delicious food and a welcoming atmosphere"; "The pine cupboards, coloured rugs, ornaments and books made the hotel feel lived in. We got the nicest room we have ever had in a ski hotel." Guests also have a large and comfortable sitting room, a sun terrace, sauna, solarium and whirlpool. Some of the larger bedrooms are divided into sleeping and sitting areas and have a balcony. More reports welcome.

Open 2 Dec–22 Apr, 24 June–10 Sept approx.
Rooms 11 suites, 4 double, 1 single – all with bath, and/or shower, telephone, radio and T V.
Facilities Lift. Lounge, bar, residents' dining room; sun terrace. Garden with children's playground. Sauna, solarium, whirlpool, massage. Evening entertainments.
Location On the mountain above Lech; take road to Oberlech. Parking.
Credit cards None accepted.
Terms [1989 rates] Half board: winter 530–1,670 Sch; summer 530–740 Sch. Set lunch 180–290 Sch, dinner 280–490 Sch. Ski packages. Reduced rates for children sharing parents' room; special meals.

MAYRHOFEN 6290 Tyrol   **Map 9**

Hotel Elisabeth   *Tel* (05285) 2929
Einfahrt Mitte 432   *Telex* 534145

High-class *Gemütlichkeit* infuses this stylish holiday hotel in a skiing and climbing resort up the Zillertal valley, some way east of Innsbruck. "We spent Christmas here", says a reader this year, "and Elizabeth Thaler-Moigg made a special effort to create a family atmosphere, while her husband in my view is one of Austria's best chefs. A hotel of highest excellence in every respect – food, service, bedrooms, leisure facilities and fellow clientele." An earlier view: "A wonderful hotel, quite pricey but worth every penny. There's a night-club in the basement, and a fitness centre and indoor pool all beautifully maintained. The 'standard' bedrooms are as luxurious as the suites, while the open-plan public rooms are spacious." British package tours pour into Mayrhofen, but it's also a centre for Innsbruck University's international holiday courses, which engender much animation and folklore activity. (*David Ball*)

Open All year except 1 month in autumn and 1 month in spring.
Rooms 2 suites, 24 double, 10 single – all with bath and/or shower, telephone, radio, TV, mini-bar.
Facilities Lift. Hall, bar, 4 restaurants; conference room; indoor swimming pool, sauna, hot whirlpool, beauty farm. Dancing. Garden with terrace, children's playground.
Location In centre of village, 68 km E of Innsbruck.
Credit cards Diners, Visa.
Terms B&B: 1,050–1,295 Sch, suite 3,450–3,885 Sch; dinner, B&B: 1,150–1,395 Sch, suite 3,750–4,185 Sch. 50% reduction for children in parents' room; special meals.

MÖSERN BEI SEEFELD 6100 Tyrol   Map 9

Hotel Lärchenhof   *Tel* (05212) 8167

The anglophone Holzer family's quiet little chalet-style hotel, four miles south-west of the big resort of Seefeld, has panoramic views of the Inn valley and makes a good centre alike for skiing and summer walking. Recently modernised, it has a welcoming ambience; log fire in the lounge, chaises-longues on the terrace. Good breakfasts; good overall value. Light evening meals available. 24 rooms, all with bath or shower. B&B 210–340 Sch. Recent nomination. More reports please.

MUTTERS 6162 Tyrol   Map 9

Hotel Restaurant Muttererhof   *Tel* (05222) 587491
Nattererstrasse 20
Mutters, bei Innsbruck

Run by twin sisters, the neat flower-girt *Muttererhof* stands on the edge of a picturesque mountain village just south of Innsbruck, facing a "most breathtaking" landscape. It was liked again this year. "Excellent Tyrolean fare, with generous breakfasts (bacon and egg)", runs a recent report; "staff and management, especially Frau Stark-Egger, all very helpful and welcoming. Rooms are not luxurious: some are attractive, some a bit basic." "The hotel's best feature is the large well-heated swimming pool, with solarium and sauna. Decor and furniture of bedrooms is uninspiring, though ours had a balcony (many of them do not, and they face north, getting no sun). Beds were comfortable. The dining room was absolutely beautiful, panelled in dark wood with ecclesiastical-style carvings. Our appetite was well satisfied by the meal, and the *carte* contained Austrian specialities."

> Report forms (Freepost in UK) will be found at the end of the Guide.

Open 23 Dec–15 Apr, 10 May–20 Oct.
Rooms 1 suite, 18 double, 1 single – all with bath and/or shower and telephone; many with balcony.
Facilities Hall, bar, *Stube*, restaurant; functions room. Indoor swimming pool, sauna and solarium. Garden.
Location 6 km SSW of Innsbruck, S of Natters, E of Gotzens.
Restriction Not suitable for &.
Credit cards Access, Amex, Visa.
Terms B&B 300–450 Sch; half board 380–580 Sch; full board 500–640 Sch. Full alc 200–220 Sch. Reduced rates and special meals for children.

PÖRTSCHACH 9210 Carinthia   Map 9

Hotel Pörtschacherhof   *Tel* (04272) 2335

This is our only entry for the beautiful and famous Wörthersee, in Carinthia, and for the large, lively and prosperous resort of Pörtschach on its north shore, much frequented by Germans. Owned and run by the Koroschetz family, it is a big white traditional villa with modern annexes: "There is a large attractive garden with a small heated swimming pool, and a pleasant lounge. We had a room with bathroom and balcony, adequately furnished. The food is good and varied, the breakfast buffet generous, the waitress service quick and friendly. When we left a pair of slippers and a nightdress behind, they were promptly posted to our home address without our asking." Modern dining room rather dull, but there's an outdoor shaded terrace by the garden.

Open May–Oct.
Rooms 53 – 24 with bath, 22 with shower; most with telephone and balcony.
Facilities Lounge, salon, TV room, restaurant; terrace. Garden with swimming pool.
Location Close to lake; Pörtschach is 13 km W of Klagenfurt.
Credit cards None accepted.
Terms [1989 rates] B&B 440–650 Sch; dinner, B&B 500–710 Sch.

SALZBURG   Map 9

Hotel Elefant   *Tel* (0662) 843397
Sigmund-Haffnergasse 4,   *Telex* 632725 ELHOT
Salzburg 5020

This typical Salzburg town house, tall, narrow and medieval, has been an inn for 400 years. It stands conveniently in the city's historic heart, on a quiet street five minutes' walk from the opera house. The area is pedestrian: you can drive your car up to load or unload, but the police may ask questions. The hotel has recently been renovated, and this year and last readers have been mainly satisfied. Most bedrooms are said to be pleasant and comfortable, though some may be rather dull and functional. The renovated restaurant has been judged attractive, and its cooking reasonable if unremarkable. "We had a top-floor double room, quiet and pretty, not at all small, with a fine view of the cathedral. Helpful front desk, and delicious buffet breakfasts." "A delightful hotel and an interesting meal." One reader this year found the staff very helpful, apart from the lack of room service, but was less happy with his room and the main meals. (*Patrick Barclay, RAL Ogston, Liz and Tom Piatt*)

Open All year.
Rooms 1 suite, 26 double, 10 single – all with bath and/or shower, telephone, radio and TV. Ground-floor rooms.
Facilities Lift. Lounge, bar, TV room, breakfast room, dining room; conference facilities.
Location Central. Municipal parking 5 mins' walk away.
Credit cards All major cards accepted.
Terms [1989 rates] B&B 425–550 Sch; dinner, B&B 580–705 Sch. Reduced rates and special meals for children.

Pension Nonntal
Pfadfinderweg 6–8
Salzburg 5020

Tel (0662) 841427 and 846700
Fax (0662) 8467006

Otto and Anna Huemer run a small and homely *pension* with a pretty garden in quiet residential south-east Salzburg, with a spectacular view of the Hohensalzburg fortress, and only ten minutes' walk from the centre. Readers recently have written of the Huemers' kindness to their guests, of the "warm family atmosphere", and of comfortable rooms with antiques; and this year again most reports have been positive. "Our room was quiet and romantic, overlooking floral gardens, and Herr Otto was an outstanding host", write Americans. "A modest but excellent pension, with imaginative menus." "A warm welcome, and home-cooked Austrian dishes in a cosy restaurant." (*Kathy and Tony Gillett, Diane and Joel Morris, Miss L Hall*) But there have also been reports of instant coffee, of tinned fruit for dessert, and of some rooms shabby or with sloping beds. Rooms in the main building are judged better than those in the annexe. More reports please.

Open All year. Restaurant closed to non-residents.
Rooms 4 suites, 10 double, 4 single – all with bath and shower and telephone. 10 with TV. 8 rooms in annexe. 2 ground-floor rooms.
Facilities Salon/breakfast room, restaurant with bar; functions room. Garden with terrace and lawns. Bicycles available.
Location In SE suburbs. Leave *Autobahn* at Salzburg-Süd, take Friedensstrasse, Hellbrunnerstrasse, Hofhaymer-Allee, Nonntaler Hauptstrasse. Frequent buses to city centre. Free transport by hotel's bus from station or airport.
Credit cards Access, Amex, Visa.
Terms [1989 rates] B&B: single 580–700 Sch, double 850–1,100 Sch, suite 1,100–1,200 Sch. Dinner, B&B double 1,200–1,400 Sch. Set dinner 185–245 Sch; full alc 345 Sch. 3 day packages in winter; ski packages. Reduced rates and special meals for children.

Hotel Schloss Mönchstein
Mönchsberg Park 26
Salzburg 5020

Tel (0662) 848555
Fax (0662) 848559
Telex 632080 MOEHO

Once the guest-house of an archbishop, now an expensive hotel, this dun-coloured creeper-covered *Schloss* stands high on the Mönchsberg just above central Salzburg, but is easy of access: a lift service, running till 2 am, whisks you up in 30 seconds from the tourist hurly-burly below. A large and pleasant garden, antiques in the halls and dining room, spacious rooms, and breakfast on a flowery terrace, are among the assets – but oddly there is no lounge. One reader this year renewed former praise for the friendly service and the tranquillity. (*PC Walker*) Another called it "the star of the journey and worth every schilling". (*C and M*

Hedoin) But yet another thought the high prices excessive, and was very critical of the service in an "unwelcoming, spartan room". We'd be glad of further reports.

Open All year.
Rooms 9 suites, 8 double – all with bath and/or shower, telephone, radio, TV and mini-bar; baby-listening on request; 24-hour room service. Some ground-floor rooms.
Facilities Lift. Hall, bar, café, restaurant; chapel for weddings; terrace with café; weekly concerts. Large garden with tennis court.
Location Above Salzburg on Mönchsberg – hotel is signposted. 3 mins by car from city centre, 7 mins by the Mönchsberg lift. Parking and garages.
Credit cards All major cards accepted.
Terms B&B: single 1,400–1,800 Sch, double 2,200–4,600 Sch, suite 4,100–5,900 Sch. Dinner, B&B 500 Sch added per person. Set lunch 300–700 Sch, dinner 500–1,000 Sch; full alc 550 Sch. Reduced rates and special meals for children.

Hotel Zistelalm	*Tel* (0662) 20104
Auf dem Gaisberg,	*from Mar 1990* (0662) 641067
Salzburg 5026	

Situated 1,000 metres up on the Gaisberg just east of the city, this gemütlich *little chalet-style mountain* Gasthaus, *owned by the Hauser family, caters for skiers in winter, walkers in summer. Good food and beer, swimming pool in a meadow, rustic decor. Closed 21 Oct–21 Dec. 30 rooms, most with bath or shower. B&B double 730–970 Sch. Full alc 285 Sch. New nomination. More reports please.*

SCHLOSS ROSENAU 3924 Lower Austria   Map 9

Museumsverein Schloss	*Tel* (02822) 8221
Rosenau	

The village of Schloss Rosenau, not far from the Czech border, lies amid quiet rolling countryside, good for walking and cross-country skiing. The yellow-fronted Schloss from which it gets its name is now partly a remarkable 18th-century Masonic museum and partly a hotel – outwardly grand-looking but offering fairly simple accommodation. Readers paying a return winter visit liked it as much as ever, "Rooms simply furnished but nicely heated, restaurant first-rate, best in the region, with very good wines. Host most attentive, carried luggage to room himself. Heated pool, delightful walks, lots of cross-country skiing." "Owners very accommodating. Best calf's liver I have ever eaten." The extensive dinner menu offers food that is tasty, plentiful, fairly imaginative and good value. *Note*: the *Schloss* has close links with the *Pension Weissenhofer* next door, and guests who book may find themselves sleeping at the *Pension*, unless they specify. (*Prof. HC Robbins Landon, Mary Clark*)

Open All year except 22 Jan – 28 Feb.
Rooms 18 double – all with shower. Guests also accommodated in Pension Weissenhofer nearby.
Facilities Lift. TV room, dining room, 2 *Stüberl*; conference and banqueting rooms; sun terrace. Masonic museum and baroque church. Park with covered heated swimming pool, sauna, 2 tennis courts and miniature golf. Riding and fishing available.

Location 8 km SW of Zwettl.
Credit cards All major cards accepted.
Terms B&B: single 380–500 Sch, double 560–800 Sch; half board: single 470–590 Sch, double 740–980 Sch. Set lunch/dinner 90–140 Sch; full alc 300–400 Sch. Reduced rates and special meals for children.

SCHRUNS 6780 Vorarlberg   Map 9

Hotel Krone   *Tel* (05556) 2255

Close to the centre of Schruns, a pleasant little market town in the Montafon valley, is this small hotel, all wood panelling, chintzy curtains and cosy *Gemütlichkeit* – "a gem", says a visitor in 1989. The Mayer family have run it for four generations, and readers continue to respond to their hospitality. "Excellent room, food and service, nice furniture." "The Mayers maintain a keen interest in the running of their hotel and the behaviour of the staff reflects their simple kindness. Our meals were beautifully planned, delightfully cooked and served with great charm." (*BJ Walter*)

Open 20 Dec–16 Apr, end May–end Oct. Restaurant closed Thur.
Rooms 8 double, 1 single – all with bath and shower, telephone and radio; TV for hire.
Facilities Lounge, bar, 2 restaurants. Garden terrace; river frontage with trout fishing.
Location 12 km SE of Bludenz. Central, near the Kronen bridge. Parking.
Restriction Not suitable for &.
Credit cards None accepted.
Terms B&B 300–450 Sch; dinner, B&B 430–530 Sch. Set lunch 150 Sch, dinner 165 Sch. Reduced rates and special meals for children.

SEEHAM 5164 Salzburg   Map 9

Hotel Walkner   *Tel* (06217) 550

A friendly modern family-run hotel in a rural setting near a lake, amid fairly flat but attractive scenery only 20 kilometres due north of Salzburg, near Mattsee. Lovely gardens with pool, wide stone-flagged terrace with views, where meals are served when fine. Goodish Austrian food, with help-yourself salads. Airy bedrooms. Open 15 May–30 Sept. 20 rooms, most with private facilities. B&B 270–380 Sch; half board 350–460 Sch [1989]. Recent nomination, endorsed this year. More reports welcome.

STRASSEN 9920 East Tyrol   Map 9

Strasserwirt   *Tel* (04846) 63540
                                                         Telex 46643

This big chalet is a lively and attractive holiday hotel in a hamlet in an East Tyrolean mountain valley between Lienz and the Italian border. Friendly family owners, the Bürglers. Good traditional cooking, plenty of Gemütlichkeit and local character such as four-poster beds (modern), plus sauna, solarium and fitness room. Parties and excursions organised (horse-trekking, river rafting), with the accent on fun and local folklore. Closed Nov–10 Dec. 30 rooms, all with bath or shower. B&B double 640–920 Sch [1989 rates]. Meals from 200 Sch. Recent nomination. More reports welcome.

VIENNA **Map 9**

Hotel Amadeus *Tel* (0222) 638738
Wildpretmarkt 5, Vienna 1010 *Telex* 111102

Praise enough to make any Salieri jealous is heaped by readers on this *Amadeus*, a modern hotel in a small street near St Stephan's. "Charming and comfortable, with very helpful service"; "Flowers everywhere, fine prints on the walls, staff all very pleasant. The bedrooms and public rooms are decorated in red and white like the Austrian flag, the hotel is fully carpeted with rich red rugs; crystal chandeliers are scattered throughout." (*H and L Mathé-Dumaine*) An earlier visitor found the atmosphere "pure Maria Theresa and delightful". Another voiced delight about breakfast – "ambrosial coffee and a basket of newly baked rolls". But a visitor this year thought the coffee far from ambrosial.

Open All year except 23–27 Dec.
Rooms 18 double, 12 single – all with bath and/or shower, telephone and radio; 22 with TV.
Facilities Breakfast room.
Location Central, down a small turning off Tuchlauben.
Restriction Not suitable for &.
Credit cards All major cards accepted.
Terms B&B: single 890–1,370 Sch, double 1,540–1,760 Sch. Extra bed for child 170 Sch. (No restaurant.)

Hotel Kaiserin Elisabeth *Tel* (0222) 515260
Weihburggasse 3 *Fax* (0222) 515267
Vienna 1010 *Telex* 112422 ELIHO

Franz Liszt, Richard Wagner and others once stayed at this demure traditional hotel in an historic building down a side-street near St Stephan's cathedral. Rooms are quiet, clean and well furnished, and a second lift has just been installed. Readers remain pleased this year: "Friendly staff and wonderful breakfast, including porridge"; "Charming, efficient staff and a delightful room with wooden beds." (*Paul Palmer, and others*) No restaurant, but *Zum Drei Hussaren* just opposite is commended.

Open All year.
Rooms 3 suites, 50 double, 12 single – all with bath and/or shower, telephone, radio, TV and mini-bar.
Facilities 2 lifts. Lobby with bar, lounge.
Location Central, in pedestrian zone near cathedral. Parking arrangement with nearby garage.
Credit cards All major cards accepted.
Terms [1989 rates] B&B: single 800–1,150 Sch, double 1,050–1,700 Sch, suite 1,950 Sch. Extra bed 260 Sch. (No restaurant.)

We asked hotels to estimate their 1990 tariffs. About a quarter of the hotels on the Continent failed to reply, so the prices we quote should not be relied upon.

König von Ungarn   *Tel* (0222) 5265200
1 Schulerstrasse 10, Vienna 1010   *Telex* 116240

Kadar may be toppled from his throne, as his country lurches towards democracy: but this "King of Hungary" has continued in 1989 to rule potently over the affections of most of our reporters: "We enjoyed the glass-domed courtyard and our dinner was excellent"; "We had a lovely room and a nice meal." "A very romantic art-nouveau-decorated hotel in the heart of old Vienna. Excellent courteous service." *Und so weiter.* It's a finely restored 16th-century building close to St Stephan's Cathedral, its inner courtyard now an attractive lounge "where an inspired variety of cocktails is served". Everyone praises the "warm and helpful" staff, also the buffet breakfasts and the rooms (those at the back are quietest). "When you go through the fine bevelled-glass doors you have the feeling of entering an exclusive club." The elegant and fashionable restaurant, under separate ownership, has been judged excellent by some, but it is very expensive. One pleasant touch is that the hotel provides its guests with daily reports, in three languages, on places to visit and other suggestions for the day. (*Ruth H and Robert D Todd, Julia and Nigel Rhodes*)

Open All year.
Rooms 70 beds – 28 rooms with bath, 4 with shower, all with telephone.
Facilities Lift. Lounge, bar, TV room, children's room, restaurant (under separate ownership).
Location Central, near St Stephan's Cathedral. Parking.
Terms [1989 rates] B&B 825 Sch; half board 925 Sch.

Pension Nossek   *Tel* (0222) 5337041
Graben 17, Vienna 1010   *Telex* 113113

Established by his grandmother 80 years ago, Dr Renato Cremona's high-ceilinged old-world *pension* is very centrally situated in one of Vienna's most fashionable streets, now a pedestrian precinct – five minutes from the Opera, the Hofburg and the Riding School – and it occupies the top floors of a stately office building. "It charmed us because it successfully mixes the ancient and modern", was one of several favourable reports this year. Another was this, from a returning regular, "Atmosphere friendly with Herr Doktor very much in evidence; service and reception worked well; constant boiling-hot water; generous breakfasts." Others have praised the large, clean and airy bedrooms, efficient staff and good value for money. Renovation now seems to have reached nearly all rooms. But there was one complaint this year about lack of ventilation, and slow service at breakfast. (*Claudia Wood, Uli Lloyd Pack, Tom & Gillian Wadden*)

Open All year.
Rooms 3 suites, 21 double, 4 single – 17 with bath, 4 with shower, all with telephone.
Facilities Lift. Reading room, breakfast room.
Location Central, but quiet. Underground carpark 1 min's walk.
Restriction Not suitable for &.
Credit cards None accepted.
Terms B&B: single 300–770 Sch, double 850–900 Sch, suite 1,100 Sch. (No restaurant.)

> We are particularly keen to have reports on italicised entries.

Hotel Römischer Kaiser
Annagasse 16, Vienna 1010

Tel (0222) 5127751
Fax (0222) 512775113
Telex 113696

Very central but in a traffic-free road, just off the Kärntnerstrasse, and built in 1684 as the private palace of the Imperial Chancellor: today it is a small, very personal and fairly luxurious hotel, with period furnishings and plenty of chandeliers. Some disturbances at night from disco revellers, and the bells of the Annakirche ring from 6.15 am. 24 rooms, 23 with bath. B&B double 1,700–2,100 Sch. No restaurant, lots nearby. Recent nomination. More reports welcome.

Hotel Sacher
Philharmonikerstrasse 4
Vienna 1015

Tel (0222) 51456
Fax (0222) 51457-810
Telex 112520 SAHOT

Heaven knows what Hapsburg ghosts are hiding behind the red velvet drapes of this famous old Viennese institution, founded in 1876. Nowadays it has slipped out of the limelight, and it fell out of the Guide four years ago for want of feedback. But we've had two favourable reports this year – one from a reader who has made over 20 visits in as many years: "Family owned and run, its Grand Hotel atmosphere is mitigated by quite a personal touch. Maybe it trades too much on its role in past Viennese history, but it has now been modernised, i.e. the hall has air-conditioning in summer. The restaurant is a bit too self-consciously Viennese, but it is good – though the much-hyped Sachertorte is actually better in other pastry shops. Decor is traditional Austrian with many original paintings. One upstairs bit of the restaurant has zither music at times, played perhaps by a distinguished professional musician on his day off. The place is expensive, but one is not rooked. And the few single rooms that still exist without bathrooms, presumably former servants' rooms, are good value. I prefer the *Sacher* to the *Inter-Continentals* of this world." "Luxury, courtesy and a romantic atmosphere. We had dinner in the Red Salon, so evocative that I expected Crown Prince Rudolph to walk in at any moment." (*FM Steiner, M and D Chambers*)

Open All year.
Rooms 7 suites, 81 double, 37 single – 122 with bath and shower, all with telephone and TV; 3 with radio.
Facilities Lift. 2 bars, 2 restaurants, 2 cafés.
Location Central, near the Opera. Garage opposite.
Credit cards All major cards accepted.
Terms B&B: single 1,400–1,750 Sch, double 2,500–2,850 Sch, suite 8,100–8,600 Sch. Set lunch 550 Sch, dinner 650 Sch; full alc 590 Sch. Children under 6 free of charge.

Pension Suzanne
Walfischgasse 4,
Vienna 1010

Tel (0222) 5132507

This *pension* close to the Opera House has an entrance next to a sex-shop, but is admired for its pleasant Viennese furnishings (handsome beds and tables, fine mirrors, decent pictures). A recent report, "What a treat! You walk up a long flight of wide marble stairs and come to a tiny office. The staff are scatter-brained and disorganised, but sweet and helpful: typical North Americans, we shocked them with our request for ice, but they let us make our own in their kitchen. The rooms are clean: ours overlooked the street but was quiet (double-glazed). Excellent coffee for breakfast in a small crowded room." One couple this year told us that their bed had collapsed: but others have reported nothing but comfort and helpfulness. (*Jeanette King, Mrs Ann Dowson*)

Open All year.
Rooms 34 beds – 16 rooms with bath, 3 with shower, all with telephone.
Facilities Lift. Breakfast room.
Location Central, near Opera House.
Restriction Not suitable for &.
Credit cards None accepted.
Terms [1989 rates] B&B 365–430 Sch. (No restaurant.)

VILLACH 9500 Carinthia   Map 9

Romantik Hotel Post   *Tel* (042 22) 26101
Hauptplatz 26   *Telex* 45723

In a town on the old Vienna-Venice road, a former 16th-century palace which has been a hotel for 250 years (Empress Marie Thérèse stayed here). Bedrooms combine character with modern comforts; good breakfast buffet and meals, which you can eat in the garden. Friendly service. 77 rooms, all with bath and/or shower. B&B double 780–1,330 Sch. Set lunch 140 Sch; full alc 220 Sch. Re-nominated this year. More reports please.

WAGRAIN 5602 Salzburg   Map 9

Hotel-Gasthof Moawirt   *Tel* (06413) 8818
Schwaighof 123

Backed by forested hills, this spruce modern flower-bedecked chalet stands just outside Wagrain, an all-year resort south of Salzburg, just off the *Autobahn* to Villach. "Quiet, comfortable and spacious. We were the only guests and did not arrive till 8.15 pm, but they opened up the kitchen for us: splendid trout and wines." That report this year follows earlier ones: "Charming owners, the Maurers; a large spotless room with balcony, and good dinners and breakfasts." The attractive countryside is perfect for summer walking and winter skiing (a chair lift is opposite the hotel). (*ECM Begg*) Traffic can be audible from front rooms.

Open All year.
Rooms 23 double, 4 single – most with bath or shower, all with telephone, radio, TV and baby-listening; many with balcony.
Facilities Lift. Lounge/bar, TV room, breakfast room, dining room; folk music once a week. Sun terrace and garden. Bathing in private lake.
Location About 75 km S of Salzburg, just off Salzburg–Villach *Autobahn*.
Credit cards Access, Amex, Diners.
Terms [1989 rates] B&B 230–450 Sch; dinner, B&B 340–610 Sch. Reduced rates and special meals for children.

All inspections are carried out anonymously.

Belgium

DIE SWAENE, BRUGES

BRUGES   Map 3

Hotel Adornes   *Tel* (050) 34.13.36
St Annarei 26   *Fax* (050) 34.20.85
Bruges 8000

Warm praise again this year for this small B&B hotel, run by a pleasant young couple, in a 17th-century house close to the *Markt*. Some rooms overlook a canal: those facing the busy street are less quiet. "Despite the modern style, the hotel has retained some of its old character, with polished wood floors and exposed beams. Our comfortable room was bright and airy. Breakfast in an attractive flower-filled room." "Quite the best small hotel we have been to abroad. Breakfast was a welter of goodies of the utmost diversity, with a log fire burning on a hearthstone." (*A Sargent, Oliver Snow, and others*)

Open All year except 2 Jan–17 Feb.
Rooms 20 double (also let as single) – all with bath, shower, telephone, radio and TV. 2 on ground floor.
Facilities Lift, ramps. 2 lounges, breakfast room.

Location Central. Go from *Markt* to theatre; hotel is signposted. Parking.
Credit cards Access, Amex, Visa.
Terms [1989 rates] B&B: single 1,900–2,700 Bfrs, double 2,100–2,900 Bfrs. Winter package including museum tickets, free bicycle. Reduced rates for children. (No restaurant.)

Hotel Anselmus
Riddersstraat 15
Bruges 8000

Tel (050) 34.13.74

A small B&B in a quiet street near the central market. It is an attractive old Flemish-style gabled house with a massive wooden door, and takes its name from an eminent humanist of Bruges who lived here and was possibly a contemporary of Erasmus. The interior has been skilfully and beautifully converted into a comfortable little hotel, again appreciated in 1989 for its large, fairly simple but very clean rooms, good breakfasts and friendly and solicitous owners, the Dutoit-Schoores. (*David Rhodes, WR Gouger*)

Open All year.
Rooms 1 suite, 8 double, 1 single – all with bath and shower, telephone, radio and TV. 2 ground-floor rooms.
Facilities Hall, lounges, breakfast room.
Location 5 mins' walk from the market square. 1 garage; street parking.
Credit cards Access, Amex, Visa.
Terms B&B: single 2,000 Bfrs, double 2,300 Bfrs, suite 3,500 Bfrs (for 3 people 3,100 Bfrs, for 4 3,500 Bfrs). 1-night bookings sometimes refused. Reduced rates for children. (No restaurant.)

Hotel Bryghia
Oosterlingenplein 4, Bruges 8000

Tel (050) 33.80.59
Fax (050) 34.14.30

A former 15th-century merchant's house, facing a quiet square and canal. Pleasant family owners, well-furnished rooms, good buffet breakfasts below a beamed ceiling (no restaurant). 18 rooms, all with bath and shower. B&B double 2,600–2,950 Bfrs [1989]. New nomination. More reports welcome.

Hotel de Orangerie
Kartuizerinnenstraat 10
Bruges 8000

Tel (050) 34.16.49
Fax (050) 33.30.16
Telex 82443 ORANGE

In the heart of Bruges, beside the Dijver canal, this 16th-century house has recently been converted into an elegant small hotel, described as "excellent" this year. "A calm oasis with simple, spacious bedrooms, spotlessly clean; nice touches like fresh flowers and hair-drier. Smashing breakfasts and quiet lounge; staff pleasant and helpful." A charming bar with open fireplace and period furniture gives the impression of a private drawing room. In the summer breakfast and drinks are served on a terrace by the canal. (*Donald Hartog, Mary Lawson*)

The *Orangerie* now has an annexe, *De Tuilerieën*, opposite, with 25 bedrooms, indoor swimming pool, jacuzzi, sauna and solarium. It is slightly pricier.

Open All year.
Rooms 5 suites, 14 double – all with bath and shower, telephone, radio, TV, mini-bar and baby-listening. Some ground-floor rooms. 25 rooms in annexe, *De Tuilerieën* opposite.
Facilities Lift. Bar, TV room, breakfast room; conference facilities. Garden and canalside terrace. Swimming pool, jacuzzi, sauna, solarium in annexe.
Location Central, near Markt. Private parking 5 mins' walk.
Credit cards All major cards accepted.
Terms B&B: single 3,950 Bfrs, double 4,250–5,250 Bfrs, suite 5,950–6,950 Bfrs. (No restaurant.)

Die Swaene	*Tel* (050) 34.27.98
Steenhouwersdijk 1	*Fax* (050) 33.66.74
Bruges 8000	*Telex* 82446 SWAENE

Still a firm guide favourite, the "quietly elegant" *Swaene* is set in a 15th-century house on a canal, almost opposite the Belfry. As a B&B it has long been liked for its "comfortable family atmosphere", and now it has a restaurant too, specialising in fish. Reports this year and last: "First-class food in an elegant dining room. A pretty garden, comfortable bedroom with balcony, and charming service." "An excellent, friendly hotel. The food is good, but the dining room a bit small and airless. Breakfasts lavish. A splendid lounge, with a piano which guests can play. My only major criticism: the slipperiness of the bath which could be dangerous for the elderly." "The predominance of pink and our rose-decorated good-sized room made me think I was staying with a maiden aunt. The staff installed a baby-alarm from our room, so we did not need a baby-sitter." The lounge, with its open fire and fine painted ceiling, is the restored meeting room of the Guild of Taylors, dating from 1779, free coffee and tea are still served here every afternoon from two till four. (*S and K Murray-Sykes, Sir Patrick Reilly, Alan Rodger and Peter Macaulay, and others*) One reader on a package weekend break was given a distinctly inferior room.

Open All year. Restaurant closed Wed, and Thur midday.
Rooms 2 suites, 19 double, 3 single – all with bath and shower, telephone, radio, TV and baby-listening; 4 ground-floor rooms.
Facilities 2 lifts. Lobby, lounge, bar, breakfast room, restaurant. Terrace and garden.
Location Central (but quiet): signposts from the market square. Garage.
Credit cards All major cards accepted.
Terms B&B: single 3,000 Bfrs, double 3,650 Bfrs, suite 6,800–7,800 Bfrs. Set lunch 900 Bfrs, dinner 1,300 Bfrs; full alc 1,900 Bfrs. Special meals for children.

****
Traveller's tale *There were five waiters of various sorts, so desperately keen to serve you that I felt hideously conspicuous, and had to sneak my bottle out of the wine bucket in order to fill up my glass when no-one was looking, or I got a look of reproach.*
****

BRUGES Map 3

Hotel Ter Duinen *Tel* (050) 33.04.37
Langerei 52
Bruges 8000

A dedicated and very friendly young couple, the Bossu-Van Den Heuvel, run this inexpensive little canalside hotel, about 800 metres from the centre. Numerous readers have again extolled it in 1988/9 – notably for its lavish breakfasts, warm ambience and pleasant newly renovated rooms. "The owners are young, enthusiastic, very much in love with their hotel, and their love for their guests is enormous. The rooms are beautiful and cosy and the view is breathtaking. The breakfast is royal." "Baskets of flowers hang everywhere. Our attractively furnished room had a balcony with canal view. Best coffee I've tasted." "Beds the most comfortable we have ever slept in." "I took a party of seven very fussy German ladies, all pleasantly surprised." "The rooms are furnished with subtle printed fabrics and period furniture. We enjoyed moonlight over the canals at night from our two big windows." Some have found the rooms facing the canal noisy, others not. (*Chava and Amira Teomi, Mr and Mrs G Dove, E Allfrey-Pizer, Sara A Price, and many others*) A connoisseur from New England adds: "Belgian wcs are the best in Europe."

Open All year.
Rooms 18 – all with bath and/or shower, telephone and TV; baby-listening on request.
Facilities Lift. Lounge/bar with TV.
Location On canal 10–15 mins' walk from centre. Street parking in front of hotel; private garage available (100 Bfrs 1st night, 50 Bfrs thereafter). Windows double-glazed.
Restriction Not suitable for &.
Credit cards All major cards accepted.
Terms B&B: single 1,800–2,000 Bfrs, double 2,050–2,900 Bfrs. Reduced rates for children. (No restaurant.)

Hotel Wilgenhof *Tel* (050) 36 27 44
Polderstraat 151
Bruges 8310

For those who would prefer to stay just outside Bruges, here is a pleasantly converted farmhouse in the quiet polder two miles to the north-east. Bright, nicely decorated comfortable rooms with modern bathrooms; good breakfasts, served in the garden when fine. No other meals. 6 rooms, all with bath and shower. B&B: single 2,400 Bfrs, double 2,800–3,200 Bfrs. Recent nomination. More reports please.

BRUSSELS Map 3

Hôtel Agenda *Tel* (02) 539.00.31
6–8 rue de Florence *Fax* (02) 539.00.63
Brussels 1050 *Telex* 63947 AGENDA

Useful in an expensive city, a small modern medium-priced hotel just off the Avenue Louise. Bedrooms are spacious, comfortable and quiet. "Its charm lies also in the genuinely warm greeting. Our room had big windows, lots of cupboards, soft chairs, and a kitchenette. Breakfast was delicious, served in a small pretty room." There are no other public rooms, and no restaurant, but *Les Cadets de Gascogne* down the block is recommended. (*Andrew Semple*)

Open All year.
Rooms 2 suites, 23 double, 13 single – all with bath and shower, telephone, TV and kitchenette. 2 ground-floor rooms.
Facilities Lounge, breakfast room. Small garden.
Location Fairly central: in side street off Avenue Louise, 700 metres S of Place Louise. Garage.
Restriction Not suitable for &.
Credit cards All major cards accepted.
Terms B&B: single 2,725 Bfrs, double 3,250 Bfrs, suite 3,750 Bfrs. (No restaurant.)

Hôtel Amigo
Rue de l'Amigo 1–3
Brussels 1000

Tel (02) 511.59.10
Fax (02) 513.52.77
Telex 21618

"Still the best hotel in central Brussels" (a report this year), and the favourite choice of many visiting diplomats, Eurocrats and tourists, the *Amigo* occupies a prime site close to the Grand-Place. It's a large, spacious place of post-war design, still liked for its very swift service, good breakfasts, and quiet rooms (especially those at the back). But some find it too impersonal to be a true *amigo*, and there has been one complaint about shortage of hot water. Some rooms have a balcony. The restaurant is wholesome rather than enterprising, but there are many exciting eating-spots in the Grand-Place area. (*C and A Daintree, Toni Citroën*)

Open All year.
Rooms 11 suites, 157 double, 26 single – 173 with bath and shower, telephone, radio and TV; baby-listening on request. Some ground-floor rooms.
Facilities Lift, ramps. Salon, TV room, bar, restaurant; conference rooms and banqueting facilities.
Location Central, behind the Grand-Place. Garage.
Credit cards All major cards accepted.
Terms B&B: single 4,750–5,850 Bfrs, double 5,200–6,400 Bfrs, suite 8,400–20,100 Bfrs. Set meals 1,190 Bfrs; full alc 1,900 Bfrs. Children under 12 sharing parents' room free; special meals on request.

COUVIN 6400 Namur

Map 3

Au Petit Chef
6 Dessus la Ville

Tel (060) 34.41.75

A modern red-walled white-shuttered restaurant-with-rooms, decorated à la *House and Garden*, with patterned floral wallpaper, and some four-poster beds; the seven bedrooms have names such as Casanova and Romeo et Juliette; the cuisine is *nouvelle*, with dishes like foie gras with raspberry sauce. The hotel is just outside a small town down by the French border west of the Meuse, with an industrial estate on one side but open country on the other. "Our room was very pretty, with white furniture and a large bathroom under the eaves. Good breakfasts. Food enjoyable though not quite of *Michelin* rosette standard." More reports please.

Open All year except 15 Feb–10 Apr.
Rooms 7 double – all with bath and shower, telephone and TV.
Facilities Salon, bar, dining room. Terrace; large grounds.
Restrictions Not suitable for &. No children under 12.
Location On edge of town which is 44 km S of Charleroi.
Credit cards All major cards accepted.
Terms B&B: single 3,600 Bfrs, double 4,800 Bfrs. Dinner, B&B: single occupancy 5,500 Bfrs, double 8,500 Bfrs. Full alc 2,250 Bfrs. Reduced rates for children sharing parents' room; special meals.

CRUPET 5332 Namur   Map 3

Hôtel Les Ramiers   *Tel* (083) 69.90.70
1 rue Basse   *Fax* (083) 69.98.68

New to the Guide this year, a delectable little restaurant-with-rooms in a rural setting by a stream, on the edge of an out-of-the-way Ardennes village between Namur and Dinant. "Charming, flower-decked, with an outside terrace for drinks. Bedrooms are in the annexe, a functional building 15 minutes' walk away, but the room was satisfactory. The restaurant, small and elegant, bore accolades on its walls that seemed richly deserved – judging by my warm chicken liver salad with poached quail's egg. Breakfast was above average, too." (*Gault Millau toque* for such dishes as sweetbreads in port.) (*Bettye Chambers*)

Open All year except 2–19 Dec and 16–25 Mar. Closed Mon and Tue.
Rooms 6 double – all with bath and/or shower, radio and TV. Rooms are in annexe 800 metres from restaurant.
Facilities Lounge. 2 restaurants; terrace where lunch is served in fine weather.
Location Crupet is 20 km S of Namur, reached either from N47 or N49.
Restrictions Not suitable for &.
Credit cards All major cards accepted.
Terms B&B: single 1,650 Bfrs, double 2,050 Bfrs. Set lunch/dinner 1,700, 2,550 and 2,950 Bfrs (including drinks). Reduced rates and special meals for children.

DURBUY 5480 Luxembourg Belge   Map 3

Hostellerie le Sanglier des   *Tel* (086) 21.10.88
Ardennes   and 21.32.62
Rue Comte Théodule d'Ursel   *Fax* (086) 21.24.65
                                                       Telex 42240 SANDUR

Set amid lovely forests in the valley of the river Ourthe, Durbuy is a pretty little village, overcrowded in summer. Here three small hotels, the *Sanglier*, the *Cardinal* and the *Vieux Durbuy*, are under the same ownership (Maurice Caerdinael) and are run jointly, with the *Sanglier* serving as the restaurant for all three. Its sophisticated cooking is reputed (two *Gault Millau toques*) and this year a reader who had truite amoureuse and tournedos de biche thought it excellent but expensive. He liked his spacious bedroom, too. Others have liked the frogs' legs and sole poached in vermouth, and have admired the bedrooms in all three hotels, and the views of the river and medieval castle. "Nicely welcomed, we enjoyed our room with its pleasant fabrics; breakfast was a dream – except for the tea." (*Endorsed by Dr A John Robertson*)

Open All year except Jan. Restaurant closed Thur.
Rooms 11 suites, 34 double – all with bath and shower, telephone and TV. Suites have radio and kitchenette. Some ground-floor rooms.
Facilities 2 Lounges, TV room, 4 restaurants; banquet room, conference facilities; terrace. The *Cardinal* has a large garden.
Location 45 km S of Liège. Hotels are central; the *Cardinal* has private parking.
Credit cards All major cards accepted.
Terms Rooms 2,200–2,700 Bfrs, suite 3,500–4,500 Bfrs. Breakfast 275 Bfrs. Set meals 1,200–1,750 Bfrs; full alc 1,600 Bfrs. Reduced rates and special meals for children.

GENT 9000 East Flanders   Map 3

Hotel St Jorishof   *Tel* (091) 24.24.24
Botermarkt 2   *Fax* (091) 24.26.40
                                                Telex 12738 SJORIS

Belgium's fourth largest town is quite industrial, but it contains also a famous medieval quarter, where the splendid cathedral of St Bavon holds Van Eyck's masterpiece *The Adoration of the Mystic Lamb*. The *St Jorishof* (or *Cour St-Georges*), in the heart of the old town, dates from the 13th century – Charles V, Napoleon and other great figures stayed there – and it has maintained in fine order many of its original public rooms, including a spacious Gothic hall. Most recent visitors have found the food excellent and impressively served, and the staff competent and friendly: but one thought his dinner expensive and pretentious. The hotel itself is said to be spacious and clean: but some rooms, especially in the new annexe, can be small, simple and noise-afflicted, and one reader this year expressed concern about the state of fire precautions. More reports welcome.

Open All year except 3 weeks in July and 3 weeks over Christmas. Restaurant closed Sun and public holidays.
Rooms 5 suites/family rooms, 26 double, 6 single – all with bath and shower and telephone; 19 with TV. 26 in annexe across road.
Facilities Lift. Bar, 3 restaurants; conference facilities.
Location Central, opposite Town Hall. Garage and carpark.
Credit cards All major cards accepted.
Terms B&B: single 1,825–3,500 Bfrs, double 2,350–3,500 Bfrs, suite 3,500–5,000 Bfrs. Set lunch/dinner 1,050–1,500 Bfrs; full alc 1,800 Bfrs. Weekend breaks. Reduced rates and special meals for children.

HERBEUMONT 6803 Luxembourg Belge   Map 3

Hostellerie du Prieuré de   *Tel* (061) 41.14.17
  Conques
Route de Florenville 176

A stylishly converted 18th-century priory, long, low and white, surrounded by neat gardens, and standing by the banks of the river Semois in the heart of the Ardennes forests. Long lawns set with apple trees run down to the curving river. And most correspondents continue to find the hotel equally delectable: "Madame was pleasant and chatty, the owner is fatherly and friendly, and service is carried out by efficient country women. Furniture is either genuine rustic or good repro, and the beamed second floor rooms ooze atmosphere (bedrooms vary in size and style). I enjoyed the food tremendously – fantastic home-smoked salmon, hot lobster salad, sensitively cooked foie de veau, good cheeses. Public rooms are comfortable and smartly furnished with antiques, and a profusion of gorgeous old ornaments and lovely old paintings. We enjoyed our stay." Others likewise have praised the elegance, good cooking, and general professionalism. But we continue to get some criticisms – of poor housekeeping upstairs, or muddles over bookings. (*Ian and Francine Walsh, William A Grant*) The owners have built a new annexe, *La Résidence* with six suites.

Open 1 Mar–1 Jan. Restaurant closed Tue.
Rooms 6 suites with TV in annexe, 8 double, 3 single – all with bath, shower, telephone and radio.
Facilities 2 salons, bar, 2 restaurants. Garden; private fishing.
Location 3 km from Herbeumont, between Florenville and Bouillon.
Restriction Not suitable for &.
Credit cards All major cards accepted.
Terms B&B: single 2,700 Bfrs, double 3,200 Bfrs, suite 4,500 Bfrs. Set lunch 1,050 Bfrs, dinner 1,750–2,200 Bfrs; full alc 1,500 Bfrs. Half board rates (min 3 days). Reduced rates and special meals for children.

MAISSIN 6852 Luxembourg Belge   Map 3

Le Roly du Seigneur   *Tel* (061) 65.50.49
Av. du Roly du Seigneur

In an Ardennes village along the main Sedan-Liège road, an extremely friendly modern hotel. Large, clean, well-equipped rooms, some with balconies; excellent food, good breakfasts. Closed Jan, and Wed (except summer). 16 rooms, all with private facilities. Dinner, B&B double 2,800 Bfrs. Set meals 600–1,300 Bfrs. New nomination. More reports welcome.

MALMÉDY 4891 Liège   Map 3

Hostellerie Trôs Marets   *Tel* (080) 33.79.17
  et Résidence   *Fax* (080) 33.79.10
2 route des Trôs Marets

In lovely rolling wooded country north-east of Malmédy, near the German frontier, this sleek modern hostelry has a neat garden set amid thick trees. Readers this year have again spoken well of the bedrooms, the welcome, the peace and quiet, and the food – especially the "delightful" breakfasts that include Ardennes ham and home-made jam. "It's immaculate, elegant and comfortably welcoming. Well-furnished bedrooms with 16 TV channels – imagine watching *Popeye* in Italian on a Sunday morning, after a swim and walk in the forest. In the beautiful dining room we had very imaginative, light little courses – cubes of warm goose-liver, turbot lasagne, quail with wild mushrooms. The design of the public rooms is of the slightly heavy Belgian country style." One reader this year found the tall trees that surround the main building a bit oppressive: the annexe, *La Résidence* on a hillside close by, has better views and more feeling of space. (*TH Nash, John W Behle*)

Open All year except 15 Nov–23 Dec.
Rooms 4 suites, 7 double – all with bath and/or shower, telephone, radio and TV; baby-sitting. Suites in garden annexe.
Facilities Lounge/bar, restaurant; conference room; indoor swimming pool and solarium. Garden, terrace.
Location At Mont, 5 km NE of Malmédy on N28 to Eupen. Parking.
Restriction Not suitable for &.
Credit cards All major cards accepted.
Terms [1989 rates] B&B: single 2,850–3,100 Bfrs, double 4,100–6,200 Bfrs, suite 7,150–15,000 Bfrs. Set lunch/dinner 1,375–2,100 Bfrs; full alc 1,850 Bfrs.

NEERIJSE 3055 LEUVEN Map 3

Kasteel van Neerijse *Tel* (016) 47.28.50
Lindenhoflaan 1 *Fax* (016) 47.23.80
Telex 20519 CASTLE

Ten kilometres south-west of the university town of Leuven (Louvain), a red-brick 18th-century mansion newly converted into a four-star hotel, set in a lovely park, with a pond and old mill nearby. Extensive conference and function facilities. Golf, riding, tennis nearby. Pleasant staff, pretty bedrooms. 30 rooms, all with bath. B&B: single 3,000 Bfrs, double 3,500–3,800 Bfrs. Set menus 1,000 Bfrs. New nomination. More reports please.

NOIREFONTAINE 6831 Luxembourg Belge Map 3

Auberge du Moulin Hideux *Tel* (061) 46.70.15
Route de Dohan 1 *Fax* (061) 46.72.81
Telex 41989 HIDEUX

Along with one or two daring notes of criticism, the eulogies have continued to pour in for this famous and luxurious country hotel in the Ardennes, near the French border. "One of the best small hotels in Europe", "a wonderful experience, as usual", "one of our favourite hotels for the past six years", "to have breakfast on the terrace on a beautiful morning is probably the nearest we'll ever get to heaven" – a selection from this and last year's postbag, mostly from returning regulars. It's a big converted millhouse by a pond, secluded in a wooded valley, and is owned and run by Charles and Martine Lahire who are steeped in the traditions of good hotel-keeping. Not only do they provide very distinguished cooking, and bedrooms with superlative modern comforts, but they and their highly trained staff know exactly how to welcome and cosset their guests, and make them feel like well-remembered friends – "When we wrote to book a return visit after two years", says a reader this year, "the Lahires sent us a note to say that the family of owls that had nested outside our bedroom last time had all survived. After a wet and tiring drive, the warmth of welcome was a delight. We had a newly refurbished bedroom with padded armchairs and *en suite* a huge triangular bath of beige marble. The set menu as usual was superb (better value than the very pricey *carte*): the cooking is both visually pleasing and full of strong positive flavours – feathery mousses, salmon in a light creamy sauce, magret with fresh figs, etc. Breakfast, served in our room, is surely one of the best in Europe." (*Padi and John Howard; Marcia and*

Dominic Chambers, K and SM-S, JF Holman and others). However, the wine mark-ups are steep, and we note that while the *Moulin* keeps its two red *Gault Millau toques, Michelin* has this year downgraded it from two rosettes to one. One new visitor, while finding rooms and dinners superb, regretted that the set menu did not change over three nights. Another found the staff snooty; he was made to feel guilty, he told us, because he did not order champagne as an aperitif.

Open Mid-Mar–mid-Nov. Restaurant closed Wed Mar–July.
Rooms 3 suites, 10 double – all with bath (2 also with shower), telephone, radio and TV.
Facilities Sitting room, loggia, restaurant. Garden with tennis court.
Restriction Not suitable for &.
Credit cards All major cards accepted.
Terms B&B: single occupancy 4,800 Bfrs, double 5,200–5,500 Bfrs, suite 7,000 Bfrs. Set meals 1,900–2,200 Bfrs. Special meals for children on request.

DE PANNE 8470 West Flanders   Map 3

Hostellerie Le Fox   *Tel* (058) 41.28.55
Walckierstraat 2

In a popular coastal resort near Ostend, a family-run restaurant-with-rooms, reputed for its fish and good regional dishes (Michelin *rosette). Good, well-equipped rooms, recently modernised and extended. Closed October, 15–31 Jan, 1 week May, restaurant closed Tue. 15 rooms, all with bath and/or shower. B&B double 1,500–2,500 Bfrs. Meals alc 1,550–2,100 Bfrs [1989]. Some noise from main road. Endorsed this year. More reports welcome.*

RENINGE 8981 West Flanders   Map 3

't Convent   *Tel* (057) 40.07.71
Halve Reningestraat 1   *Fax* (057) 40.11.27

A short drive inland from either Ostend or Dunkerque, this idiosyncratic hotel "really a medieval barn in a field" has bedrooms ranging in style from Louis XVI to Provençal, some with four-poster beds. "Ours was small but beautiful, with wood panelling and velvet drapes", says a reader this year, "we were welcomed warmly, and food and service were brilliant during one of their 'gastronomic weekends' - seafood, foie gras, salmon mousse, pigeon, presented with style." (*Sandra E Garrick*) Others have written: "We had most unusual rooms, outrageously decorated but great fun. Ours looked on to a pasture with cows whose heavy breathing woke me in the night. The loft bar for drinks is charming, and the meal was a delight, served efficiently by shy young girls." "The meal was superb, especially in its visual appeal: our neighbours photographed each course as it arrived." "Some rooms are fairly small, but others are bigger and retain a convent flavour: canopied painted bed, stone floor, icons and other such medieval trinkets, and a bathroom like a private chapel with the basin in an arched alcove."

Open All year except Feb and last week of Aug. Restaurant closed Tue evening and Wed.

Rooms 7 double – all with bath, telephone. All in annexe 50 metres from restaurant. Some ground-floor rooms.
Facilities Bar, restaurant; conference facilities. Terrace.
Location On edge of village, 15 km NW of Ieper (turn off N65 at Oostvleteren).
Credit cards All major cards accepted.
Terms [1989 rates] Rooms: single 1,500 Bfrs, double 2,000–2,500 Bfrs. Breakfast 250 Bfrs. Alc 1,700–2,180 Bfrs (excluding wine).

RONSE 9681 East Flanders   Map 3

Hostellerie Shamrock	*Tel* (055) 21.55.29
Ommegangstraat 148	*Fax* (055) 215683
Maarkedal, Ronse	*Telex* 86165 SHAMRO

Just to the north-east of Ronse, a textile town between Brussels and Lille, amid rolling wooded country, is this smart and stylish restaurant-with-rooms that seems to be of mixed English and French inspiration (let alone its Irish name). Up a long drive in a well-kept garden, it has the air of a private house in mock-Tudor style, but the large and airy bedrooms are furnished à la Louis XV. It dropped out of the last Guide through lack of news, but visitors in 1989 thought it "one of the very best hotel/restaurants in Belgium" (*Michelin* gives it a rosette, and *Gault Millau* two red *toques*, for its modern French cooking). "A comfortable, welcoming and relaxed atmosphere, with expert and charming service. The rooms have recently been refurbished and are now brighter and lighter, with sumptuous bathrooms. The food we found better than ever." The main staircase with carved wooden balcony descends directly into the elegant dining room, giving residents the opportunity for spectacular entry. (*Pat and Jeremy Temple*) Wine prices have been called "fiendishly" high.

Open All year except 15–31 Jul. Closed Sun evening to Tue midday except public holidays.
Rooms 1 suite, 4 double – all with bath and shower, telephone and TV.
Facilities Salon, bar, restaurant; small conference room. Garden.
Location 5 km NE of Ronse, off N62, near Louise-Marie.
Restriction Not suitable for &.
Credit cards All major cards accepted.
Terms [1989 rates] B&B: double 4,200 Bfrs, suite 5,200 Bfrs. Set meals 1,500–2,700 Bfrs; full alc 1,700–2,700 Bfrs.

TILFF-SUR-OURTHE 4040 Liège   Map 3

| Hôtel du Casino | *Tel* (041) 88.10.15 |
| 3 place du Roi Albert | *Fax* (041) 88.33.16 |

In the winding valley of the Ourthe, just south of the Liège industrial conurbation, a restaurant-with-rooms nominated this year, "A charming, small family-run hotel with reasonable prices. The building, a former brasserie dating from 1622, has been lovingly restored by the owners, the Claes. Our good-sized room was tastefully decorated in French country style, with beamed ceiling, silk-covered walls, and windows overlooking the river. Our only complaint: the usual one of inadequate light for reading. The food was delicious – terrine of rabbit, lobster mousse, breast of wild pigeon. Breakfast, too, was excellent, including cheese and baked apples." (*John and Connie Partridge*)

Open All year except 15 Dec–15 Jan. Restaurant closed Mon.
Rooms 6 double – 5 with bath and shower, all with telephone.
Facilities Salon, bar, 2 restaurants.
Location 11 km S of Liège.
Restrictions Not suitable for &.
Credit cards None accepted.
Terms [1989 rates] B&B: single 1,400 Bfrs, double 1,900 Bfrs. Set lunch/dinner 1,750 Bfrs; full alc 2,000–2,500 Bfrs. Reduced rates for children; special meals on request.

Denmark

STEENSGAARD HERREGÅRDSPENSION, MILLINGE

COPENHAGEN Map 1

Hotel d'Angleterre	*Tel* 33.12.00.95
Kongens Nytorv 34, Copenhagen	*Fax* 33.12.11.18
1050	*Telex* 15877

"Recommending the *Hotel d'Angleterre* is a bit like urging travellers to discover the *Connaught* in Britain" a reader once wrote. It is the epitome of a grand hotel, and also something of a national institution, having first opened its doors in 1755. It is close to the harbour, the royal palace and the state theatre, and is at one end of the famous street, Strøget. It has a fine restaurant (speciality: canard à la presse), and a brasserie with the longest bar in Copenhagen. A reader this year, re-nominating the *d'Angleterre* (which was in earlier editions) writes, "To book in at 'the white lady of Copenhagen' you sit at an individual desk and are welcomed with that discreet but warm courtesy that is the hallmark of the service here. Imagine a room that has been furnished with a mixture of first class repro and genuine antiques, a large bathroom where all the fittings are luxurious antique reproductions (allied with a telephone) and you have the ultimate in comfort and efficiency. Scandinavian breakfast (do they eat the rest of the day?) arrived on a trolley delivered by a cross between Ursula Andress and Marilyn Monroe, who apologised for waking me up! The brasserie claims 'reasonable prices' but you won't get out for under £20 a head, and more with wine, though the food is good. The prices in the restaurant are astronomical – but compared with London, it is a bargain." (*Braham Murray*)

Open All year.
Rooms 28 suites, 81 double, 21 single – 127 with bath and shower, 3 with shower, all with telephone, radio, TV.
Facilities Lifts. Lobby, bar, 2 restaurants.
Location Central, opposite the Royal Theatre.
Credit cards Probably all major cards accepted.
Terms Room: single 1,600–1,800 Dkr, double 1,800–2,000 Dkr, suite 2,600–10,000 Dkr. Breakfast 90 Dkr.

Hotel Ascot	*Tel* 33.12.60.00
57 Studiestræde	*Fax* 33.14.60.40
Copenhagen 1554	*Telex* 15730

On quiet pleasant street close to Tivoli, the air terminal, railway station, and Strøget, Copenhagen's famous pedestrian area. 18th-century facade, old-fashioned beautiful red-carpeted winding stairway; contemporary colour schemes in bedrooms, some of which are small, others of which are in suites with kitchenette, terrace, sitting room. Attractive breakfast room, no restaurant. 10 suites, 55 double, 35 single, all with bath or shower. B&B: single 520–690 Dkr, double 690–1090 Dkr. In Guide previously, dropped when house-keeping standards were criticised, re-nominated after recent renovation. More reports please.

---

71 Nyhavn Hotel	*Tel* 33.11.85.85
Nyhavn 71, Copenhagen 1051	*Fax* 33.93.15.85
	Telex 27558 NYHHOT

Hans Christian Andersen lived next door to this converted early 19th-century warehouse on the *Nyhavn* (New Harbour) in the heart of the old city. Readers have enjoyed especially the "lively bustle" (though no traffic noise) and the adjacent canal with its mixture of restaurants and bars. The building was restored about 20 years ago as a smart hotel, with the sea motif much in evidence. Its *Pakhuskælderen* restaurant has an excellent reputation, with its smörgåsbord specially recommended. The cheapest bedrooms are very small (thick walls and low beams have obviously imposed restraints on room space); the dearer ones have a view over the canal. Staff are helpful and welcoming. A visitor this year writes, "A charming conversion with comfortable rooms, friendly service and a good breakfast. My only caveat would be that the double room I occupied at the maximum single person rate was on the small side for *two*, though nice for one. Otherwise highly recommended." (*Anthony Land*)

Open All year. Restaurant closed 24–26 Dec.
Rooms 6 suites, 39 double, 37 single – all with bath and/or shower, telephone, radio and TV; baby-listening on request.
Facilities Lift. Lounge, bar, restaurant; 2 conference/function rooms.

Location In town centre, near Royal Opera and Royal Castle, facing Nyhavn Canal and harbour. Parking for 8 cars.
Restriction Not suitable for ໄ.
Credit cards Probably all major cards accepted.
Terms B&B: single 825–1,125 Dkr, double 1,075–1,375 Dkr, suite 1,850–2,250 Dkr. Set lunch 170 Dkr, dinner 300 Dkr. Reduced rates 18 June–13 Aug; weekend reductions 1 Oct–30 Apr. Children under 12 sharing parents' room free; special meals on request.

Hotel Vestersøhus
Vestersøgade 58
Copenhagen 1601

Tel 01.11.38.70
Telex 15708

"First-rate; this is one of our favourite hotels, with modest but well-furnished rooms and extremely pleasant staff." "I had a spacious sixth-floor room with lobby, large bedroom overlooking the canal, and kitchen/dining area with balcony overlooking the other side – well equipped and clean. Good to be able to cook where dinner can be very expensive." The centre of the old town is within ten minutes' walk, and the nearest train station, with frequent trains to the suburbs and about half of Zeeland, is even closer. Breakfasts are praised (buffet style) and joggers will like the nearby paths along the Skt Jørgens Lake. The Vestersøgade has fast traffic during the day; not a problem with double-glazing in the winter, but rooms at the rear probably quieter during the summer (though they lack the view). (*Robert W Phillips, Mary E Hanson*) A room on the sixth floor is said to have low water pressure and irregular hot water.

Open All year.
Rooms 15 apartments, 37 double, 7 single – all with bath or shower, telephone; some with radio and TV; baby-sitting service.
Facilities Lift. Salon, breakfast room; roof garden.
Location 10 mins' walk from centre, on W edge of old town. Parking.
Credit cards All major cards accepted.
Terms [1989 rates] B&B single 750–850 Dkr, double 850–975 Dkr. (No restaurant.)

FALSLED 5642 Funen
Map 1

Falsled Kro
Tel 62.68.11.11
Telex 50404

Jean-Louis Lieffroy is a great French chef working in Denmark at a charming inn on the south-west coast of the central island of Funen. Readers of the Guide have been enjoying his restaurant and hotel for many years. "Utterly charming," begins a report this year, "the last word in luxury and our meal was superb (which it should have been, at the price)." Meals are taken seriously here: "langoustines in a cream sauce, monkfish au beurre blanc, moist breast of guinea-fowl". Breakfasts have been praised as well: "crème fraiche with honey, freshly squeezed orange juice, quails' eggs served on bacon and endless excellent coffee!" During the 15th century the hotel was a smugglers' inn; it is now a cluster of old thatched buildings round a small cobbled courtyard with a fountain. The "enchanting" bedrooms – some with Spanish floor tiles, and some with four-poster beds – are in outbuildings and cottages across the road. The garden runs down to the sea and the yacht harbour. Expensive, yes, but recommended nonetheless, "given the beauty of the hotel". Criticisms have been few: a small uncurtained window in a bedroom; a smell of stagnant water, possibly from the marina during one visit. More reports please.

Open All year except Jan, Feb, Christmas and New Year. Restaurant closed Mon in low season.
Rooms 3 suites, 9 double, 2 single – 12 with bath, 2 with shower, all with telephone and TV. Suites, with lounge and mini-bar are in *Ryttergården* farmhouse opposite the hotel. Some ground-floor rooms.
Facilities Lounge, salon with TV, bar, café, restaurant. Garden. Sea 100 metres.
Location 10 km NW of Millinge; S of Odense on Fåborg–Assens road.
Restriction Not suitable for &.
Credit cards All major cards accepted.
Terms [1989 rates] Rooms: single 630 Dkr, double 1,100 Dkr, suite 1,650 Dkr. Breakfast 105 Dkr. Set lunch 210 Dkr, dinner 250–630 Dkr. Special meals for children on request.

MILLINGE 5642 Funen   Map 1

Steensgaard Herregårdspension   *Tel* 62.61.94.90
Steensgård 4   *Fax* 62.61.78.61
Millinge, Fåborg

"Would appeal to those in search of the genuine country house atmosphere rather than a grand country house hotel", begins a report this year on the beautiful half-timbered 14th-century manor house on the middle island of Funen (Fyn), north-west of Fåborg. Many people consider the countryside here to be the prettiest in Denmark – an area of hills and fields dotted with long low farmhouses. The hotel is situated in one of three buildings round a cobbled courtyard; on one side is a working farm, on the other a tennis court and an enclosure with deer and wild boar. The rooms are furnished with many antiques – Louis XIV, Italian rococo and English.. There are several spacious lounges, a library lined with leather-bound volumes, and a grand hall decorated with hunting trophies. "A very beautiful place. The feeling of space and privacy abundant. We thought the food was good – wholesome and not too rich. It was nice for a change to have food simply presented." Dinner (three courses) is served in the candle-lit dining room promptly at 7 o'clock. (*JD Monteith; BJ Walter*) *Warning*: the stable clock chimes every half-hour throughout the night – "the wrong number of rings too!"

Open All year except Feb.
Rooms 3 suites, 10 double, 2 single – 13 with bath and/or shower, all with telephone and mini-bar. Some in annexe.
Facilities Hall, 5 salons, library, dining room; billiards, piano, chess. Large park with deer and wild boar; lake (fishing), tennis and riding. Rocky beach 2 km.
Location NW of Millinge, between Assens and Fåborg on the Middlefart road.
Restriction Not suitable for &.
Credit cards All major cards accepted.
Terms [1989 rates] Rooms: single 310–520 Dkr, double 510–950 Dkr. Breakfast 60 Dkr. Set lunch 135 Dkr, dinner 240 Dkr. Reduced rates for 3 or more nights; reduced rates for children.

We asked hotels to estimate their 1990 tariffs some time before publication so the rates given are often arbitrary. Please always check terms with hotels when making bookings.

NYBORG 5800 Funen   Map 1

Hotel Hesselet
Christianslundsvej 119

Tel 65.31.30.29
Fax 65.31.29.58
Telex 9297122

Low-built modern hotel thirty kilometres from Odense, with views of the sea to the east. "The architect has been strongly influenced by Japanese tradition, and it looked somewhat forbidding from outside. Inside, however, everything was lovely – helpful staff, good food, beautiful swimming pool, free bicycle hire – in fact everything 'laid on'." International/French cuisine. Hotel does substantial conference business. Closed 2 weeks Christmas/New Year. 46 rooms, all with bath and shower. Dinner, B&B 800–1,130 Dkr. New nomination. More reports please.

RIBE 6760 Jutland   Map 1

Hotel Dagmar
Torvet 1

Tel 75.42.00.33
Fax 75.42.36.52

Ribe, with its 800-year old cathedral, nesting storks and narrow cobbled streets, is an old town of great charm lying on the flat windy west coast of Jutland. The *Dagmar*, a hotel of great character, built in 1581, looks across the main square to the cathedral. The ground floor rooms are hung with splendid paintings, and filled with antique and repro furniture. Front bedrooms have tiny windows overlooking the church. Several readers have had rooms without a view, but have not minded: most have lovely paintings and are quiet. A visitor this year praised the "attentive staff" and "elegant food: we chose to eat in the more casual cellar restaurant and were surprised by the quality and quantity. Breakfast was 'serve yourself' and there was no way that you could go away hungry." Other readers have enjoyed the candle-lit restaurant and, in summer, the arrival of the night watchman "dressed in black, carrying a lantern and singing his watchman's song". Guests are invited to join him on his traditional nightly rounds. Mr. Petersen, the former owner, has sold the hotel this year but remains as manager. "No changes", we are assured. (*K and J Beal, and others*)

Open All year, except Christmas and New Year.
Rooms 50 double – all with bath and/or shower, telephone, radio, TV, and mini-bar.
Facilities Lounge, bar, 3 restaurants; conference facilities; music and dancing on Fri and Sat in July. Fishing 3 km.
Location Central; Ribe is 34 km SE of Esbjerg.
Restriction Not suitable for &.
Credit cards All major credit cards accepted.
Terms [1989 rates] B&B: single 450–550 Dkr, double 650–750 Dkr. Set menu 95 Dkr, full alc dinner 300 Dkr. Reduced rates and special meals for children.

Hotel Restaurant Weis Stue   *Tel* 75.42.07.00
Torvet

A tiny inn, also in the medieval town centre, and exuberantly nominated last year as a much cheaper alternative to the *Dagmar*: "Denmark is the best-kept holiday secret of Europe, Ribe of Denmark, and the *Weis Stue* of Ribe – the sort of place to enthral many Guide readers. As the *Blue Guide* states, it is perhaps the finest of Ribe's old buildings, and its early 18th-century interior contains some notable furniture. Our room, the Panel Room, is the showpiece, its two longer walls covered in magnificent medieval panelling; the windows, with tiny ancient panes, looked out onto the cathedral. The twin beds were comfortable. We managed to get into this room by bending low and almost crawling, with our heads bowed beneath innumerable beams (if you were Falstaff, they would hoist you in through the window). There is no lounge, but three dining rooms each stuffed with antiques, plus a courtyard and banqueting hall. The food was superb, our best meal in Denmark, though breakfast was modest by Danish standards. Service was efficient, but a little impersonal." (*Rev. Michael Bourdeaux*) The manager tells us that personal service can now be guaranteed, as the owners themselves take part in the serving of guests.

Open All year except 24/25 Dec.
Rooms 4 double, 1 single.
Facilities Restaurant, banqueting hall; small courtyard. 200 metres from river.
Location Central, in old town.
Restriction Not suitable for &.
Credit cards None accepted.
Terms Rooms: single 150 Dkr, double 300 Dkr. Full alc 180–200 Dkr. Extra bed for child 75 Dkr; special meals.

SØNDERHO 6720 Fanø   **Map 1**

Sønderho Kro   *Tel* 75.16.40.09
Kropladsen 11

"Certainly the most exciting thing on the island of Fanø, which is really only a long sand dune", writes a reader this year. The inn is at one end, in the picturesque old fishing village of Sønderho; it is one of the oldest inns in Denmark, dating from 1772. It has been owned by the same family for three generations (Olga and Erik Jensen until recently, now their daughter and son-in-law Birgit and Niels Steen Sørensen). Modern comforts have not been overlooked – there is a new extension where the bedrooms are large and very comfortable. The entrance hall has an open fireplace with a roaring fire in cold weather; antiques and modern paintings abound. "My husband was most taken with the waitresses, all blond bombshells, very helpful and friendly, and spoke good English. The food was delicious and the service fast and efficient. The puddings were decorated imaginatively with all manner of exotic fruits, most of which I couldn't name. Breakfasts, too, were superb, with an excellent selection of home-made jam." The innkeepers have written to us this year to say: "Our cooking is 100% *ecological* (without poison). It is Danish, natural, with French influence, and local produce if possible." (*JD Monteith*)

Open All year except 8 Jan–10 Feb. Possibly closed Christmas.
Rooms 7 double – all with bath and/or shower. 5 ground-floor rooms.
Facilities Hall, salons, restaurant. Garden. By sea with sandy beach and safe bathing; golf and tennis nearby.
Location 20 mins by ferry from Esbjerg. In SE part of Sønderho, on left by church.
Credit cards Access, Diners, Visa.
Terms B&B: single 450–570 Dkr, double 610–850 Dkr. Set lunch 125 Dkr, dinner 270 Dkr, full alc 338 Dkr. Half- or full-board only certain times of year. Reduced rates for children; special meals.

France

HÔTEL - RESTAURANT
GEORGES BLANC, VONNAS

AIRE-SUR-LA-LYS 62120 Pas-de-Calais Map 3

Hostellerie des Trois *Tel* 21.39.01.11
  Mousquetaires *Fax* 21.39.50.10
Château du Fort de la Redoute

The Venet family run a very popular *hostellerie* where you need to book. It's a small late 19th-century château in a garden beside a pond, 40 miles from Calais and with easy access to the motorway. And therefore it gets *very* full of the British – to the detriment of its French ambience, some readers feel. This, and the often slow service, have been the main criticisms this year, but otherwise there's been little but praise, especially for the rooms in the new wing. "Very charming atmosphere, the family are most welcoming", say returning regulars in 1989; "breakfast was good, the large lounge bar is attractively furnished, and the new wing has been built with great taste" (one of the rooms is "furnished in the Japanese style with maize-coloured grass wallpaper and antiques"). Another new report, "Service before dinner was a bit chaotic, but we then enjoyed our truite aux baies sauvages, jugged pork and the farandole of desserts". A reader who stayed on till lunch the next day found that all his fellow-countrymen had gone – "We were now surrounded by French families enjoying a relaxed Sunday lunch. It was one of the best meals we've ever had in France, complemented by charming waitresses." (*NA and JM Rhodes, Philippa Herbert, Kay and Neville Varley*)

Open 20 Jan–20 Dec. Closed Sun evening, and Mon.
Rooms 1 suite, 26 double – all with bath and/or shower and telephone; 24 with TV. 3 in pavilion in park.
Facilities 2 salons, bar, TV room, garden room in summer, 2 restaurants. 1-acre grounds.
Location On N43 between St-Omer and Lillers, 2 km from centre of Aire on Arras side. Private parking.
Restriction Not suitable for &.
Credit cards All major cards accepted.
Terms [1989 rates] Rooms 200–400 frs. Breakfast 35 frs. Set lunch/dinner 79, 122, 184 and 264 frs; full alc 280 frs. Reduced rates and special meals for children.

AIX-EN-PROVENCE 13100 Bouches-du-Rhône   Map 5

Hôtel "Le Mozart"   *Tel* 42.21.62.86
49 cours Gambetta

A modern and cleverly designed hotel, inexpensive, spacious and quiet, on a boulevard less than a kilometre from the city centre. Comfortable bedrooms – most have a balcony with views; dull breakfast room. Garage. 48 rooms, all with bath and/or shower. B&B double 264–284 frs. No restaurant, but lots nearby. Recent nomination. More reports welcome.

AJACCIO 20000 Corsica   Map 5

Eden Roc   *Tel* 95.52.01.47
Route des Sanguinaires   *Telex* 460486

This fairly smart family-run hotel above the sea, beside the coast road west of Ajaccio, has been much admired again this year: "A delightful choice for our two weeks' holiday. The hotel is set into the hillside, and from our balcony (all rooms face seaward) there's a magnificent view of the varying shades of blue of the bay. Meals (food was excellent) are taken on a beautiful terrace above a lovely garden in which is a swimming pool. Staff were all most courteous and helpful, and the ambience is totally relaxed, and breakfast included marvellous coffee. Rooms are air-conditioned. Just across the quiet road is a small sandy rock-girt cove from which one can swim in the clear, clean blue water." (*Diane and Keith Moss*) A fitness centre has just been completed.

Open May–Sept.
Rooms 40 – most with bath and/or shower, telephone and TV; many with balcony.
Facilities Lift. Lounge, restaurant, terrace. Garden with swimming pool.
Location 8 km W of Ajaccio. Parking.
Credit cards All major cards accepted.
Terms [1989 rates] Rooms 720–920 frs. Breakfast 60 frs. Half board 620–750 frs per person. Set meals 200–480 frs. Special meals for children.

ALBERTVILLE 73200 Savoie · Map 4

Hôtel Million
8 place de la Liberté

Tel 79.32.25.15
Telex 306022 HOTMILLION

This dullish sub-alpine town will be hosting the 1992 Winter Olympics. Just off its main street is this sophisticated hostelry, where Philippe Million's "original cooking in the modern style" (e.g. lake fish with snails) is rated among the finest in Savoy (two *Michelin* rosettes, two red *Gault Millau toques*). Our latest reports consider the bedrooms adequate if unexciting, the waiters friendly, and the fixed price meals "magnificent and extremely good value". An earlier view, "Traditional atmosphere with modern comforts. Rooms not very large but pleasantly decorated: most are in a modern extension behind the building. There is a comfortable lounge and bar. Plentiful breakfasts, and a good wine list with delicious local Savoy wines at low prices." The savoury pastries, sweets and chocolates are especially praised. In summer you can dine in elegance on a flowery terrace facing the small and pretty garden. Around the hotel, alas, are new apartment blocks, obscuring the outlook. But 20 minutes' walk up the hill is the medieval walled hill-village of Conflans, where the views are superb." (*Dave Watts*)

Open All year except 24 Apr–8 May, 18 Sept–2 Oct. Restaurant closed Sun evening and Mon.
Rooms 26 double, 2 single – 27 with bath and/or shower, all with telephone and 26 with TV.
Facilities Lift. 3 lounges, bar, breakfast room, dining room. Small garden, terrace for dining.
Location Central. Parking. Albertville is 45 km SE of Annecy.
Credit cards All major cards accepted.
Terms Rooms: single 200–350 frs, double 280–550 frs. Breakfast 50 frs. Set lunch/dinner 150, 250 and 450 frs. Special meals for children.

ALBI 81000 Tarn · Map 4

Hostellerie Saint-Antoine
17 rue St-Antoine

Tel 63.54.04.04
Telex 520850

A former monastery in the town centre where the Rieux family have run an inn since 1734. An inspector this year "liked the feel of the place" and enjoyed the food. Other recent views: "Not long ago the fine 18th-century building was pulled down and a characterless new one put up. But much old furniture remains, and spaciousness; also a garden at the back with big trees; and total silence, despite its being a stone's throw from the centre. Good food indeed." "A little impersonal, but it provides elegance and comfort. In the pleasant dining room, food expensive but adequate" (*Gault Millau* red *toque* however for its "modern regional cooking"). Bedrooms have been found "charmingly pretty". It is advisable to ask for garden-facing rooms.

Open All year. Restaurant closed Sun Nov–Mar.
Rooms 6 suites, 34 double, 10 single – all with bath and shower, telephone, TV and tea-making facilities. 4 in annexe.
Facilities Lift. 3 lounges, bar with TV, restaurant. Garden. Guests have access to swimming pool and tennis court at *La Réserve* (under same management) 3 km away.
Location Central. Parking.
Credit cards All major cards accepted.

Terms B&B: single 350–500 frs, double 490–750 frs, suite 850–950 frs. Set lunch/dinner 140–200 frs; full alc 220 frs. Reduced rates and special meals for children.

St-Clair   *Tel* 63.54.25.66
Rue St-Clair   *Telex* 521605

In the pedestrian quarter of the old town, near the cathedral, here is a cheaper but still comfortable alternative to our other Albi entry. Most rooms face a courtyard and are quiet. No bar or lounge, but adequate breakfasts, including some fresh fruit. Open Easter–Oct. 12 rooms, all with bath and shower. B&B double 240–290 frs. No restaurant, lots nearby.

LES ANDELYS 27700 Eure   Map 3

Hôtel de la Chaîne d'Or   *Tel* 32.54.00.31
27 rue Grande

This 18th-century *auberge* had an entry in earlier editions, now, after a change of ownership it is welcomed back. It enjoys a spectacular position on a loop of the Seine above Rouen; most of the bedrooms, the dining room and the breakfast room overlook the shimmering river and the island opposite. At night it is quiet save for passing barges but they don't operate very late. Bedrooms are large; most are freshly decorated and well furnished; bathrooms are not their strongest point and an inspector reports a dowdy and poorly lit back room and a casual reception "but dinner was a very different matter: a beautiful beamed dining room, tables well spaced with fresh flowers and candle, exemplary service, not slow, not rushed, not standoffish, not fulsome, and the 200 franc menu [1989], with exciting new tastes, could not be faulted." The old part of Les Andelys is a pictureque village, dominated by the ruins of Richard Coeur de Lion's Château Gaillard; it is only 15 minutes by car from Giverny, with Monet's lovely garden. (*Gillian Seel, PA Catling, and others*)

Open 2 Feb–31 Dec. Closed Sun evening and Mon.
Rooms 11 double, 1 single – 5 with bath, 2 with shower, all with telephone.
Facilities Dining room, breakfast room, functions room. Courtyard.
Location In Petit Andelys, on the river. Parking. (Village is 39 km SE of Rouen).
Restriction Not suitable for &.
Credit card Visa.
Terms [1989 rates] Rooms: single 240 frs, double 390 frs. Breakfast 45 frs. Set meals 130, 200 and 320 frs.

ANTIBES 06600 Alpes-Maritimes   -   Map 5

Mas Djoliba   *Tel* 93.34.02.48
29 avenue de Provence   *Telex* 461686

In a quiet street in the southern suburbs, near the beach, a villa hotel in a lovely garden, with a little of the air of a private house, but not smart. Simple, pretty bedrooms. Meals served in a vine-arbour when fine. Swimming pool. 15 rooms, 14 with bath and/or shower. Dinner, B&B double 510–630 frs. New owners this year, "friendly and charming". More reports welcome.

ARDRES 62610 Pas-de-Calais   Map 3

Grand Hôtel Clément   *Tel* 21.82.25.25
91 esplanade du Maréchal Leclerc   *Telex* 130886 RES CLEMENT

On the edge of a small town near Calais, a family-run hotel much frequented by the British. Garden with swings, log fire in bar in winter. Beautiful well-known restaurant, with nouvelle-ish *cooking (Gault Millau* red *toque) done by the son of the house, François Coolen. Some bedrooms are attractive, but many others tend to be sub-standard: small, dingy, fusty, unkempt. Closed 15 Jan–15 Feb and Mon. 17 rooms, 16 with bath and/or shower. B&B double 244–344 frs. Set meals 100–300 frs. Continued 1988/9 criticism of bedrooms, but restaurant again admired by readers. Back rooms are quietest.*

ARLES 13200 Bouches-du-Rhône   Map 5

Hôtel d'Arlatan   *Tel* 90.93.56.66
26 rue du Sauvage   *Telex* 441203 ARLATAN

Located down a quiet street in the heart of old Arles, this lovely 15th-century building (with later additions) was the ancestral home of the Counts of Arlatan, and its pleasant little garden is enclosed on one side by the high wall of the palace of Constantine. "The best place to stay in Arles", says one recent visitor. "It has a Proustian discretion to it, as rooms open out of each other into shady courtyards." "You enter through a fine courtyard with palm trees and an interesting stone fountain. The public areas and bedrooms carry out the theme of old Provence, with antiques, colourful print fabrics and art objects." This ever-popular hotel is owned by the "warm and helpful" M. Desjardin, "quite a character", and run by his family. Its vaunted charms may have pitched expectations too high, for again in 1988/9 reports have varied. Most readers have stressed the friendly staff, good breakfasts and pleasant rooms, but one thought breakfast too basic and the staff impersonal, while some others have found their rooms a little too small and basic. (*PJ Borrett, Shelley B Andrews, JA*) No restaurant, but try the *Vaccarès* or excellent *L'Olivier*, both upper-medium-priced.

Open All year.
Rooms 7 suites, 32 double, 5 single – all with bath and/or shower and telephone; 36 with mini-bar, suites with TV.
Facilities Lift. Bar, reading room, salons; conference room. Garden with patio for outdoor refreshments.
Location Central, near place du Forum, but quiet (rooms overlook garden and patio). Garage parking (with a charge).
Restriction Not suitable for &.
Credit cards All major cards accepted.
Terms Rooms: single 298–385 frs, double 385–598 frs, suite 850 frs. Breakfast 40 frs. (No restaurant.)

Hôtel Le Calendal   *Tel* 90.96.11.89
22 place Pomme

Mistral's epic poem about fishermen has given its name to this modest but pleasant little B&B hotel near the Roman theatre and arena. Rooms simply but well furnished; lovely shady garden where drinks and breakfast are served. Closed 15 Nov–31 Jan. 27 rooms, all with bath and shower. Rooms 150–270 frs. Breakfast 26 frs. Hostellerie des Arènes *and* Le Grillon *are good inexpensive restaurants nearby. Recent nomination endorsed this year. More reports please.*

ARNAY-LE-DUC 21230 Côte-d'Or   Map 4

Chez Camille   *Tel* 80.90.01.38
1 place Edouard-Herriot

Fondue of snails with Brussels sprouts, and cream of frogs' legs with Japanese pearls (but these dishes do sound more convincing in French) are just two of the delights that have won owner-chef Armand Poinsot a *Michelin* rosette and two *Gault Millau toques.* His converted 16th-century posthouse in a small Burgundy town, now a *soigné* little hotel, was commended again in 1989 for its comfortable rooms, good food and charming Madame, thus endorsing last year's report, "Our room was furnished with antiques and it was rather like staying in a friend's house. The restaurant is pretty, in a glassed courtyard, where one has full view of the kitchen – almost a distraction from the food, which was excellent light Burgundian. Madame presides over a fleet of well-trained young waitresses." Outdoor summer dining under parasols or by torchlight. Vegetarians well catered for. (*Tony and Harriet Jones, Stanley Burnton*)

Open All year except Christmas Eve.
Rooms 3 suites, 11 double – all with bath, telephone, TV and baby-listening. 3 doubles in house 6 km away.
Facilities 2 lounges, dining-room; sauna.
Location Central. Town is on N6, 28 km SE of Saulieu.
Restriction Not suitable for &.
Credit cards All major cards accepted.
Terms [1989 rates] Rooms: double 385 frs, suite 550–750 frs. Breakfast 45 frs. Dinner, B&B 470 frs per person. Set lunch/dinner 160 frs. Special meals for children.

ARPAILLARGUES 30700 Gard   Map 5

Hôtel d'Agoult, Château   *Tel* 66.22.14.48
    d'Arpaillargues   *Telex* 490415
Arpaillargues, Uzès

Three miles west of fascinating Uzès (q.v.), on the edge of the village of Arpaillargues, stands this 18th-century château, formerly the home of the d'Agoult family (Marie d'Agoult was a mistress of Liszt). It is now a stylish country hotel, beautifully modernised and maintained, with a library, park, and views over the rolling hills. "Luxurious and restful", runs a report this year; "the pool and tennis facilities were excellent, the dining in the garden delightful and the service friendly." Another visitor enjoyed breakfast in the privacy of his balcony, and the lunchtime restaurant by the pool, but thought the cooking "too adventurous for the chef's abilities" (the French guides do not rave either). "A finely furnished room, more like a suite, and a perfect dinner that included terrine de rascasse and magret de canard." (*Anna Steiger, Dave Watts, Denis Tate*)

Open 15 Mar–2 Nov. Restaurant closed Wed in low season.
Rooms 25 – all with bath or shower and telephone.
Facilities Salon, library, restaurant; conference facilities; courtyard. Large grounds with tennis courts and swimming pool.
Location 4.5 km W of Uzès.
Credit cards All major cards accepted.
Terms [1989 rates] Rooms 420–690 frs. Breakfast 45 frs. Half board 415–680 frs per person. Set lunch/dinner 185 frs. Special meals for children.

ARRAS 62000 Pas-de-Calais   Map 3

Hôtel Univers   *Tel* 21.71.34.01
3 place Croix-Rouge

A finely restored 18th-century monastery, down a cobbled road off a main shopping-street. All rooms, newly refurbished (some have four-posters), look onto the central cloister. Walls are thin, but food and service are excellent. 36 rooms, all with bath or shower, 285–335 frs. Breakfast 32 frs. Set menus 88–205 frs [1989]. Re-nominated. More reports please.

AUVILLERS-LES-FORGES 08260 Ardennes   Map 3

Hostellerie Lenoir   *Tel* 24.54.30.11

Jean Lenoir's comfortable restaurant-with-rooms, in a village near the Belgian frontier, is reputed to be one of the best in the Ardennes, but expensive (*Michelin* rosette, two *Gault Millau toques*, for such dishes as mousse of pigeon with foie gras). It used to be a modest café run by M. Lenoir's parents, in the pre-war days when he was born in a room above the bar. Now it has some pretensions – as our nominator reports, "Each course is accompanied by a different bunch of flowers, varying with the colour of your car: ours was a red Mercedes, so we were welcomed by red roses, served on a silver tray. It's a charming little hotel, with attentive service, nice decor, and a fountain next door. The elegant and cosy dining room is lined with diplomas" (M. Lenoir is a member of the Order of the Dynasty of Hong Kong, *inter multa alia*). Another visitor this year found it "quiet and exquisitely furnished", and the food "expensive but very good". (*Dr Christine Herxheimer and Gabriele Berneck, EM Jacob*)

Open 1 Mar–1 Jan. Closed 24 Dec evening, and Fri except public holidays.
Rooms 21 – 12 with bath, 6 with shower, all with telephone, 18 with radio, 3 with TV; baby-listening on request. All rooms in building across terrace from restaurant; some on ground-floor.
Facilities Lift. 2 Lounges, bar, 2 dining rooms; functions room. Terrace, garden.
Location 14 km SW of Rocroi, on D 877 to Laon.
Credit cards All major cards accepted.
Terms [1989 rates] B&B: single 173 frs, double 201–325 frs, suite 421 frs; dinner, B&B 265–400 frs per person. Set lunch/dinner 150–390 frs. Reduced rates and special meals for children on request.

In all continental European and Scandinavian countries except Denmark, France, Hungary, Malta, Spain and Turkey, the dialling codes begin with a 0. Omit this when dialling from outside the country in question. Spanish codes begin with a 9, which should also be omitted.

AUXERRE 89000 Yonne   Map 4

Le Parc des Maréchaux   *Tel* 86.51.43.77
6 avenue Foch   *Telex* 800997

"An attractive little place, staffed by people who seem to enjoy working in a hotel", runs a 1989 report on what an inspector has called "this idiosyncratic little bed-and-breakfast hotel", in a quiet street of a dignified cathedral city. "It is run in an appealing and very personal way by its *patronne*, Espérance Hervé, a doctor's wife. The genteel 1856 mansion is set in its own big garden amid lovely and unusual trees. This was formerly known as the Parc des Maréchaux, so the comfortable bedrooms are now all named after French marshals such as Lyautey (but not Pétain). The American bar, all plush red velvet, is called L'Araucaria, after the 100-year-old Chilean monkey-puzzle tree in the garden. These may be gimmicks, but there is nothing forced about the private house atmosphere, especially in the comfortable sitting room where under chandeliers I took a pleasant breakfast to the strains of Chopin. Breakfasts and drinks are served on the lawn in summer." Visitors in 1989, arriving late, were offered a cold supper in their room – pretty good, for a B&B hotel. (*MR Freeman*)

Open All year.
Rooms 4 triple, 20 double, 1 single – all with bath and shower, telephone, TV and baby-listening. 3 ground-floor rooms.
Facilities Lift, ramps. Lounge, bar, breakfast room, tea room; conference room. Garden.
Location 500 metres W of town centre. Private parking.
Credit cards Access, Amex, Visa.
Terms B&B: single 234–239 frs, double 319–364 frs, suite 379–404 frs. No charge for children under 7. (No restaurant.)

Hôtel de Seignelay   *Tel* 86.52.03.48
2 rue du Pont

Suitable for a stop-over, this modest hotel in the town centre consists of a group of old buildings around a tiled patio where drinks and meals can be taken. The restored half-timbered facade adds a picturesque touch. A reader this year had a comfortable modernised room, and enjoyed "large helpings of solid Burgundian food", cheerfully served. (*Jill Thomas*) Front rooms facing a narrow street can be noisy; courtyard rooms are quieter.

Open All year except 4 weeks Jan/Feb. Closed Mon Nov–July.
Rooms 16 double, 5 single – 5 with bath, all with telephone, 14 with TV.
Facilities Lounge with TV, 2 dining rooms. Patio.
Location Central. Garage nearby.
Credit cards Access, Visa.
Terms [1989 rates] Dinner, B&B 191–218.50 frs. Full alc 150 frs.

AVALLON 89200 Yonne   Map 4

Les Capucins   *Tel* 86.34.06.52
6 avenue Paul-Doumer

Little Avallon, a charming and typical old Burgundy town, has far more than its share of good hotels. This recent recruit to our own short-list is a villa in a tree-

lined boulevard, with a friendly staff, and a pleasant garden at the back. Bedrooms newly modernised, but the beamed dining room is rustic style: good food, nouvelle-ish but with generous portions (menu changes little, so short stay might be best). Closed Wed; Tue evening in low season, 15–20 Oct, 15 Dec–20 Jan. 8 rooms, 7 with bath and shower. Rooms 250 frs. Set menus 110–270 frs [1989]. New nomination. More reports welcome.

Le Relais Fleuri
Route de Saulieu

Tel 86.34.02.85
Telex 800084

A modern motel-type place on the Saulieu road, providing a useful alternative to our more "picturesque" entries for this much-visited and much-hotelled town. "A cut above other main-road stop-over hotels. Originally an old *auberge*, it has recently been extended. Our large well-equipped room faced fields and was very quiet. The hotel has comfortable seating areas, a bar and a smoke-soaked card room. The large and attractive new restaurant is nicely lit and has a welcoming feel: friendly multilingual waiter, an open fire in October, and a good, reasonably priced meal. Open-air solar-heated swimming pool with pleasant poolside bar." OK, but nothing special, says a reader this year.

Open All year except 24 and 31 Dec.
Rooms 48 double – 45 with bath and shower, 3 with shower, all with telephone, radio and TV. All on ground-floor, 2 specially equipped for &.
Facilities 2 lounges, bar, restaurant; 3 conference rooms. Garden with heated swimming pool; 2 tennis courts.
Location 4 km E of Avallon on N6 to Saulieu.
Credit cards All major cards accepted.
Terms Rooms: single 280–310 frs, double 310–380 frs. Breakfast 35 frs. Set lunch/dinner 100–175 frs; full alc 210 frs.

Le Moulin des Templiers
Vallée du Cousin

Tel 86.34.10.80

An idyllically situated old watermill, attractively converted into a small bed-and-breakfast hotel beside the quiet-flowing Cousin, in a pastoral valley outside Avallon. Breakfast served on a terrace by the water's edge or in a tiny but pretty salon. Bedrooms, though charming, are very small and washing facilities cramped: best for a night stop, not a long stay. Open 15 Mar–31 Oct. 14 rooms, all with bath and/or shower. Rooms 190-280 frs. Breakfast 27 frs [1989 rates]. More reports please.

AVIGNON 84000 Vaucluse
Map 5

Hôtel d'Europe
12 place Crillon

Tel 90.82.66.92
Fax 90.85.43.66
Telex 431965

This former 16th-century aristocrat's house was already an inn when Napoleon stayed here in 1799, and it has far more character than the average modern Avignon hotel. It is in a small square just inside the old city walls, close to the Papal Palace. "Tranquil and cool, elegantly

FRANCE

furnished, staff very helpful"; "a lovely hotel: dinner in the charming courtyard was perfectly served" – two reports this year that endorse an earlier view. "The courtyard and public rooms, filled with flowers and antiques, are a feast to the eye and spirit." However, readers warn that a few of the bedrooms are "poky", and that those at the back can suffer from traffic noise. The Provençal cuisine in the hotel's *Vieille Fontaine* restaurant is admired. You can eat in a rather formal dining room or, preferably, under the plane trees beside a fountain in the graceful courtyard – "a magical experience". (*Simon Small, Bettye Chambers, WG Frick*)

Open All year.
Rooms 3 suites, 47 double – all with bath, shower, telephone, radio and TV.
Facilities Lift. 2 salons, bar, TV room, restaurant; conference facilities. Courtyard. 5 mins' walk from Papal Palace.
Location By Porte de l'Oulle on W side of city. Private garage (40 frs).
Restriction Not suitable for &.
Credit cards All major cards accepted.
Terms Rooms 420–975 frs, suite 1.500 frs. Breakfast 55 frs. Set lunch 160 frs, dinner 210 frs; full alc from 300 frs. Reduced rates for children; special meals on request.

BARBAZAN 31510 Haute-Garonne   Map 4

Hostellerie de l'Aristou   *Tel* 61.88.30.67 and 61.88.37.55
Route de Sauveterre

Barbazan is a spa village in the central Pyrenean foothills, within striking distance of the big resort of Luchon and of the ancient walled hill-town of St-Bertrand-de-Comminges, first built by the Romans, whose ruins survive (Herod the Tetrarch was exiled here by Caligula). Exile today to the stylish but far from expensive *Aristou* could be most agreeable, according to our reporter, "Without a doubt the nicest of the hotels we have used during the past three years of touring in France. It is on a hill above the village, with good views. Beds are very comfortable. Service was good *and* charming. We were warmly welcomed by the *patron*-chef, M. Geraud, whose food is excellent and plentiful. Breakfast included freshly squeezed orange juice and a basket of apricots, peaches and oranges. Nice furnishing and decoration." This latter is very *soigné* in its Victorian boudoir manner, with chintzy wallpaper and some antiques. The hotel is a low white traditional building, with tables and chairs in an attractive patio. More reports would be welcome.

Open All year.
Rooms 1 suite, 5 double, 1 single – 7 with bath and shower, all with telephone, radio and TV.
Facilities Lounge/bar, 2 restaurants; conference facilities. Terrace, garden.
Location On edge of village, 13 km SW of St-Gaudens.
Restriction Not suitable for &.
Credit cards All major cards probably accepted.
Terms B&B: single 290–330 frs, double 330–360 frs; Set lunch/dinner 95–220 frs. Children under 7 free; special meals.

The 1991 Guide will appear in the autumn of 1990. Reports are particularly useful in the spring, but need to reach us by May 1990 if they are to help the 1991 edition.

BARBIZON 77630 Seine-et-Marne   Map 3

Hôtellerie du Bas-Bréau   *Tel* 60.66.40.05
22 rue Grande   *Telex* 690953 BABRÉAU

A well-known traditional auberge, *very luxurious, frequented by rich Parisians, in a village near Fontainebleau that once had an important artists' colony. Commended this year for its charming peaceful atmosphere, beautiful garden, tennis court, and excellent food* (Michelin *rosette, two* Gault Millau *toques*). *Closed Jan. 8 suites, 12 double, all with bath and shower. B&B double 1,350 frs. Alc from 260 frs. New nomination. More reports needed.*

LE BARROUX 84330 Vaucluse   Map 5

Hôtel Les Géraniums   *Tel* 90.62.41.08

A new nomination this year: "Le Barroux is an out-of-the-way hill-village, topped by an old castle, amid glorious country up near Mont Ventoux. This old stone building, pleasantly converted but still quite simple, is the kind of authentic local *auberge* that is becoming harder to find in touristy Provence: you need to go right up into the wilder hinterland, as here. The charming young *patronne* supervises the meals, served in a beamed *salle* or out on the terrace, facing the view. Good local cuisine: tripes provençales, fresh apple pie; local wine a bit rough. The best bedrooms, with modern bathrooms, are in the new annexe. As befits the hotel's name, there is plenty of pink in the decor." (*JA*)

Open 10 Feb–5 Jan. Restaurant closed Wed in low season.
Rooms 22 double – 8 with bath, 14 with shower, all with telephone. 9 in nearby annexe
Facilities Salon with TV, bar, restaurant; 2 terraces. Garden. Solarium, table-tennis.
Location Le Barroux is 12 km N of Carpentras. Parking.
Restrictions Not suitable for ♿.
Credit cards All major cards accepted.
Terms Rooms 160–200 frs. Breakfast 25 frs. Dinner, B&B 170–250 frs per person. Set meals 60, 110, 140 and 200 frs; full alc 150 frs. Reduced rates and special meals for children.

BAUDUEN 83630 Var   Map 5

Auberge du Lac   *Tel* 94.70.08.04

In upper Provence, just west of the mighty Gorges du Verdon: three old houses in the village have been joined into one, to form this pleasant unassuming auberge, *directly overlooking the large lake of Ste-Croix (bathing, sailing, fishing). Comfortable rooms with old furniture, good classic cooking, friendly service. Open 15 Mar–15 Nov. 10 rooms, all with bath and shower. B&B double 350–400 frs. Set menus 100–240 frs. New nomination. More reports please.*

> We asked hotels to quote 1990 prices. Not all were able to predict them in the late spring of 1989. Some of our terms will be inaccurate. Do check latest tariffs at the time of booking.

LES BAUX-DE-PROVENCE 13520 Bouches-du-Rhône   Map 5

Oustaù de Baumanière   *Tel* 90.54.33.07
                                                           Telex 420203

This ruined hill-village-cum-castle, on a rocky spur of the Alpilles, is one
of the show-places of Provence. In the Middle Ages it was the seat of a
great feudal family and a leading "court of love" where troubadours
played. Then it came under the rule of a sadistic viscount who would
kidnap his neighbours and laugh as he forced them to jump to their
deaths from the clifftop. In 1632 Richelieu had the castle demolished.
Today it is a ghost realm, where coach parties daily pick their way across
the jagged rocks of bauxite (named after Les Baux) and through the
spooky remains of medieval grandeur. It is best visited by moonlight.

The renowned *Baumanière*, in the valley below the village, is owned by
that doyen of great French chefs, Raymond Thuilier, who is aged 92 but
last year was still present in the restaurant most evenings in his white hat,
mixing with his guests. His grandson runs the place. Their chef Alain
Burnel still wins *Michelin*'s top rating of three stars and five red knives
and forks, and he is now beginning to innovate with new dishes in a
restaurant that had long held out against the *nouvelle* tide. Prices are in
the top bracket, and, as you would expect, not everyone is sure that they
are worth it: some readers this year found service a shade aloof, and one
minded being put without warning in an annexe 800 metres from the
main building. But many have been impressed alike by the luxurious
bedrooms, the splendid breakfasts, and the very real beauty of the place.
"A large garden with peach, fig and olive trees, roses and a plethora of
flowers. Breakfast was served in our own garden." "At night, the crescent
moon, starlight and floodlit château, the eerie white rocks, the discreetly
lit pool . . ." "As near to perfection as one is likely to get in an imperfect
world." (*Marie and Dominic Chambers*) More reports welcome on the
kitchen's break with classic tradition.

Open All year except 15 Jan–2 Mar. Closed Wed, and Thur afternoon 1 Nov–
15 Mar.
Rooms 12 suites, 12 double – all with bath, telephone, TV and air-conditioning.
14 in 3 annexes. 8 ground-floor rooms.
Facilities Salon, arcaded restaurant. Garden, swimming pool, tennis courts, riding
stables.
Location 19 km SW of Arles; 86 km NW of Marseilles.
Credit cards All major cards accepted.
Terms Rooms: single 700 frs, double 820 frs, suite 1,120 frs. Breakfast 75 frs.
Dinner, B&B double 2.100–2,400 frs. Set lunch/dinner 500–600 frs; alc 600 frs.

La Benvengudo   *Tel* 90.54.32.54

This creeper-covered farmhouse, in the valley south-west of the village, is
far cheaper than the *Baumanière* but quite glamorous in its own way:
dinners are served in a cosy room with antiques or on a floodlit patio, and
there is a large and lovely swimming pool in a big garden. "The great
romantic-looking crags of the Alpilles rise above the garden. I found the
food excellent: cooking very fresh and individual, e.g. a delicious
combination of moules and escargots. The service was good and prompt,
and breakfast first-class. Madame seemed a little sharp at first, but we
came to like her, especially when she padded round gardening in bare

feet." Others have found it "very comfortable and friendly", "peaceful and civilised". This year, two readers admired the beautiful setting and "lovely rooms"; one had a very good meal, but another thought the food "not above average" – a view we have heard more than once. (*N D'Emden and H Osman, G Evans*)

Open 15 Feb–11 Nov. Restaurant closed lunchtime and Sun evening.
Rooms 3 suites, 17 double – all with bath or shower, and telephone; suites have kitchenette. 10 (with terrace and TV) in annexe. Ground-floor rooms.
Facilities Salon, TV room, restaurant. Garden with terrace, swimming pool and tennis court.
Location 2 km SW of Les Baux, off D78. Parking.
Credit card Visa.
Terms Rooms 370–470 frs, suite 700–750 frs. Breakfast 50 frs. Dinner, B&B double 860 frs. Set dinner 230 frs.

BAYEUX 14400 Calvados   Map 2

Hôtel d'Argouges   *Tel* 31.92.88.86
21 rue St-Patrice   *Telex* 772402

"Exactly as provincial France should be - owners delightful", writes a visitor this year to this 18th-century private town house, now converted into a charming and elegant little family-run B&B hotel, warm and welcoming, with beamed bedrooms, an attractive lounge, and a small garden. It is also quiet, being set back from the street behind a courtyard, opposite the market square, and has private parking. The cathedral and that tapestry are 600 metres away. (*Mr and Mrs George R Staton, Mary Hanson, Peter and Ann Jones, Peter Hill*) *Warning:* "Tall people should beware of the ceilings on the staircase."

Open All year.
Rooms 2 suites, 20 double, 3 single – 20 with bath, 5 with shower, all with telephone, radio and baby-listening; 19 with TV. 12 in building in garden.
Facilities Salon, breakfast room; courtyard. Garden.
Location Central. Parking.
Restriction Not suitable for &.
Credit cards All major cards accepted.
Terms B&B: single 188–348 frs, double 208–348 frs, suite 350–518 frs. Reduced rates for children. (No restaurant.)

BEAULIEU 06310 Alpes-Maritimes   Map 5

La Réserve   *Tel* 93.01.00.01
Boulevard Maréchal Leclerc   *Telex* 470301

This famous pink palace beside the rocky shore was one of the most fashionable venues of pre-war Riviera society. Greta Garbo, Virginia Woolf and of course Scottie all stayed or dined here; today regular guests include Robert Maxwell. It dropped out of the Guide in 1987 for lack of feedback (probably few of our readers fancy its prices). But an inspector returned this year: "Still much the same, save that it's just been renovated and has a new chef, Joël Garault, who I think deserves his two *Gault Millau toques*, judging by my poissons crus marinés, carré d'agneau aux aromates and hot lemon soufflé. You can dine on the terrace by the sea, or in an elegant paved patio. Period furniture and a tinkling piano recall the old days. The piscine is heated in winter, or you can bathe from the rocks. Most rooms, suitably luxurious, face the sea." M. Maria, the "charming manager", has retired after 12 years, but we are assured that the team otherwise remains the same and will continue the traditions of *La Réserve*. More reports please.

Open 23 Dec–20 Nov.
Rooms 3 suites, 50 double – all with bath and shower, telephone, radio and TV.
Facilities Lift. Salon, bars, restaurant; terrace. Garden with swimming pool. Sauna, solarium.
Location On seafront. Parking.
Restrictions Not suitable for &. No children under 10 in July and Aug.
Credit cards Amex, Diners, Visa.
Terms [1989 rates] Rooms: single 710–1,280 frs, double 960–2,100 frs, suite 2,300–4,350 frs. Breakfast 85 frs. Set lunch/dinner 330–440 frs; full alc 550 frs.

BEAUNE 21200 Côte-d'Or   Map 4

Hôtel le Cep   *Tel* 80.22.35.48
27 rue Maufoux   *Telex* 351256 CEPHOTL

Recently extended and modernised, this beautiful 17th-century house in the centre of Burgundy's wine capital has antique furnishings and continues to be admired. One reader this year enjoyed breakfast in the garden courtyard with its elegant tables and chairs, and thought the staff "exceptionally kind". Last year's view, "A charming little hotel. Dinner was very good, in the lovely restaurant that bears the name of its chef, Bernard Morillon." Each bedroom is named after a *Grand Cru* wine of the Côte d'Or vineyards; the modern ones, though nice, have less character than the old rooms; front rooms could be noisy. (*Deborah F Reese, Joe Van der Sneppen*)

Open All year. Restaurant closed Feb.
Rooms 49 – all with bath and/or shower, telephone and TV. 5 suites in courtyard annexe. 1 room equipped for &.
Facilities Lift. Lounge, bar, restaurant; functions facilities; courtyard. Garden.
Location Central, near Hôtel-Dieu. Garage parking.
Credit cards All major cards accepted.
Terms [1989 rates] Rooms: single 450 frs, double 550–800 frs. Breakfast 50 frs. Set lunch/dinner 160–320 frs. Special meals for children.

La Closerie   *Tel* 80.22.15.07
61 route de Pommard   *Fax* 80.24.16.22
                                                   Telex 351213

A modern purpose-built hotel in the quiet southern outskirts, just off the N74 to Chalon. Spacious foyer, modern bedrooms, and plenty of creature comforts, including large garden, pleasant swimming pool and lido. Closed 25 Dec–14 Jan. 32 rooms, all with bath or shower. B&B double 400–424 frs. No restaurant. Recent nomination. More reports please.

> Our italicised entries indicate hotels which are worth considering, but which, for various reasons – inadequate information, lack of feedback, ambivalent reports – do not at the moment warrant a full entry. We should particularly welcome comments on these hotels.

BEAUREPAIRE 38270 Isère   Map 4

Hôtel Restaurant Fiard   *Tel* 74.84.62.02
Avenue des Terreaux

In a small town south-east of Vienne, off the Rhône valley, a quite smart, newly refurbished restaurant-with-rooms: gracious hostess, attractive modern furniture, excellent classic cooking and Côte-du-Rhône wines. Closed 1 Jan–14 Feb. 15 rooms, all with bath and shower. B&B double 320–370 frs. Set menus 110–380 frs. New nomination. More reports please.

LE BEC-HELLOUIN 27800 Eure   Map 2

Auberge de l'Abbaye   *Tel* 32.44.86.02

Peacefully situated on a village green, this old half-timbered Norman *auberge* has simple but clean rooms at modest prices, and a dining room with low-beamed ceilings, providing good food. Our readers remain content: one had a room "furnished with lovely antiques" and a fine breakfast, while others have admired the cooking, though one this year found it expensive. Le Bec-Hellouin was the home of one of Europe's great Benedictine monasteries, and no fewer than three archbishops of Canterbury came from here in medieval times. The monastery, formerly a ruin, has now been substantially restored and once again houses a religious community. The Gregorian chant in the abbey is worth hearing: but its resonant bells do start ringing early. (*Lynne and David Allen, and others*) The hotel asks you to take one meal in the hotel for each night you stay and strongly recommends that you use its courtyard parking.

Open 23 Feb–8 Jan. Closed Mon night and Tue out of season.
Rooms 1 suite, 7 double – all with bath and shower, and telephone.
Facilities TV lounge, 3 dining rooms; courtyard.
Location 5 km from Brionne; SW of Rouen, W of N138. Parking.
Restriction Not suitable for &.
Credit cards Access, Diners, Visa.
Terms Rooms 300–500 frs. Breakfast 30 frs. Dinner, B&B: double 560 frs, suite 760 frs. Set lunch/dinner 100, 175 and 250 frs; full alc 195 frs.

BELLEGARDE-SUR-VALSÉRINE 01200 Ain   Map 4

Hôtel Le Fartoret   *Tel* 50.48.07.18
Éloise

Set amid fine scenery on a hillside near the Swiss frontier, this old country auberge has expanded considerably and become grander, losing some of its former simple charm. Still run jovially by the Gassilloud family, it has small but pretty and comfortable rooms with nice views, a sheltered swimming pool, Savoyard furnishings and cuisine. 40 rooms, all with bath and/or shower. Rooms 190–350 frs. Breakfast 35 frs. Set menus 95–250 frs [1989]. Food, service and ambience criticised this year: more reports please.

> We don't lack *Michelin*-rosetted hotels in France but would be glad of more nominations at the more modest end of the price scale.

BÉNODET 29118 Finistère   Map 2

Hôtel Menez-Frost   *Tel* 98.57.03.09
4 rue J Charcot

Bénodet is an attractive resort in south-west Brittany, at the mouth of the
quiet river Odet studded with pleasure-boats. It is busy with French
families in August, but the season ends in early September when many
amenities close, even if the hotels stay open longer. This one has been
commended again this year as perfect for a family holiday. A devotee
explains, "it has so many facilities – heated outdoor swimming pool,
tennis, ping pong – and is near very good beaches. Our bedroom had dull
decor but a balcony overlooking the pool; in our building the rooms were
grouped in pairs, useful for a family. Breakfast was very good, apart from
the packaged butter and jams. The manager was wonderful, keeping an
eye on everything in a charming fashion." Many rooms face the pool, but
are not noisy. No restaurant, which some families might find a handicap,
but there are plenty of good eating-places near by.

Open Easter–Oct.
Rooms 7 suites, 30 double, 23 single – all with bath and shower, telephone and
baby-listening; some with balcony. 12 ground-floor rooms. 5 self-catering
apartments.
Facilities Salon, bar, TV room, reading room; conference facilities; billiards and
table tennis. Garden with heated swimming pool (lessons available), solarium and
sauna; tennis.
Location Central, near post office, port and ferry. Parking.
Credit card Access, Visa.
Terms Rooms: single 260–390 frs, double 280–450 frs, suite 460–700 frs. Breakfast
30 frs. (No restaurant.)

BEUZEVILLE 27210 Eure   Map 2

Auberge du Cochon d'Or and   *Tel* 32.57.76.08 and 32.57.70.46
  Le Petit Castel
Place du Général-de-Gaulle

This old Norman *auberge* and adjacent modern hotel, in a small town near
Honfleur, are both owned and run by the Folleau family. Most guests
sleep at the *Castel*, a *Logis de France*, recently renovated and as well liked
as ever: visitors this year had a pleasant room facing the quiet walled
garden (those at the front, by the main road, might be noisier). The
welcome is friendly. As for the *Cochon d'Or*, where you eat, again this year
readers felt that it well deserves its *Michelin* red "R" for good value (one
couple enjoyed truite farcie and tripes au calvados). Earlier views:
"Normandy cooking at its best"; "an enjoyable meal in a relaxing
atmosphere – guinea-fowl in a grapefruit and orange sauce." One reader
who liked the food thought the hotel itself a bit ordinary. (*Jack B Ainslie,
Peter and Ann Jones*) It is recommended that you book in advance.

Open 15 Jan–15 Dec. Restaurant closed Mon.
Rooms 21 double – 17 with bath, 4 with shower; 16 with telephone; 7 with TV.
16 at *Le Castel*.
Facilities 2 lounges (1 at *Le Castel*), TV room, restaurant; 2 conference rooms.
Garden.
Location In centre. Quietest rooms in *Petit Castel*. Beuzeville is 15 km SE of
Honfleur, just N of Paris–Caen motorway. Parking.

Credit cards Access, Visa.
Terms B&B: single occupancy 195 frs, double 305 frs. Set meals 90, 140 and 190 frs; full alc 200 frs.

BEYNAC 24220 Dordogne   Map 4

Hôtel Bonnet   *Tel* 53.29.50.01

We are grateful to the readers this year who responded – all favourably – to our appeal for new reports on this charming and unpretentious little hotel with its flowery creeper-covered terrace, in a village above a curve in the Dordogne where four medieval castles are in view. "A superb hotel with wonderful food". "Madame Bonnet is always cheerful. The rooms in the annexe are particularly nice, being quieter and away from the main road" (this road is the hotel's main drawback, making some front rooms noisy). (*Josephine Barratt, J Alan Thornton, Mary Connolly and Fred Sweet, LH*)

Open 14 Apr–15 Oct.
Rooms 21 double, 1 single – all with bath and/or shower and telephone. Some rooms in annexe.
Facilities Lounge, restaurant, terrace. Garden.
Location 10 km W of Sarlat.
Credit cards Access, Visa.
Terms Rooms: single 120–160 frs, double 185–240 frs. Breakfast 26 frs. Half board: single 250–279 frs, double 520–550 frs. Set lunch/dinner 110–200 frs. Special meals for children.

BIOT 06410 Alpes-Maritimes   Map 5

Hôtel-Galerie des Arcades   *Tel* 93.65.01.04
16 place des Arcades

An idiosyncratic 15th-century inn/café/bistro/art gallery in the arcaded main square of a picturesque hill-village behind Antibes. Engagingly Bohemian *patron*, André Brothier, has lined the dining room with Braques and Miros, and he attracts a lively clientele of local fellow-Bohemians. Bedrooms are olde worlde, but the plumbing is not. The inn's hyper-relaxed atmosphere may not suit all tastes: pop music may resound from the café while you eat your aıoli or sardines farcies. Restored to the Guide this year after a period of no news: "Typically and rustically French. The rooms were perfectly acceptable, but as we all know the French see food as more important. On our visit, my charcuterie and soup could have fed the whole restaurant, and standards were superb. Madame was charming." (*David Lees, JA*)

Open All year. Restaurant closed 15 Nov–8 Dec.
Rooms 12 double – all with bath (7 also have shower) and telephone; 7 with TV.
Facilities Bar, TV room, 2 restaurants. Patio.
Location Central, some garages. Biot is 8 km NW of Antibes.
Restriction Not suitable for &.
Credit cards None accepted.
Terms [1989 rates] Rooms 180–350 frs. Breakfast 30 frs. Set lunch/dinner 140 frs; full alc 170 frs. Reduced rates for children.

We depend on detailed fresh reports to keep our entries up-to-date.

BLOIS 41000 Loir-et-Cher   Map 2

Anne de Bretagne   *Tel* 54.78.05.38
31 avenue Jean-Laigret

Useful for a night's stop in the Loire valley: a clean and comfortable little hotel in the upper town, near the castle, well above the river. Madame is friendly. Pleasant bar, and patio for drinks and breakfast. Closed 19 Feb–12 Mar. 29 rooms, most with bath and/or shower. Double rooms 195–330 frs [1989]. Breakfast 22 frs [1989]. No restaurant: plenty in town. Recent nomination. More reports please.

BONNEVAUX-LE-PRIEURÉ 25620 Doubs   Map 4

Le Moulin du Prieuré   *Tel* 81.59.21.47

Another French charmer new to our pages this year. It's secluded in the glorious Brême valley, a green winding cleft in the Jura, near picturesque Ornans where Courbet was born and painted (museum). "The scenery is grandiose and the silence complete," says our 1989 nominator; "the hotel is a converted water-mill, and parts of its mechanism can still be seen; the bedrooms are in separate modern chalets. Guests prepare their own breakfasts in their rooms, a system developed with fishermen and walkers in mind, who want to start at crack of dawn. Monsieur deals mostly with the fishing (season begins in May), while Madame looks after the restaurant in regal manner. Innovative dishes of high quality, with menus changing seasonally." *Gault Millau toque.* Public rooms are gracefully furnished in local style. (*AF Thomas*)

Open 15 Mar–20 Dec. Closed Sun evening and Mon, 15 Mar–1 May and 1 Oct–20 Dec.
Rooms 8 double – all with bath/shower, telephone and TV.
Facilities Lounge, restaurant. Garden. Fishing.
Location 8 km NE of Ornans by D67 and D280.
Credit cards All major cards accepted.
Terms [1989 rates] Rooms 300–325 frs. Breakfast 25 frs. Alc meals 180–330 frs (excluding wine). Special meals for children.

BONNIEUX 84480 Vaucluse   Map 5

Hôtel L'Aiguebrun   *Tel* 90.74.04.14

In a narrow upland valley of the lovely and curious Luberon hills, north of Aix (the church at Bonnieux village, four miles from the hotel, has remarkable 15th-century German paintings). Here Roger Chastel, a gentle Parisian, artist and former couturier, has taken over a small 19th-century manor beside a stream, which he runs more like a private home than a hotel. "Lovely, lovely place. The countryside is wild, with nothing to be heard but birdsong and the waterfall. The lounge was so inviting, with its country antiques, fresh flowers, original oil paintings (some by M. Chastel) and a fire crackling in the great stone fireplace. Comfortable bedrooms, also with country antiques, plus modern tiled bathrooms. You can breakfast on a terrace above the river. Food was delicious." "We arrived to find the air full of garlic and oil paints, and a Mozart concerto playing. The pigtailed M. Chastel runs the hotel very professionally and the food is superlative." This year, however, a reader was disappointed – poor upkeep, and food overpriced, he felt.

Open 19 Mar–1 Nov. Restaurant closed for lunch on Mon.
Rooms 7 double, 1 single – all with bath and telephone.
Facilities Salon, restaurant. Riverside garden where meals are served in summer.
Location Just off D943, 6 km SE of Bonnieux which is 48 km N of Aix.
Credit cards None accepted.
Terms [1989 rates] Rooms 380–420 frs. Breakfast 35 frs. Set meals 190 frs.

BOURBON-L'ARCHAMBAULT 03160 Allier   Map 4

Hôtel des Thermes   *Tel* 70.67.00.15
Avenue Charles Louis Philippe

"The rooms are most comfortable, and an exquisite dinner was served in an atmosphere of old-fashioned courtesy and cherishing: the brothers Barichard deserve highest praise for civility of the grave kind", writes a Brigadier this year. Indeed the brothers have already won First Prize for Welcome and Friendliness in the Allier *département,* in their sedate and spruce little hotel: it is set in a spa town of northern Auvergne where Talleyrand used to take a cure for rheumatism. An earlier report: "M. Barichard gave us a memorable dinner of omelette, sole meunière and steak in a special sauce" – he wins a *Michelin* rosette for the kind of orthodox dishes that *curistes* probably prefer. The hotel has a garden-terrace facing the cure centre and a private lake for fishing. One visitor had a spotless room with a large tiled bathroom, overlooking a flowery patio. But another found front rooms noisy, for they face a main road: rear ones are quieter. (*Brig. Laurence and Fran Fowler, ME Chamberlain*)

Open 24 Mar–31 Oct.
Rooms 1 suite, 17 double, 4 single – 10 with bath, 6 with shower, all with telephone. 4 in annexe.
Facilities Salon with TV, dining room. Large grounds with terrace, garden and private lake; fishing.
Location 100 metres from town centre. Town is 23 km W of Moulins. Garage.
Restriction Not suitable for &.
Credit cards All major cards accepted.
Terms B&B: single 145 frs, double 280 frs, suite 306 frs; full board 270–320 frs per person. Set lunch/dinner 82, 142 and 189 frs. Special meals for children on request.

LE BOURGET-DU-LAC 73370 Savoie   Map 4

Hôtel Ombremont   *Tel* 79.25.00.23
                                            Fax 79.25.25.77
                                  Telex 980832 CHAMBERY

The large Lac du Bourget is Lamartine's *Le Lac* where he mourned his lost love – and one reader, maybe caught by the poet's volatile moods, found it "pleasant only when the sun shines, otherwise black, vast and unfriendly". But the *Ombremont* shares none of these three epithets – a handsome gabled country house, run sympathetically by its young owners, and secluded in its big garden by the lake, just outside the smart resort of Le Bourget. One report this year criticises food and room upkeep, but others have again been quite lyrical: "Elegantly furnished bedrooms, superb views from the dining room's open balcony, food of good quality. The owner was actively involved in serving every table." "The menu at 320 frs [1989] was innovative and exquisite – roquefort terrine, and coconut mousse in dark chocolate with mango" (*Michelin* rosette, two red *Gault Millau toques* for such dishes as ravioli of frogs legs with fresh herbs). But the stairs are numerous and the swimming pool not easy of access. (*David Grant, FW Hulton, and others*)

Open All year except 2 Jan–5 Feb. Restaurant closed Sat midday except Jul and Aug.
Rooms 4 suites, 16 double – all with bath and shower, telephone, radio and baby-listening; some with TV. 2 in chalet in park.
Facilities 2 salons, billiard room, restaurant; conference facilities; terrace. Garden, with swimming pool, leading down to lake; rocky beach with lifeguard; fishing.
Location 2 km N of Le Bourget, on N504.
Restriction Not suitable for &.
Credit cards Access, Visa.
Terms [1989 rates] Rooms 425–750 frs. Breakfast 46 frs. Set lunch 175 frs, dinner 420 frs. Reduced rates and special meals for children.

BRANTÔME 24310 Dordogne   Map 4

Le Châtenet   *Tel* 53.05.81.08

Brantôme, on the river Dronne north of Périgueux, is a beautiful but trippery little town. Just outside it, away from the crowds and by the river, stands this delightful little 17th-century ranch-like manor, all mellow brown stone, with creepers and outdoor galleries. It was converted by its English-speaking owners, the Laxtons, and has again won a torrent of praise this year. "This lovely comfortable hotel feels like a home, and Mrs Laxton is a charming lady. Bedrooms are spacious: most overlook the garden." "A perfect hotel, with beautiful swimming pool, extensive grounds with a bar in the club-house. Bedrooms were elegant: ours even had an electric mosquito-killer. Delicious breakfast, including eggs, served on Limoges china." Bed-and-breakfast only: but there are no fewer than three *Michelin*-rosetted restaurants nearby (see Champagnac-de-Belair), while the Laxtons will recommend good cheaper places too. (*Eileen Broadbent, Judy Smith, Patricia and Christopher Bevan, and others*) There is a new garden room specially equipped for the disabled.

Open All year, except possibly a short while in low season (1 Nov–1 Apr).
Rooms 2 suites, 8 double – all with bath and shower, and telephone; TV and baby-listening on request. 1 ground-floor room equipped for & with electrically manned bed and special fittings (20% reduced rate for &). 2 rooms in cottage with lounge and kitchenette.
Facilities Ramps. Lounge; club house with bar, billiards; terrace. 10-acre grounds with swimming pool heated 20 Apr–15 Oct, tennis court, children's' playground, areas for bowls and cricket, river frontage, fishing.
Location 1/2 m W of Brantôme, off D78.
Credit cards Access, Visa.
Terms Rooms 300–430 frs, suite 500–620 frs. Breakfast 45 frs. Extra bed 50 frs. (No restaurant.)

> Deadlines: nominations for the 1991 edition should reach us not later than 1 May 1990. Latest date for comments on existing entries: 1 June 1990.

BRESSON 38320 Isère   Map 4

Chavant   Tel 76.25.15.14

"Within 20 minutes' drive of the centre of Grenoble, yet in the unspoilt
setting of a quiet village, this delightful old auberge is today smart and
sophisticated, but is still run with unaffected personal warmth by the
Chavant family who have owned it for three generations: Émile Chavant
was in the 1930s a disciple of the then aged Escoffier, and Jean-Pierre
Chavant still provides the best food in the Grenoble area (*Michelin*
rosette). Each of the seven bedrooms is pretty and cosy, with period
furnishings. Ours had blue-and-pink matching fabrics and a large
carpeted balcony/sun-terrace with views of the Vercors massif; we awoke
to birdsong. The old building has beamed ceilings and Louis XIII decor;
meals in winter are served in a spacious panelled room before a log fire.
Our visit was in June and we lunched under the chestnut trees in the
idyllic flower-filled garden. A large lunch-party of the local *haute
bourgeoisie* was in progress (*Chavant* is Grenoble's most chic venue for
such events) but this did not affect the service. The cooking is rich and
classic rather than *nouvelle*: especially superb were the escalope de foie
gras de canard with nuts, and the coquilles St-Jacques aux girolles in a
cream-and-wine sauce – vive Escoffier! Much play is made of the local
noix de Grenoble (walnuts): they even get into the pain aux noix,
delicious. A splendid range of old armagnacs, too."

Open All year except 25–31 Dec. Restaurant closed Sat lunch and Wed.
Rooms 7 – all with bath and shower, telephone and TV.
Facilities Lift. Salon, restaurant; conference room. Garden. Swimming pool.
Location 8 km S of Grenoble: go to Eybens and turn right (signposted).
Credit cards All major cards accepted.
Terms [1989 rates] Rooms 380–720 frs. Breakfast 45 frs. Set meals 158 frs.

BRIGNOGAN-PLAGES 29238 Finistère   Map 2

Hostellerie Castel-Regis   Tel 98.83.40.22
                                                    Telex 940941

*In a beautiful rocky setting on the North Brittany coast, only 36 km west of
Roscoff and its ferries, a spruce and quite elegant little hotel where you can
drink or dine by the water's edge, with fine views. Most rooms are in bungalow
style; pleasant service, and very good local fish dishes (Gault Millau toque).
Heated sea-water swimming pool. Open 8 Apr–30 Sept. 21 rooms, all with bath
and shower. B&B double 275–380 frs. Set menus 110-175 frs. New nomination.
More reports please.*

BRIOUDE 43100 Haute Loire   Map 4

Hôtel Le Brivas   Tel 71.50.10.49
Avenue du Velay   *Telex* 392589

Midway between Le Puy and Clermont-Ferrand, Brioude is a good centre
for touring the Massif Central – a market town with narrow medieval
streets and a fine 12th-century romanesque basilica. Here on the broader
main road to Le Puy, on the town's edge, is one reader's "find of the

year". He goes on: "It is modern and very much a concrete slab, for all that the owners are trying to soften its harshness with ivy and creepers. The garden terrace in front blocks out all traffic noise from the road. Bedrooms are large, comfortable and well furnished in the modern idiom. The large and airy restaurant has fine views of the mountains. The chef, son of the owners, is obviously working on his reputation, with his own specialities: he appears at the end of dinner and is willing to debate with you the mysteries of his trade." "Service friendly, food ample and well cooked." There is now an outdoor heated swimming pool.

Open All year except 17 Nov–27 Dec, Fri evening 27 Dec–7 Apr and 5 Oct–Dec; restaurant closed Sat midday in low season.
Rooms 30 – all with bath or shower, telephone, and TV.
Facilities Lift. Salon, bar, restaurant; conference facilities. Garden with swimming pool.
Location Outskirts, on N 102 to Le Puy. Brioude is 69 km S of Clermont-Ferrand.
Credit cards All major cards accepted.
Terms [1989 rates] B&B double 310 frs; dinner, B&B 235–315 frs per person. Set lunch/dinner 80, 110 and 140 frs; full alc 155 frs. Reductions for long stays. Children under 7 free in parents' room; special meals.

Hôtel de la Poste et Champanne
1 boulevard Docteur Devins

Tel 71.50.14.62

On the main street, a down-to-earth and very traditional hotel, run "with tremendous verve and atmosphere" by the octogenarian Albertine Barge and her family. Recently enlarged and modernised, it has lost some of its rough-and-ready simplicity and Madame Barge's grandchildren provide "considerable panache", even if not fine frills. But again this year several readers have been content, "A smiling welcome, a decent modern bedroom and balcony, a good dinner and breakfast"; "M. Barge is a wonderful character. Good plain peasant-style cooking, in contrast to the mouthwatering and beautifully presented sweets"; "the menu of regional dishes was a delight". *Michelin* and *Gault Millau* concur, by awarding their "good value" red print for the cheaper set menus (local dishes such as potée de lentilles and tripoux d'Auvergne) which are preferred to the dearer ones. Rooms in the new annexe are best. (*RA Mayor, Sara Price, William A Grant, BW Ribbons*)

Open All year except 1–15 Jan and Sun evening Oct–May.
Rooms 20 double – 10 with bath and shower, 4 with shower, all with telephone. 14, with balcony, in nearby annexe.
Facilities 2 lounges (1 with TV), bar with terrace, 4 dining rooms. Small garden.
Location Central; annexe has parking.
Credit cards None accepted.
Terms Rooms 100–200 frs. Breakfast 20 frs. Half board 170 frs per person; full board 220 frs. Set lunch/dinner 60, 85 and 140 frs. Reduced rates for children.

BUSSIÈRES 71960 Saône-et-Loire

Map 4

Relais Lamartine
Tel 85.36.64.71

Modern hotel on edge of quiet village west of Mâcon, where Lamartine lived. Large terrace with views of vineyards, sparklingly clean but "with old-fashioned values". Warm praise for five-course dinners, and breakfasts with home-made apricot and blackberry jams. Open 15 Jan–1 Dec; restaurant closed

Sun evening and Mon in low season. 8 rooms, all with bath and shower, 210–310 frs. Set meals 95–250 frs. Sadly Madame Gacon died at the end of 1988 but her husband plans to continue the business as before. More reports please.

CABASSON 83230 Var   Map 5

Hôtel Les Palmiers   Tel 94.64.81.94

West of Le Lavandou, secluded in woodland yet near to sandy beaches – not an easy combination on this crowded coast. A cheerful well-modernised hotel in local style, fairly smart yet not pretentious, run with style by the Guinets (he reserved, she charming). Bedrooms and cooking both approved. 21 rooms, some with shower, 460–700 frs. Set menus 120–220 frs [1989]. Was in very early editions of the Guide. Now re-nominated. More reports welcome.

CABOURG 14390 Calvados   Map 2

Pullman Grand Hôtel   Tel 31.91.01.79
Promenade Marcel Proust   *Telex* 171364

"As my teeth bit lovingly into the madeleine that all guests here are served at breakfast, and as my gaze wandered out through the picture windows of the huge *belle époque* dining room that Proust called 'the aquarium', to the broad sandy beach where his hero first glimpsed Albertine with her brilliant, laughing eyes and her black polo-cap, I fell to musing what this great white wedding-cake of a seaside hotel in a once-so-fashionable Normandy resort (today the *Grand* mostly hosts business seminars) must have been like in the 1880s when Proust came on the first of his many long visits, listening to the same surging of the waves that lulled me to sleep last night, mesmerised by the same shifting colours of the sunlight on the sea that he described so poetically in his novel, which transmuted Cabourg into Balbec, for though much today is taken, much abides, including the same marble pillars and chandeliers in the vast foyer, and though no one knows exactly which was Proust's bedroom (in fact he had several, and today the hotel has been totally remodelled inside, and has only 70 rooms, against 200 in his day), still you can if you wish, ask for the '*chambre* Marcel Proust' which has *belle époque* furnishings including a big brass bedstead and old-fashioned taps on the bath (but, oddly, a modern telephone), and you can enjoy as I did a rather good gigotin de turbot and panachée de quatre viandes in the intimate winter restaurant that of course is called *Le Balbec*, while reflecting that Pullman have done quite a good job of restoration, to provide nostalgic Proustians with an experience that can only be called (to use an overworked word) "Proustian", even though one disappointed visitor this year felt the hotel was "living on its past", but then we might ask what is more Proustian than to live on the past, while at the same time requesting further insights from correspondents, please. (*JA with more than a nod to MP*)

Open All year.
Rooms 70 – all with bath, shower, telephone, radio and TV; baby-listening on request.

Facilities Lift. Salon, bar, restaurant; conference rooms. Casino.
Location Central, by the beach. Free parking. Cabourg is 24 km NE of Caen.
Restriction Not suitable for &.
Credit cards All major cards accepted.
Terms Rooms 440–1,010 frs, suite 1,270–1,690 frs. Breakfast 62 frs. Half board 645–860 frs per person. Set lunch/dinner 170–230 frs. Reduced rates and special meals for children.

CABRERETS 46330 Lot
Map 4

La Pescalerie
Tel 65.31.22.55

This 18th-century Quercy country house, restored and decorated in exquisite taste (many bedrooms have antiques), stands alone at the foot of a rocky hill, just outside the village . A large semi-formal garden stretches away to the wooded banks of the Célé where you can swim if you wish and where jays call and kingfishers arrow through the shadows. "The atmosphere", suggests a reader, "is rather like that of an English country house hotel with French overtones. We were all made very welcome by Hélène Combette and her surgeon husband. Our room was small but the cream marble bathroom was palatial. Food good and different, and the ambience in the dining room one of total enjoyment." "Breakfast on the terrace, attended by a friendly cat, was a joy – fresh orange juice, honey in the comb." "The luxury of the bedrooms was almost sinful, the elegance of breakfast on the terrace under a huge magnolia tree, with oleanders in bloom, was unforgettable." This year, one reader found dinner "delicious", but another thought it only average, and the welcome judged to be a bit too nonchalant. (*Lynne and David Allen, Minda Alexander*)

Open 1 Apr–1 Nov.
Rooms 10 double – all with bath and shower, and telephone; TV on request.
Facilities Lounge with TV, bar, dining room; breakfast terrace. Garden leading to river with swimming, fishing, boating.
Location At La Fontaine de la Pescalerie, 2.5 km NE of Cabrerets on D41 to Figeac.
Restriction Not suitable for &.
Credit cards All major cards accepted.
Terms [1989 rates] Rooms 600 frs. Breakfast 50 frs. Dinner, B&B 685 frs per person. Set lunch/dinner 195–230 frs.

LA CADIÈRE-D'AZUR 83740 Var
Map 5

Hostellerie Bérard
Rue Gabriel Péri
Tel 94.90.11.43 and 94.90.14.98
Telex 400509

Though only five miles from the busy coast at Bandol, La Cadière is a fairly unspoilt hill-village. In its narrow main street, above the valley, stands this 19th-century *auberge*, today much modernised and smartened up but still sympathetic. An inspector this year found it unchanged, endorsing his 1988 report, "A family venture by René and Danièle Bérard – he, rather shy, does the cooking, while she is the exuberant front-of-house. The Bérards have ambitiously turned their *auberge* into quite a sophisticated place, catering for business seminars out of season, and the homely touch has possibly been muted in the process. But prices are still reasonable, and all is attractively done – new beamed ceilings and tiled floors, a spacious and cosy lounge/bar, and a bright dining room with wide views of hills and valley. The menu du terroir (135 francs, 1988) offers Provençal specialities such as pieds-et-paquets; other dishes, more expensive, lean towards the *nouvelle*, such as loup en croûte à la sauce champagne. We thought the results very good and the service charming. But the breakfast coffee was poor. Bedrooms, comfortable and well equipped, are mostly in a nearby annexe: ours was in a converted monastery, above the pool and sun-terrace." "Enjoyable." Some rooms can be noisy. Many guests are British. (*JA and KA; Janet and Dennis Allom*)

Open All year except 5 Jan–18 Feb.
Rooms 3 suites, 37 double – all with bath and/or shower, telephone and TV; baby-listening on request. All in 3 different buildings. Some ground-floor rooms.
Facilities 2 salons, bar, TV room, games room, dining room; conference room. Terrace, small garden with heated swimming pool. Sandy/rocky beaches 7 km.
Location 9 km N of Bandol: if coming from Marseilles, leave *autoroute* at Les Lecques, go through St-Cyr village. Garage parking.
Restriction Not suitable for &.
Credit cards Access, Amex, Visa.
Terms Rooms: single 355–405 frs, double 405–484 frs, suite 525–580 frs. Breakfast 42 frs. Set lunch/dinner 140, 190 and 290 frs. Reduced rates and special meals for children.

CAEN 14000 Calvados   Map 2

Le Dauphin   *Tel* 31.86.22.26
29 rue Gémare   *Telex* 171707

Two Bath hoteliers returned this year to their "magic find" in the centre of Caen near the castle and liked it as much as the year before, "Listed in *Michelin* as a three-*couverts* restaurant 'avec chambres' (always the best value in *Michelin*, we feel), it forms part of an ancient priory in a quarter which miraculously escaped the 1944 devastations. Owner-chef Robert Chabredier offers numerous fish specialities, including an excellent barbue à l'oseille, and St-Jacques in a light Calvados sauce. We have lasting memories, too, of a really gamey game terrine, a fine classic poulet vallée d'Auge and a tender young partridge in a cider sauce. The cheese-board (including Livarot) vies with Normandy's best, while the apple and pear tarts come with that delicious ivory-coloured Normandy cream. House claret superb and ridiculously inexpensive. The dining room, with a log fire, is full of atmosphere, whilst the bar has a full array of farmhouse Calvados. Breakfast, with home-made breads, stewed and fresh fruit, Norman cream cheese, is the best we have found in France. The bedrooms, which vary in size, are less exciting, but they are now being renovated, and our new one had fine beds." (*Malcolm and Jean Seymour*)

Open All year except 17 Jul–8 Aug and Christmas Eve. Restaurant closed Sat.
Rooms 21 double – all with bath and/or shower, telephone and TV. 7 in annexe next door.
Facilities Lift in annexe. Bar, restaurant.
Location Central; signposted from château. Rooms in main building are quiet, the others are sound-proofed. Private parking; garage nearby.
Restriction Not suitable for &.
Credit cards All major cards accepted.
Terms [1989 rates] Rooms 170–320 frs. Breakfast 30 frs. Set meals 80, 140, 195 and 280 frs; full alc 260 frs. Special meals for children on request.

CALVI 20260 Corsica   Map 5

Hôtel Résidence "Les Aloës"   *Tel* 95.65.01.46
Quartier Donatéo

The old fortified port of Calvi, now a popular summer resort, has one of Corsica's most spectacular settings – a big sandy bay, guarded by an old Venetian citadel, with a back-drop of high snow-capped mountains. An ideal spot for viewing all this is the peace and cool of the *Aloës*, an unpretentious modern (1965) B&B hotel above the town and away from the noise. "Rooms are small, but all are quiet and some have a superb view of the bay", says a reader this year; "we took breakfast on our own small terrace" (rooms at the back facing the maquis are especially quiet). Others have referred to the "helpful management", but one visitor thought the plumbing "bizarre". A good choice of restaurants down by the port. (*Christian Draz*)

Open May–Oct.
Rooms 26 – all with bath and/or shower, and telephone. 5 with terrace in annexe.
Facilities Salon, bar, T V room, library. Terrace and garden. Beach 1 km.
Location 1 km SW of town centre: take route d'Ajaccio or route de l'Usine Électrique. Parking.
Credit cards All major cards accepted.
Terms Rooms: single 170 frs, double 240–400 frs. Breakfast 26 frs. 1-night bookings sometimes refused in high season. (No restaurant.)

CAMBRAI 59400 Nord   Map 3

Hôtel Beatus   *Tel* 27.81.45.70
718 avenue de Paris   *Telex* 820597

A low white building set back from the road, a mile out of town on the N44 to St-Quentin. Very friendly and helpful owners; quiet and comfortable rooms furnished in Louis XV/XVI styles; elegant little bar; good breakfast; private parking. No restaurant, but there are several in town. 26 rooms, all with bath or shower. B&B double from 340 frs. Re-nominated in 1989, but we'd welcome fuller reports.

CARCASSONNE Aude   Map 4

Domaine d'Auriac   *Tel* 68.25.72.22
Route St-Hilaire, 11009   *Telex* 500385

An imposing creeper-covered 19th-century mansion, lying peacefully amid its own woodlands two miles outside Carcassonne, and just across the motorway (out of earshot) from the medieval hilltop fortress. An elegant dining room with a blazing fire in winter; terrace for alfresco meals in summer; dishes such as cassoulet approved. Most bedrooms pleasant and spacious. Closed Sun evening and Mon midday. 23 rooms, all with bath and shower. Rooms 450–950 frs. Set menus 160–300 frs [1989]. Some criticism of food and service this year. More reports please.

Hôtel du Donjon   *Tel* 68.71.08.80
2 rue du Comte-Roger, La Cité, 11000   *Telex* 505012

*Of our two new 1990 entries within the walled medieval fortress, this Logis de
France is the smarter – a beautifully converted ancient building with red tiled
floors, rough stone walls (but all mod cons) and a charming rear garden where
you can escape from the tourist mob, and eat out in summer. Affable welcome,
good local dishes such as cassoulet. Restaurant closed Sun night. 36 rooms, all
with bath and/or shower, 260–380 frs. Set menu (dinner only) 100 frs. New
nomination. More reports please.*

Hôtel des Remparts   *Tel* 68.71.27.72
3 place du Grand Puits, La Cité, 11000

*In a relatively secluded part of the much-visited medieval Cité, an old house
with friendly owners and a fine 14th-century spiral staircase; but the bedrooms
are modern. 18 rooms, all with bath and shower. B&B double 290 frs. New
nomination. No restaurant, but try the Donjon (above).*

CARSAC-AILLAC 24200 Dordogne   Map 4

Le Relais du Touron   *Tel* 53.28.16.70

*Plenty of unaffected Dordogne rural charm is to be found at this 19th-century
gentilhommière, on the outskirts of a small village 9 km east of Sarlat,
tastefully converted and recently opened as a hotel by its charming Belgian
owner, Claudine Carlier. Food good value (lots of regional specialities), staff
friendly, swimming pool a joy. Open 15 Mar–15 Nov. 12 rooms, all with bath or
shower. B&B: double 234-350 frs. Set menus 60-180 frs [1989]. New nomination.
More reports welcome.*

CASTELPERS 12170 Aveyron   Map 4

Château de Castelpers   *Tel* 65.69.22.61

In deep countryside far from anywhere, off the main N88 from Rodez to
Albi, an old stone mansion turned into a small unpretentious hotel/res-
taurant by the family who have owned it for generations. "We spent two
enjoyable days," say recent visitors. "The château is at the bottom of a
heavily forested ravine, beside a river, in a lovely park with friendly
sheep and stunning conifers. The interior is still furnished like the family
home it was, with portraits on the stairs. There is a magnificent lounge
with baronial open fireplace; our bedroom had two four-poster beds and
windows rimmed with red stained glass, giving a cosy feel. We were
welcomed by an enthusiastic collie and Madame, who had put an electric
radiator on 'in case the baby might be cold'. We had dinner in front of a
blazing fire: the menu was not very exciting, but service was friendly.
There were swings in the grounds, and a children's menu. The place has
all the makings of a classic Guide entry: they just need to throw away the
long menu and make a couple of simple dishes each day and it would be
fine." Your views, please, on this idyll.

Open 1 Apr–1 Oct. Restaurant closed Tue to non-residents.
Rooms 2 suites, 7 double – all with bath and/or shower, and telephone; 8 with
TV. 1 equipped for &.
Facilities Salon with TV; 2 dining rooms. Garden bordered by 2 rivers with
fishing.
Location 12.5 km SE of Naucelle by D10, down road to Requista.
Credit cards Access, Visa.
Terms B&B double 260–400 frs. Dinner, B&B 185–260 frs per person. Set
lunch/dinner 90–195 frs; full alc 206 frs. Reduced rates and special meals for
children.

CÉRET 66400 Pyrénées-Orientales	Map 4

La Terrasse au Soleil	*Tel* 68.87.01.94

Route de Fontfrède

Splendidly situated in the Pyrenean foothills south of Perpignan, this
small modern hotel built in local Catalan style has fine views of the
mountains and distant sea. Bedrooms are large, modern and comfortable,
notably those in the new annexe. "The ladies of the house were friendly,
and we had a fine view from our balcony", says one reader this year, "but
the food was nothing special and service was slow." Another visitor
thought the hotel "wonderful", with *nouvelle*-ish food generously served;
a third judged the food "adequate rather than brilliant", and found the
tables too close-packed. (*Sara Price, Mrs JE Lyes, Dave Watts*)

Open 10 Mar–10 Jan.
Rooms 1 suite, 25 double – all with bath, telephone and TV. 14 in 2 annexes.
Ground-floor rooms.
Facilities 3 salons, bar, 2 restaurants; terrace. Garden with swimming pool, golf
practice and ping-pong.
Location Céret is 31 km SW of Perpignan.
Credit cards Access, Visa.
Terms Rooms 380–410 frs. Breakfast 45 frs. Dinner B&B 565–820 frs. Full alc
250 frs. .pa

CHABLIS 89800 Yonne	Map 3

Hostellerie des Clos	*Tel* 86.42.10.63
Rue Jules Rathier	*Telex* 351752 HOSCLOS

Patron-chef Michel Vignaud's elegant and select hotel/restaurant, a
converted almshouse in a well-known wine town, is now firmly
established as one of the best in North Burgundy, winning a *Michelin*
rosette and two red *Gault Millau toques* for such regionally inspired dishes
as pike cooked in Chablis, and kidneys and grapes also cooked in
Chablis. Our earlier nomination, from a connoisseur, "It's a restaurant
that is totally professional, serving light creative cookery perfectly
complementing the great wines of Chablis. The rooms are carefully
decorated and furnished in the modern style." This year, others have
largely agreed: "Modern, comfortable and friendly, with beautiful food";
"Excellent food, and breakfast included anything from poached pears to
home-made fruit loaf. Our spacious room had a view over the flower-
filled courtyard." The only complaint (from a Britisher): "Too many
British guests." (*C Carter, Simon Small, Peter and Ann Jones*)

Open All year except 10 Dec–10 Jan. Closed Wed, Thur midday except 1 May–30 Sep.
Rooms 26 double – all with bath, telephone, radio, and TV. 2 specially adapted for &.
Facilities Lift. Salon, bar, restaurant; conference room; garden.
Location Central, parking. Chablis is 19 km E of Auxerre.
Credit cards All major cards accepted.
Terms Rooms: single occupancy 180–240 frs, double 215–470 frs. Breakfast 42 frs. Dinner, B&B 420–470 frs per person. Set lunch/dinner 140, 238 and 340 frs; full alc 320 frs. Extra bed for child 50 frs; special menus.

CHAGNY 71150 Saône-et-Loire   Map 4

Château de Bellecroix   Tel 85.87.13.86

Two kilometres south of Chagny, a turreted castle of medieval origin, set in its own park, with a heated swimming pool and tables under the trees for drinks. Large and charmingly-furnished bedrooms; excellent classic cooking in the panelled dining room; friendly staff. Closed 1 Jan–1 Feb, and Wed. 19 rooms, all with bath and/or shower. Rooms 400–650 frs. Set menus 95–280 frs. [1989] Recent nomination warmly endorsed this year.

Hôtel Lameloise   Tel 85.87.08.85
36 place d'Armes   Telex 801086

Jacques Lameloise's elegantly converted 15th-century mansion is renowned for its cuisine, arguably the best in Burgundy (three *Michelin* rosettes and three *Gault Millau* red *toques*). It stands in the main street of a dullish little town amid woods and vineyards. "There's not much to say about it because it's all perfect", says one of this year's visitors and others are equally laconic, "As good as ever: cuisine superb, staff splendid, bedrooms luxurious"...and so on. Terrine de foie gras aux artichaux and a warm apple tart with sharp sorbet have been singled out. Recently returning visitors found a smart new lift to all floors, and renovations in the bedrooms which have superb bathrooms. Others have spoken of "the best cuisine we've had in France", "elegant rooms, with antiques, beamed ceilings and fireplaces", "a quietly luxurious atmosphere, attentive and courteous service", and "the top *sommelier* of France, Georges Pertuiset, is a charming and modest man". (*Rosamund Hebdon, Alan F Thomas, Aaron Esman, Jeff and Karen Nebel*)

Open All year, except 20 Dec–19 Jan and 1 May. Closed Wed, and Thur midday.
Rooms 21 double – all with bath and shower, telephone, radio and TV.
Facilities Lift. Salon, bar, restaurant.
Location Central. Garage parking.
Credit cards Access, Visa.
Terms Rooms 280–980 frs. Breakfast 60 frs. Alc meals (excluding wine) 290–450 frs.

Set dinner refers to a fixed price meal (which may have ample, limited or no choice on the menu). Full alc is the hotel's own estimated price per person of a three-course meal taken à la carte, with a half-bottle of house wine.

CHÂLONS-SUR-MARNE 51000 Marne   Map 3

Hôtel d'Angleterre et Restaurant   *Tel* 26.68.21.51
  Jacky Michel   *Telex* 842078
19 place Monseigneur Tissier

This traditional hotel in the town centre, small but very *soigné*, and newly modernised, is praised above all for owner Jacky Michel's innovative cooking (*Michelin* rosette, *Gault Millau toque*). Dropped from last year's Guide for lack of feedback, it has been liked by several visitors this year. "It's been recently renovated and we found it delightful – exceptional value for very high quality. The welcome was smiling and friendly, the furnishings and decor are attractive, and the bathrooms super. The cooking is superb, especially the 155-franc set menu available on weekdays, and the food is beautifully presented in modern style. The wine list includes 12 pages of champagnes alone." You can take drinks on a pretty terrace. (*Pat and Jeremy Temple; ML Dodd*)

Open 8 Jan–30 Jun and 23 Jul–20 Dec. Closed Sun; restaurant also closed Sat lunch.
Rooms 18 double – all with bath and/or shower, telephone and TV.
Facilities Lounge with TV, bar, restaurant. Small terrace where meals are served in summer.
Location Central; near Notre Dame en Vaux. Parking.
Credit cards All major cards accepted.
Terms Rooms 300–520 frs. Breakfast 38 frs. Dinner, B&B: single 490–690 frs, double 700–900 frs. Set meals 155, 225 and 350 frs; full alc 350 frs. Special meals for children.

CHALON-SUR-SAÔNE 71100 Saône-et-Loire   Map 4

Hôtel St-Georges   *Tel* 85.48.27.05
32 avenue Jean-Jaurès   *Telex* 800330

The idea of a commercial hotel next to the station in a biggish town would not make mouths water in Britain or the US: but this is France, and readers in 1988/9 have again warmed to young Yves Choux's "non-eccentric *nouvelle* cooking" (e.g. vinaigrette de rougets, pot-au-feu de la mer) which wins a *Michelin* rosette and *Gault Millau* black *toque*. "Ideal for a stopover. Plain rooms with excellent modern bathrooms, and fine cuisine." "A civilised hotel with tremendously friendly welcome, *un*patronising waiters, best dinner of our whole holiday." (*Mary Hanson*)

Open All year except Christmas Eve.
Rooms 3 triple, 45 double – 17 with bath, 31 with shower, all with telephone, radio, TV, mini-bar and air-conditioning.
Facilities Lift. Bar with TV, restaurant; conference facilities.
Location Central, near railway station. Garage.
Credit cards All major cards accepted.
Terms Rooms: single 230–290 frs, double 280–330 frs. Breakfast 36 frs. Set lunch/dinner 105, 170, 195 and 380 frs; full alc 320 frs. Reduced rates for children sharing parents' room; special meals.

> Always let a hotel know if you have to cancel a booking, whether you have paid a deposit or not. Hotels lose thousands of pounds and dollars from "no-shows".

CHAMONIX 74400 Haute Savoie   Map 4

Hôtel Albert Premier   *Tel* 50.53.05.09
119 impasse du Montenvers   *Telex* 380779

Long popular with readers, this sizeable chalet-type ski-hotel stands in its
own big garden near the middle of the resort. Latest reports: "Incredible
value. We had a lovely room with a view of Mont Blanc. Fantastic
breakfasts and dinners." "Our room was impeccably clean with lovely
furnishings and a balcony with view. The dining room with fresh flowers
and beautiful china was the perfect setting for the superb meal – salmon
with basil butter." Others have praised the ambience and professionalism
and have enjoyed using the pool, jacuzzi and sauna. "A roomy and
comfortable hotel, full of well-heeled skiers enjoying their *après-ski*. Log
fire and piano in the salon." In the large sophisticated dining room, the
interesting and ambitious cooking by the son of the *patron*, Pierre Carrier
(*Michelin* rosette, two red *Gault Millau toques*), is mostly much admired.
When fine, it's well worth taking the *téléphérique* (the world's highest,
they claim) to a point just below the summit of Mont Blanc.

Open All year except 2–22 May, 22 Oct–5 Dec. Restaurant closed Wed midday in
low season.
Rooms 5 suites, 24 double, 3 single – all with bath and shower, telephone, TV and
mini-bar.
Facilities Lift. Bar, lounge, 3 dining rooms, table-tennis room; sauna, whirlpool,
solarium. Large garden with tennis court, swimming pool (heated in summer),
children's play area. Winter sports, walking.
Location In side road, 150 metres from station; 500 metres from town centre.
Parking and garages.
Credit cards All major cards accepted.
Terms B&B: single 450–530 frs, double 560–820 frs; dinner, B&B 390–630 frs per
person; full board 460–700 frs. Set meals 150–380 frs; full alc 380 frs. Reduced
rates and special meals for children.

CHAMPAGNAC-DE-BELAIR 24530 Dordogne   Map 4

Moulin du Roc   *Tel* 53.54.80.36
                                                  Telex 571555

Solange Gardillou, wife of the *Moulin*'s owner, is the most highly reputed
woman chef in France (two *Michelin* rosettes). She and her husband run a
very trendy operation in a gracefully converted 17th-century walnut mill,
set quietly beside a stream in a Périgord village near Brantôme. An earlier
account paints the picture: "Tiny hotel, small rooms, flowers everywhere,
objets, old walnut-mill equipment. Our room with four-poster bed. Silver-
tray breakfast: strawberries, home-made jams. View from our window of
maids rinsing a bin in the millstream." Mme Gardillou's forte is variations
on local dishes, e.g. foie gras poêlé à la ciboulette. This, and the idyllic
setting, has led the *Moulin* to be much publicised in the glossy press and
the rich international tourists are still flocking in. But most of our readers
remain contented. A report this year, "Every year more flowers, and now
the addition of a swimming pool reached by a 'celestial bridge'. M.
Gardillou in yet another new jacket, and a well-drilled corps (slightly
lacking in humour) serving to perfection." However, another visitor, who
thought the set 190 fr menu [1989] "the best value in France", found it
unchanged the next night and felt that the *Moulin* might be resting on its

glossy laurels. (*DAC Cartwright, I and N Pressnell*) And *Mrs C Smith*, who otherwise liked the place a lot, reports a muddle over her room booking because "three couples all called Smith" were arriving on the same day. . .

Open All year except 15 Nov–15 Dec and 15 Jan–15 Feb. Restaurant closed Tue, and Wed midday.
Rooms 4 suites, 10 double – all with bath, telephone, radio and TV.
Facilities Salons, restaurant. Small garden. Swimming pool and tennis court
Location 6 km NE of Brantôme by D78 and D83. Parking.
Restriction No smoking in dining room.
Credit cards All major cards accepted.
Terms [1989 rates] Rooms 380–550 frs, suites 620 frs. Breakfast 50 frs. Set lunch/dinner 190–350 frs. Reduced rates and special meals for children.

LA CHARTRE-SUR-LE-LOIR 72340 Sarthe   Map 2

Hôtel de France   *Tel* 43.44.40.16
20 place de la République

A pleasant little market town between Tours and Le Mans, just west of the Ronsard country where the poet lived and loved; also near the strange hill village of Trôo where some English writers and others live in cunningly modernised caves in the tufa cliffside. The *France* is an unpretentious hostelry on the main square, breezily described to us: "Madame is dead brisk but v. amiable and proved happy to stay up after all the waiters had gone home. The hotel is obsessed with motor-racing – toy cars and photos of heroes in the public areas. Our long meal was OK, good solid stuff, jolly attempts at presentation (the caneton had a bandage, the escalopes came with sort-of horseshoe rosettes). The place was full of Brits, which does tend to slow down service. You need to be able to bark out your order very fast, as in New York delis. Nice room, comfy, quite pretty. Very short fat bath, just about fitted me after three weeks pigging French food." Rooms in the annexe are said to be less good than those in the main building. More reports please.

Open All year except 15 Nov–15 Dec.
Rooms 26 double, 2 single – 22 with bath, 4 with shower, all with telephone; 22 with TV. 12 in annexe.
Facilities 2 salons, bar, restaurant; conference facilities. Garden on river Loir.
Location In main square; parking. Town is 40 km N of Tours.
Restriction Not suitable for &.
Credit cards Probably Access, Visa.
Terms Rooms: single 110 frs, double 170–210 frs. Breakfast 22 frs. Set lunch/dinner 62, 95, 170 and 220 frs.

CHÂTEAU-ARNOUX 04160 Alpes-de-Haute-Provence   Map 5

La Bonne Étape   *Tel* 92.64.00.09
Chemin du Lac   *Fax* 92.64.37.36
                                                Telex 430605 BONETAP

Some of the best cooking in Provence (two *Michelin* rosettes, three red *Gault Millau toques*) is provided by the anglophile Gleize family (father created the restaurant at the *Capital* in London, son worked at the *Connaught*) at their elegantly converted and fairly expensive 17th-century coaching-inn. The setting is a bit cramped, on the main Grenoble-Marseilles highway, in a small town in a dull part of the Durance valley: but there are open fields at the back, and some rooms have a balcony facing these, over the swimming pool. Front rooms can be noisier. "A wonderful place, with charming rooms", say visitors this year; "in the beautiful dining room we enjoyed roast pigeon, wild boar with raisins and pignon nuts, and stuffed courgette flowers." Try also the local herb-fed lamb. (*Lynne and David Allen*)

Open 15 Feb–26 Nov, 4 Dec–5 Jan. Closed Sun evening and Mon out of season. Restaurant closed 24 Dec.
Rooms 7 suites, 11 double – all with bath and shower, telephone, radio and TV.
Facilities Salon, bar, 2 dining rooms; small conference room. Garden with heated swimming pool and patio. Lake 200 metres.
Location Near town centre, which is 14 km S of Sisteron. Parking.
Restriction Not suitable for &.
Credit cards All major cards accepted.
Terms Rooms: single 400 frs, double 600 frs, suite 850 frs. Breakfast 70 frs. Dinner, B&B 725–850 frs per person. Set lunch/dinner 190, 320, 370 and 390 frs; full alc 300 frs. Special meals for children on request.

CHÂTEAUNEUF 21320 Côte d'Or   Map 4

Hostellerie du Château   *Tel* 80.49.22.00

This well-modernised little rural hotel has a dramatic hilltop location in a medieval fortified hill-village west of Dijon. Reports last year: "A charming hostelry, carefully converted, with lots of rough stonework, exposed beams, and a small terrace for drinks. Dinner excellent." "A pretty garden, and an excellent meal in the unpretentious restaurant." "Comfortable, well run and well equipped". The suite and the larger bedrooms are in the annexe, *La Résidence*, a 16th-century house 50 metres from the hotel. This year, some readers found the setting delightful and the food good (*Janet and Dennis Allom, and others*): but another, while admiring the cooking, severely criticised the "patronising" Madame and slow, unsmiling, unhelpful service, so we'd welcome further reports.

Open 15 Mar–12 Nov. Closed Mon evening and Tue 1 Oct–15 Jun.
Rooms 1 suite, 16 double, 2 single – all with bath and/or shower, 11 with WC, all with telephone; 3 with radio. Suite, 5 doubles in annexe.
Facilities Salon, bar, 2 restaurants; banqueting room. Small garden with swings for children.
Location 10 km SE of Pouilly-en-Auxois. Take Pouilly exit from A6 motorway, take Arnay-le-Duc turning (N494), turn left down Beaune road (D977 bis), left again via Vandenesse to Châteauneuf.
Restriction Not suitable for &.
Credit cards Access, Amex, Visa.
Terms [1989 rates] Rooms: single 135–155 frs, double 450–500 frs, suite 500 frs. Breakfast 30 frs. Set lunch/dinner 125–260 frs. Special meals for children.

CHÂTILLON-SUR-SEINE 21400 Côte-d'Or   Map 3

Hotel de la Côte d'Or   *Tel* 80.91.13.29
Rue Charles Ronot

Châtillon is a small town on the upper Seine between Troyes and Dijon, noted for its museum of antiquities which include gold and silver Grecian artefacts of the 6th century BC, found in 1953 at nearby Vix, in the tomb of a Gallic princess. Not quite in that class of distinction, but very pretty and charming, is the ivy-covered *Côte d'Or*, new to the Guide this year, "A favourite stop-over point for me. Dinner – ah, dinner! – is served out in the courtyard (when fine), under vast rustling chestnut and sycamore trees, filled with cooing doves. A fountain plays gently, lights in the trees come on as the afterglow fades from the skies, the service is friendly and prompt but not hurried. The *menu régional* at 115 frs [1989] was excellent value: the vast array of cheeses went well with the delicious walnuted brown bread. My little room had a comfortable bed, two elegant chairs, a tiny antique desk, fresh flowers – but a gigantic spider leapt out of the folds when I drew the curtains." (*Hilary Swenson*) More reports welcome on this only slightly tarnished idyll.

Open All year except 18 Dec–23 Jan. Closed Sun evening and Mon except Jul and Aug.
Rooms 10 – 9 with bath and/or shower. all with telephone and TV.
Facilities Salon, bar, restaurant. Garden.
Location Central, near river. Parking. Town is 64 km SE of Troyes.
Restriction Not suitable for &.
Credit cards All major cards accepted.
Terms Rooms: single 170 frs, double 255–460 frs. Breakfast 35 frs. Dinner, B&B 80 frs added per person. Set meals 80–220 frs; full alc 180 frs.

CHÂTEAUNEUF-DU-PAPE 84230 Vaucluse   Map 5

Hostellerie Château des Fines   *Tel* 90.83.70.23
  Roches   *Fax* 90.83.78.42

This creeper-covered neo-Gothic pile with crenellated towers, former home of the Marquis de Baroncelli, stands isolated amid its own vineyards on a low hill above the plain north of Avignon. Readers have admired it (with reservations) for some years, and our inspector reports, "From the outside it looks massively mock-feudal, but inside the public rooms are small and intimate, though still 'baronial'. Soothed by piped classical music and seated on leather chairs, we took drinks in a salon lined with antique books; of the two tiny, elegant dining rooms, one is in modern style, but the other has a log fire and baronial emblems. Service we found deft but impersonal, otherwise all was as sleek and *soigné* as you'd expect in a small superior high-priced château hotel. Our cosy bedroom was well furnished and equipped, with antique bed-lamps, matching fabrics, hair-drier, tiled bathroom, even a trouser-press. The main set menu has limited choice and the cooking was uneven: but it is served with style and just about merits its *Michelin* rosette and *Gault Millau toque*. The wine list is mainly local C-du-P, including some from the hotel's own vineyards. Breakfast, including iced fresh orange juice, was excellent, though marred by piped pop music which had replaced the classical. In summer it is served more peacefully out on the panoramic terrace." A reader this year found the owners unfriendly – as did our inspector.

Open All year except Christmas–end-Feb, hotel closed Sun evening and Mon in low season. Restaurant closed Mon.
Rooms 7 double – 5 with bath, 2 with shower, all with telephone and TV.
Facilities 2 lounges, bar, 2 dining rooms.

Location 3 km S of Châteauneuf (by D17) which is 18 km N of Avignon, 13 km S of Orange.
Restriction Not suitable for ᴖ.
Credit card Access, Visa.
Terms [1989 rates] Rooms 520–720 frs. Breakfast 60 frs. Set lunch/dinner 195 frs.

CHAVOIRES 74290 Haute-Savoie

Map 4

Pavillon de l'Ermitage

Tel 50.60.11.09

The Tuccinardi family's white villa beside the lovely lake of Annecy is a formally elegant restaurant whose Bressane cooking (e.g. fish soufflé) is judged to be well deserving of its *Michelin* rosette and *Gault Millau toque*. "Yes, the cuisine is indeed distinguished, with portions dauntingly large," runs one report this year; "but the bedrooms with their faded decor are serviceable rather than attractive." Others tend to agree, though one recent visitor did have "a lovely room with a view over the lake, and a palatial pink marble bathroom." Back rooms with balconies facing the lake are best: front ones face the main road. "Everyone was cheerful and welcoming and the food excellent." In summer you can dine by the water's edge on a smart terrace under the trees. (*Alex Liddell, PJ Forrest, Peter and Ann Jones*)

Open Mar–end Oct.
Rooms 2 suites, 8 double – all with bath and telephone.
Facilities Lounge, bar, restaurant. Terrace and lakeside garden.
Location 3 km E of Annecy on Lake Annecy, near *téléphérique*.
Restriction Not suitable for ᴖ.
Credit cards All major cards accepted.
Terms Rooms: double 280–450 frs, suite 500–550 frs. Breakfast 40 frs. Dinner, B&B 350–520 frs per person. Set lunch/dinner 190, 250 and 380 frs; alc 350 frs (excluding wine).

CHEFFES 49125 Maine-et-Loire

Map 4

Château de Teildras

Tel 41.42.61.08
Telex 722268 TEILDRA

A visitor this year had a "wonderful" stay at this elegant little 16th-century château on the edge of a quiet village beside a pretty stretch of the river Sarthe, north of Angers. It is the family home of the Comte de Bernard du Breil, who some years ago decided that the best way to preserve his estate was to turn it into a hotel. This he has done, meticulously, and is helped by his wife and two daughters, one of them married to an American writer. You can ride, fish or go for walks in the large park. "We sipped tea in the rose garden and enjoyed an elegant room with high beamed ceiling and royal blue floral wallpaper. It had a view across the fields. Dinner was expensive but well prepared." That report this year echoes earlier enthusiasm: "Magnificent atmosphere, delicious food." "The public rooms are beautifully decorated with tapestries, paintings and plants, and the lighting is subdued. Our bedrooms had antiques, and its windows looked on to the park with its lovely trees and three cows munching in the sunlight." However, one visitor this year thought the grounds poorly maintained and the local wines of poor quality. (*Nancy P Barker, TD Baxendale*)

Open Hotel: 1 Feb–31 Dec. Restaurant 1 Apr–2 Nov. Both closed Tue, Wed morning.
Rooms 11 double – all with bath and shower, telephone and TV.
Facilities 2 salons, bar, 2 dining rooms. Wooded park. Golf, tennis, swimming nearby.
Location 19 km N of Angers. Turn out of Cheffes towards Juvardeil; château is signposted.
Credit cards All major cards accepted.
Terms B&B: single 470–774 frs, double 670–999 frs. Dinner, B&B single 730–880 frs, double 1,280 frs. Full alc 250 frs. Children under 12 sharing parents' room free; special meals.

CHÊNEHUTTE-LES-TUFFEAUX 49350 Maine-et-Loire   Map 4

Hostellerie du Prieuré   *Tel* 41.67.90.14
Telex 720379 PRIEURE

A priory dating from the 12th century is now a smart and well-known hostelry, set in a splendid position on a bluff above the Loire, amid 60 acres of private wooded park. "Lovely location, friendly and attentive staff, attractive pool, large room with usual French flock wallpaper, but comfortable." "The multiple terraces and flower gardens are wonderful. Not all bedrooms overlook the Loire, but ours did and the view was superb. The room itself was delightfully furnished with matching materials, and well equipped. The dining room and lounge also look over the river. Here the food was just a little 'over the top' and *too* highly priced: delicious, but fussily garnished". Another visitor has agreed – and we note that *Michelin* has now withdrawn its rosette, though the two red *Gault Millau toques* remain. One reader this year enjoyed the food and lovely setting, but thought that the hotel did not quite merit such prices. (*ATW Liddell, Edwin Prince*) The rooms facing the river are subject to some noise disturbances: express trains and gravel dredgers. One reader recommends the bungalows in the oak and pine woods, slightly less luxurious, but cheaper. It is worth visiting the nearby caves in the tufa rocks. Some are used for growing mushrooms (300 tons per day!), some have ancient sculptures recently discovered, and some are still occupied as troglodyte dwellings (open to tourists).

Open All year except early Jan–3 Mar.
Rooms 2 suites, 33 double – 32 with bath, 3 with shower, all with telephone; 21 with TV. 15 in pavilion in park.
Facilities Lounge, bar with TV, restaurant. Large grounds with mini-golf, tennis court, heated swimming pool; fishing in the Loire.
Location 7 km NW of Saumur off D751.
Restriction Not suitable for &.
Credit cards Access, Diners, Visa.
Terms B&B: single 558–708 frs, double 696–1,316 frs, suite 1,116–1,566 frs. Set lunch/dinner 270, 340 and 390 frs; full alc 400 frs. Reduced rates and special meals for children.

> Hotels often book you into their most expensive rooms or suites unless you specify otherwise. Even if all room prices are the same, hotels may give you a less good room in the hope of selling their better rooms to late customers. It always pays to discuss accommodation in detail when making a reservation.

CHINON 37500 Indre-et-Loire   Map 4

Hôtel Diderot   *Tel* 47.93.18.87
4 rue Buffon

This modest B&B, run by a friendly Cypriot, Theodore Kazamias, is in a lovely old town near the Loire, with a famous half-ruined hilltop castle, where Joan of Arc first met the Dauphin. It has long been a Guide favourite. The house is attractive, built of pale stone, much of it covered by a vine, with a wrought-iron balcony on the second floor, reached by a spiral staircase. Inside are exposed beams, and a welcoming salon. Breakfasts, taken communally, are notable for the huge choice of home-made preserves. A great bonus is the courtyard, closed at night, where cars can be safely parked. Some rooms are spacious, others quite small; courtyard-facing ones are the quietest. The hotel went through a slightly rocky patch in 1988, but we are glad to hear from recent readers of immaculate rooms, freshly decorated, and attractive new bathrooms. As before the consensus is that the *Diderot* is "tremendous value for money". (*Jo and Mick Féat, JM Pictet, Nancy P Barker, Peter Nicholls, and others*)

Open All year.
Rooms 24 double – all with bath and/or shower, and telephone; TV on request. 3 in annexe. 4 on ground floor are suitable for &.
Facilities Lounge, bar with TV, breakfast room; limited conference facilities. Courtyard.
Location Near place Jeanne d'Arc; hotel is well signposted. Parking in courtyard.
Credit cards All major cards accepted.
Terms B&B: single 185–265 frs, double 250–350 frs. (No restaurant.)

Château de Marçay   *Tel* 47.93.03.47
                                                   Fax 47.93.45.33
                                                   Telex 751475 MARCAY

Set in open country south of Chinon, here's a familiar Loire valley species – a 15th-century stone château approached by an impressive chestnut-tree-lined gravel drive, with neat pepper-pot towers and formal garden, converted into a smart and stylish hotel, and consecrated by *Michelin* with its full panoply of rosette, red gables and red rocking-chair. "Very seductive", "Large rooms furnished with antiques, and restaurant beautifully appointed", are among this year's comments. Other reports: "Quite a friendly reception. We had a pleasant room in the pavilion annexe. Rather snooty dining room, with so many staff; food very good, but rather a lot of noisy banging of kitchen doors." "Our vast room occupied an entire floor in one of the towers, beds were turned down at night and luxury chocolates left on the bedside tables. Dinner on the terrace was near perfect – the food leans towards *nouvelle* with very few vegetables. Both the maitre d' and the sommelier were young ladies, smart and charming. Prompt yet unhurried waitress service. Breakfast just about adequate though 25 frs extra for orange juice seemed extortionate." (*ATW Liddell, Victoria P Turner, Minda Alexander, Ian and Francine Walsh*) Rooms in the annexe are considerably cheaper than those in the château.

Open Mid-Mar–mid-Jan.
Rooms 3 suites, 35 double – all with bath and/or shower, and telephone; 12 with radio and TV. 11 in pavilion annexe.

Facilities Lift. 2 salons, TV room, bar, restaurant; conference/functions facilities; 2 terraces. Gardens with tennis court, heated swimming pool and children's playground.
Location 7 km S of Chinon by D116.
Credit cards All major cards accepted.
Terms Rooms: château 780–1,350 frs, pavilion 495–850 frs. Breakfast 54 frs. Dinner, B&B 610–1,010 frs per person. Set lunch/dinner 200 and 320 frs; alc (excluding wine) 350–400 frs. Reduced rates and special meals for children.

CHONAS L'AMBALLAN 38121 Isère   Map 4

Domaine de Clairefontaine

Tel 74.58.81.52
Fax 74.58.84.18
Telex 308132 CLAIRGI

A cheaper alternative to the *Marais St-Jean* (see below), but equally pleasant: a big stone 18th-century mansion on the edge of the village, in a lovely rural setting, converted into "the nicest kind of French country hotel, family-run, very unpretentious, slightly down-at-heel, reasonably priced", as an inspector relates. "We had breakfast on the terrace amid birdsong, facing vistas of meadows and rolling hills. A big garden and lovely lawn, a pond, a farm-like feeling – idyllic. The house, which once belonged to the bishops of nearby Vienne, is now run by charming petite Madame Girardon and her two sons, who trained chez Outhier at La Napoule. Their cooking is not in that class, but good (poulet à l'ail, truite au fenouil); menus have limited choice and change little, so a short stay might be best. Friendly service by local girls in a high-ceilinged too-brightly-lit dining room. Some rooms in main building, others in converted outhouse, simple but fairly comfortable." Endorsed this year: "Food was delicious"; "Full of kindness: we arrived when the restaurant was closed, but the son of the house made us a scratch meal which was perfection." (*Peter Dingley, Paul Van Broekhoven*) However, a reader who had one of the simpler rooms found it decidedly uncomfortable, and thought the service a bit chaotic, too.

Open All year except Dec and Jan. Closed Mon midday and Sun evening out of season.
Rooms 18 double – 12 with bath and/or shower; 16 with telephone. 6 in annexe next to main building. 4 ground-floor rooms.
Facilities Salon, 2 dining rooms; terrace. Garden, tennis court.
Location Off N7, 9 km S of Vienne; turn off A7 motorway at Vienne Sud. Parking.
Credit card Visa.
Terms Rooms 90–330 frs. Breakfast 28 frs. Set lunch/dinner 95, 130, 160 and 220 frs. Special meals for children.

Hostellerie Le Marais St-Jean   *Tel* 74.58.83.28

Christian and Suzette Heugas own and run a very stylish modern hotel, in a big pink converted farmhouse set amid pretty country near the Rhône, south of Vienne. "This was the jewel in the crown – what a treat!" runs one recent report; "attractive pieces of old France everywhere, beautiful flowers and lovely antiques. The bedrooms were spacious and comfortable, the view from our room was like a postcard. Dinner was the best meal I have ever had in France, beautifully presented, and breakfast was special too, with bowls of home-made jams. The Heugas are that lovely combination of a dedicated, enthusiastic and modest couple." Others, too, have much enjoyed the food (*Gault Millau toques*) – e.g. duck in a sharp fruit sauce and "real country soups" – as well as the beamed ceiling and tiled floor of the cool and sober dining room, and the luxurious bedrooms. "Our teenage children had great fun with the owners' dogs." One visitor this year thought the rooms nice but the food overpriced; another, who suffered a flight delay, was put out to find that her room had not been kept despite a written confirmation.

Open All year except 1–10 Nov, Feb, Tue evening and Wed.
Rooms 10 double – all with bath, shower and telephone. 1 ground-floor room with easy access.
Facilities 2 salons, bar, restaurant; conference room. Garden with terrace for alfresco meals.
Location Turn off A7 motorway at Vienne Sud; village, well-signposted, lies to W of N7, 9 km S of Vienne.
Credit cards All major cards accepted.
Terms B&B: single 505 frs, double 550 frs. Set lunch/dinner 150, 240 and 290 frs; full alc 250 frs. Reduced rates and special meals for children.

CLUNY 71250 Saône-et-Loire · Map 4

Hôtel de Bourgogne · *Tel* 85.59.00.58
Place de l'Abbaye

A rambling but dignified old hotel in the main square of this picturesque medieval town, facing what remains of the mighty Romanesque abbey that in the Middle Ages was one of Europe's leading religious, artistic and intellectual centres. The well-kept *Bourgogne* has been an inn since the 18th century (Lamartine often stayed here and guests can still sleep in his bed). Most of its bedrooms "ours was the size of a small flat" look out on to green hills or to the towers of the abbey. One reader this year had "an ambitious dinner served by charming novices" and found the Gosse family owners "most cordial". Others agree: the "delicious food" merits its *Michelin* rosette, though one visitor thought the *nouvelle cuisine* preparation rather affected. (*William A Grant*)

Open 10 Feb–15 Nov. Closed Tue except high season; restaurant also closed Wed midday.
Rooms 2 suites, 14 double – 9 with bath, 4 with shower, all with telephone; 2 with TV.
Facilities Ramps. Salon, bar, restaurant. Small courtyard where drinks and breakfasts are served in fine weather. Films, concerts.
Location On N79, 25 km NW of Mâcon. Hotel is opposite the abbey (back rooms quietest). Garage parking.
Credit cards All major cards accepted.
Terms Rooms: double 328 frs, suite 720 frs. Breakfast 40 frs. Set lunch/dinner 110–350 frs; full alc 200–300 frs. Reduced rates and special meals for children.

COLLIOURE 66190 Pyrénées-Orientales · Map 4

Hôtel Madeloc · *Tel* 68.82.07.56
Rue Romain-Rolland

Ten minutes' walk up a steepish hill from the quayside of the picturesque and popular fishing-port-cum-trendy-resort, south-east of Perpignan, is this modern B&B hotel in local Catalan style, cool and welcoming, set in its own garden;

*many rooms have balcony or terrace; upper ones have views over the hills.
Pleasant decor, efficient bathrooms. Open Easter–15 Oct. 21 rooms, all with
bath or shower and balcony. B&B: single 240 frs, double 302–380 frs. No recent
feedback. More reports welcome.*

COLLONGES-LA-ROUGE 19500 Corrèze   Map 4

Relais de St-Jacques de   *Tel* 55.25.41.02
Compostelle   *Telex* 283155

Many fine buildings including a 12th-century church grace this beautiful
16th-century village, built of local purple-red stone, carefully restored
and set in lush green valleys a few miles north of the Dordogne. The
ruined château of the Vicomte de Turenne, former lord of the region,
stands just to the west. The *Relais*, more popular than ever this year,
offers inexpensive bedrooms that, although very clean, may be too basic
for some tastes: but it also has "delightfully friendly" owners, the
Castéras, whose cooking earns a *Michelin* red "R" for good value. "A
most delectable place", runs one report this year; "the bedrooms may be
simple, but the restaurant's ambience is one of rural sophistication, with
expert service (uniformed waiters hover). The food is amongst the best we
have had anywhere - tremendous platters of hors d'oeuvre, massive
helpings of stuffed lamb, superb goats' cheeses. Breakfast similarly
civilised." "Madame slightly disorganised but very welcoming, bedrooms
spotless and rather sweet, a very cosy salon and a marvellous dinner."
"M. Castéra loves to chat with his guests after dinner, even if their French
is poor." Be warned, however, that the bedrooms are small, the shower-
rooms can be minuscule, and lavatories are not numerous. (*Melanie
Worrall, Minda Alexander, Dr P Blackwell-Smyth*)

Open 1 Feb–30 Nov. Closed Tue evening and Wed in low season.
Rooms 11 double, 1 single – 5 with bath, 2 with shower, all with telephone. 5 in
annexe.
Facilities Salon, bar, 2 dining rooms, dining terrace.
Location 21 km SE of Brive; follow signs to Meyssac. Hotel is central. Parking.
Restriction Not suitable for &.
Credit cards Access, Diners, Visa.
Terms [1989 rates] Rooms 100–240 frs. Dinner, B&B 160–230 frs per person. Set
lunch/dinner 90–220 frs; full alc 250 frs. Reduced rates and special meals for
children.

COLY 24120 Dordogne   Map 4

Manoir d'Hautegente   *Tel* 53.51.68.03 and 53.51.60.18

Set amid deep country near Terrasson, some 20 kilometres north of
Sarlat, this fine creeper-covered mansion has been owned by the Hamelin
family for 300 years and they have now converted it into a small hotel. It
makes an appealing Guide debut this year: "The house is beautiful, amid
water-gardens, streams, fields and woods, and the interior has been
furnished and decorated with imagination. The bedrooms (more are
about to be built in the granaries) are all different and all lovely, with
antiques and big, comfortable beds. In the salon, a log fire blazes when
the evenings get cool. Dinner, a five-course set meal, is cooked by

Madame Hamelin, using her own foie gras, confit de canard, cèpes – and it is excellent. It has a strong regional bias, but there are some lighter, more innovative dishes too. Breakfasts are a delight. A peaceful place and the family are charming, though never intrusive." (*Jennifer Harte*)

Open 1 Apr–31 Oct. Dining room closed for lunch.
Rooms 10 double – all with bath and telephone. 1 ground-floor room.
Facilities Lounge, dining room. Garden. River with private fishing.
Location 19 km N of Sarlat. Parking.
Credit cards Access, Visa.
Terms Dinner, B&B 420–600 frs. Set dinner 200 frs; full alc 280 frs. Reduced rates and special meals for children.

COMBEAUFONTAINE 70120 Haute-Saône   Map 3

Le Balcon   *Tel* 84.92.11.13

In a village on the Langres-Vesoul road, north-east of Dijon, a friendly family-run Logis de France *with rustic decor and excellent food* (Gault Millau toque). *Rooms at back are quietest. 20 rooms, all with bath and/or shower. Rooms 110–350 frs. Breakfast 28 frs. Set meals 130–280 frs [1989]. New nomination. More reports welcome.*

COMBLOUX 74920 Haute-Savoie   Map 4

Aux Ducs de Savoie   *Tel* 50.58.61.43
Le Bouchet   *Telex* 319244 AUXDUCS

This big modern chalet, where most rooms have a balcony facing Mont Blanc, is the leading hotel of a sizeable skiing and summer resort near Megève. Warm, friendly and well run, with large bedrooms; food good, but choice limited. Open-air pool, heated in summer. Open 10 Jun–25 Sep, 18 Dec–25 Apr. 50 rooms, all with bath. B&B double 406–496 frs. Set menus 130–190 frs. New nomination. More reports please.

COMBREUX 45530 Loiret   Map 3

L'Auberge   *Tel* 38.59.47.63

On the edge of a village in flat but pleasant woodland country east of Orléans, this creeper-covered *auberge* dates from 1847 and has been liked by several readers. An inspector reports, "Quite unsmart, it is run in a friendly, casual way by its civilised bourgeois owners, Madame Gangloff and her niece. There is a cosy pub-like lounge with log fire, a beamed dining room, and a small rather unkempt garden at the back, with swings and ping-pong; tennis-court and swimming pool are across the road, next to open fields and a bedroom annexe. Rooms are simple but comfortable, good value. All in all, a sympathetic place – save that the classic home cooking (tête de veau, râble de lièvre, tarte tatin) is somewhat overpriced for its only average quality. Nice service by local girls, and good breakfasts." "Good food (e.g. salmon in sorrel sauce), and superior bathrooms."

Open All year except 20 Dec–20 Jan.
Rooms 21 – all with bath and/or shower, and telephone. Some in annexe.
Facilities Lounge, bar, restaurant; conference room. Garden with swimming pool and tennis court.
Location 35 km E of Orléans, 13 km N of Châteauneuf-sur-Loire. Parking.
Credit cards Access, Visa.
Terms [1989 rates] Rooms 250–300 frs. Breakfast 30 frs. Half board 270–330 frs per person. Set lunch/dinner 90–200 frs. Special meals for children.

COMPIÈGNE 60200 Oise   Map 3

Hostellerie du Royal-Lieu   *Tel* 44.20.10.24
9 rue de Senlis

Joan the Maid was captured and sold to the English in this historic town with its huge royal palace; then the Germans in 1918, and later the French in 1940, signed ignominious armistices in a clearing in the nearby forest. In today's happier age, British, French and German tourists rub shoulders in this "excellent hotel" just outside the town. It is not cheap, but offers quality. Apart from one reader this year who liked the bedrooms but had a poor meal, all new reports have been favourable. "It makes a great first night in France because it reminds you of all the things the French do better than us in hotels – delicious food, making their guests feel looked after in an unservile way, an unfussed view of children in public places. We had a superb meal. The rooms are small and cluttered with heavy repro furniture, but all look out onto greenery and a little flock of doves." "An efficient and warm welcome, and superb cooking." "Comfortable, but bed-lighting poor." The main road in front is ugly, but at the back all is calm and green. (*Jeremy Raymond, Carolyn and Gary Smith, Mrs RB Richards*)

Open All year.
Rooms 3 suites, 15 double, 2 single – all with bath and/or shower, telephone and TV. 1 ground-floor room, suitable for &.
Facilities Salon, bar, restaurant; terrace for meals in fine weather. Garden.
Location 3 km SW of town, on Senlis road (D932A).
Credit cards Access, Diners, Visa.
Terms Rooms 300–420 frs. Breakfast 30 frs. Set lunch/dinner 180 and 280 frs. Special meals for children.

CONDRIEU 69420 Rhône   Map 4

Hôtellerie Beau Rivage   *Tel* 74.59.52.24
                                                    Telex 308946

An old creeper-covered hotel beside the *beau rivage* of the Rhône, in Côte du Rhône vineyard country. In summer you can take drinks under white parasols on the "wonderful" terrace right by the river, or dine out on the stone-flagged patio. The hotel was dropped from the 1989 Guide during a period of ownership reshuffle, but the Humann family are now firmly at the helm, and many readers have spoken well of them this year, and of the *Michelin*-rosetted food. "We had a splendid room with fabric-covered walls and fine furniture. The public areas are spacious and the gardens lovely. The service had a flourish, and the dinners were amongst the best of our holiday." "We were delighted at the standards of cuisine, welcome and service – we found the porter polishing all the guests' cars' windscreens, quite unasked." "A typically French hotel with slightly higgledy-piggledy room arrangements." "The meal was a gastronomic masterpiece." There's a petro-chemical works half a mile away, whose low throbbing can be heard at night. (*Mrs JB Priestley, Stephan and Kate Murray-Sykes, Sarah Curtis, John RL Cook, Carolyn and Gary Smith, and others*)

Open 15 Feb–15 Jan.
Rooms 2 suites, 22 double – all with bath and shower, telephone, radio, TV and baby-listening.
Facilities Salon, bar, 2 restaurants. Terrace restaurant overlooking the Rhône. Garden, fishing.
Location 40 km S of Lyon, on N86. Leave A7 at Condrieu exit (coming from N), or Chanas exit (coming from S).
Restrictions Not suitable for &.
Credit cards All major cards accepted.
Terms B&B: single 557 frs, double 614–834 frs, suite 904 frs. Set meals 250–370 frs.

CONQUES 12320 Aveyron   Map 4

Hôtel Sainte-Foy   *Tel* 65.69.84.03

This famous old village between Figeac and Rodez was a leading staging-post on the pilgrimage to Santiago. It straggles along a steep wooded hillside above a gorge, and its slate-roofed houses and cobbled streets surround a massive and awesome abbey church, renowned for the Romanesque stone carving on the west doorway and for its rich gold and silver treasure. The *Sainte-Foy* is called after the martyred girl whose weird gold relic is still to be seen in the abbey museum. It's a fine medieval house facing the abbey, with handsome old furniture in the public rooms; and in 1988/9 readers have again enjoyed its comforts, food and service, especially "dining in the leafy courtyard, gently floodlit". The food is traditional and regional, very well cooked ("delicious tripoux"). The staff, all female, are helpful and charming, and the atmosphere is restful. Readers warn that some upper rooms are small and thin-walled (but well fitted, apart from one account of a sagging bed) and that plumbing and church clocks can be noisy at night. (*D and L Allen, Dr RL Holmes and Dr MW Atkinson*)

Open Easter–1 Nov.
Rooms 1 suite, 18 double, 2 single – 11 with bath, 10 with shower, all with telephone.
Facilities Reading room, TV room, bar, dining room; conference facilities; interior patio.
Location Off D601 and not far from N662 between Figeac (54 km) and Rodez (37 km). Hotel is central, opposite cathedral. Garage and car park.
Restriction Not suitable for &.
Credit cards Access, Visa.
Terms [1989 rates] Rooms 180–380 frs, Breakfast 34 frs. Dinner, B&B 310–370 frs per person. Set lunch/dinner 108–175 frs. Special meals for children.

LES CONTAMINES-MONTJOIE Haute-Savoie 74170   Map 4

Hôtel Gai Soleil   *Tel* 50.47.02.94

An old farmhouse, modernised into a spruce and friendly little holiday hotel, set on the edge of a ski and summer resort at the foot of Mont-Blanc, south of St-

Gervais. Small but comfortable rooms with good lighting and bathrooms. A leafy garden with deck-chairs, where you can take drinks. Home cooking, simple and without choice, but good; generous breakfasts. Guests almost all French. Open 16 June–18 Sept, 18 Dec–16 Apr. 19 rooms, some with bath and shower. Dinner, B&B 215–260 frs. Set menus 80–150 frs. Recent nomination. More reports please.

CORDES 81170 Tarn Map 4

Hôtel Le Grand Écuyer *Tel* 63.56.01.03
Rue Voltaire

This "lovely hotel", a former hunting-lodge of the Counts of Toulouse, is a select little place with fine antiques and spacious rooms. It stands inside a famous old ramparted hilltop village, whose streets today are lined with boutiques and craft shops. It was built by the Counts in the 13th century as a defence against Simon de Montfort and his cruel anti-Cathar crusaders. "A wonderful way to bid farewell to the Cathars," writes one north-bound visitor this year; "a bedroom with a comfortable four-poster, pleasant carpets, a high timbered ceiling, and the best-appointed bathroom I've met outside Paris. A good, relaxed meal, capped by the virtuoso dessert production" (*Michelin* rosette and two red *Gault Millau toques*). Other correspondents were even more ecstatic: "When I die, dear Lord, please send me to *Le Grand Écuyer*. The staff were the best of any hotel in France. The food was wonderful, the desserts fabulous. I have such a poignant memory of rising in the morning and opening the shutters to find myself floating on a sea of mist sunk in the valley while the sun sparkles on the green hills above. There is a knock on the door and the breakfast tray full of breads and croissants, fresh juice and aromatic tea and coffee is set before us on a table by the window. Surely this must be heaven." (*TH Nash, Lynne and David Allen*)

Open 17 Mar–31 Oct. Restaurant closed Mon except July and Aug.
Rooms 1 suite, 12 double – all with bath, telephone, radio and TV.
Facilities 2 lounges, bar, 3 dining rooms. Terrace.
Location In centre of village which is 25 km NW of Albi. Public parking down the hill, crowded in high season.
Restriction Not suitable for &.
Credit cards All major cards accepted.
Terms Rooms 500–750 frs, suite 1,200 frs. Breakfast 50 frs. Dinner, B&B 520–620 frs per person. Set lunch/dinner 180–360 frs. Special meals for children on request.

Hostellerie du Vieux Cordes *Tel* 63.56.00.12
Rue St-Michel *Telex* 530955

Warmly nominated this year as a cheaper alternative to the *Grand Écuyer*, this newly redecorated and very stylish *Logis de France* stands next to a medieval church: you can dine on the terrace, or in a delightful courtyard under a huge ancient wistaria. "The best hotel of our week's touring, a friendly welcome, and a lovely view of the valley from our room. Much of the old building remains, though the bedroom decor disguises this with a fabric wall cover. The menus range in price and style from traditional to modern: ours was in the middle of both, and was excellent and charmingly served. Breakfast too was the best of our trip." (*CR; John and Rita Newnham*)

Open All year except Jan.
Rooms 21 double – all with bath and/or shower, and telephone; 10 with TV.
Facilities Lounge, bar, TV room, restaurant. Small garden, courtyard.
Location Central; parking nearby.
Restriction Not suitable for &.
Credit cards All major cards accepted.
Terms B&B: single 295–405 frs, double 360–465 frs; dinner, B&B: single 350 frs, double 520 frs. Set meals 70–240 frs; full alc 180 frs. Reduced rates and special meals for children.

CORDON 74700 Haute-Savoie   Map 4

Hôtel des Roches Fleuries   *Tel* 50.58.06.71

In a small ski-resort west of Chamonix, this pleasant, spacious and informal chalet-style hotel faces across the valley to Mont Blanc, with spectacular views; many bedrooms have their own balcony. The new owners, the Picot family, continue to please most of our readers, who praise the well-furnished, comfortable rooms and warmth of hospitality. Most of them like the food, too, though one couple thought the medium-price set menu rather poor. The smaller of the two dining rooms is the more attractive. A heated swimming pool has now been installed.

Open 20 Dec–15 Apr, 1 June–25 Sep.
Rooms 27 double, 1 single – all with bath and shower, telephone and TV. 2 in annexe.
Facilities 2 lounges, bar, restaurant. Garden, heated swimming pool.
Location 4 km SW of Sallanches on D113. Parking.
Restriction Not suitable for &.
Credit cards Access, Amex, Visa.
Terms B&B double 305–345 frs; dinner, B&B 260–340 frs per person. Set lunch/dinner 120–240 frs; full alc 250 frs. 1-night bookings probably refused in high season. Reduced rates and special meals for children.

CORPS-LA-SALETTE 38970 Isère   Map 4

Hôtel de la Poste   *Tel* 76.30.00.03
Place de la Mairie

At this scenic village along the Route Napoléon, high up on the winding Grenoble to Gap highway (N85) in the Dauphiné Alps, Bonaparte rested on his journey from Elba to Paris and Waterloo. Many tourists today pass this way too, en route to or from Provence, and the highly traditional *Poste* is again much liked by several readers this year: "A busy and bustling hotel with superb food and always full – justifiably so. No *nouvelle cuisine* here – vast helpings (*Michelin* red "R"), a very pleasant dining room, and the best breakfast we had in France. Our room was Victorian (apart from the bathroom) but comfortable." Another 1989 visitor, on a return trip, also found the food enjoyable and copious, but noted a shortage of hot water and a mistaken over-charging for two beers; she felt that the owner's attitude to his guests was a little offhand, maybe due to over-popularity. Of the two annexes across the road, one is "rather basic", the other has smartly decorated rooms giving onto a private courtyard with tables and chairs. One reader had a room with walls "covered in gold silk damask and the shower room was all new in lilac pink with gold taps". (*Philippa and Peter Herbert, Lt. Col. BAS Barnes; also EP Bazalgette*)

Open All year except 31 Nov–1 Feb.
Rooms 19 double, 1 single – all with bath/shower and telephone; 15 with TV. 4 in annexe opposite. 2 ground-floor rooms.
Facilities Salon, TV room, bar, restaurant; terrace. Lake with sailing and fishing 500 metres.
Location In centre of village. Garage parking.
Credit cards Access, Visa.
Terms B&B: single 185–195 frs, double 250–270 frs; dinner, B&B 205–273 frs per person. Set meals 80–200 frs; full alc 200 frs. Reduced rates and special meals for children.

COTIGNAC 83850 Var — Map 5

Hostellerie Lou Calen   *Tel* 94.04.60.40
1 cours Gambetta   *Telex* 400287

This much-visited village in the hilly Var hinterland is oddly situated at the foot of a brown cliff holed with caves, some of them once inhabited. The *Lou Calen* (Provençal for "the place of the oil-lamp"), a small family-run place, "friendly and amateurish but nice", has again been enjoyed this year, by readers who liked dining on the terrace with its wide view, and thought the food well cooked and generously served. Rooms are furnished in local country style, but have modern plumbing. Previous visitors have found the Provençal cooking always reliable and sometimes excellent: one has enthused over the "fantastic array of help-yourself hors d'œuvre with delicious dressings", another over the "pieds et paquets and sinful great hunks of tarte aux fraises" on the cheaper menu. The large swimming pool, not always perfectly tended and sometimes crowded, is reached through a small garden. Only drawback: some traffic noise at night, heard in front rooms. Much of interest to visit in the area: the majestic Gorges du Verdon, the lovely Cistercian abbey of Thoronet and, less well known, the château at Entrecasteaux, housing a most original museum (and which is now a B&B with an entry in the Guide this year). (*Philippa Herbert, Dave Watts, Kay and Neville Varley, and others*)

Open 8 Apr–1 Jan. Restaurant closed Wed in low season.
Rooms 8 suites, 8 double – all with bath and shower, telephone , TV and tea-making facilities. 2 suites in garden annexe.
Facilities Salon with TV, bar, 2 restaurants; conference facilities. Garden with terrace and swimming pool.
Location On Route des Gorges du Verdon. For Cotignac take exit Brignoles or Le Luc-Toulon off N7. Central (3 rooms might have traffic noise). Parking.
Restriction Not suitable for &.
Credit cards All major cards accepted.
Terms Rooms 230–410 frs. Breakfast 39 frs. Set lunch/dinner 105, 183 and 238 frs; full alc 300 frs. Special meals for children.

> If you are nominating a hotel, please do make sure that you tell us enough to convey its character and quality. We can't make good bricks without plenty of straw.

COULANDON 03000 Allier   Map 4

Le Chalet   *Tel* 70.44.50.08

"An oasis of rural calm, with charm, comfort and good, simple food." "A spacious, elegant bedroom in the annexe, efficient staff, and a blissful dinner overlooking the park." So run reports this year and last on this former hunting lodge set peacefully (it is a *Relais du Silence*) in its own spacious park with a pond full of fish. Offering rural tranquillity at modest prices, it stands half-way between the market town of Moulins and the village of Souvigny with its fine priory church. "Good value in the old style; a lush pastoral setting with nightingales." Some rooms have exposed beams, and there's even a comfortable library – what a rarity in a modest French hotel. The cheaper menus are "plain but adequate". "The amazing Gallic chinoiserie wallpapers are all Sandersons." (*RHW Bullock, Mr and Mrs RM Booth, JP Berryman*) One reader was disturbed by traffic noise from the main road and recommends the annexe rooms as quieter; another was disappointed by the food.

Open 1 Feb–31 Oct. Restaurant closed midday.
Rooms 25 double – all with bath and/or shower and telephone; 15 with TV. Some in annexe.
Facilities Lounge, dining room with terrace, library. Large park with pond.
Location 6 km W of Moulins, down side-road just off D945 towards Souvigny.
Restriction Not suitable for &.
Credit cards All major cards accepted.
Terms B&B: single 200–280 frs, double 270–390 frs; dinner, B&B 185–345 frs per person. Set lunch/dinner 70 and 110 frs; full alc 160 frs. Special meals for children.

COULON 79510 Deux-Sèvres   Map 4

Le Central   *Tel* 49.35.90.20
4 rue d'Autremont

In the 'Venise Verte' of the Marais Poitevin with its many canals, here's a white-walled geranium-bedecked small restaurant-with-rooms whose cooking wins a Michelin red "R" for good value, and is served with skill. Lively and congenial atmosphere, happy staff. Clean, efficient bedrooms. Closed 15 Jan– 4 Feb, 24 Sept–14 Oct, Sun night and Mon. 7 bedrooms, all with bath or shower. Rooms 160–180 frs. Breakfast 20 frs. Set menus 75–162 frs. Recent nomination. More reports please.

CRÈCHES-SUR-SAÔNE 71680 Saône-et-Loire   Map 4

Hostellerie du Château   *Tel* 85.37.12.04
de la Barge

"A handsome creeper-covered 17th-century manor in south Burgundy has been tactfully converted into a pleasant country hotel, graceful but informal, slightly old-fashioned, and exuding Burgundian well-being. The two salons have comfortable period furnishings; some bedrooms are large, also in period style, others are smaller but good value. In the large lovely dining room, with its pink table linen, a log fire burns in winter and big windows look on to the garden; drinks, breakfast and lunch can be served out on its terrace in summer. The cooking, mainly Burgundian but with some inventive touches, we thought excellent: e.g. terrine de brochet in a rich tarragon sauce, and saumon frais aux deux beurres. Admirable desserts and cheeses. We took those tiny hard chèvres which are known as 'boutons de culottes' (fly-buttons) – "Well, we *are* in the Clochemerle country here," said the motherly but very expert and knowledgeable head waitress. Coffee at breakfast was poor; and the hotel's setting is unpromising, on the edge of a dull village south of Mâcon. But it would make a good base for touring south Burgundy and the Beaujolais – including the village of Vaux that was the original for Chevalier's *Clochemerle* and today exploits this full-tilt with tourist-geared oh-là-là ribaldry. It has even built a new *pissotière*. A surly receptionist was encountered this year.

Open All year except 25 Oct–3 Nov, 19 Dec–5 Jan. Restaurant closed Sat, Sun in low season.
Rooms 2 suites, 21 double – 16 with bath, 5 with shower, all with telephone. 2 ground-floor rooms.
Facilities Lift. Salon, TV room, restaurant. Garden with children's playground.
Location In village (follow signposts for Gare TGV) which is on N7 8 km S of Mâcon.
Credit cards All major cards accepted.
Terms [1989 rates] Rooms: single 206 frs, double 226 frs. Breakfast 21 frs. Dinner, B&B 226 frs per person. Set lunch/dinner 72, 123 and 160 frs; full alc 135 frs. Reduced rates and special meals for children.

CREST 26400 Drôme — Map 4

Grand Hôtel　　　　　　　　　　　　　　　　*Tel* 75.25.08.17
60 rue de l'Hôtel de Ville

In a little town south-east of Valence on the road to Nice, with a ruined hilltop fortress above the river Drôme, this Logis de France has a touch of faded grandeur, with marble pillars and a ramshackle garden. But prices are pleasantly lacking in grandeur, while the large bedrooms are comfortable and the staff friendly, and food is inexpensive, varied and excellent (Michelin red "R" for good value). Closed 23 Dec–23 Jan. 22 rooms, 14 with bath and/or shower. B&B double 350 frs. Set menus 70–200 frs. New nomination. More reports welcome.

DIJON 21000 Côte-d'Or — Map 4

Hôtel La Cloche　　　　　　　　　　　　　　　*Tel* 80.30.12.32
　Restaurant Jean-Pierre Billoux　　　　　　　*Telex* 350498
14 place Darcy

A large, imposing hotel, traditional but well modernised, and centrally located on a big square. "Rooms are all double-glazed, so there is no noise. There is a garage, a quiet garden, a cosy bar, and a lounge which has changing art exhibitions. Our split-level room was large, with good views; lighting could have been better, but the bathroom was huge. The main attraction is the magnificent restaurant in the old cellars (two *Michelin* rosettes, three red *Gault Millau toques*) which Jean-Pierre Billoux, one of Burgundy's best young chefs, rents from the hotel: cooking is traditional Burgundian with modern overtones and wines are of course superb. Lunch is also served in a small conservatory. Very good service." (*Pat and Jeremy Temple*)

Open All year. Restaurant closed Feb.
Rooms 4 suites, 76 double – all with bath, telephone, radio and TV.
Facilities Lifts. Lounge, bar, restaurant; conference facilities; conservatory. Garden.
Location Central (rooms are double-glazed). Garage.
Credit cards All major cards accepted.
Terms [1989 rates] Rooms: single 460 frs, double 540 frs, suite 1100 frs. Breakfast 45 frs. Reduced rates for children. Set menus 230–400 frs.

DIVONNE-LES-BAINS 01220 Ain Map 4

Château de Divonne *Tel* 50.20.00.32
Route de Gex *Fax* 50.20.03.73
Telex 309033

The casino at this fashionable spa resort has a bigger turnover than any other in France (Monaco is another country), being much frequented by wealthy international punters from Geneva, only 12 miles away. Many of them make also for the luxurious *Château*, a handsome white building amid parkland, admired by one of our most discriminating correspondents, "This excellent 19th-century reproduction of a Loire Valley château sits on a hill above the charming little town, down a winding drive through trees, with its own helipad by the gate. The marble hall, breathtaking, harbours magnificent modern sculptures; public rooms are smartly furnished in period style.

"On a summer evening, dinner on the terrace was pure ecstasy, the pale-yellow-stone facade floodlit, tables lit by oil-lamps and Mont-Blanc 50 miles away glowing pink in the sunset. The cooking well deserves its *Michelin* rosette and two red *Gault Millau toques* for its beautiful presentation and subtle flavours – chaud-froid de homard et foie gras, two sorts of contrasting lake fish, and fantastic chocolate puddings. Superb wine-list, not over-priced. Breakfast on the sunlit terrace was also splendid, and included delicious goats' cheese. The hotel's young and enthusiastic owners have the knack of choosing caring, charming and very hard-working staff, and the ambience is warm and individual; nor is the place over-expensive – by Geneva standards. Bedrooms are spacious and characterful, with genuine antiques; ours had the same superb view as from the terrace. If you leave your room very untidy, as we did, it is cleared up swiftly and totally." Warmly endorsed this year by *Neil and Jacqueline Britton*.

Open Early-Mar–early Jan. Restaurant closed Tue, and Wed midday in low season.
Rooms 5 suites, 15 double, 7 single – 26 with bath, 1 with shower, all with telephone and TV. 3 ground-floor rooms.
Facilities Lift, ramps. Salon, bar, 2 restaurants; conference facilities. Park with terrace, tennis, table-tennis and helipad.
Location On road to Gex, on W side of Divonne, which is 19 km N of Geneva (leave Lausanne motorway at Divonne-Coppet).
Credit card Visa.

Terms Rooms: single 380–475 frs, double 595–970 frs, suite 970–1,580 frs. Breakfast 60 frs. Set lunch/dinner 215, 305 and 405 frs; full alc 380 frs. Reduced rates and special meals for children.

DOMME 24250 Dordogne   Map 4

Hôtel de l'Esplanade   *Tel* 53.28.31.41

This well-known showpiece village on a cliff above the Dordogne has been tastefully restored in the tradition of Viollet-le-Duc, and is full of expensive antique shops and foie gras. In the daytime in summer it is horribly crowded, but then it quietens when the trippers have gone – "On a midsummer evening, when you stroll along the clifftop path, magic is in the air". The *Esplanade*, a medium-priced *Logis de France*, is worthy of this setting, and is run with style by *patron*-chef René Gillard and his friendly wife. A visitor this year enjoyed her "blue-rose-covered attic room" and her 105-franc dinner. Bedrooms are individually decorated in a variety of floral wallpapers. "Our room had an enchanting small balcony overlooking the wonderful valley. Superb food (try the salmon stuffed with mousseline of trout)." One visitor, while praising the view and the decor, thought the owners and staff cool and churlish. (*Caroline Currie, Mr and Mrs R Porter, P Talbot Smith, and others*)

Open 15 Feb–15 Nov. Closed Sun evening and Mon Feb–Apr.
Rooms 19 double – 15 with bath, 4 with shower, all with telephone; some with balcony. 4 in annexes.
Facilities Salon with TV, bar, restaurant; terraces.
Location 13 km S of Sarlat.
Restriction Not suitable for &.
Credit cards Access, Amex, Visa.
Terms [1989 rates] Dinner, B&B 265–370 frs; full board 365–470 frs. Full alc 310 frs.

DONZENAC 19270 Corrèze   Map 4

Relais du Bas Limousin   *Tel* 55.84.52.06 and 55.84.54.62

Usefully placed by the main N20 Limoges–Toulouse highway (at Sadroc, 6 km north of Donzenac), but quiet, here is a cheerful and efficient family-run auberge, just right for a night's stop. All very clean and well kept, with good bedrooms at low prices and first-rate traditional country cooking. 24 rooms, most with bath or shower. B&B double 146–266 frs. Set menu 60–200 frs. Recent nomination. More reports please.

DUCEY 50220 Manche   Map 2

Auberge de la Sélune   *Tel* 33.48.53.62
2 rue St-Germain

A neat little hotel with garden and terrace above the river, in a dullish Norman village not far from Mont-St-Michel. Bedrooms are said to be clean and pretty: the best are those at the back, facing garden and river. Some readers this year, but not all, have again been full of good words: "Lovely welcome from Mme Girres, an attractive dining room, and very good food, notably the truite duceyne." "Wonderful food, charming garden." (*Minda Alexander, C Head, Martin Davis, Mr and Mrs G Buckland*) However, some have found the welcome less than warm and the service far less than perfect, with preferential treatment for regulars. More reports, please.

Open All year except mid-Jan–mid-Feb. Closed Mon Oct–Mar.
Rooms 18 double, 1 single – 19 with bath and shower, all with telephone and TV. 3 in garden pavilion.
Facilities Lounge, bar, 3 restaurants; 2 seminar rooms. Garden with terrace.
Location On N176, 11 km SE of Avranches (garden rooms quietest). Carpark.
Restriction Not suitable for &.
Credit cards Access, Diners, Visa.
Terms Rooms 203–230 frs. Breakfast 25 frs. Set lunch/dinner 63, 90, 120 and 145 frs.

DURAVEL 46700 Lot   Map 4

Auberge du Baran   *Tel* 65.24.60.34

In the lovely Lot valley west of Cahors, Roger and Letitia Washbourne, from Bath, run a simple village inn (*Logis de France*) which, says our nominator this year, "has become a meeting place for locals to drink. They seem to have set up a very 'French' place here, gaining acceptance from both natives and tourists" – a plus for Euro-integration and the ideals of 1992. "From the road it doesn't look especially inviting, but inside and at the back all is changed. Our ground-floor room had french windows opening onto a little terrace and a pretty 'wild' garden with beautiful views of the fine Romanesque village church. The room was cool and comfortable, furnished in pale blue and cream. The summer dining room is a delightful terrace covered in wistaria and tobacco plants, with a glorious view. Food and service were both excellent: omelette au fromage frais, chicken in garlic sauce, delectable cassis sorbet. Breakfast is taken in the bar." (*David and Melanie Worrall*)

Open All year. Restaurant closed mid-Jan–mid-Mar.
Rooms 7 double – all with bath and shower, and telephone.
Facilities Bar, TV room, restaurant; 2 terraces. Garden.
Location In village, on D911 12 km E of Fumel.
Restrictions Not suitable for &.
Credit cards Access, Visa.
Terms B&B 125 frs; dinner, B&B 210 frs; full board 270 frs. Set meals 60, 85, 130 and 195 frs; alc 120 frs. Reduced rates and special meals for children.

ELINCOURT-STE-MARGUERITE 60157 Oise   Map 3

Château de Bellinglise   *Tel* 44.76.04.76
                                                              Fax 44.76.54.75
                                                              Telex 155048

North of Compiègne, an imposing rose-coloured château, part 16th-century, set beside a big lake in its 600-acre grounds. Its new owners, a Belgian hotel group, run it partly as a rather grand conference centre: it won't appeal to all our readers' tastes, but might suit those seeking a touch of formal grandeur on their way from Calais to Paris. For example, a reader this year thought both the cooking and the bedrooms "excellent" and enjoyed the views, while others wrote last year: "Architecturally it's a gem. My room in the courtyard, one of the cheaper ones, was finely furnished (modern) and well equipped. In the beautiful and spacious dining room, with its panelling and chandeliers, I had the best dinner of my trip." "We found the decor in the public areas rather opulent, if florid: the spacious halls and staircase have walls of yellow marble and gold silk damask. The formal dining room was attractive, and the menu good value, but service was slow." The new chef is a pupil of the great Robuchon, but he has not yet won laurels from the French guides.

Open All year.
Rooms 47 – all with bath and/or shower, telephone and TV.
Facilities Lift. Lounge, TV room, bar, restaurant; 6 conference rooms. Large grounds with tennis court, riding, golf.
Location 15 km N of Compiègne, on D142 to Lassigny. Parking.
Credit cards All major cards accepted.
Terms [1989 rates] Rooms 400–1,000 frs. Breakfast 50 frs. Dinner, B&B 565–740 frs per person. Set lunch/dinner 175–260 frs. Special meals for children.

ENTRECASTEAUX 83570 Var   Map 5

Château d'Entrecasteaux   *Tel* 94.04.43.95

This unusual bed-and-breakfast venture, new to the Guide, occupies part of a Provençal château with a very odd history. It's an austere 17th-century hulk, on the edge of an unspoilt village in a valley west of Draguignan and not far from the lovely Cistercian abbey of Le Thoronet. The château belonged to local lords, one of whom in the 18th century killed his young wife and then vanished into a Portuguese jail. This brought the family into such disgrace that gradually their château fell into ruin – till in 1974 it was bought and carefully restored by the amazing Ian McGarvie-Munn, avant-garde painter, Scottish nationalist, soldier and adventurer, ex-commander-in-chief of the Guatemalan navy and married to the grand-daughter of a former president of that country. He died in 1981; the building is now run by his son Lachlan as a delightfully informal and varied museum (Scottish bagpipes, pre-Columbian ceramics, Murano goblets, Provençal kitchenware, etc) which you enter via the family kitchen. There are many temporary exhibitions, and classical concerts on the lovely terrace in summer: but it's a pity that Lachlan has hidden away his father's surreal pornographic paintings, judged too shocking for local taste. He now lets out three rooms: one has a vast colonnaded Roman-style bathroom, designed by his father. "One room is divinely large with parquet floor and huge antique Provençal bed. Breakfast was a treat, and the owner very friendly and kind." (*Clare Enders, JA*)

Open All year except 5 days in early Aug, Christmas Eve.
Rooms 1 suite, 2 double – all with bath (1 also has shower) and telephone; 2 with tea-making facilities.
Facilities Museum. Terrace. Garden (designed by Le Nôtre) with swimming pool.
Location 8 km S of Salernes.
Restrictions Not suitable for &.
Credit card Amex.
Terms B&B: double 600–900 frs, suite 1,200 frs. (No restaurant.)

Please make a habit of sending a report if you stay at a Guide hotel.

L'ÉPINE 51460 Marne   Map 3

Aux Armes de Champagne   *Tel* 26.66.96.79
Telex 830998

An old coaching-inn, restored and modernised, in the square of a village
east of Châlons-sur-Marne. The dining room and most bedrooms face the
huge, floodlit basilica of Notre Dame, a place of pilgrimage in the Middle
Ages. Above all it's the food that matters here, not cheap, but awarded a
rosette by *Michelin* and a *toque* by *Gault Millau* (for e.g. salad of courgettes
and truffles with foie gras). One reader in 1989 thought the cuisine
uninspired, especially the vegetables and sweets, but another has written
of "refined French cooking at its best", and praised also the "friendly
greeting, flowers everywhere and well-groomed little garden". Noisy
lorries sometimes pass the dining room, but bedrooms are quiet,
especially those at the back and in the new annexe. "The picturesque
garden at the back, with a small stream, is an ideal spot for an aperitif."
"Clean and comfortable, without the firework-night-in-Hawaii wallpaper
which usually tells you that you are in a French hotel." The proprietor
has his own champagne vineyard, and the long wine list is devoted
mainly to bubbly. (*Dr Peter Woodford, Mrs S Groves, and others*)

Open All year except 7 Jan–12 Feb.
Rooms 39 double – 27 with bath, 12 with shower, all with telephone; 13 with T V.
16 in 2 annexes 150 metres from main building. Some ground-floor rooms.
Facilities Bar, T V room, 2 restaurants; functions facilities; concerts in summer.
Small garden with mini-golf.
Location Central; village is 8.5 km E of Châlons, on N3. Parking.
Credit cards Access, Amex, Visa.
Terms [1989 rates] Rooms 400–460 frs. Breakfast 36 frs. Set lunch/dinner 90, 165,
235 and 320 frs; full alc 320 frs. Reduced rates and special meals for children.

ÉTOILE-SUR-RHÔNE 26800 Drôme   Map 4

Château de Clavel   *Tel* 75.60.61.93

The stately Napoleon III château in the Rhône valley south of Valence,
has been restored by its new owner, Xavier Wernert, and now opened as a
fairly smart hotel. "Peacefully located in a large park amid green
countryside, it has an elegant staircase and square-well with chandelier.
Our split-level bedroom was *gigantic*, furnished finely with antique-
looking bureaux and chairs. M. Wernert is a delightful man, rather vague
and seemingly eccentric, but all in all the hotel functions well. The staff
were cheerful and the food excellent, including the breakfasts. The lake
has many frogs and a swan which M. Wernert told us was a priest, i.e.
celibate. He fed it every day. We enjoyed the horses. . ." (*Kenneth E Smith*)
More reports please.

Open 1 Apr–31 Dec.
Rooms 6 suites, 17 double – all with bath and shower, telephone and T V. 7 in
annexe.
Facilities Lounge with T V. Garden with swimming pool and tennis court. Lake,
river, golf, riding nearby.
Location Turn E off N7, 12 km S of Valence.
Restriction Not suitable for &.
Credit cards Access, Amex, Visa.

Terms [1989 rates] Rooms 300–350 frs, suites 450–500 frs. Breakfast 32 frs. Set lunch/dinner 120–280 frs; full alc 170–180 frs. Reduced rates and special meals for children.

EUGÉNIE-LES-BAINS 40320 Landes   Map 4

Les Prés d'Eugénie   *Tel* 58.51.19.01
  et le Couvent des Herbes   *Telex* 540470

Michel Guérard's very superior establishment, in a Second Empire mansion north of Pau, is world-famous as the home of *cuisine minceur*. But robust appetites are catered for too. In the main restaurant the cuisine is *gourmande* rather than *minceur*, quite different from the diets devised by this three-star chef for his health farm next door. Alas, no reader has reported to us this year, though from a food writer we've heard news of a dish of pasta and wild mushrooms, in a redolent sauce, that "encapsulated mushroomness". One recently visiting connoisseur has had mixed feelings: "The food prepared for the wealthy gourmets is totally exquisite, and its accent is on subtlety of taste, not calorie control. Presentation is impeccable, and service is on oiled castors by waiters clearly proud of the masterpieces coming from the kitchen. This said, the place seems to have serious flaws as a hotel. The bedrooms are comfortable and spacious, but they are not serviced properly and have lacunae that seem odd amid so much expensive luxury. Breakfast is idiosyncratic and expensive. Staff are cheerful and relaxed, but reception was somewhat casual." Top ratings in the French guides, needless to say. More reports badly needed, both on the existing hotel and on the new six-room annexe, a renovated 18th-century convent, *Le Couvent des Herbes*, opening in 1990.

Open 13 Feb–10 Dec.
Rooms 7 suites, 28 double – all with bath, telephone and TV.
Facilities Lift. Salon, billiard room, TV room, gallery, bar, dining rooms, restaurant. Beauty salon, thermal baths, sauna. 2 tennis courts, *boules*, unheated swimming pool. Garden and river. 6 more rooms in annexe opening in 1990.
Location Off D944 St-Sever–Aubagnan, 53 km N of Pau.
Credit cards Amex, Diners, Visa.
Terms [1989 rates] Rooms 1,173 frs, suite 1,357–1,403 frs. Breakfast 80 frs. *Menu minceur* (residents only) 230–330 frs. Set lunch/dinner 370–470 frs. Reduced rates and special meals for children.

ÉVIAN-LES-BAINS 74500 Haute-Savoie   Map 4

La Verniaz et ses Chalets   *Tel* 50.75.04.90
Route de l'Abondance   *Telex* 385715

Our first-ever entry for France's leading lakeside spa is quite small but luxurious, with four red *Michelin* gables and a rosette, plus more red print for its chalet-suites secluded amid greenery. Its Californian nominator is enthusiastic, "A perfect mix of charming informal service and elegance. I have been to plenty of hotels whose pool attendants acted like head waiters and vice versa, but here is a balance to be envied. The hotel is up a steep and tortuous drive from Évian, but the reward for that is the view of Lac Léman, Lausanne, the Swiss Alps and Mont Blanc. The peace and quiet is broken only by the faint plonk of tennis balls. The gardens are a riot of colour, the rooms spacious and homey, with balconies that afford both privacy and a fine lake view. The restaurant is the crowning glory – grilled rack of lamb with basil, fresh fish from the lake, game-fowl in local style and superb soufflés. Wines are fairly priced, but I wish they wouldn't chill the port. On fine days you can dine outdoors. The front desk staff are helpful. The Verdier family owners have been hoteliers for generations and can point proudly to some old sepia-toned pictures that document their past. Those ancestors must also be looking down proudly from the walls on the current establishment." (*H Richard Foss*)

Open All year except end Nov–early Feb.
Rooms 5 chalet-suites, 35 double – all with bath/shower and telephone; TV on request; many with balcony.
Facilities Lift. Salons, bar, restaurant; conference facilities; terrace. Garden with swimming pool and tennis court.
Location 2 km SE of centre of Évian. Parking.
Credit cards Access, Amex, Visa.
Terms [1989 rates] Rooms: single 350–550 frs, double 500–950 frs, suites 1,500–2,500 frs. Breakfast 45 frs. Half board 450–885 frs per person. Set lunch/dinner 220–240 frs. Special meals for children on request.

EYNE 66800 Pyrénées-Orientales   Map 4

Auberge d'Eyne   *Tel* 68.04.71.12

Eyne is an unspoilt village up on the glorious Cerdagne plateau near Saillagouse (q.v.): here this beautiful old rural *auberge*, newly restored, with bedrooms in period style, makes its Guide debut. "The ski resorts are rather an eyesore in the Cerdagne but can be avoided. The *auberge* could be called 'up-market rustic'. Quiet and comfortable, run by an ambitious young patron, it has a good lounge with log fire, and friendly staff. Pension dinners were excellent. Very good value." (*John Mainwaring*)

Open All year except Nov. Restaurant closed Mon.
Rooms 11 double – all with bath/shower and telephone. Ground-floor rooms.
Facilities Lounge, bar, reading room, 3 dining rooms. Garden.
Location 6 km E of Saillagouse, 85 km W of Perpignan.
Credit cards Access, Diners, Visa.
Terms Rooms 375 frs. Breakfast 40 frs. Set lunch/dinner 99–150 frs; full alc 185 frs. Reduced rates and special meals for children.

LES EYZIES-DE-TAYAC 24620 Dordogne   Map 4

Hôtel Cro-Magnon   *Tel* 53.06.97.06
                                                        Telex 570637

Les Eyzies, France's leading "centre of prehistory", is dominated by steep cliffs riddled with palaeolithic caves. It is bedlam at the height of the tourist season, though it quietens down in the evening. In its outskirts is this handsome creeper-covered old hotel – "a traditional family-run place with plenty of atmosphere, good value", runs one report this year. Its chief drawback is proximity to the railway and main road, causing some noise even at night: quietest rooms are those in the pleasant annexe, set in a large garden with a swimming pool on the other side of the railway. The *demi-pension* meals are described this year as "good but not inspirational" (the inspiration is maybe reserved for *à la carte* dishes such as salade périgourdine which earn the *Michelin* rosette). This earlier description remains valid: "The entrance hall has an English coaching inn feel, with wood-panelled walls, pretty flowers, brasses polished daily; there is a delightful and quiet residents' lounge upstairs. Our room was a fair size, spotless, furnished and wallpapered in rustic style; plumbing noises were the only snag. The hotel's family owners, Jacques and Christiane Leyssales, chat warmly with their guests. The ambience is friendly and personal." (*Willis G Frick, N and I Pressnell, and others*) The hotel prefers its residents to dine at the hotel.

Open End-Apr–mid-Oct. Restaurant closed Wed for lunch.
Rooms 4 suites, 20 double – all with bath and shower, and telephone; 4 with TV. 8 in annexe by swimming pool.
Facilities 2 lounges, 2 dining rooms. Garden restaurant. 5 acres of parkland with heated swimming pool and river.
Location 600 metres W of town centre. Parking.
Restriction Not suitable for &.
Credit cards All major cards accepted.
Terms B&B: double 380–480 frs, suite 630–780 frs; dinner, B&B 300–400 frs per person. Set lunch/dinner 110–300 frs; full alc 200–300 frs.

Les Glycines   *Tel* 53.06.97.07

The creeper-covered *Glycines*, by a river about ten minutes' walk from the village, is regarded by some readers as a better bet than the *Cro-Magnon* above, partly because it is further from the noisy railway. It has won a stint of praise again this year: "The garden is an informal heaven – chairs and loungers under a willow or by the pool, or on lush grass, with farmland beyond. Chic, blonde Madame smiles, the staff are most helpful. Meals were very good – small and delicious helpings, with all vegetables crisp (*à point*) and fresh. The baby deer was pink and juicy – a shame when we'd seen them in the woods that day." "Superb comfortable rooms with lovely views, outstanding cuisine, and a large new swimming pool. The Mercats look after their guests very well." "There is a vine-shaded terrace for drinks or lunch. Our room in the new annexe was quiet but small, with doors opening onto our own table and chairs in the sunny courtyard; rooms in the main building may be a little dark and cramped." (*Mr and Mrs Wilmot-Allistone, Mr and Mrs R Porter*)

Open Mid-Apr–1 Nov.
Rooms 25 – all with bath and telephone. 2 rooms accommodating 4 in separate building in garden. 5 ground-floor rooms.
Facilities 2 salons, bar, restaurant; terrace for alfresco meals. Large garden with swimming pool.
Location On road to Périgueux, by the river. Parking.
Credit cards Access, Amex, Visa.
Terms Rooms 285–318 frs. Breakfast 38 frs. Dinner, B&B 314–344 frs per person; full board 387–417 frs. Set lunch/dinner 105–300 frs; full alc 230 frs. Reduced rates for children under 5; special meals on request.

Le Moulin de la Beune   *Tel* 53.06.94.33

"Just the kind of hotel that should be in the Guide" is one 1989 verdict on this big converted mill, tastefully restored: it stands next to the National Museum of Prehistory and beside the river Beune which flows through its garden. "Owners friendly, breakfast good, bedrooms attractive with good modern plumbing." "There is a large old fireplace in the lounge/reception which is attractively furnished as are the bedrooms. Inviting breakfast room, with glass doors leading out to tables by the river. Breakfast exceptional, with home-made jams, hot croissants, coffee *ad lib*. Smart chairs in the garden. Warm welcome from the owners, the Dudicourts." No restaurant, but readers speak highly of the one in the millwheel building (*Au Vieux Moulin*), under separate management. (*DG Randall, and others*)

Open End Mar–early Nov.
Rooms 20 double – 14 with bath, 6 with shower, all with telephone. 4 ground-floor rooms with separate entrance.
Facilities Salon, bar, TV room, breakfast room. Garden. River (fishing), swimming pool and tennis nearby.
Location Central, near the National Museum of Prehistory. Parking.
Credit cards All major cards accepted.
Terms [1989 rates] Rooms: single 190 frs, double 265 frs. Breakfast 30 frs. (No restaurant.)

ÈZE 06360 Alpes-Maritimes   Map 5

Château de la Chèvre d'Or	*Tel* 93.41.12.12
Rue du Barri	*Fax* 93.41.06.72
	Telex 970839 CHEVDOR

The best-known and most touristy of all the Côte d'Azur's hill-villages stands in a spectacular site beside the Middle Corniche, on a rocky outcrop almost sheer above the sea (Èze-Bord-de-Mer, see next entry, is just below). It has been scrupulously restored, and its many souvenir shops are not too vulgar; when the trippers have departed, it can be hauntingly quiet at night. There is no motor traffic, but a short walk along its main alley leads to the celebrated *Chèvre d'Or* ("a jewel," writes a recent American visitor), a medieval château artistically converted into a small luxury hotel run with suave efficiency. Soft music plays as you sip your champagne cocktails by the pool, gazing at Cap Ferrat far below; even the telephones in the lavishly furnished bedrooms are Edwardian museum-pieces. If some bedrooms are cramped, blame the 11th-century architect, though the 20th-century redesigners have done their ingenious best. Rooms near the kitchens may be noisy. The panoramic restaurant, frequented by famous and beautiful people, wins a well-deserved *Michelin* rosette and two *Gault Millau toques* for such dishes as hot oysters in champagne. But we'd be glad of up-to-date reports, please.

Open 1 Mar–30 Nov. Restaurant closed Wed in Mar.
Rooms 3 suites, 11 double – all with bath and shower, telephone and TV. All in different buildings 4–10 metres from main building.
Facilities Bar/salon, restaurant, grill room. Garden with terrace and 2 swimming pools; alfresco meals in summer. 10 mins' drive to sea.
Location 10 km E of Nice on "Moyen Corniche" road.
Restriction Not suitable for &.
Credit cards All major cards accepted.
Terms [1989 rates] Rooms 1,160 frs–1,950 frs, suite 2,050 frs. Breakfast 75 frs. Alc meals (excluding wine) 340–480 frs. Reduced rates for children; special meals on request.

> If you have kept brochures and tariffs for Continental hotels, do please enclose them with your reports.

ÈZE-BORD-DE-MER 06360 Alpes-Maritimes   Map 5

Le Cap Estel
                                   Tel 93.01.50.44
                                            Fax 93.01.55.20
                                        Telex 470305

For years only *Tom and Rosemary Rose* reported to us on this Italianate villa, now an elegant family-run luxury hotel, on a promontory between Beaulieu and Monaco. They visited it annually, reported each year that it was just as good as ever, and praised the excellent bedrooms, all with terrace or loggia and air-conditioning, the comfortable public lounge and poolside bar, the excellent buffet lunches, and the dinners. Last year another reader endorsed the entry with even greater enthusiasm: "If hotel perfection ye seek, here it be. A magnificent position, excellent food and brilliant service by a young highly trained team who would do credit to the Brigade of Guards. Room service arrived in a flash, the lad looking after the open-air swimming pool had a mattress and towels spread out on your poolside bed when he saw you coming. A lovely building in a lovely setting." A 1989 visitor is more cautious in his praise: "Yes, it *is* excellent – but of course not perfect. They allow smoking in the dining room, decoration sometimes borders on kitsch, we had one or two maintenance problems. But it's pretty good!" Half board is obligatory.

Open 1 Mar–31 Oct.
Rooms 8 suites, 40 double – all with bath and shower, telephone, terrace or loggia and air-conditioning.
Facilities Lift. Bar/salon, restaurant, grill room. Garden with terrace; alfresco meals in summer. Indoor and outdoor swimming pool.
Location 10 km E of Nice on "Moyen Corniche" road.
Credit cards Access, Visa.
Terms [1989 rates] Dinner, B&B 1,700–2,550 frs. Full board 250 frs added.

LA FAVÈDE 30110 Gard   Map 4

À l'Auberge Cévenole   *Tel* 66.34.12.13

A hamlet just off the N106, in the attractive southern foothills of the Cévennes (but be warned that the approach up the industrial valley from Alès, to the south, is not so attractive). Here the *Auberge Cévenole* is a neat, white-walled red-roofed building in local style, sprucely and prettily decorated. It wins *Michelin*'s red rocking chair and two red gables for secluded tranquillity and pleasant charm, and from one reader the comment: "Charming and peaceful, with a lovely and very clean pool. The staff were attentive, the setting elegant and traditional, but the food on the set menu did not quite live up to its promise." Others this year have again approved the well-kept garden and well-furnished rooms, and have enjoyed the food: but charges for extras are said to be very high. Not a hotel, incidentally, for those who want to escape from fellow-Brits on holiday. (*GE Samson, Peter L Aston*)

Open 15 Mar–30 Nov. Possibly Christmas and New Year.
Rooms 2 suites with mini-bar, 18 double – all with bath or shower, telephone; 4 with TV. 8 in bungalows with ground-floor rooms.
Facilities Salon, TV room, dining room. Terrace where meals are served. Garden with swimming pool, mini-tennis.
Location 3 km W of La Grand-Combe, on D283.

Credit cards Access, Visa.
Terms [1989 rates] Rooms 250–350 frs. Breakfast 45 frs. Dinner, B&B 300–550 frs
per person. Set lunch 150–250 frs. Special meals for children.

FAYENCE 83440 Var   Map 5

Moulin de la Camandoule   *Tel* 94.76.00.84
Chemin de Notre-Dame des Cyprès

*Beautifully restored old olive-mill in delightful Provençal setting amid
meadows below hill-village of Fayence; garden, pretty stream, big swimming
pool (barbecues in summer). Owned since 1986 by former film-director and
novelist Wolf Rilla and his wife Shirley, from London. Rooms recently renovated
in traditional Provençal style. Recent reports, while appreciating ambience, find
fault with details of room upkeep and general management. Shirley Rilla has
now taken over control in the kitchen. 11 rooms, all with bath and/or shower,
175–485 frs. Breakfast 35 frs. Set dinner 155 – 250 frs. More reports please.*

FÈRE-EN-TARDENOIS 02130 Aisne   Map 3

Hostellerie du Château   *Tel* 23.82.21.13
                                                                  Fax 23.82.37.81
                                                                  Telex 145526

A luxurious manor house, part Renaissance, part 19th-century, that
stands in its own sizeable park within a forest, 45 km west of Reims,
owned, run and cooked for by the Blot family. Rooms vary greatly: older
ones in the main house have more personality, but attic ones are very
small; newer ones in the modern annexe are plainer but larger, with
superior bathrooms (some suites have a jacuzzi). "Very peaceful and
relaxing," say visitors this year; "we had a warm welcome and were
shown to a large, attractive room. Dinner was excellent" (serious *nouvelle
cuisine*, awarded *Michelin* rosette and two red *Gault Millau toques*). (*Pat
and Jeremy Temple*)

Open All year.
Rooms 9 suites, 14 double – all with bath and shower, telephone and TV.
Ground-floor rooms. 1 specially adapted for &.
Facilities Salon, bar, 3 restaurants; conference facilities. Large grounds with golf
and tennis.
Location 3 km N of Fère-en-Tardenois, on road to Fismes.
Credit cards All major cards accepted.
Terms Dinner, B&B: single 1,300 frs, double 1,900 frs, suite 3,300 frs. Set meals
2900–430 frs.

FLAGY 77940 Seine-et-Marne   Map 3

Hostellerie au Moulin   *Tel* (1) 60.96.67.89
2 rue du Moulin

A 13th-century millhouse, beautifully converted into a rustic-style
restaurant-with-rooms, in a pretty village south-east of Fontainebleau.
There's a pleasant lounge with some of the old mill-wheels and pulleys,
and in summer you can eat out under weeping willows beside a stream,

with the murmur of rushing water close by. This idyllic and peaceful setting has again been much admired this year, as have the little beamed bedrooms (with modern bathrooms), the staff, and the Scheideckers who own the place: "The owner is a most urbane and courteous man, and his taste must account for the meticulous attention to detail in the pretty little bedrooms and romantic dining room by the river." (*Sharon Gutman, Deborah Reese, Lorraine Carlson, RHW Bullock, and others*) Several visitors this year have been critical of the cooking – we'd welcome more reports on this.

Open All year, except 9–21 Sept, 20 Dec–22 Jan, Sun evening and Mon (Mon evening and Tue at Easter and Whitsun).
Rooms 3 triple, 7 double – all with bath and shower, and telephone; 3 with TV.
Facilities Lounge, bar, restaurant. Garden beside river; fishing (permit obtainable in village).
Location 23 km S of Fontainebleau by N6 (18 km); turn right onto D403, and immediately left onto D120.
Restriction Not suitable for &.
Credit cards All major cards accepted.
Terms Rooms: single 170–190 frs, double 210–370 frs. Breakfast 32 frs. Dinner, B&B 251–324 frs. Set lunch/dinner 130 frs; full alc 220 frs. Reduced rates and special meals for children.

FLORIMONT-GAUMIERS 24250 Dordogne   Map 4

La Daille   *Tel* 53.28.40.71
Florimont-Gaumiers, Domme

Several eulogies have reached us this year for this secluded farmhouse south of Domme that Derek and Barbara Brown now run as a tiny four-bedroom hotel-restaurant – a stirring example of the British love-affair with the Dordogne. Set in the hills above the Céou valley, the house is built in local stone with an external stone staircase and pigeon tower, but internally it has been sensitively modernised, with new bathrooms. "The Browns strike just the right balance of friendliness and professionalism and the food was excellent; the rooms enjoy a splendid view across the valley"; "the whole atmosphere was peaceful and relaxed". No lunches are served, but you can buy your own delicatessen and wines and enjoy them under the walnut trees in the pretty garden. (*Dr and Mrs James Stewart, EA and BM Prower, and others*)

Open 1 May–15 Oct. Restaurant closed for lunch.
Rooms 3 double, 1 single – 3 bath, 1 with shower. Single room in annexe.
Facilities Restaurant. Garden, terrace.
Location La Daille is signposted from Gaumiers village, which is just W of the D46, 13 km S of Domme and 5 km NW of Salviac.
Restrictions Not suitable for &. No children under 7.
Credit cards None accepted.
Terms Dinner, B&B (min 3 days) 288–325 frs. Set dinner (by reservation only) 120 frs.

Do you know of a good hotel or country inn in the United States or Canada? Nominations please to our sibling publication, America's Wonderful Little Hotels and Inns, PO Box 150, Riverside Avenue, Riverside, Conn. 06878, USA.

FONTAINEBLEAU 77300 Seine-et-Marne Map 3

Hôtel Aigle Noir
27 place Napoléon

Tel (1) 64.22.32.65
Fax (1) 64.22.17.33
Telex 694080

Fontainebleau's grandest hotel, in the centre, facing the gardens of Napoleon's favourite palace. Classic Louis XVI and Empire decor plus mod cons. Some bedrooms are lavishly Victorian in style, others plainer; service is good, but room upkeep can be faulty. Food mostly admired: Michelin rosette *and* Gault Millau toque *for such dishes as caneton rouennais aux groseilles. 6 suites, 51 rooms, all with bath or shower. B&B double 940–1,090 frs. Set menus 200–280 frs [1989]. Endorsed this year, but some recent criticisms. Further reports welcome.*

FONTGOMBAULT 36220 Indre Map 4

Auberge de l'Abbaye
Tel 54.37.10.82

Exuding authentic rural Frenchness, this Guide newcomer stands in a village of the Creuse valley between Poitiers and Châteauroux: "An enchanting place: five 16th-century cottages grouped round a shady courtyard (where you take breakfast) have been sympathetically convert-ed into a small comfortable hotel. The *patron* is a man of talents who even mends cameras. The food was delicious, served in the stone-flagged entrance hall. The monastery up the road does a nice Gregorian chant. Front bedrooms suffer from early traffic noise." Madame writes to us: "C'est moi qui fait la cuisine, plûtot du type traditionnel, et nous fabriquons nous-mêmes charcuterie, sauces, pâtisseries. Nous aimons les clients qui aiment la maison et qui apprécient les petits coins tranquilles de campagne. L'été, nous servons le repas le plus souvent sur la terrasse, à l'ombre d'un gros tilleul. À 50 mètres coule une belle rivière. Nous pouvons louer des bicyclettes pour visiter la région." (*Ann Mary Bishop*) Des avis supplémentaires, SVP.

Open All year.
Rooms 4 double, 1 single – 3 with shower (2 have WC).
Facilities Bar, dining room; terrace where meals are served. River 50 metres.
Location 8 km NW of Le Blanc towards Chattelerault.
Restriction Not suitable for &.
Credit card Visa.
Terms [1989 rates] Rooms 90–175 frs. Breakfast 20 frs. Set meals 60 and 85 frs. Reduced rates for children sharing parents' room.

FONTVIEILLE 13990 Bouches-du-Rhône Map 5

Auberge La Régalido
Rue Frédéric Mistral

Tel 90.54.60.22
Telex 150451

Daudet's windmill (not the real one actually, but that's another story) stands on a hill outside this tiny town in the foothills of the Alpilles, near Arles. Admired as much as ever this year, *La Régalido* is a former oil-mill in a side street, now converted into a most welcoming little *auberge*, luxurious yet unpretentious. It is run by the Michel family: Madame's hand is evident in the flowers which grace all the rooms, and Monsieur's in the cooking (*Michelin* rosette), which our readers continue to find excellent (try the gratin de moules aux épinards or gigot d'agneau en casserole). Latest reports: "A friendly, welcoming hotel, with enthusiastic owner. Wines of particular interest." "A superb lunch with perfect service." "A wonderful place with *really* charming staff. Mme Michel a powerhouse of efficiency and strikingly beautiful; Monsieur a delight, amiable, the perfect host. Not cheap, neither *should* it be." A visitor in October found "a fire blazing in the sitting-room". Bedrooms have individual charm, and there is a flowery garden. (*Mrs JB Priestley, PH Wainman, Ellen & John Buchanan*)

Open All year except Dec and Jan.
Rooms 14 double – all with bath and/or shower, telephone, radio and TV, most air-conditioned. 1 on ground-floor.
Facilities Lounge, TV room, bar, restaurant; function room. Garden, terrace.
Location 5 km NE of Arles. Leave *autoroute* A7 at Cavaillon, direction St-Rémy-de-Provence, or at Nîmes, direction Arles. Parking.
Credit cards All major cards accepted.
Terms Rooms: single 390–500 frs, double 800–1,150 frs. Breakfast 65 frs. Dinner, B&B: single 710–820 frs, double 1,450–1,800 frs. Set lunch/dinner 250, 290 and 380 frs; full alc 300 frs. Special meals for children on request.

FROENINGEN 68720 Haut-Rhin   Map 3

Auberge de Froeningen   *Tel* 89.25.48.48
2 route d'Illfurth

In a village 9 km southwest of Mulhouse, an elegant restaurant-with-rooms (oriental carpets in the red-walled dining room), in a spruce modern house built in local style with flower-decked balconies. Cosy bedrooms, convivial ambience, excellent food. Large grounds. 7 rooms, all with bath and shower. Rooms 260–320 frs. Breakfast 30 frs. Set menus 100–295 frs. New nomination. More reports please.

FUTEAU 55120 Meuse   Map 3

L'Orée du Bois   *Tel* 29.88.28.41

This most seductive hotel, a low white building, stands on a wooded hillside in the pretty Argonne countryside where Lorraine meets Champagne. "We were again delighted", say returning visitors whose nomination last year ran: "The charming and helpful young owners, Paul and Roselyne Aguesse, have been there about four years and obviously enjoy running their little hotel. Its bedrooms are in a new annexe: ours was very clean, freshly decorated, with pretty pink-and-apricot bedspreads, and was good value. The cosy rustic-style bar had a beamed ceiling and roaring log fire; so indeed did the spacious dining room whose long windows afforded glorious views over the countryside. On each table, fresh flowers and lit candles. The food was not cheap, but really excellent (*Gault Millau toque*). The meal takes time, as all is cooked to order. Breakfast was good too, served by a motherly soul in a room where a fire was already crackling. As we left, M. Aguesse was sweeping the drive. I have never seen an owner-chef take such an active part in keeping his hotel spick and span – long may the enthusiasm last." (*Padi and John Howard*) This year, eating from the *carte*, the Howards especially enjoyed the foie gras chaud, salade de homard, and "the best pigeon dish I've ever eaten. I enthused so much about it that M. Aguesse came out of the kitchen to talk to me about cooking game."

Open All year except Jan. Restaurant closed Tue.
Rooms 7 – all with bath, telephone, TV and tea-making facilities.
Facilities Lounge, bar, TV room, restaurant. Terrace, garden.
Location 1 km S of Futeau, which is 13 km E of Ste-Ménehould (turn S off N3 at Les Islettes).
Credit cards Access, Visa.
Terms Rooms: single 220 frs, double 240 frs. Breakfast 35 frs. Half board 300–360 frs per person. Set lunch/dinner 100, 150 and 280 frs; full alc 320 frs.
Reduced rates for children sharing parents' room; special meals.

GÉMENOS 13420 Bouches-du-Rhône   Map 5

Relais de la Magdeleine   *Tel* 42.82.20.05

"Mozart tends to pervade this well-lit hotel in the evening. There is open-air chess and dining by candle-light under the trees. The proprietor is charming and has a superb collection of paintings and tapestries" – an enticing recent report on the sophisticated and much admired *Relais de la Magdeleine*, described also as "a charming 17th-century *bastide*, set in a large walled garden with lovely bathing pool – a peaceful and luxurious oasis on the outskirts of the small town of Gémenos" (which is within easy reach of the coast at Cassis or Marseilles, and the wild and strange *massif* of La Sainte-Baume). "The owners, the Marignanes, made us feel like welcome guests in their own home. The service was faultless, by charming young girls, and the food was delicious, with good breakfasts too." "The public rooms and large bedrooms were attractively furnished with antiques; the beds were high quality. The dining rooms were cool and spacious, with some walls covered with silk or damask. But in spite of this luxury there was nothing pretentious or formal about the atmosphere, which was friendly and happy. There was an aura of peace, especially on the terrace in the early evening when drinks were served under floodlit plane trees. Provençal cooking, plus a large selection of pâtisseries and wonderful cheese. At breakfast, freshly made hot brioches." Two strong endorsements this year, but a third reader was slightly disappointed. The hotel welcomes children. (*Peter L Aston, Sarah Curtis*)

Open 15 Mar–1 Nov.
Rooms 3 suites, 17 double – 18 with bath, 2 with shower, all with telephone and TV.
Facilities 2 salons, 2 restaurants. Garden with swimming pool.
Location On outskirts of Gémenos, which is 23 km E of Marseilles. Exit Pont de l'Étoile from Aix–Toulon motorway.
Restriction Not suitable for ♿.
Credit cards Access, Visa.
Terms B&B: single 415–480 frs, double 435–640 frs, suite 840 frs. Dinner, B&B 415–650 frs per person. Set lunch/dinner 150–180 frs; full alc 220–240 frs.
Reduced rates and special meals for children.

We depend on detailed fresh reports to keep our entries up-to-date.

GÉRARDMER 88400 Vosges   Map 3

Grand Hôtel Bragard   *Tel* 29.63.06.31
Place du Tilleul   *Telex* 960964

Within 500 metres of the lovely lake in this big, popular Vosges resort, a sizeable old-fashioned hotel renovated and given a fresh lease of life by its new owners. Pleasant service and bedrooms, comfortable lounge, and excellent food (Gault Millau toque). *Large garden with small swimming pool. 61 rooms, all with bath and shower. B&B double 370–570 frs. Set menus 90–250 frs. New nomination. More reports please.*

LES GETS 74260 Haute-Savoie   Map 4

Hôtel Mont Chéry   *Tel* 50.79.74.55

In a pretty skiing village devoid of modern concrete buildings, 25 miles south of Lake Geneva, here close to the ski-lifts and ski-school is a friendly chalet-style ski hotel, family-run and ideal for families. Very good food. Garden for summer. Open 15 Dec–20 Apr, 1 July–31 Aug. 26 rooms, all with bath. B&B double 280–490 frs. Set menus 78–240 frs [1989]. Recent nomination. More reports please.

GIEN 45500 Loiret   Map 4

Hôtel du Rivage   *Tel* 38.67.20.53
1 quai de Nice   *Telex* 375974 BOX RIVAGE

"A splendid old Loire-side town with floodlit castle and church. A friendly welcome, open fire, dining room well filled with locals, food superb and service delightful. Beds comfortable but bath rather small." "The best chicken liver pâté I've ever eaten, champagne sorbet, a wonderful tuna steak in a cream sauce, delicious desserts – all for 135 francs" [1989]. So run two of the four endorsements this year for this very spruce modern hotel just off the main road, close to the river. *Michelin* awards the food a rosette, and *Gault Millau* a toque. Everyone praises the service and comfort: one reader had "a charming room overlooking the Loire". There were earlier reports of noisy front rooms, but the owners this year write that all now have double-glazing, and all have been modernised. (*Capt. JS Stewart, SHD Johnson; also Dr John Cliffe and Annie Stott*)

Open All year. Restaurant closed 5 Feb–8 Mar.
Rooms 5 suites, 15 double, 2 single – all with bath, shower, telephone and TV.
Facilities Salon, piano-bar, dining room. Terrace.
Location On road to Nevers, on banks of the Loire (double-glazing). Parking.
Restriction Not suitable for &.
Credit cards All major cards accepted.
Terms Rooms: single occupancy 245 frs, double 300 frs, suite 600 frs. Breakfast 35 frs. Set lunch/dinner 140, 175 and 280 frs; full alc 350 frs. Reduced rates and special meals for children.

We are particularly keen to have reports on italicised entries.

GIGONDAS 84190 Vaucluse   Map 5

Les Florets   *Tel* 90.65.85.01
Route des Dentelles

An attractive small country hotel outside Gigondas, near to some of the best Côtes du Rhône vineyards and just below the spectacular Dentelles de Montmirail. "It consists", says a recent visitor, "of a smallish main house and an annexe on the hill behind, all gravel yard, blossom and sunshine. The service is pleasant, the food a bit boring, but the glory of the place is the deliciously tree-dappled, fountain-rilled, Pernod-supplied, chaise-longued terrace, which looks over vineyards and mountains, and is absolutely silent except for the clinking of ice in glasses." Others this year have endorsed that report, save that one visitor thought the management less than friendly. And the reference to boring food has been indignantly refuted by a regular patron of the *Florets'* restaurant for the past 20 years, "The food is always a delight, and the menu is regularly changed too."(*Peter L Aston, AG Catchpole*) The owners write to say that they also possess a Gigondas vineyard.

Open All year except Jan and Feb. Closed Wed; also Tue evening Nov–Mar.
Rooms 13 double, 2 single – 13 with bath and/or shower, all with telephone.
4 bungalows 50 m from hotel.
Facilities Salon/bar, restaurant, TV room; terrace. Garden.
Location 1.5 km E of Gigondas, which is 18 km E of Orange.
Restriction Not suitable for &.
Credit cards All major cards accepted.
Terms [1989 rates] Rooms 225–260 frs. Breakfast 32 frs. Dinner, B&B 230–260 frs per person. Set meals 110–170 frs. Reduced rates and special meals for children.

GIVRY 71640 Saône-et-Loire   Map 4

Hôtel de la Halle   *Tel* 85.44.32.45
Place de la Halle

The charming Renard family run a modest but friendly little hotel, well suited for an overnight stop, in a pleasant Burgundy village west of Chalon; it is a venerable building with a fine spiral staircase, facing the former market hall. Reports this year and last have again pointed to its qualities and its faults: front rooms a bit noisy, some rooms rather small and basic, but: "Splendid value", "excellent old-fashioned Burgundian food", and: "Bedrooms though simple are spotlessly clean, and have an interesting conflict of different textile patterns. We had a warm reception from the Renards. It was a pleasure to sit in their good restaurant watching the locals come and go, most of them close friends of the family, judging by all the kissing going on." There are local wine tastings just opposite. (*PA Catling, GC Brown*)

Open All year except 21–28 Aug, 13–27 Nov, 1–7 Jan, Sun evening and Mon.
Rooms 10 double – 2 with bath, 3 with shower, all with telephone.
Facilities Lounge, restaurant. Garden.
Location Givry is 9 km W of Chalon-sur-Saône on D69. Hotel is central (front rooms may be noisy). Parking.
Restriction Not suitable for &.
Credit cards All major cards accepted.
Terms [1989 rates] Rooms 100–165 frs. Breakfast 22 frs. Set lunch 55, dinner 165 frs.

GORDES 84220 Vaucluse   Map 5

La Mayanelle   *Tel* 90.72.00.28

Near the centre of the much-visited hill-village of Gordes (a summer resort for the Parisian intelligentsia), M. Bayard's friendly little hotel is perched on a cliff and has fine views over hills and valley from many bedrooms and from the broad stone dining-terrace. Bar with antique decor. Rooms vary in size and some lack a view. Good traditional Provençal cooking. Closed 4 Jan–28 Feb. 10 rooms, all with bath or shower, 200–300 frs. Breakfast 38 frs. Full alc 130–190 frs [1989]. Few recent reports. More welcome.

GOSNAY 62199 Pas-de-Calais   Map 3

La Chartreuse du Val St-Esprit   *Tel* 21.62.80.00
1 rue de Fouquières   *Telex* 134418

This useful stop-over hotel on the way to Calais has an unusual history – it's a former monastery where Princess Isabel of Portugal died in 1471, later rebuilt in classic château style and recently turned into a rather elegant hotel. It lies slap amid the now defunct Pas-de-Calais coal-mines – not the most lyrical of settings, but the Béthune motorway exit is conveniently close. More reports this year: "Comfortable and friendly, with food of a high standard"; "reasonably good value for money, a staff that tries hard to please, but the place has too 'new' a feel and lacks atmosphere." "Great pleasure to walk up the attractive staircase in classic château style. Our room was of imposing elegance, but service was a bit hectic and breakfast disappointing." "A perfect weekend; the food was brilliant." The restaurant is doing well locally, and a swimming pool is planned. (*P Gill, Dr FP Adler, RP Wynings, GB and Dr CH*)

Open All year.
Rooms 23 – all with bath and shower, telephone, TV and mini-bar. Some ground-floor rooms; special bathroom for &.
Facilities Ramps. Lounges, restaurant; conference and functions rooms. Garden with tennis court.
Location 5 km SW of Béthune. Leave A26 motorway at Béthune exit and make for Bruay-en-Artois.
Credit cards Access, Amex, Visa.
Terms [1989 rates] Rooms: single occupancy 290 frs, double 420 frs. Breakfast 38 frs. Set meals 110–320 frs. Reduced rates and special meals for children.

GOUMOIS 25470 Doubs   Map 4

Hôtel Taillard   *Tel* 81.44.20.75

"A typical French country hotel, looking a little seedy from outside but with a large terrace which must be lovely in mid-summer. The food is French country cooking at its best with very ample portions – we remember especially the poached salmon." So runs one recent report on the Taillard family's spacious and gracious chalet, much reputed for its cooking (*Michelin* rosette); it is secluded on the slopes of a wooded valley, close to the Swiss border between Belfort and Neuchâtel. Many rooms have a balcony, fine views and "not a sound all night save the gurgling of the little stream in the gardens". This year, one reader thought the rooms nice and the food good, but another found it patchy. And one affectionate regular visitor, on her umpteenth return visit, found the hotel's charms beginning to wane, "Madame Taillard, who has run the hotel with a firm hand since we started going there, has sadly retired, and her nephew and his wife are now in charge. Some of their new additions seemed out of place to us: notably the modern seating area that's replaced the old rustic bar. Some rooms are lovely, but some at the back are small and cramped. The dinner was enjoyable as ever, e.g. warm foie gras and the truite belle goumoise, but the main dishes had rich cloying sauces. Breakfast was exceptionally good." (*Stephen Ruell, Padi and John Howard*) Some other recent reports have been critical, and we'd welcome more, please.

Open Early Mar–mid-Nov. Closed on Wed Mar, Oct and Nov.
Rooms 4 suites, 13 double – 10 with bath, 5 with shower, all with telephone and TV.
Facilities TV room, bar, 2 dining rooms; terrace. Garden with swimming pool. River nearby with trout fishing and canoeing.
Location 50 km SE of Montbéliard, 18 km E of Maiche on D437A and D437B. Leave *autoroute* A36 at Montbéliard Sud exit. The hotel is near the church. Parking.
Restriction Not suitable for &.
Credit cards All major cards accepted.
Terms Rooms 150–230 frs, suite 290–310 frs. Breakfast 32 frs. Dinner, B&B 250–295 frs per person, full board 300–345 frs. Full alc 250 frs. Reduced rates and special meals for children.

GRENOBLE 38000 Isère   Map 4

Park Hôtel   *Tel* 76.87.29.11
10 place Paul-Mistral   *Fax* 76.46.49.88
                                                          Telex 320767

A connoisseur of Grenoble writes, "This large, booming and industrial/ university city has remarkably few good hotels, and the *Park* is its most stylish and comfortable. It faces onto the big central park, and some rooms have views of the surrounding mountains. The dark oak panelling and deep easy chairs in the foyer set the pampered tone, for the bedrooms are panelled too (we were less enamoured of the purple velvet linings to the corridor walls). Some rooms have minitels, the videotex computers that are France's favourite new gimmick. Service is deft and friendly, and a good breakfast was served us in the hotel's *Taverne de Ripaille*." More reports please.

Open All year except 29 Jul–21 Aug, 24 Dec–2 Jan. Restaurant closed Sun midday.
Rooms 4 suites, 56 double or single – all with bath and/or shower, telephone, TV and air-conditioning.
Facilities Lift. Lounge, bar, restaurant; conference facilities.
Location Central. Free public parking beside hotel.
Credit cards All major cards accepted.
Terms [1989 rates] Rooms 610–910 frs. Breakfast 40 frs. Alc meals 120–200 frs (excluding wine).

We need feedback on all entries. Often people fail to report on the best-known hotels, assuming that "someone else is sure to".

GRIMAUD 83310 Var   Map 5

Hostellerie du Coteau Fleuri   *Tel* 94.43.20.17
Place des Pénitents

Grimaud is a fashionable hill-village behind St-Tropez, its ancient stone houses neatly converted into summer homes for the Parisian intelligentsia. The *Coteau Fleuri*, on the outskirts, is an old building modernised as a neo-Provençal auberge with tiled floors, and it is as flower-decked as its name implies. New owners, the Minards, took over in 1988, and three recent reports are so complimentary that we restore the hotel as a full entry (after previous criticisms): "A very friendly atmosphere and delicious cooking, e.g. gigot de lotte aux lentilles", writes a Swiss reader. "Meals on the terrace, with a marvellous view, are of high quality – exquisite langoustines. The maids are efficient, the bedrooms small but comfortable." A piano for guests to use, a log fire for chilly days, a spacious lounge and rambling garden slope, plus superb views over the wooded Maures hills. But some bedrooms are *very* small. (*Jean-Michel and Monique Pictet; also M Neale, John and Rita Newnham*) *Note*: it is essential to reserve a table for dinner even if you are resident.

Open All year except Jan. Restaurant closed 2 weeks in Dec and Tue except Jul and Aug.
Rooms 14 double – all with bath/shower and telephone.
Facilities Salon, bar, restaurant. Terrace.
Location 10 km from St-Tropez. On edge of village. Parking.
Restriction Not suitable for &.
Credit cards All major cards accepted.
Terms [1989 rates] Rooms 300–450 frs. Breakfast 45 frs. Set lunch 130 frs, dinner 180 frs; full alc 250–300 frs.

GUÉTHARY 64210 Pyrénées-Atlantiques   Map 4

Hôtel Pereria   *Tel* 59.26.51.68
Rue de l'Église

This old Basque house in a big, slightly unkempt garden has been liked again this year: "An uncomplicated holiday hotel catering mainly for French families – a plus point, in our book. Tasty meals, outstanding value." It is "run by youngish, good-looking and friendly owners, with an attractive and demure staff". The annexe, across a busy road, is possibly more comfortable than the hotel itself, and bedrooms in both are large. Recent visitors have enjoyed the friendly efficiency and the good meals (e.g. ttoro, a Basque fish soup) served out on the terrace. You can view the hills and the distant sea, and can watch the sunset from the outdoor dining terrace. (*Helen and Charles Priday; JAG Stonehouse*)

Open 1 Mar–1 Nov.
Rooms 28 double, 2 single – 26 with bath, all with telephone. 11 in annexe across road.
Facilities Salon, 2 restaurants; terrace where meals are served. Garden with *boules* and swings. Beach nearby with swimming, wind-surfing, sailing and fishing.
Location On the coast between Biarritz and St-Jean-de-Luz.
Restriction Not suitable for &.
Credit cards Access, Visa.
Terms B&B: single 70–150 frs, double 245–250 frs. Set lunch/dinner 70, 105 and 150 frs; full alc 100 frs. Reduced rates and special meals for children.

HAUT-DE-CAGNES 06800 Alpes-Maritimes   Map 5

Le Cagnard   *Tel* 93.20.73.21
Rue du Pontis-Long   *Telex* 462223

The sizeable town of Cagnes-sur-Mer is divided, like Caesar's Gaul, into three parts: the ugly sprawling resort of Cros-de-Cagnes; just inland, Cagnes-Ville, unremarkable save for the inspiring Renoir museum on its outskirts; and, higher up, Haut-de-Cagnes, one of the region's most sophisticated hill villages (fascinating museum in the château). Here *Le Cagnard*, a well-known and very smart little hotel – "delightful and distinguished", "very romantic", say readers – has been artfully converted out of some 13th-century houses by the ramparts and virtually clings to the side of a cliff. Devotees returning this year admired the newly extended terrace restaurant with its superb hand-painted ceiling. Here there are fine views; you can also eat in a graceful candle-lit room, former guardroom of the château, where sometimes there is guitar music. The food, say readers, is "delicious": it wins a *Michelin* rosette and two *Gault Millau toques* for inventive adaptation of local dishes. Despite these *nouvelle* influences, portions are large. The set menu is expensive, but they do not mind if you take a light snack from the *carte*.

"Our room was the whole floor of a medieval house, with superb antique furniture and a picture window." Rooms, however, vary considerably in size and comfort: for example, Nos 18 and 19 are said to be far nicer than No 22, just above the hotel entrance and a bit noisy. It is worth asking for a room with a view of the coast (but these may be the costlier ones). Parking is a nightmare; it is best to park in the new carpark just below the village, or else leave parking to the hotel. (*Pat and Jeremy Temple, Dr John Cliffe*)

Open All year. Restaurant closed 1 Nov–20 Dec, and Thur midday.
Rooms 10 suites, 8 double, 2 single – all with bath and/or shower, telephone; 16 with TV. Suites in annexe.
Facilities Lift. Salon, bar, 2 restaurants. Small garden and terrace. Sandy beach 6 km.
Location On the ramparts, 2 minutes from château. Parking.
Restriction Not suitable for &.
Credit cards All major cards accepted.
Terms Rooms: single occupancy 300–410 frs, double 350–600 frs, suite 730–1,000 frs. Breakfast 50 frs. Set lunch/dinner 340 and 430 frs; full alc 420 frs. Extra bed 120 frs. Special meals for children on request.

HESDIN-L'ABBÉ 62360 Pas-de-Calais   Map 3

Hôtel Cléry   *Tel* 21.83.19.83
     Telex 135349

This newly opened country-house hotel just south of Boulogne is already proving popular with British visitors; it's a *Relais du Silence*, and is brought to the Guide by an inspector this year, "Set in five acres of parkland and approached by a tree-lined avenue, this 18th-century château has a splendid facade, and the entrance hall is appealing with a lovely curving Louis XV wrought-iron staircase. The Osselands, who bought the house recently, are helpful and friendly. Our room had prettily painted modern furniture, and decor in soft pastel shades. Reception rooms are well furnished and homely. In the smallish, prettily decorated dining room, service was a trifle erratic but the food good, very professionally cooked in the *nouvelle* manner – salmon with fennel sauce, duck slightly pink, superb marquise au chocolat, etc – and good breakfast too. A pleasant hotel, well suited to a short break." More reports welcome.

Open All year except 15 Dec–15 Jan.
Rooms 19 – all with bath and/or shower, telephone and TV.
Facilities Lounges, bar, restaurant; conference room. Park with tennis court.
Location 9 km SE of Boulogne, off N1.
Credit cards Access, Amex, Visa.
Terms [1989 rates] Rooms 270–480 frs. Breakfast 55 frs. Dinner, B&B 295–510 frs per person. Set lunch/dinner 140–240 frs.

HONFLEUR 14600 Calvados   Map 2

Ferme de la Grande Cour   *Tel* 31.89.04.69
Côte de Grace

An offbeat idyll for those who love rural Normandy – a farmhouse restaurant-with-rooms, set amid apple orchards just west of picturesque but trippery Honfleur. Courteous young staff, simple but comfortable bedrooms, quite good food served in a beamed dining room or on the lawn. Open 1 Feb–31 Dec. 14 rooms, all with bath and/or shower. B&B double 182–352 frs. Set meals 100–195 frs [1989]. More reports welcome.

IGÉ 71960 Saône-et-Loire   Map 4

Château d'Igé   *Tel* 85.33.33.99
                                                         Fax 85.33.41.41
                                                         Telex 351915

Igé is a small Burgundy village away from the main roads, amid pleasant country lanes. Here the former hunting lodge of the Dukes of Mâcon, "a beautiful little medieval castle", is now a luxurious hotel set beside a stream on the edge of the Mâcon hills: "A proper castle with rounded turrets, grey ivy-covered walls and stone-flagged floors and staircases." One visitor this year enjoyed breakfast on the terrace "with families of ducks to watch", and found the service friendly but slow; another relished the sense of *noblesse*, enhanced by Vivaldi; a third liked her turret room. Other recent visitors have had a suite of rooms full of antiques, or have praised the home farm's goat's cheese and enjoyed being able to select their own trout from a holding pond. Food, not cheap, is straightforward rather than fancy modern. (*Prof. AS Douglas, Peter and Ann Jones, Jeff and Karen Nebel*)

Open 1 Mar–15 Nov.
Rooms 6 suites, 6 double – all with bath and shower, telephone, TV.
Location 6.5 km N of N79; 14 km NW of Mâcon, 11 km SE of Cluny.
Restriction Not suitable for &.
Credit cards All major cards accepted.
Terms [1989 rates] Rooms 360–550 frs, suite 650–900 frs. Breakfast 50 frs. Set lunch/dinner 180–330 frs. Special meals for children.

> Hotels are dropped if we lack positive feedback. If you can endorse an entry, please do so.

ILLHAEUSERN 68150 Haut-Rhin   Map 3

Hôtel La Clairière   *Tel* 89.71.80.80
Route de Guémar

The Haeberlin family's celebrated *Auberge de l'Ill* (three *Michelin* rosettes) does not qualify for the Guide, as it has no bedrooms; the *Clairière*, in the same Alsatian village north-west of Colmar, has no restaurant. So they complement each other conveniently: you can eat at one, stay at the other, as our nominator suggests this year: "A fairly new modern building, just outside the village amid fields and woods. We had a warm welcome, joined by four assorted dogs. The hotel is smartly furnished and well kept, with some antiques, lovely pictures, an attractive small lounge. Our enormous bedroom had hessian wallpaper, pretty bedlights, dark oak furniture, beds with heavy wooden frames and pinky-red Paisley-design drapes: the beds, though lumpy and creaky, were comfortable. A huge bathroom with greeny-brown tiles. Breakfast nicely served in the bedroom. Staff friendly." (*John and Padi Howard*)

Open 1 Mar–1 Jan.
Rooms 4 suites, 24 double – all with bath (4 also with shower), telephone, TV and baby-listening. Ground-floor rooms.
Facilities Lift. Lounge with TV.
Location Village is 17 km NW of Colmar. Parking.
Credit cards Access, Visa.
Terms Rooms: single 390 frs, double 430 frs, suite 800–1,000 frs. Breakfast 45 frs.

JOIGNY 89300 Yonne   Map 3

À la Côte Saint-Jacques   *Tel* 86.62.09.70
14 faubourg de Paris   *Fax* 86.91.49.70
                                                 Telex 801458 SAINJAC

We continue to receive breathlessly ecstatic accounts of this old coaching inn beside the river Yonne, where *patron*/chef Michel Lorain and his son Jean-Michel win the top ratings of four red *Michelin* gables and three rosettes, and four red *Gault Millau toques*, for their fine cooking in luxury surroundings with bedrooms and prices to match. They have recently created some opulent rooms from old houses facing the river, across the noisy N6, and to provide access they have made a paved tunnel under this road, decorated with Roman remains from the excavation. Readers have stayed there in 1989:

"This is a very sexy place, as only the French can do it. The luxurious new bedrooms are sexy, and the whole set-up slightly outrageous. The dining rooms have gaudy flower arrangements, paintings of scantily dressed girls, candle-light, and very sensuous food. It all works, because it is totally professional – and fun. The entire Lorain family greeted us for dinner, and absurd smiles of ecstasy were on our faces as we ate terrine of marinated sardines and tapenade, quail egg in truffle juice, exquisitely delicate skate in a lemon sauce, grilled lobster in a Sauternes sauce, and more. Our only complaint: in one room the tables are set too closely – nasty if your neighbours smoke. Our bedroom had a combination of antique and contemporary furnishings, with dark beams, Berber carpets over plank floors, a huge marble bathroom. In this new building one is totally unaware of the N6; you overlook the lovely Yonne. I have never been so conscious of being surrounded by beauty, peace and comfort." This was no Xanadu-like dream that flees on waking, for others this year have echoed the praise in more down-to-earth terms: "Delicious light cooking, very good breakfast, faultless service, fittings of the highest quality." "An enjoyable atmosphere. The bedrooms are probably among the finest in France." (*Sharon Gutman; Rosamund Hebdon*)

Open All year except 2 Jan–2 Feb. Restaurant closed for lunch at weekend.
Rooms 3 suites, 11 double – all with bath, shower, telephone and TV; baby sitting on request. All in annexe linked to main building by tunnel.
Facilities Lift. Salon, bar, breakfast room, 3 restaurants; conference room; indoor heated swimming pool, sauna. Garden.
Location 27 km NW of Auxerre on N6; leave at Sens exit.
Restriction Not suitable for &.
Credit cards All major cards accepted.
Terms Rooms: 980–1,550 frs, suite 1,550–2,450 frs, triple 1,920–2,800 frs. Breakfast 80 frs. Set lunch 240 frs (not served on weekends); dinner 520 frs. Special meals for children.

JOUÉ-LÈS-TOURS 37300 Indre-et-Loire — Map 2

Hôtel du Château de Beaulieu — *Tel* 47.53.20.26
1 rue de l'Épend

A modernised 18th-century manor on the south-west outskirts of Tours. "Sadly", says an admirer, "they have sold their land to the local council, and the *jardins à la française* are now municipal tennis courts. But it remains an impressive building, inside and out, with huge stone staircase and panelled restaurant. The latter draws a smart and demanding clientele from miles around and was full on our visit. We greatly enjoyed our meal. Our mansarded first-floor bedroom was vast and a bit stark, despite flowery wallpaper, but was comfortable, clean and spacious. We spied more attractive rooms in the annexe. Prices were reasonable, service efficient, breakfast copious and promptly served." Other recent visitors, too, have enjoyed the "excellent" food (mussel soup with puff pastry, duckling served as two courses), as well as the river views (but Tours skyscrapers are also in view). Guests are expected to dine in the hotel between April and the end of October.

Open All year except Christmas Eve.
Rooms 19 double – 18 with bath, 1 with shower, all with telephone, TV and mini-bar. 10 in pavilion.
Facilities Salon, TV room, 2 restaurants; conference room. Large garden.
Location 4 km SW of Tours, by D86 and D207.
Restriction Not suitable for &.
Credit cards Access, Diners, Visa.
Terms Double room 350–600 frs. Breakfast 40 frs. Dinner, B&B double 700–930 frs; full board 930–1,210 frs. Set lunch/dinner 165–380 frs. Reduced rates Nov–Mar.

LA JOUVENTE 35730, Ile-et-Vilaine — Map 2

Manoir de la Rance — *Tel* 99.88.53.76

Beautifully set above the boat-filled Rance estuary, 7 km south-east of Dinard, a converted manor with clean rooms, excellent breakfasts, obliging owners, and decor and furnishings in a mixture of styles, some more sympathetic than others.

Closed Jan, Feb. 7 rooms, most with bath and/or shower. B&B double 330–550 frs [1989]. No restaurant. New nomination. More reports please.

| KAYSERSBERG 68240 Haut-Rhin | Map 3 |

Hôtel Résidence Chambard	*Tel* 89.47.10.17
13 rue de Général de Gaulle	*Fax* 89.47.35.03
	Telex 880272

Albert Schweitzer was born in this picturesque Alsatian wine village, and in its main street is a small museum devoted to him. Down the road is *patron*/chef Pierre Irrmann's smartish restaurant-with-rooms (*Michelin* rosette, two red *Gault Millau toques*), converted from two old buildings with pretty facades. It was dropped from the 1989 Guide for want of feedback, but is restored by a reader this year, "Dinner was costly but excellent; room was comfortable with good view of vineyards." The food is *nouvelle*-ish but not too much so, and such dishes as marinated raw salmon and garlicky ragout of lamb have been admired. The Alsatian wines are reasonably priced. But an inspector thought that the bedroom annexe lacks the personality of a hotel. It might be worth paying extra to secure the special room with a big canopied bed and a quaint round salon in a 15th-century tower. (*LC Foreman*)

Open All year except 1–21 Mar and 21 Dec–4 Jan. Restaurant closed Mon and Tue midday.
Rooms 2 suites, 20 double, 9 single – 20 with bath and shower, all with telephone, radio and TV. Ground-floor rooms.
Facilities Lift. Lounge, bar, restaurant; cellar for conference/functions.
Location 11 km NW of Colmar. Central, but quiet. Parking.
Credit cards All major cards accepted.
Terms: Rooms 400–550 frs. Breakfast 50 frs. Set lunch/dinner 200–340 frs; full alc 400 frs.

| LACAVE 46200 Dordogne | Map 4 |

| **Le Pont de l'Ouysse** | *Tel* 65.37.87.04 |

Not far from Rocamadour, a restaurant-with-rooms in a fine situation by a river, with a château looming above and a tree-shaded dining terrace for fine weather. "It's charming, and the rooms are delightful with a light, elegant garden look", says a reader this year, backing up last year's view: "A gem. Quiet, friendly and beautifully furnished, with tasteful bedrooms and bathrooms. The service is helpful and the food 'exquisite' but rather too rich for a long stay." Another visitor has spelt this out, "Family run, but by a family of chic urbanites – rooms utterly chic. Food very urban and *nouvelle*-ish, not cheap and portions not large" (*Gault Millau* bestows a red *toque* for variations on regional dishes, such as sautéed foie gras with capers). The dog, Sacha, likes to go on walks with guests – "he came with us to Rocamadour and back and seemed to know the ropes – I should think he does this every day in season."

Open 1 Mar–11 Nov. Closed Mon in low season.
Rooms 1 suite, 12 double – all with bath, telephone, radio and TV. 5 in annexe.
Facilities Lounge, dining room. Terrace, garden with swimming pool. River, fishing nearby.

Location 10 km NW of Rocamadour.
Restriction Not suitable for &.
Credit cards All major cards accepted.
Terms Rooms double 400 frs. Breakfast 35 frs. Dinner, B&B 400 frs per person.
Set lunch/dinner 150, 250 and 300 frs; full alc 280 frs. Reduced rates and special
meals for children.

LAMASTRE 07270 Ardèche   Map 4

Hôtel du Midi/Restaurant   *Tel* 75.06.41.50
  Barattéro
Place Seignobos

Steady praise again this year for owner-chef Bernard Perrier's serious,
well-run hotel/restaurant – "a gem" – in the market square of a pleasant
little town west of Valence, on the edge of the Rhône valley: "An
excellent family-run place, with Madame Perrier very much in evidence.
The food is very good, fully justifying its *Michelin* rosette and two red
Gault Millau toques, and the menus are a splendid mixture of old and new
– including old favourites such as poularde de Bresse en vessie. Despite
the *nouvelle* influences, portions are more than adequate. The wine list is
good on local Rhône wines, weak if you want to look further afield. The
hotel is in two parts, its beautifully cared-for garden and most bedrooms
being 30 metres away from the restaurant. Our rooms at the back were
pleasant and clean." Another visitor wrote of this annexe (where the
rooms are also said to be the quietest), "It looks from outside like a house
of correction, very austere, but is beautiful inside: our room was large,
with a sumptuous bathroom. Our friends were in the main building,
beautiful outside, not as nice as ours within, but OK. Restaurant splendid,
with chestnuts featuring in quite a few dishes. All the staff were
charming." (*Roger Bennett; also Mr & Mrs RM Booth*) One warning: "The
wine list is fairly short and concentrates on high quality, but rather
expensive, bottles; not really for 'quaffers'."

Open 1 Mar–15 Dec. Closed Sun evening and Mon except July, Aug, and public
holidays.
Rooms 18 – 15 with bath and/or shower, all with telephone; 5 with TV.
1 ground-floor room. Some rooms in annexe.
Facilities 2 salons, 3 restaurants. Garden.
Location Central. Parking.
Credit cards All major cards accepted.
Terms Rooms: single 150–250 frs, double 200–300 frs. Breakfast 40 frs. Set
lunch/dinner 140–320 frs; full alc 300 frs. Reduced rates and special meals for
children.

Château d'Urbilhac   *Tel* 75.06.42.11
Route de Vernoux

Totally different from the *Midi* (above), here is a finely converted 19th-
century château in Renaissance style, complete with pepperpot tower, set
high on a hillside in its own 150-acre wooded park just outside the town.
Three reports this year have used the words "delightful" and "magnificent", notably this one: "After our fourth visit, this has become one of
two top favourite hotels in France. The food used to be dull, but Madame
now has a new chef and it's lovely, though the wine list is disappointing.

Breakfasts are copious. Rooms, some with antique furniture, are all comfortable. And the pool is the best you'll find anywhere, superbly situated amid classic scenery, with modern sun-loungers." "A charming châtelaine". (*PA Catling, Brenda Gape, FM and CN Grist*) Best for a short stay as the menu seldom changes.

Open 1 May–10 Oct.
Rooms 11 double, 3 single – all with bath or shower and telephone. 2 in pavilion. 1 ground-floor room.
Facilities Bar, salon, 2 dining rooms; terrace. Garden, heated swimming pool, tennis.
Location 2 km S of Lamastre on D2 to Vernoux.
Credit cards All major cards accepted.
Terms Rooms: single 350 frs, double 500 frs. Breakfast 50 frs. Dinner, B&B 450–500 frs per person. Set lunch/dinner 160, 195 and 250 frs; full alc 200 frs.

LANGEAIS 37130 Indre-et-Loire

Map 2

Hôtel Hosten et Restaurant "Le Langeais"
Tel 47.96.82.12

2 rue Gambetta

In a small Loireside town west of Tours with a fine 15th-century château, *patron*-chef Jean-Jacques Hosten's attractive creeper-covered hostelry is introduced to the Guide this year by two reports: "The food richly deserves its *Michelin* rosette (and *Gault Millau toque*) and service is obliging. Our bedroom, though overlooking the main road, was comfortable." "The best hotel we found during three weeks in France. Restaurant outstanding, especially fish dishes. Breakfast hard to beat, with six different types of brioche, croissant, etc." We are told that the salon is being rebuilt after a lorry ran into it. (*Janet and Dennis Allom, and others*)

Open All year except 10 Jan–10 Feb, and 20 Jun–10 Jul.
Rooms 1 suite, 9 double – all with bath and TV.
Facilities Bar, 2 dining-rooms.
Location Central, parking. Langeais is 25 km W of Tours.
Restriction Not suitable for &.
Credit cards All major cards accepted.
Terms Rooms: single 230 frs, double 310 frs, suite 520 frs. Breakfast 35 frs. Full alc 180–280 frs.

LANGRES 52200 Haute-Marne

Map 3

Grand Hôtel de l'Europe
Tel 25.87.10.88

23-25 rue Diderot

Langres, an interesting old town on a high ridge with a cathedral and ancient ramparts, makes a useful stop on the way to Switzerland. Near its centre is this traditional stone-fronted hostelry, down-to-earth and inexpensive, liked again this year for its simple comforts and good fare. Rooms vary in size and amenities: front ones are best, but all are quiet. One new account, "The restaurant was busy, more like a *relais routier* than an elegant place: many of the diners were enormous, as were the portions. Parking one's car in the tight space provided was an entertainment in itself, as enthralled onlookers watched the harassed

drivers trying to obey the arm-waving instructions of the receptionist."
(*Joan Powell, Stephen Ruell*)

Open All year except 23 Apr–8 May and 8–31 Oct. Closed Sun evening.
Restaurant closed Mon midday in season, all day Mon in low season.
Rooms 2 suites, 25 double, 1 single – some with bath and/or shower, all with
telephone; 17 with T V. 8 in annexe.
Facilities Salon, bar, 2 restaurants.
Location Between Chaumont (35 km) and Dijon (66 km). Hotel is central (rooms
overlooking garden are quietest). Garage facilities for 20 cars.
Restriction Not suitable for &.
Credit cards All major cards accepted.
Terms Rooms 100–190 frs. Breakfast 24 frs. Set lunch/dinner 58, 80, 85 and
145 frs; full alc 210 frs.

LANSLEVILLARD 73480 Savoie   Map 4

Les Prais   *Tel 79.05.93.53*
                                                              Telex 309983

*In a high ski-resort just below Mont Cenis, a typical little chalet-style ski-hotel
amid meadows beside the ski-lifts, liked for its good and plentiful food and
friendly staff. Most rooms have mountain views, some have balconies.
Swimming pool. Piano bar for après-ski. Open 18 Jun–15 Sep, 23 Dec–23 Apr.
25 rooms, most with bath or shower. Also annexe with apartments. Dinner,
B&B 220–320 frs. Set menus 72–145 frs. New nomination. More reports
welcome.*

LAPALISSE 03120 Allier   Map 4

Hôtel Galland   *Tel 70.99.07.21*
20 place de la République

*In a small town in the Bourbonnais, near Vichy, quietly located beside a park
and a pond just off the N7 Lyon–Paris highway, here is a very spruce little hotel
whose attractive restaurant wins a Michelin red "R" for good value. Bedrooms
are simple and clean, Madame is pleasant and efficient. 8 rooms, 6 with bath
and/or shower. B&B double 282 frs. Set menus 65–230 frs. Recent nomination.
More reports welcome.*

LAPOUTROIE 68650 Haut-Rhin   Map 3

Hôtel-Restaurant Les Alisiers   *Tel 89.47.52.82*

*Unlike our other Alsatian entries, mostly smart, this Logis de France is rustic
and modestly priced: an old farmhouse with beamed ceilings, secluded up in the
Vosges, but only 19 km from Colmar. Friendly patron, simple cooking served in
a new panoramic dining room; buffet breakfast. Comfortable rooms, some small,
others bigger with glorious mountain views. Open 1 Jan–15 Mar, 22 Mar–
22 Jun, 29 Jun–30 Nov, 24–31 Dec. 15 rooms, 13 with bath or shower. B&B
double 310 frs. Set meals 100–148 frs. Some criticisms this year, of food and lack
of hot water: more reports please.*

LESTELLE-BÉTHARRAM 64800 Pyrénées-Atlantiques Map 4

Le Vieux Logis   *Tel* 59.71.94.87
Route des Grottes

Near to Lourdes and not far from Pau and the high Pyrenees, this simple flower-girt country *auberge* could make a useful excursion centre. A visitor this year was delighted, "Monsieur et Madame Gaye have created a charming place, with a park where you can sit under the trees listening to the tinkle of cowbells. A huge courtyard where peacocks strut and two creaky old Pyrenean dogs bound up to welcome you. A sunny terrace with parasols for drinks, but no salon. The cuisine is exceptional (*Michelin* red 'R'), endorsed by the many locals who come to eat here – very good trout from the river, and the lightest crêpe I've ever eaten. The five attractive wooden chalets were full, so we had a huge room in the house, with Pyrenean blue-and-white blankets." (*Eileen Broadbent; JAG Stonehouse*)

Open 1 Mar–15 Nov. Restaurant open 1 Mar–10 Jan. Only restaurant open Christmas and New Year.
Rooms 15 double – all with bath, shower, telephone and TV. 5 chalets in the park.
Facilities Restaurant; 4 functions rooms. Garden; terrace.
Location 12 km W of Lourdes and 3 km E of Lestelle-Bétharram, on N637.
Restriction Not suitable for &.
Credit cards Access, Amex, Visa.
Terms B&B: single 185 frs, double 210–250 frs; dinner, B&B: single 255 frs, double 350–390 frs. Set lunch/dinner 80–170 frs; full alc 245 frs.

LEZOUX 63190 Puy-de-Dôme   Map 4

Château de Codignat   *Tel* 73.68.43.03
Bort-l'Étang

The small town of Lezoux, east of Clermont-Ferrand, was an important ceramics centre in Roman and Gallo-Roman days, as the local museum bears witness. At Bort-l'Étang, eight kilometres to the south-east, on a wooded hill above a valley, stands this handsome 15th-century château, rather fancifully converted (suits of armour, four-poster beds, etc). Bedrooms are in the towers and turrets, reached by winding stairways. A recent account, "It is delightfully run by a middle-aged lady and her personable young son. Our bedroom was nicely furnished with either genuine antiques or excellent replicas. There is a good swimming pool with jacuzzi and large gardens. We had an excellent five-course set dinner." An earlier visitor was equally captivated, "A riot – the castle belonged to the Obolenskys, was bought in a state of collapse by the present owners who did it up in rather camp baroque: even the walls are carpeted. But it's also a gem, absolutely peaceful and very clean and comfortable, with real chic. Service admirable. Found proprietors scrubbing out the lavatories – always a sign that standards are high." More reports welcome.

Open 19 Mar–2 Nov. Restaurant closed Tue and Thur midday except holidays.
Rooms 3 suites, 11 double – all with bath and/or shower (suites also have jacuzzi), telephone and TV. 1 ground-floor room.

115

Facilities Salon, 3 restaurants; banqueting room. Large grounds with swimming pool, health and beauty centre, putting-green.
Location At Bort-l'Étang, 8 km SE of Lezoux which is 27 km E of Clermont-Ferrand.
Credit cards All major cards accepted.
Terms [1989 rates] Rooms 650–980 frs, suite 1,500. frs. Breakfast 55 frs. Dinner, B&B 605–890 frs per person. Set lunch/dinner 245–305 frs. Reduced rates and special meals for children.

LYON   Map 4

La Cour des Loges   *Tel* 78.42.75.75
6 rue du Boeuf   *Telex* 330831
Lyon 69005

France's second city is as short on really attractive hotels as it is rich in excellent restaurants. But a high-class hostelry of unusual character recently opened: it is down a narrow street in the St-Jean quarter of Vieux-Lyon, across the Saône from the town centre and behind the Palais de Justice where the Barbie trials were held. An inspector reports: "It has been formed by restoring four adjacent Renaissance mansions. The main one is built round a galleried four-storey courtyard that forms the hotel's lofty foyer, hung with drapes of Lyon silk, cleverly lit and much festooned with foliage: the overall effect is breathtaking. The owners and architect, all local, have done a tasteful job, though I wish they had been less lavish with their modern gimmicks. But it's all great fun – even the top hat in the lift. The small heated swimming pool is really a large jacuzzi. In the cellar is a wine club with church pews. No restaurant, but there are lots of good ones close by (notably *La Tour Rose*, run by a pupil of Bocuse), and the hotel has its own *tapas* bar with a stream of water running down a trough on the counter. This part of Vieux-Lyon is now a sort of St-Germain-des-Prés, bursting with a youthful night-time animation that belies the city's staid image." "A major new asset to Lyon. The contemporary decor works well with the simple lines of this old building." "Service exemplary. One of the best hotels I've ever stayed in." However, a reader this year found the high-tech gadgetry "nightmarish" and inefficient (the air-conditioning did not work), "When we protested, the manager nodded and told us they were suing the architects!" For unloading luggage, you can just about drive your car down the alley to the front door, where the porter will arrange for its garaging and retrieval. (*Jeremy Round*)

Open All year.
Rooms 10 suites, 53 double – all with bath and/or shower, telephone TV and mini-bar. Some ground-floor rooms.
Facilities Lift. Lounge, bar, *tapas* bar, wine club; conference rooms. Terraced gardens. Small indoor pool, sauna, jacuzzi and fitness room.
Location: 1 km from main station. Garaging.
Credit cards All major cards accepted.
Terms [1989 rates] Room 950–1,300 frs. Breakfast 80 frs. Snacks in *tapas* bar 160 frs.

We get less feedback from smaller and more remote hotels. But we need feedback on all hotels: big and small, far and near, famous and first-timers.

MAILLY-LE-CHÂTEAU 89660 Yonne   Map 4

Le Castel   *Tel* 86.40.43.06
Place de l'Église

This *Relais du Silence* between Auxerre and Avallon, "a rather run-down
19th-century house in a very quiet village", has again been recommended
for a short visit: "Good, rich food, and a comfortable, pleasantly old-
fashioned room." "We enjoyed Madame's efficient running of the
attractive dining room. The countryside is lovely." Others have praised
such dishes as snails in garlic butter with chopped hazel-nuts, and calves'
liver in a cream sauce. Decor is attractive, but bedrooms vary greatly in
size (some are said to be suitable for elves) and the service can be slow.
(*Dr RL Holmes, MW Atkinson, Sarah Curtis*)

Open 15 Mar–15 Nov. Closed Wed in low season.
Rooms 2 suites, 10 double – most with bath and/or shower, all with telephone.
2 ground-floor rooms.
Facilities Lounge, restaurant; functions facilities. Garden with terrace.
Location 30 km S of Auxerre, 30 km NW of Avallon. Turn off N6 at either of
these towns or at Nitry. Hotel is in centre of quiet village. Parking.
Credit cards Access, Visa.
Terms Rooms: single 140–280 frs, double 180–290 frs, suite 330–345 frs. Breakfast
28 frs. Set lunch 72 frs, dinner 145 frs; full alc 210–230 frs. Reduced rates and
special meals for children.

LA MALÈNE 48210 Lozère   Map 4

Manoir de Montesquiou   *Tel* 66.48.51.12

*Once a residence of the aristocratic Montesquiou family, this 15th-century stone
manor house at the foot of a cliff in the Tarn gorge has been most gracefully
preserved and converted. Old-world charm includes four-poster beds and spiral
stairways, but comforts are modern. Good regional food and courteous staff.
Garden. Open Apr–end Oct. 12 rooms, all with bath or shower, 255–450 frs.
Breakfast 30 frs. Half board 295–395 frs per person [1989]. Recent nomination.
More reports welcome.*

MARSEILLE Bouches-du-Rhône   Map 5

Le Petit Nice and Restaurant   *Tel* 91.52.14.39
  Passédat   *Fax* 91.59.28.08
Anse de Maldormé   *Telex* 401565 PASSEDA
Corniche JF Kennedy
Marseille 13007

*Small, stylish and hugely expensive hotel, owned and run since 1917 by lordly
Passédat family. Though right inside the city, it is secluded on a rocky headland
below the coastal corniche road, with fine views across bay. Restaurant, in
richly decorated Hellenic-style villa with lovely garden, serves just about the
finest food in Marseille (two Michelin rosettes); elegant classical-style
bedrooms including two new suites in adjoining building. Very superior
clientele. Closed Jan. 18 rooms, all with bath and shower. Rooms 800–1,000 frs.
Breakfast 70 frs. Set menus 290–550 frs [1989]. Few recent reports. More please.*

Hôtel Pullman Beauvau *Tel* 91.54.91.00
4 rue Beauvau, Marseille 13001 *Telex* 401778

The recent opening or refurbishment of middle-sized hotels of true individual character, in large provincial cities hitherto bereft of them, has been an encouraging new development in France (see our entries for the *Cour des Loges*, Lyon, and the *Opéra*, Toulouse). The *Beauvau*, a famous old hostelry long moribund, falls into this class and has been recently nominated: "Chopin and George Sand (together), and Cocteau and Mistinguette (separately), are among the past habitués of this 18th-century *relais de poste* which is right in the heart of things beside the Vieux Port, at the foot of La Canebière. Newly restored by its Pullman Group owners after a long decline, it is a hotel of genuine warmth and elegance, still patronised by celebrities such as the singers who perform at the nearby Opéra. The restoration has been finely done and our bedroom was cosy and inviting, in period style (double glazing keeps out the noise and air-conditioning the Midi heat). Service was good. The dark-panelled 'English style' bar was a little claustrophobic for our taste, but the buffet breakfast was excellent and you can get light meals served in the bar or your room till 1 am."

Open All year.
Rooms 71 – all with bath and/or shower, telephone, radio, TV, mini-bar and air-conditioning.
Facilities Lift. Lounge, breakfast room; 3 conference rooms.
Location Central. Garage 800 metres.
Restriction Not suitable for &.
Credit cards All major cards accepted.
Terms Rooms 550–700 frs. Breakfast 50 frs. (No restaurant.)

MARTIN-ÉGLISE 76370 Seine-Maritime Map 3

Auberge du Clos Normand *Tel* 35.82.71.01 and 35.82.71.31
22 rue Henri IV

Just inland from Dieppe, on the edge of a forest, this former 16th-century *relais de poste*, now a restaurant-with-rooms, is as redolent of Normandy as its name implies. The bedrooms are in a separate vine-covered building, once stables or a hayloft, with a romantic garden which has a pavilion for eating out in summer, and a stream; it's very quiet except for farmyard noises. The accommodation used to be defiantly unmodernised, and we got reports of sagging beds, gouty chairs, even flooding toilets and rotten balconies. But all that seems to have changed, for the bedrooms have been renovated: this year, it's true, one uncomfortable bed has been slept in, but other visitors in 1988/9 have been happy: "The newly modernised rooms are very attractive"; "Ours was lovely, with pink bedspreads, clean and well appointed"; "The refurnishing has been done with taste and style."

Dinner has long been admired – generous helpings of Norman cooking (e.g. duck terrine and sole meunière) with lashings of cream, butter and Calvados. "Food was delicious", says one 1989 visitor, "and we liked Madame's leisurely personal service", though some have found her shy and reserved. Above all, the setting delights – "We woke to look out on a charming lush garden and stream", "farmhouse sounds and smells", and "a selection of cats, a stick-retrieving dog and the river abounding in young frogs". (*Susan E Rayner, J Guest*)

Open All year except 15 Dec–31 Jan. Closed Mon evening and Tue.
Rooms 1 family, 8 double – all with bath and/or shower and telephone. All in separate building in garden.
Facilities Lounge with mono TV, restaurant; functions room/ballroom. Garden with large lawn and stream; pavilion for outdoor summer meals.
Location 5 km from Dieppe; off D1 to Neufchatel.
Restriction Not suitable for &.
Credit cards All major cards accepted.
Terms [1989 rates] Rooms 200–310 frs. Breakfast 25 frs. Alc 180 frs (excluding wine). Guests are expected to dine in the restaurant.

MAUSSANE-LES-ALPILLES 13520 Bouches-du-Rhône   Map 5

Hostellerie l'Oustaloun   *Tel* 90.97.32.19
Place de l'Église

A new nomination, "Unusual and charming: it's a converted 16th-century chapel, in the small main square of an untouristy Provençal village just south of ultra-touristy Les Baux. Owned and run by an affable Bolognese, Robert Bartoli, and his shy French artist wife, Emma, whose pictures adorn the main rooms. The ambience is personal, intimate, cosy, but quite sophisticated – and the clientele likewise. Yet prices are most reasonable. Small, pretty bedrooms with period furniture. Three small, attractive dining rooms with unusual decor, and a short *carte* of mostly regional dishes, quite good. The help-yourself buffet that opens the 130-franc [1990] set menu includes the best tapenade and anchoiade I've ever tasted. Hurry, for the Bartolis might retire before long." (*JA*)

Open All year.
Rooms 9 – all with bath or with shower.
Facilities 3 dining rooms.
Location Central, parking. Maussane is 19 km E of Arles.
Restriction Not suitable for &.
Credit cards All major cards accepted.
Terms [1990 rates] B&B double from 275 frs. Set lunch/dinner 130 frs; full alc 120 frs. Special meals for children.

MERCUREY 71640 Saône-et-Loire   Map 4

Hôtellerie du Val d'Or   *Tel* 85.45.13.70
Grande Rue   *Telex* 800660

Renewed praise in 1988/9 for this tidy traditional hostelry in a village producing one of Burgundy's great wines (there are several *caveaux de dégustation* close by). The "courteous and efficient" Cogny family provides locals as well as tourists with generous helpings of mainly traditional local cuisine (*Michelin* rosette, *Gault Millau toque*, for such dishes as fillet of rabbit and parsleyed ham). One recent visitor especially enjoyed the middle-priced menu and had a small but pretty room with a balcony over the garden. Others, too, have found the rooms comfortable and charmingly decorated, if a little cramped. Light and colour in the garden, armchairs in the salon, and sociable chatter in the attractive restaurant with its stone-tiled floor, flowers and lamps, and log-fire in winter. "Splendid" Mercurey wines – but expensive. The hotel is on a busy main street. (*Peter and Ann Jones, and others*)

Open All year except late Aug–early Sep and 17 Dec–17 Jan; closed Mon and Tue midday.
Rooms 10 double, 1 single – 5 with bath, 6 with shower, all with telephone and T V.
Facilities Reception, salon, bar, 2 restaurants. Garden, swings.
Location 13 km from Chalon-sur-Saône. Leave *autoroute* at Chalon Nord and take D978 Autun–Nevers road, then turn right to Mercurey. Parking.
Restriction Not suitable for &.
Credit card Access.
Terms [1989 rates] Rooms: single occupancy 130 frs, double 350 frs. Breakfast 35 frs. Set lunch/dinner 140, 200 and 320 frs; full alc 300 frs. Reduced rates and special meals for children.

MEYRUEIS 48150 Lozère   Map 4

Château d'Ayres   *Tel* 66.45.60.10

An old creeper-covered château, originally a 12th-century monastery, now much rebuilt, standing alone in open country outside Meyrueis on the edge of the limestone *causses* and the Cévennes National Park, close to the Jonte and Tarn gorges. Large bedrooms overlook a park of giant sequoias, chestnuts and cedars. A devotee returning this year sets the tone, "The owners, the Comte and Comtesse de Montjou, make you feel that you are not so much hotel guests as family friends staying in their home. The staff, too, are all smiles and courtesy. Huge, comfortable rooms, beautiful breakfasts, more than adequate cuisine, and an air of peace and elegance." That was from *Colin Pilkington*, who last year wrote, "It is in the evening that the hotel's charm best manifests itself: small tables and chairs are set under the sequoias in the park, with candles on each table, and subtle floodlighting tints the château's facade and the trees beneath the hillside, creating perfect reflections in the ornamental pool." We'd be glad of more details, please, about this "more than adequate cuisine".

Open 1 Apr–15 Oct.
Rooms 3 suites, 20 double, 1 single – 22 with bath, 2 with shower, all with telephone and T V; baby-listening on request.
Facilities 2 salons, T V room, 2 dining rooms. Garden with tennis.
Location 1.5 km SE of Meyrueis.
Restriction Not suitable for &.
Credit cards All major cards accepted.
Terms Rooms double 270–330 frs, suite 550 frs. Breakfast 40 frs. Dinner, B&B double 550–830 frs. Set lunch/dinner 116–230 frs; full alc 260 frs. Low season rates. Reduced rates and special meals for children.

MIMIZAN 40200 Landes   Map 4

Au Bon Coin du Lac   *Tel* 58.09.01.55
34 avenue du Lac

The long flat Atlantic coast south-west of Bordeaux has splendid sandy beaches, lined by a number of dullish resorts. Just inland are freshwater lakes amid the Landes forests, also with resort facilities, and here is *Au Bon Coin du Lac*. Its main emphasis is on cuisine (*Michelin* rosette, two red *Gault Millau toques*), and readers again this year thought the food "excellent", endorsing last year's verdicts: "One of the most arresting places we have ever stayed at. It is edged by well-kept public gardens, with woods and beaches beyond, and it has rowing-boats for hire (free to residents). Our bedroom above the restaurant was most luxurious, with repro antique furniture, lace bedspread, huge bathroom. Dinner was a delightful affair, served with panache and humour by efficient young waiters; even the cheapest menu was delicious, and supreme value for money. Gorgeous china, impeccable napery, silver candlesticks. Blissful peace at night in the flowery lakeside gardens, and then a good breakfast." "The atmosphere is excellent, with a smiling Madame Caule leading a friendly team. The only sound to disturb us at night was a cat-fight." Rooms in the annexe are equally luxurious. (*Ian and Francine Walsh, EH, PW Arnold*)

Open All year except Feb. Restaurant closed Sun evening and Mon in low season.
Rooms 3 suites, 5 double – all with bath (5 also have shower, telephone, TV and mini-bar. Suites, with kitchenette, in annexe 100 metres from hotel. Some ground-floor rooms.
Facilities Lounges, bar, dining room; functions rooms; terrace. Garden. Lake with fishing, rowing boats. Sea 4 km.
Location 1 km N of Mimizan, which is 111 km SW of Bordeaux.
Credit card Visa.
Terms [1989 rates] Rooms double 480–560 frs. Breakfast 55 frs. Dinner, B&B 400–520 frs per person. Set lunch/dinner 130-350 frs; full alc 350 frs. Reduced rates and special meals for children.

MIONNAY 01390 Ain   **Map 4**

Alain Chapel   *Tel* 78.91.82.02
                                                                    Telex 305605

Alain Chapel is sometimes regarded as the greatest of all the great modern French chefs, and his elegant restaurant-with-rooms, on the edge of a village north of Lyon, wins *Gault Millau's* highest rating of 19.5 out of 20, as well as the expected three *Michelin* rosettes. He is a serious, rather austere man, not at all a flamboyant showman like his rival Paul Bocuse down the road; a perfectionist and tireless innovator, he changes his menu with the season and the market, creating superb new tastes from simple high-quality products, in the light modern manner. Of course his prices are high (and one reader has judged them excessive): but this year two expert travellers have endorsed ("better than ever") this 1988 inspector's report: "It's an old rural *auberge*, much extended and now very grand and spacious, with stone-flagged halls and patios and a floodlit garden. Chapel tries to keep the rural touch, but he does cheat: one dining annexe with ancient beams looks like a medieval barn but was built in 1987! You eat in a series of small discreet flower-filled rooms, where tables are well spaced and the ambience is quiet and dignified (save for the tourists taking snapshots of their meal). We especially liked the écrevisses in a spicy dark-green coriander sauce, the pigeon à la presse and the very ripe cheeses. Oddly poor bread, but truly friendly service. Quaint loos (the ladies' has a piano). The few bedrooms are not large but pretty and cosy." "Our room was bright and cheerful, with fresh flowers (some road noise at 7 am). Excellent food, notably the strawberry soufflé. Monsieur Chapel was very formal but not unfriendly." (*Pat and Jeremy*

FRANCE

Temple) Only one criticism: a seriously sub-standard breakfast, served badly and slowly. Seven new rooms are planned for 1990.

Open All year except Jan and Mon. Restaurant closed Tue midday except public holidays.
Rooms 13 double – all with bath, telephone and TV.
Facilities 3 lounges, bar, restaurant. Small garden where meals are served in fine weather.
Location 17 km N of Lyons, on N83. Coming from Paris on A6, take first exit after Villefranche, then D51 to Neuville, then Montanay. Parking.
Credit cards All major cards accepted.
Terms Rooms 600–750 frs. Breakfast 75 frs. Set lunch/dinner 460, 600 and 750 frs; full alc 500 frs. Reduced rates and special meals for children.

MOLINES-EN-QUEYRAS 05350 Hautes-Alpes   Map 4

Hôtel l'Équipe   *Tel* 92.45.83.20
Route de St-Véran

"Fantastic value for money", "delightful and charming" – two examples of the enthusiasm engendered by this unpretentious little chalet-hotel in a beautiful Alpine setting. It stands in a broad high valley south-east of Briançon, with ski-slopes and wooded hills all round. Nearby is the 13th-century fortress of Château-Queyras, and the isolated village of St-Véran, which at 2,040 metres claims to be the highest in Europe. "The hotel is simple but well furnished and equipped, and managed with charm and discretion by the Catalins. Our dinner was original, well produced and, unusually for France, served at speed." "The owners were warm and helpful, the meal delicious, the view spectacular." "We had a comfortable bedroom with a balcony giving magnificent views." "There's no night life around here, but interesting 'happenings' in season, such as folk-singing, and firework displays on the hills. Monsieur leads excursions into the mountains." Sometimes the Catalins throw the guests together for a fondue party. (*Endorsed this year by Pat and Brian Lloyd*)

Open 20 Dec–16 Apr, 3 June–18 Sept.
Rooms 22 – all with bath (3 also with shower) and telephone. 11 with 2–4 beds in annexe.
Facilities Salon, TV room, bar, restaurant. Terrace; garden on river. Winter sports (ski lifts 50 metres).
Location 1 km from Molines on road to St-Véran.
Restriction Not suitable for ර.
Credit cards All major cards accepted.
Terms [1989 rates] B&B double 244 frs; dinner, B&B 215 frs per person; full board 265 frs. Set lunch/dinner 55, 84, 113 frs; full alc 130 frs. Reduced rates and special meals for children.

MOLITG-LES-BAINS 66500 Pyrénées-Orientales   Map 4

Château de Riell   *Tel* 68.05.04.40
                                                   Fax 68.05.02.91
                                                   Telex 500705

Specialising in skin and lung diseases, the imposing spa buildings of Molitg-les-Bains stand beside a small lake in a hollow of the Pyrenean foothills, west of Perpignan and close to Prades where the Spanish cellist Pablo Casals spent his exile (there is still an annual music festival in his honour). Set on a hillside above the spa, the very smart *Château de Riell* is owned and run by Biche Barthélemy, sister-in-law of Michel Guérard (*see* Eugénie-les-Bains), and its quirky sophistication is clearly in his tradition – as our nominator quirkily reports, "A sudden tower in a more or less vertical wood in the mountains. The architecture (early Gothic revival, 1829) owes more to Sir Walter Scott, we suspect, than to certain medieval buildings in the valley below. The interior, quite new, is devilish stylish: the tiger-skin bar, the carpet-lined lift *and* lift-shaft, strange plastic linings to the dining room which speak of Gaudi, the cushions piled here and there on the floor in your bedroom and – believe it or not – in the public rooms while you are having dinner. The luxury is absolute, the service unconditional, the basins and the bath furniture copper, and the price, though very high, no more than commensurate. A double bed is vast. As to the cooking (*Michelin* rosette, two red *Gault Millau toques*), it is dramatic, careful, perhaps a bit over-complicated: lots of unexpected bits not on the menu turn up to keep you going between courses." The hotel's elegant brochure, written in the quaintest of purple English prose, gives glimpses also of a pretty tiled courtyard for drinks, and lounges by a swimming pool under the trees. The chef, Marc Baudry, was trained by Guérard, and adds his own Catalan flourishes. Thermal and beauty cures are available, but there does not appear to be the same accent on dieting as at Eugénie. More reports please.

Open 1 Apr–5 Nov.
Rooms 3 suites, 18 double – all with bath, shower, telephone, radio, TV. 7 in 3 houses (with kitchenette) in castle grounds.
Facilities 2 lifts. Lounge, salon with TV, bar, dining room; private club; conference centre; terrace. Park with 2 swimming pools, 2 tennis courts. Fitness centre with sauna and beauty cures. Access to lake with beach, fishing.
Location On edge of spa, which is 7 km NW of Prades. Garage.
Credit cards Access, Amex, Visa.
Terms Rooms: single 875 frs, double 1,030 frs, suite 1,355 frs. Breakfast 74 frs. Set lunch 270 frs, dinner 400 frs; full alc 380 frs. Reduced rates and special meals for children.

MONTFORT-EN-CHALOSSE 40380 Landes   Map 4

"Aux Touzins"   *Tel 58.98.60.22*

A mile outside the village of Montfort on the southern fringe of the Landes forest, amid pleasant rolling Gascony countryside, is this unpretentious white-walled auberge. *Comfortable modern bedrooms, nicely decorated, some with balconies and views; smiling staff; good regional cooking, popular with locals. All excellent value. Closed 15 Jan–15 Feb. 20 rooms, 13 with bath or shower. Dinner, B&B double 250–320 frs. Set menu from 90 frs* [1989 rates]. *New nomination. More reports welcome.*

MONTPELLIER 34000 Hérault   Map 4

Hôtel Le Guilhem   *Tel 67.52.90.90*
18 rue J-J Rousseau

An inspector reports this year, "Montpellier used to be a sleepy place, but it's now the fastest-growing boom-town in France, an upstart rival to

Toulouse and Grenoble, with some monumental new architecture by Ricardo Bofill. None of this has spoilt the charm of the *vieille ville*, to my mind as lovely as Aix or Arles; and here in a narrow street is this brand-new little B&B hotel, converted from an old building by a former Parisian accountant and his wife, the Charpentiers, both friendly. Rooms are inevitably small, but very well equipped (hair-drier, good reading lights); breakfast comes copiously with flowers, eggs, newspaper, etc. A lovely terrace for summer, amid greenery. Parking is hard." For restaurants, see under *Noailles*, below.

Open All year.
Rooms 22 double, 2 single – all with bath and/or shower, telephone and T V; baby-sitting.
Facilities Lift. Breakfast room, salon. Terrace.
Location Central, in pedestrian zone; follow signs for "centre historique". Public parking 600 metres away.
Restriction Not suitable for &.
Credit cards All major cards accepted.
Terms Rooms 200–400 frs. Breakfast 35 frs. (No restaurant.)

Hôtel de Noailles   *Tel* 67.60.49.80
2 rue des Écoles-Centrales

"Lovely comfortable hotel on a quiet street"; "charming, with good breakfasts" – two recent verdicts on this 17th-century mansion, graceful in a cool classical style. It is not easy of access by car (without a good street map, at least), for it lies in the heart of the network of quiet alleys, some closed to traffic, that forms the kernel of this beautiful southern city. Readers have found the staff caring and the contrast with modernism quite blissful. But there are warnings that front rooms can be noisy, especially from the bell tower next door. No restaurant, but you can eat well nearby at the *Louvre* (medium price) or cheaply at many places in the charming and lively little squares of the old town. More reports please.

Open 15 Jan–21 Dec.
Rooms 20 double with bath, 10 single with shower, all with telephone and T V.
Facilities Reception, salon/T V room where breakfast is served.
Location Central, near church of Notre Dame de Tables. Look for signs: "centre historique". Nearby parking not easy; use underground carpark in Place de la Comédie, entrance opposite Monoprix (300 metres S).
Restriction Not suitable for &.
Credit cards All major cards accepted.
Terms Rooms: single 300 frs, double 350–380 frs. Breakfast 30 frs.
(No restaurant.)

MONTPINCHON 50210 Manche   **Map 2**

Château de la Salle   *Tel* 33.46.95.19

Within an hour's drive of Cherbourg, between St-Lô with its national stud and Coutances with its sublime cathedral, a handsome 18th-century stone mansion is now a most elegant country hotel. It is new to the Guide this year: "Peaceful surroundings, lovely bedroom beautifully furnished, and superb food" (a mixture, it seems, of *nouvelle* and *ancienne*: traditionalist *Michelin* awards a rosette for ris de veau braisé *à l'ancienne*, modernist *Gault Millau* picks out lobster in truffle vinaigrette, when bestowing its red *toque*). A huge roaring fire, elegant furniture, some four-poster beds, and a lovely garden where you can take breakfast. (*Mrs D Goodey*) More reports welcome.

Open 16 Mar–5 Nov.
Rooms 1 suite, 9 double, 1 single – 10 with bath, 1 with shower, all with telephone and TV.
Facilities Lounge, 3 dining rooms. Garden.
Location Montpinchon is 12 km E of Coutances, by D7 and D73.
Restrictions Not suitable for &.
Credit cards Access, Diners, Visa.
Terms B&B: single 528 frs, double 676–726 frs, suite 856 frs; dinner, B&B: single 758 frs, double 1,136–1,186 frs, suite 1,316 frs. Set lunch/dinner 155–230 frs. Reduced rates and special meals for children by arrangement.

MONTREUIL 62170 Pas-de-Calais   Map 3

Château de Montreuil   *Tel* 21.81.53.04
4 chaussée des Capucins   *Telex* 135205 HOTEUIL

Large old house in lovely walled garden, near ruined citadel in quiet part of medieval hilltop town; stylish and ambitious. Many guests, like the patronne, *are British. Rooms vary greatly in size and style; some have been severely criticised for decor and upkeep in 1988/9, as has the food – despite its* Michelin *rosette, and the service. But recent reports are more favourable – "beautiful, newly refitted garden room, food superb"; could we have more feedback please? Closed 10 Dec–early Feb, Thurs midday except July/Aug. 14 rooms, all with bath or shower, 380–580 frs. Breakfast 45 frs. Alc meals (excluding wine) 250–350 frs [1989].*

MONT-ST-MICHEL 50116 Manche   Map 2

Hôtel La Mère Poulard   *Tel* 33.60.14.01
     Telex 170197

No other site in France outside Paris attracts more tourists than Mont-St-Michel, linked to the coast by a causeway at low tide and capped by its towering Benedictine monastery. An overnight stay is well worth it, for then you can appreciate the aura of the place when the day trippers have left, and visit the abbey early the next morning before they arrive. *La Mère Poulard*, just inside the rampart gates, has character and tradition and is much frequented by Americans. Its restaurant has been famous for its omelettes for exactly 101 years, and under a new chef is continuing to provide good classic Norman and Breton cooking (*Gault Millau toque*). A report since that change, "Worth the high prices, and deserves to get back its *Michelin* rosette – we enjoyed salmon, magret de canard in a rich sauce, and more cheese than Brussels could subsidise. A pianist tinkles. The *patron* is charming, the service slick and the rooms comfortable." An earlier view, "The experience of staying Easter Saturday and visiting the Abbey at midnight for the service was perfectly complemented by the hotel. Service was excellent." The hotel has just been renovated, but it's still not a place for the elderly as the stairways to the rooms are steep and narrow. (*Paul Palmer, Victoria Turner*) The late Rita Hayworth and Emperor Hirohito were among past guests, while in December 1988

President Mitterrand entertained Mrs Thatcher here, to scallops, lamb, and dessert omelette flambée.

Open All year.
Rooms 1 suite, 26 double – 24 with bath, 3 with shower, all with telephone and TV. 14 rooms in nearby annexe.
Facilities Lounge, TV room, games room, restaurant, omelette room. Fishing and bathing nearby.
Location Just inside walls of Mont St-Michel. Large car park across causeway.
Restrictions Not suitable for &. No babies in restaurant.
Credit cards All major cards accepted.
Terms [1989 rates] Rooms 450–750 frs. Breakfast 50 frs. Set lunch/dinner 120–300 frs. Special meals for children.

MORLAIX 29210 Finistère   Map 2

Hôtel de l'Europe   *Tel* 98.62.11.99
1 rue d'Aiguillon   *Telex* 941676

In the centre of this North Breton market town, a classic and dignified hostelry with fairly simple, modestly priced rooms, many of them spacious and overlooking a quiet courtyard. Excellent, innovative cooking in a Second Empire style brasserie (there is also a restaurant under separate management). 70 rooms, most with bath and shower. B&B double 304–344 frs. Set menus in brasserie 60 and 70 frs. New nomination. More reports welcome.

MUZILLAC 56190 Morbihan   Map 2

Domaine du Château de   *Tel* 97.41.69.27
Rochevilaine   *Telex* 950570
Pointe de Pen Lan

Two of the Guide's ace reporters recount their poetic discovery on the south coast of Brittany this year: "This old manor stands on a rocky headland just above the sea. Its many outbuildings, ranging from the medieval to the modern, are scattered in well-tended gardens dotted with ancient Breton sculptures and crosses; these pavilions, each with a private lounge, can be taken by a whole family. Our room was palatial, and all the hotel's furniture is ancient Breton and superb: the huge chest, creaky carved wardrobe and writing desk in our room were of the kind one drools over in antique shops. Bedroom service is impeccable and the breakfast copious. Dinner in the cavernous dining room under its ancient beams can be somewhat noisy, but the view of the sun setting on the sea takes your breath away. Cooking is *soigné*, exploiting the catch of the day, and the table d'hôte offers good value (two red *Gault Millau toques* for e.g. palourdes in truffle vinaigrette). You can take lunch in the modern courtyard. There's a small outdoor swimming pool above the rocks for those who do not fancy the nearby rocky or sandy beaches; and the hotel is about to build a thalassotherapy centre. At high tide, the sea rose right up to our bedroom on the rocks: here, leaving windows and curtains open, we woke bathed in the beams of the rising sun at dawn, to the purr of fishing vessels sailing out. At night, the magical darkness, dotted with distant lights, was undisturbed save for the gentle swish of the waves below. It was the most striking memory of our trip – that amazing room at the edge of the world, with nothing beyond but the sea and the stars." (*Francine and Ian Walsh*)

Open All year except Jan and Feb. Closed Sun evening and Mon midday in low season.
Rooms 27 – all with bath and/or shower and telephone; some with TV. Rooms in pavilions in garden.
Facilities Lounge, restaurant; conference facilities. Courtyard where meals are served; garden, swimming pool. Tennis, riding, golf nearby.
Location At Pointe de Pen Lan, 4.5 km S of Muzillac which is 25 km SE of Vannes.
Credit cards All major cards accepted.
Terms [1989 rates] Rooms 380–920 frs. Breakfast 48 frs. Dinner, B&B 460–730 frs per person. Set lunch/dinner 180–330 frs.

NAJAC 12270 Aveyron   Map 4

Hôtel Miquel: l'Oustal del Barry   *Tel* 65.29.74.32
Place du Bourg

In this remote but scenic part of the Massif Central, Najac is a beautiful medieval village above the Aveyron gorges, with an old castle high on a hill above the river. The *Miquel* is on the village square, yet also has a private garden for sunbathing, with a children's playground. Some rooms have a balcony, and there are wonderful views. An inspector this year had an "amazingly generous" lunch with "really good provincial cooking, not *nouvelle*-ish, served very professionally but with enthusiasm". And another visitor found Madame Miquel "friendly, caring and attentive". Rooms vary in size and quality as the hotel has been converted from several different old houses. (*HR, John Gray*)

Open Apr–end Oct. Closed Mon Apr and Oct except holidays.
Rooms 4 suites, 13 double, 4 single – all with bath and/or shower, telephone and TV. 7 in annexe. Some ground-floor rooms.
Facilities Lift. Salon, TV room, bar, 2 restaurants; 2 terraces. Large garden with play area for children.
Location Coming from Villefranche de Rouergue or Cordes on D122 hotel is on right at entrance of village. Parking.
Credit cards Amex, Visa.
Terms Rooms: single 165 frs, double 195–220 frs, suite 240 frs; dinner, B&B 220–250 frs per person. Set lunch/dinner 100, 180 and 250 frs; full alc 250–280 frs. Reduced rates and special meals for children.

NARBONNE 11100 Aude   Map 4

Hôtel la Résidence   *Tel* 68.32.19.41
6 rue du Premier Mai   *Telex* 500441 SOMARES

In a quiet street in the shadow of Narbonne's great fortified cathedral, here's an unusual but sympathetic small hotel in Victorian boudoir style: Louis XV furniture, gilt mirrors, silk flowers in vases. "Run by very friendly local people, really quite jovial; it is slightly quaint and theatrical, with decor verging on the kitschy. In the corridors, old chests, velvet drapes, red candles on silver sticks. Some of the rooms are in this style too, but ours had plainer decor. It was comfortable and cosy. Adequate breakfast, taken in one of three spruce and elegant little salons." "Breakfast served on pretty china, with an accompanying rose-bud that opened and lasted 11 days." No restaurant, but some good ones close by. (*Endorsed in 1989 by Mrs VA Preston.*)

Open All year except 3 Jan–3 Feb.
Rooms 1 suite, 23 double, 2 single – all with bath/shower, telephone and TV. 4 ground-floor rooms.
Facilities 2 salons, TV room.
Location Central, near cathedral and canal. Parking.
Restriction Not suitable for &.
Credit cards Access, Visa.
Terms Rooms: single occupancy 265–290 frs, double 300–390 frs. Breakfast 32 frs. (No restaurant.)

NICE 06300 Alpes-Maritimes   Map 5

Hôtel La Pérouse   *Tel* 93.62.34.63
11 quai Rauba-Capeu   *Fax* 93.67.59.41
                                                       Telex 461411

Of Nice's 350 hotels, nearly all of them dull, the upper-medium-priced *La Pérouse* is possibly the most attractive (apart, of course, from the super-luxury *Negresco*). Its setting is its star feature, for it is perched half-way up the castle rock at the east end of the promenade, with "breathtaking" views of the bay. "More super than ever," say inspectors returning recently; "we enjoyed our lunch on the terrace under the lemon trees: food is just basic grills, but plentiful and nicely served. Idyllic swimming pool under high rocks. The hotel has white marble corridors, bedrooms with cool white decor and marble bathrooms (rooms vary in price, but even the cheaper ones without sea views are well furnished and comfortable). A really lovely bar with comfy chairs and a log fire in winter. The civilised young manager, Roland Muntzer, runs one of the pleasantest city hotels in France. No restaurant, but there are scores of candle-lit bistros close by in the Vieille Ville." Readers this year have been pleased, though one of them thought the beds too short and found the staff less than helpful when sorting out a muddle over booking. (*M and L Piper, ML and MM Gravelle*)

Open All year.
Rooms 2 suites, 60 double, 3 single – all with bath and shower, telephone, radio and TV.
Facilities Lifts. Bar/lounge, terrace, conference facilities. Sauna. Garden with patio; 2 swimming pools. Beach across road.
Location At E end of Promenade des Anglais, by château. Paid parking nearby.
Credit cards All major cards accepted.
Terms Rooms 295–1,020 frs, suite 1,030–1,700 frs. Breakfast 40–45 frs. Reduced rates for children. (No restaurant but light snacks and room service.)

NIEUIL 16270 Charente   Map 4

Le Château de Nieuil   *Tel* 45.71.36.38
                                                       Telex 791230

Originally used as a hunting-lodge by François I, this moated Renaissance château stands in its own huge wooded park north-east of Angoulême. It has fine antiques and an imposing marble staircase – and of course it is not cheap. Visitors continue to appreciate its beauty and comfort, as well as the kindliness of M. Bodinaud, the owner, but again this year they are not entirely sure whether the cooking, though good, quite merits its *Michelin* rosette and two red *Gault Millau toques*. This earlier report remains entirely valid, "The gardens are lovely, and the château bears the stamp of several generations of French nobility. Yet the atmosphere is not pretentious. It is both friendly and sophisticated. Dinner in the panelled dining-room was a mixture of trad and modern, with generous helpings, imaginative salads, and a choice of 15 different fruit tarts. Each course was decorated with fresh flowers. We were somewhat embarrassed, however, by M. Bodinaud's gimmick of putting the flag of the appropriate nation on each guest's table. M. Bodinaud is also an art buff, and in the former stables he exhibits and sells expensive prints, modern paintings and sculptures." (*DG Randall, FW*)

Open End Apr–early Nov.
Rooms 3 suites, 12 double – 11 with bath, 2 with shower, all with telephone; T V and baby-listening on request; many with minibar. 1 in tower 40 metres from main building. 2 ground-floor rooms suitable for &.
Facilities Salon/bar with T V, restaurant; conference facilities. 350-acre wooded park with swimming pool, tennis court, fishing in pond, archery and art gallery.
Location Off D739, between Nieuil and Fontagie; 42 km NE of Angoulême.
Credit cards All major cards accepted.
Terms [1989 rates] Dinner B&B: single 675–925 frs, double 1,010–1330 frs. Set meals 190–245 frs. Reduced rates and special meals for children on request.

NÎMES 30000 Gard   Map 4

Hôtel Imperator Concorde   *Tel* 66.21.90.30
Quai de la Fontaine   *Telex* 490635

An imperially classic turn-of-the-century hotel, newly renovated, in a good position between the Maison Carrée and Jardin de la Fontaine. Courteous service, pleasant walled garden, most bedrooms modernised; nouvelle cuisine *not quite up to its pretensions. 62 rooms, all with private facilities. B&B double 460–760 frs. Set menus 165–350 frs. New nomination. More reports welcome.*

NONTRON 24300 Dordogne   Map 4

Grand Hôtel Pélisson   *Tel* 53.56.11.22
3 place Alfred Agard

Between Angoulême and Périgueux, in the so-called "Périgord Vert", an old walled hilltop town where this former coaching-inn, quite modest and unsmart, stands on the main square. Very good simple country cooking, copiously served. Friendly, helpful people. Rooms comfortable, but they vary in size and furnishings are sombre. Parking in large rear courtyard. 26 rooms, most with bath or shower. B&B double 200–270 frs. Set menus 60–220 frs. More reports please.

There are many expensive hotels in the Guide. We are keen to increase our coverage at the other end of the scale. If you know of a simple place giving simple satisfaction, please write and tell us.

NOVES 13550 Bouches-du-Rhône   Map 5

Auberge de Noves   *Tel* 90.94.19.21
                                                    Fax 90.94.47.76
                                                    Telex 431312

A 19th-century manor amid pleasant open country south-east of
Avignon, owned and run by André Lalleman as a stylish and luxurious
hotel, well known for its cuisine (*Michelin* rosette, two red *Gault Millau
toques*). An inspector returning this year found it as superb as ever,
"Glorious floodlit patio, some new bedrooms of stunning luxury, with
lovely decor; some have balconies with pastoral views," and others have
concurred, "Breakfast delicious, food consistently good and generous. To
listen to M. Lalleman discuss in French, English or German the ordering
of the meal is an education and entertainment in itself." Earlier views: "A
friendly and helpful atmosphere. M. Lalleman proved an amusing,
intelligent and multilingual host. Excellent antiques in the bedroom,
elegant pink-marble bathroom – but we could have done with a mini-bar
in the heat!" "We can recommend the duck en papillote. M. Lalleman
personally advised us on our choice of dishes. The waitresses treat you
like honoured guests. The hotel even has its own well, with refreshing
spring water; but the pool and gardens were untidy and the public rooms
have too much flowery wallpaper." One gripe this year about food and
service. And not all rooms are air-conditioned. (*Endorsed by Joy and
Raymond Goldman*)

Open All year except Jan, Feb, Wed midday.
Rooms 4 suites, 18 double – all with bath and shower, telephone, and TV; some
with balcony; baby-listening on request. Ground-floor rooms.
Facilities Lift. Salon, dining room; conference facilities. Garden with swimming
pool and tennis court.
Location Off D 28, 2 km NW of Noves, which is 13 km SE of Avignon.
Credit cards Probably all major cards accepted.
Terms [1989 rates] Rooms 900–1,150 frs. Breakfast 70 frs. Dinner, B&B 880–
1,005 frs per person. Set lunch/dinner 300–400 frs. Reduced rates and special
meals for children.

PARIS   Map 3

Hôtel de l'Abbaye St-Germain   *Tel* (1) 45.44.38.11
10 rue Cassette, 75006

This *Relais du Silence* is on a busy little street near St-Sulpice, but even
front rooms are quiet. It is a former monastery, nicely restored with
simple elegance: bedrooms are well furnished, and windows open onto a
little flagged courtyard with palms, pot-plants and flowers, where
breakfast or refreshments can be taken. For these qualities, the *Abbaye*
continues to be admired – "beautiful" and "excellent" are among this
year's epithets. (*Phillip Gill, FM and CN Grist*) However, some rooms are
very small, and more than one recent visitor complains of imperfect
housekeeping and maintenance.

Open All year.
Rooms 4 suites, 44 double – all with bath and telephone, suites with terrace.
Facilities Lift. 2 salons, TV room, bar. Interior courtyard/garden.
Location Central, near St-Sulpice church. (Métro St-Sulpice.)

Restriction Not suitable for &.
Credit cards None accepted.
Terms B&B: double room 650–850 frs, suite 1,500–1,800 frs. (No restaurant.)

Hôtel de l'Angleterre
44 rue Jacob
Paris, 75006

Tel 42.60.34.72
Fax 42.60.16.93

Once upon a time the British Embassy (hence its name), this spruce and popular little hotel near St-Germain-des-Prés has some elegance (antiques and deep sofas in the foyer). Hemingway once lived in Room 14. Comfortable rooms, some with old beams: the quietest face the inner patio. 29 rooms, all but 1 with bath and shower. Rooms 650–900 frs. Breakfast 30 frs [1989]. No restaurant. Endorsed this year, but further reports welcome.

Hôtel de Banville
166 boulevard Berthier, 75017

Tel 42.67.70.16
Telex 643025 H BANVIL

"The *Banville* calls itself 'the cheapest three-star hotel in Paris', which at under 500 frs a night may well be so. It is also one of the nicest in its class, family-run by very pleasant people, with a friendly staff and warm inviting atmosphere – not always so common in Paris. It fills up with regular clients, mostly French provincials, so needs to be booked well in advance. Bedrooms are comfortable and cosy, exceptional value, and the big foyer is cosy too, as well as elegant, with lots of flowers and pretty fabrics. One snag is the location, on a broad boulevard in the unglamorous *17e*, with few good restaurants nearby. The Métro is quite close, however." (JA) It is also handy for the air terminal. More reports please.

Open All year.
Rooms 40 double – 33 with bath and shower, 7 with shower, all with telephone, radio, TV. Baby-sitting.
Facilities Lift. 2 lounges, breakfast room.
Location 2 minutes' walk from Porte de Champerret, 10 minutes from Étoile. Underground parking nearby. (Métro Porte de Champerret and Pereire.)
Restriction Not suitable for &.
Credit cards Access, Amex, Visa.
Terms Rooms 470–490 frs. Breakfast 30 frs. (No restaurant.)

Hôtel Châtillon
11 square de Châtillon, 75014

Tel (1) 45.42.31.17
Fax 45.42.72.09

This cheap and mildly eccentric little hotel is about four kilometres south of central Paris, in the totally untouristy Alésia district, and useful for access to the motorways. A devotee returning this year found the place mercifully unchanged under new owners, as "delightful" as the previous ones, and endorses his previous encomium: "The whole place reeks of Frenchness. The rooms are spacious with wonderful views of the neighbours – we cannot believe what people wear to go to bed. I far prefer it to *EastEnders*. A charming and quiet place where we awoke to birdsong in the trees. The floorboards creak, the furniture is nothing special, but the staff are delightful, the beds comfy, and breakfast deliciously fresh." Others, too, have approved the bedrooms and modern bathrooms. (*Paul Palmer*)

Open All year.
Rooms 2 for 4, 29 double – 30 with bath and/or shower, telephone and TV. 1 ground-floor room.
Facilities Lift, salon, bar, breakfast room.
Location Near Porte de Châtillon and Porte d'Orléans. Underground parking nearby. (Métro Alésia.)
Credit card Visa.
Terms Rooms 230–350 frs. Breakfast 22 frs. (No restaurant.)

Hôtel Duc de Saint-Simon   *Tel* 45.48.35.66
14 rue de Saint-Simon   *Fax* 45.48.68.25
          Telex 203277

The sophisticated little *Duc de Saint-Simon* (formerly just the *Saint-Simon*) could be bracketed with the *Abbaye St-Germain* and the *Résidence du Bois* (q.v.) as being perhaps the most stylish of the city's small hotels. Centrally but quietly located down a side-street just off the boulevard St-Germain, it is usually booked up months ahead. Here is an inspector's recent view, "The tiny cobbled forecourt, with its shrubs and trellis-work, gives it a somewhat rural air. Converted from a 17th-century mansion, it is now owned and run by a civilised Swedish couple who have filled it with the antiques they love collecting. Tiled walls, old beams and rough stone walls add to the effect, and there's a small and pretty rear garden for breakfast and drinks in summer. My room was small and unremarkable, but many others are larger and better. The former cellars are now a network of little bars and salons, elegant certainly but a trifle claustrophobic; nor did I like the mindless piped music, not even classical. Clients tend to be reasonably well-off travellers who prefer Left Bank old-world charm to a luxury palace. I can see why they like this place, but I found it slightly snobbish and lacking in warmth, though certainly the staff are efficient." Others have judged it "utterly charming", "very beautiful".

Open All year.
Rooms 5 suites, 29 double – all with bath and/or shower, and telephone; TV on request. 5 in annexe.
Facilities Lift. 2 lounges, bar.
Location Central. (Métro Rue du Bac.)
Restriction Not suitable for &.
Credit cards None accepted.
Terms [1989 rates] Rooms 800–1100 frs, suites 1,250–1,500 frs. Breakfast 45 frs. (No restaurant.)

Hôtel des Grands Hommes   *Tel* (1) 46.34.19.60
17 place du Panthéon, 75005   *Telex* 200185 PANTEON

André Breton and other Surrealist painters and writers are "great men" who used to stay at this little hotel of character, though the hotel is named for the even greater men (Voltaire, Victor Hugo, Rousseau et al) entombed in the Panthéon across the street. Its claim to be the place where Surrealism was created has just been formally recognised by the city with a marble plaque. The hotel was commended again this year, by Americans, for its cleanliness and friendly staff – save for one unwelcoming woman serving breakfast, (which you take in an 18th-century vaulted cellar). Rooms are furnished in period style. "Ours had a stylish canopy bed, and its view of the lighted dome of the Panthéon was the most beautiful nightlight we've ever had." (*Georgene Smith, E and L Marder*)

Open All year.
Rooms 32 double (also let as singles) – all with bath, telephone and radio. 1 ground-floor room.
Facilities Lounge with bar, breakfast room. Small garden.
Location Opposite Panthéon. Underground paying car park 100 metres. (Métro Luxembourg.)
Restriction Not suitable for &.
Credit cards All major cards accepted.
Terms [1989 rates] Rooms: single 400–530 frs, double 500–600 frs. Breakfast 30 frs. Reduced rates in low season. (No restaurant.)

Hôtel La Louisiane
60 rue de Seine, 75006

Tel (1) 43.29.59.30

This simple little Left Bank hotel must be just about the most famous cheap hotel in Europe, for it is hallowed in literary and artistic history. Hemingway, Connolly and others used to stay here (it's mentioned in *The Unquiet Grave*); Sartre here wrote *L'Être et le Néant* during the war, when Simone de Beauvoir was staying here too (in a separate bedroom). Today the plumbing may be better and the geniuses, alas, far fewer: but basically it's unchanged, and it continues to appeal to readers in search of blissful Rive Gaucherie at low cost. Americans write: "The ambience was wonderful – sort of artistic, bohemian and decidedly friendly. We met good people at breakfast and we all shared a love of this little hotel. It has its drawbacks – if you're finicky, then a hotel that has the sounds of the street market waking you up at 6 am, offers glimpses down narrow and often dirty (but secretly so romantic) alleys, may not be for you. But I felt I really was in Paris, far more than I would in some luxury hotel." "This is not a place for those seeking chic, and you may be put off by the cramped foyer and tiny lift: but the young staff are affable and the bedrooms and bathrooms, though *very* plain, are modernised, of a good size, for Paris, and have proper baths. Front rooms look straight on to the colourful Buci street market; but there's double glazing, and upper or back rooms are very quiet." The multinational clientele are always amusing: "A group of precocious child fashion-models were demanding croissants" – this was because the help-yourself breakfast (in a *very* drab room) features not croissants but a kind of brown soda-bread. (*Endorsed this year by Rev. M Bourdeaux, PW Brereton, and by our Continental Editors JA and KA whose regular Paris pad this is*)

Open All year.
Rooms 79 – all with bath and/or shower, and telephone.
Facilities Lift. Breakfast room.
Location Near St-Germain-des-Prés. Underground parking nearby. (Métro St-Germain-des-Prés, Odéon.)
Credit cards Access, Diners, Visa.
Terms B&B: single 300 frs, double 450–600 frs. (No restaurant.)

If you are nominating a hotel, please err on the side of saying too much. Many suggestions have to be rejected only because they are too brief.

Hôtel des Marronniers
21 rue Jacob, 75006

Tel (1) 43.25.30.60

Near the heart of hectic St-Germain-des-Prés, but quiet, for it lies at the back of a courtyard: most rooms, well modernised, face this or the tiny garden where you can breakfast on fine days. Some period furniture; staff friendly. But bathrooms are small and walls can be thin. 37 rooms, all with bath, 460–575 frs [1989]. Re-nominated this year. More reports welcome.

Pavillon de la Reine
28 place des Vosges, 75003

Tel (1) 42.77.96.40
Telex 216160

An elegant old building on one of Paris's most beautiful squares, sympathetically converted into a charming little luxury hotel, with white marble bathrooms. The quietest rooms overlook a flower-filled patio. 23 suites, 30 other rooms, all with bath and shower. Double room 900–2,200 frs. No restaurant. New nomination. More reports please.

La Résidence du Bois
16 rue Chalgrin, 75116

Tel (1) 45.00.50.59

An 1860s mansion in a quiet residential street off the stately avenue Foch, near the Étoile. It is very expensive, but arguably the most delightful of all Paris's smaller hotels – de luxe and exclusive, its salons and bedrooms tastefully furnished with period pieces, silks and satins. Readers this year were again entranced: "We could hardly believe we were in the heart of Paris when we heard the doves cooing and saw the lovely little garden. Madame is so kind – it really is like staying with good friends in an elegant house." "Our wonderful large room looked on to the garden, the staff were pleasant and the breakfasts nice." A couple arriving with a baby found the owner and staff charming, but report that the room walls are thin and the plumbing lively. Light meals served on request. (*M and D Chambers, N and V Elton*)

Open All year.
Rooms 3 triple, 15 double, 2 single – 18 with bath, 2 with shower, all with telephone and TV; baby-listening on request. 1 room in annexe.
Facilities Salon, bar. Garden.
Location Central (near Arc de Triomphe). Parking nearby. (Métro Argentine.)
Restriction Not suitable for &.
Credit cards None accepted.
Terms [1989 rates] B&B: 1,040–1,530 frs, suite 2,375 frs. (No restaurant.)

Hôtel des Saints-Pères
65 rue des Saints-Pères, 75006

Tel 45.44.50.00
Fax 45.44.90.83
Telex 205424

A pleasant upper-middle-price Left Bank hotel, centrally situated, with chic modern decor and a charming inner courtyard where you can take breakfast. Rooms are not large. Front desk helpful. 37 rooms, all with bath and/or shower. Rooms 400–1,100 frs. Breakfast 40 frs [1989]. No restaurant. Recent nomination. More reports welcome.

Hôtel de Suède   *Tel* (1) 47.05.00.08
31 rue Vaneau, 75007   *Telex* 200596 HT SUEDE

Again approved in 1988/9 for its "courteous and helpful staff", as well as
for its quiet, comfort and good value (for Paris), this small medium-priced
hotel lies in the heart of the old Faubourg St-Germain, aristocratic in
Proust's day, governmental in ours (rooms at the back overlook the
gardens of the Hôtel Matignon, the Prime Minister's residence and office,
and other ministries close by). "Stylish in a somewhat formal way, and
with a discreet, private feel to it. An adequate breakfast is served in the
big salon, furnished in Directoire style with yellow-green upholstery.
Here you can also get 'mini-snacks' such as omelettes. Clientele of young
men in modish dress." (*JA*) "An interior courtyard where they serve
breakfast and drinks in summer. The armed police in the street may not
exactly create a holiday atmosphere, but they do make this a very safe
part of Paris at night." (*Endorsed by William Bentsen, M and L Piper, AE
Eldon-Edington*)

Open All year.
Rooms 1 suite, 33 double, 7 single – 36 with bath and/or shower, all with
telephone; TV, baby-sitter on request. 7 in pavilion in courtyard.
Facilities Lift. Lounge where drinks and snacks are served 6.30 am–10 pm. Small
garden.
Location 10 mins' walk from Seine and St-Germain-des-Prés. (Métro Varenne.)
Credit cards Access, Amex, Visa.
Terms [1989 rates] B&B: single 445 frs, double 490 frs, suite 860 frs. (No
restaurant.)

Hôtel de l'Université   *Tel* (1) 42.61.09.39
22 rue Université, 75007   *Telex* 260717 OREM 310

This converted 17th-century town house near the Seine, intimate and
stylish, continues to be one of the most popular of our Paris hotels.
Reports this year: "A delight, and great value for money"; "Small, refined
and quiet, with an electronic safe in each room for storing valuables";
"Our room was spacious enough, restfully decorated in a soft silvery
green". The public rooms are decorated with antiques and tapestries, and
breakfast is taken at small marble tables looking out onto a charming tiny
courtyard. Back rooms are quietest, and one reader this year found the
decor "slightly gloomy". (*Willis G Frick, Mrs RB Richards, and others*)

Open All year.
Rooms 1 suite, 17 double, 10 single – 20 with bath, 8 with shower, all with
telephone and TV; baby-sitters available.
Facilities Lift. Lounge, bar.
Location 5 mins from St-Germain-des-Prés. Underground parking nearby. (Métro
Rue du Bac.)
Restriction Not suitable for &.
Credit cards None accepted.
Terms [1989 rates] Rooms: single 400 frs, double 780 frs. Breakfast 40 frs. 1-night
bookings refused in high season. Reduced rates for children sharing parents'
room. (No restaurant, but snacks served in bar.)

If you have had recent experience of a good hotel that ought to be in
the Guide, please write to us at once. Report forms are to be found at
the back. Procrastination is the thief of the next edition.

Hôtel de Varenne
44 rue de Bourgogne, 75007

Tel 45.51.45.55
Telex 205329

"Highly recommended" again this year, a converted mansion with a pretty courtyard, near the Invalides. Earlier praise: "Peaceful, with a friendly and efficient staff. Nice comfortable rooms. Breakfast on patio or in lounge area." "Lovely to hear early morning birdsong, but beware the occasional late-night disco party nearby." (*Seymour Sachs*) One reader this year was critical of *accueil* and bedroom furnishings.

Open All year.
Rooms 20 double, 4 single – all with bath, shower, telephone and TV.
Facilities Lift. Lounge, patio.
Location Within walking distance of the Champs-Élysées and St-Germain-des-Prés. Parking in quiet street, 5 mins' walk away. (Métro Varenne.)
Credit cards Amex, Visa.
Terms Rooms: single 320 frs, double 470 frs. Breakfast 30 frs. (No restaurant.)

PASSENANS 39230 Jura   Map 4

Auberge du Rostaing
Tel 84.85.23.70

No fewer than six reports, all favourable, have arrived this year for this modest but charming rural *auberge* that is fast becoming a Guide favourite. All stress the excellent value for money, the good, straightforward cooking, (though the microwave is kept busy) and the friendly helpfulness of the Franco-Swiss owners, the Eckerts (she cooks, he hosts). The hotel is tucked away in unspoilt countryside, on the outskirts of a sleepy village between the Jura hills to the east and the rich farmlands of Bresse to the west: yet it is not hard to reach, for major tourist routes are near by. "It's good walking country – and walking is what many of the guests do. Then they come drifting in to sit in the courtyard under a tree or parasol, sipping a drink. The white 18th-century main building contains a spacious dining room with open fireplace, large peasant cupboards and modern art, and a 'parlour' upstairs with a piano, records, books and games. Some of the rooms are in an attractive vine-balustraded building with an outside staircase and open walkway balcony. Rooms are simple but pleasant; excellent showers and even an electric hair-drier." That earlier report remains valid. One reader this year thought the food "delicious", with good salads and cheeses, and home-made jams for breakfast. Swiss dishes such as fondue and raclette are sometimes offered – "and the Swissness of the place shows up with the long list of admonitions to guests. We liked the one urging visitors to take their showers on sunny days in view of the solar heating." (*E Newall, Mrs Lucy Slater, Group Capt and Mrs HB Verity, and others*)

Open 1 Feb–30 Nov. Closed Tue except school holidays.
Rooms 10 double – 6 with bath and/or shower, 3 with WC; baby-listening.
Facilities Salon with library, 2 dining rooms. Courtyard, garden. Bicycles for hire.
Location Off N83, 11 km S of Poligny, which is where the Dijon–Geneva road crosses the Lyon–Besançon road.
Restriction Not suitable for &.
Credit cards Access, Diners, Visa.
Terms Rooms: single 75–139 frs, double 83–152 frs. Breakfast 18 frs. Dinner, B&B: single 126–196 frs, double 189–268 frs. Set lunch/dinner 52–132 frs. 1-night bookings sometimes refused. Reduced rates and special meals for children.

PEILLON 06440 Alpes-Maritimes   Map 5

Auberge de la Madone   *Tel* 93.79.91.17

Only 19 kilometres from Nice, yet remote in the silent hills, this attractive family-run *auberge* stands on the edge of one of the most striking *villages perchés* of the area. Reports this year: "Our room had a balcony overlooking the village and valley, where breakfast came with hot toast. A glorious garden, and a beautiful terrace for meals and drinks. The food was delicious and the service friendly, but dinner was a bit rushed so as to finish by 9.30 pm." "A bedroom with tiled floor and typical French country furniture. The terrace was idyllic but the food was uninspired." Others have commented on the warm ambience created by the Millo family, and the good regionally based dishes such as daube de boeuf à l'orange et aux cèpes. (*Caroline Thomson and Roger Liddle, Philippa Herbert*)

Open 20 Dec–15 Oct. Closed Wed.
Rooms 3 suites, 16 double – 15 with bath and shower, all with telephone; 3 with TV.
Facilities Salon with TV, dining room; conference facilities. Large garden.
Location 18 km NE of Nice on D21.
Restriction Not suitable for &.
Credit cards None accepted.
Terms Dinner, B&B: double 360–480 frs, suite 520 frs. Set lunch/dinner 130, 190 and 260 frs; full alc 300 frs. Reduced rates and special meals for children.

LA PEINIÈRE-ST-DIDIER 35220 Ille-et-Vilaine   Map 2

Hôtel Pen'Roc   *Tel* 99.00.33.02
                                                      Telex 741457

Renewed praise this year for the "marvellous hospitality" and "delicious fish dishes" at the attractive modern *Pen'Roc*: built in local Breton style, it lies quietly amid meadows, beside a little romanesque church, just off the main road from Rennes to Vitré. "The staff showed warmth and kindness." "The cuisine is refined and imaginative (notably the fishermen's choucroute), the setting is beautiful and the staff charming. Pity about the bedroom decor – someone clearly has a penchant for mauve, purple and brown." An earlier impression, "It's used during the day for business gatherings, but in the evening we found it delightful and peaceful. Family-run by the Frocs. Madame is tall and (even at 8 am) as elegant as the dishes her husband produces." Bedrooms are "large and comfortable". Another Froc speciality is "méli-mélo de la mer à la badiane". (*Robyn Morton, Jack B Ainslie, G Buckland*)

Open All year except 2 weeks Feb. Restaurant closed Sun evening.
Rooms 1 suite, 23 double, 2 single – 11 with bath, 10 with shower, all with telephone, radio and TV. 1 ground-floor room.
Facilities Lift. Lounge, bar, 3 dining rooms; conference facilities. Garden with children's play area.
Location 6 km E of Châteaubourg. Turn off D857 at St-Jean-sur-Vilaine, towards St-Didier, then right to La Peinière.
Credit cards All major cards accepted.
Terms B&B: single 237 frs, double 283 frs, suite 500 frs; half board 237–326 frs per person. Full alc 240 frs. Reduced rates and special meals for children.

PÉROUGES 01800 Ain   Map 4

Ostellerie du Vieux Pérouges   *Tel* 74.61.00.88
                                                            Telex 306898

This medieval hilltop village north-east of Lyon, with its ramparts, cobbles and half-timbered houses, is so well preserved that historical feature films (e.g. *The Return of Martin Guerre*) are often shot here. The hotel, converted from 13th-century buildings, is part of the decor, forming one side of the village square. Its studied folksiness is not to all tastes, but many readers continue to like it. One of them "felt transported back into the Middle Ages," and goes on, "The rooms are period-perfect, and the dining room – with its costumed waitresses – is also a delight with a wood-fire burning. We had an enormous ground-floor suite with medieval furnishings and paintings" (but bathrooms are modern). Others have enjoyed "climbing to our room by way of a winding stone tower" and "breakfast in a private garden". Another visitor was more sceptical, "Rather gimmicky, e.g. the large rolls of parchment on which menus are presented." But most people like the cuisine, e.g. écrevisses pérougienne, duck with green pepper, and the celebrated local griddle cake with raspberries. More reports please.

Open All year except Wed in low season.
Rooms 3 suites, 25 double – all with bath, telephone and TV. 1 ground-floor room.
Facilities Lounges, bar, restaurant; conference facilities. Gardens.
Location In town square. Parking. Pérouges is 39 km NE of Lyon.
Restriction Not suitable for &.
Credit cards Visa.
Terms [1989 rates] Rooms 450–750 frs, suite 850 frs. Breakfast 60 frs. Set lunch/dinner 150–320 frs; full alc 300 frs.

PERPIGNAN 66000 Pyrénées Orientales   Map 4

Park Hotel et Restaurant Le   *Tel* 68.35.14.14
Chapon Fin   *Telex* 506161
18 bvd Jean-Bourrat   *Fax* 68.35.48.18

Downtown Perpignan's premier hotel: smart and modern, it faces gardens on the inner ring boulevard, but is quiet (double glazing). Period Catalan furniture, polite service, very good food (Michelin rosette, two Gault Millau toques). 67 rooms, some suitable for &, all with bath and/or shower. B&B double 316–476 frs. Set menus 170–350 frs. New nomination. More reports please.

LA PETITE PIERRE 67290 Bas-Rhin   Map 3

Hôtel aux Trois Roses   *Tel* 88.70.45.02
                                                            Telex 871150

A fine 18th-century *auberge*, white-walled, flower-bedecked, all cosy inside, and admired again in 1989. It is in the main street of an ancient hilltop Alsatian village (front rooms can be noisy), with remains of ramparts, and hilly forests all around; the dining room has a fine view of the castle, romantic on summer evenings when it is floodlit. Run hectically by the Geyer family and a whole bevy of other Alsatians, it is a sympathetically informal and lively place, very much a local social centre, less in the French than in the Central European tradition – several comfy salons, and a big *Stübe* where snacks and cakes are served all day.

Some bedrooms in the old building are a bit cramped and shabby, but a modern wing has been built down the hillside, and this is preferred by readers (*Michelin*, too, gives it three gables, while the rest of the hotel gets two). The dining room has also been extended, and there is a new outdoor patio. "We had a suite with pleasant views from the balcony", says one reader this year, while another much enjoyed the food (e.g. help-yourself hors d'oeuvre and trout in riesling). Breakfast, formerly criticised, has now improved and is a German-style buffet. (*K and S Murray-Sykes, K and N Varley*)

Open 6 Feb–6 Jan. Restaurant closed Sun evening and Mon.
Rooms 16 suites, 21 double, 9 single – all with bath and shower, telephone and TV; 16 with radio. Some in annexe.
Facilities 2 lifts. 3 lounges (2 with TV), bar, 5 dining rooms; indoor swimming pool. Garden with terrace, children's play area, tennis.
Location 60 km NW of Strasbourg; hotel is central. Parking.
Credit cards Access, Visa.
Terms Rooms: single 80–350 frs, double 160–435 frs, suite 350–435 frs. Breakfast 52 frs. Dinner B&B 185–350 frs per person. Set lunch/dinner 85–198 frs; full alc 230 frs. Reductions for children under 8; special meals on request.

PLÉHÉDEL 22290 Côtes-du-Nord   **Map 2**

Château Hôtel de Coatguélen
Tel 96.22.31.24
Telex 741300

Seven kilometres from the sea and quite near to good North Brittany beaches, this elegant little 19th-century château stands in its own 170-acre park of woods, lakes and meadows – not to mention a nine-hole golf-course. Dropped from the 1989 Guide for lack of news, it is now reinstated by a reader who found it "superb", with "marvellous" food, and by another more restrained report, "We were quite pleased. It's still owned by the Marquis de Boisgelin, but run by the friendly Le Roys: Louis has written books on modern cookery (his own cuisine gets a deserved two red *toques* in *Gault Millau*), and his wife Nicole, front-of-house, is not only charming, stylish and vivacious but arranges remarkable art exhibitions. Bedrooms have been attractively decorated (ours overlooked the golf-course) and there's much old furniture: the drawing room contains lovely antiques, a gorgeous grand piano and spectacular pictures. The dining room has windows overlooking the lake and the food is interesting – baked oysters, lobster steamed in seaweed en vessie, excellent sauces. The service was very willing, but sometimes erratic and inexperienced. There was a down-at-heel character in reception every evening. Was he a gardener or odd-job-man? My guess is that it was the Marquis in mufti, keeping an eye on the place." (*Francine and Ian Walsh; Helmut Schoen*)

Open 15 Mar–15 Nov, 15–31 Jan.
Rooms 2 suites, 14 double – all with bath and/or shower and telephone.
Facilities Salon with TV, bar, restaurant; conference rooms; children's playroom. Large park with unheated swimming pool, tennis, children's play area, horses, ponies, trout fishing, 9-hole golf course. Beach 7 km.

Location 11 km S of Paimpol, on D7 to Lanvollon. Parking.
Credit cards All major cards accepted.
Terms [1989 rates] Rooms 415–1,300 frs. Breakfast 55 frs. Dinner, B&B 565–790 frs per person. Set meals 200–300 frs.

LE POËT-LAVAL 26160 Drôme   Map 4

Les Hospitaliers   *Tel* 75.46.22.32

A variety of ecstatic admiration in 1988/9 for "this secret paradise", "this divine hotel", "our favourite in France". It stands on a hilltop in a medieval village, above fine wooded countryside where the foothills of the Alps descend to the Rhône valley, on the borders of Dauphiné and Provence. Here the owner Yvon Morin has sensitively restored an old building, with a ruined 12th-century chapel towering above, and a swimming pool facing the glorious panorama. "We dined on an enchanting terrace with tables around a magnificent tree and a superb view over the valley. The owners were most friendly and dinner extremely good" (*Michelin* rosette, two red *Gault Millau toques*). "We had a huge room with balcony overlooking the ruined chapel. The lounge is magnificent – vaulted, beamed, a roaring fire (in March), interesting paintings and M. Morin's personal collection of sculptures. Food was excellent." "M. Morin is a marvellous host, hard working and courteous. Delightful pantomime of tasting each bottle of wine." "The best service I have seen anywhere." "The pool is a delight." The foie gras, carré d'agneau, potage of wild mushrooms and the grilled goats' cheese are much praised. Only quibbles: an unchanging set menu, and pool furniture a bit worn. (*Lynne and David Allen, Tom and Rosemary Rose, PA Catling, Mr and Mrs RM Booth, and others*)

Open 1 Mar–15 Nov.
Rooms 1 suite, 21 double – 21 with bath and shower, 1 with shower, all with telephone. 3 annexes adjacent to main building.
Facilities Salon, TV room, bar, 2 restaurants; conference facilities. Garden with terraces and heated swimming pool.
Location On D540, E of La Bégude-de-Mazenc; Montélimar 25 km.
Restriction Not suitable for &.
Credit cards All major cards accepted.
Terms Rooms: double 440 frs, suite 750 frs. Breakfast 65 frs. Set lunch/dinner 200–390 frs; full alc 500 frs. Special meals for children.

POLIGNY 39800 Jura   Map 4

Hostellerie des Monts de Vaux   *Tel* 84.37.12.50
Monts de Vaux   *Telex* 361493

On the N5 from Dijon to Geneva, in a hamlet just south-east of Poligny, here's a rather smart coaching inn, dating from 1793 but with modern extensions. The site, on the edge of a cliff above Poligny, is lovely. Charming family owners, comfortable rooms, excellent food, sophisticated ambience. Garden with tennis court. Closed end Oct to end Dec and Tue, Wed evening in low season. 10 rooms, all with bath and shower. Dinner B&B: single 640 frs, double 900–1,400 frs. Alc (excluding wine) 180–300 frs [1989]. New nomination. More reports much desired.

PONS 17800 Charente-Maritime — Map 4

Auberge Pontoise   *Tel* 46.94.00.99
23 avenue Gambetta

This medieval town above the river Seugne, near the *autoroute* down to
Bordeaux, has a castle with a vast keep and a hospice once used by
pilgrims Compostela-bound. Our own voyagers mostly – but not all –
approve the *Pontoise*, which returns to the Guide this year with these
reports: "Modest, clean and comfortable, with a helpful front desk and
superbly executed cuisine – a model of what a *Michelin* one-rosette
restaurant should be." "Lovely cream stone courtyard, entrance hall
beautiful with Persian rugs on stone floors, much well-polished brass.
Chic petite Madame smiles a welcome. Bedroom gently old-fashioned.
Dining room full of locals, with black-and-white tiled floor, gleaming
glasses and silver. Dinner was magic – home-cured smoked salmon,
delicious fish soup, langoustines with pasta." (*WG Frick, Minda Alexander*)
However, another visitor this year, while finding the room comfortable,
strongly criticised the decor, "pretentious" food, and glum service. More
reports needed.

Open 30 Jan–21 Dec. Closed Sun evening and Mon 15 Sept–1 Jul.
Rooms 1 suite, 21 double – all with bath and/or shower, telephone and TV.
1 ground-floor room.
Facilities Lounge, bar, 2 dining-rooms.
Location Central. Parking. Pons is 96 km N of Bordeaux.
Restrictions Not suitable for &.
Credit cards Access, Visa.
Terms Rooms 200–280 frs, suite 550 frs. Breakfast 40 frs. Set lunch/dinner 160–
250 frs; full alc 300–350 frs.

PONT-AUDEMER 27500 Eure — Map 2

Auberge du Vieux Puits   *Tel* 32.41.01.48
6 rue Notre-Dame du Pré

Three 17th-century timbered houses around a courtyard make up this
very picturesque restaurant-with-rooms, which remains popular with
many readers, though it comes in for criticism, too. "Beautiful buildings,
delicious cooking, friendly service, a very small but comfortable room";
"The warmest of welcomes. The menu doesn't change, ever: but if I can
eat truite Bovary and canard aux griottes there once a year, I don't
complain." Thus two reports this year, following on last year's, "We were
warmly welcomed by Madame Foltz and shown to a pretty and
comfortable room in the new wing. The inn is beautifully maintained
with fresh flowers in the rooms, and the courtyard has a pretty garden
where people gather for aperitifs on fine evenings." The eight original
bedrooms by the courtyard are pretty but small, and one visitor this year
found their plumbing noisy. The six newer rooms have more comfort: but
one recent report called them "soulless and motel-like". (*Mrs RB Richards,
E Newall, PF*) One reader this year regretted that the menus do not change
– and we note that *Michelin* has now withdrawn its rosette.

Open 18 Jan–2 Jul, 11 Jul–16 Dec. Closed Mon evening and Tue.
Rooms 12 double – 6 with bath and shower, 5 with shower, 9 with WC, all with telephone; 6 with TV. 2 ground-floor rooms, accessible for &.
Facilities 2 small salons, 2 restaurants. Small garden.
Location 300 metres from town centre (hotel is signposted), but quiet. Parking.
Credit cards Access, Visa.
Terms Rooms 150–350 frs. Breakfast 32 frs. Set lunch 150 frs, dinner 250 frs; full alc 230–290 frs. Guests expected to dine at the hotel.

PONT-DE-BRIQUES 62360 Pas-de-Calais   Map 3

Hostellerie de la Rivière   *Tel* 21.32.22.81
17 rue de la Gare

We are always glad of new nominations near the Channel ports, and owner/chef Jean Martin's country-style restaurant-with-rooms just south of Boulogne, close to the N1 to Paris, sounds promising: "The expensive menus are excellent value. For 260 francs I had pâté de foie gras, an astonishing (but only semi-successful) shrimps folded into a cabbage leaf bathed in a raspberry (!) sauce, carré d'agneau and a magnificent selection of cheeses. Nice little garden. Quiet – only the river speaks. Our room charge, 110 francs [1988], was less than an eighth of the final bill. But M. Martin says they will be 'rebuilding' the hotel." *Michelin* rosette. *Gault Millau*'s *toque* is in black for 'traditional' cuisine, rather than red for 'inventive' - despite the *Rev. M Bourdeaux*'s raspberry sauce. More reports welcome.

Open All year except 16 Aug–10 Sept and 10 days in Feb. Closed Sun evening and Mon, and Christmas night.
Rooms 7 double, 1 single – 3 with bath and shower, all with telephone; 2 with TV.
Facilities Bar, restaurant.
Location 5 km S of Boulogne, close to N1.
Credit cards Access, Visa.
Terms Rooms: single 250 frs, double 270–330 frs. Breakfast 30 frs. Set lunch/dinner 130, 195 and 260 frs; full alc 300–350 frs.

PONT-DE-VAUX 01190 Ain   Map 4

Le Raisin   *Tel* 85.30.30.97
2 place Michel-Poisat

A pleasant little town just east of the Saône, between Tournus and Mâcon; here Gilles Chazot's warmly decorated restaurant-with-rooms offers excellent traditional Bressane cooking at very fair prices (Michelin rosette, Gault Millau toque). Above-average breakfasts, and simple but comfortable rooms. Closed Jan, Sun evening and Mon. 7 rooms, all with bath or shower. B&B double 210 frs. Set menus 72–230 frs [1989]. New nomination. More reports please.

In all continental European and Scandinavian countries except Denmark, France, Hungary, Malta, Spain and Turkey, the dialling codes begin with a 0. Omit this when dialling from outside the country in question. Spanish codes begin with a 9, which should also be omitted.

PORQUEROLLES 83540 Var   Map 5

Mas du Langoustier   *Tel* 94.58.30.09

A most seductive Guide newcomer, secluded in its own 75-acre pine-
wooded park beside the sea, at the eastern and virtually uninhabited end
of a very lovely island, which is mostly a national park (no cars, no
smoking outside the village, bike trails with virtually no tarmac, sandy
beaches, wooded cliffs). It's a handsome old yellow-walled manor,
converted and modernised with some sophistication, and warmly
recommended by retired hoteliers: "An outstanding hotel, three-star, but
more like four-star. Meals are served on a large terrace: the food is of the
highest quality (two red *Gault Millau toques*), the service excellent and the
bedrooms well appointed. A new wing of 21 bedrooms blends superbly
into the old style of this lovely building. There are new tennis courts, and
two sandy beaches three minutes' walk away. Free buses go to the village
and port of Porquerolles every hour. Eighty per cent of the clients are
French, and the hotel is almost unknown to the British" – quite a rarity in
France today. Full board terms only. (*Sally and Curtis Wilmot-Allistone*)
More reports welcome.

Open 15 Mar–15 Nov.
Rooms 3 suites, 62 double – all with bath and/or shower, telephone and TV.
Ground-floor rooms.
Facilities 2 lounges, bar, restaurant; conference facilities; terrace. Park with
tennis, boules, sandy beach, sailing, windsurfing.
Location 3.5 km E of port of Porquerolles which is 15 mins by boat from La Tour
Fondue (frequent services). No cars allowed on island. Free bus service from port
to hotel.
Credit cards All major cards accepted.
Terms [1989 rates] Full board 762–1,162 frs. Set lunch/dinner 200–440 frs. Special
meals for children.

Relais de la Poste   *Tel* 94.58.30.26
Île de Porquerolles

*M. and Mme Ghiglion's modern and spotless B&B hotel is in the only village of
this beautiful island. Eccentric library, sturdy bikes for hire. No restaurant, but
salad lunches available. The church clocks chime all night. Auberge Arche de
Noé recommended for best food on the island. 30 rooms, all with bath or
shower. B&B 250–450 frs. Recent nomination. More reports please.*

LE PORT BOULET 37140 Indre et Loire   Map 4

Château des Réaux   *Tel* 47.95.14.40
Le Port Boulet, Bourgueil

*Small 15th-century castle on an island, peaceful apart from the occasional
passing train, belonging to Château Accueil group. Elegant salon and dining
room, small but attractively furnished bedrooms, bathrooms functional; annexe
rooms, not on the island, and nearer the railway are simpler and cheaper.
"Individual and civilised; excellent food, welcoming hosts." 4 suites, 600–900
frs, 12 double rooms, 300–600 frs. Breakfast 40 frs [1989]. New nomination.
More reports please.*

PORTICCIO 20166 Corsica

Map 5

Le Maquis

Tel 95.25.05.55
Fax 95.25.11.70
Telex 460597

A beautiful and sophisticated hotel with more than a touch of glamour, right by the sea across the bay from Ajaccio. Family-run (Madame Salini is usually dressed in leather), it has been described as "small, very French and absolutely marvellous". It has a smart swimming pool and its own private beach, overlooked by some bedrooms; white walls, black beams and red-tiled floors lend style to the interior decor. "If you have a ground-floor room, your balcony literally meets the sand. The food is good, especially the huge help-yourself hors d'oeuvre table. One of our happiest memories will be eating lunch on the terrace – pink tablecloths, umbrellas, silver, fine china and glass and the bright blue sky and sea below, wonderful fresh seafood and delicious Corsican wines." However, a reader this year found the ambience somewhat mercenary and questions value for money.

Open All year. Restaurant closed Feb.
Rooms 7 suites, 22 double, 1 single – all with bath and/or shower, telephone, TV and video, mini-bar and air-conditioning. Some ground-floor rooms.
Facilities Lift, lounge, bar, dining room; terrace for alfresco meals. Indoor swimming pool. Garden with tennis court, heated swimming pool, and children's play area. On private beach with safe bathing.
Location On the coast 15 km SE of Ajaccio, on the D55. 12 km from airport.
Credit cards All major cards accepted.
Terms [1989 rates] Dinner, B&B: single 980–1,500 frs, double 1,300–2,200 frs, suite 1,870–3,330 frs. Set meals from 200 frs. Reduced rates and special meals for children.

PORTICCIOLO 20228 Corsica

Map 5

Hôtel Le Caribou

Tel 95.35.02.33

The Catoni family's "delightful" hotel, with its "house-party atmosphere" and "cornucopia of food", lies on the road north from Bastia to Cap Corse, in a colourful garden of flowers and trees. Those few readers who report to us on this Eden are always ecstatic. "The welcome from the Catonis – he grizzled, she statuesque – is exceedingly warm. The place glows with atmosphere and we made many friends, fellow guests and staff alike. Guests are an interesting mixture of old regulars and young families with children who mingle with the Catonis' grandchildren, giving the place an ambience of informality. The rooms are old-fashioned and plainly furnished, but comfortable, with good plumbing. And the food is outstanding. For the main dish, you choose from Monsieur's oral selection, but first you have to resist plate after plate of hors d'oeuvre, pâtés, melon and water melon, local smoked ham, langoustines, mussels, home-made pasta. . ." Another view: "As you go up the steep drive, you find a swimming pool set into the garden. Splendid old trees have been interlaced with vines to make a cool shady place for aperitifs or coffee. Our suite across the road, overlooking the sea, was one of several *pavillons* built into the rocks just above the water's edge, each with a small sun-terrace. Fresh flowers had been put in our room when we retired for a siesta."

Open 25 June–25 Sept.
Rooms 1 suite, 29 double – all with bath (6 also have shower), and telephone; some with balcony. Also 13 bungalows, with kitchen, for 3–8 people, let by the week.
Facilities Lounge, bar, TV room, restaurant; terraces. Sauna, fitness room. Swimming pool, 2 tennis courts. Private harbour, fine sandy beach with bathing, water skiing, windsurfing, sailing, fishing, skin diving and volley-ball.
Location On east coast, off N198.
Credit cards All major cards accepted.
Terms Rooms 400–700 frs. Dinner, B&B: single 600–700 frs, double 1,200–1,500 frs. Set meals 280 frs; full alc 300 frs. Reduced rates and special meals for children.

PORT-MANECH 29139 Finistère   Map 2

Hôtel Restaurant du Port   *Tel* 98.06.82.17
30 rue de l'Aven

Superb fish dishes (but not much meat) are on offer at this unpretentious and inexpensive modern inn by the harbour, in a south Brittany fishing-village. Kindly owners, good breakfasts. Simple rooms, some with fine coastal views; the annexe, which is cheaper and has been criticised as "basic", has been upgraded. Open Easter–end Sept. Restaurant closed Mon lunchtime. 35 rooms, 6 with bath, 25 with shower. Dinner, B&B 230–250 frs. Set meals 80–170 frs. Endorsed this year, but past criticisms of room upkeep. More reports welcome.

QUESTEMBERT 56230 Morbihan   Map 2

Le Bretagne   *Tel* 97.26.11.12
Rue St-Michel   *Telex* 951801

Located in a small town east of Vannes, here is Brittany's most distinguished restaurant (*patron*-chef Georges Paineau wins two *Michelin* rosettes, three red *Gault Millau toques*), but maybe because it has only six bedrooms it's not been reported to us before. Now it's described with awe and wonder by two of our keenest sleuths: "The ivy-clad exterior is pretty standard, but within the archway surprise followed surprise – not least the spacious garden with lovingly chosen shrubs, populated by a large number of lean oriental cats adding to the exotic feel. Bedrooms are not palatial but smart and very comfortable. Ours had a huge double bed: it was vaguely exotic, because of the palmed net curtains, imitation bamboo tables, adorable wooden Japanese dolls. The bathroom was amazing, giving the feel of a hot South Sea island, in vivid rainbow hues, with cotton kimonos provided.

"This wild exuberance is reflected throughout the hotel. The Paineaus have travelled widely, buying what took their fancy, and installing these objects side-by-side with Breton antiques regardless of the dictums of so-called 'good taste'. And it works, this colourfully varied tour-de-force. Of the two dining rooms, one is a beautifully panelled expanse of golden wood lit by antique lamps, the other a large glass conservatory straight out of the *1001 Nights*, with a colourful screen painted in 'naïve' style by the *patron* himself. The sitting room is dark and dramatic. And the same bravura is evident in Georges Paineau's forceful style of cooking: sauces are deceptively simple but a delight, presentation is superb, with each dish appearing on an appropriate plate of rare porcelain. We enjoyed hot oysters in cream, melting terrine de foie gras, fantastic pigeon cooked in a shell of rock salt. Service is swift and impeccable. Breakfast included hot brioche slices with apple, and superlative coffee. M Paineau is a fine figure of a man with a splendidly bushy moustache, adept at charming compliments; his wife Michèle is also flamboyant, like an explosive orchid." (*Ian and Francine Walsh*) Prices are remarkably reasonable. If you, too, visit this Xanadu, please don't fail to tell us.

Open All year. Closed Christmas, Sun evening and Mon except Jul, Aug and bank holidays.
Rooms 6 double – all with bath and shower, telephone, radio and TV.
Facilities 2 lounges, restaurant. Garden. Swimming pool 300 metres.
Location 27 km E of Vannes. Central, parking.
Restriction Not suitable for &.
Credit cards Amex, Visa.
Terms B&B: single 420–520 frs, double 520–630 frs. Dinner, B&B 780–880 frs per person. Set lunch/dinner 150–420 frs; full alc 380 frs. Reduced rates and special meals for children.

RABASTENS 81800 Tarn   Map 4

Hostellerie du Pré Vert   *Tel* 63.33.70.51
54 promenade des Lices

In the centre of a small town between Toulouse and Albi, a handsome old creeper-covered 18th-century house with a big shady garden, now making its Guide debut: "Rabastens is a sleepy old town, time-warped, unspoilt by tourism (don't miss the 12th-century church of Notre-Dame-du-Bourg), and the hotel is likewise – not at all smart, but welcoming, and the local girls are friendly in a non-professional way. Meals are served in an old-fashioned drawing-room with a cosy ambience: here our meal was thoroughly satisfactory and amazing value at 95 francs [1989]. Bedrooms too are good value." "Helpful owners; large rooms furnished in a solid, old-fashioned way." (*HR, Diana Holmes*)

Open All year except Dec. Restaurant closed Sun evening; also Mon midday in low season.
Rooms 12 double, 1 single – 4 with bath and shower, 8 with shower, all with telephone.
Facilities Bar, TV room, 2 dining rooms. Terrace where meals are served. Garden.
Location Central, parking. Rabastens is 37 km NE of Toulouse.
Restrictions Not suitable for &.
Credit cards Access, Visa.
Terms Rooms: single 150 frs, double 160–240 frs. Breakfast 23 frs. Set lunch/dinner 57–150 frs; full alc 185 frs. Reduced rates and special meals for children.

RAGUENÈS-PLAGE 29139 Finistère   Map 2

Hôtel Chez Pierre   *Tel* 98.06.81.06

This old Guide favourite, a most sympathetic family hotel, stands right next to good sandy beaches and is within easy reach of Concarneau and

Pont-Aven (where Gauguin painted). Old Madame Guillou has recently died, but her family are keeping up the standards – and readers remain pleased, with the caveats that rooms in the modern annexe are better than the older ones, and that standards may drop a bit in August when the crush is on. Xavier Guillou's cooking (*Michelin* red "R" for good value) has again been much admired this year, "Very good classical fish dishes with often quite rich sauces. The five-course half-board menu is outstanding value. And if you want to splurge one night, the lobster with tarragon is delicious. As M. Guillou does all the fish dishes and sauces himself, some long waits are inevitable." "A spacious room in the annexe and a cordial reception. Madame Guillou Jr was charm itself, making sure our needs were met." "Garden a bit run-down, in a pleasant informal way." Attractive courtyard, bar and lounge. Service sometimes erratic: the reception desk is not always manned. And this is not a place for those who want to avoid their fellow-Britons on holiday. (*John and Helen Wright, and others*)

Open 24 Mar–12 Apr, 29 Apr–26 Sept. Restaurant closed Wed 21 Jun–6 Sept.
Rooms 29 – 21 with bath and shower, all with telephone. 8 in annexe. 1 ground-floor room.
Facilities Salon, bar, TV room, 2 dining rooms. Garden.
Location 12 km SW of Pont-Aven. Parking.
Credit cards Access, Visa.
Terms [1989 rates] Rooms: single 158 frs, double 310 frs. Breakfast 22 frs. Dinner, B&B 182–265 frs per person. Set meals 80–200 frs. Reduced rates and special meals for children.

RAMATUELLE 83350 Var   Map 5

Hostellerie Le Baou   *Tel* 94.79.20.48
Avenue Georges Clémenceau   *Telex* 462152

The charming hill-village of Ramatuelle stands close to the best St-Tropez beaches; the noble elm in its main square was planted in 1598, and Gérard Philipe lies buried in its cemetery. Plenty of film stars and other trendy people visit this fabled peninsula, and many of them make for *Le Baou*, a very smart hotel on a hillside, with fine views over woods and vineyards to the sea. It has been revived by new owners, the Sarraquignes, who "treat their guests with care", and whose young chef Claude Taffarello worked with Roger Vergé at Mougins and wins two red *toques* from *Gault Millau*. "The food was exquisite, the flavours fresh and unusual", comments one recent visitor. Most rooms have a balcony, and from these and the dining terrace there are lovely views. Grills are served during the day by the pleasant swimming pool. More reports welcome.

Open 6 Apr–14 Oct.
Rooms 2 suites, 39 double – all with bath and shower, telephone, radio and TV; some with private garden.
Facilities Lift. 2 lounges, 2 bars, 2 restaurants; conference facilities; indoor garden. Garden with terrace, grill, swimming pool, jacuzzi, solarium. Sea 3 km.
Location At entrance of village. Garage and parking.
Restriction Not suitable for &.
Credit cards All major cards accepted.
Terms B&B: single occupancy 610–860 frs, double 660–1,190 frs, suite 1,450–1,750 frs. Set lunch/dinner 180, 250 and 380 frs; full alc 380 frs. 360 frs; full alc 350 frs. Reduced rates and special meals for children.

RASTEAU 84110 Vaucluse   Map 5

Hôtel Bellerive   *Tel* 90.46.10.20

An ultra-modern *Relais du Silence* with a bright interior and friendly vibes. It lies amid Côtes-du-Rhône vineyards, in open country beside the river Ouvèze, with fine view of the hills; Orange and Vaison-la-Romaine are both quite near. Recent verdicts: "Superb food and local wine, an excellent swimming pool, and a comfortable room with a balcony and fine view." "Good comfortable rooms and a relaxed atmosphere. The dining room is attractive and the food has been improving. The pool gets crowded on Sundays." (*Endorsed this year by JA*)

Open All year except 2 Jan–18 Mar.
Rooms 20 double – all with bath, telephone and balcony; TV on request; some with kitchenette. Some ground-floor rooms.
Facilities Salon with TV, restaurant. Large garden with swimming pool; river bathing and fishing nearby.
Location Leave A7 motorway at Orange, take N575 towards Vaison, then turn right on D69, then left for hotel. Parking.
Credit cards None accepted.
Terms [1989 rates] Rooms 290–320 frs. Breakfast 35 frs. Dinner, B&B 280–300 frs per person. Set lunch/dinner 105–260 frs. Special meals for children.

RECQUES-SUR-HEM 62890 Pas-de-Calais   Map 3

Château de Cocove   *Tel* 21.82.68.29
                                                       Telex 810985

Usefully located near the autoroute south-east of Calais, a grey-fronted 18th-century château in a large park, newly opened as a fairly smart hotel. "Bedrooms light and airy, simply but comfortably furnished." The stone-walled restaurant serves food which some guests (but not all) have called "impeccable". Closed Christmas. 24 rooms, all with private facilities. Rooms 295–550 frs. Breakfast 35 frs. Set meals 99, 150, 190 and 250 frs. New nomination. More reports please.

REIMS Marne   Map 3

L'Assiette Champenoise   *Tel* 26.04.15.56
40 avenue Paul Vaillant-Couturier   *Fax* 26.04.15.69
Tinqueux, Reims 51430   *Telex* 830267

Jean-Pierre and Colette Lallement previously owned a much-laureated restaurant of this same name in a village near Reims: in 1988 they moved to this larger 1920s mansion in the western suburb of Tinqueux – and with them come their *Michelin* rosette and two red *Gault Millau toques*. As they now have bedrooms, they qualify for our Guide, too, and this year's nominators find them worthy of it: "It's an unprepossessing area, but the large park-like grounds mean that you hardly notice. Despite the relative grandeur of the main building and the 'interior designed' look of the public rooms, there's a homely family feel – Madame was working as receptionist, and her young son carried our suitcases. Our room was prettily decorated and furnished, with white wood and pastel finishings.

Breakfast was above average, and dinner was of a high standard, with a strong emphasis on fish. Service was good, with a human touch." (*Kate and Stephan Murray-Sykes*) More reports please.

Open All year.
Rooms 2 suites, 28 double – all with bath and shower, telephone and TV; baby-listening on request. 1 ground-floor room.
Facilities Lounge with TV, bar, restaurant; conference facilities. Garden; terrace.
Location 3 km W of centre of Reims; well signposted. Parking.
Credit cards All major cards accepted.
Terms Rooms 450 frs, suite 950 frs. Breakfast 42 frs. Set lunch/dinner 250–380 frs. Special meals for children.

Boyer "Les Crayères"	*Tel* 26.82.80.80
64 boulevard Henri-Vasnier	*Fax* 26.82.65.52
Reims 51100	*Telex* 830959

Gérard Boyer's awesomely superior little hotel is much patronised by the magnates of the leading Reims champagne houses, who use it to wine, dine and lodge their more important guests and clients. It is thus aiming at the very highest standards, with prices to match, and our readers tend to judge it accordingly. And no-one questions that the *cadre* is supremely elegant, in its own manner. *Les Crayères* is a beautiful cream-coloured château in the south-east suburbs, approached through massive wrought-iron gates, its proportions blending with the mature trees and sweeping lawns of its park; the imposing foyer and staircase are in pale beige marble, and hung with huge tapestries. Readers have enjoyed the airy and "palatial" bedrooms with their huge windows facing the park. Most of them also admire the luxurious cooking, which continues to dazzle the French pundits (three *Michelin* rosettes, and four red *Gault Millau toques*)

Last year one reader criticised his bathroom – "had all the character of an aeroplane first-class section. A beautiful and luxurious hotel, but a little too cool and detached." Another wrote, "There is an unstated sense of aristocracy, but allied to very strong, modern, pragmatic, vulgar touches – *Relais et Châteaux* brochures everywhere. The identity of the hotel gets a bit lost, and you start to think you are in the home of Monsieur Relais and Madame Château, the one concession to tourism being the room temperature raised to Bermudan heights." This year most readers have praised both the bed and the board, though one lamented the absence of a salon in which to mingle with fellow-guests before and after dinner. There is a small dark green bar which gets crowded when the restaurant is busy; some tables can be reserved in advance. Another, commenting on the absence of set menus, tells us that you can order half-portions at half prices and so compose your own *menu gastronomique*. (*Rosamund Hebdon, Stefan and Yvette Wiener, Rosemary Smith and David Lawrence, Elaine Cole-Shear, Kate and Steve Murray-Sykes*)

Open All year except 21 Dec–16 Jan. Restaurant closed Mon, and Tue midday.
Rooms 3 suites, 16 double – 11 with bath (8 also have shower), telephone, radio, TV and baby-listening. 3 in annexe.
Facilities Lift. Hall, bar, restaurant; private dining room. Park with gardens, tennis, helipad.
Location Leave motorway at St-Rémy exit. Travel towards Luxembourg for ½ km, then towards Châlons-sur-Marne on N44. Hotel is 3 km from town centre. Parking.
Credit cards All major cards accepted.

Terms Rooms 980 frs, suite 1,590 frs. Breakfast (served only in bedrooms) 70 frs. Full alc 600–650 frs. Special meals for children.

REPLONGES 01750 Ain   Map 4

La Huchette   *Tel* 85.31.03.55
                                                          Telex 800787

A quite sophisticated old *auberge* outside a village east of Mâcon, ornately decorated in warm colours and admired for its friendly welcome, regional cuisine and pretty dining room. It has broad lawns with tall trees and a large swimming pool with mattress loungers. And we are grateful to readers who brought us up-to-date views on it this year, enabling us to restore a full entry: "The rooms and bathrooms are spacious, airy and spotless, the service quietly efficient, the à la carte excellent, the wines good but expensive." "A large bedroom beautifully decorated, overlooking the pool." Some traffic noise during the day. A disabled reader was especially pleased: "Not a single step of even an inch to inhibit my chair." (*Denis O'Mulloy, Mr and Mrs AL Fraser*)

Open All year except 10–22 Jan.
Rooms 1 suite, 11 double, 1 single – all with bath and shower, telephone, TV. Ground-floor rooms.
Facilities 2 lounges, dining room. Garden with swimming pool. Golf 500 metres.
Location 4 km E of Mâcon off N79. On edge of village. Parking.
Credit cards All major cards accepted.
Terms Rooms: single 350 frs, double 450–550 frs, suite 750 frs. Breakfast 50 frs. Set dinner 160 frs; full alc 200 frs. Reduced rates and special meals for children.

RIBEAUVILLÉ 68150 Haut-Rhin   Map 3

Le Clos Saint-Vincent   *Tel* 89.73.67.65
Route de Bergheim

The "delicious" breakfast and fine views have been singled out for praise by *Bettye Chambers* this year for this sophisticated chalet-style restaurant-with-rooms, superbly set among Riesling vineyards, and backed by three ruined castles. Earlier comments: "Expensive, but an idyllic place to stay, with management and staff constantly attentive." "Wonderful rooms, superb meals, though the wines are very dear and the menus stay unchanged too long." The hotel's interior is spacious and elegant, with decor in soft muted golds and browns. "Our room was large and airy, with french windows opening on to a small terrace and attractive gardens, with views of the gently rolling countryside and the lights of Colmar in the distance."

Open 15 Mar–15 Nov. Restaurant closed Tue/Wed.
Rooms 3 suites, 8 double – all with bath and shower, telephone and TV; many with terrace or balcony. Ground-floor suites.
Facilities Lift. Salon, bar, restaurant. Garden.
Location In NE outskirts of town, which is 15 km N of Colmar. Parking.
Credit cards Access, Visa.
Terms [1989 rates] B&B: single 520–612 frs, double 570–865 frs, suite 840–988 frs. Set lunch/dinner 200–250 frs; full alc 250 frs. Reduced rates and special meals for children.

RIGNY 70100 Haute-Saône   Map 4

Château de Rigny   *Tel* 84.65.25.01
                                                      Telex 362926

"Outstanding – like staying in some well-kept Scottish castle with old-style furniture and exotic bedrooms. Remembered six months later for the very good food, the tranquillity and lovely gardens." (*Brian MacArthur*) That 1989 encomium from a Scot is endorsed by *Gault Millau's toque*, and by *Michelin's* three red gables, for the attractive charm of this select 13th-century château rebuilt in its present form under Louis XIII. Recently renovated, it is set quietly in its own grounds bordering the Saône and has a 12-acre *jardin anglais* and a large baronial salon. Another comment, "Rooms vary in size but all are well furnished (ground-floor ones in the annexe look the best). Jacques and Brigitte Maupin are excellent hosts."

Open All year except 2–31 Jan and Christmas.
Rooms 24 double – all with bath and shower, telephone and TV. 11 in annexe. 4 ground-floor rooms.
Facilities Salon, bar, dining room; conference/function facilities. 12-acre park with tennis court and swimming pool, pond for fishing, access to Saône river.
Location 4 km NE of Gray on Rigny road; Gray is 45 km NE of Dijon. Parking.
Credit cards All major cards accepted.
Terms Rooms: single occupancy 280 frs, double 350–480 frs, suite 600 frs. Breakfast 40 frs. Set meals 180–280 frs.

LA ROCHE-BERNARD 56130 Morbihan   Map 2

Auberge des Deux Magots   *Tel* 99.90.60.75

In a village just off the Nantes–Vannes highway, a charming and very soignée little family-run auberge, with clean, neat bedrooms, and a pretty panelled dining room where good local dishes (notably fish) are served at moderate prices. Closed Sun evening and Mon out of season. 14 rooms, 9 with shower. B&B double 270–310 frs. Set menus 80–320 frs. New nomination. More reports welcome.

ROCHEGUDE 26790 Drôme   Map 5

Château de Rochegude   *Tel* 75.04.81.88
                                                      Telex 345661 ROCHGUD

A gracefully restored stone château, dating in part from the 12th century, set in its own park on a rocky bluff above the vineyards of the Rhône plain north of Orange. It is now a smart and very expensive hotel, again much liked this year, "Friendly staff, faultless cuisine, lovely grounds for strolling, a spacious room with four-poster and sympathetic lighting – but in September the pool was unheated." Earlier views: "Our room, furnished with antiques, overlooked the vast plain. A large pool at which one could have a light but lingering lunch. Breakfast served out in a small courtyard was delicious. Madame was even weeding the garden while we were having it"; "Service impeccable, like being in a private house. They make their own wine and olive oil, and food was the best I've had in France." (*Michelin* rosette and *Gault Millau toque*). (*Caroline and Gary Smith*)

151

Open 1 Mar–2 Jan. Restaurant closed Tue and Wed midday.
Rooms 4 suites, 23 double, 2 single – all with bath and shower, and telephone; 25 with TV. Some ground-floor rooms.
Facilities Lift, ramps. Salon, TV lounge, bar, restaurant; conference facilities. Large grounds with heated swimming pool and tennis court.
Location 14 km N of Orange. From N leave A7 motorway at Bollène and go towards Carpentras. From S leave at Orange and go towards Gap on N7.
Credit cards All major cards accepted.
Terms [1989 rates] B&B: single 460 frs, double 600–1,380 frs, suite 1,700–2,000 frs. Dinner, B&B: single 760 frs, double 1,200–1,980 frs, suite 2,300–2,600 frs. Set lunch 170 frs, dinner 300 frs.

LA ROCHE-L'ABEILLE 87800 Haute-Vienne · Map 4

Moulin de la Gorce · *Tel* 55.00.70.66
La Roche-l'Abeille, St-Yrieix-la-Perche

"Ah, this is a lovely place. A sweet small lake with ducks in it, kind and skilful staff, delectable food (especially the desserts), delightful French people dining out and mercifully few English." That's one among many recent plaudits for Jean Bertranet's enchanting millhouse in a hamlet in pleasant hilly Limousin country between the two porcelain centres of Limoges (large and ugly) and St-Yrieix-la-Perche (small and lovely). The *Moulin*, also small and lovely, is the kind of place that warmly appeals to lovers of French rural simplicity plus high gastronomic complexity (two *Michelin* rosettes and two red *Gault Millau toques*). Very quiet and off the beaten track, it consists of two old buildings; six of the nine bedrooms are in the old mill, beside a small lake with waterfall. The bedrooms have antiques; in one is a fine four-poster bed.

"An enchanting setting, especially if you can watch the sun rise over the lake. Our small room was comfortable and the bathroom luxurious. Breakfast was expensive but wonderful – home-made jam, croissants and rolls straight from the kitchen. Food magnificent." "Dinner was delicious, service impressive. Expensive, but value for money." But you will need a degree in engineering to master the modern high-tech system of mixer taps in the bathrooms. (*Endorsed this year by ME Ricca and BH Jenkinson*)

Open All year except Feb. Closed Sun night and Mon Oct–Apr.
Rooms 9 double – all with bath and shower, telephone and TV. 6 in annexe. 2 ground-floor rooms
Facilities Salon, dining room. Garden with stream; fishing.
Location 12 km NE of St-Yrieix, off the D704. 2 km S of La Roche off D17. Parking.
Restriction Not suitable for &.
Credit cards All major cards accepted.
Terms B&B: single 325 frs, double 510 frs; dinner, B&B: single 800 frs, double 1,200 frs. Set lunch/dinner 250 and 320 frs; full alc 355 frs. Special meals for children.

LA ROCHELLE 17000 Charente-Maritime · Map 4

Hôtel les Brises · *Tel* 46.43.89.37
Chemin Digue Richelieu · *Telex* 790821

An efficient and stylish modern hotel, upper-medium price, in a prime position right by the sea, just outside the harbour: it overlooks the islands and estuary, and is a ten-minute walk from the heart of La Rochelle, one of the loveliest old towns in France ("a kind of maritime Bruges", an inspector has called it). "Comfort and quiet; polite and very helpful staff; best breakfast I've had in France for years." So runs one 1989 report. Other recent ones: "Stunning views over the bay, friendly people, firm bed"; "a vast terrace on which one can sun oneself over a drink, and two luxurious lounges." It is essential to ask for a room with a sea view. A reader this year warns that a nearby foghorn and revolving foglight make sleep difficult on foggy nights. No restaurant: you can eat very well, but expensively, at *Richard Coutanceau*, and there are goodish cheaper places along the quayside. (*Elizabeth Nines, Victoria P Turner, AF Thomas, and others*)

Open All year.
Rooms 46 – all with bath and/or shower, telephone, TV and baby-listening.
Facilities Lift. TV lounge, reading room, bar; terrace with direct access to sea and rocky beach.
Location On sea front 1½ km from town centre. Underground garage and carpark.
Restriction Not suitable for &.
Credit cards Access, Visa.
Terms [1989 rates] Rooms 340–480 frs. Breakfast 35 frs. Reductions for children. (No restaurant.)

---

33 rue Thiers	*Tel* 46.41.62.23
33 rue Thiers	*Fax* 46.41.64.87
	Telex 790821

This remarkable "find" in 1989 is an 18th-century town house in the heart of a lovely old city: "Maybelle Iribe and her *33 rue Thiers* are WONDERFUL. She is welcoming, eternally helpful (she even lent us her and her son's bikes). And she has created a sensational bed-and-breakfast out of this old mansion: six huge guest rooms all with wonderful bathrooms, all decorated differently. Ours, overlooking the tiny interior garden, was decorated with Maybelle's collection of Mexican folk art. The rooms are furnished with pieces from the local auction house. Everywhere you look there is style, character, whimsy and love. Breakfast included delicious scrambled eggs with hot herbs (Maybelle has written several cookbooks)." Cocktails and canapés are served in the garden or the library, and picnic baskets are on offer in summer." (*Lynne and David Allen*) More reports eagerly awaited.

Open All year except 15 Jan–15 Mar.
Rooms 6 double – all with bath and/or shower, 2 with radio.
Facilities Lounge, TV room. Courtyard garden.
Location Central. Parking.
Credit cards None accepted.
Terms B&B: single 300–380 frs, double 380–400 frs, suite 400–450 frs. Dinner, B&B 100 frs added per person. Picnic lunch 60 frs.

LES ROCHES-DE-CONDRIEU 38370 Isère	**Map 4**

Hôtel Bellevue	*Tel* 74.56.41.42

More approval this year for the good food and "excellent" wines at this pleasant modern creeper-covered hotel, set in a village beside the majestically curving Rhône, south of Lyon; vine-clad hills rise behind.

The restaurant, with its picture windows facing the river, is very popular locally. Bedrooms are modestly comfortable, some on the small side: try to get the one with a big balcony. (*L Sinker, Grania Little*)

Open All year except 1–12 Aug and 6–28 Feb. Closed Mon, Tue midday and Sun evening.
Rooms 18 – 9 with bath, 9 with shower, all with telephone. 3 in annexe. 1 ground-floor room.
Facilities Salon, restaurant; conference facilities.
Location 12 km SW of Vienne.
Credit cards Access, Diners, Visa.
Terms Rooms 180–250 frs. Breakfast 25 frs. Set meals 100–250 frs; full alc 230 frs.

ROLLEBOISE 78270 Yvelines   Map 3

Château de la Corniche   *Tel* 30.93.21.24
5 route de la Corniche   *Telex* 695544 CHAROL

Rolleboise is a village on the Seine between Paris and Rouen, some 12 kilometres from the splendid Monet museum and garden at Giverny. The *Château de la Corniche*, built by Leopold II of Belgium, stands splendidly in its large gardens above a bend in the river (front bedrooms have fine views of countryside and river). Each bedroom is different, and the restaurant, which shares the view, is done in pretty pink napery with bouquets of flowers on each table. The food includes artfully arranged salads and superlative desserts" (*Gault Millau* awards a red *toque* for these and for such dishes as fricassée of winkles). One recent visitor has commended the swimming pool. More reports please.

Open All year except Christmas week. Closed Sun evening and Mon in low season.
Rooms 1 suite, 37 double – all with bath and/or shower, telephone, TV and mini-bar. 17 in 2 separate buildings in grounds.
Facilities Lift. Salons, bar, TV room, 2 restaurants; conference facilities; terrace. 5-acre grounds with swimming pool and tennis court.
Location Just W of Rolleboise, overlooking the Seine. Leave A13 to Rouen at Bonnières exit.
Restriction Not suitable for &.
Credit cards All major cards accepted.
Terms [1989 rates] Rooms 260–600 frs, suite 1,200 frs. Set lunch/dinner 200 and 350 frs; full alc 400–500 frs.

ROMANÈCHE-THORINS 71570 Saône-et-Loire   Map 4

Les Maritonnes   *Tel* 85.35.51.70
      Telex 351060

A fairly sophisticated little hotel at the foot of the vine-clad slopes of the Beaujolais, between Fleurie and the N6 highway. Visitors this year and last have again much enjoyed the parasols and lilos around the swimming pool in its flowery garden, and the Burgundian cuisine in the *Michelin*-rosetted restaurant (e.g. crayfish soufflé and escalope of salmon cooked in Fleurie) as well as the fine local wines. "Delicious food, Guy Fauvin a splendid owner-chef"; "beautifully furnished rooms and a warm welcome from Madame Fauvin". Some rooms are on the small side, and light sleepers may be upset by the nearby railway. (*M and L Piper*)

Open All year except mid-Dec–end Jan, Sun evenings, Mon 15 Oct–15 Apr.
Restaurant closed Mon, and Tues midday 16 Apr–14 Oct.
Rooms 20 double – 18 with bath, 2 with shower, all with telephone and TV.
Facilities Lounge, bar, restaurant. Garden with heated swimming pool.
Location Near station. Parking.
Restriction Not suitable for ப.
Credit cards All major cards accepted.
Terms B&B: single 380–400 frs, double 450–520 frs. Set lunch/dinner 180,
230 and 320 frs.

LES ROSIERS 49350 Maine-et-Loire   Map 4

Auberge Jeanne de Laval   *Tel* 41.51.80.17
Route Nationale

"Dining room very plush. Food excellent, especially the rillettes and
delicious local fish" – a recent report on this much reputed restaurant-
with-rooms where *patron*-chef Michel Augereau specialises in local beurre
blanc fish dishes and wins a *Michelin* rosette and two *Gault Millau toques*.
It is a handsome creeper-covered house in a pretty garden, all very *soigné*
inside, both the public rooms and bedrooms; simpler, more rustic
bedrooms (and at least one uncomfortable bed) are in a nearby annexe,
the *Ducs d'Anjou*, a converted manor. "We stayed very pleasantly in the
annexe, a short car ride from the hotel: it is a pretty house in a big walled
garden, and the rooms were attractively decorated. Breakfast, with good
home-made jam, was taken by an open window facing the garden." More
reports please.

Open All year except 8 Jan–17 Feb. Closed Mon except public holidays.
Rooms 12 double – some with bath or shower, all with telephone. 8 in annexe,
Ducs d'Anjou, nearby.
Facilities Restaurant; functions facilities. Garden. Tennis, swimming, riding, golf
nearby.
Location 15 km NW of Saumur, on banks of the Loire.
Credit cards All major cards accepted.
Terms [1989 rates] Rooms 330–500 frs. Breakfast 44 frs. Dinner, B&B 450–520 frs
per person. Set meals 260–320 frs. Special meals for children.

ROUEN 76000 Seine-Maritime   Map 3

Hôtel de la Cathédrale   *Tel* 35.71.57.95
12 rue St-Romain

A slightly shabby but efficient and friendly hotel of some character,
centrally situated on a pedestrian walkway near the cathedral. A reader
this year found her room warm and clean, if a bit run down, and thought
the building charming. An earlier view, "From the moment you go
through the heavy wooden doorway and into the courtyard with its
geranium pots, busy lizzies and bits of statuary, you feel the delicious
Frenchness of it all. Our room with flowered wallpaper overlooked the
courtyard with a view of the cathedral spire; comfortable beds and very
quiet at night. Good coffee for breakfast but no croissants. No restaurant,
but we had a good fairly priced meal at the popular *Petite Auberge*
nearby." (*Georgene Smith, PF*)

Open All year.
Rooms 24 double – 8 with bath, 5 with shower, all with telephone.
Facilities Entrance hall, salon. Courtyard.
Location Central. Public carpark nearby.
Credit cards Access, Visa.
Terms B&B: single 160–254 frs, double 226–318 frs. (No restaurant.)

RUFFIEUX 73310 Savoie   **Map 4**

Château de Collonges   *Tel* 79.54.27.38

A château hotel an easy drive from Annecy and Aix-les-Bains is warmly
nominated: "It glows in the memory, not only for outstanding food but
also for heart-warming views across the valley to the mountains beyond.
Our stay was memorable for several reasons: the château itself, with
circular stone staircase, sumptuously furnished with antiques, spotlessly
clean and with great atmosphere. Small but ample swimming pool
overlooking the valley below a beautiful garden where chickens strut
(and serve as an alarm call in the morning), and where the owner relaxed.
He was anxious for silence from the children, and insistent that we should
eat on the dot of 7.30, only – as we discovered – so that we could admire
the magnificent sunset over the mountains from the terrace where meals
are served in summer. In cool weather dinner is served in the comfortably
furnished dining room in the cellars." "Virtually perfect. Cool stone
interior, atmosphere of calm and charm. Large and beautiful bedroom
with comfortable beds; large bathroom. Beds turned down at night.
Breakfast with real orange juice and *two* pots of coffee. Food excellent,
service impossible to fault. Expensive, but worth every penny." (*Brian
MacArthur, Anthony Hinds*)

Open All year except Jan and Feb. Closed Mon in low season; restaurant closed
Tue midday.
Rooms 9 – all with bath and shower, telephone and TV.
Facilities Salon, dining room, terrace. Park with swimming pool. Golf, water
sports, winter sports nearby.
Location 21 km N of Aix-les-Bains.
Restriction Not suitable for &.
Credit cards All major cards accepted.
Terms [1989 rates] Rooms 470–570 frs. Breakfast 45 frs. Set meals 175–400 frs.
Half board 450–510 frs per person. Special meals for children.

SABRES 40630 Landes   **Map 4**

Auberge des Pins   *Tel* 58.07.50.47
Route de la Piscine

This attractive half-timbered chalet, built in local style with a low sloping
roof, is in a village in the heart of the vast Landes pine-forests. In the
hands of the Lesclauze family it has won first prize for the best flower-
decked hotel in Aquitaine. Visitors this year found it friendly and good
value, "One end of the ground floor is a plastic-tabled local villagers' bar,
the other is a lovely restaurant with good local food. Specialities include
woodpigeon cassoulet, and all parts of a duck's anatomy – livers, hearts,
whole, etc." Plenty for children – sandpit, swings, ping-pong – and a
mini-rail takes you to the local outdoor ecology museum. (*Elizabeth Jones*)

Open All year except 15–30 Nov and 2–15 Jan. Closed Mon in low season.
Rooms 14 double – 4 with bath, 8 with shower, all with telephone; 6 with TV.
4 in annexe.
Facilities Lounge with TV, restaurant; conference facilities. Garden.
Location 35 km NW of Mont-de-Marsan.
Credit card Visa.
Terms Rooms 100–240 frs. Set lunch/dinner 70, 130 and 220 frs; full alc 150 frs.
Special meals for children.

SAILLAGOUSE 66800 Pyrénées-Orientales   Map 4

Auberge Atalaya   *Tel* 68.04.70.04
Llo

The Cerdagne, an hour's drive from Andorra and two from Perpignan, is
one of the most appealing corners of France – an upland plain of
meadows and pine forests, backed by the snowy Pyrenees. It is
surprisingly lush and pastoral for such an altitude (1,066 metres) and has
France's highest sunshine level. There's much of interest – the fortress of
Mont-Louis, the big ski-resort of Font-Romeu, and the strange black
Romanesque Madonna at l'Hermitage.

"A charming little *auberge* in a delightful setting, with enjoyable food
and tastefully decorated rooms." So runs a recent report on the *Atalaya*, a
converted farmhouse in the hamlet of Llo, just outside the resort of
Saillagouse, run by Hubert Toussaint, London born and bred. The menu
might feature such dishes as fillet of rascasse with fennel. "Very attractive
– a stone building with dark wood but light and spacious bedrooms. Ours
had a balcony. The Toussaints have a civilised attitude to their guests. A
quiet and relaxing place to stay – out of season at least." Just one adverse
report, however, last year. More reports welcome.

Open 20 Dec–5 Nov. Restaurant closed Mon, Tue midday in low season.
Rooms 1 suite, 9 double – 7 with bath and shower, 3 with shower, all with
telephone, radio, TV and mini-bar.
Facilities Lounge, bar, restaurant. Garden.
Location In Llo, on D33 2 km E of Saillagouse, which is 91 km W of Perpignan.
Restriction Not suitable for &.
Credit cards Access, Visa.
Terms Double rooms 390–498 frs. Dinner, B&B 720–830 frs; full board 980–
1,090 frs. Breakfast 39 frs. Set lunch 130 frs; full alc 250 frs. Reduced rates and
special meals for children.

ST-CHARTIER 36400 Indre   Map 4

Château de la Vallée Bleue   *Tel* 54.31.01.91
Route de Verneuil

Here you are in the heart of the George Sand country. St-Chartier with its
high-walled romantic castle is where she set *Les Maîtres sonneurs* and the
wedding in *La Mare au Diable*, and just to the south is her family château
at Nohant where she lies buried under a yew tree. Her dining-room table
is set with place-names for Flaubert, Turgenev, Liszt, etc (people she
entertained here). So it is appropriate that the bedrooms in the nearby
Château de la Vallée Bleue should be likewise named – "Our room was
called Flaubert", says our 1989 nominator who "really loved" this family-
run *Logis de France*: "Set quietly in a large park, it's a fine 18th-century

FRANCE

house, full of light and sunshine, run by the charming Gasquets. Our bedroom had style – two antique chairs, blissfully comfy beds, pale-green watered silk bedheads, marvellous reading lights. Charming lounge where a log fire was lit. Lots of polished wood – obviously first-rate housekeeping. Lots of lovely flowers. The cooking is tilted towards the *nouvelle*, but not over the top – delicious lapin en sauce courte à l'estragon. The house was busy with French guests, including business executives who always know the best places." (*Eileen Broadbent*) More reports welcome.

Open All year except Feb. Closed Sun evening and Mon Oct–mid-Apr.
Rooms 1 suite, 12 double, 1 single – 5 with bath, 8 with shower, all with telephone, radio and T V. 3 ground-floor rooms. 3 rooms in rustic-style annexe.
Facilities Ramps. Lounge, 2 dining rooms; terrace. 10-acre grounds with children's playground.
Location 9 km N of La Châtre on D918, then D69. Parking.
Credit cards Access, Amex, Visa.
Terms B&B: single 215 frs, double 340–475 frs, suite 540 frs. Dinner, B&B 260–370 frs per person. Set lunch/dinner 110, 175 and 265 frs; full alc 250 frs. Reduced rates and special meals for children.

ST-CIRQ-LAPOPIE 46330 Lot   Map 4

Hôtel de la Pélissaria   *Tel* 65.31.25.14

If we held a readers' referendum on their favourite small country hotel in France, this might well win. It is in a famous *village perché*, set dramatically on a cliff high above the river Lot. One of the old houses is now this tiny hotel, lovingly restored by its delightful owners, the Matuchet family; and yet again this year it has evoked rapturous praise from numerous readers – "a perfect place", "all is excellent", "paradise indeed", "this most lovely hotel in idyllic surroundings", and so on. It is on such a steep slope that the entrance is at the top and bedrooms are on the floor below. These, cool and spacious, have tiled floors, white walls, old beams, pine doors, rough-woven white curtains and bedspreads, and they look out onto the old church, the apple orchards and the river Lot beyond. M. Matuchet, "a man of infinite charm", is a musician and singer and will sometimes play the tapes he has made of his own setting of the poems of Ronsard or de Nerval. This music is not obtrusive, and is typical of the hotel's elegance. "The village is spectacular", says one visitor this year, "and the views from the rooms magical. The dining room with its beamed ceiling is intimate and relaxing, like a private dining room. And Madame Matuchet's food is quite, quite delicious." "The Matuchets excelled themselves in making us feel totally at home; rooms very clean and comfortable, with personal touches such as fresh flowers. The cooking was easily the best we have tasted in France" (trout soufflé and brochette of beef in pepper sauce have been singled out). (*Dr Anthony Winterbourne, Mr and Mrs J Alan Thornton, Caroline Currie, Sheila Newman, GE Samson, Eileen Broadbent, and others*) One audacious dissenter writes of unremarkable food and poor value for money.

Open 1 May–15 Nov. Restaurant closed midday.
Rooms 1 suite, 5 double, 2 single – 4 with bath, 4 with shower, all with telephone. Suite, 1 double, with private terrace, in garden.
Facilities Salon, dining room. Music and poetry evenings. Garden.

158

Location Central. Parking at some distance from hotel. Village 30 km E of Cahors.
Restriction Not suitable for ♿.
Credit cards Access, Visa.
Terms Rooms: single 220 frs, double 290 frs, suite 350 frs. Breakfast 30 frs. Set dinner 120 frs. Special meals for children.

ST-DYÉ-SUR-LOIRE 41500 Loir-et-Cher   Map 4

Manoir Bel Air   *Tel* 54.81.60.10

A low creeper-covered manor house now an unpretentious country hotel, set by the banks of the broad Loire near Blois and Chambord. It is not smart, and one reader this year thought it "scruffy", but others continue to enjoy it for its large, comfortable rooms and good regional cooking. "We had the grandest bedroom, big enough to play cricket in, with a beautiful bathroom and five huge windows. A house martin flew in and out of them. Lovely view of river. Food excellent, served in a beautiful big dining room with pink cloths and lovely plates. Good local wines." "The honest bourgeois food, lots of it, was fabulous value. Served in a delightful dining room, packed with locals at lunchtime, and with wonderful views over the river." Some have found the reception friendly, others less so. Poor housekeeping has also been reported. Charming exterior stone staircase. (*Victoria P Turner, Josephine Barratt, David V Lees, and others*) At certain times of year there are swarms of midges on the river banks making after-dinner strolls uncomfortable.

Open All year except 15 Jan–20 Feb.
Rooms 2 suites, 38 double – all with bath, telephone and TV.
Facilities Salon with bar, TV room, restaurant; conference facilities. Garden.
Location 200 metres from village which is 4 km W of Chambord.
Credit cards Access, Visa.
Terms [1989 rates] Rooms 200–320 frs. Breakfast 25 frs. Half board 280–300 frs per person. Set lunch/dinner 90–180 frs. Reduced rates and special meals for children.

ST-EMILION 33330 Gironde   Map 4

Hostellerie Plaisance   *Tel* 57.24.72.32
Place du Clocher

A former monastery has been converted into a graceful and "delightful" little hostelry, well befitting medieval St-Emilion and its famous wines. The site is most curious, atop a sandstone cliff that contains a troglodytic church dating from the 9th century and a mass of other caves. "The hotel's terrace", says a recent visitor, "juts out to the edge of the cliff, providing a superb view over the town, the castle and the vineyards. The food, and of course the cellar, have been famous in the district for many years, but the new management have recently modernised the bedrooms which are now first-rate." *Gault Millau toque* for such dishes as magret à la vapeur, served in an elegant setting. Very crowded during wine festivals. (*Endorsed this year by Paul A Hoffstein*)

Open All year except 2–31 Jan.
Rooms 11 – all with bath and shower, and telephone.
Facilities Salon, bar, restaurant; conference facilities. Garden.
Location Central, near Syndicat d'Initiative. Open parking.

Restriction Not suitable for &.
Credit cards All major cards accepted.
Terms [1989 rates] Rooms 400–600 frs. Breakfast 40 frs. Set lunch 100 frs, dinner 215 frs. No charge for children under 12 sharing parents' room; special meals.

Le Logis des Remparts
Rue Guadet

Tel 57.24.70.43

An old building in the village, newly renovated and prettily decorated, backing onto vineyards. Garden, private parking. No restaurant, but the nearby Francis Goullée *is admired. Closed 21 Dec–7 Jan. 15 rooms, all with bath and/or shower. B&B double 316–456 frs. New nomination. More reports please.*

ST-ETIENNE-DE-BAIGORRY 64430 Pyrénées-Atlantiques   Map 4

Hôtel Arcé

Tel 59.37.40.14

Only five miles from the Spanish border, this charming and typical Basque village up in the hinterland has a Roman bridge and a fine old church – as well, of course, as a *fronton* for *pelote* and an old smuggling tradition, now on the wane. The riverside *Arcé*, backed by green hills, has been in the hands of the same family for five generations and its fine traditions are by no means waning, as a recent visitor reports, "Its restaurant, *Le Trinquet*, has had a rosette in *Michelin* for over 25 years (pipérade is a speciality). It is a modest hotel of quiet charm: vulgarisation has passed it by, though modern comforts are not lacking. Set beside the fast-flowing river Nive, its firm-bedded rooms have small terraces from which the beauty of the valley can be savoured. The hotel is a bookman's delight, with a multilingual library. There is a heated swimming pool, across the river, and an air of unassuming professionalism at every level." Another visitor appreciated the setting, the pool and the food, but found the reception cool and the service inexperienced.

Open Mid-Mar–mid-Nov.
Rooms 5 suites, 19 double, 1 single – all with bath and/or shower, telephone; TV on request. 3 in annexe by river. 1 ground-floor room.
Facilities Lounge, library, billiard room, 2 restaurants. Gardens and terrace; outdoor swimming pool. River fishing.
Location 11 km W of St-Jean-Pied-de-Port; hotel is near church. Garage and parking.
Credit cards Access, Visa.
Terms [1989 rates] Rooms 300–800 frs. Breakfast 37 frs. Dinner, B&B 270–600 frs per person (3 nights min.). Set meals 90–220 frs; full alc 300 frs. Reduced rates and special meals for children.

****

Traveller's tale *Someone somewhere – Brussels no doubt – has created the Euro breakfast. Slices of prepackaged shiny ham, slices of processed cheese, salami, bread rolls that the armies of Garibaldi could have used as ammunition, all await your pleasure. Reconstituted orange juice or orange drink and hot coffee-flavoured liquid complete the feast. Blindfolded you could be marched in, and apart from the napkins (paper of course) you could be anywhere.*

****

ST-FÉLIX-LAURAGAIS 31540 Haute-Garonne   Map 4

Auberge du Poids Public   *Tel* 61.83.00.20
                               Telex 532477

An attractive village of timbered houses, perched on a hill in the rolling countryside east of Toulouse. The view from it is magnificent, taking in the snowy Pyrenees to the south and the darker Dordogne hills to the north. The *Poids Public*, admired as ever in 1988/9 ("everything perfect – room, welcome, cuisine"), is a low building much extended from the original village inn where produce was weighed (hence its name) before the proceeds were split between landlord and tenant. "The joy of this place is its complete lack of pretentiousness. Restaurant excellent, even on New Year's night." "Our rooms though small were tastefully furnished, the bathrooms pleasant. We dined on the terrace overlooking the lovely countryside with the smell of lavender in the air." "Interesting pictures everywhere. *Patron*-chef Bernard Augé is a bit of a showman, but produces wonderful food based on local produce (red *Michelin* 'R' and *Gault Millau* laurels for regional cuisine) – our five-course 95-franc [1989] menu included brochet mousseline with walnut sauce and his grand-mère's way of dealing with pig's trotters (interesting!). We sat at our window table watching the setting sun light up houses in Puylaurens 20 kilometres away. The fresh flowers on the table were all wild." "M. Augé is fun in a larger-than-life way and his wife is a poppet." One visitor thought his room "charming but ultra-twee". (*Curtis and Sally Wilmot-Allistone, Mrs VA Preston*)

Open All year except 6 Jan–10 Feb. Closed Sun evening 15 Oct–15 Mar.
Rooms 13 double – all with bath and shower, and telephone.
Facilities Bar, TV lounge, restaurant; terrace. Garden.
Location On N622 43 km E of Toulouse. Back rooms quietest.
Restriction Not suitable for &.
Credit cards Access, Amex, Visa.
Terms Rooms 225–260 frs. Breakfast 35 frs. Dinner, B&B 230–265 frs per person, full board 280–315 frs. Set lunch/dinner 95-170 frs; full alc 180–200 frs. Reduced rates for children sharing parents' room; special meals on request.

ST-FLORENTIN 89600 Yonne   Map 3

Les Tilleuls   *Tel* 86.35.09.09
3 rue Descourtive

A pleasant Logis de France, *making a useful, inexpensive alternative in this small Burgundy town. Warm welcome, charming service, excellent value on the cheaper menus* (Michelin red *"R"*). *Near centre but not noisy. Small garden. 10 rooms, all with bath or shower. B&B: single 207–242 frs, double 254–319 frs. Set menus 70–220 frs. New nomination. More reports welcome.*

> We don't lack *Michelin*-rosetted hotels in France but would be glad of more nominations at the more modest end of the price scale.

> The length of an entry does not necessarily reflect the merit of a hotel. The more interesting the report or the more unusual or controversial the hotel, the longer the entry.

ST-GERMAIN-EN-LAYE 78100 Yvelines   Map 3

Cazaudehore et La Forestière   *Tel* 34.51.93.80 and 39.73.36.60
1 avenue du Président Kennedy   *Fax* 39.73.73.88
    Telex 696055

Within 20 kilometres of Paris, in the heart of the forest of St-Germain, the Cazaudehore family run a fashionable restaurant that bears their name, and next door, in a wooded garden, a stylish little hotel that a reader this year thought "wonderful". It has tasteful modern rooms and suites, elegantly decorated with antiques and prints. Tiled bathrooms, friendly service, and a pleasant outlook on to the oak and beech forest. The restaurant has fresh flowers, gleaming silverware, an interesting menu, and draws a sophisticated clientele – especially at weekends when you need to book, even if you have a room reserved. (*DJ Harden*) *Michelin* is lavish with its red print for style and beauty, but has this year withdrawn its rosette for cuisine. We'd be glad of more reports.

Open All year. Restaurant closed Mon (light meals available for hotel guests).
Rooms 6 suites, 24 double – all with bath and shower, telephone, radio, TV and mini-bar.
Facilities Lift. 2 salons, restaurant; conference facilities. Garden.
Location 1.5 km NW of St-Germain, by N 284 and route des Mares.
Restriction Not suitable for &.
Credit cards Access, Visa.
Terms Rooms: single 560 frs, double 650 frs, suite 820 frs. Breakfast 45 frs. Full alc 300–350 frs. Reduced rates for children sharing parents' room; special menu.

ST-GIRONS 09200 Ariège   Map 4

Hôtel Eychenne   *Tel* 61.66.20.55
8 avenue Paul-Laffont   *Telex* 521273

Down a side street in a small town in the Pyrenean foothills south of Toulouse, a very spruce and attractive hostelry, white-walled, blue-shuttered, creeper-festooned, owned and run by the Bordeau family for six generations. Readers this year have again extolled the warm, friendly ambience, solicitous proprietor and excellent regional cooking (*Michelin* rosette, *Gault Millau toque*), nicely served in a large red-walled dining room well patronised by locals. "Fish first class, good local wines, and a pleasant room with balcony overlooking courtyard and garden." Rooms by the courtyard are quieter than those on the street. (*Peter Stattersfield, TH Nash*)

Open All year except 22 Dec–31 Jan.
Rooms 2 suites, 42 double, 4 single – 22 with bath, 20 with shower, all with telephone and TV; some with balcony.
Facilities Lounge, TV room, 2 bars; conference facilities. Garden with heated swimming pool.
Location Central; parking. St-Girons is 99 km S of Toulouse.
Restriction Not suitable for &.
Credit cards All major cards accepted.
Terms B&B: single 273 frs, double 451 frs, suite 461 frs. Dinner, B&B: single 381–473 frs, double 573–662 frs. Set lunch/dinner 103, 160 and 260 frs; full alc 240 frs. Children sharing parents' room free; special meals on request.

ST-JEAN-DU-BRUEL 12230 Aveyron   Map 4

Hôtel du Midi   *Tel* 65.62.26.04

The Papillon family's unpretentious *Logis de France*, in the western
Cévennes, vies with the *Pélissaria* at St-Cirq (q.v.) as our most popular
rural entry for central France. It is in an old village on the river Dourbie
between Millau and Le Vigan, a good centre for walking holidays or for
visiting the Gorges du Tarn. Tributes this year: "The Papillons' charm,
and the remarkable value they offer, make this the best French hotel of its
kind that we know. How do they do it at the price (red 'R' in *Michelin*)?
Part of the answer lies in M Papillon's skill with unusual ingredients –
tripe, gizzards and sheep's feet, for example: his feuilletée aux gésiers is
delicious. The combination of scenery and hotel is irresistible." Service is
swift and personal. The no-choice but varied menu for residents is far
better than what guests *en pension* normally get given in France –
excellent soup ad lib, home-made charcuterie, main courses that may
include quail, civet de chevreuil, cassoulet, confit de canard aux lentilles.
"Rooms are simple, but food is marvellous, and the whole place is
warmed by the Papillon family: Madame never ceases to be utterly kind."
"Madame was an elegant bundle of energy." "Our plain but adequate
room was in an adjacent building with a fine stone turret stair." Some
rooms are modern and pretty; some are a bit cramped and less
comfortable. British and German guests are much in evidence. "This is
splendid walking country, best in spring when regulars come for the
display of wild flowers covering the *causses*. In the evenings, the polyglot
conversation between dinner tables is full of botanical Latin." (*JP
Berryman, Jack B Ainslie, Jean Seymour, AG Catchpole, BW Ribbons, and
others*) Floreat Papillonia.

Open 7 Apr–11 Nov.
Rooms 17 double, 2 single – 15 with bath and/or shower, all with telephone.
2 pairs of communicating rooms in nearby annexe.
Facilities Salon, TV room, bar, restaurant; terrace. On banks of river Dourbie;
bathing, fishing.
Location 40 km SE of Millau on D991; 20 km E of N9. Garage and open parking.
Restriction Only restaurant suitable for &.
Credit cards Access, Visa.
Terms B&B: single 87 frs, double 122–208 frs; half board: single 163–173 frs,
double 274–380 frs; full board: single 191–201 frs, double 330–436 frs. Set
lunch/dinner 63–168 frs; full alc 135 frs. Reduced rates for children under 6;
special meals.

ST-JEAN-DU-DOIGT 29228 Finistère   Map 2

Le Ty-Pont   *Tel* 98.67.34.06
Plougasnou

A down-to-earth seaside hotel in northern Brittany, offering remarkable
value. Readers this year hugely enjoyed the five-course *en pension* meals,
especially lunch (the main meal of the day) and the local fish. They had a
comfortable room, and loved the "stunningly beautiful" coastline. A
family of regular devotees have written lyrically: "The food was
staggering: honest cooking and the freshest possible ingredients. Lunch
might start with crab-claws and slices of melon, then a fish in a delicate
sauce, then a meat course (perhaps guinea-fowl), then cheese, fromage

blanc or yoghurt, then ice-cream (home-made) or a good selection of fresh fruit or crème caramel. The scene in the dining room was astonishing – working-class French families, a baby drinking potage out of its bottle, a two-year-old having fromage blanc spooned into it. It was very noisy, but the young waitresses were never flustered. Bedrooms were adequate. There is a garden by a stream, where you can sit in the sun and recover from *la bouffe*. St-Jean is an attractive village amid farmlands, with good views and a pretty church. Lovely beach at Primel-Tregastel nearby." There are good amenities for children, but some adults might find the hotel, though very clean, a bit basic. (*Mrs Lucy Slater*)

Open Easter–31 Oct. Closed Sun evening and Mon, except 1 June–30 Sept.
Rooms 26 double, 6 single – 2 with bath, 18 with shower; 17 with telephone.
Facilities Salon, bar, TV room, 2 restaurants. Garden with children's playground. Sandy beach 700 metres.
Restriction Not suitable for &.
Location 17 km NE of Morlaix, 1.5 km E of Plougasnou village.
Credit cards None accepted.
Terms Rooms 90–165 frs. Breakfast 20 frs. Full board 160–193 frs. Set lunch/dinner 48–190 frs. Reduced rates for children.

ST-JEAN-PIED-DE-PORT 64220 Pyrénées-Atlantiques   Map 4

Hôtel des Pyrénées	*Tel* 59.37.01.01
Place du Général de Gaulle	*Telex* 570619

St-Jean, at the foot of the Roncesvalles pass into Spain, is one of the most picturesque of Basque towns (15th-century ramparts, hilltop citadel) and a capital of Basque folklore (summer festival and *pelota* championships). It used to be a major resting-place for Santiago-bound pilgrims about to cross the Pyrenees. And today many of our readers choose to halt there, seeking out this distinguished *auberge* which has been owned and run by the Arrambide family for four generations. One report this year, "Their glorious restaurant fully deserves its two stars in *Michelin* and three red *Gault Millau toques*. My meal started with a magnificent foie gras de canard, then a whole grilled local salmon, most delicious, then stuffed hare, and chocolate desserts. Our first-floor room was more than adequate, but there was some noise from a courtyard below. When the bill came I marvelled at its reasonableness – this place is very good value." Several others recently have extolled the cooking – "It is rumbustious and copious, no *cuisine minceur* here. And we loved the Arrambides, warm friendly people with the simple charm of the working French. Their traditional hostelry has no pretension to elegance, and evokes the *cossu bourgeois* of the 1950s rather than 1980s flair and panache." Rooms have been remodelled this past year; there are some luxury suites with lavish bathrooms on the first floor, and readers have enjoyed them. Back rooms are quietest, but lack a view. (*Roger Bennett; also Willis Frick, Stanley Burnton*)

Open All year except 5 –26 Jan, 20 Nov–20 Dec. Closed Tue except 1 July–15 Sept.
Rooms 2 suites, 18 double – all with bath/shower, telephone and TV.
Facilities Lift. 2 salons, 2 dining rooms; conference rooms; terrace.
Location 54 km SE of Bayonne on D933. Parking.
Credit cards Access, Amex, Visa.

Terms Rooms 460 frs, suite 750–800 frs. Breakfast 40 frs. Dinner, B&B 470 frs per person; full board 670 frs. Set lunch/dinner 165–380 frs. Reduced rates for children sharing parents' room.

ST-LATTIER 38840 Isère   Map 4

Le Lièvre Amoureux
Tel 76.36.50.67
from late 1989 76.64.50.67
Telex 308534 LIEVRE

This "amorous hare" is a pleasant old creeper-covered *auberge* in the Isère valley between Valence and Grenoble, and both *Michelin* and *Gault Millau* give it their red print for attractiveness. The cooking is regional, served outside in summer on a candle-lit terrace under lime-trees, or indoors in a panelled room where a fire blazes in winter. "An excellent hotel with comfortable rooms tastefully furnished and a very good swimming pool," runs a recent report; "Madame Hannelore Breda, the *patronne*, conducted the service of dinner like a stage director and the food and wine were superb and not over-priced." An earlier visitor stayed in the new annexe by the open-air heated pool, "These rooms are quiet and well appointed with sliding 'patio' windows. Though we were staying *en pension*, we were allowed the run of all the menus including the *carte* at no extra cost. The food was excellent, especially the local trout. Breakfasts included optional orange juice, yoghurt and eggs at no extra charge. The staff were competent and friendly, and on our last evening we received a free bottle of champagne over dinner." Rooms in the old building are smaller and simpler but have pretty views through the trees to the Vercors mountains. There is a railway nearby, but trains are few and not too noisy; the plumbing in the newer section is said to be noisy. New reports welcome.

Open All year except 18 Dec–15 Jan. Closed Sun evening and Mon Oct–Apr.
Rooms 14 double – 12 with bath and shower, all with telephone; 5 with radio; 5 with TV. 5 in annexe. 2 on ground floor.
Facilities Salon, bar (in summer), 2 restaurants. Garden with terrace for meals in summer, swimming pool and bar.
Location Halfway between St-Marcellin and Romans on N92.
Credit cards All major cards accepted.
Terms [1989 rates] Rooms 300–400 frs. Breakfast 40 frs. Set meals 195 frs; full alc 225 frs. Reduced rates and special meals for children.

ST-MALO 35400 Ille-et-Vilaine   Map 2

Hôtel Le Valmarin
7 rue Jean XXIII
Tel 99.81.94.76

A clean and friendly hotel, modernised from a beautiful 18th-century house in the suburb of St-Servan, just south of St-Malo harbour. "A bit formal for my taste, but very good"; "warm welcome, helpful staff"; "civilised, with a discreet atmosphere. The proprietor brings you a glass of chilled Muscadet on a silver tray, covered with lace, while you sit in the impressive gardens." One reader had a room beautifully decorated in white, green and gold, but another found his bed too soft and a third reported a lack of comfortable chairs throughout the house. No restaurant, but there are several good cheap fish places in the harbour area. The nearby beach is said to be insalubrious. More reports welcome.

Open 1 Mar–24 Dec.
Rooms 10 double – all with bath, telephone, radio and T V.
Facilities Salon bar. Garden. 300 metres from sandy beach.
Location Centre of St-Servan near Port Solidor; 2 km from old St-Malo. Parking.
Restriction Not suitable for &.
Credit cards Access, Amex, Visa.
Terms Rooms 330–510 frs. Breakfast 32 frs. (No restaurant.)

ST-MARTIN-VALMEROUX 15140 Cantal   Map 4

Hostellerie de la Maronne   *Tel* 71.69.20.33
Le Theil

"An immaculate hotel in a lovely setting, with excellent food," says a reader who appreciated the Auvergnat rural charm of this modest hostelry outside the hamlet of Le Theil. It stands in its own informal garden, in the lush upper valley of the Maronne, quite close to the lovely Renaissance hill-village of Salers. "The engaging but slightly eccentric" Alain de Cock and his Malagasy wife provide comfort and a choiceless evening meal (e.g. rêve d'escargots and tripoux flambés au cognac, but some dishes have been judged more "prosaic" than these). "Our room in the cottage annexe small but comfortable", says a reader this year. Others have enjoyed swimming in the pool and have had very good food. *Note:* dinner is not served after 8 pm. (*Diana Holmes, John and Rita Newnham*)

Open 20 Apr–15 Oct. Restaurant closed for lunch.
Rooms 25 – all with bath and shower, telephone and mini-bar. 8 in annexe.
Some ground-floor rooms.
Facilities Salon, games room, dining room. Garden with heated swimming pool, tennis.
Location 3 km E of St-Martin-Valmeroux on D37 to Fontanges.
Credit cards Access, Visa.
Terms [1989 rates] Rooms 230–310 frs. Breakfast 30 frs. Half board 230–310 frs per person.

ST-PAUL-DE-VENCE 06570 Alpes-Maritimes   Map 5

La Colombe d'Or   *Tel* 93.32.80.02
                                                   Fax 93.32.77.78
                                                   Telex 970607

"A beautiful hotel in a marvellous setting. Our balcony overlooking the mountains and valley was wonderful, the room and bathroom were spacious and clean. The food was satisfactory and the atmosphere in the dining room was tops." So runs one of several recent plaudits for this famous little luxury hotel in a show village behind Nice. But some other readers are more critical (the food is generally judged mediocre) and undoubtedly *La Colombe* suffers from its popularity as a tourist attraction in its own right: it houses a private collection of modern art that would be the envy of any museum – Braque and Calder by the swimming pool, César and Miró in the lounge, Matisse, Picasso and Utrillo in the dining room, and much else. Many of these works were given to the former owner, the late Paul Roux, in payment by artists who stayed or ate there.

It's a beautiful old house, with many fine pieces of furniture, and is still owned and run by the Roux family. Some rooms have their original beams, others are all in white stucco with window-seats overlooking gardens; many have a terrace and outside bathroom. There is an idyllic veranda, decorated with a fine Léger mural, where lunch is served; dinner is taken indoors in a large rustic dining room. The swimming pool is surrounded by cypress trees. But not everyone will like the high-class tourist ambience, and the service has sometimes been found erratic or aloof.

Open All year except 10 Nov–15 Dec.
Rooms 10 suites, 15 double – all with bath, telephone, radio and TV; many with terrace. 1 ground-floor room.
Facilities Lift. Salon, bar, restaurant; terrace for lunch or refreshments. Garden with swimming pool. 10 km from sea.
Location 20 km W of Nice; take road to La Colle and Hauts de St-Paul. Parking.
Credit cards All major cards accepted.
Terms [1989 rates] Rooms 850 frs, suite 1,050 frs. Breakfast 40 frs. Dinner, B&B 620 frs per person. Alc (excluding wine) 195–390 frs. Reduced rates and special meals for children.

Le Hameau *Tel* 93.32.80.24
528 route de La Colle

Many of the small idyllic hotels in the Nice/Cannes hinterland have become marred by the overkill of trendy tourism. This one, just outside St-Paul, remains remarkably unspoilt and rural – a white-walled 18th-century farmhouse, imaginatively converted. A recent visitor adored it: "Its low white buildings are on several levels on a hillside, with doors opening on to terraces, some right out of bedrooms. We enjoyed breakfast on the largest terrace, amid flower-beds, trellised arbours and citrus trees, and were invited to pick oranges, tangerines and grapefruit whenever we wished. The main building holds a spacious comfortable lounge with big stone fireplace; there are tables for playing games, and lots of books in both English and French. The white-walled bedrooms are attractively furnished in country style, with many antiques. Rooms vary in size and shape, some being a bit low-ceilinged and dark. Management and staff were all helpful and friendly. Some traffic noise (a main road is nearby), but it did not continue all night." No restaurant, but among the many in St-Paul you could do worse than eat Danish (Lapland reindeer etc) at *La Brouette*.

Open 15 Feb–16 Nov and 25 Dec–8 Jan.
Rooms 2 suites, 13 double, 2 single – 13 with bath, 3 with shower, 16 with telephone and mini-bar.
Facilities Lounge with TV, breakfast room. Terraces and garden.
Location 1 km SW of St-Paul on road to La Colle.
Restriction Not suitable for &.
Credit cards Access, Amex, Visa.
Terms [1989 rates] Rooms: single 220–260 frs, double 260–390 frs, suite 490 frs. Breakfast 33 frs. (No restaurant.)

> Our italicised entries indicate hotels which are worth considering, but which, for various reasons – inadequate information, lack of feedback, ambivalent reports – do not at the moment warrant a full entry. We should particularly welcome comments on these hotels.

ST-PÉE-SUR-NIVELLE 64310 Pyrénées-Atlantiques   Map 4

Hôtel de la Nivelle   *Tel* 59.54.10.27

"A friendly and unassuming little *auberge*, truly Basque", at one end of
the main street of a village between Cambo (don't miss Edmond
Rostand's flamboyant Villa Arnaga) and St-Jean-de-Luz. "Madame
Berrotaran's family have owned the hotel for generations. She and her
husband are sweet and welcoming, and his regional cooking we found
excellent, at fair prices – pipérade, ttoro (Basque fish soup) and caneton
farci on the main menu, and good fish specialities on the *carte*, such as
fillet of brill in a subtle wine sauce. A garrulous party of trendies from
Biarritz just failed to spoil the ambience in the quaint beamed dining
room; breakfast (good coffee) is served in the equally quaint bar, where
locals gather. The bedroom area could do with a facelift, and rooms are
small and simple. Front ones could suffer from morning traffic noise, so it
might be better to opt for the modern annexe, 200 metres away across
fields. Nearly all rooms have peaceful views of Basque hills and
farmland."

Open All year except Feb.
Rooms 35 double – all with bath and/or shower. 15 in annexe.
Facilities Salon, TV room, bar, 2 restaurants; banqueting facilities. Garden.
Location Village is 13 km E of St-Jean-de-Luz. Parking.
Credit cards Access, Visa.
Terms Rooms 200 frs. Breakfast 25 frs. Dinner, B&B 210 frs per person. Set lunch
90 frs, dinner 130 frs; full alc 100–250 frs. Reduced rates and special meals for
children.

ST-PONS-DE-THOMIÈRES 34220 Hérault   Map 4

Château de Ponderach   *Tel* 67.97.02.57
Route de Narbonne

This splendid 17th-century manor stands in its own 400-acre wooded
park, just outside the pleasant old town of St-Pons (fine 12th-century
cathedral). It is on the edge of the wild heavily forested hills of the Haut
Languedoc nature reserve. For the past 300 years it has been in the
aristocratic family hands of the present owner, Madame Counotte. It was
dropped from the 1989 Guide purely from lack of news, but a report this
year brings it back, "The fact that it's run by a woman shows in many
small points – a pot of detergent in our bathroom, flowers in unlikely
places. Madame Counotte is an accomplished pianist and her daughter
plays professionally: any music in the dining room is always good. The
food is decent and plentiful, and the wines reasonably priced. Bedrooms
have balconies overlooking the park: some English people staying longer
than us were enchanted with the quiet beauty of the hotel. And it's the
cheapest of its château-type that I've seen." (*Alan F Thomas*)

Open 1 Apr–early Oct.
Rooms 11 – all with bath and/or shower and telephone.
Facilities Salon with TV, bar, restaurant; conference facilities. Large garden where
meals are served in good weather.
Location 1.2 km S of town on Narbonne road.
Credit cards All major cards accepted.
Terms [1989 rates] Rooms 355–405 frs. Breakfast 60 frs. Dinner, B&B 565–570 frs
per person. Set lunch/dinner 160–330 frs. Special meals for children.

ST-QUENTIN 02100 Aisne   Map 3

Grand Hôtel et Restaurant   *Tel* 23.62.69.77
  Le Président   *Fax* 23.62.53.52
6 rue Dachery   *Telex* 140225

Picardy's second largest town, itself a humdrum place, is worth visiting for the Quentin de la Tour portraits in the Lécuyer museum. And it has other surprises in store – as nominators of the *Grand* found this year: "The town centre and the *Grand* were a revelation – the former for its super reconstructed buildings, the latter for an inspired re-creation. From the outside, despite the floodlighting, it looks like just another turn-of-the century facade in a dull street near the station: but the interior has been gutted and replaced by a central atrium with a glass roof, glassed-in balconies and a glass lift, all very modern and tasteful. In the modern marble foyer, a receptionist sat at a Louis XV repro table. Our large and pleasant bedroom had a marble bathroom *en suite*. To cap it all, *Le Président* restaurant, very popular locally, fully deserves its *Michelin* rosette" (*and* it has three *Gault Millau* red *toques* for its inventive dishes, some of them Picard in inspiration). (*David and Angela Stewart*)

Open All year. Restaurant closed Christmas, New Year and Aug.
Rooms 24 double – all with bath and shower, telephone, radio and TV.
Facilities Lift. Bar, breakfast room, restaurant.
Location Central. Parking.
Credit cards Amex, Diners, Visa.
Terms [1989 rates] Rooms: single 380 frs, double 480 frs, suite 550 frs. Breakfast 50 frs. Set lunch/dinner 185 and 320 frs; alc (excluding wine) 400–500 frs. Reduced rates for children sharing parents' room.

ST-RÉMY-DE-PROVENCE 13210 Bouches-du-Rhône   Map 5

Hôtel Les Antiques   *Tel* 90.92.03.02
15 avenue Pasteur   *Telex* 431146

In the southern suburbs of this typical small Provençal town is the mental home of St-Paul-de-Mausole where Van Gogh spent a year as a patient after cutting off his ear in Arles; nearby are the curious Roman remains of Glanum, known also as Les Antiques. Hence the name of this hotel near the town centre, a gracefully converted 19th-century mansion. You can stay in the main building, or in a *pavillon* with its own terrace. "One of my favourite hotels", says a devotee this year, "a great welcome, grounds and pool attractive, atmosphere delightful". Other regulars, too, have endorsed an earlier view, "Lovely people, charming atmosphere: it was like being guests in a private home. Beautiful gardens, and a grand entrance with marble floors, tapestries, Italian painted ceiling." (*Mrs RB Richards; also Ellen and John Buchanan*) No restaurant, but the *France* and the *Arts* in town are both good value. A September visitor found "carnival noises non-stop, bulls running through the streets and bicycle races, and a fun-fair just opposite" – to her, a nightmare, but maybe to others a good reason for visiting joyous Provence.

Open 7 Apr–15 Oct.
Rooms 26 double, 1 single – all with bath, shower, and telephone. 10 in bungalow in park. 2 ground-floor rooms with ramps.
Facilities 2 salons, TV room. Large grounds with unheated swimming pool.

Location In town centre. Parking.
Credit cards Amex, Diners, Visa.
Terms (Excluding tax) B&B: single 388 frs, double 490 frs. (No restaurant.)

Hôtel Château de Roussan
Route de Tarascon

Tel 90.92.11.63

"Still one of our favourite places in Europe: we'd probably go here for a second honeymoon" – a recent letter that typifies many readers' feelings about this stately pink 18th-century château, secluded outside St-Rémy in its own big park. It has been the country home of the Roussel family for over a century; today they accept bed-and-breakfast clients to keep it going. Many visitors find it an unusual and civilised experience, more like being the house-guests of cultured friends than staying in a hotel. "Breakfast with the peacocks and doves is a treat under the huge plane trees with the sound of the small fountains." "Our enormous room was full of antiques." "An ideal place for writing. You can set your table and chair in a far corner of the park and be disturbed only by the house dogs who take a well-behaved interest when picnic lunchtime has arrived." Bathrooms are modern, but the rooms are in careful period style, with Louis XV furniture. "Louis Roussel was a courteous host, showing us the 16th-century farmhouse in the grounds where Nostradamus once lived and inviting us to browse in his library." No restaurant, but try the *Café des Arts* or the *France* in town, both quite cheap. (*Endorsed this year by JA –* "*as delightful as ever*".)

Open 15 Mar–31 Oct.
Rooms 4 suites, 10 double, 3 single – all with bath and/or shower, telephone and tea-making facilities. 2 ground-floor rooms.
Facilities Lounge, TV room, library. Large park.
Location 2 km W of centre of St-Rémy, off Tarascon road. Parking.
Credit cards Access, Visa.
Terms [1989 rates] Rooms: single 300 frs, double 500 frs. Breakfast 48 frs. (No restaurant.)

Domaine de Valmouriane
Petite route des Baux

Tel 90.92.44.62
Fax 90.49.01.79
Telex 431169 DOMVAL

An old stone Provençal *mas* in the rocky foothills of the wild Alpilles, just south of town, which has been exquisitely converted into a small luxury hotel, owned by an Englishwoman, Catherine McHugo, and run by her in association with Jean-Claude Aubertin who was chef at the *Auberge* at Noves (q.v.) and at *Ma Cuisine* in Chelsea. The *Domaine* opened only in 1988 but already has two red *toques* in *Gault Millau* (and four red gables in *Michelin*). Cool white walls, tiled floors, a sense of space and grace, much admired by our nominators this year: "Lovely bedrooms and bathrooms: ours was very stylish. A large sitting room with open fireplace, and a small panelled bar. In the pleasant restaurant with its huge windows, opening onto the terrace, the food was excellent" – and highly inventive in its posh way, e.g. foie gras with peaches and ginger, and fricassée of lamb's foot with truffles. (*Pat and Jeremy Temple*) More reports please.

Open All year.
Rooms 12 – all with bath and/or shower, telephone, TV and mini-bar.

Facilities Lounge, reading room, bar, restaurant; terrace where meals are served. Garden with swimming pool and tennis court.
Location 4.5 km S of St-Rémy, by D27 (petite route des Baux). Parking.
Credit cards Access, Amex, Visa.
Terms [1989 rates] Rooms: single 650–1,000 frs, double 850–1,200 frs. Breakfast 55 frs. Half board 200 frs per person added. Special meals for children.

ST-SERNIN-SUR-RANCE 12380 Aveyron   Map 4

Hotel Carayon   *Tel* 65.99.60.26
Place du Fort   *Telex* 531917 CARAYON

"A real find," says this year's nominator of a country hotel in a thinly populated area well off the main north-south tourist routes: it's in a village on the Albi–Millau road, just south of the lovely valley of the Tarn. "Pierre Carayon, ebullient and enthusiastic, spent some years at the Dorchester and Savoy in London, and is now transforming the family hotel/restaurant into a larger enterprise: fifteen new rooms have just been built into the hillside in a sympathetic way. There's a garden with diversions for children. Our small but neat room in the old part of the hotel had a splendid view across the valley. The food (*Michelin* red 'R') was fantastic value – our 78-franc [1989] dinner included two terrines, a whole trout, quail flamed in brandy and home-made sorbet. Very much a family affair, with *grandpère* and two small boys all in evidence, and elegant Madame supervising the dining room." (*Diana Holmes*) More reports welcome, especially on the new rooms.

Open All year. Closed Sun evening and Mon in low season.
Rooms 5 suites, 40 double – all with bath and/or shower; 40 with telephone, 20 with TV, some with balcony.
Facilities Lift. Lounges, 2 TV rooms, bar, 3 dining rooms. Disco. Terrace. Garden with children's playground and table tennis.
Location St-Sernin is 50 km E of Albi on D999. Hotel is central; parking.
Credit cards All major cards accepted.
Terms [1989 rates] Rooms 99–260 frs. Breakfast 24 frs. Set meals 59–239 frs; full alc 200 frs. Reduced rates and special meals for children.

ST-SYMPHORIEN-LE-CHÂTEAU 28700 Eure-et-Loir   Map 2

Château d'Esclimont   *Tel* 37.31.15.15
St-Symphorien-le-Château   *Telex* 780560 ECLIMON

"C'est mon plaisir", is the motto of La Rochefoucauld on the facade of this stately moated Renaissance château, standing in a 150-acre wooded park between Chartres and Rambouillet. An American visitor this year found the pleasure hers, too, "Fairytale vintage, with its period moats, crenellated towers, stone sculptures. I was charmed by our two-storeyed room, and found the *nouvelle cuisine* good, but expensive; lunch or drinks can be taken on the terrace, overlooking a garden and lovely lake with swans." (*Victoria P Turner*) An earlier view, "Truly glorious, luxuriously appointed. Even on a bitter winter's day, everywhere was deliciously warm. The views are amazing, over park, river and woods; the food is delicious and served in generous portions from an inspired menu (two *Gault Millau toques*). Two recent visitors found the welcome and ambience cool.

Open All year.
Rooms 6 suites, 48 double – all with bath and shower, telephone and TV. 24 in 3 separate buildings.
Facilities Salon, bar, 4 dining rooms; conference facilities. Wooded park with small lake, river, tennis court, heated swimming pool and helipad.
Location 6 km NW of Ablis. Leave A11 or N10 at Ablis; go towards Prunay; turn left on D101.
Restriction Not suitable for &.
Credit card Visa.
Terms Rooms: single occupancy 520 frs, double 825–1,210 frs, suite 1,430–2,100 frs. Breakfast 75 frs. Set lunch/dinner 260–430 frs; full alc 450 frs. Special meals for children.

ST-THIBÉRY 34630 Hérault   Map 4

Château de Nadalhan   *Tel* 67.77.87.93
Route de Valros

An Italianate mansion in its own big park, set on the vine-clad Languedoc plain halfway between the lovely Renaissance town of Pézenas, where Molière often performed, and the huge new bathing resort of Agde. "A small pretty château amid vineyards, run as a restaurant *avec cinq chambres* by a pleasant young couple, the Théronds. We had a spacious 18th-century room with a good big bathroom; hand-hemmed linen sheets, two tall arched windows. All spotless. Food well and imaginatively cooked, though the set menu offered limited choice and began to pall after ten days. Piped music during the meal, but we managed to get the cassettes changed to suit our taste. Service cheerful and personal."

Open All year except Jan.
Rooms 1 for 4, 4 double – all with bath; telephone on request.
Facilities Salon, 3 dining rooms. Park. Sea 10 km.
Location On D125 between St-Thibéry and Valros, 7 km SW of Pézenas.
Credit cards Access, Visa.
Terms B&B: single 230–260 frs, double 310–360 frs; dinner, B&B: single 310–340 frs, double 510–560 frs. Set lunch/dinner 105, 150, 180 and 250 frs; full alc 220 frs. Reduced rates and special meals for children.

ST-TROPEZ 83990 Var   Map 5

Le Mas de Chastelas   *Tel* 94.56.09.11
Route de Gassin   *Telex* 462393 CHASTA

Once used for silkworm breeding, this converted 17th-century farmhouse stands secluded in vineyards a little west of St-Tropez and 500 metres from the sea. Guests tend to include French stars of stage, screen and fashion, fleeing the *paparazzi* of the frenzied port area. "A bit of a poseur's paradise" is one view, but for another reader this year it is "a wonderful combination of taste, luxury and informality, very clean and comfortable, with helpful staff and superb *nouvelle cuisine*", while regular visitors concur: "Still pretty, calm and casually elegant, it is a quiet, restful and superior oasis in a crowded area. The *accueil* is warmer, service is unobtrusively good, though occasionally a little amateurish. Dinner was excellent. Our suite in an annexe in the woods was luxurious; flowers were changed daily. Fine breakfast, with cherries and brioches; good food pleasantly served by the pool, but the menus don't change often enough." Others have admired the buffet lunches by the heated pool, the dinners served on a candle-lit terrace, and the pine furnishings. The new chef, Michel Gaudin, wins two red *toques* from *Gault Millau* for some very fancy fish dishes. Some visitors are enthusiastic, but one was critical, particularly of the waiters. (*William G Frick, Stefan and Yvette Wiener*)

Open Easter–early Oct. Restaurant closed to non-residents for lunch.
Rooms 10 suites, 21 double – all with bath and/or shower, telephone; 11 with TV. Suites in separate building with private garden.
Facilities Lounge, TV room, indoor and outdoor restaurant; terrace. Garden with heated swimming pool, jacuzzi, 4 tennis courts. Beaches 10 mins by car.
Location 3 km SW of St-Tropez, just off Gassin road.
Restriction Not suitable for &.
Credit cards All major cards accepted.
Terms [1989 rates] Rooms 500–1,100 frs, suite 1,575–1,800 frs. Breakfast 65 frs. Set dinner 350 frs. Special meals for children.

Les Palmiers   *Tel* 94.97.01.61
26 boulevard Vasserot   *Telex* 970941

Much more centrally located than our other St-Tropez entry: five minutes' stroll from the harbour, and facing the place des Lices with its famous trendy-bohemian bar-bistrots, the Café des Arts *and* Bistrot des Lices. *A simple family-run B&B hotel, now getting an overdue face-lift; patio garden, good breakfasts; decent rooms, very good value for a town that Michael Frayn has called 'St-Trop' (the saint of excess). 22 rooms, most with bath and/or shower, 220-330 frs. Breakfast 25 frs [1989]. New nomination. More reports welcome.*

ST-VAAST-LA-HOUGUE 50550 Manche   **Map 2**

Hôtel de France et des Fuchsias   *Tel* 33.54.42.26
18 rue Maréchal Foch

An old oyster-breeding port east of Cherbourg, where Edward III landed his troops before the battle of Crécy. Today troupes of Britons continue to land at this popular family-run hotel, which preserves its exuberant charm even though it is run to something of a formula and has become "a kind of club for the English middle classes". Many readers enjoy the look of the place – very pretty, much festooned indeed with red fuchsias – and admire the garden, cobbled courtyard and thatched canopy, as well as the

****
* **Traveller's tale** *The town of Dreux (Eure et Loire) has no good hotels so* *
* *the Unwary Traveller, looking for a bed for the night, follows the* *
* *roadsigns to Môtel St-Georges. The signs are official, not advertisements,* *
* *so it is clearly an establishment of some importance. Exhaustive search* *
* *fails to locate it. The U. T. asks a villager who, before replying, fetches his* *
* *mates out of the café to witness the fun. A verbose explanation in patois* *
* *then ensues from which one gathers that the Môtel commence au pont* *
* *et finit à l'église. We are therefore right in the middle of it. (Gallery* *
* *laughter.) After much wordplay it is revealed that there is no motel as* *
* *such. Môtel St-Georges est le nom du village. Howls of mirth all round.* *
* *They should be sick of the joke by now.* *
****

"superb" meals (the plates and curtains in the dining-room also have fuschia patterns). A recent verdict: "Welcome friendly, rooms unpretentious but well furnished and very comfortable, food superbly cooked and presented, staff charming and efficient." No main lounge, but plenty of sitting space. We should welcome more reports.

Open 1 Mar–2 Jan. Closed Mon except school holidays.
Rooms 3 suites, 26 double, 3 single – 29 with bath and shower, 2 with shower, all with telephone and TV. 12 in annexe.
Facilities Bar, 2 salons, reading room, 2 dining rooms. Garden. Bicycle hire. Sandy beach nearby.
Location Central (some windows double-glazed, quietest rooms overlook garden). Small parking place.
Restriction Not suitable for &.
Credit cards All major cards accepted.
Terms Rooms 235–320 frs. Breakfast 30 frs. Dinner, B&B 198–295 frs per person; full board 265–365 frs. Set lunch/dinner 65–180 frs; full alc 190 frs. Children under 8 sharing parents' room half-price; special menu.

STE-ANNE-LA-PALUD 29127 Finistère   Map 2

Hôtel de la Plage   *Tel* 98.92.50.12
Plomodiern   *Telex* 941377

Not far from the lovely old village of Locronan, the beachside chapel of St Anne is the venue of one of the largest and most colourful of Breton *pardons*, held on the last Sunday of August. Near this chapel is the *Plage*, not an ordinary seaside hotel as its *Hulot*-ish name might imply, but stylish and expensive – and strongly admired again in 1989, especially for its cuisine (*Michelin* rosette, two red *Gault Millau toques*): "A lovely place, oozing atmosphere, with its paintings of seascapes and waitresses in Breton costume. The demi-pension menu includes oysters, grilled salmon, and char-grilled lobster which you eat with a special pinny draped tenderly round you by a maternal waitress. A picturesque thatched cottage houses a bar. Bedrooms comfortable and tasteful." Earlier paeans: "A very well-run hotel on a beautiful sandy beach, long and uncrowded. Good and friendly service. At dinner, predominance of fish, always fresh and large portions. Classic puddings, incredibly sweet; cheeses fresh and local; a wonderful platter of fruits de mer at lunch; and delicious croissants, brioches and home-made jams for breakfast." "A good tennis court, and a stunning situation, especially with the light of the setting sun reflected on the wet low-tide sands." Some front rooms can be noisy, and a few may suffer from cess-pit smell in the heat; and one reader points out that though the beach is on the doorstep the sea is often a long way away, owing to the tides, and that the hotel does not have much in the way of facilities for small children. (*Francine and Ian Walsh; Pamela M Zargarani, Philip Carter, BH Jenkinson, and others*)

Open 24 Mar–10 Oct.
Rooms 4 suites, 28 double, 2 single – most with bath and shower, all with telephone; 16 with TV. 2 ground-floor rooms.
Facilities 2 lifts. Salons, bar, TV room, restaurant; conference facilities. Garden with tennis court and swimming pool. Safe, sandy beach.
Location On coast, 16 km NE of Douarnenez.
Credit cards All major cards accepted.
Terms [1989 rates] Rooms 500–700 frs, suite 950 frs. Breakfast 48 frs. Half board 550–680 frs per person. Set lunch 170 frs, dinner 300 frs.

SAINTES 17100 Charente-Maritime   **Map 4**

Relais du Bois St-Georges   *Tel* 46.93.50.99
Rue de Royan   *Telex* 790488 STGEOR

Saintes, with its ruined Roman amphitheatre and fine Romanesque
churches, is one of the most attractive and historic towns of south-west
France. The *Bois St-Georges*, well placed in its own big garden near the
autoroute, in the western outskirts, is by contrast very modern – in an
elegantly unusual way, as readers tell us this year. "The indoor heated
swimming pool has a grand piano, statuary, and large windows
overlooking the lawns." "An excellent hotel with a superb pool. My room
was very individual, being on several floors with its own staircase and a
good supply of French books. Food and service are excellent. The garden
with its lake and fountains is an example of the care and enthusiasm
lavished by the owner, very much in evidence and clearly proud of his
achievement." "Swimming pool in the dining room" (sic). Bedrooms are
said to be tastefully decorated. (*DJ Harden, Peter Aston, AF Thomas, Victoria
P Turner*) There is some traffic noise – and a reader warns against taking a
chalet room by the lake if it is too near the pool's noisy refiltration plant.

Open All year.
Rooms 3 suites, 27 double – all with bath and shower, telephone, radio, TV and
baby-listening. Some with balcony. 6 ground-floor rooms specially adapted for &.
Facilities Lounge, 2 bars, TV room, restaurant; indoor swimming pool; terrace
where meals are served in season. 14-acre grounds with lake.
Location On W outskirts – 1.5 km from exit 25 of *autoroute* A10. Garage parking.
Credit cards Access, Visa.
Terms Rooms: single occupancy 290–410 frs, double 380–570 frs, suite 740–
880 frs. Breakfast 55 frs. Dinner, B&B double 395–459 frs per person. Set
lunch/dinner 130 frs; full alc 180–280 frs. Special meals for children.

LES STES-MARIES-DE-LA-MER 13460 Bouches-du-Rhône   **Map 4**

L'Étrier Camarguais   *Tel* 90.47.81.14
Chemin bas des Launes   *Telex* 403144

On the edge of the Camargue, just north of Les Saintes-Maries, the *Étrier*
("stirrup") is one of several modern ranch-like holiday hotels here that
cater mainly for riders: it has its own herd of white Camarguais horses
which it hires to guests by the hour (not cheap). It is a spacious, breezy
and youthfully informal place, slightly shabby, with log-cabin decor; the
simple bedrooms, in chalets in the garden, have patios where you can
breakfast in privacy. A family wrote to us this year, "The swimming pool
and gardens were attractive, the staff were friendly, and we enjoyed the
horse-rides. The dinners were mostly good – on one evening, a
magnificent buffet with smoked and fresh salmon, crab, all sorts of
shellfish, an array of delicious salads and other delights. Pity that lunch
was a full three-course affair, with no chance of just snacks round the
pool. Breakfast was adequate." (*JA, and others*) The nearby disco (just out
of earshot) is not cheap. Les Saintes-Maries' famous Gypsy festival, every
23–27 May, is well worth seeing.

> Don't let old favourites down. Entries are dropped when there is no
> endorsement.

Open 1 Apr–15 Nov.
Rooms 27 double – all with bath, telephone and TV. Ground-floor rooms.
Facilities Bar, restaurant, disco; conference facilities. Terrace, garden with swimming pool and tennis court. Sandy beach 2 km.
Location 3 km N of the town, just off N570 to Arles.
Credit cards All major cards accepted.
Terms Dinner, B&B: single 605 frs, double 795 frs; full board: single 755 frs, double 1,095 frs. Set lunch/dinner 150–200 frs.

Hôtel Le Mas de la Fouque

Tel 90.47.81.02
Fax 90.47.96.84
Telex 403155

The *Mas de la Fouque* is similar in style to the *Étrier* (above) but smaller and much more up-market – a modern whitewashed ranch, very comfortable, set in the Camargue with wildlife all around and a stable full of white horses. "We had a big beautiful room, an amazing bathroom and our own veranda at the edge of a small lake where we saw water-rats, carp, heron and other beautiful birds. The food was mainly straightforward Camargue roasts, and there was no choice for the main course on the daily menu *pension*. Breakfast delicious, but service a bit haphazard." "The pool is lovely, heated but not over-heated, with good beach chairs. The hotel is in superb good taste, and the welcome from owner Jean-Paul Cochat is warm. His wife runs the kitchen, his daughter the bar and dining room (food satisfactory). It is all very informal and relaxed. If one is lucky, one sees flights of white flamingos around sunset taking off from the marsh, and in the morning the white horses will come thundering down the narrow path outside one's bedroom – a wonderful sight."

Open All year except 2 Jan–20 Mar. Restaurant closed Tue.
Rooms 1 for 4, 13 double – all with bath and shower, telephone, TV and mini-bar. Ground-floor rooms.
Facilities Salon, bar, 2 restaurants; terrace with café. Garden with heated swimming pool, tennis, putting. Fishing. Large sandy beach with safe bathing 2 km.
Location 4 km NW of Les Saintes-Maries by D38.
Credit cards All major cards accepted.
Terms Dinner, B&B: double 1,700 frs, suite 2,030 frs. Full board 2,130 frs. Set lunch/dinner 210–320 frs; full alc 245 frs. Reduced rates and special meals for children.

SALON-DE-PROVENCE 13300 Bouches-du-Rhône   Map 5

Abbaye de Sainte-Croix
Route du Val de Cuech

Tel 90.56.24.55
Telex 401247 STECROI

A venerable 12th-century abbey on a hillside north-east of Salon, sumptuously restored as a luxury hotel. It has a wooded park, and a dining room giving onto a terrace with a fine view across the plain; at night it is cande-lit. "The position is spectacular, and wholly tranquil", writes an inspector this year; "we had their nine-course *menu dégustation* which was perhaps not as *haute* as the view but wholly agreeable. The outdoor pool is well maintained." Bedrooms tend to be small (many are former monks' cells) but some have a balcony. (*HR*)

> We are particularly keen to have reports on italicised entries.

Open 1 Mar–31 Oct. Restaurant closed Mon midday.
Rooms 5 suites, 19 double – all with bath and/or shower, and telephone; radio on request.
Facilities Bar, TV room, restaurant; functions facilities. Garden with swimming pool. Tennis 200 metres.
Location 5 km NE of Salon, off D16.
Credit cards Access, Diners, Visa.
Terms B&B: single from 615 frs, double from 680 frs, suite from 1,120 frs. Dinner, B&B: single 905 frs, double 1,140 frs, suite 1,570 frs. Set lunch/dinner 180–420 frs; alc 350 frs. Special meals for children on request.

SARLAT-LA-CANÉDA 24200 Dordogne   Map 4

La Hoirie   *Tel* 53.59.05.62

Just south of Sarlat, this former hunting lodge is now a friendly Relais du Silence, *with swimming pool and garden. Efficient staff, pleasant rooms (those in main house better than annexe); good Périgourdin food, copiously served. Open 15 Mar–14 Nov. 15 rooms, all with bath and/or shower. B&B double 520 frs. Set menus 170–260 frs. New nomination. More reports please.*

Hostellerie de Meysset   *Tel* 53.59.08.29
Route des Eyzies

Périgourdine *douceur de vivre* suffuses this very pleasant rural hotel, built in local style and set on a hill outside the town, in its own park: from its terrace there are wide views over two valleys. Plenty of red print in *Michelin,* and a black *Gault Millau toque* for good regional cooking, back up the report of our nominator who brings it to the Guide this year: "Comfortable, and efficiently run. Madame Brottier is bandbox smart, Monsieur is friendly and likes a joke. Our ground-floor room had french windows opening onto a tiny private lawn. In the well-appointed dining room the atmosphere was relaxing and the five-course *menu pension* was varied: excellent soups." Meals are served on the terrace when fine; the furniture is suitably rustic in style. (*Ann Webber*) More reports welcome.

Open 27 Apr–7 Oct.
Rooms 31 – all with bath or shower and telephone.
Facilities Lounge, restaurant. Large terrace. Garden.
Location 3 km NW of town, off Les Eyzies road (D67). Parking.
Credit cards All major cards accepted.
Terms [1989 rates] Rooms 310–360 frs, suite 565 frs. Breakfast 40 frs. Dinner, B&B 330–355 frs per person. Set lunch 160 frs, dinner 190 frs.

SAULIEU 21210 Côte d'Or   Map 4

Hôtel de La Côte d'Or   *Tel* 80.64.07.66
2 rue d'Argentine   *Telex* 350778

A noble old coaching-inn, on the main street of a dullish little Burgundy town on the old Paris-Lyons highway (N7). It was long famous, for its former owner Alexandre Dumaine was one of the great French chefs of his day (***Michelin). Then it fell into eclipse, with Dumaine's death and the coming of the *autoroute* which stole most of the through traffic. Today, despite its unpromising location, it is again in form under a new *patron-*

chef, Bernard Loiseau, who has brought it up to the standard where it wins two *Michelin* rosettes and no fewer than four red *Gault Millau toques* – endorsed by one expert reader this year, "I was enthusiastic about the 'cleanness' and intensity of flavour which is characteristic of M. Loiseau's *cuisine à l'eau*; my husband was less so. The inn has been beautifully restored, with masses of fresh flowers and well-polished antique furniture." Others have echoed this: "The cooking, modern and light, is soundly based on old Burgundy dishes. The wine list, mostly expensive, contains some house wines at reasonable prices." Room furnishings are a little heavy, but the lavish new suites are said to be excellent. (*Rosamund V Hebdon; also T and R Rose, Jeff and Karen Nebel, Denis Tate*)

Open All year.
Rooms 10 suites, 13 double – all with bath and/or shower, telephone, tea-making facilities and baby-listening; 10 with radio, 17 with TV. Ground-floor rooms.
Facilities 2 lounges, 3 dining rooms. Garden. Near Morvan National Park with tennis, riding, lakes, fishing and water sports.
Location Central. Garage parking.
Credit cards All major cards accepted.
Terms B&B 330–970 frs per person; suites 1,570–1,870 frs. Set lunch 250 frs, dinner 390 frs; full alc 600–650 frs. Special meals for children.

SAUTERNES 33210 Gironde   Map 4

Château de Commarque   *Tel* 56.63.65.94
Langon

Few names are sweeter than Sauternes – and we are glad to welcome this Guide debutant, a handsome English-owned wine-producing château amid the vineyards, 40 kilometres south-east of Bordeaux. Dr Nigel Reay-Jones and his wife recently bought it to restore the neglected vineyards, and they have now planted eight acres with young vines. They have also converted the outbuildings into self-contained studio apartments, each with an independent entrance opening onto a courtyard, where one reader stayed this year, "An ideal family holiday hotel, excellent value for money. The Reay-Jones were most helpful. They welcome children, and have five well-behaved ones of their own. There's no high luxury, but the basic amenities are there, including a swimming pool. A Basque chef gives a flavour of the south-west with his regional dishes: the 'turbot sur commande' is a must. Dr Reay-Jones, an ex wine-importer, has an unusual, well-chosen wine-list – especially the Sauternes." Meals are served in the former *chai*, probably 17th-century. Local wine tours can be arranged. And the literary-minded might care to know that this is also the Mauriac country: his family home, Malagar, is just across the Garonne at Vergelais, north of Langon, and his boyhood summer home at St-Symphorien, south-west of Sauternes, was the setting for *Thérèse Desqueyroux* and *Le Mystère Frontenac*. (*Stephen and Samantha Pollock-Hill*)

Open All year except Feb. Restaurant closed to non-residents Wed in low season.
Rooms 8 suites with small sitting room, suitable for 4 people (2 grouped together), 1 double – all with shower. 1 ground-floor room.
Facilities Restaurant. 30-acre grounds; garden with swimming pool, vineyard.
Location 40 km SE of Bordeaux. Leave A62 at Langon. Follow road to Sauternes; château is signposted.
Credit cards Access, Visa.

Terms Rooms: double 120–150 frs, suite 180–250 frs. Breakfast 24 frs. Set lunch/dinner 70, 110 and 165 frs; full alc 150 frs. Half board rates (min 4 nights). 50 frs added for use of sofa bed in sitting rooms. Special meals for children.

SAUVETERRE-DE-COMMINGES 31510 Haute-Garonne   Map 4

Hostellerie des Sept Molles   *Tel* 61.88.30.87 and 61.88.31.36
Gesset   *Telex* 530171

This captivating hotel is a large white villa, quite smart and most gracefully furnished, secluded in a verdant wooded valley of the Pyrenean foothills. *"Molle"* is a local word for *moulin*, as the brochure lyrically explains: "On the slopes of the hills overlooking the valley, seven joyous watermills used to cling to the meanderings of the capricious stream flowing from the plateaux. The locals came down on Sundays to fetch sacks full of white flour and drink their fill of mirth. Sadly, times have changed ... but the seven mills were retrieved by the management and now adorn our gardens." Several readers this year and last have drunk their fill of mirth at the Ferran family's hostelry: "A luxurious hotel run by a young and friendly couple, with innovative high-class food and memorable breakfasts." "We took two of their cheapest rooms, which proved to be comfortable and nicely decorated. The only sound was of cowbells. Service and public rooms were as you'd expect from *Relais et Châteaux*, but informal. A swimming pool and tennis court in the lawned garden; table tennis in the gazebo; and children are entertained by the proprietors' small daughter. Nice touches like poached quails' eggs as appetisers and baskets of fruit in the bedrooms. Menus were imaginative, using local ingredients (rabbit and pigeon) and *nouvelle* in presentation" (*Gault Millau* red *toque*). (*Helen and Charles Priday, Paul A Hoffstein*)

Open Mar–Oct and Dec.
Rooms 2 suites, 17 double – all with bath and shower, telephone and TV; some with balcony.
Facilities Lift. Salon, bar, 2 restaurants. Garden with swimming pool and tennis court.
Location At Gesset, 2 km SE of Sauveterre, 13 km SW of St-Gaudens.
Credit cards All major cards accepted.
Terms Rooms: single 280–450 frs, double 380–520 frs, suite 680–850 frs. Breakfast 40 frs. Set lunch/dinner 140–220 frs; full alc 250 frs. Reduced rates and special meals for children.

SÉGURET 84110 Vaucluse   Map 5

La Table du Comtat   *Tel* 90.46.91.49

This picturesque old village, on a hillside above the Rhône vineyards, is within easy reach of Orange and Roman Vaison, and has fine views of the startling jagged peaks of the Dentelles de Montmirail; it's also a centre of Provençal folk culture, with a Christmas church pageant and craftsmen making *santons*. Here this fine old 15th-century house, now a sophisticated restaurant-with-rooms (*Michelin* rosette and *Gault Millau toque*), is splendidly situated just above the village - "one of our favourite little hotels in France", say readers in 1989. An inspector has been impressed this year too, "The view's the thing, so it's best to eat by daylight, taking advantage of the big windows of the dining room, a bit dull and formal after dark. Service is outstandingly stylish and courteous, and Madame Gomez is friendly though reserved (her husband cooks). The cuisine is superbly done in its more-or-less *nouvelle* way – an *amuse-gueule* of salmon mousse with oyster, superb lamb and lotte au pistou, good cheeses – they are strong on chèvres – and a fine local white Séguret, better than the Gigondas red, also local. Smart international clientele, classical piped music. Rooms comfortable, many with views: mine was well equipped, including even a shoebrush, so new-looking that I used it as a hairbrush, having left mine in my *gîte*. The small piscine, floodlit at night, below its high rock is a stunner – as are the toilets whose unisex basin area is right against the naked rock of the cliff into which the hotel is built." (*Endorsed by David and Lynne Allen*)

Open Mar–21 Nov, 7 Dec–end Jan. Closed Tue evening and Wed except Christmas and Easter.
Rooms 8 double – all with bath, (4 also with shower), and telephone.
Facilities Salon, dining room; terrace. Small garden with unheated swimming pool.
Location 8 km S of Vaison-la-Romaine off the D23; at entrance to Séguret; hotel is signposted. Parking.
Restriction Not suitable for &.
Credit cards All major cards accepted.
Terms Rooms: single 380 frs, double 410–560 frs. Breakfast 50 frs. Set lunch/dinner 210, 270 and 400 frs, full alc 350–400 frs. Special children's menu.

SEPT-SAULX 51400 Marne   Map 3

Hôtel Restaurant le Cheval   *Tel* 26.03.90.27
   Blanc   *Telex* 830885 CHEBLAN
2 rue du Moulin

A pleasant old creeper-covered coaching inn, run by the Robert family for five generations. It is liked especially for its food (*Michelin* rosette, *Gault Millau toque*), and for its pastoral setting beside a big garden and a stream (it straddles the main road of a village south-east of Reims). "Excellent food, magnificent rooms, and we relaxed in garden hammocks and rocking chairs amid trees and murmuring streams," is a report this year. Earlier ones: "A warm atmosphere, Madame Robert very charming, dinner excellent especially poulet de Bresse in a tarragon sauce." "We were delighted with the food and excellent breakfast. Service competent if not swift – but who wants to rush a good French meal?" The warm attentiveness of the Roberts and their staff is generally praised, though one dissenter this year found the reception cool and thought the food overpriced. Be warned, too, that party walls are thin, making neighbours' night noises audible; and rooms on the road side, where lorries lumber by, hardly justify the hotel's rating as a *Relais du Silence*. (*Prof. AS Douglas, Brian MacArthur, J Masters*)

Open All year except 15 Jan–15 Feb.
Rooms 3 suites, 18 double – all with bath and/or shower, telephone, TV and mini-bar. All on ground floor in building opposite restaurant.
Facilities Hall, salon, restaurant, breakfast room; functions room. Terrace. Large park bordered by river Vesle; tennis, mini-golf, volleyball, fishing.
Location On D37 off N44 in direction of Châlons.
Credit cards All major cards accepted.

Terms Rooms: single 250 frs, double 450 frs. Breakfast 38 frs. Dinner, B&B 490–550 frs per person; full board 610–675 frs. Set lunch/dinner 170, 270 and 370 frs; full alc 300 frs.

SERRES 05700 Hautes-Alpes · Map 4

Hôtel Fifi Moulin · *Tel 92.67.00.01*
Route de Nyons

Somewhat coyly named (who anyway was Fifi?), this in fact is a solid down-to-earth hostelry on the main Grenoble to Provence road. It continues to be popular with readers, especially for its restaurant (*Michelin* red "R" and *Gault Millau toque*) which is strongly patronised by locals. "Delightful, inexpensive meals, dynamic and charming host, excellent rooms with mountain views." "Pleasing fabrics, remodelled bathrooms, pretty dining room, good food especially the cheeses." So run two recent reports. "The hotel is on several levels, with kitchens next to guest bedrooms: for this reason, some rooms may be a little noisy in late evening. Terrace and back bedrooms on upper levels have views over the mountains, with blocks of flats in the foreground." Upper rooms at the back are best.

Open 15 Mar–30 Nov. Closed Wed except in season.
Rooms 25 double – all with bath/shower and telephone. 12 in annexe.
Facilities Bar, restaurant; terrace. Large garden with swimming pool. Near river with bathing and fishing.
Location 107 km S of Grenoble, 64 km from Nyons on N75.
Credit cards All major cards accepted.
Terms Rooms 200 frs. Breakfast 30 frs. Dinner, B&B 220 frs per person. Set lunch/dinner 90 and 150 frs.

SEURRE 21250 Côte d'Or · Map 4

Le Castel · *Tel 80.20.45.07*
20 avenue de la Gare

Set in a small town on the Beaune-Dole road, this attractive Logis de France has comfortable rooms with modern bathrooms. No lounge but a bar and flowery terrace. Big, bright dining room: excellent local cooking at reasonable prices by the patron-chef, who worked for 13 years in England. Closed 2 Jan–5 Feb. 20 rooms, most with bath. Rooms 190–220 frs. Set meals 95–250 frs. Endorsed this year by its original nominators, but another reader warns of train noises.

SOMMIÈRES 30250 Gard · Map 4

Auberge du Pont Romain · *Tel 66.80.00.58*
2 rue Émile-Jamais

Converted from a 17th-century carpet factory, this somewhat unusual hotel has a riverside setting in a large and attractive Languedoc village. Big bedrooms with tiled floors, shady garden new swimming pool, pleasant staff, but owner a bit domineering. Good if somewhat rich food, including sole Lawrence Durrell, named after Sommières' most famous resident, an habitué. Open 15 Mar–

31 Dec. 18 rooms, all with bath and/or shower. B&B double 260–380 frs. Set menus 140–205 frs [1989]. Some criticisms. More reports welcome.

SOUSCEYRAC 46190 Lot　　　　　　　　　　　　　　Map 4

Au Déjeuner de Sousceyrac　　　　　　　　　　*Tel 65.33.00.56*

A rustic *auberge* in a remote village south of the upper Dordogne: under its previous owners, the Espinadel family, it so much delighted one *académicien*, Pierre Benoit, that he wrote a book about it, *Au déjeuner de Sousceyrac*, and the inn then took that name. Some of our own readers in the mid-1980s were equally thrilled: but then Pierre Espinadel retired and it lost its place in the Guide. Now it has been bought by Richard Piganiol, Paris-trained but a local man, and already he's won a *Michelin* red "R" and *Gault Millau* red *toque* for dishes such as paupiette de pigeon au foie gras. Our own re-nomination this year, "I doubt if the bedrooms have changed – ours was cramped but adequate. The dining room decor was freshly done, about right for this simple hotel, and the cuisine is excellent, with more than a touch of the *nouvelle*. Some French fellow-guests were high in its praise and clearly knew what they were talking about."(*Jack B Ainslie*) If you do too, please give us further news.

Open 1 Mar–1 Jan.
Rooms 10 – 3 with bath, 7 with shower.
Facilities Salon, restaurant; terrace.
Location In centre of village, which is between St-Cère and Aurillac, on D673 and D653. Parking.
Credit card Visa.
Terms Rooms: single 110 frs, double 140 frs. Breakfast 30 frs. Dinner, B&B 200–300 frs per person. Full alc 270 frs. Reduced rates and special meals for children.

STRASBOURG 67000 Bas-Rhin　　　　　　　　　　Map 3

Nouvel Hôtel Maison Rouge　　　　　　　　*Tel 88.32.08.60*
4 rue des Francs-Bourgeois　　　　　　　　　　*Telex 880130*

Most Strasbourg hotels are expensive, but this medium-priced one is both quiet and very central, 30 metres from the main square, the place Kléber. It has just been renovated in "modern 1930s" style and is again approved by several readers this year, notably for its spacious, comfortable rooms and generous buffet breakfasts ("mouth-watering croissants"). Most reports commend the multilingual staff as efficient and friendly, but some have found them impersonal. The hotel caters heavily for groups but retains its character – even down to the grand piano, for guests' use, on one upper landing. "Our high room at the back was quiet and overlooked the rooftops of old Strasbourg." No restaurant, but you can eat very well all over Strasbourg – for example, expensively at the *Crocodile*, medium-pricewise at *l'Ancien Horloge* and cheaply at *l'Ancienne Douane*. (*Dr FP Woodford, Lynne and David Allen, GB Brook, and others*)

Open All year.
Rooms 1 suite, 131 double, 3 single – 125 with bath, 10 with shower, all with telephone; some with radio and TV.
Facilities 2 lifts. TV room, bar, breakfast room; conference facilities.

Location In town centre (hotel is sound-proofed). Underground parking in place Kléber nearby.
Credit cards All major cards accepted.
Terms [1989 rates] Rooms: single 320 frs, double 460 frs. Breakfast 40 frs. (No restaurant.)

Hôtel des Rohan   *Tel* 88.32.85.11
17 rue Maroquin   *Telex* 870047

"This charmer" (to quote a recent American visitor) is small and family-run, in a discreet traditional style, but is also well modernised. And it lies in the heart of the old quarter, in a cobbled pedestrian area beside the cathedral. Readers this year have again found it friendly, efficient and quiet (apart from some cathedral chimes). Though modern, it has "repro" furniture in the current French taste and is warm and comfortable. They will send a bell-boy to bring your bags from the nearby public parking. The Sunday breakfast with Kugelhopf cakes is commended. (*Prof. Sir Alan and Lady Cook, GB Hart, John Grammer, Kathy and Tony Gillett*)

Open All year.
Rooms 36 – all with bath and/or shower, telephone, radio and TV. Baby-sitter on request.
Facilities Lift. Salon with TV, 2 breakfast rooms.
Location Central, near cathedral. Parking nearby.
Credit cards Access, Visa.
Terms Rooms: single 260–485 frs, double 275–520 frs. Breakfast 35 frs on weekdays, 50 frs on Sun. (No restaurant.)

Hôtel Royal   *Tel* 88.32.28.71
3 rue du Maire Kuss   *Telex* 871 067

This well-modernised B&B hotel on a main street near the station could make a useful alternative to the Rohan and Maison Rouge, both often full. Friendly and helpful staff, excellent breakfasts (continental or buffet), bedrooms and bathrooms well equipped and quiet. Patio garden, health club (sauna, jacuzzi, etc). Open all year. 50 rooms, all with bath and shower. B&B: single 330–380 frs, double 395–500 frs. No restaurant. Recent nomination. More reports please.

TALLOIRES 74290 Haute-Savoie   **Map 4**

Hôtel de l'Abbaye   *Tel* 50.60.77.33
                                                        Telex 385307 ABBAYE

"A lovely hotel, expensive, yes, but not over-priced", says a visitor this year to this gracefully converted old abbey, idyllically situated beside the Lake of Annecy; it has a fine cloister, vast oak-panelled rooms, and a charming garden and shady dining terrace by the water. Some rooms are small, being former monks' cells, but others are much larger, with sofas and balconies. The food, and the "outstandingly agreeable" owner, are commended. "Ultimate luxury, and a superb setting, peaceful and relaxing. We were delighted by the quality of the food and service, down to the beachboy who looks after the hotel's private jetty. Most water

183

sports are available next to the hotel." Modernised regional cooking: e.g. trout with cabbage, duck with raspberries – and even scrambled eggs with frogs' legs. (*Mrs C Smith, Prof. AS Douglas*)

Open All year except 15 Dec–15 Jan. Restaurant closed Sun evening and Mon midday in low season.
Rooms 2 suites, 28 double, 2 single – all with bath and shower, and telephone; TV on request. 1 ground-floor room.
Facilities Salon, TV room, library, bar, restaurant; conference facilities; concerts and exhibitions in cloisters; medical centre with hydrotherapy, whirlpool, massage, etc. Garden and terrace; private lakeside beach, windsurfing.
Location On E shore of Lake Annecy, 12 km SE of Annecy.
Restriction Not suitable for &.
Credit cards Access, Visa.
Terms [1989 rates] Rooms: single 580 frs, double 1,065 frs. Breakfast 50 frs. Dinner, B&B 530–775 frs per person. Set lunch/dinner 200–350 frs. Reduced rates and special meals for children.

Hôtel Beau-Site   *Tel* 50.60.71.04

This pleasant and unpretentious hotel offers an alternative to the high prices of the famous *Père Bise* and the *Abbaye*, and is also set serenely by the shores of the glorious lake of Annecy, with lovely views. Two reports this year: "A most enjoyable stay, in a large comfortable room; the food uniformly good and M. Conan an attentive and pleasant host. But the lounge is small." "The five-course 130-franc [1989] menu is marvellous value, apart from disappointing soups, and service is friendly." One reader found rooms in the venerable old annexe a bit austere. And there are hints this year of a slight drop in standards (for example, garden somewhat neglected), maybe because it seems that M. Conan is now running the hotel on his own, and his wife and daughter have moved to the *Prés du Lac* (see below). (*GE Samson, GB Hart*) More reports please.

Open 15 May–Oct.
Rooms 1 suite, 27 double, 1 single – 23 with bath, 6 with shower; 18 with TV. 10 in annexe in garden.
Facilities Lift. 3 salons, dining room; terrace. Garden with private beach on lake; tennis court.
Location Central, on Lake Annecy. Parking.
Credit cards All major cards accepted.
Terms B&B: single 247–300 frs, double 370–590 frs, suite 730–880 frs; dinner, B&B 310–575 frs per person. Set lunch/dinner 130, 170 and 235 frs; full alc 270 frs. Reduced rates and special meals for children.

Hôtel Les Prés du Lac   *Tel* 50.60.76.11
Clos Beau-Site   *Telex* 309288 PRESLAC

A select and expensive little villa of ultra-modern design, cool and bright, with lawns in front that stretch to its private beach. Pleasant welcome, good views; rooms have patios and terraces, and new annexes are being added. Open 4 Feb–11 Nov. 9 rooms, all with bath and shower. B&B double 616–1,016 frs [1989]. No restaurant, but meals can be taken at Beau-Site *(above), owned by same family. No recent reports. More welcome.*

If you think we have over-praised a hotel or done it an injustice, please let us know.

TAMNIÈS 24620 Dordogne   Map 4

Hôtel-Restaurant Laborderie   *Tel 53.29.68.59*

An attractive modern hotel in a truly rural setting, on the edge of a tiny hilltop village between Les Eyzies and Sarlat, facing out over rolling wooded country. The facade is of yellowish stone; inside are beamed ceilings and a log fire in winter. "Excellent hotel with fantastic food and a lovely swimming pool", says a reader this year. Others have referred to the "exceptional value", "pleasant" staff and "good rustic Périgourdin food" served in large helpings, especially on the four-course *demi-pension* menu (but one reader thought there was too much Périgourdin emphasis on duck and goose). Rooms are comfortable: some prefer those in the annexe, but one reader this year thought them a bit small and noisy. "It is a popular eating-place for locals, many of whom were being greeted as old friends." "A warm welcome from the Laborderie family, who are good with children. Bar and lovely terrace." (*Jo and Mick Feat, Diana Holmes, FR Bishop*)

Open 1 Apr–11 Nov.
Rooms 31 double – 24 with bath, 7 with shower, all with telephone. 16 in garden annexe.
Facilities Bar, 2 salons, TV room, 2 dining rooms; functions rooms; terrace. Garden with swimming pool. Lake nearby with swimming, fishing, windsurfing, sandy beach.
Location In centre of Tamniès which is 14 km NE of Les Eyzies. Parking.
Restriction Not suitable for &.
Credit cards Access, Visa.
Terms Double room 160–320 frs. Breakfast 25 frs. Half board 200–290 frs per person; full board 250–340 frs. Set lunch/dinner 85, 105, 150 and 240 frs; full alc 110 frs. Reduced rates for children.

TARDETS-SORHOLUS 64470 Pyrénées-Atlantiques   Map 4

Hôtel du Pont d'Abense   *Tel 59.28.54.60*
Abense-de-Haut

The old Basque medieval charades (pastorales *and* mascarades), *with their richly costumed characters, are still sometimes performed at this village southwest of Pau, where this clean, quiet and inexpensive little family-run hotel offers efficiency and friendliness, good food (some local dishes), and real value for money. Attractive small shady garden, where you can eat out in summer. Open 16 Jan–14 Nov, closed Fri out of season. 12 rooms, some with bath and shower, 130–195 frs. Breakfast 20 frs. Set menus 60–170 frs [1989]. Endorsed this year, but further reports welcome.*

THIONVILLE 57100 Moselle   Map 3

L'Horizon   *Tel 82.88.53.65*
50 route du Crève-Coeur   *Telex 860870*

This ivy-covered hostelry, smart and appealing, is an "unlikely find" on the edge of an ugly industrial town amid the decaying Lorraine steel mills, beside the Luxembourg border. But *Michelin* gives it red print for pleasantness, and our readers agree, "It is in a quiet position up on a hillside above the town, with wide views over the countryside as well as industry. We entered through wrought-iron gates, past well-kept gardens ablaze with flowers. The house is very attractive, with an elegant paved terrace at the back where you can have tea or drinks. The light and spacious hall had fresh flowers, plus a ceiling looking like something out of the *Arabian Nights*, but it was very pretty when lit up at night. Our large bedroom had French windows with wide views, and excellent lighting, but some of the fittings were a little worn. The attractive dining room had velvet drapes and a tapestry, fresh flowers and elegant table appointments. The set menu was mostly excellent, including an unusual apple sorbet between meat courses. Though quite expensive, the place has the feeling of a family-run hotel and all the staff were pleasant."

Open All year except early Jan.
Rooms 6 double, 4 single – all with bath and shower, telephone and TV. 3 in annexe
Facilities Salon, bar, TV room, breakfast room, restaurant; conference facilities; terrace. Garden.
Location 2 km NW of Thionville: follow signs to Bel-Air or Crève-Coeur. Garages.
Restriction Not suitable for &.
Credit cards All major cards accepted.
Terms Rooms 300–580 frs. Breakfast 45 frs. Set lunch 175 frs, dinner 195 frs.

TOULOUSE 31000 Haute-Garonne   Map 4

Grand Hôtel de l'Opéra   *Tel* 61.21.82.66
1 place du Capitole   *Fax* 61.23.41.04
                                        Telex 521998 ESPI

This is our only downtown entry for France's fourth largest city, capital of the European aviation and aerospace industries. Its medieval rose-pink kernel is the 18th-century place du Capitole, and here stands one of the most beautiful city hotels in the French provinces, with a superb restaurant, too. "Recently converted from a 17th-century convent, it is set back in a leafy courtyard – a haven of peace and grace in this hectic town – and is run with a personal touch by its local owners who have furnished it in period style. Most bedrooms are inviting and cosy – the best is the rococo 'Suite 1260' with its lovely pale murals. The restaurant well deserves its high ratings (two *Michelin* rosettes, two red *Gault Millau toques*): its chef and co-owner, Dominique Toulousy, local boy made good, serves delicious regional-based cuisine that is inventive without being chi-chi (pigeon with crayfish, ravioli with truffles, and an unusual cassoulet). His wife is a charming hostess. On fine days you eat under awnings in the flowery patio, beside an ornamental pool that is also the hotel's tiny swimming pool (bathers are forbidden at meal-times, as they would splash the diners)." "The restaurant has several small rooms, some of whose walls are mirrors: one has all four walls made of mirrors – a narcissist's paradise." Others have concurred: but an inspector this year felt that his room in the 700-franc bracket lacked character; and he disliked the breakfast, even more so the loud musak served with it.

> In your own interest, always check latest tariffs with hotels when you make your bookings.

Open All year. Restaurant closed 2 weeks Aug.
Rooms 15 suites, 39 double, 9 single – 61 with bath and shower, 2 with shower, all with telephone, radio, TV, and air-conditioning; most with 24-hour room service; baby-sitting on request. 4 in annexe.
Facilities Lift. Lobbies, salon, bar, restaurant, brasserie; conference facilities; sports room with sauna and whirlpool. Garden with terrace, restaurant and swimming pool.
Location Central (windows double-glazed). Underground carpark in square.
Credit cards All major cards accepted.
Terms Rooms: single 400–750 frs, double 700–750 frs, suite 980–1,150 frs. Breakfast 60 frs. Set lunch/dinner 280–380 frs (c. 150 frs in brasserie); full alc 400 frs (c. 170 frs in brasserie). Reduced rates for children sharing parents' room.

TOURNUS 71700 Saône-et-Loire   Map 4

Hotel de la Paix   *Tel* 85.51.01.85
9 rue Jean-Jaurès

In the town centre, near the Saône, an unassuming little Swiss-owned hotel, very well run, with comfortable carpeted rooms and good food. Closed 5 Jan – 1 Feb, 15–24 Apr, 21–30 Oct, Tue in winter. 23 rooms, many with bath and/or shower. Rooms 205–278 frs. Breakfast 22 frs. Set menus 68–138 frs [1989]. New nomination. More reports welcome.

Le Rempart   *Tel* 85.51.10.56
2 avenue Gambetta   *Telex* 351019

On the main street of a beautiful old town by the Saône, with a fine ancient abbey, here is a modernised hotel with unremarkable decor but bright and comfortable rooms (double-glazing keeps out the noise) and affable service. Pretentious-looking menu, but excellent regional cooking (frogs' legs in garlic, etc.), deserving its rosette and toque. Open all year. 38 rooms, all with bath. B&B: single 300–330 frs, double 490 frs. Set menus 150–350 frs. Recent nomination. More reports welcome.

TOURS 37000 Indre-et-Loire   Map 2

Hôtel Colbert   *Tel* 47.66.61.56
78 rue Colbert

A small family-run B&B hotel, in a narrow shopping street near the cathedral and within walking distance of the pleasantly restored Vieux Tours quarter, full of bars and little restaurants. Clean and comfortable, efficient and friendly. 18 rooms, most with bath and/or shower. B&B 208–306 frs. No restaurant. Recent nomination. More reports welcome.

Hôtel Royal   *Tel* 47.64.71.78
65 avenue de Grammont   *Telex* 752006 LE ROYAL

On a main street close to the centre of Tours, but quiet: a useful modernised hotel with Louis XV and XVI 'repro' furnishings, good bathrooms and breakfasts, friendly service, and garage. No restaurant, but lots nearby. 35 rooms, all with bath and shower, 265–312 frs. Breakfast 29 frs. New nomination. More reports welcome.

TOURTOUR 83690 Var   Map 5

La Bastide de Tourtour   *Tel* 94.70.57.30
                                                              Telex 970827

The medieval hill-village of Tourtour is today a fashionable residential
centre and a showpiece: its lovely facades of golden-brown stone have
been scoured clean. There are wide vistas on all sides, and the Gorges du
Verdon are quite close. *La Bastide*, smart and expensive, was custom-built
in the 1960s in mock-château style, and stands in its own wooded garden
on the edge of the village. An enthusiastic report this year refers to the
"calm, relaxing atmosphere amongst the fragrant pines", as well as to
"courteous service and excellent cuisine – the pension menu was different
on all eight nights of our stay." Last year, another reader was also
pleased, "I had a large and cheery room with cloth-covered walls and
matching bed-covers. First-floor balcony rooms face the big swimming
pool and are just above the outdoor dining terrace. This makes for some
noise and lack of privacy, and I'd rather recommend the second-floor
rooms which also have a better view. The food was superb (*Michelin*
rosette), especially the ravioli stuffed with goats' cheese and the
sweetbreads in a wine sauce. The dining room is intimate and romantic,
with doors open to the terrace. Etienne and Francine Laurent, the owners,
work hard to give their guests a perfect stay." They also enjoy showing
their rare collection of 200 peasant bonnets and hats. (*M and D Chambers,
Susan Schmidt*)

Open 15 Mar–31 Oct. Restaurant closed Tue midday, Mon in low season.
Rooms 23 double, 2 single – all with bath and shower, telephone and TV.
Facilities Lift. Lounge, bar, restaurant; exercise room and jacuzzi. Garden with
swimming pool and tennis court.
Location 500 m SE of Tourtour on road to Draguignan (20 km). Parking.
Credit cards All major cards accepted.
Terms Rooms: single 350–450 frs, double 400–1,100 frs. Breakfast 60 frs. Set
lunch 150 frs (except Sun) 250 and 330 frs; dinner 250 and 330 frs; full alc 350 frs.
Reduced rates and special meals for children.

TRÉBEURDEN 22560 Côtes-du-Nord   Map 2

Hôtel Ti al-Lannec   *Tel* 96.23.57.26
Allée de Mézo Guen   *Telex* 740656

Few other seaside hotels in France are more warmly liked by readers than
this handsome grey-and-white mansion, set high above the sea in its
quiet garden on the edge of a pleasant family bathing resort; it's on an
especially delightful stretch of the North Breton coast, where rocks in
strange shapes alternate with sandy coves. "A marvellous hotel with
excellent food and charming staff; our beautifully furnished room had
panoramic views over the bay"; "a superb meal and luxurious lounges".
Those two 1988/9 reports echo many earlier ones. The large balconies,
immaculate gardens, and attentive owners are all praised. Some rooms
have four-poster beds. A big light dining room with sea views; snug,

---

Don't trust out-of-date Guides. Many hotels are dropped and new
ones added every year.

---

elegant lounge with period decor; white tables and chairs under parasols and trees on the lawn. Rare for a summer seaside hotel, the cooking (seafood especially) wins a red *Gault Millau toque*. (*Mrs JP Holwell, ECM Begg, BH Jenkinson, and others*) Also recommended this year is another very select hotel in Trébeurden, the *Manoir de Lan-Kerellec* (telephone 96.23.50.09), rather more expensive and with possibly even better food (*Michelin* rosette): we'd be glad of reports on that too.

Open 17 Mar–12 Nov. Restaurant closed Mon lunchtime 18 Sept–12 Jun.
Rooms 21 double, 2 single – all with bath and shower, and telephone; TV on request.
Facilities Salon, TV/games room, bar, restaurant; conference facilities. Garden with outdoor chess, table tennis and boules; path leading down to sandy beach, safe bathing and fishing.
Location In centre of village. Signposted from Lannion.
Restriction Not suitable for &.
Credit cards Access, Amex, Visa.
Terms [1989 rates] Rooms: single 295 frs, double 540 frs. Breakfast 42 frs. Dinner, B&B 375–455 frs per person. Set lunch/dinner 155–285 frs. Reduced rates for children under 8; special menus.

TRÉGUIER 22220 Côtes-du-Nord   Map 2

Kastell Dinec'h   *Tel* 96.92.49.39

Tréguier is an old grey Breton town with a fine cathedral, not far from the beaches of Perros-Guirec and Trébeurden. Just outside it, liberally daubed in red print by the French guides, is this promising Guide newcomer: "A charming little hotel set quietly down a country lane. It's an old farmhouse in a pretty garden (with small swimming pool); the comfortable rooms, nicely decorated in Laura Ashley-ish prints, are in the main house and a converted stable block. The food deserves its *Michelin* red 'R': we enjoyed salmon with sorrel sauce, a cassolette of lobster tails, chicken with morels, scallops in Pernod sauce. Good breakfasts, too, and friendly service. Not the place to avoid fellow-Brits." (But where is, in northern France these days?) (*Mrs J Thomas*)

Open 15 Mar–12 Oct, 27 Oct–31 Dec. Closed Tue evening and Wed in low season. Restaurant closed for lunch
Rooms 15 – most with bath and/or shower.
Facilities Lounge, restaurant. Garden with small swimming pool.
Location 2 km SW of Tréguier, off the Lannion road.
Credit cards Access, Visa.
Terms Rooms 220–350 frs. Breakfast 35 frs. Dinner, B&B 240–320 frs per person. Set dinner 90–240 frs.

TRÉMOLAT 24510 Dordogne   Map 4

Hôtel Panoramic   *Tel* 53.22.80.42
Route du Cingle de Trémolat

In a superb position overlooking a great loop in the Dordogne river, just outside Trémolat village (where Chabrol set and filmed Le Boucher*), this old stone mansion is now an unpretentious hotel where the welcome is warm, the rooms plain but pleasant, and the food excellent, including breakfast; terrace for drinks and meals, with that fine view. Closed Jan, maybe also Dec. 24 rooms, most with* *private facilities. B&B double 296 frs. Set menus 60–195 frs. Newly nominated for good value. More reports welcome.*

TRIGANCE 83840 Var   **Map 5**

Château de Trigance   *Tel* 94.76.91.18

We've had a mixed bag of reports in 1988/9 for this "most idiosyncratic hotel" – a boldly battlemented medieval pile on a hilltop above the village of Trigance, only about ten kilometres from the dramatic Gorges du Verdon in upper Provence. Access is not easy, by a steep rocky path and stone stair, but you are rewarded by wide views over the encircling rocky hills, where one reader "felt a great sense of pastoral peace" as he watched a flock of sheep being herded. The castle is owned by Jean-Claude Thomas, a Paris ex-businessman, who has turned it into a small hotel. "The physical setting is dramatic and M. Thomas is a superb and entertaining host. I find myself chuckling whenever I recall our stay." "Very imposing from a distance. Warm personal welcome – it's worth staying just to converse with the owner. Rooms are severe and dark, but reasonably priced. Dining room and bar charming; food average. A unique place full of heart." "The only noises to disrupt us were the sheepbells and the cuckoos. But the food was pretentious and disappointing." Some readers have enjoyed the "romantic vaulted restaurant", but one has disliked its "medieval chamber music"; some have warmed to the "lovely canopied beds", but others have found the rooms a bit oppressive. (*David and Lynne Allen, William A Grant, and others*) A new entrance is planned, eliminating the steep steps – "pity, for the access is part of the charm."

Open 18 Mar–11 Nov. Restaurant closed Wed midday in Mar, Apr, Oct, Nov.
Rooms 2 suites, 8 double – all with bath and shower, telephone and TV.
Facilities Salon, dining room, large terrace.
Location 20 km SW of Castellane, 12 km NW of Comps-sur-Artuby.
Restriction Not suitable for &.
Credit cards All major cards accepted.
Terms B&B: double 500–660 frs, suite 730 frs. Set lunch/dinner 160, 220 and 300 frs. Reduced rates for children; special meals on request.

UZÈS 30700 Gard   **Map 4**

Hôtel d'Entraigues   *Tel* 66.22.32.68
8 rue de la Calade

In the rolling *garrigue* country north of Nîmes, an enchanting old town of narrow streets and lofty towers: the tallest belongs to the massive turreted ducal castle. Secluded in one of the alleys below is the *Entraigues*, a 16th-century mansion once the home of a general. Its conversion into a select little hotel is supremely aesthetic but not cosy – soft-hued stone and dim-lit low-vaulted ceilings. It is under the same ownership as the *Château* at Arpaillargues (q.v.) and could provide a useful and cheaper alternative. You can eat out on a terrace. "Comfortable and very good value: croissants delicious", is one report this year. Uzès has a classical music festival in July, and quaint country fairs in the main square throughout the year – e.g. pig fair in February, garlic fair in June.

Open All year. Restaurant closed midday on Tue and Wed in season, all day Tue, Wed midday in low season.
Rooms 17 double, 1 single – all with bath, shower, telephone; some with TV. Some in annexe.
Facilities Salons, TV room, bar, restaurant.
Location Central, opposite cathedral, but quietly situated. Uzès is 25 km N of Nîmes. Parking.
Restriction Not suitable for &.
Credit cards All major cards accepted.
Terms [1989 rates] Rooms 225–350 frs. Breakfast 25 and 30 frs. Half board 135 frs per person added to room rates. Set lunch/dinner 75 and 130 frs; full alc 210 frs. Extra bed in room 70 frs. Special meals for children on request.

VALENCE 26000 Drôme
Map 4

Restaurant Pic
285 avenue Victor-Hugo
Tel 75.44.15.32

In a tree-lined street on the edge of dusty Valence, in the Rhône valley, Jacques Pic and his charming wife run one of France's most renowned restaurants: he earns three *Michelin* rosettes, just as his father did here in the 1930s. As well as a shady garden and just four pretty bedrooms, they offer *nouvelle cuisine* at its least affected, fully worth the high prices. One recent visitor found the meal "elegant" and had a "marvellous" room with oriental rugs and marble bathroom. An American reader adds, "Splendid food, perfect and charming service. We were invited to the kitchen after dinner." "Helpful staff, incredible (but simple) comfort in the bedrooms and total luxury in the dining room. The whole place is so undaunting, the atmosphere is charming and there's no snootiness by anyone, in contrast to what happens at many other prestigious places. Breakfast a dream of warm fresh lemon brioche." (*Ed and Meg Raftis, CM*)

Open All year except Aug and 1 week in Feb. Closed Wed, and Sun evening.
Rooms 2 suites, 2 double – all with bath and shower, telephone and TV.
Facilities Sitting room, dining room. Courtyard and garden.
Location 1 km S of town centre. Take *autoroute* exit for Valence Sud, follow "Victor Hugo" sign. Parking.
Restriction Not suitable for &.
Credit cards All major cards accepted.
Terms Rooms: double 400–420 frs, suite 550–700 frs. Breakfast 50 frs. Set lunch 400–500 frs; full alc 500-600 frs. Special meals for children.

VALLIÈRES 37230 Indre et Loire
Map 2

Manoir du Grand Martigny
Tel 47.42.29.87

Friendly and inexpensive guest house in 16-acre park, five kilometres west of Tours in 16th-century manor lovingly restored by M. and Mme Desmarais who speak excellent English. "Makes no pretence of being commercially run; atmosphere relaxed and warm; excellent breakfasts. Ideal for Loire sightseeing." Open Mar–Nov, by arrangement in winter. 7 rooms, all with private facilities. B&B double 370–500 frs [1989]. Evening meals not normally served, but dinner en famille *by arrangement for minimum of 6, 160 frs with wine. New nomination. More reports please.*

VAL SUZON 21121 Côte d'Or

Map 4

Hostellerie du Val Suzon and
Chalet de la Fontaine aux Geais
Val Suzon Fontaine-lès-Dijon

Tel 80.35.60.15
Telex 351454

This hamlet north-west of Dijon is a good base for visiting the city – and here you will find Burgundian rusticity at more moderate prices than in most of our entries for this sophisticated Dijon/Beaune area. It is a double entry – a restaurant-with-rooms and a small chalet-hotel close by, both owned by the same family. A reader suggests, "The best bet is to book a room at the *Chalet*, a two-minute walk up the hill above the *Hostellerie*: its rooms are quieter and more spacious, and have a nice outlook across the gardens to the hills beyond. The grounds are well manicured and contain two aviaries (*geai*=jay). The *Hostellerie* is the restaurant for both buildings; the food is almost one-rosette standard, far better than at many similar country places around, and you can eat outside on fine days or by the fire in winter. The whole place has an air of unpretentious efficiency and relaxed charm." Readers this year have commented on the attractive setting, friendly owners and staff, good value and good cooking (*Gault Millau* gives it two *toques* for such dishes as ravioli of morilles with foie gras). (*ME Chamberland, PJ Robinson, Michel Bourdrez*)

Open 15 Jan–15 Nov. Closed Wed and Thur lunchtime 15 Jan – 30 Apr.
Rooms 16 double, 1 single – 9 with bath and shower, 8 with shower, all with telephone. 10 in the *Chalet*.
Facilities Lounge, bar, 2 dining rooms. Garden.
Location 16 km NW of Dijon, just off N71 to Châtillon.
Restriction Not suitable for &.
Credit cards All major cards accepted.
Terms Rooms: single 220 frs, double 340 frs. Breakfast 40 frs. Dinner, B&B: single 440 frs, double 700 frs. Set lunch/dinner 140, 200 and 320 frs; full alc 300 frs. Reduced rates and special meals for children.

VANNES 56000 Morbihan

Map 2

Le Roof
Presque'île de Conleau

Tel 97.63.47.47
Telex 951843

In a pleasant waterside setting on the Gulf of Morbihan, just south of Vannes, this spruce white-walled hotel with its odd franglais *name has an outdoor dining terrace facing the bay, and serves good fish. Large bar, smallish bedrooms. Rebuilding and enlarging in progress, 1989. 43 rooms, all with bath and shower. B&B double 360–460 frs. Set menus 70–300 frs. New nomination. More reports welcome.*

VELLERON 84740 Vaucluse

Map 5

Hostellerie de la Grangette

Tel 90.20.00.77

A beautifully converted manor house, alone in the open country of the Vaucluse plain, just off the main D938 from L'Isle-sur-Sorgue to Carpentras. Semi-wild grounds with pool and tennis; ornate bedrooms with oak beams, antiques, draped curtains, and views of the Provençal hills. Willing staff, and good sophisticated food (not cheap) in a lovely dining room. 17 rooms, all with bath and or shower. B&B double 500–710 frs. Set menus 139–375 frs. Recent nomination. More reports please.

VENCE 06140 Alpes-Maritimes   Map 5

Relais Cantemerle   *Tel* 93.58.08.18
258 chemin Cantemerle

In a peaceful setting on the southern outskirts of much-visited Vence, this smart little modern hotel in local Provençal style, lyrically attractive, consists of a sequence of self-contained split-level apartments, set around a swimming pool and garden, beautifully landscaped, with lawns well manicured. Breezy modern decor with traditional touches. A report this year, "An enormous room with a lovely antique bureau, very good dinner (perfect noisettes d'agneau), well-groomed staff, maybe a bit too laid-back, a peaceful, friendly ambience and fantastic value for money". (*K Jardine-Young*)

Open 15 Mar–end Oct. Restaurant closed Wed.
Rooms 19 – all with bath, shower, telephone, TV, mini-bar and terrace.
Facilities Lounge, bar, restaurant. Garden with unheated swimming pool; terrace, where meals are served.
Location 1 km S of Vence. Parking.
Restriction Not suitable for &.
Credit cards All major cards accepted.
Terms Rooms [1989 rates] 550–790 frs. Breakfast 60 frs. Dinner, B&B 250 frs per person added. Set lunch/dinner 200 frs; full alc 300 frs. Reduced rates and special meals for children.

Hôtel Diana   *Tel* 93.58.28.56
Avenue des Poilus

Several returning regulars have again enjoyed this well-run modern hotel near the centre of a busy little Provençal town. Bowls of flowers, helpful staff – just one gripe about inadequate dusting of rooms. Not all rooms are spacious, but they are nicely designed and furnished, with well-equipped *cuisinettes* (washing up is part of the hotel's service). The underground garage is not easy to operate: take advice. Breakfasts are variously described as "generous" or "adequate". The hotel has no restaurant, but it will prepare snacks such as omelettes, while not far away the inexpensive *Farigoule* is again commended. Do not miss Matisse's lovely Chapel of the Rosary in Vence itself (open Tuesdays and Thursdays only), nor the mountain drive to the north, the *circuit des clues*. (*Philippa Herbert, Kay and Neville Varley*)

Open All year.
Rooms 25 double – all with bath and telephone; 15 with kitchenette.
Facilities Lift. 2 salons with TV, bar, library, 2 breakfast rooms. Terrace; solarium.
Location 100 metres from town centre. Garage.
Restriction Not suitable for &.
Credit cards All major cards accepted.
Terms Rooms 300 frs. Breakfast 35 frs. (No restaurant.)

VERVINS 02140 Aisne   Map 3

La Tour du Roy   *Tel* 23.98.00.11
45 rue du Général Leclerc   *Telex* 155445

A converted manor house, built on the ramparts of a small town near the
Belgian border, in an area of orchards and streams. It is run with warmth
and skill by Annie Desvignes, who is also chef – and the food (*Michelin*
rosette) and service have again been admired this year. "Annie's robust
and enthusiastic presence was obvious, and Monsieur, too, was full of
bonhomie, while the staff were cheerful and attentive, especially with
children. We have memories of a delicious light monkfish mousseline
with prawn sauce, mixed fish with ginger sauce, and a cheese trolley that
sent you to bed dreaming." Another reader also liked the food and Annie,
but thought her room "fairly basic". Not all are basic, however, as
witness this earlier account: "When we asked for a 'nice' room, Madame
said, 'We will put you in the Tower', and opening our front door we
found ourselves in an enormous circular bathroom with large near-
circular bath, and a toilet which was literally a throne, made of decorative
porcelain, with chair back and arm rests. We then climbed the spiral
staircase to another circular room with a high-domed ceiling, a small
decorative sink, and our bed. It was kitschy but comfortable." The hotel is
exceptionally kind to children, and it has a pretty garden. (*Diana Cooper*)
Front rooms can be noisy.

Open All year except 15 Jan–15 Feb.
Rooms 1 triple, 13 double, 1 single – all with bath and/or shower, telephone,
radio, TV, mini-bar and baby-listening. 2 ground-floor rooms in bungalow annexe.
Facilities Salon, bar, TV room, restaurant; functions room.
Location Vervins is off N2, 71 km N of Reims. Hotel is central. Parking.
Credit cards All major cards accepted.
Terms Rooms: single 200–250 frs, double 200–380 frs, suite 450 frs. Breakfast 40
frs. Dinner, B&B: single 390 frs, double 680 frs. Full alc 325 frs. Reduced rates and
special meals for children.

VÉZAC 24220 Dordogne   Map 4

Rochecourbe   *Tel* 53.29.50.79

A small manor house amid lush meadows and gentle wooded hills, in one
of the loveliest parts of the Dordogne valley, between Beynac and
Domme. "We were delighted with this charming old house", runs a letter
this year; "we had a large, comfortable room and liked the beautifully
furnished salon – such comfortable antiques are rare in French hotels.
Service friendly and attentive." Others have spoken of the charm of the
owners, the Rogers. "The old house has been restored with great care.
Our spacious room looked out on three castles. Breakfasts are excellent."
A spiral staircase in the tower leads from the garden (reclining chairs for
drinks) up to the bedrooms. This quiet rural setting is slightly marred by a
nearby road and railway, but "they do not intrude unduly". No
restaurant, but Madame will serve residents with light meals to order:
"Excellent cooking, especially the warm salads of smoked duck breast,
crisp skinned trout and luscious puddings." (*Mrs JW Makinson, David Lees*)

Open Probably 1 May–31 Oct.
Rooms 1 suite, 4 double – all with bath and shower, and telephone.

Facilities Salon with TV, breakfast room. Garden.
Location 8 km SW of Sarlat on D57.
Credit cards Access, Visa.
Terms B&B: double 350 frs, suite 450 frs. (No restaurant.)

VÉZELAY 89450 Yonne   **Map 4**

L'Espérance   *Tel* 86.33.20.45
St-Père   *Fax* 86.33.26.15
                                                        Telex 800005

Just as the hilltop Romanesque basilica of Vézelay, in northern Burgundy,
is one of France's 20 finest buildings, so Marc Meneau's *Espérance* is one
of its 20 finest restaurants (three *Michelin* rosettes, four red *Gault Millau
toques*). Small and very chic, it lies in a valley just east of the little town,
on the Avallon road. Antique furniture, strikingly pretty bedrooms; a
garden with a rose arbour and a stream lit up at night. Many bedrooms
are in the nearby converted mill. With some caveats, approval this year
has again been intense: "Very expensive, but value for money; as near
perfect a French hotel/restaurant as I know. Our suite in the mill
displayed impeccable taste and luxury, the bathroom being the ultimate
for any sybarite (it included a huge cactus). An immense basket of fruit
was delivered. Service and reception are very welcoming and friendly,
the food needless to say is superb (never has one been so overwhelmed
with chocolates at the end of a meal), and breakfast (with scrambled eggs,
etc) is the best one has had in France." "An attractive suite in the mill,
with expensive if rather heavy rustic-style decor. In the dining room,
looking onto the attractive garden, we enjoyed oysters in watercress
aspic, brilliant salmon in apple sauce, but the puddings are lack-lustre."
The restaurant is in three big glass pavilions full of house plants. Earlier
reports: "Sipping drinks on the terrace or in the glass-domed cocktail bar
to the sound of a grand piano is a delight. Marc Meneau greets diners
with a modest charm. (*Phillip Gill, Helen and Charles Priday, Rosamund
Hebdon and others*) One couple begged to differ, feeling that the hotel had
become very commercial since their last visit – tour coaches, a gift shop
selling purses (!) and staff less friendly than before.

Open All year except early Jan–early Feb. Restaurant closed Tue and Wed
midday.
Rooms 4 suites, 17 double – all with bath and shower, telephone, radio and TV;
babysitter on request. 8 in annexe.
Facilities Lounge, bar, restaurant. Garden.
Location 3 km E of Vézelay on D957.
Credit cards Amex, Diners, Visa.
Terms [1989 rates] Rooms 600–950 frs. Breakfast 90 frs. Set lunch 280 frs, dinner
520 frs.

Résidence Hôtel Le Pontot   *Tel* 86.33.24.40
Place de la Mairie

A fine 15th-century stone house, with 18th-century additions, situated
near the town centre with superb views over the rooftops and the rolling
countryside below. It has long been the home of Charles Thum, an
American architect, who has converted it into a select and charming bed-
and-breakfast hotel, managed by Christian Abadie. An inspector has

written recently: "We were treated with great courtesy, as though we had come to stay in a private house. You enter through an arched doorway into a delightful small walled garden; a stone-flagged spiral stairway leads up to the bedrooms which share a small pleasant lounge. Our suite of two rooms and bathroom was ideal for a couple with children; it was comfortable, furnished with a mixture of antiques and simple modern pieces. Breakfast, beautifully presented with blue and gold Limoges china, can be taken in the garden or in a blue-panelled Louis XV salon; coffee and croissants were excellent. "Superb bedroom and breakfasts. Messieurs Thum and Abadie were attentive and erudite hosts, and the measures of drinks were gigantic, served in attractive glassware."

Open 17 Mar–Nov.
Rooms 3 suites, 7 double – 9 with bath, 1 with shower, all with telephone, radio and coffee-making facilities. 1 suite in separate wing.
Facilities Entrance hall with boutique, lounge, bar, breakfast room. Walled garden with breakfast and bar service in fine weather. Canal trips, hot-air ballooning by prearrangement.
Location Central. "Ignore signs at entrance to town inviting tourists to walk. Drive straight up main street to Place de la Mairie and park."
Restriction Not suitable for &.
Credit cards Access, Amex, Visa.
Terms Rooms: double 450–600 frs, suite 550–750 frs. Breakfast 50 frs. Extra bed 100 frs for children sharing parents' room. (No restaurant).

VIEILLE-TOULOUSE 31320 Haute-Garonne   Map 4

Hôtel de la Flânerie   *Tel* 61.73.39.12
Route de Lacroix-Falgarde   *Telex* 531666

An unusual little hotel six miles south of Toulouse along D4, on a hillside with a splendid view over the curving Garonne just below. The cosy bedrooms are got up in kitschy boudoir style, with a nicely naughty flavour. Period furnishings, affable and very helpful owners, sleek lounge (with questionable decor), and a lovely terrace above the river where drinks and the (very good) breakfasts can be served. Central Toulouse is 15 minutes by car, more at rush hour. 12 rooms, all with bath or shower. Rooms 175–290 frs, breakfast 36 frs [1989]. No restaurant (but TV *suppers served). Recent nomination. More reports would be welcome.*

VILLEFRANCHE-SUR-MER 06230 Alpes-Maritimes   Map 5

Hôtel Welcome et Restaurant   *Tel* 93.76.76.93
  St-Pierre   *Telex* 470281
1 quai Courbet

Villefranche is a lively and colourful old fishing-port on a deep bay – remarkably unspoilt, seeing that Nice and Monte Carlo are both so close. The *Welcome*, a classic and dignified hotel recently modernised, stands on the harbour opposite the tiny fishermen's chapel decorated by Cocteau. In the past its name has sometimes been judged inappropriate, but this year a reader found the staff "charming" – and the food excellent. "Rooms reasonable, with harbourside balconies; the smaller ones at the top, though without bath, are the most quiet and pleasant." "A few faults, such as broken lamp-bulbs, but the food at the delightful ground-floor *St-*

Pierre restaurant was exceptional, especially fish in a variety of ways" (if you want a cheaper and less smart alternative for a meal, try *Ste-Germaine* down the quay, says a reader). Night noises may include some trains, and: "The US Navy was in town and 'Jingle Bells' outside the door at 2 am was not 'Welcome'." (*Peter Wade, Brian MacArthur*)

Open All year except 25 Nov–18 Dec.
Rooms 35 – all with bath and/or shower, telephone, mini-bar and air-conditioning; TV on request.
Facilities Lift, ramps. Breakfast room, bar with TV, restaurant. Terrace. 600 m from beach; windsurfing, scuba diving etc.
Location Central, on quai. Parking nearby.
Credit cards All major cards accepted.
Terms [1989 rates] Rooms 490–770 frs. Breakfast 35 frs. Dinner, B&B 290–525 frs per person. Set lunch/dinner 145–310 frs. Reduced rates and special meals for children.

VILLENEUVE-DE-RIVIÈRE 31800 Haute-Garonne   Map 4

Hostellerie des Cèdres   *Tel* 61.89.36.00

In a village just west of St-Gaudens, near the Pyrenean foothills, a stylishly converted 17th-century manor with cedars and palms in its wide courtyard. Garden with swimming pool. Large, pretty rooms (the lightest have shower, not bath). Good regional cooking (Gault Millau toque). 18 rooms, all with bath and/or shower. B&B double 356–526 frs. Set menus 120–265 frs. Attractive new nomination. More reports welcome.

VILLENEUVE-LEZAVIGNON 30400 Gard   Map 5

Hostellerie le Prieuré   *Tel* 90.25.18.20
7 place du Chapitre   *Fax* 90.25.45.39
                                                     Telex 431042

The town of Villeneuve contains almost as much of interest as Avignon itself, directly across the Rhône. Relics of the great age when the popes held sway in their palace include the gigantic Chartreuse, the Fort St-André, the municipal museum (superb painting by Enguerrand Charonton) and the church of Notre-Dame with its remarkable carved ivory statuette of the Virgin. Next to this church is the *Prieuré*, a 14th-century priory, well converted and run with panache by the Mille family as an elegant and sophisticated little hotel. It looks out over fields and an ugly school building.

"I judge this to be the nearly perfect hotel", says a returning admirer this year; "it is larger and grander than when I knew it in the old days, but the Milles have managed to keep an air of informality, and service is excellent. The garden is pleasant and the big shady terrace delightful. The food is not of the highest flight but good and reliable." (*Jacquetta Priestley*) Others have written: "A superb place, expensive but not unfairly so. We had lovely rooms in a new block, with balconies facing the pool. Dinner by candle-light on the lawn under the plane trees is most romantic." "A very special place. The public rooms and gardens are delightful, the service faultless. We preferred the rooms in the old building to those in the new extension." "Beautiful, desirable and totally romantic." (*M and D*

Chambers; also SJ) You can choose between a "characterful" bedroom in the old building (antiques, but modern bathrooms) or a larger, more expensive one in a new annexe (wide balcony, big sofas). Noise from a nearby railway has irritated some readers.

Open 10 Mar–8 Nov. Restaurant closed 1 May.
Rooms 10 suites, 19 double, 7 single – all with bath, shower, telephone, radio, T V, double glazing, air-conditioning. 17 rooms in annexe. Some have access for &.
Facilities Lift. 2 salons, bridge room, library, bar, breakfast room, dining room and dining patio. Large garden with 2 tennis courts and swimming pool.
Location 3 km N of Avignon. In village centre, behind the church. Carpark.
Credit cards All major cards accepted.
Terms B&B: single 525 frs, double 930–1,130 frs, suite 1,350–1,700 frs; dinner, B&B: single 785 frs, double 1,450–1,650 frs, suite 1,870–2,220 frs. Set lunch/dinner 220–380 frs; full alc 360 frs. Special meals for children on request.

VONNAS 01540 Ain   Map 4

Hôtel-Restaurant Georges Blanc   *Tel* 74.50.00.10
                                                                  Fax 74.50.08.80
                                                          Telex 380776 GEBLANC

"In our opinion, easily the best of France's three-rosette establishments", is the weighty judgment of two of our most trusty connoisseurs of the French scene, who have again revisited M. Blanc's famous and sophisticated little hotel-restaurant. Half-timbered and pink-bricked, it stands in pretty countryside beside the river Veyle on the edge of a quiet *village fleuri* between Mâcon and Bourg-en-Bresse. "Our dinner was superb, the hotel is always immaculate, the staff welcoming and friendly: when I arrived for lunch with my jacket soaked in a storm, Madame Blanc immediately dried and pressed it." Her husband retains his top-level rating of three rosettes and four red gables in *Michelin*, and four red *toques* in *Gault Millau*, and our readers remain *d'accord* as ever. "They are always happy to serve just one or two light courses, if you are staying for lunch *and* dinner and two full meals are too much." "Better than ever, with new recipes and puddings", is another comment this year; "and the sommelier, who is English, knows his job to perfection". "Georges Blanc *is* Vonnas, with two shops in the village selling his provisions and souvenirs. But there's a refreshing candour about his enterprise. His chefs can be seen at work as you walk through the kitchen to the large elegant dining room with its beamed ceiling, antiques and tapestries." Rooms vary in grandeur, some are small and plain, some huge with marble bathroom. A "winter garden" – a bar/lounge area, which can become a riverside terrace in summer, but with a roaring log fire in winter – has recently been added. (*Pat and Jeremy Temple, M and D Chambers, David Grant*) An 11-room annexe, *La Cour aux fleurs*, was being added in 1989.

Open All year except 2 Jan–9 Feb. Restaurant closed Wed and Thur (except 15 June–15 Sept when open Thur evening).
Rooms 6 suites, 35 double – all with bath and/or shower, telephone, T V, mini-bar and air-conditioning. 11 in annexe.
Facilities Lift. 2 lounges, breakfast room, bar, dining room; conference room; winter garden, terrace on river Veyle. 2½-acre grounds with tennis court, putting-green, swimming pool and helipad.
Location 20 km E of Mâcon. From N leave *autoroute* at Mâcon Nord; from S leave *autoroute* at Villefranche, then direction Châtillon-sur-Chalaronne, Neuville-les-Dames and Vonnas.

Credit cards All major cards accepted.
Terms Rooms: double 450–1,000 frs, suite 1,900 frs. Breakfast 65 frs. Set meals 350 and 540 frs; full alc 540 frs. Special meals for children.

WIERRE-EFFROY 62720 Pas-de-Calais   Map 3

Ferme-Auberge du Vert   *Tel* 21.92.82.10

A number of French farms nowadays have turned themselves into small *auberges* while retaining their farming activities. This one, just off the Boulogne to Calais road, in a truly rural setting, provides visitors with an opportunity to move straight from the hassle of hovercraft and ferries into the bosom of French peasant life – into a real farmyard full of ducks and geese. And a number of readers in 1988/9 have again been enthusiastic. It is not exactly a hotel, and the pine-clad rooms fashioned from converted barns are fairly small and a bit basic, but they are very clean and good value. One reader adored sleeping in a modernised hayloft, another found the early cries of geese an acceptable alarm clock. Everyone likes the charm and skilful management of the Bernard family. They have now handed over the restaurant to separate management, and it gets very crowded with local French at weekends, but the food is still approved by readers as sound and unpretentious, not aiming at high gastronomy. Recent comments: "A delightful place, with total peace"; "M. Bernard is a genial host and his prices absurdly reasonable"; "Breakfast was as substantial as required, with coffee drunk in traditional bowls. A really warm welcome with lots of handshaking." Bicycles are for hire. (*Jo and Mick Feat, BN Turvey, H Schon, PJ Robinson, HR, and others*)

Open All year. Restaurant closed 15 Dec–31 Jan.
Rooms 1 suite, 13 double, 1 single – 2 with bath and shower, 13 with shower, all with telephone; suite has TV. 12 in 2 farm buildings. 4 ground-floor rooms.
Facilities Salon with TV, bar/restaurant, breakfast room.
Location Off N1 between Calais (N) and Boulogne (S); SE of Marquise. Follow signs "Ferme H** Auberge" from Marquise and from Hypermarket Auchan.
Credit card Visa.
Terms B&B: single 250 frs, double 400 frs. Set lunch/dinner 80–150 frs. Reduced rates and special meals for children.

****
Traveller's tale *Through the whole south of France, the inns are cold, damp, dark, dismal and dirty; the landlords equally disobliging and rapacious; the servants awkward, sluttish and slothful; and the postillions lazy, lounging, greedy and impertinent. If you chide them for lingering, they will continue to delay you the longer; if you chastise them with sword, cane, cudgel, or horse-whip, they will either disappear entirely, and leave you without resource; or they will find means to take vengeance by overturning your carriage. The best method I know of travelling with any degree of comfort is to allow yourself to become the dupe of imposition, and stimulate their endeavours by extraordinary gratifications.*
Tobias Smollett (Travels through France and Italy, 1766)
****

Germany

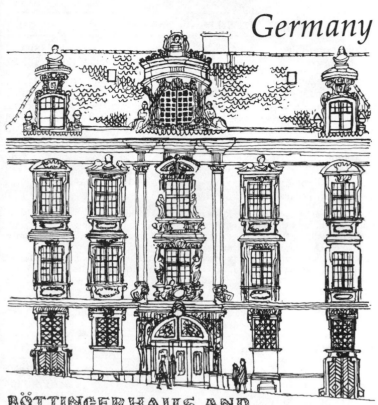

BÖTTINGERHAUS AND GÄSTEHAUS STEINMÜHLE, BAMBERG

ALFDORF 7077 Baden-Württemberg Map 7

Haghof Hotel-Restaurant Tel (07182) 5 45
Telex 7246712

In pleasant Swabian countryside east of Stuttgart, near Schwäbisch Gmünd, a modern purpose-built hotel whose spacious rooms have balconies and local-style wooden furniture; very good Swabian cooking (Michelin red "Karte" for good value) and buffet breakfast. Swimming pool; golf-course next door. 50 rooms, all with bath. B&B double 125–135 DM. Full alc 33–60 DM [1989]. New nomination. More reports welcome.

We asked hotels to estimate their 1990 tariffs. About a quarter of the hotels on the Continent failed to reply, so the prices we quote should not be relied upon.

ALT-DUVENSTEDT 2371 Schleswig-Holstein   Map 7

Hotel Töpferhaus   *Tel* (04338) 3 33
Am Bistensee   Restaurant (04338) 2 22

Approved again this year for its "excellent" main meals and breakfasts, and its "kindly proprietor", this stylish rural hotel lies in the pleasantly pastoral Schleswig plain just east of the Hamburg–Flensburg *Autobahn*. Reached down a drive through woods, it is an attractive white-painted building with thatched roof, on a bluff above a lake. Inside, there are Persian rugs on the floor, a very comfortable lounge, and sizeable bedrooms. An inspector's "faultless meal" included labskaus, the traditional sailors' dish of North Germany – a hash of pickled meat, herring and potato with fried eggs, tasting a bit like a pickled shepherd's pie. (*Russell W Field Jnr, TH Monteith*)

Open All year except 2–30 Jan. Restaurant closed Mon.
Rooms 8 double, 4 single – 10 with bath, 2 with shower, all with telephone.
Facilities Hall, lounge, breakfast room, restaurant in annexe. Garden with terrace and lawns. On lake; swimming and sailing; riding and golf nearby.
Location 12 km N of Rendsburg; leave *Autobahn* at Rendsburg-Nord if coming from S, at Owschlag if coming from N. Hotel is at S end of Bistensee. *Note:* do not go towards town of Bistensee on N side of lake.
Credit cards None accepted.
Terms [1989 rates] Rooms: single 60–85 DM, double 130–150 DM. Breakfast 12 DM. Meals 25–50 DM. Reduced rates and special meals for children.

AUERBACH 8572 Bayern   Map 7

Romantik Hotel Goldener Löwe   *Tel* (09643) 17 65
Unterer Markt 9   *Telex* 631404

"This ordinary little North Bavarian town used to be an iron-mining centre", writes our nominator this year, "and the theme is assertively reflected in the decor of this pleasant traditional inn: an old black mining cart stands in the foyer, and one part of the restaurant has been done up to look like a mine-shaft, with mining lamps hanging from the ceiling, and the back wall actually made of rough iron-ore. A gimmick, if you like, but a true reflection of local tradition. It's claimed that an inn has stood on this spot since 1144, almost since the Iron Age! – but today this Golden Lion is nicely modernised, with comfortable rooms, and heavy furnishings in the Bavarian style. The friendly Ruder family have owned the place only since 1847. Service by local girls is smilingly willing, if not always expert; the local cuisine very good, if hardly sophisticated – smoked trout, Schweinbraten with dumplings, etc. The local Franconian wines, though reputed, are not to my taste, and I opted instead for a sweetish, fizzy Ahr red that looked – and tasted – a bit like Campari soda. But I *like* Campari soda." (*JA*)

Open All year.
Rooms 2 suites, 16 double, 5 single – all with bath and shower, telephone, radio, TV and mini-bar.
Facilities Lift. 3 dining rooms, bar; conference facilities.
Location Central. Parking. Auerbach is 42 km SE of Bayreuth.
Restriction Not suitable for &.
Credit cards All major cards accepted.

Terms B&B: single 104 DM, double 158 DM, suite 226 DM; dinner, B&B 30 DM
added per person. Set lunch/dinner 38–75 DM; full alc 50 DM. Reduced rates and
special meals for children.

AYING 8011 Bayern   Map 7

Brauereigasthof Aying   *Tel* (08095) 7 05
Zornedinger Strasse 2   *Fax* (08095) 88 50

*A big creeper-covered pub, very traditional, right next to a famous brewery in a
picturesque flower-decked village south-east of Munich, where commuters and
dairy-farmers rub shoulders. Large airy bedrooms with Biedermeier furniture;
walloping great breakfasts, served with beer if you wish. Good food served
indoors or in the courtyard: some delicate dishes, as well as the usual hefty
pork-based Bavarian ones. And beer, beer, beer... Closed mid-Jan–early Feb.
19 rooms, most with bath or shower. B&B double 150–175 DM. Meals 29–
68 DM [1989]. New nomination. More reports welcome.*

BAD BERGZABERN 6748 Rheinland-Pfalz   Map 7

Hotel-Pension Pfälzer Wald   *Tel* (06343) 10 56
Kurtalstrasse 77

Fine Renaissance buildings and a modern spa centre are features of this
neat little town at the southern end of the Pfalz *Weinstrasse*, just east of
the strange red crags of the Wasgau (the ruined clifftop castles of Altdahn
are not to be missed). The *Pfälzer Wald*, a small traditional family hotel,
stands alone beside a lake, with green hills behind, and has been liked
again this year: "A good base for a comfortable holiday, and excellent
value. Our room was spacious, clean and quiet, the cooking was plain but
good, buffet breakfasts were copious." Other visitors have found the
welcome warm and the staff helpful, though some rooms are said to be
small and not too well equipped. (*Ronald S McNeill; Mary Clark*) *Warning*:
the hotel faces a busy main road.

Open All year except Feb.
Rooms 17 double, 10 single – all with shower, telephone and TV.
Facilities Lounge, TV room, wine bar, dining room, restaurant; functions room;
terrace. Large garden by lake.
Location About 1 km W of town centre; 38 km NW of Karlsruhe. Parking.
Restriction Not suitable for &.
Credit cards Some accepted.
Terms B&B 30–55 DM; half board 47–72 DM. Set lunch/dinner 20–30 DM.
Reduced rates and special meals for children.

BAD HERRENALB 7506 Baden-Württemberg   Map 7

Mönchs Posthotel   *Tel* (07083) 74 40
Doblerstrasse 2   *Telex* 7245123

The first hotel that our Continental Editor and his wife ever visited
together remains blissfully unchanged, as they found this year. Nor are
they its only admirers. "Expensive but worth the cost, with a superb
restaurant"; "Elegant, yet intimate and cosy. And better than ever." So

run reports this year and last, on this smart and stylish old half-timbered flower-decked post-hotel, at a crossroads in the centre of a Black Forest spa town. The setting is less urban than this may suggest, for the hotel also has an outdoor swimming pool and large and graceful gardens leading to a river. "Our large bedroom was superbly equipped. The lovely dining room has beamed ceilings, wood panelling and several discreet alcoves. The food, beautifully prepared and presented, tends towards *nouvelle cuisine* and is worthy of its *Michelin* rosette. Service was smooth and affable. The breakfast buffet was the most lavish we have found in Germany – and that's saying something. All in all, a romantic place – despite the prevalence of rich businessmen." But front rooms facing the noisy road should be avoided, and service can be slow. (*William A Grant; JA and KA*)

Open All year.
Rooms 2 suites, 23 double, 14 single – 24 with bath, 15 with shower, all with telephone, most with radio and TV. 14 in adjoining annexe.
Facilities Lift. Salon, TV room, bar, restaurant, breakfast terrace; conference facilities; beauty parlour. Garden with heated swimming pool. Tennis and 9-hole golf course nearby.
Location Central. (Road-facing rooms can be noisy.) Parking.
Restriction Not suitable for &.
Credit cards Access, Amex, Diners.
Terms B&B 97–218 DM; half- and full-board rates (3 days min). Set lunch 35–45 DM, dinner 40–70 DM; full alc 50–70 DM. Reduced rates and special meals for children.

BAD HERSFELD 6430 Hessen	Map 7

Romantik Hotel Zum Stern	*Tel* (06621) 7 20 07
Am Markt	

This sizeable spa town close to the Kassel-Würzburg *autobahn* contains the ruins of a Benedictine monastery; the *Zum Stern*, now in the spa's pedestrian zone, was once part of that monastery, used to house its secular guests. It returns to the Guide this year: "A hotel of real class, its neat flowery window-boxes overlooking the market square. Our room was in the old building, with antique furniture; the modern extension, leading deep behind, includes the covered swimming pool. Welcome slightly impersonal, but the meals were excellent, especially salmon soup with caviare and côte d'agneau en croûte. A feast of a breakfast served in a warren of tiny rooms." (*Rev. Michael Bourdeaux*)

Open All year. Restaurant closed Fri midday.
Rooms 3 suites, 30 double, 15 single – 49 bath and/or shower, all with telephone, and radio; most with TV. 3 with baby-listening. 1 room suitable for &.
Facilities Lift. Lounge with TV, 2 restaurants; conference facilities. Indoor swimming pool.
Location Central, in pedestrian area. Parking. Bad Hersfeld is 69 km S of Kassel.
Credit cards All major cards accepted.
Terms B&B: single 95–100 DM, double 168–192.50 DM. Dinner, B&B: single 125–130 DM, double 228–252.50 DM. Reduced rates and special meals for children.

We asked hotels to quote 1990 prices. Not all were able to predict them in the late spring of 1989. Some of our terms will be inaccurate. Do check latest tariffs at the time of booking.

BAD MERGENTHEIM 6990 Baden-Württemberg   Map 7

Haus Bundschu   *Tel* (07931) 30 43
Cronbergstrasse 15   *Fax* (07931) 30 46

Bad Mergentheim is an important spa centre on the "Romantic Road"
south-west of Würzburg, in the Tauber valley; it has a 16th-century castle
of the Teutonic Order. Our inspector's 1989 nomination, "The delightful
Bundschu naturally has its share of the *Kurgäste* who go in their millions to
popular spa resorts such as this: the Germans are the world's most
assiduous spa-cure addicts. But we found this far removed from the usual
image of a spa hotel: it's cosy, inviting, informal, run very cheerfully by
the kindly Bundschu family, Swabians all, and in summer it gets lots of
ordinary tourists too. It's a *Relais du Silence*, set in the outskirts of the
town beside fields and woods, a spacious, rambling modern building – no
beauty – but the rooms are very comfortable (with unusual brass
bedlamps, resembling old gas-lamps), and the big rustic-style dining
room is pretty. Good *Maultaschen* soup and other Swabian dishes (a red
'*Karte*' in *Michelin* for good value, equivalent of its 'R' in France) and a
sumptuous buffet breakfast. The hotel has its own spa facilities, such as
fango."

Open 15 Feb–15 Jan. Restaurant closed Mon.
Rooms 5 suites, 20 double, 40 single – all with bath and shower, telephone, radio
and TV. Some ground-floor rooms.
Facilities Lift. Bar, restaurant, TV room; functions room. Garden. Spa cure
facilities.
Location In outskirts, parking. Town is 53 km SW of Würzburg.
Credit cards All major cards accepted.
Terms B&B 65–80 DM; dinner, B&B 18 DM added. Set dinner 25–50 DM.
Reduced rates and special meals for children.

BADEN-BADEN 7570 Baden-Württemberg   Map 7

Hotel "Der Kleine Prinz"   *Tel* (07221) 34 64
Lichtentaler Strasse 36   *Telex* 781433
(entrance Du-Russel Strasse)

A Victorian building in the town centre, now probably the most elegant
and appealing of Baden Baden's many small hotels: it is owned and run
by a charming and sophisticated couple, Norbert and Edeltraud Rade-
macher, who spent 22 years in the US (he was catering director of the
New York Hilton and *Waldorf Astoria*), and today many guests are
cultivated Americans travelling individually. Three satisfied customers
this year restore it to full entry: "We adored this lovely hotel, whose
owners truly care about their guests. Dinner was outstanding." "Our
supper party went superbly, and the pillows were the most comfortable
we slept on in Europe". "Intimate and classical, with pleasant modern
touches, such as the charming *motif* of the carrot-mopped, blue-cloaked
Kleine Prinz that appears in every room – but the hotel has *no* connection
with St-Exupéry; its name was chosen at random by the Rademachers.
Elegant decor in the little salon and restaurant, where food and service
are both very stylish. We had a lovely suite, with bathroom in grey
marble and the thickest bath-foam I've ever seen, covering us so that we
emerged from the bath looking like Alps!" (*JA and KA, and others*) A new

GERMANY

tunnel under the town now diverts through-traffic: the hotel is in a pedestrian zone, and quiet.

Open All year.
Rooms 10 suites, 15 double, 6 single – all with bath and/or shower, telephone, radio and TV; some with whirlpool.
Facilities Lift. Lounge, bar, restaurant.
Location Central. Some parking.
Credit cards All major cards accepted.
Terms B&B: single 125–200 DM, double 200–275 DM, suite 300–350 DM. Set lunch 40 DM, dinner 60 DM; full alc 60 DM. Reduced rates and special meals for children.

BAMBERG 8600 Bayern   Map 7

Böttingerhaus and   *Tel* (0951) 5 40 74
  Gästehaus Steinmühle   *Telex* 662946 BOETT
Judenstrasse 14

This jewel lies in the old quarter of Bamberg, one of the loveliest of Bavarian towns, its narrow streets and Baroque palaces unscathed by wartime bombing. The *Böttingerhaus* is itself a Baroque mansion of great beauty (built in 1713 as the home of a rich merchant and diplomat) recently acquired and renovated by a Hamburg architect and now run by his daughter, Maria, and her Parisian husband, Victor Orsenne, as a distinguished restaurant and cultural centre. They have also renovated a lovely old mill house on the river close by, and run it as a guest house annexe, the *Steinmühle*. Our nominator has returned this year, endorsing her previous field dispatch:

"A dream hotel in a dreamy maze of cobbled streets, wonderful churches, enchanting old houses, antique shops and delicious *Konditorei*. When you stay at the *Steinmühle*, you have superb views of the 15th-century Rathaus set on its tiny island; light sleepers who might be disturbed by the roar of the millstream can take rooms facing the street. Our room, though smallish, was charming and elegantly furnished. All meals – including the generous buffet breakfast – are taken amid the splendours of the *Böttingerhaus*. Dishes from the menu were delicious and beautifully served, not at all heavy and over-copious as is often the case in Bavaria. Windows look out on to ancient roofs, or on to the delightful terrace garden where you can take aperitifs; the sound of Mozart drifts gently in the distance." The cuisine includes local Franconian specialities with French influences coming from M. Orsenne; there is also an informal bistro for lighter meals. Live piano music at weekends and classical concerts fill out the scenario, as do official banquets of all kinds. A second, very comfortable bedroom annexe, the *Molitor Haus*, next to the *Steinmühle*, with an integral garage, opened in 1988. (*Eileen Spencer, EW Smallwood*)

Open All year.
Rooms 5 suites, 23 double – all with bath, shower, telephone, radio and TV; kitchenette in suites; babysitter on request. All in 2 houses about 80 yds from main building. 2 ground-floor rooms suitable for ð.
Facilities Lift. Lounge, restaurant, bar, tea room, wine cellar (piano player nightly); conference facilities. Garden terrace, children's playground.
Location Central. Garages.
Credit cards All major cards accepted.

Terms [1989 rates] B&B: single 95–110 DM, double 160–260 DM, suite 350 DM. Meals: restaurant 48–66 DM, wine cellar 33–51 DM. Reduced rates and special meals for children.

Hotel Sankt Nepomuk
Obere Mühlbrücke 9

Tel (0951) 2 51 83

Very close to the *Böttingerhaus* (see above), and almost equally delightful, this "most original and magic hotel" stands on stilts on the river Regnitz between the rushing millraces, and was again much liked by inspectors this year. It belongs to an affluent Catholic foundation which has managed the conversion with fastidious taste. Everything is stylishly open-plan, notably the big restaurant on two floors, with handsome fireplace, curving stone stairway, and picture-windows facing the river. This year's report, "We enjoyed fresh tomato soup with mushrooms and gin (sic), roast leg of lamb with herbs, and excellent vegetables. The cooking remains ambitious but not pretentious, with generous helpings, and is delightfully and skilfully served by young people. The staff are exemplary." Try Bamberg's curious 'smoky beer' made from smoked malt. The bedrooms are in light modern Scandinavian style, and vary in size. "The special glass of our bathroom window gave out a dazzling prismatic light effect; glow-worms darted and shone above the river; and we were lulled to sleep by the therapeutic roar of the millrace – to awaken next day to a sumptuous buffet breakfast, served in a lovely room with cheerful modern murals of local scenes." (*JA and KA, Eileen Spencer*)

Open All year except Christmas Eve.
Rooms 10 double, 2 single – all with bath and/or shower, telephone, radio, TV and mini-bar.
Facilities Lift. Bar, café, 2 restaurants; conference facilities.
Location Central. Do *not* try to drive car up to hotel (narrow streets); leave it in public car park in Geyerswörthstrasse just across river.
Credit cards Access, Diners, Visa.
Terms B&B: single occupancy 80–90 DM, double 130–150 DM. Set lunch/dinner 65–70 DM; full alc 55–60 DM. Special meals for children on request.

BARGUM 2255 Schleswig-Holstein   Map 7

Andresen's
Gasthof-Friesenstuben

Tel (04672) 10 98

An inn on the edge of a small village near the flat and windswept west coast of Schleswig, on Route 5 between Husum and Niebüll (Nolde museum). Delicious North German cooking (Michelin rosette) and good service in the lovely dining room with its beamed ceilings. Comfortable rooms facing a garden and fields. Closed 3 weeks Jan, 2 weeks Sept; restaurant closed all Mon, Tue midday. 5 rooms, all with shower (8 more planned for 1990). B&B double 135 DM. Set menus 90–110 DM. Recent nomination. More reports welcome.

Hotels often book you into their most expensive rooms or suites unless you specify otherwise. Even if all room prices are the same, hotels may give you a less good room in the hope of selling their better rooms to late customers. It always pays to discuss accommodation in detail when making a reservation.

BAYRISCHZELL 8163 Bayern

Map 7

Romantik Hotel Die Meindelei
Michael-Meindl Strasse 13

Tel (08023) 3 18

Bayrischzell is a pleasant hiking and skiing resort in the Bavarian Alps, at the foot of the rocky Wendelstein peak (go up it by cable-car for roof-of-the-world views). The *Meindelei*, in a quiet location backed by pinewoods, comes new to the Guide: "A fairly typical Romantik Hotel, named after a local writer, Herr Meindl, now dead, and run by his perfectionist, fiercely hardworking daughter and her quieter husband. The heavily kitschy Bavarian decor might not suit all tastes (lots of painted cupboards, china stoves, folk objects; in the dining room, bowls of plastic fruit, even a crucifix), but it's very comfortable, spruce and well run. First-class, sophisticated cooking by the Swabian son-in-law of the owners (paprika soup with cream, delicious mixed salad with pine-nuts, rare roast venison – and an oyster au gratin offered as an *amuse-gueule*), all daintily presented but not too *nouvelle*. Lavish breakfast buffet, including various types of fruit salad. Some rooms are in the main buildings, others in bungalows in the big tree-filled garden. A small heated pool is free to guests, and there's a bigger public one across the road. A very good hotel in its own way." (*JA and KA*)

Open All year except 2 weeks in Mar/Apr and 15 Oct–22 Dec. Restaurant closed for lunch and Tue.
Rooms 17 – all with bath and/or shower and telephone. 5 bungalows in garden.
Facilities Lounge, bar, restaurant. Indoor swimming pool and sauna. Garden; terrace where meals are served.
Location Fairly central; parking. Bayrischzell is 77 km SE of Munich.
Credit cards All major cards accepted.
Terms [1989 rates] B&B: single 85–95 DM, double 135–165 DM. Meals 30–65 DM.

BAYREUTH 8580 Bayern

Map 7

Bayerischer Hof
Bahnhofstrasse 14

Tel (0921) 2 20 81
Telex 642737

A post-war building near the station, outwardly dull-looking but probably the best of Bayreuth's hotels, owned by the Seuss family since 1918. Large, quiet, well-furnished rooms; fine heated indoor pool; rooftop bar and restaurant with outdoor terrace, serving local dishes; pleasant staff and good breakfasts. Restaurant closed Sun. 62 rooms, all with bath and shower. B&B double 110-210 DM. Meals 35–63 DM [1989]. Few recent reports. More welcome.

BAYREUTH-SEULBITZ 8580 Bayern

Map 7

Waldhotel Stein

Tel (0921) 90 01

Seulbitz is an attractive village just east of Bayreuth (you can see the floodlit *Festspielhaus* from your window). Here Frau Stein's peaceful modern family hotel has again been liked this year, for its "above average" cooking (most of the ingredients are organically produced locally) and spacious rooms – some are bedsitters with balcony, some are in bungalows in the large garden. Swimming pool; very efficient service.

A new bungalow with a luxurious bridal suite has just been built and further expansion is planned. (*Philip A True*)

Open Jan–end Nov.
Rooms 5 suites, 48 double, 6 single – all with bath and/or shower, telephone, radio and TV. 4 with kitchenette. Most rooms in bungalows. Some on ground floor.
Facilities Lounge, breakfast room, 2 restaurants; conference facilities. Indoor heated swimming pool, sauna, solarium, massage. Large grounds. Tennis 3 km.
Location 6 km E of Bayreuth, near Seulbitz village; follow signs for Eremitage. Parking.
Credit cards All major cards accepted.
Terms B&B: single 58–180 DM, double 98–280 DM, suite 200–1,200 DM (prices increase hugely during opera festival period). Set lunch/dinner 25–48 DM; full alc 45 DM. Reduced rates and special meals for children.

BEILSTEIN 5591 Rheinland-Pfalz   Map 7

Hotel Haus Lipmann   Tel (02673) 15 73

Metternich was the last overlord of this very picturesque old village in the Mosel valley, and his castle stands on the hill above. To the south is the wooded plateau of the Hunsrück where Edgar Reitz set and filmed his 16-hour masterpiece *Heimat*. "Very characterful and atmospheric", says a visitor this year to the *Lipmann*, a cheap and unpretentious little family-run half-timbered *Gasthof*, in the main square. "Our rooms were quaint, but comfortable, and our window opened on to a wonderful view of the river." Some rooms are in a modern annexe amid trees; others, newly renovated but smaller, are in the charming old *Alte Zollhaus* annexe. Interesting dishes such as smoked Mosel eel with scrambled eggs are served generously in a baronial hall, while opposite is the hotel's lovely old vaulted pub where you can drink wine with locals. (*Mrs AJ Goodwin, JA and KA*)

Open 15 Mar–15 Nov.
Rooms 20 double, 4 single – 1 with bath, 23 with shower. 18 in 2 annexes.
Facilities Restaurant; conference/functions facilities; wine cellar (wine tastings held); terrace on Mosel.
Location Central, near market place. Parking.
Credit cards None accepted.
Terms B&B: single 45–65 DM, double 70–85 DM; dinner B&B (min stay 4 days) 12 DM per person added; full board 20 DM added. Full alc 25–55 DM. Special meals for children on request.

BERCHTESGADEN 8420 Bayern   Map 7

Hotel Krone   Tel (08652) 6 20 51
Am Rad 5

Few German resorts are more teemingly popular than Berchtesgaden. Hitler's eyrie has been rased to the ground, and only its ghosts remain; but the mountains and alpine lakes are gorgeous, and a guided tour of the extraordinary salt-mines is not to be missed. The unpretentious *Krone*, attractively white-walled and blue-shuttered, and furnished in local rustic style, stands on a hill just outside the town, aloof from the madding throng. It now makes its Guide debut: "In a town where all other hotels seem large and package-tour orientated, here's just the kind of small, idiosyncratic but wholly delightful place that should appeal to readers. All its good rooms away from the road open onto communal balconies facing the valley and hills. Ours was fairly small, but snug and wood-panelled, and the house is full of Bavarian hand-painted furniture. The Grafe family gave us a warm welcome, and they provide good home cooking. Frau Grafe dresses quite naturally in Bavarian costume as she serves in the dining room." (*Angela and David Stewart*) More reports please.

Open All year except Nov–20 Dec. Restaurant closed for lunch; dinner for residents only.
Rooms 28 – most with bath and/or shower, telephone and TV.
Facilities Lounge, restaurant; terrace.
Location 1 km N of town centre, off Salzburg road. Parking.
Credit cards None accepted.
Terms [1989 rates] B&B: single 65–77 DM, double 120–150 frs. Half board: 12 DM per person added.

BERGISCH GLADBACH 5060 Nordrhein-Westfalen Map 7

Waldhotel Mangold *Tel* (02204) 5 40 11
Am Milchbornsberg 32

Set in the midst of rolling hills, next to a forest and running stream, this "woodland hotel" (*Michelin* red print for pleasantness) is in some ways very rural. Yet it is only ten miles from Cologne, just beyond the eastern fringe of its urban sprawl. A long low white building, it has been in the hands of the Mangold family since 1927. "Rooms both in the annexe and in the main building are large, clean, comfortable and well furnished. The large reception area is furnished with antique clocks and pictures. The small restaurant has a terrace for summer: cooking is imaginative, using high-quality fresh ingredients. Good breakfast."

Open All year except 3 weeks in Jun/Jul. Restaurant closed for lunch and on Mon, Sun and public holidays.
Rooms 20 – all with bath and/or shower, telephone and TV; some with balcony.
Facilities Lounge, salon with open fireplace, restaurant; conference facilities. Terrace.
Location 17 km E of Cologne: leave *Autobahn* E40 at Bergisch Gladbach/Bensberg exit, follow sings to Bensberg. Parking.
Credit cards None accepted.
Terms [1989 rates] B&B: single 100–135 DM, double 150–180 DM. Meals 46–72 DM.

BERLIN 1000 Map 7

Hotel Belvedere *Tel* (030) 826 10 77
Seebergsteig 4, Grunewald
Berlin 33

Some three miles west of the city centre, the smart residential suburb of Grunewald, aptly named, is next to a forest that leads to the big Havel lake. It's a setting that puts paid to the false image of West Berlin as a claustrophobic city without space or greenery (in fact, it has 80 farms). Here, in a quiet and leafy side-street, this turn-of-the-century villa in its own garden was liked again this year. Reports have praised the buffet breakfasts, the thickness of the feather duvets and the welcome to small children: but while some rooms are large and sunny, basement ones may be dark. One was "adorable but tiny". "Stylish bedrooms with antique cane and wood furniture. Public rooms have the air of a bourgeois private house. Peaceful, relaxed, unpretentious. Breakfast in a funny conservatory-like annexe". (*EW Smallwood, Stephanie and Bryan Lorge*) No restaurant, but there are some nearby such as the lakeside *Chalet Corniche*. Or bus 19, five minutes' walk, will take you to the city centre. Visit the fabulous Dahlem museums, quite near by.

Open All year. Restaurant open to residents only.
Rooms 12 double, 7 single – 10 with bath, 2 with shower, all with telephone, radio and TV.
Facilities Salon with TV, breakfast room. Garden.
Location In Grunewald, 4 km SW of city centre.
Restriction Not suitable for &.
Credit cards Access, Diners, Visa.
Terms [1989 rates] Rooms: single 55–100 DM, double 85–140 DM. Breakfast 8 DM. Reduced rates for children.

BONN 5300 Nordrhein-Westfalen   **Map 7**

Haus Hofgarten   *Tel* (0228) 22 34 82
Fritz-Tillmann Strasse 7

In a residential street close to the university and the traffic-free heart of old Bonn, well away from the modern Regierungsviertel, *here is a tiny, friendly hotel with lots of wood panelling and good pictures, and huge old-fashioned bedrooms, comfortable and well equipped. Breakfast, complete with the day's newspapers, served in a room facing the garden. 15 bedrooms, some with bath and/or shower. B&B double 85–145 DM [1989]. No restaurant, but lots nearby. Restored to Guide. More reports please.*

Schlosshotel Kommende   *Tel* (0228) 44 07 34
  Ramersdorf
Oberkasseler Strasse 10
Bonn 3-Beuel

Just across the Rhine from Bonn, some three kilometres from the city centre and government area, this massive ancient *Schloss* stands incongruously in the middle of a motorway network (but the traffic is not audible). Parts date from 1220, but most is 19th-century neo-Gothic. Dropped from the 1989 Guide for lack of feedback, it is restored by two reports this year: "A delight. Our large room was furnished with antiques, and a plentiful breakfast was served in a charming room." "We arrived at 10.30 pm but were kindly cosseted with a cold meal. The good service compensated for the worn carpets and other shabbiness. Incredibly cheap by German standards." Part of the *Schloss* is a museum of furniture, paintings, etc, and some items are for sale. (*Claire W Enders, J Thérèse Simon*) Reports on the cooking would be welcome.

Do you know of any good budget hotels in Berlin?

Open All year. Restaurant closed 4 weeks in Jul/Aug and Tue.
Rooms 10 double, 8 single – all with bath and shower, telephone and radio; some with TV.
Facilities Bar, TV room, breakfast room, restaurant; terrace-café.
2 functions/conference rooms. Courtyard and garden.
Location Take A59 motorway in direction of Königswinter, leave it at
Niederholtorf exit; turn left, and after 300 metres left again.
Restrictions Not suitable for &.
Credit cards All major cards accepted.
Terms [1989 rates] B&B: single 85–120 DM, double 150–170 DM. Meals 46–
70 DM.

BOPPARD AM RHEIN 5407 Rheinland-Pfalz   Map 7

Klostergut Jakobsberg   *Tel* (06742) 30 61
Im Tal der Loreley   *Telex* 426 323

Readers this year endorse last year's picture of this large and remarkable
Rhineland hotel: "In 1157 Frederic I Barbarossa founded a monastery 'für
Mönche und Nonnen' high on the hills above Boppard, overlooking a
magnificent stretch of the Rhine. This had a chequered history and even
became a school for French émigré children during the Revolution.
Finally the owner of the Harribo sweets empire bought it and converted it
into a smart hotel, adding a number of new buildings, complete with
superb indoor sports centre, pool and tennis. The courtyard at dusk with
its fountain and scores of sculptured glass lanterns is impressive.
Reception rooms are vast and comfortable, decked out with modern
bronze sculptures, antique wooden statues, stained-glass windows. All
bedrooms are individual, with genuine paintings, modern wooden
furniture. Some have a sun balcony; ours overlooked a rocky wooded
escarpment. It was very cosy, and the bathroom had a ceiling-to-floor
mosaic. All is beautifully maintained by a charming staff. There are two
bars (one in the old wine cellars) and two restaurants, one with views
over the trees to the Rhine. Food is interestingly presented (excellent
quails, lobster tails, veal in cream) and many ingredients come fresh from
the adjacent home farm. Breakfast was superb and lavish, and service
quick and pleasant: we saw one waitress taking particular care over single
old ladies. At the weekend the hotel was full of families with children;
during the week, of businessmen and conference guests. English and
Americans prefer the old part for its atmosphere." (*TH Nash, Miss D
Tunstall*)

Open All year.
Rooms 110 – all with bath and/or shower, telephone and TV.
Facilities Lift. Lounge, 2 bars, 2 restaurants; conference facilities. Large garden
with children's playground. Indoor swimming pool, sauna and solarium. Indoor
and outdoor tennis, squash and bowling alley. Rifle range. Chapel for weddings.
Location 12 km N of Boppard: turn off B9 Rhineside main road at Spay, take
Rheingoldstrasse turning.
Credit cards Probably all major cards accepted.
Terms [1989 rates] B&B: single 110–180 DM, double 160–280 DM; half board
40 DM added per person, full board 60 DM added.

> When hotels have failed to return their questionnaire, we have
> quoted 1989 prices, with a note to that effect.

BREITNAU 7821 Baden-Württemberg   **Map 7**

Hotel Kaiser's Tanne-Wirtshus   *Tel* (07652) 15 51
Am Wirbstein 27   *Fax* (07652) 15-07

Set in rolling pastoral country a few miles away from the big resort of
Hinterzarten, and thus secluded from the main tourist crowds, here is a
welcoming chalet-style Black Forest hotel, all gables and flowery
balconies outside, all folksy *Gemütlichkeit* within. "Beautifully decorated,
very ornate, full of antiques and pictures and homely touches making it
one of the most pleasant hotels I have visited in Europe. Very friendly
staff. Bedroom and bathroom clean and airy. Excellent duvets. If you
arrive in time do not miss the tea downstairs, which is a real treat.
Excellent dinner and first class buffet breakfast." Many bedrooms have a
balcony with peaceful rural views which include cows to-ing and fro-ing.
Indoor swimming pool and attractive garden. (*John Moseley, and others*)

Open All year except mid-Nov–mid-Dec. Restaurant closed Mon.
Rooms 2 suites, 24 double, 5 single – all with bath, shower, telephone, radio and
TV.
Facilities Lift. Lounge, bar, 2 restaurants, indoor heated swimming pool and
sauna; terrace. Garden, playground for children.
Location Just SW of Breitnau, which is 30 km E of Freiburg, off route 500.
Credit cards None accepted.
Terms B&B 70–100 DM. Dinner, B&B 105–135 DM.Set lunch 25–40 DM, dinner
35–70 DM; full alc 45 DM. Reduced rates and special meals for children.

BÜSINGEN 7701 Baden-Württemberg   **Map 7**

Alte Rheinmühle   *Tel* (07734) 60 76
Junkerstrasse 93   *Telex* 793788 HOTEL

*The village of Büsingen is a German enclave inside Switzerland near
Schaffhausen (either Swiss or German currency can be used). Here this
converted 17th-century mill on the Rhine serves some of the best food in Baden-
Württemberg (Michelin rosette). The beamed dining room is large but cosy, and
overlooks the river. Bedrooms (some have four-posters and painted wooden
wardrobes) are scattered on various levels, in a random but homely fashion.
Closed 20 Dec–15 Jan. 16 rooms, all with bath or shower. B&B double 130–
180 DM. Meals from 30 DM [1989]. Few recent reports. More please.*

CELLE 3100 Niedersachsen   **Map 7**

Fürstenhof Celle – Restaurant   *Tel* (05141) 20 10
  Endtenfang   *Fax* (05141) 20 11 20
Hannoversche Strasse 55   *Telex* 925293 CEHOG

This pink-fronted mansion, a stylish and rather formal hotel, stands on a
main road near the centre of an historic old city where the Guelph princes
ruled (imposing baroque *Schloss*, lovely *Altstadt* of ancient timbered
houses). "We've tried four different rooms", say devotees this year, "and
all have been pleasant, with a balcony overlooking the garden where
drinks are served. This separates the older part of the hotel, a 17th-
century palace, from the new bedroom wing. Service is impeccable, the

breakfast buffet is good, and excellent duck is served in the hotel's *Endtenfang* restaurant (*Michelin* rosette). We haven't tried its cheaper *Kutscherstube*. The comfortable lounge is in baroque style." (*Stephan and Kate Murray-Sykes*)

Open All year. *Kutscherstube* closed midday and Sun.
Rooms 3 suites, 75 double or single – all with bath and shower, telephone, radio, TV and baby-listening.
Facilities Lift. Lounge, bar, beer-cellar, 2 restaurants; conference and function facilities; indoor swimming pool, solarium, sauna. Garden and terrace.
Location Central, near *Schloss*. Parking.
Credit cards Access, Amex, Diners.
Terms [1989 rates] B&B: single 98–190 DM, double 180–380 DM, suite 400 DM. Meals: *Kutscherstube* 33–52 DM; *Endtenfang* 85–125 DM.

COCHEM 5590 Rheinland-Pfalz Map 7

Hotel "Alte Thorschenke"   *Tel* (02671) 70 59 and 39 31
Brückenstrasse 3   *Fax* (02671) 42 02

Cochem, with its painted houses and neat gardens along the river, and its high-pinnacled hilltop feudal castle, is the most picturesque town on the Mosel – and this Guide newcomer, in an old gabled house dating from 1332, is worthy of it, "The entrance opens onto an ancient carved circular wooden staircase, leading to rooms in the old building. Behind is a post-war bedroom extension, fitted out with splendid antique pictures and furniture. Here we slept deliciously well in a vast family heirloom of a bed, all massive carved oak. The bathroom was somewhat clinical but adequate. The welcome was warm yet professional, and dinner in a superb baronial dining room included the best game we've ever had." (*Angela and David Stewart*)

Open 15 Mar–5 Jan. Restaurant closed on Wed 15 Nov–5 Jan.
Rooms 38 double, 6 single – 34 with bath and shower and radio; 22 with telephone; TV on request. 4 in nearby annexe.
Facilities Lift. Hall, restaurant, *Weinstube*. Terrace.
Location Central, parking. Cochem is 51 km SW of Koblenz.
Credit cards All major cards accepted.
Terms B&B: single 55–115 DM, double 125–180 DM; half board 28 DM per person added; full board 48 DM added. Full alc 50–60 DM. Reduced rates and special meals for children.

COLOGNE 5000 Nordrhein-Westphalen Map 7

Hotel Spiegel   *Tel* (02203) 6 10 46
Herman-Löns-Strasse 122, Porz-
Grengel

The Guide's search for good hotels in Cologne is rarely successful, so this newcomer is welcome: a small family-run gasthof in the south-eastern outer suburb of Porz-Grengel, conveniently near the airport, but set peacefully by a forest. Good food, and a personal touch. Closed 3 weeks in summer. 19 rooms, all with bath or shower. B&B double 130–180 DM. Alc 50–65 DM. New nomination. More reports please.

DAHLEM-KRONENBURG 5377 Nordrhein-Westfalen   Map 7

Eifelhaus   *Tel* (06557) 295
Burgbering 12

In a hilltop village south-west of Dahlem, in the lovely but little-known Eifel massif, quite near the Belgian border, a white-walled old building has been converted into a modest but appealing little hotel; vaulted dining room, terraced garden, helpful owners, clean, simple rooms and good food. Amazingly low prices. Lake and castle nearby. 19 rooms, all with bath and/or shower. B&B 30–35 DM. Set menus 9.50–25 DM [1989]. New nomination. More reports eagerly requested.

DAUN 5568 Rheinland-Pfalz   Map 7

Schloss-Hotel Kurfürstliches   *Tel* (06592) 30 31
Amtshaus   *Fax* (06592) 49 42
Auf dem Burgberg   *Telex* 4729310

Daun is a resort in the lovely rolling volcanic hills of the Eifel, west of Koblenz. On a hill in the village centre, this handsome yellow-walled 18th-century schloss has been converted into a stylish and fairly expensive hotel, admired by several readers this year. Public rooms and most bedrooms have bracing views of the surrounding woods, hills and ski-slopes. The decor and furnishings are somewhat baronial, with heavy oak chests, etc. "Most of the decor is what we call 'pseudo-Germanic semi-kitsch', though others might call it 'altdeutsch'. But the main restaurant is inviting and intimate, and here we had a wonderful meal, with sophisticated haute cuisine (tomato mousse with smoked breast of goose, fried quail with quince sauce, date ice-cream with apple sauce, etc) and excellent service. The high-quality table accessories included fresh roses in December. Our comfortable room had a view of an old chapel and fir trees. Rich buffet breakfast with lots of unusual extras." Another reader thought the meal good but the service slow. Inspectors report, "The heated swimming pool is almost as hot as a sauna, for its water comes from the local volcanic springs; it has red and green alcoves and is chiselled out of the volcanic rock. The garden terrace contains barbecue facilities. Bedrooms are smallish but pleasant. One of the splendid suites, the Fürstensuite, contains a famous bed acquired from the Government's hotel at the Petersberg in Bonn, where it was slept in by Brezhnev, the Shah of Iran, etc. It is now covered in fancy orange drapes and an orange silk canopy, and the bath *en suite* is triangular. All this for only 320 DM [1990]. A snip." (*GB and Dr CH, Mrs CM Hunter*)

Open All year except 3 days early Jan.
Rooms 1 suite, 25 double, 17 single – 8 with bath, 34 with shower, all with telephone, radio, TV and mini-bar; baby-listening on request.
Facilities Lift. Lounge, bar, 2 restaurants, conference facilities. Garden; terrace. Indoor swimming pool, sauna.
Location Central, parking. Daun is 70 km W of Koblenz.
Credit cards All major cards accepted.
Terms B&B: single 95–105 DM, double 160–220 DM, suite 320 DM. Dinner, B&B 38 DM per person added. Set lunch 39–52 DM, dinner 64–94 DM; full alc 75 DM. Reduced rates and special meals for children. 2 nights minimum stay at weekends.

DEIDESHEIM 6705 Rheinland-Pfalz
Map 7

Romantik Hotel Deidesheimer Hof   *Tel* (06326) 18 11
Am Marktplatz   *Telex* 454675

Chancellor Kohl comes from Mainz, the nearby *Land* capital, and his local connections led him to select this stylish and well-known hotel for his summit meeting with – guess who? – on 30th April 1989. They sat at a white table and argued fruitlessly about short-range nuclear missiles, after which Mrs T. drank the local white wine and confided to the TV cameras, *"Very* dry, with just a *touch* of sweetness"*, (giggles all round). This however is not why we are now restoring the *Hof* to the Guide, from which it was dropped in 1988 purely through lack of feedback. An inspector this year has admired the wood-panelled *Weinstube*, full of Germanic warmth and prettiness, and an American has written: "A real joy! Cheerful, helpful staff, exceptional food. Despite the crowds in the food rooms and front terrace, the back bedrooms are quiet – and beautifully decked out" (rooms do vary). Run by the Hahn family, leading local vinegrowers, the hostelry stands on the busy main street of a picturesque little wine-town on the Pfalz *Weinstrasse* (its balustraded *Rathaus* has a wine museum). (*SR Holman, JA and KA*) More reports please.

Open All year except 4–15 Jan. *Schwarzer Hahn* restaurant closed midday, Sun, and in low season.
Rooms 27 – all with bath and/or shower, telephone and TV.
Facilities 2 restaurants; conference facilities. Terrace.
Location Central, parking. Deidesheim is 23 km SW of Mannheim.
Credit cards All major cards accepted.
Terms [1989 rates] B&B: single 57–118 DM, double 88–179 DM. Meals: *Weinstube* 37–67 DM, *Schwarzer Hahn* 58–87 DM.

DÜSSELDORF 4000
Map 7

Hotel Schnellenburg   *Tel* (0211) 43 41 33
Rotterdamerstrasse 120   *Telex* 8581828 BURG
Düsseldorf 30

Recommended again in 1989, especially for its bedrooms and its fine position beside the Rhine, this is a pleasantly unusual place in a big commercial city full of dull hotels. A low white building with iron grilles on the windows, it looks more Spanish than German. "A light room where it was easy to work, and a first-class breakfast, and smiling service." The restaurant, newly renovated with lots of brass and marble, has a good view of the river.

Open All year except Christmas and New Year.
Rooms 3 suites, 35 double, 11 single – all with bath, shower, telephone, radio, TV.
Facilities Lounge, residents' bar, restaurant (under separate management). Small garden.
Restriction Not suitable for &.
Location 4 km N of city centre, opposite Nord Park, on the Rhine. Parking.
Credit cards All major cards accepted.
Terms B&B: single 125–190 DM, double 160–260 DM, suite 220–360 DM. Full alc 35 DM. Reduced rates and special meals for children.

> Please make a habit of sending a report if you stay at a Guide hotel.

FEUCHTWANGEN 8805 Bayern   Map 7

Greifen-Post   *Tel* (09852) 20 03
Marktplatz 8   *Fax* (09852) 48 41
                                                  Telex 61137

A solidly down-to-earth coaching inn, spacious and rambling, with parts
dating back to 1450 or earlier. It stands in the main square of this pleasant
little north Bavarian town (interesting Frankish folk museum) and has
been owned by the Lorentz family for three generations. "Friendly
greeting, lovely rooms and fine food", runs one recent report. Others
have relished the Frankish specialities served in an old beamed dining
room, the buffet breakfast, and the owners' personal touch. Wide
corridors full of antiques are part of the charm. Most bedrooms are well
modernised, though some definitely need attention. Those in the front
may be noisy; those in the newer annexe are quieter but have less cachet.
The pool, done up in the style of Roman baths, is much commended
"like swimming in a Roman grotto".

Open All year. Restaurant closed 2 Jan–15 Feb.
Rooms 3 suites, 35 double, 6 single – all with bath and shower, telephone, radio
and TV; baby-listening on request. 3 in annexe.
Facilities Lift. Bar, breakfast room, 3 restaurants; conference facilities; indoor
heated swimming pool, sauna, solarium; garden terrace.
Location Central. Garage parking.
Credit cards All major cards accepted.
Terms B&B: single 85–115 DM, double 125–200 DM, suite 250–380 DM. Set
lunch 42 DM, dinner 89 DM. Reduced rates and special meals for children.

FRANKFURT-AM-MAIN 6000 Hessen   Map 7

Westend   *Tel* (069) 74 67 02 and 74 50 02
Westendstrasse 15, Frankfurt 1

"A very pleasant contrast to the concrete monstrosities I normally have to
stay in on business trips," runs one recent report on this small and select
hotel of charm and character, most unexpected in downtown Frankfurt. It
is in a quiet residential district that has somehow survived the metallic
frenzy of post-war rebuilding; yet it is very central, only five minutes'
walk from the Fair centre, the *Hauptbahnhof* and the banking district. One
reader this year found reception discourteous, but others have enjoyed
the serenity and cordial efficiency, confirming this earlier view, "The late
20th century has been carefully excluded from the *Westend*, which is
tastefully furnished throughout with antiques and old pictures; gracious
old-world service by discreet middle-aged men in black suits who address
lady guests as 'Gnädige Frau' ('Esteemed Madame'). Very comfortable
rooms; lavish German breakfasts; light evening meals on request; a leafy
garden for summer; prices very reasonable for central Frankfurt." A lift
has just been installed: and the hotel promises that almost all rooms will
have private bath or shower by the end of 1989.

Open All year except Easter holidays, Christmas and New Year.
Rooms 20 – 8 with bath, 2 with shower, all with telephone and mini-bar.
Facilities Lift. 3 lounges (1 with TV). Garden and terrace where light meals and
drinks are served.

Location Central; 5 mins' walk from station. By car approach from Westkreuz.
Private parking.
Credit cards Access, Amex, Visa.
Terms Rooms: single 75-150 DM, double 150–200 DM, triple 280 DM. Breakfast
14 DM. (No restaurant, but light evening meals served on request.)

FREIBURG IM BREISGAU 7800 Baden-Württemberg   Map 7

Zum Roten Bären   *Tel* (0761) 3 69 13
Oberlinden 12   *Fax* (0761) 3 69 16
    Telex 7721574 BAER

Blue-and-pink diamond-shaped designs adorn the painted facade of this
famous and very *gemütlich* old inn, dating back 600 years, and set near
the centre of a lovely old university city on the edge of the Black Forest. It
has also been comfortably modernised, its newer parts skilfully integrated
into the old ones; old prints line the walls, fresh flowers are everywhere.
One reader this year found dinner "divine", and an inspector fared well,
too: "Good traditional cooking, e.g. Tafelspitze (boiled beef), but the local
'Freiburger Festtagsuppe' was boringly unfestive. Staff wear local Baden
tracht, including – incongruously – our deft Pakistani waiter. A good but
expensive Baden Bürgheimer red. It's a hotel that breathes confident well-
being, nicely supervised by its jolly and expansive *Wirtin*, Monika
Hansen." Others have approved braised venison and the breakfast buffet.
One reader found her bathroom unkempt. Parking is difficult.

Open All year. Restaurant closed 24 Dec.
Rooms 3 suites, 17 double, 5 single – all with bath, shower, telephone, radio and
TV.
Facilities Lift. Reception, lounge, TV room, restaurant; conference room.
Courtyard and boulevard café.
Location Central; in old part of city. Underground carparks. From Basle highway
take exit Freiburg Mitte; follow signs for Stadtmitte, Schwabentor, *Hotel Bären*.
Credit cards All major cards accepted.
Terms B&B: single 125–145 DM, double 170–190 DM, suite 280–300 DM; dinner,
B&B 30 DM per person added. Set lunch 26 DM; full alc from 45 DM. Reduced
rates and special meals for children.

FREUDENSTADT 7290 Baden-Württemberg   Map 7

Hotel-Restaurant Gut Lauterbad   *Tel* (07441) 74 96
Dietrichstrasse 5, Lauterbad

Freudenstadt, one of the larger Black Forest resorts, lies on a pine-clad
plateau astride the old hill-road from Stuttgart to Strasbourg, amid
excellent hiking country. After destruction in 1945, it was completely
rebuilt in its former 17th-century style: note its curious church, with the
aisles set at right-angles. The admired *Gut Lauterbad*, a modern building in
local style, lies just outside the town, amid meadows, woods and streams;
it has a garden terrace beside a trout pond. "We had an excellent room,
spacious and comfortable, and very good food in ample portions on the
set menus. Staff friendly." More reports welcome.

Open All year except 15 Nov–15 Dec and 10 Jan–1 Feb. Restaurant closed Wed.
Rooms 1 suite, 16 double, 4 single – all with bath and shower, telephone, radio
and TV. 1 suite, 4 double in annexe.

Facilities Lounge, bar, TV room, restaurant; conference room; indoor heated swimming pool. Park with children's playground, small lake and stream; trout-fishing.
Location 3 km SE (B294) of centre; follow directions to Freiburg then to Dietersweiler/Lauterbad. Hotel is at end of road on left. Garage and parking.
Restriction Not suitable for &.
Credit cards All major cards accepted.
Terms B&B: single 48–58 DM, double 78–106 DM, suite 150 DM; dinner, B&B 21.50 DM per person added. Set lunch/dinner 21.50–35 DM; full alc 38–50 DM. Children under 2 free; under 12, 50% reduction; special meals.

FRIEDRICHSRUHE 7111 Baden-Württemberg　　　　　　**Map 7**

Wald-und Schlosshotel　　　　　　　　　*Tel* (07941) 6 08 70
　Friedrichsruhe　　　　　　　　　　　*Fax* (07941) 6 14 68
Öhringerstrasse 11　　　　　　　　　　*Telex* 74498 WAFRI

A large white-walled red-roofed mansion in the hilly and wooded Hohenlohe country, built in 1712 by the *Fürsten* of that ilk and still owned today (after conversion in 1953 into a very superior hotel) by the Prinz Kraft zu Hohenlohe-Öhringen. His chef/manager, Lothar Eiermann, runs it in lordly style and provides some of the most ambitious cooking in Germany (a second *Michelin* rosette added in 1989). Rooms are in the old mansion or, along with the restaurant, in a modern and stylish extension. "The best hotel we stayed at in Germany. A lovely room, excellent food", say some readers this year. "Germany's answer to England's *Priory* in Bath (q.v.)." (*Robert and Ruth Todd*) But others were inclined to endorse a more ambivalent view recorded last year. Reception: pleasant but a bit cool. Their room: large and very comfortable but showing signs of wear and tear, and lighting no more than adequate. No complaints about the bathroom, or the service or the breakfast ("delicious"). As for the dinner, it was good – but not *that* good in view of the prices; the wines (the Perrier too!) had in their view an excessive mark-up. More reports welcome, especially on the food.

Open All year. Restaurant closed Mon.
Rooms 13 suites, 26 double, 11 single – all with bath, shower and telephone; radio, TV and baby-listening on request. 22 rooms in hunting lodge.
Facilities Lifts. Lounge/bar, 2 restaurants; functions room. Large grounds with outdoor and covered swimming pools, tennis court, 9-hole golf course, children's playground.
Location 30 km E of Heilbronn; leave the Nürnberg motorway at Öhringen exit, drive through Öhringen till Friedrichsruhe is signposted.
Credit cards All major cards accepted.
Terms B&B: single 170–300 DM, double 260–400 DM, suite 400–800 DM. Set lunch 110 DM; full alc 120 DM. Reduced rates for children; special meals on request.

FULDA 6400 Hessen　　　　　　　　　　　　　　**Map 7**

Hotel "Zum Kurfürsten"　　　　　　　　*Tel* (0661) 7 00 01
Schlosstrasse 2

The old city of Fulda near the East German border, has a cathedral where St Boniface, an 8th-century English missionary to Germany, lies buried, having anointed Pippin the Short as king and then himself been murdered. The life of the Zum Kurfürsten *has also been eventful, for it was built in 1737 as a palace of the Prince Bishop; later Queen Victoria, Bismarck,* et al, *stayed in it. It is now a sleek, well-run hotel in the classic style, with good food. 68 rooms, 40 with bath or shower. B&B: single 49–90 DM, double 90–150 DM. Set menus from 30 DM* [1989]. *New nomination. More reports please.*

FÜSSEN-WEISSENSEE 8958 Bayern   Map 7

Seegasthof Weissensee   *Tel* (08362) 70 95

In a lakeside village just west of the old town of Füssen, and quite near the Royal Castles, this pleasant little Gasthof *has fine mountain views. Two modern buildings with alpine decor (lots of stripped pine); spacious bedrooms, cordial staff, lavish breakfasts, average main meals (good for fish). Closed 11 Jan–11 Feb, 16 Nov–19 Dec. 22 rooms, all with bath and shower. B&B double 102–138 DM. Set meals 25–45 DM. Endorsed this year, but fuller reports welcome.*

GEISLINGEN AN DER STEIGE 7340 Baden-Württemberg   ap 13

Burghotel   *Tel* (07331) 4 10 51
Burggasse 41
Weiler ob Helfenstein

Down a winding road in the rolling hills of the Schwäbische Alb, north-west of Ulm, an attractive modern building in superior motel style. Pleasant owners, nice rooms with balconies, varied breakfasts, indoor pool plus jacuzzis, and a large garden. No restaurant, but the Burgstüberl *close by has been found excellent. Closed 3 weeks in summer, also Christmas/New Year. 23 rooms, all with bath and shower. Rooms: single 50–100 DM, double 98–145 DM. Breakfast 8–20 DM. No recent reports: more welcome.*

GRAINAU 8104 Bayern   Map 7

Hotel Alpenhof   *Tel* (08821) 80 71
Alpspitzstrasse 22

Grainau, just west of Garmisch, is a popular village-resort at the foot of the high Alps. The *Alpenhof*, down a quiet side-road, is a big modern chalet in typical local style. Many rooms have a flower-decked balcony looking on to the craggy Zugspitze massif. The hotel has a pleasant garden and sun-terrace with yellow parasols, and a good indoor swimming pool. Reports this year have again been enthusiastic: "A delightful hotel in a lovely setting. Good honest German food very well presented; staff friendly and helpful; our room large and comfortable." "The meals were wonderful." Buffet breakfasts include a heated covered dish of bacon, scrambled eggs and sauté potatoes. (*Dr RH Freeman, Diane and Joel Morris*)

Open All year except 3–30 Apr and 10 Nov–17 Dec.
Rooms 29 double, 7 single – all with bath and shower, telephone, radio and TV; some with balcony.

Facilities Lift. Salon with open fireplace, TV room, restaurant; banqueting room. Indoor heated swimming pool and sauna. Garden and terrace.
Location 6 km SW of Garmisch-Partenkirchen. Hotel is central, but quietly situated. Parking.
Credit cards Access, Amex, Diners.
Terms [1989 rates] Dinner, B&B: single 78–120 DM, double 180–240 DM. Reduced rates and special meals for children.

GUTACH IM BREISGAU 7809 Baden-Württemberg   Map 7

Hotel-Restaurant Adler   *Tel* (07681) 70 22
Landstrasse 6

There are two Black Forest villages called Gutach, quite close to each other, and this is the less well known of the two, on the main Freiburg–Elzach road. The *Adler* is a new building in traditional rustic style, with oak-beamed ceilings and tiled floors. The staff are friendly, and the food has again been enjoyed this year, notably the soups and vegetables. An earlier view that still holds good: "Our bedroom was airy and attractive, furnished in repro rococo style with pretty pictures. It was at the back, quiet, looking on to a steep pine-clad hillside with huge rocks. The gardens are well tended: you can eat outside on warm days. One dining room has an open log fire and beautiful Victorian oil-lamps. The other has an original 19th-century mechanical organ with moving military statuettes, playing hum-pah-pah music. We enjoyed the frogs' legs, wild duck, venison with spätzle. Good Bodensee wine. Dogs permitted in restaurant: we were treated to a howling concerto for poodle, dachshund and mongrel."

Open All year except 2 weeks in Jan. Closed Sun, and Mon until 5 pm.
Rooms 1 suite, 10 double, 3 single – 13 with bath, 2 with shower, all with telephone; some with radio and TV.
Facilities Lounge/bar, TV room, 2 restaurants. Garden terrace with outdoor meals and barbecues in summer.
Location 21 km NW of Freiburg, just W of D294 to Elzach.
Credit cards None accepted.
Terms [1989 rates] B&B: single 60–80 DM, double 78–120 DM. Meals 31–70 DM.

HAGNAU 7759 Baden-Württemberg   Map 7

Erbguth's Landhaus   *Tel* (07532) 62 02 and 90 51
Neugartenstrasse 39   *Telex* 733811 ERBHA

Lake Constance (Bodensee) is a busy holiday area. Wisely, the Germans have put the accent here on smallish hotels of character rather than big lakeside palaces, and this *Landhaus* (country house) is typical – a converted private house, newly renovated, on the edge of a pretty lakeside village. It is a hotel of much personality, run with flair by a young couple, the Erbguths (he cooks, she hostesses). An inspector's recent assessment: "The elegant white marble hall leads to an equally elegant and small restaurant, newly decorated in soothing blue tones. Our comfortable bedroom had a small terrace and solid wooden furniture – more the feeling of a guest house than a luxury hotel. The welcome was warm. We took the 98 DM [1989] 8-course menu and judged it to be borderline *Michelin* rosette standard – excellent salad with sweetbreads.

Good buffet breakfast." An earlier view: "You dine by candle-light, amid flowers and modern 'antiques'. Much of the food was smoked and preserved in their own kitchens – e.g. superb home-smoked caviar. Frau Erbguth has panache and artistry: she dresses smartly, is charming, modern and slick, and the same could be said of her clientele. Not a cheap place, but the quality is superb." A *Jugendstil* villa by the lake, with four bedrooms, has just opened.

Open All year except 4 Jan–1 Mar. Restaurant closed Tue.
Rooms 16 double, 4 single – all with bath and/or shower, telephone, radio and TV. 5 in lake-side annexe 5 mins away. Some ground-floor rooms.
Facilities Lounge, TV room, bar, 2 restaurants; fitness room with sauna and solarium. Gardens and terraces. Private beach on lake.
Location On Lake Constance (Bodensee), just E of Meersburg. Parking.
Credit cards All major cards accepted.
Terms B&B: single 65–150 DM, double 110–320 DM; half board 35 DM per person added; full board 48 DM added. Set lunch/dinner 38–50 DM; full alc 45–50 DM. Reduced rates for children sharing parents' room.

HAMBURG 2000   Map 7

Hotel Abtei   *Tel* (040) 44 29 05 and 45 75 65
Abteistrasse 14, Hamburg 13   *Telex* 2165645 ABHA

An elegant little B&B hotel in a quiet residential district two miles north of the centre, near the Alster. Large, attractive rooms with good bathrooms; interesting breakfasts; small garden. Light meals provided on request. 18 rooms, all with bath and/or shower. B&B double 180 DM. No recent reports. More welcome.

Hotel Hanseatic   *Tel* (040) 48 57 72
Sierichstrasse 150
Hamburg 60

The very select *Hanseatic*, a pink-fronted patrician villa in a residential area north of the big Alster lake, is said to be Hamburg's smallest hotel, with just 13 rooms. But lucky are those who, by booking well ahead, are privileged to share in the very personal atmosphere created by owner-manager Wolfgang Schüler. "Herr Schüler's dedication and courtesy make this small hotel a rare jewel", "truly magnificent bedrooms", are two reports this year. Last year's: "He was exceedingly gracious and charming, takes great pride in his intimate hotel and should receive the 'Host of the Year' award. Fresh flowers in our room and a plate of fresh fruit on beautiful old Rosenthal china, plus big white towelling bathrobes. Breakfast was wonderful, served in a beautiful room hung with old oil paintings. The antique sterling coffee service gleamed." "He makes his own breads and marmalades, and serves his superb breakfasts personally in a high style verging on the camp." Some film, theatre and opera people visiting Hamburg prefer to stay here rather than at the larger and more expensive *Vier Jahreszeiten* (q.v.). (*H Langenberg, Jeremy and Anthea Larken*)

Open All year.
Rooms 1 suite, 2 studios, 10 double – all with bath and shower, telephone, radio and TV; baby-sitting on request. Ground-floor rooms

Facilities Lounge/bar, breakfast room; fitness room and sauna. Small garden. Alster lake and city park both 2 blocks away.
Location In Winterhude, 4 km N of city centre. Parking in street, but difficult.
Credit cards Access, Amex, Diners.
Terms Rooms: single occupancy 150–170 DM, double 180–250 DM, suite 250–350 DM. Breakfast 20 DM. Children under 12 sharing parents' room free. (No restaurant.)

Hotel Prem	*Tel* (040) 24 54 54
An der Alster 9	*Fax* (040) 28 03-851
Hamburg 1	*Telex* 2163115 PREM

Facing the Alster on its eastern shore, a mile from the city centre, this smallish and elegant hotel, not cheap, has again been liked in 1988/9. "Service is friendly and efficient," write Americans; "we had a wonderful meal, and took the breakfast buffet in their lovely garden." Others have spoken of "a charming flower-filled hotel with a courteous staff" and "large, airy, colourfully decorated rooms". Rooms however do vary in size: some look over the lake, some over gardens, and those facing the street can be noisy. The hotel's French restaurant, *La Mer*, has a good reputation; its garden restaurant serves German food. (*David and Patricia Hawkins, Russell W Field, JR Welby and others*)

Open All year.
Rooms 40 double, 11 single – all with bath and/or shower, telephone and TV. Some ground-floor rooms.
Facilities Lift. Lounge, TV room, bar, restaurant, *Stüberl*; conference facilities. Garden with restaurant. Garage.
Location On SE shore of Alster lake, 10 mins' walk from city centre and station.
Restriction Not suitable for &.
Credit cards All major cards accepted.
Terms B&B: single from 140 DM, double from 220 DM. Set lunch 65 DM, dinner 100 DM; full alc 145 DM. Reduced rates and special meals for children.

Hotel Vier Jahreszeiten	*Tel* (040) 3 49 40;
Neuer Jungfernstieg 9-14	*Reservations* (040) 3 49 46 93
Hamburg 36	*Fax* (040) 3 49 46 02
	Telex 211629

We are sorry to have received no reports this year on one of Europe's most famous and gracious luxury hotels, which faces Hamburg's inner lake, the Binnen Alster. Founded in 1897, it has no connection with the other *Vier Jahreszeiten* hotels (e.g. in Munich), it is privately owned and run by the Haerlin family who have carefully amassed its antique furnishings over the years. Despite its splendour it avoids pretentiousness, and although fairly large, with conference facilities, it is neither bustling nor impersonal, but has something of the calm atmosphere of a private club. The elegant rooms have antiques and splendid tapestries. Some, with balcony, look over the lake. "Nice extras included a shoehorn, and a thermometer for checking the bathwater – but you might well expect this at 300 DM a night." "Super-efficient German service dished up with a smile. Huge classy rooms with glittering chandeliers and gilt carved mirrors – all thoroughly plush and decadent. Best venison I've ever eaten – the restaurant (*Michelin* rosette) is one of Hamburg's best." The restaurant is beautiful, in a modern style; so is the *Konditorei Condi* that serves light lunches. Could recent visitors bring us up to date, please?

Open All year.
Rooms 11 suites, 75 double, 86 single – all with bath and shower, telephone, radio and TV.
Facilities Lounge, 2 bars, tea-room, 4 restaurants; conference and functions facilities; night club, barber's shop, wine shop.
Location Central, on W side of Alster lake. Parking.
Restriction Not suitable for &.
Credit cards All major cards accepted.
Terms Rooms: single 275–355 DM, double 375–545 DM, suite 650–930 DM. Set lunch/dinner 60-125 DM; full alc 80–100 DM.

Hotel Wedina   *Tel* (040) 24 30 11
Gurlittstrasse 23,
Hamburg 1

Very modestly priced for Hamburg but quite central (in a quiet side-street near the southern end of the Alster lake), the useful Wedina offers pleasant spacious bedrooms and good German breakfasts, plus the bonus of a small garden, with outdoor heated pool and sauna. Street parking. Open 10 Feb–12 Dec. 23 rooms, most with bath or shower. B&B: single 60–90 DM, double 88–120 DM [1989]. No restaurant. Recent nomination, endorsed in 1989, but we'd like more reports please.

HEIDELBERG 6900 Baden-Württemberg   **Map 7**

Hotel Alt Heidelberg   *Tel* (06221) 91 50
Rohrbacher Strasse 29   *Fax* (06221) 164272
                                            Telex 461897

Ten minutes' walk from the heart of the *alt* part of town (the university library, former students' prison, and Friedrich-Ebert museum are all worth a visit), this Guide debutant is a neat, well-modernised hotel on a main street (but quiet), whose *Graimberg* restaurant serves some of the best food in town – "a French chef doing wonders with German dishes" (e.g. venison with spätzle, warm röte grütze, both enjoyed in 1989). "Charming, cosy and friendly", says a regular. But another visitor found service erratic. Some rooms are spacious and modern; others smaller, with antiques. (*Reginald B Vaughan, Eileen Spencer, JA and KA*) Live jazz on Fridays in the basement bar: but it's more fun to visit one of the uproarious old student pubs in the old town, such as *Scnookeloch*, or *Seppl* where you sit round big tables and beer is drunk communally out of giant glass boots.

Open All year. Restaurant closed Sat till 6 pm.
Rooms 80 – all with bath and shower, telephone, radio and TV.
Facilities Lift. Hall, restaurant, bar; conference facilities. Sauna.
Location Central. Parking.
Credit cards All major cards accepted.
Terms [1989 rates] Rooms: single 95–130 DM, double 125–165 DM, suite 185 DM. Breakfast 15 DM. Alc 35–60 DM. Children under 12 sharing parents' room free.

HELLENTHAL 5374 Nordrhein-Westfalen   Map 7

Haus Lichtenhardt   *Tel* (02482) 614

In the northern part of the Eifel massif, not far from the enchanting old town of Monschau and the absorbing open-air museum of rural life at Kommern, this unpretentious modern hotel is in a quiet hilly setting outside the village. Comfortable rooms, friendly and personal service, modest prices. Indoor pool. Closed 17–27 Dec. 19 rooms, most with bath and/or shower. B&B double 65–90 DM. Set menus 13–31 DM [1989]. New nomination. More reports welcome, especially on the food.

HINTERZARTEN 7824 Baden-Württemberg   Map 7

Pension Hotel Sassenhof   *Tel* (07652) 15 15
Adlerweg 17

"This very superior yet friendly *pension* is just what you might expect to find in one of the smartest of Black Forest resorts, popular alike with skiers and walkers. It's a modern gabled building, flower-decked, facing the wide village green, with views of the hills. Elegant public rooms, and a big indoor swimming pool with picture windows facing the lake and woods." "Fabulous!" runs another report this year; "a romantic garret room, delicious and copious breakfast, proprietors charming." (*JA and KA, Bettye Chambers*)

Open All year except 20 Nov–20 Dec.
Rooms 6 suites, 7 double, 10 single – all with bath and/or shower, telephone, radio, TV and tea-making facilities.
Facilities Lift. Hall, lounges, TV room, breakfast room. Indoor swimming pool, sauna, solarium. Terrace; garden.
Location. Central, parking. Hinterzarten is 26 km E of Freiburg.
Restriction No children under 3.
Credit cards All major cards accepted.
Terms B&B: single 50–90 DM, double 60–80 DM per person, suite 70–90 DM. (No restaurant.)

HOFGEISMAR 3520 Hessen   Map 7

Burghotel Dornröschenschloss   *Tel* (05678) 10 52
 Sababurg   *Fax* (05678) 10 32
Hofgeismar-Sababurg

An inspector's discovery this year, on the rolling wooded plateau west of the Weser valley: "A self-consciously romantic old 14th-century schloss, whose twin green cupolas tower up through the oakwoods. It was long a country home of the princes of Hessen: the brothers Grimm were invited here for hunting parties, and it is said to have been the model for the castle in *Dornröschen* (*The Sleeping Beauty*). Today it capitalises on these fairy-tale associations: statuettes of Puss in Boots and Cinderella stand by

---

Please write and confirm an entry when it is deserved. If you think that a hotel is not as good as we say, write and tell us.

the entrance, and the garden shop will sell you some rather grim Grimm Kitsch. Off-putting, maybe: but the hotel itself is delightful, a stylish conversion, very well run by its cultivated owner, Karl Koseck. Lovely rooms in the tower with canopied beds; lovely views, too, from rooms and restaurant; good food, especially the pheasant and venison in season. Sometimes, Grimm tales are read aloud during meals; in summer, there are concerts and fairy-tale plays in the medieval courtyard. It is much liked by Americans and very popular for functions (five wedding parties were in progress on the day of our visit). For further good measure, the 120-hectare zoo on the Sababurg estate is Germany's oldest (1571). It has buffaloes, bears, penguins, even Exmoor ponies – but no Frog Prince."

Open All year except Jan and Feb.
Rooms 17 double, 1 single – 8 with bath, 10 with shower, all with telephone and radio; 8 with TV.
Facilities Salon with TV, dining rooms; conference/functions facilities; museum. Courtyard. Garden. Zoo adjacent.
Location 14 km NE of Hofgeismar, 30 km N of Kassel.
Restrictions Not suitable for &.
Credit cards All major cards accepted.
Terms B&B: single 80–150 DM, double 150–240 DM. Set lunch/dinner 55– 70 DM; full alc 45–60 DM. 1-night bookings refused at weekends. Special meals for children.

HOLZAPPEL 5409 Rheinland-Pfalz   Map 7

Altes Herrenhaus zum Bären   *Tel* (06439) 70 14
Hauptstrasse 15

This most stylishly decorated restaurant-with-rooms stands in a village square amid pleasant wooded country between Koblenz and Limburg: "The half-timbered 17th-century hotel, small and intimate, is a gem inside, with pleasant furnishings, bowls of flowers, and a cared-for atmosphere. Our room was well equipped, the owners were helpful and informative, and the food was some of the best we have eaten in Germany, making the most of fresh ingredients. Breakfast was a feast, including raspberries and omelettes. Each departing guest gets a packet of fruit." The delightful annexe, the *Goethehaus*, once visited by the poet, houses all the bedrooms (ten are new this year) and has a wine cellar.

Open All year except Jan.
Rooms 10 suites, 10 double, 4 single – all with bath and shower, telephone, radio TV and baby-listening. Ground-floor rooms. All in *Goethehaus*.
Facilities Lift. Restaurant, wine cellar; 2 conference rooms. Terrace. Garden.
Location In village, 16 km W of Limburg, on road to Bad Ems. Parking.
Credit cards All major cards accepted.
Terms [1989 rates] B&B: single 49.50–95 DM, double 98–165 DM, Set meals 30– 35 DM; full alc 70 DM. Reduced rates and special meals for children.

HOPFEN AM SEE 8959 Bayern   Map 7

Hotel Alpenblick   *Tel* (08362) 70 18
Uferstrasse 10   *Telex* 541343 ABLIK

As its name indicates, there are views of the Allgaü Alps (and of the lake) from the front-room balconies of this spruce flower-decked chalet-style hotel, modern

*but in traditional style, set beside a lake in a pleasant little Bavarian resort
north of Füssen. Large airy rooms, friendly staff, better-than-average food.
46 rooms, most with bath and shower. B&B double 126–156 DM. Meals 25–
55 DM [1989]. New nomination. More reports welcome.*

HÖRSTEL-RIESENBECK 4446 Nordrhein-Westfalen Map 7

Schlosshotel Surenberg *Tel* (05454) 70 92
Surenberg 13 *Telex* 94586 SUREN

This appealing Guide newcomer, a *Relais du Silence*, lies in a little-known
part of Germany – the opulent farming country of northern Westphalia,
flat but pleasantly pastoral, not unlike Norfolk: "The name is misleading,
for it's not a converted castle but a modern sporty ranch-hotel on the
estate of a moated *Wasserschloss*, the home of the influential president of
the German farmers' union. He owns this lovely, spacious hotel, and it is
run for him with breezy efficiency by jovial Klaus Trottier, a Huguenot,
who also cooks: in his big open-plan restaurant, very popular locally, we
enjoyed a good meal, especially the foie gras salad and braised
vegetables. Service by local girls was remarkable, even by high German
standards, for its smiling stylish courtesy. Our large bedroom was rather
bare in decor, but well equipped, with french windows opening onto a
flowery balcony and the wide grounds. The hotel is much used for sporty
weekends: as well as a fine heated indoor pool, and various games, it has
large riding stables where many local people keep their horses. The
restaurant's wide panoramic windows give straight onto the main indoor
riding hall, so that you can watch the riders and horses while you eat.
We've never seen this in a hotel before."

Open All year except 9–22 Jan.
Rooms 23 – all with bath and/or shower, telephone and TV; many with balcony.
Facilities Restaurant; conference facilities. Indoor swimming pool, sauna, fitness
centre. Large grounds with stables; children's playground, minigolf; bicycles for
hire.
Location 6 km SW of Hörstel which is 44 km N of Münster.
Credit cards Access, Amex.
Terms [1989 rates] B&B: single 83–94 DM, double 139–160 DM. Meals 34–65 DM.

ISMANING 8045 Bayern Map 7

Hotel Fischerwirt *Tel* (089) 96 48 53
Schlosstrasse 17 *Fax* (089) 96 35 83

*In an attractive commuter town on the northern edge of Munich, set back in a
quiet courtyard, this typical modern German inn is clean, friendly and efficient.
Nice lounge, small garden; lavish breakfasts; good restaurant. Closed Christmas
and New Year. 44 rooms, all with bath or shower. B&B double 78–165 DM.
Latest reports vary between "very good" and "overpriced". More welcome.*

If you are nominating a hotel, please do make sure that you tell us
enough to convey its character and quality. We can't make good
bricks without plenty of straw.

KETTWIG 4300 Nordrhein-Westfalen   Map 7

Hotel Schloss Hugenpoet   *Tel* (02054) 1 20 40
August-Thyssen-Strasse 51   *Fax* (02054) 1 20 450

The winding valley of the river Ruhr is not an industrial blackspot but quite rural and idyllic (the big mines and steelworks are a few miles to the north); and here on its banks, within the borders of the Essen residential suburb of Kettwig, is this moated 16th-century castle, now a luxurious hotel. Its newly renovated bedrooms and *Michelin*-rosetted cuisine have been again admired this year, endorsing these 1988 views: "The atmosphere is warm and welcoming, with the open fire and stately furnishings. Our room was large, with a curtained-off sleeping area, newly re-covered antique and modern chairs, and a large marble-tiled bathroom." "A fine black-marble staircase with red carpet in the foyer, reception staff very thoughtful, wonderful afternoon tea, and interesting French cooking." The hotel and restaurant cater for functions, but these are not usually obtrusive. (*Derek and Annette Lambert*) The grandiose Krupp family mansion in Kettwig, Villa Hügel, now a museum, is worth visiting; and do not miss the Folkwang museum of local history in Essen. Both provide poignant insights into the splendours and horrors of the Ruhr's mighty past.

Open All year except 24 Dec.
Rooms 1 suite, 13 double, 5 single – all with bath and shower, telephone, radio TV, and mini-bar.
Facilities Lift. Large hall, salon, wine cellar, restaurant; conference facilities; chapel for weddings and christenings; terrace. Large grounds with garden and tennis court.
Location 11 km SW of Essen off A52, near A2 and A3 motorways. Parking.
Credit cards All major cards accepted.
Terms B&B: single 190–255 DM, double 245–365 DM, suite 410 DM. Alc (excluding wine) 100–130 DM. Reduced rates for children sharing parents' room.

KOBLENZ 5400 Rheinland-Pfalz   Map 7

Zum schwarzen Bären   *Tel* (0261) 4 40 74
Koblenzer Strasse 35,
Koblenz-Moselweiss

This city at the confluence of the Rhine and the Mosel has been largely rebuilt since wartime bombing: it contains few buildings of note save the massive Ehrenbreitstein citadel, but it remains a good base for exploring these two rivers. The "Black Bears", a small modern winehouse-with-rooms, which has been in the same family since 1810, is in the suburb of Moselweiss, west of the city centre. "Rooms are comfortable but basically furnished, the bathrooms all have a shower, not a bath. There is a spectacular lack of mirrors – just as well, for the lighting is appalling. But the hotel's real strength lies in the warmth of the welcome provided by the Kölsch family and Peter Kölsch's superlative cuisine – e.g. stuffed breast of chicken poached in white wine, pigeon with truffles in a whisper of pastry, apple pancakes with cinnamon ice cream. He cooks with love, and tells you where you're going wrong when choosing your meal." An endorser this year laments the lack of comfortable chairs. (*Marion Godfrey and Judy Smith; also NR Measey*)

Open All year except 2 weeks in Feb and 2 weeks in Aug. Restaurant closed Sun evening and Mon.
Rooms 10 double, 3 single – 1 with bath, 12 with shower; all with telephone; TV on request. 8 in annexe. Some ground-floor rooms.
Facilities Lounge, *Bierstube*, TV room; conference facilities; terrace.
Location 1.5 km W of Koblenz. Parking.
Credit cards All major cards accepted.
Terms B&B: single 60 DM, double 95 DM. Set lunch 26–48 DM, dinner 45–98 DM; full alc 40 DM. Reduced rates and special meals for children.

KRONBERG IM TAUNUS 6242 Hessen   Map 7

Schlosshotel Kronberg   *Tel* (06173) 7 01 01
Hainstrasse 25   *Fax* (06173) 70 12 67
                    Telex 415424 SHLO

This vast grey towered and gabled *Schloss*, eminently Victorian, was built for Queen Victoria's eldest daughter after the death of her husband, Kaiser Friedrich III. It is now a classy hotel (still sometimes also used privately by visiting royalty) but is no more expensive than the leading hotels in central Frankfurt, 17 kilometres away. This year the management changed, but regulars returning in 1989 felt that standards had improved, if anything, as a result. Guests are now given gift-wrapped ashtrays as a "welcome" present! "For comfort and style, still our favourite hotel in the Frankfurt area," is their view; "our bedroom overlooking the beautiful grounds was lovely. The public rooms are imposing, with wood panelling and huge tapestries. Service can be a little slow, but staff are polite; the dining rooms are attractive and the food good. Lavish breakfasts." Male guests must wear jacket and tie for dinner. (*Stephan and Kate Murray-Sykes*) The grounds contain an 18-hole golf course.

Open All year.
Rooms 7 suites, 24 double, 26 single – all with bath and/or shower, telephone, radio and TV.
Facilities Lift. Lobby, lounge, bar, restaurant; functions facilities. Park with 18-hole golf course.
Location 15 mins' walk from centre of Kronberg. Open parking.
Restriction Not suitable for &.
Credit cards All major cards accepted.
Terms Rooms: single 220–325 DM, double 340–530 DM, suite 630–1,400 DM. Breakfast 23 DM. Set lunch 49.50 DM, dinner 125 DM; full alc 116 DM. Special meals for children on request.

LEMGO 4920 Nordrhein-Westfalen   Map 7

Auf dem Brokhof   *Tel* (05261) 44 82
Zur Behrensburg 19, Lemgo-
Lüerdissen

"A delightful surprise", say this year's nominators. "The charming Wittigs, retired farmers in their early 60s, have converted their farmhouse into a very sympathetic guesthouse, set in open rolling country just north of the fine old Hanseatic town of Lemgo, near Bielefeld. Pleasant, unforced touches, such as an old cartwheel for garden decor. Bedrooms in the new annexe are very spacious; the main building has smaller ones.

Furniture is modern utility, but serviceable. The Wittigs provide hearty, wholesome rural fare, such as home-made soups, braised pork, and big breakfasts. Prices are absurdly low. This would be an ideal base for a quiet country holiday in a little-known part of North Germany where there's much to see: Lemgo itself has a superb Altstadt of medieval gabled houses, and a museum of torture inflicted on witches." (*JA and KA*)

Open All year.
Rooms 6 rooms, 3 apartments, all with bath and/or shower.
Facilities Sitting room with piano, 2 dining rooms (one for non-smokers), playroom with ping-pong, swings. Garden.
Location 4 km N of Lemgo, in suburb of Lüerdissen.
Terms B&B 26–30 DM. Dinner 10 DM.

LENZKIRCH 7825 Baden-Württemberg　　　　　　　　　Map 7

Hotel Ursee　　　　　　　　　　　　　　　　　*Tel* (07653) 7 81
Grabenstrasse 18

Set amid rolling wooded country just outside the popular resort of Lenzkirch, in the southern Black Forest near Titisee: a big modern chalet, mixing the smart and cosy in true local style. Spacious rooms (with clashing decor), excellent food including buffet breakfast. Closed early Nov–mid-Dec. Restaurant closed Mon. 49 rooms, most with bath and/or shower. B&B double 98–138 DM. Meals 30–60 DM [1989]. New nomination. More reports please.

LIMBURG AN DER LAHN 6250 Hessen　　　　　　　　　Map 7

Hotel Zimmermann　　　　　　　　　　　　*Tel* (06431) 46 11
Blumenröderstrasse 1　　　　　　　　　　　　*Fax* (06431) 4 13 14

Dull-looking from outside, but inside richly furnished with antiques, this modern hotel behind the station is only a short walk from Limburg's picturesque old quarter and hilltop Gothic cathedral. Triple glazing ensures quiet. Prices moderate, owner friendly, service very thoughtful; dinner for residents only. 30 rooms, all with bath and/or shower, double 98–220 DM [1989]. Endorsed this year, but further reports welcome.

MARKTHEIDENFELD 8772 Bayern　　　　　　　　　　　Map 7

Hotel Anker　　　　　　　　　　　　　　*Tel* (09391) 40 41
Obertorstrasse 6–8　　　　　　　　　　　*Telex* 689608 DEPAN

In a small wine-growing town on the Main west of Würzburg, this enticing Guide newcomer is a smart modern white building, stylishly furnished in good taste (red print in *Michelin*), owned by the Deppisch family who also have the elegant *Weinhaus Anker* restaurant just opposite. "A delightful family-run place. Much care and pride has been lavished on the rooms. Herr Deppisch owns extensive vineyards round the hotel, and you can buy his excellent Franconian wines. The *Weinhaus* well deserves its *Michelin* rosette: all food, including butter and cheese, comes from their local farm. The perfect combination of a hotel and restaurant run by people who really care for their guests." (*Judy and Gordon Smith*) Though they are central most rooms are quiet as they overlook a courtyard. More reports welcome.

Open All year. Restaurant closed Mon and Tue midday.
Rooms 3 suites, 22 double, 13 single – 30 with bath, 8 with shower, all with telephone, radio, TV; baby-sitting on request. Ground floor rooms suitable for &.
Facilities 2 lifts, ramps. Lounge, TV room, breakfast room, restaurant, cellar (wine tastings); conference facilities. Courtyard where meals are served.
Location Central, next to church. Garage (8 DM). Town is 29 km W or Würzburg on B8.
Credit cards Access, Amex. (Diners in restaurant only).
Terms B&B: single 85–95 DM, double 135–175 DM, suite 250 DM. Set lunch 40 DM, dinner 50 DM; full alc 90 DM. Reduced rates and special meals for children.

MEERSBURG 7758 Baden-Württemberg   Map 7

Hotel-Gasthof zum Bären   *Tel* (07532) 60 44
Marktplatz 11

The prettiest town on Lake Constance has half-timbered houses, a romantic old castle and a newer pink baroque one, all crowded together in the *Altstadt* on a hill above the lake. Here in the lovely market square is the *Hotel-Gasthof zum Bären*, a stunning old building with flower-pots and carvings on its quaint corner-tower, an inn since the 17th century, now owned and run by the charming Gilowsky family. Readers this year have again liked this "unpretentious guesthouse with its creaking wooden floors", and its warm family welcome. "The restaurant is a delight; I was asked if I would mind sharing a table, and this seemed to be the status quo. An excellent meal of baked perch from the lake and fine cheeses." Others have admired the beamed ceilings, Alpine furniture and cheerful rooms: "A spacious, comfortable room facing the square, with a charming sitting-alcove in the quaint old tower." Be warned that the stairs are fairly steep and there is no lift; also the quieter back rooms lack a view. (*Dr FP Woodford*)

Open 20 Mar–15 Nov. Restaurant closed Mon.
Rooms 13 double, 3 single – all with shower. 1 double in annexe.
Facilities 2 restaurants.
Location Central (back rooms quietest). 15 garages.
Restriction Not suitable for &.
Credit cards None accepted.
Terms B&B: single 52 DM, double 98–108 DM. Set lunch/dinner 22–32 DM; full alc 37–47 DM. Extra bed for child in parents' room 20 DM; special meals.

MUNICH 8000 Bayern   Map 7

Hotel Biederstein   *Tel* (089) 39 50 72
Keferstrasse 18, Munich 40

A spruce little hotel, modern but with some good classic furniture, in a residential street between the Englischer Garten and the raffish night-club quarter of Schwabing, Munich's Chelsea-cum-Soho: the city centre is two miles to the south. Service mainly efficient, bedrooms clean and comfortable; no restaurant, but light meals on request. Garage. Some redecoration has taken

*place this year. 31 rooms, all with bath and shower, and balcony. B&B: single
110–125 DM, double 135–165 DM. Restored to Guide after earlier criticisms.
More reports still needed.*

Gästehaus Englischer Garten .
Liebergesellstrasse 8
Munich 40

Tel (089) 39 20 34

*Only 4 km from the city centre, a creeper-covered 18th-century millhouse
beside a stream at the edge of the Englischer Garten in Schwabing, popular with
artists and writers. Garden, old furniture, helpful staff, family owners. Cosy
rooms in main building: those in annexe less attractive. 37 rooms, 20 with bath
and shower. B&B double 99–172 DM. No restaurant. Some criticisms. More
reports please.*

Marienbad Hotel
Barerstrasse 11, Munich 2

Tel (089) 59 55 85
Fax (089) 59 82 38

Centrally and quietly located near the Alte Pinakothek, this little B&B
hotel has few frills or graces but is friendly and serviceable and continues
to have its fans. A report this year: "Perfectly quiet, and the better rooms
at least are quite large and well equipped. More wattage would be
appreciated. Breakfast room gloomy: but an ample breakfast will be
brought to your room." (*Dr FP Woodford*)

Open All year.
Rooms 16 double, 11 single – 22 with shower, all with telephone.
Facilities Lift. Salon with TV.
Location Central, but very quiet; approach from Karolinenplatz. Parking nearby.
Credit cards None accepted.
Terms B&B: single 65–120 DM, double 160 DM. Reduced rates for children
sharing parents' room. (No restaurant.)

Hotel an der Oper
Falkenturmstrasse 10
Munich 2

Tel (089) 22 87 11
Telex 522588

Down a small side-street off the famous and fashionable Maximilian-
strasse, this bed-and-breakfast hotel is much frequented by visitors to the
nearby Opera – as its name implies. "Very good value," is an inspector's
judgement; "the white-walled bedrooms are plain (apart from the
ubiquitous chandeliers) but comfortable, with modern bathrooms. The
green-leather armchairs and sofas in the lobby were comfortable, and
newspapers on wooden handles were available in the best Mitteleuropa
tradition. Service was helpful and personal, especially with regard to
carrying luggage. Breakfast was adequate. The elegant, intimate and
expensive *Bouillabaisse* restaurant is in the same building: its French
cooking did not greatly impress us, but there are many cheaper and better
places nearby" (e.g. the huge, bustling *Franziskaner*).

Open All year.
Rooms 55 – all with bath and/or shower, telephone and radio.

Facilities Lift. Lounge, TV room, breakfast room.
Location Central, near Opera House.
Restriction Not suitable for &.
Credit cards Access, Amex, Diners.
Terms [1989 rates] B&B: single 110–125 DM, double 170–190 DM. (No restaurant.)

Trustee Parkhotel　　　　　　　　　　　*Tel* (089) 51 99 50
Parkstrasse 31, Munich 2　　　　　　　*Fax* (089) 51 99 54 20
　　　　　　　　　　　　　　　　　Telex 5218296 TRUP

A new upper-medium-priced hotel, west of the city centre and close to the main station, exhibition centre and Theresien park (where the Oktoberfest is held). "I had an enormous room, beautifully furnished," says a recent visitor. "Cheerful and efficient service, first-class welcome with fresh fruit in the room, good food, and every facility for the business traveller." The hotel is quiet, built around its own courtyard; some rooms have a balcony. (*Endorsed this year by Garry and Janette Collier*)

Open All year except Christmas and New Year.
Rooms 36 – all with bath and shower, telephone, radio and TV. Ground-floor rooms.
Facilities Lift. Lounge, bar, restaurant; conference facilities. Garden.
Location 1 km SW of central station. Parking.
Credit cards All major cards accepted.
Terms Rooms: single 185–250 DM, double 220–290 DM, suite 300–390 DM. Breakfast 18 DM. Set lunch/dinner 35 DM; full alc 50 DM. Children under 12 free of charge; special meals.

MÜNSTER 4400 Nordrhein-Westfalen　　　　　　　　　　**Map 7**

Hotel Schloss Wilkinhege　　　　　　　*Tel* (0251) 21 30 45
Steinfurter Strasse 374

The area around Westphalia's historic capital is well known for its numerous *Wasserburgen* – old castles girt by broad moats or even by lakes. These watery surrounds were originally defensive, but are now ornamental. Some of the castles are still lived in by descendants of the original owners in this very aristocratic part of Germany; others are now colleges, or museums. This one in the city's north-west outskirts, dating from the 16th century, is a fairly smart hotel, brought to the Guide by two reports this year: "A lovely peaceful setting with a golf course behind. Ducks, geese, peacocks, etc, strut in the courtyard within the moat. We stayed in a modern room in the annexe, converted from the stables. The food was excellent and the young staff were pleasant." "We got a friendly welcome and a huge family suite. There's an atmospheric *Schlosskeller*, but we dined out on the terrace – a relaxed ambience, thoughtful service and the best food we had in Germany (but not cheap). The very pretty chapel is open to guests." (*Dr Carolyn A Cooper, Mary Hanson*)

Open All year.
Rooms 4 suites, 38 double and single – all with bath and shower, telephone, TV and mini-bar.
Facilities Lounge, 3 restaurants, conference and banqueting facilities; terrace. Park with tennis courts and golf course.
Location 2 km NW of city centre, just off B54. Parking.
Credit cards All major cards accepted.

Terms [1989 rates] B&B: single 115–160 DM, double 165–180 DM, suite 280 DM. Meals 58–79 DM.

NECKARGEMÜND 6903 Baden-Württemberg   Map 7

Hotel zum Ritter   *Tel* (06223) 70 35
Neckarstrasse 40   *Telex* 461837

In a pretty part of the Neckar valley, just east of Heidelberg, here's an old hunting lodge dating from 1579, well modernised but with folksy touches such as suits of armour. Rooms with riverside views; good breakfasts. 39 rooms, all with bath or shower. B&B double 98–180 DM. Set menus 45–55 DM. New nomination. More reports please, especially on the food.

OBERAMMERGAU 8103 Bayern   Map 7

Gasthof "Zur Rose"   *Tel* (08822) 47 06
Dedlerstrasse 9

Those keen to see the much-contested 32-year-old mother-of-two Virgin Mary in the 1990 *Passion Play* had better book quick for the *Zur Rose*, as for any other hotel in this about-to-be-crowded-out little town. Even outside Passion Play Year (once a decade), it's an unashamedly touristy place, with every other shop a *Holzschnitzerei* selling wood carvings, mostly of a religious or religiose character. But in any year it is also a good centre for hiking or cross-country skiing, and for exploring the Bavarian alps. The *Zur Rose* "is the quintessence of the *gemütlich* – a fine example of a friendly Alpine inn, and has been in the Stückl family for two generations. They speak good English and are warmly hospitable. The rooms, well heated, are simple but not spartan. In the big attractive dining room, meals are substantial meaty affairs; public rooms are full of fine furniture and old paintings (family heirlooms)." Admired again this year for its "excellent food, simple comfort and friendly owners". (*Stephen Ruell*)

Open All year except 1 Nov–15 Dec.
Rooms 24 double, 4 single – 4 with bath, 2 with shower. 10 self-catering units for 2–6 people with shower, kitchenette, telephone and TV.
Facilities Salon, dining room. Garden.
Location In town centre. Parking. Oberammergau is 19 km N of Garmisch.
Credit cards All major cards accepted.
Terms B&B: single 30 DM, double 58 DM. Dinner, B&B 18 DM added per person. Full alc 30 DM. Reduced rates and special meals for children.

OBERWESEL 6532 Rheinland-Pfalz   Map 7

Burghotel-Restaurant Auf   *Tel* (06744) 70 27
  Schönburg   *Telex* 42321 BURG

Visitors this year were mightily impressed: "Upstream from Koblenz, towering high above the west bank of the Rhine, the massive medieval stronghold of the Dukes of Schonburg is three fortresses in one, each with its own keep. One is now used as a Catholic holiday and social centre, but the others have been tastefully converted into as delightful a hotel as any that we have visited recently in Germany. It is owned and run by a friendly and civilised young couple, the Hüttls. While the *Burg*'s outward aspect is severe, inside all is intimate and cosy – small beamed courtyards and dining rooms, a handsome library, slightly twee bedrooms with four-posters (best are those with balconies in the old tower). It's the kind of obviously super-romantic place that foreign tourists would adore, yet is no phoney tourist-trap, for it's all done with such taste and unaffected grace. Of course the view over the river is superb. The Hüttls have painted one of the outer walls bright red, because that's how it was in the 16th century, when painted walls were a sign of wealth." "Attractively furnished with antiques; beautiful restaurant with a sense of intimacy, excellent food and service." (*ECM Begg, and others*)

Open 1 Mar–30 Nov. Restaurant closed Mon.
Rooms 1 suite, 17 double, 3 single – 12 with bath, 8 with shower, all with telephone, radio and T V.
Facilities Lift. Small library, 3 dining rooms; courtyard where meals are served in fine weather.
Location 2 km S of Oberwesel, which is 42 km S of Koblenz.
Restriction Not suitable for &.
Credit cards Access, Amex, Visa.
Terms B&B: single 85–90 DM, double 130–220 DM, suite 240 DM; dinner, B&B 50 DM per person added. Set lunch/dinner 40–85 DM; full alc from 70 DM. Reduced rates and special meals for children.

OFFENBURG 7600 Baden-Württemberg   **Map 7**

Hotel Sonne   *Tel* (0781) 7 10 39
Hauptstrasse 94

Commended again in 1989, this old coaching-inn makes a useful stopover. Industrial Offenburg is close to Strasbourg, the Black Forest and the Frankfurt–Basel *Autobahn*. The Schimpf-Schöppner family claims to have been running an inn here since 1350, and though much rebuilt in the 19th century, the hotel still has many earlier antiques. Napoleon stayed here, and you are shown the pewter tureen he used. "Despite this weight of history, the *Sonne* is utterly unpretentious; no foyer, the front door leads straight into the big beamed *Stube*, which today is very much a social centre. At its big round *Stammtisch*, elderly local worthies were tippling and speechifying in true German style, while we enjoyed sound Baden cooking and local wine from the Schimpfs' own vineyards." "Good value, with wholesome, unsophisticated cooking; the rooms in the new part are fairly spartan, but adequate", runs a report this year. Rooms vary, some being old and full of charm, but unmodernised; some newer, but duller.

Open All year. Restaurant closed Sat and Christmas.
Rooms 2 suites, 14 double, 21 single – 7 with bath, 13 with shower, all with telephone; 3 with T V.
Facilities T V room, 2 dining rooms.
Location Central; in pedestrian zone in old part of town. Parking.
Restriction Only restaurant suitable for &.
Credit cards Access, Amex, Visa.
Terms B&B: single 46–62 DM, double 65–88 DM; dinner, B&B: 14 DM added. Full alc 18–35 DM. Reduced rates for children.

Report forms (Freepost in UK) will be found at the end of the Guide.

PEGNITZ 8570 Bayern   Map 7

Pflaums Posthotel   *Tel* (09241) 72 50
Nürnberger Strasse 14   *Fax* (09241) 404
                                                Telex 642433 PPP

The Pflaum family have run this old post house in a small town between
Bayreuth and Nuremberg since 1707. It is now a stylish and fairly
expensive hotel. This year a returning regular has renewed her eulogies,
"All Pflaums hospitable as ever. They gave us a delicious room full of
colour, armchairs, desk, lots of lights, even a CD set-up. The lay-out of
breakfast is pure theatre – five round tables laid out with *everything*. The
staff used to be in *Tracht* but now look slinky and *moderne* in pretty
blouses and skirts." This reader's earlier view, "If you like a country-
house-style hotel with an international and musical flavour, this one is
very much worth a detour, though during the Bayreuth Festival or the
Nuremberg trade fairs it is hard to find a room. One brother Pflaum is the
charming manager of house and another is considered one of the best
chefs in Germany (*Michelin* rosette). Delicious food in the two restaurants
(kid and game are specialities). Drinks by the fire in winter, with pretty
little curved sofas to sit on; in summer, coffee out in the sunshine with the
fountains playing, or strawberry cake for tea."(*John and Eileen Spencer*)
Some rooms are in a modern extension. The Pflaums also offer Bayreuth
Wagner operas on a large screen.

Open All year.
Rooms 25 suites, 25 double – all with bath and shower, telephone, radio and TV.
1 ground-floor suite.
Facilities Lift. Lounge, bar, 2 restaurants; conference facilities. Indoor swimming
pool and health club, massage, sauna; indoor golf. Garden with terrace for dining.
Location 1 km SW of Pegnitz, 33 km N of Nuremberg.
Credit cards All major cards accepted.
Terms Rooms: single 135–240 DM, double 168–490 DM, suite 290–1,150 DM.
Buffet breakfast 18 DM. Set lunch/dinner 32 DM and 140 DM; full alc 110 DM.
Reduced rates and special meals for children.

RAVENSBURG 7980 Baden-Württemberg   Map 7

Romantik Hotel Waldhorn   *Tel* (0751) 1 60 21
Marienplatz 15   *Telex* 723211 WHORN

*In an attractive old Swabian town, a family-run hotel of some character, in an
old building with panelled public rooms. Pleasant bedrooms, excellent local
dishes* (Michelin *rosette), good buffet breakfasts in a cosy room. 40 rooms, all
with bath. B&B single 88–125 DM, double 130–180 DM. Set menu 28 DM. New
nomination. More reports please.*

REICHENAU (Insel) 7752 Baden-Württemberg   Map 7

Romantik Hotel Seeschau   *Tel* (07534) 2 57
Schiffslände 8   *Fax* (07534) 78 84

Reichenau is a pastoral low-lying island in the western part of the
Bodensee (Lake of Constance) , linked to the mainland by a causeway. In

the Middle Ages it was a major monastic centre, and two glories survive from that time: the late 9th-century Carolingian church of St-George (amazing wall paintings of *c*. AD 1000), and the Romanesque abbey at Mittelzell. Today the island is given over to market gardening and tourism, and its best hotel is the *Seeschau*, a gabled building by the water's edge, run by the Winkelmann-Roser family for 60 years. A report this year, "A charming and friendly little place, quite spruce and smart – panelled walls, old framed prints, uniformed waitresses. Bedrooms a bit small, but most have lake views. Good local fish, prepared by Horst Winkelmann in a somewhat *nouvelle* style, just about deserving its *Michelin* rosette. Lovely setting by the little landing-stage, but very trippery in summer." (*JA and KA*)

Open All year except 6–25 Jan and 15 Oct–20 Dec. Restaurant closed Sun night and Mon.
Rooms 11 double – all with bath or shower, telephone and TV.
Facilities Salon, 2 restaurants; conference facilities. Garden, terrace.
Location 10 km W of Konstanz. Reached by ferry or causeway. Parking.
Restriction Not suitable for &.
Credit cards Access, Amex, Diners.
Terms B&B: single 75–100 DM, double 150–180 DM. Set lunch 35 DM, dinner 70 DM; full alc 65 DM. Special meals for children.

RETTENBACH 8449 Bayern   Map 7

Kurhotel Gut Schmelmerhof   *Tel* (09965) 189-0
St-Englmar–Rettenbach

About 15 minutes' drive from the Schwarzach exit of the Regensburg–Passau motorway, Rettenbach is a small village amid the hilly pine-wooded landscapes of eastern Bavaria, between the Danube and the Czech border. On its outskirts, the *Gut Schmelmerhof* is a large chalet-style building owned by the Schmelmer family since 1630; its sporting facilities include indoor and outdoor pools, jacuzzi and sauna. "A beautiful situation and a restful atmosphere. Though family-owned it lacks personal intimacy, but the service is very courteous; the food is good, without the helpings being too overwhelming. A regular and mostly older clientele, but there's a children's playground." The Bavarian room furnishings include wood panelling and hand-made rugs; fillet of wild hare has been commended on the large menu in the restaurant with its low-vaulted ceiling – good buffet breakfast, too.

Open All year.
Rooms 7 suites, 17 double, 10 single – all with bath and/or shower, telephone, radio and TV. 5 holiday apartments 150 metres from main building.
Facilities Lounge, TV room, bar, restaurant; conference facilities. Heated indoor swimming pool, jacuzzi, fitness room and sauna. Garden with swimming pool and children's playground.
Restrictions Not suitable for &.
Location 4.5 km SE of St-Englmar, 15 km N of Schwarzach. Parking.
Credit cards None accepted.
Terms [1989 rates] B&B 52–86 DM. Dinner, B&B 22 DM per person added; full alc 43 DM. Reduced rates and special meals for children.

If you have difficulty in finding hotels because our location details are inadequate, please help us to improve directions next year.

ROTHENBURG OB DER TAUBER 8803 Bayern   Map 7

Hotel-Gasthof Glocke   *Tel* (09861) 30 25
Am Plönlein 1   *Telex* 61318

Our only surviving entry for this much-visited medieval ramparted town on the Romantiker Strasse. Central, but fairly quiet and off the main tourist circuit; good food, wine and service. Closed 23 Dec–11 Jan. 28 rooms, 22 with bath or shower. B&B double 136–150 DM. Meals 15–45 DM. Few recent reports. More welcome.

RÜDESHEIM-ASSMANNSHAUSEN 6220 Hessen   Map 7

Hotel Krone   *Tel* (06722) 20 36
Rheinuferstrasse 10   *Fax* (06722) 30 49
                                   Telex 413576 RAST

Hoffmann von Fallersleben composed *Deutschland über Alles* in 1841 at this famous old Rhineside inn which dates from 1541 and has long been a haunt of writers and musicians. It is now a fairly big and grand hotel in two buildings: many bedrooms have a balcony overlooking the gardens and river. Many reports have reached us this year, nearly all favourable. "Even more wonderful than last time. We were given a sumptuous room, close to the secluded, beautiful swimming pool, surrounded by climbing roses. The view of the Rhine from the vine-covered dining terrace is unforgettable, and the food is masterly – start your meal with the local red Sekt and you will be at peace with the world. Whether or not because of the previous Guide entry, I found the head porter's manners greatly improved." Thus spake a devotee this year, who earlier had written, "Don't be put off by the stags' antlers and gloom of the 19th-century furnishings in the main halls. The bedrooms are clean, new and well plumbed. And how lovely to watch the westering sun in peaceful isolation." The rooms in the main annexe are heavily furnished in pompous Victorian style, but comfortable. "We had a room with circular turret and elegant marble bathroom." "Super classical food as always." One reader claims that the foliage on the terrace is not vines but jacaranda. And you should be warned of some night noise from the railway. (*Dr FP Woodford, JA and KA, Ruth and Robert Todd, ND Bain, and others*)

Open 1 Mar–31 Dec.
Rooms 7 suites, 38 double, 12 single – 51 with bath, 6 with shower, all with telephone, radio and TV; many with balcony, 5 with jacuzzi. Most rooms in annexe. Some ground-floor rooms.
Facilities Lift. Salon, TV room, bar, restaurant; riverside terrace/restaurant; conference facilities. Garden with lawn and swimming pool.
Location On the Rhine; parking. Assmannshausen is 5 km W of Rüdesheim, 36 km W of Wiesbaden.
Restriction Not suitable for &.
Credit cards Access, Diners, Visa.
Terms Rooms: single 90 DM, double 190 DM, suite 340 DM. Breakfast 18 DM. Set lunch 45 DM, dinner 75–98 DM. Reduced rates and special meals for children.

Give the Guide positive support. Don't just leave feedback to others.

SCHARBEUTZ 2409 Schleswig-Holstein   Map 7

Kurhotel Martensen – Die Barke   *Tel* (04503) 71 17
Strandallee 123   *Fax* (04503 7 35 40
          Telex 261445 KAMA

Just north of elegant Travemünde, the Deauville of the Baltic, where
Thomas Mann used to stay and set parts of *Buddenbrooks*, Scharbeutz is a
less prestigious but lively family bathing resort; and the *Martensen*, white-
walled and red-roofed, is the best of its many holiday hotels along the
beach. "We had a spacious room in the old part, with generous balconies
facing the smiling Baltic", says a reader this year; "helpful staff, a dinner
of good solid bourgeois fare, and a superb covered swimming pool." The
buffet breakfast with Holstein specialities has also been commended.
(*Rev. Michael Bourdeaux; Eleanor Hope*)

Open 1 Mar–15 Nov.
Rooms 3 suites, 20 double, 15 single – all with bath and shower, telephone, radio
and tea-making facilities; many with balcony.
Facilities Lift. Lounge, TV room, restaurants. Indoor swimming pool, sauna,
massage. Garden.
Location On seafront. Parking. Scharbeutz is 26 km N of Lübeck.
Restriction Not suitable for &.
Credit cards Access, Diners, Visa.
Terms [1989 rates] B&B: single 85–125 DM, double 150–200 DM. Dinner, B&B
22 DM added per person; full board 37 DM added. Set lunch/dinner 25–35 DM;
full alc 40–50 DM. Reduced rates and special meals for children.

SCHLESWIG 2380 Schleswig-Holstein   Map 7

Strandhalle   *Tel* (04621) 2 20 21
Strandweg 2 (am Jachthafen)   *Telex* 221327

Northern Germany is still rather sparsely represented in the Guide, so we
were glad to hear about this "unusual and attractive" modern hotel in an
ancient city that looks on the map as if it is well inland, but in fact is
linked to the Baltic by a long inlet, the Schlei. Among its many maritime
souvenirs is the remarkable Nydam Boat, an Anglo-Saxon oaken craft of
the 4th century displayed in a building beside Gottorf Castle. The
Strandhalle and its pleasant café terrace face a marina on the Schlei: "I
could not decide whether it was a hotel in a museum or a museum in a
hotel. It's a sailor's dream, with model boats of every sort, figureheads
(including Lord Howe's), framed sailors' knots and a diver's helmet. My
small room (cabin?) was comfortable, the food good and the atmosphere
friendly."

Open All year.
Rooms 28 – all with bath and/or shower, telephone, radio, TV and mini-bar.
Facilities Salons, restaurant; conference facilities. Café-terrace and garden. Indoor
and outdoor swimming pools, sauna.
Location Central; by yacht harbour. Parking.
Credit cards All major cards accepted.
Terms [1989 rates] B&B: single 72 DM, double 120 DM. Meals alc.

SCHÖNWALD 7741 Baden-Württemberg   Map 7

Hotel Zum Ochsen *Tel* (07722) 10 45
Ludwig-Uhland Strasse 18   *Telex* 792606

"Elegant rustic" is how visitors this year describe this typical chalet-style
Black Forest hotel, set amid rolling woods and meadows just outside the
resort-village of Schönwald, south of Triberg. Owned by the Martin
family for generations, it has recently been rebuilt in a style at once smart
and folksy, with lots of light new wood and pale carpets. The ambience
too is informal yet sophisticated, appealing to "the classier kind of hiker"
– you could arrive in an old jersey with a rucksack or dressed by Lagerfeld
and feel equally at ease. Good Baden-cum-Alsatian cooking (soupe aux
escargots, foie gras maison, etc) served by waitresses in Baden costume,
on the patio in summer, by a log fire in winter. Musical evenings and
excursions are organised. Pleasant indoor hexagonal pool. "Good food,
and Frau Martin a welcoming hostess", says another visitor this year. (*JA
and KA, Mr and Mrs RW Beacroft*)

Open All year. Restaurant closed Tue and Wed.
Rooms 4 suites, 30 double, 6 single – 4 with bath, 36 with shower, all with
telephone and TV.
Facilities Lounge, 4 restaurants; terrace. Indoor heated swimming pool, sauna
and solarium. Large grounds with tennis court and lake with fishing. Bicycles.
Location 8 km S of Triberg. Just outside village. Parking.
Restriction Not suitable for &.
Credit cards All major cards accepted.
Terms B&B: single 57–101 DM, double 104–176 DM, suite 96–109 DM; Dinner,
B&B 78–135 DM per person. Set lunch/dinner 35–50 DM; full alc 65 DM.
Reduced rates for children.

SCHWANGAU 8959 Bayern   Map 7

Schlosshotel Lisl und Jägerhaus *Tel* (08362) 8 10 06
Neuschwansteinstrasse 1–3   *Telex* 541332
Hohenschwangau

The Bavarian royal castles in their glorious mountain setting – Mad
Ludwig's high-pinnacled fairytale Neuschwanstein, and Hohenschwangau – are both close to this hotel. One recent visitor had an excellent
venison dinner, a good spacious room with a view of one of the castles,
and found the staff efficient and courteous. Readers have always
emphasised the castle theme: "What a romantic spot to spend the night –
silent Neuschwanstein bathed in light and all the daytime crowds gone."
"We had a comfortable if idiosyncratic room, with lavish use of wood,
figured velvet carpet on the floor and half the walls ditto, presided over
by an engraving of the impossibly handsome King Ludwig. The dining
room's immense windows had Hohenschwangau castle in full, floodlit
view."

Open All year except 6 Jan–21 Mar.
Rooms 45 double, 11 single – 26 with bath, 19 with shower, all with telephone
and radio; some with TV. 21 in annexe.
Facilities Lift. Lounge, TV room, 5 dining rooms.
Restriction Not suitable for &.
Location 6 km SE of Füssen.
Credit cards All major cards accepted.

Terms B&B 40–110 DM. Full alc 45 DM. Reduced rates and special meals for children.

SCHWARZWALD-HOCHSTRASSE 7580   Map 7
Baden-Württemberg

Höhen-Hotel Unterstmatt   *Tel* (07226) 2 04 and 2 09
Bühl 13

The Black Forest High Road winds along the hillcrest south from Baden-Baden, with fine views over the Rhine plain below. This friendly and informal ski-hotel is circled by meadows and deep pine forests, and has the bonus of superb food (*Michelin* rosette). It has been owned and run since 1905 by the Reymanns, and caters for families who come to ski in winter or hike in summer. "Very well run", says a reader this year, "I had a superb meal in the more formal restaurant, clad in collar and tie, but also enjoyed eating in the cosy cellar Stube wearing my walking gear, and I felt at home in both." Returning inspectors this year have also been delighted: "Quite unchanged. The lively Stube has harmonica music and singing, and attracts locals. Superb local smoked ham, served with kirsch and crispy country bread by dirndl'd waitresses. Bedrooms are simple, in rustic style, with bright colours; some have four-posters and Baden painted cupboards. The hotel's own ski-slope (for beginners) rises from its back terrace: this is floodlit for night-skiing and has a snow-machine using up to 100,000 litres of water a day." (*Trevor Lockwood*)

Open All year except 1 Nov–15 Dec and Tue.
Rooms 1 suite, 12 double, 5 single – 16 with bath and shower, all with telephone.
Facilities Hall, bar, 2 restaurants. Music on Fri evening. Garden with terrace, where meals are served
Location 15 km S of Baden-Baden.
Credit cards All major cards accepted.
Terms [1989 rates] B&B 55–90 DM; dinner, B&B 25 DM per person added; full board 45 DM added.

SEEG 8959 Bayern   Map 7

Pension Heim   *Tel* (08364) 2 58
Aufmberg 8

This quiet family-run *pension* is a modern building in white-washed Bavarian style, set on a small hilltop north of Füssen and the royal castles. It has views of the Allgäu Alps to the south and over lakes and forests to the north; south-facing rooms have balconies. A report this year, "A luxurious version of the homely style, with solid carved furniture, both in the room and on the balcony, with its ravishing view of the Alps beyond nearby lush meadows. The single-choice evening meal can be hampering, especially if you don't like pork, but they cooked up a huge omelette on request." (*Dr FP Woodford*) Others, too, have found the cooking a little plain – but you can eat out in the village if you prefer. Apart from this one drawback, several readers have stressed the comfort of the rooms, the "superb" breakfasts, the idyllic rural setting. "Charming host and hostess, sparkling cleanliness." There is a pleasant lounge; some of the carved furniture is Herr Heim's own work.

Open 20 Dec–1 Nov. Restaurant closed for lunch.
Rooms 14 double, 4 single – 3 with bath, 15 with shower, all with telephone; some with balcony; TV on request.
Facilities Salon, restaurant, Allgäuer Stube, TV room; sauna. Terrace.
Location On hilltop outside Seeg, which is 15 km NW of Füssen.
Restrictions Not suitable for &.
Credit cards None accepted.
Terms B&B: single 55 DM, double 100 DM. Reduced rates for children.

STUTTGART 7000 Baden-Württemberg   Map 7

Gaststätte zum Muckenstüble   *Tel* (0711) 86 51 22
Solitudestrasse 25
Stuttgart 31–Weilimdorf

A bare ten kilometres from the city centre, yet on the edge of deep country just below the hilltop Schloss Solitude that an 18th-century Duke of Württemberg built for one of his mistresses. An inspector this year again enjoyed the "excellent Swabian cuisine" (e.g. Stuttgartertopf, and roast sucking-pig with spätzle) which is served at modest prices, on a garden terrace or in the rustic-style *Stüble*, at this unpretentious family-run inn, a modern building in traditional half-timbered style. Bedrooms are plain and fairly small, but newly modernised; there's a garden with kids' playground. "We were so close to the big industrial city, yet seemed to be in the heart of rural Swabia. If you have a car, an ideal alternative to the soulless downtown hotels."

Open All year except Jul. Restaurant closed Tue.
Rooms 25 – all with shower and telephone; many with balcony.
Facilities Lift. TV room, restaurant. Garden with terrace and children's play area.
Location In suburb of Weilimdorf. 10 km W of city centre. Parking.
Credit cards None accepted.
Terms [1989 rates] B&B: single 60 DM, double 100 DM. Meals 24–42 DM.

TIEFENBRONN 7533 Baden-Württemberg   Map 7

Ochsen Post   *Tel* (07234) 80 30
Franz-Josef Gall-Strasse 13   *Telex* 783485

Tiefenbronn (its ancient Gothic church deserves a visit) is a big village near Pforzheim, at the heart of a wealthy area devoted to jewellery-making. Here the Jost family's *Ochsen Post* is suitably lavish and ornate – an old 17th-century inn, black-beamed and flower-girt outside, opulently folksy inside in the south German manner, and with modern comforts. Recent visitors enjoyed an excellent lunch in the light and summery conservatory (filet of salmon-trout, venison with spätzle: *Michelin* rosette). Earlier views: "Tables were set for dinner with silver platters edged with gold, silver cutlery and crystal glass. The cosy bedrooms all have wooden beams, chintzy drapes and solid furniture; one has a four-poster honeymoon bed. A new cocktail bar does not fit in with the hotel's character: but on warm evenings you can sit in the courtyard with a cool beer." "Irritatingly pretentious in some ways, but the food *is* first-rate and the welcome genuinely warm." More reports welcome.

> We depend on detailed fresh reports to keep our entries up-to-date.

Open All year except Jan. Restaurant closed Mon midday and Sun.
Rooms 12 double, 7 single – 7 with bath, 12 with shower, all with telephone, radio and TV.
Facilities Lounge, bistro/bar, restaurant, winter garden.
Location Leave *Autobahn* A8 (E52) at Heimsheim exit. Continue to Heimsheim and turn right at Tiefenbronn sign. Hotel is central; parking.
Restriction Not suitable for &.
Credit cards All major cards accepted.
Terms [1989 rates] B&B: single 69–98 DM, double 98–138 DM. Meals 57–83 DM.

TRIBERG IM SCHWARZWALD 7740 Baden-Württemberg   Map 7

Parkhotel Wehrle   *Tel* (07722) 8 60 20
Gartenstrasse 24   *Telex* 792609

"For a combination of facilities, service, atmosphere and food this hotel must be hard to beat," writes a devotee of this fairly luxurious and sumptuously furnished old hostelry, owned and run by the Wehrle/Blum family since 1707. It is in the centre of Triberg, a leading Black Forest resort known also for its cuckoo-clock-making and local costumes (the Schwarzwald folk museum is fascinating). Some rooms are in the old building, where party walls are thin; others are in two more modern ones beside a garden. The cooking (*Michelin* rosette) has this year been judged "excellent" by one visitor, though another thought it lacked flair. It is *nouvelle*-ish, but helpings are not stinted; trout is a speciality, prepared in 20 different ways. "Claus Blum is a warm and civilised host and imparts a cultivated atmosphere; service is skilled and stylish. Delightful outdoor and indoor swimming pools. Many rather grand people, such as groups of Arab sheikhs or Stuttgart tycoons, come here for special occasions." "Scrupulously managed in old-fashioned style but with plenty of space-age plumbing facilities." (*Angela and David Stewart, WG Francis*)

Open All year.
Rooms 2 suites, 43 double, 14 single – 58 with bath and shower, all with telephone, radio and TV. 20 in annexe.
Facilities Lounge, TV room, dining rooms, billiard room; conference room. Indoor and outdoor heated swimming pools; sauna, solarium, massage. Large garden.
Location Central, near market place (quietest rooms overlook garden). Parking.
Restriction Only dining rooms suitable for &.
Credit cards All major cards accepted.
Terms B&B: single 85–135 DM, double 150–250 DM. Half board 30 DM per person added. Set lunch 36 DM, dinner 52–72 DM; full alc 58 DM. Reduced rates and special meals for children.

TRIER 5500 Rheinland-Pfalz   Map 7

Petrisberg Hotel   *Tel* (0651) 4 11 81
Sickingenstrasse 11-13

Trier is not only the centre of the Mosel wine trade and the town where Karl Marx was born (his house is a museum), but under the Emperor Diocletian it was the capital of Gaul, and this past grandeur is today evoked by the Porta Nigra, finest Roman relic in Germany, and by the Imperial Baths. One great merit of the *Petrisberg*, a modern family-run bed-and-breakfast hotel, is that it stands in a splendid position amid vineyards, high on a hill above the city with a view of those Roman ruins – and rooms facing the city have a balcony. This year once again it has been much admired – for the view, the spacious rooms, the "bountiful" breakfasts (sometimes including bacon and egg), and the personal service by the "gracious" owner, Herr Pantenburg. He has leased his vineyards to the Bishop of Trier who then sells this Riesling wine back to the hotel – "the best Mosel we tasted in the region". (*Dr FP Woodford, E Allfrey-Pizer, Ruth and Robert Todd, and others*)

Open All year.
Rooms 3 suites, 28 double, 1 single – all with bath, shower and telephone; many with balcony. 14 in annexe. 3 ground-floor rooms.
Facilities Salon, TV room, breakfast room, wine bar. Garden and terraces. Forest nearby.
Location 20 mins' walk from town centre (near Roman amphitheatre). Parking area and garages (5 DM).
Restriction Not suitable for &.
Credit cards None accepted.
Terms B&B: single 75 DM, double 120 DM, suite 180 DM. Reduced rates for children sharing parents' room. (No restaurant, but light evening meals available.)

Hotel Villa Hügel   *Tel* (0651) 3 30 66
Bernhardstrasse 14

An attractive alternative to the Petrisberg: a white chalet-like Jugendstil villa, on a hillside with good views of the city. Helpful hosts, tasteful furnishings, large rooms, simple but well-prepared food. 23 rooms, all with bath and/or shower. B&B double 95–135 DM. Full alc 25–45 DM. New nomination. More reports please.

WANGEN IM ALLGÄU 7988 Baden-Württemberg   **Map 7**

Romantik Hotel Alte Post   *Tel* (07522) 40 14
Postplatz 2   *Telex* 732774 APOST

After three years absence, this old Swabian coaching-inn – much modernised – is restored to the Guide by an inspector's report. "Wangen, quite near the Bodensee and the Allgäu Alps, is a picturesque old town of painted facades; it also has some quirky modern sculptures in its main streets – we especially liked the scattered bronze piglets in the Marktplatz. The centrally situated *Alte Post*, dating from 1409, is well run by the Veile family; the bedrooms, full of character, are reasonably priced. Ours had a four-poster canopied Himmelbett, sofas, hairdrier, chintzy curtains, and a rafter inscribed '1610'. The dining room is elegant in a restrained way, entirely lacking the heavy kitsch you find across the Bavarian border. We were nicely served by a polite young man in *Tracht* . The à la carte dishes we thought too bland and dull, but the Swabian ones were fine, including beef braised in cider, accompanied by a version of Spätzle known as Buabenspitzle which means literally 'little boys' penises'. That's just what it looks like, too."

Open All year. Restaurant closed Sun evening Nov–Mar.
Rooms 3 suites, 17 double, 8 single – all with bath or shower, telephone, radio and TV. 9 rooms in annexe.
Facilities Lounge, TV room, 2 restaurants. Garden. Golf nearby.
Location Central, parking. Wangen is 20 km NE of Lindau.
Restriction Not suitable for &.

Credit cards Access, Diners, Visa.
Terms B&B: single 80–90 DM, double 130–150 DM, suite 180–250 DM. Dinner, B&B double 186–206 DM. Set lunch 25–45 DM, dinner 25–90 DM; full alc 50 DM. Reduced rates and special meals for children.

WEIKERSHEIM 6992 Baden-Württemberg   Map 7

Hotel Laurentius   *Tel* (07934) 70 07
Marktplatz 5

This attractive little town on the Romantic Road, 42 kilometres south of Würzburg, is built round a 17th-century Hohenlohe castle beside the Tauber, worth seeing for its splendid Knights' Hall (it also hosts an international music school). Here the *Laurentius* is a recently opened hotel in an old building where Goethe's ancestors lived; it overlooks the pretty market square. "The rooms are cosy and comfortable, individually decorated; the management is helpful and friendly, and we took dinner on the quiet terrace." "Dinner was perhaps the best of our trip." "Our roomy bedroom overlooked the *Marktplatz*." You eat in an old vaulted cellar, and can take drinks and breakfast on a flowery patio.

Open All year except Feb.
Rooms 10 double, 2 single – all with bath and/or shower, telephone and radio; TV on request.
Facilities Lift. Lounge, restaurant, breakfast room, café; conference room; terrace.
Location Central. Parking.
Credit cards Access, Diners, Visa.
Terms B&B: single 65–75 DM, double 100–120 DM. Set meals 27.50–72 DM; full alc 40 DM. Reduced rates and special meals for children.

WEITENBURG 7245 Baden-Württemberg   Map 7

Hotel-Restaurant Schloss   *Tel* (07457) 80 51
  Weitenburg

This large 16th-century hilltop castle has "a marvellous rural setting" and "most romantic views" over the Neckar valley between Horb and Tübingen. Owned since 1720 by the Barons of Rassler, it is one of a number of *Schlösser* in this area that have been turned into hotels by their baronial owners as the best way of keeping the family estates together. It is run by a manager, but the baron still lives there and is much in evidence, a charming and cultivated man and a great hunter. He has sensibly kept the hotel in its original style, modernising only those aspects that need it (e.g. bathrooms). Recent visitors have especially enjoyed the indoor swimming pool, the food (with a few reservations) and the large bedrooms furnished with antiques (but some rooms could do with a spot of paint). Chris, the English head waiter, has been found to be very helpful. "A sophisticated hotel, very good value." It is in extensive grounds, with a riding school and sauna as well as the pool. There is a balcony over the valley where you can have drinks and meals. The dining room is massive. More reports welcome.

Open All year except 24–25 Dec.
Rooms 1 suite, 20 double, 18 single – 13 with bath and shower, 18 with shower, all with telephone and radio.

Facilities Lift. Hall, 4 lounges, bar, TV room, dining room; chapel for weddings and christenings; conference facilities; large balcony for drinks and meals. Park with riding school, golf, heated covered swimming pool, sauna and solarium.
Location 7 km N of Starzach; from A81 motorway take Rottenburg exit, drive 5–10 mins in the direction of Ergenzingan then follow signposts to Weitenburg.
Credit cards Access, Diners, Visa.
Terms [1989 rates] B&B: single 60–90 DM, double 110–160 DM. Full board 110–142 DM per person. Meals 36–72 DM. Reduced rates and special meals for children.

WERTHEIM-BETTINGEN 6980 Baden-Württemberg　　　　Map 7

Hotel-Restaurant Schweizer	*Tel* (09342) 30 70
Stuben	*Fax* (09342) 3 07 55
Geiselbrunnweg 11	*Telex* 689190 CHSTU

"Wonderful! The food, service and surroundings were all first-class and nothing could be faulted", enthuses a 1988 visitor to this modern, spacious and luxurious restaurant-with-rooms, to which *Michelin* awards two rosettes and four red gables. Built in chalet style, it stands beside open fields on the edge of a village by the Main, west of Würzburg, and has pleasant views of the river valley. "Our bedroom in the main building (others are in a villa 200 metres away) was large, elegant and comfortable. The food in the main restaurant, *nouvelle cuisine*-ish in style, deserves its rosettes – but the cost! My God! – 511 DM for two! The more countrified *Schober* restaurant is *much* cheaper, and the food nearly as good, though less elaborate." Visitors this year enjoyed veal marinaded in crushed olives, "exquisitely delicate" lobster mousse and grand marnier crêpes with blood oranges, but thought the wine mark-ups excessive. Others have had a room with painted country furniture, and a breakfast that included quails' eggs with smoked salmon. (*Stephan and Kate Murray-Sykes*) One reader this year thought the welcome poor and the cooking over-ambitious. A new wing, the *Landhaus*, has just opened, with a third fancy restaurant, this time Italian.

Open All year. *Schweizer Stuben* restaurant closed Jan; Mon, Tue for lunch. *Schober* restaurant closed Tue, Wed for lunch.
Rooms 2 suites, 30 double – all with bath and/or shower, telephone, radio and TV. Some in villa in garden. Ground-floor rooms.
Facilities Salon, 3 restaurants; conference facilities. Garden with tennis park (indoor and outdoor court and school); swimming pool, sauna.
Location 6 km E of Wertheim; 3 km from *Autobahn* (exit Wertheim).
Credit cards All major cards accepted.
Terms B&B: single 200–345 DM, double 250–395 DM, suite 450–950 DM. Dinner, B&B 190–540 DM per person.

Greece

HOTEL ALIKI, SIMI

ATHENS   **Map 11**

Clare's House   *Tel* (01) 9222.288 and 9220.678
24 Sorvolou Street, Mets

This small, friendly, cheap and simple B&B featured in early editions of
the Guide when it was in an old mansion in the Plaka. It is readmitted
this year, having moved to a modernish house on a hill in a residential
area southwest of the Akropolis, near the Temple of Zeus. ''To arrive on a
hot and dusty afternoon is bliss. The entrance has a cool marble floor with
a minimum of good modern furniture. My bedroom was simply but well
furnished with nice lamps and varnished wood, pictures on the white
walls and an efficient modern bathroom. The balcony overlooked the
small garden and had a grape-vine trailing from top to bottom – I was told
I was welcome to pick the grapes. The location is very quiet; taxi-drivers
find it elusive, but the hotel has printed instructions in Greek to help
them. Breakfast is simple but the bread (except on Sunday when it was
dry) was some of the best I have found in Greece. The coffee pot was
bottomless. I cannot praise enough the helpfulness of the staff when I had

problems with a delayed flight. Manos Anglias, the owner, speaks perfect English and employs an English receptionist; he is a mine of information on the Greek islands and has a wonderful collection of up-to-date guides." (*JS Jenkinson*) Some of the rooms have a private shower, some adjoining rooms share a shower and can be let as a family suite. Mr Anglias writes engagingly: "We are a family-run pension where the emphasis is to provide good – no frills – accommodation at reasonable rates. We are clean, quiet, have *hot* water and know people by their names. If the opportunity arises I invite them for a drink in my flat or go out to dinner with them. In the off-season we let rooms on a monthly basis at about 50,000 drs a month and provide basic cooking facilities for long-term guests." More reports please.

Open All year.
Rooms 20 double (also let as single) – most with shower, all with telephone.
Facilities Lift. Lounge with TV, breakfast room.
Location 1 km from Syntagma Square. Garage for 3 cars.
Restriction Not suitable for &.
Credit cards None accepted.
Terms B&B: single 3,000–4,000 drs, double 4,500–6,000 drs. Monthly rates Oct–Mar.

Herodion Hotel   *Tel* (01) 923.6832
Rovertou Galli 4   *Telex* 219423 HERO
Makrigiani

The cradle-city of Western civilisation hardly distinguishes itself by its hotels (just see how few entries we have). The *Herodion*, an unbeautiful modern cube in a quiet street quite near the Akropolis, is better than most. It has a patio garden where drinks are served beneath the trees, and a roof terrace with views of the Akropolis. And it has been well liked this year: "Cool, comfortable and clean, with quite pleasant rooms and willing and friendly staff. The inclusive breakfast was standard international, but adequate. We didn't try the restaurant since the lively Plaka is so close, and about the best place in Athens for good medium-priced eating, the *Dionysius*, is just up the road." (*Elizabeth Stanton*)

Open All year.
Rooms 4 suites, 77 double, 9 single – all with bath and/or shower, telephone, radio, TV, air-conditioning.
Facilities Lounge, bar, restaurant. Patio, rooftop terrace.
Location Central; near Plaka and Akropolis.
Restriction Not suitable for &.
Credit cards All major cards accepted.
Terms B&B: single 7,200–10,500 drs, double 9,400–13,700 drs. Set lunch/dinner 1,900 drs; full alc 4,000 drs.

St George Lykabettus Hotel   *Tel* (01) 729.0710
Kleomenous 2, Platia Dexamenis   *Fax* (01) 729.0439
                                                    Telex 214253 HEAM

A modern hotel, luxury class but not too expensive by British standards, in the fashionable Kolonaki district, on the foothills of Lykabettus hill and ten minutes on foot from Constitution Square. A regular visitor again liked it a lot this year: "Views from the bedrooms vary from good to sensational. It has recently been refurbished and the air-conditioning now works well. Staff are helpful and efficient. There's a rooftop restaurant, and another pleasant open-air one serving light meals. The hotel is used by some tour groups but not taken over by them." Similar praise last year: "The location is magnificent: from the bedroom balconies you look across to the Parthenon. The rooms are comfortable rather than opulent, but they have good bathrooms. The rooftop swimming pool is a rarity in Athens, and the roof-level restaurant serves excellent food and also has a view of the Akropolis." Some rooms, however, have been judged too small, or imperfect in upkeep, and front ones may suffer from traffic noise. (*Sir William Goodhart*)

Open All year.
Rooms 4 suites, 124 double, 21 single – all with bath, telephone, radio, tea-making facilities and air-conditioning; some with balcony; TV on request. Some ground-floor rooms.
Facilities Lift. Lounge, TV room, bar, restaurant, grill room; roof garden and swimming pool; nightly entertainment in restaurant; dancing on roof.
Location At foot of Lykabettus hill. Large garage.
Credit cards All major cards accepted.
Terms [1989 rates] Rooms: single 7,150–13,500 drs, double 8,600–15,000 drs, suite 18,000–31,500 drs. Breakfast 800 drs. Set lunch/dinner 1,900 drs.

CHANIA Crete   Map 11

Hotel Contessa   *Tel* (0821) 57437
Theofanous 15, Palio Limani

With its mix of Turkish and Venetian architecture, Chania is probably Crete's most attractive town. Here, in a maze of pretty streets by the harbour, an old family house has been carefully converted into a tiny bed-and-breakfast hotel, admired again this year apart from being a bit noisy. "The hospitality and atmosphere were all the Guide promised," ran a report last year, "and breakfast was really good and elegantly served. I'd advise asking for a front room with a view (one has a lovely painted ceiling), for ours at the back was rather airless. Tasteful decor and a courteous owner. It may be hard to persuade taxi-drivers to enter the old town with its narrow streets, but we phoned the hotelier and he helped us solve the problem." (*Col. TCH Macafee*)

Open 1 Apr–end Oct.
Rooms 2 triple, 4 double – all with shower, telephone and radio; baby-listening on request. All in annexe.
Facilities Breakfast room. Swimming pool at *Xenia* hotel nearby. 15 mins' walk to beach.
Location Overlooking old Venetian harbour; 1 km from town centre. Parking 150 metres.
Restriction Not suitable for &.
Credit card Diners.
Terms B&B double from 7,200 drs. (No restaurant.)

We badly need more entries for hotels in Athens.

If you have had recent experience of a good hotel that ought to be in the Guide, please write to us at once. Report forms are to be found at the back. Procrastination is the thief of the next edition.

CHIOS Aegean Islands	Map 11

Villa Argentikon *Tel* (271) 31599 and 31465
Chios *Telex* 294135

"Just about the most sophisticated hotel in all Greece," says a recent visitor. It lies on the plain of Campos in the southern part of the island of Chios, just off the Turkish coast. Chios used to play a key maritime role in the Aegean, and its rulers from 1346–1566, the Genoese, have left a legacy of many fine buildings. One of them is the *Villa Argentikon* which the Argenti family from Genoa built in the 16th century and still own today. Together with two adjacent mansions of the same period, all in patterned marble, they have turned it into an elegant hotel whose recent guests have included the Princess of Savoy and the former American president, Jimmy Carter. There are flowered colonnades, beautiful gardens, bedrooms gracefully furnished in period style, with marble bathrooms. You can dine by candle-light in the floodlit gardens, where good food, expensive by Greek standards, is elegantly presented.

Open 28 May–15 Oct.
Rooms 4 suites – all with bath or shower, and terrace or patio.
Facilities Restaurant. Garden. Horse riding and motor sailing can be arranged.
Location About 5 km S of town of Chios.
Terms On application.

DELPHI Central Greece	Map 11

Hotel Pan *Tel* (0265) 82294
53 Vassileos Pavlou

In a peaceful location at the quieter end of town, but only a short walk from the main shops and restaurants, an unassuming and hospitable little family-run B&B hotel, with glorious views from the balconies of rooms facing the valley. Clean, simple bedrooms; cheerful breakfast room. 30 rooms, all with bath and shower. B&B double 4,800 drs. New nomination. More reports please.

FERMA Crete	Map 11

Coriva Village *Tel* (0842) 61263
Ierapetra *Telex* 262508 CORV

Not far from the port of Ierapetra, and just outside the village of Ferma, here is a quiet hotel and not-too-large bungalow complex on the south coast of Crete where new hotels are sprouting fast. Recent visitors have liked it a lot, singling out the restaurant, the large clean swimming pool, the "friendly owners" and the "beautiful tropical garden". Many rooms are in bungalows surrounded by flowering shrubs. The beach is not impressive, but nearby are small secluded coves excellent for swimming.

Open March–Nov.
Rooms 35 double – all with bath and/or shower, telephone and air-conditioning. 11 in main house, 24 in bungalows with terrace.
Facilities Salon with TV, bar, taverna, restaurant. Garden with swimming pool; private beach with water sports; Cretan evenings once a week.
Location 8 km E of Ierapetra; 1 km from Ferma. Parking.

Restriction Not suitable for &.
Credit cards None accepted.
Terms [1989 rates] Rooms: single 7,000 drs, double 10,000 drs, suite 15,000 drs. Breakfast 1,000 drs. Set lunch/dinner 2,000 drs.

FIRA Santorini, Cyclades   Map 11

Atlantis Hotel   *Tel* (0286) 22232 and 22111
Fax (0286) 22821
Telex 293113 ATRA

The volcanic island of Santorini is a striking crescent shape. You sail into a wide bay, thought to be the crater of a volcano which erupted in Minoan times, throwing up the spectacular cliffs of pumice and lava that surround the bay. The white-washed town of Fira is perched on the cliffs, 800 steps up from the harbour: you can ride up by mule or take a cable car. Perched above it is the *Atlantis*, whose elegant facade of white arches is visible from afar. It has been admired for its comfortable rooms in one recent report. Other visitors had a large and spacious room, and a big balcony with a fine view of the town, the sea and the island of Nea Kamani, the only live volcano in Greece. The hotel has an airy lounge with the same view, and a helpful staff. More reports welcome.

Open 1 Apr–31 Oct.
Rooms 19 double, 8 single – 6 with bath, 21 with shower, all with telephone and radio; most with balcony.
Facilities Lounge, TV room, bar, breakfast room; meeting room; terrace. Beach 6 km.
Location Central. Parking.
Credit cards All major cards accepted.
Terms [1989 rates] Rooms: single 8,733–10,538 drs, double 12,049–14,486 drs. Breakfast 780 drs. (No restaurant.)

GALAXIDION Central Greece   Map 11

Hotel Ganimede   *Tel* (0265) 41328
Euthumiou Blamis 6

"Quiet, relaxed, informal, all-round idyllic, the sort of place one dreams of finding in Greece but never does", has been one comment on this idiosyncratic Italian-owned *pensione* in a tiny ancient town on the Gulf of Corinth, near Delphi. It is formed by two houses back-to-back, one a 19th-century captain's house, the other a modern facsimile, with a large garden-cum-patio in between – trees, flowers, comfortable chairs. "It's in a quiet part of town, almost suburban, though in itself it is nearly louche. The house has been beautifully kept and furnished, and has a marble tiled hall and fine woodwork. The ambience is somewhat precious. We were warmly welcomed. You can take drinks (listed on a blackboard) in the garden with its central fountain. The two best bedrooms, 1 and 2, are on the first floor front. They have tall panelled doors, coffered ceilings and lovely old wooden furniture. The breakfast room is also pretty, but covered with ikons, pictures, home-made preserves for sale, and postcards from patrons saying how lovely their stay had been. Breakfast is very generous (for Greece), and includes good fig jam, and eggs poached, scrambled and even 'mumbled', whatever that might be." An earlier visitor has written: "If Bruno Perocco, the owner, does not like the look of you, you will not get a room. In winter he runs courses on making ikons. The British and American embassies have found the place, but he is careful to spread the nationalities." Others have considered the rooms "comfortable, dark and cool". No restaurant, but *To Steki* and *To Galaxidi* are good harbourside tavernas. (*DM*)

Open 1 Mar–31 Oct.
Rooms 6 double, 1 single – 2 with shower.
Facilities Lounge. Courtyard. 10 mins' walk to sea.
Location Central; Galaxidion is 33 km SW of Delphi, via Itea and the coast road. Parking.
Restrictions Not suitable for &. No children under 10.
Credit cards None accepted.
Terms [1989 rates] Rooms: single 3,070 drs, double 4,995 drs. Breakfast 875 drs.

HERMOUPOLIS Syros, Cyclades — Map 11

Hotel Vourlis   *Tel* (0281) 28440 and 23750
Mavrogordatou 5   *Telex* 293206 MIT

The capital of the Cycladean island of Syros is a picturesque town of predominantly neo-classical architecture, with houses that rise in tiers on the slopes of two hills. The *Hotel Vourlis* is a 19th-century mansion in this neo-classical style, transformed into a gracious little private hotel, beautifully furnished. It is owned by Alexandra Mavrogordatou Petritzh, a well-known Greek artist, and recent visitors have endorsed this earlier praise: "A real oasis and sheer luxury. We were warmly welcomed and given two very elegant rooms in pink and blue, with lots of space and beautiful pictures. The bathroom was big, and we found chocolates and Metaxa brandy by the bed. Service was excellent and breakfast superb, including fruit salad and scrambled eggs." No restaurant, but snacks available, and plenty of tavernas nearby.

Open All year.
Rooms 1 suite, 5 double, 1 single – all with bath and/or shower, and telephone. 3 ground-floor rooms.
Facilities Hall, lounge/breakfast room, bar. Small front garden and patio. 100 metres from shingle beach with safe bathing and fishing. Windsurfing, water skiing, sailing, tennis and mini-golf nearby.
Location Hermoupolis is capital of Syros, capital of the Cyclades. Daily boat connections from Piraeus and Rafina. Hotel is central. Parking.
Credit cards All major cards accepted.
Terms [1989 rates] Rooms: single 3,500–4,800 drs, double 4,500–7,000 drs.

HYDRA Hydra, Saronic Gulf — Map 11

Hotel Miranda   *Tel* (0298) 52230

Hydra town, on the island of Hydra, has a beautiful harbour where the houses rise in tiers. Up one of these steep narrow streets is this finely converted 18th-century mansion with hand-painted ceilings and parquet floors; now a most select little hotel, it is furnished with genuine local antiques and run in a somewhat lordly way. Its own regular clientele (smart Athenians) keep it often full. No restaurant: good tavernas nearby. Closed Nov–Feb. 14 rooms, all with shower. B&B double 6,500–11,000 drs [1989]. Recent nomination. More reports please.

IOS Cyclades **Map 11**

Ios Palace Hotel *Tel* (0286) 91269 *and* (*in Athens*)
(01) 413.7406
Telex 213315

Homer is said to have died on the Cycladean island of Ios, now heavily colonised by students and other youthful back-packers from northern Europe and North America; discos abound. The fairly expensive and sophisticated Ios stands on the edge of a wide sandy beach, a mile from the island's main village. Rooms in bungalow style; sea-water swimming pool; water sports. Open 1 May– 10 Oct. 46 rooms, all with bath and shower. B&B double 5,868–14,000 drs. Set menus 1,000–1,300 drs [1989]. Recent nomination. More reports please, especially on the food.

LIA Epirus **Map 11**

Hotel Lia *Tel* (0664) 31208
Lia, Nr Filiates

This brand-new hotel in the wilds of Epirus, up near the Albanian border, must be one of the most remote in this book. It has an unusual genesis, too, as its nominator reports, "A marvellous hotel. It was established by Nicholas Gage, the *New York Times* reporter who wrote *Eleni*, the story of his family caught in the Greek civil war in Lia – his mother was executed for helping her children to escape. The book is what led us to Lia in the first place. Each bedroom has a balcony looking over the village and wooded mountains. The manager has worked for years in hotels in Brussels and has returned to his homeland well equipped. His wife cooks and gave us an excellent evening meal. Dozens of local villagers were in the restaurant." (*Patricia Peterson*)

Open 15 May–15 Oct.
Rooms 1 suite, 9 double – 6 with bath, 4 with shower.
Facilities Lounge, bar, TV room, restaurant. Garden with children's playground.
Location 40 km N of Filiates.
Restrictions Not suitable for &.
Credit card Access.
Terms [1989 rates] Rooms: double 3,500 drs, suite 4,500 drs. Set lunch/dinner 800 drs; full alc 2,100 drs. Special meals for children on request.

METSOVO Epirus **Map 11**

Hotel Egnatia *Tel* (0656) 41263 and 41485
L. Tossitsa

An appealing new discovery this year, in a small town on the main road over the mountains from Kalambaka (Meteora) to Ioannina: "The drive to Metsovo takes one up the spine of the Pindus range, over what not long ago must have been a road of hair-raising difficulty and which still affords spectacular views. Metsovo is a small, prosperous town hidden in a mountain valley; it is being developed as a ski resort, but still retains its

253

tradition and integrity, and has a rich heritage of handicrafts (needlework, copperwork, wood-carving). Many of the older women still wear the traditional costume on a daily basis, which adds to the local charm. The *Egnatia*, on the main road in the town centre, has a somewhat alpine exterior (flowerpots and balconies), but the interior is traditional Greek. The public rooms have warm wooden panelling, coffered wooden ceilings beautifully carved, and lovely old brass lamps. The lobby is lined in the old style with benches covered with rich red weavings and intricately designed cushions; above the fireplace is a wild boar's head. The bedrooms are simple but comfortable, and their balconies afford delightful views of the town and hills. We met a warm and genuine welcome." (*Dr SL Martin*) We'd be glad of reports on the hotel food. You can also eat at the *Victoria* (see below).

Open All year.
Rooms 2 suites, 24 double, 8 single – all with bath and shower; many with balcony.
Facilities Lounge, TV room, bar, restaurant. Garden. Winter sports 2 km.
Location Central. Metsovo is 50 km E of Ioannina.
Credit cards All major cards accepted.
Terms [1989 rates] B&B: single 3,150–3,983 drs, double 4,100–5 100 drs, suite 6,050–7,883 drs. Set meals 800–1,000 drs.

Hotel Victoria   *Tel* (0656) 41771 and 41761

Slightly more expensive, and on the town's outskirts overlooking the deep valley, here's another new entry this year for Metsovo, from a reader who has also been struck by local craft traditions: "The hand-carved ceiling of the spacious dining room, the hand-carved chairs, hand-woven cushions and wall decorations make a stay at this hotel a visit to a living museum. It is family-run, and the multilingual staff are friendly and helpful. The meals included local dishes not normally available in restaurants, such as mountain sausage and a kind of feta soup. Good local red wine. A highly recommended hotel." (*Patricia Peterson*) Metsovo also has a museum of local arts and crafts, and an interesting monastery.

Open All year.
Rooms 34 double, 3 single – all with bath and/or shower and telephone.
Facilities Lounge, bar, restaurant. Nightclub. Winter sports 2 km.
Location On W outskirts. Parking.
Terms [1989 rates] B&B: single 3,650–4,300 drs, double 4,750–5,520 drs; half board: single 4,950–5,600 drs, double 7,350–6,120 drs.

MONEMVASSIA Peloponnesus   **Map 11**

Hotel Malvasia   *Tel* (0732) 61113 and 61435

Several old houses with barrel-vaulted ceilings have been most attractively converted into a hotel of character, with a real sense of history; in wonderful position in an ancient town with a famous 6th-century castle in the south-east of the Peloponnese. Spacious rooms, nicely furnished lounge. Bar and café; plenty of restaurants close by. Very quiet (town is closed to car traffic), but not midge-free. 28 rooms, all with shower. B&B 6,000 drs. Few recent reports; more welcome.

MYRINA Lemnos, Aegean Islands   Map 11

Hotel Akti Myrina
Myrina Beach

Tel (0254) 22681
Telex 297173 MYRI
in winter: Athens
Tel (01) 72191591
Telex 216324

Long admired by readers, the *Myrina* is a large, fairly luxurious and quite original holiday venture, set above a bay just outside Myrina, the tiny capital of the lovely island of Lemnos. Spread over the hillside are 125 bungalows, with everything you could desire – air-conditioning, good lighting and linen, lots of hot water, efficient room service – each hidden by greenery from its neighbours. Most have a little patio/garden with a view, "idyllic for one's breakfast or evening drink". The central services (pool, beach) are all within two minutes' walk. "Must be a strong candidate for the most attractive hotel on the Mediterranean. Set in a garden of flowering shrubs; if you are lucky enough to be in the front row of the bungalows your garden looks straight over roses and grapes down to the sea. You can have delicious Greek yoghurt with honey and wholemeal toast for breakfast as well as the more ordinary continental fare, eggs etc. For dinner you can choose between buffet type restaurants and one serving a more conventional five-course meal. For lunch you can eat in a small taverna or at another restaurant serving a great variety of salads and hot dishes. The sea is shallow for a long way out and the beach is very clean. Service is efficient and courteous." "The hotel is a paradise for young children (you can leave your kids in their cots while you dine)". Others have praised the lunchtime garden buffet, the poolside bars for snacks and drinks, and the beach sports and caïque excursions. "Firm management – everything ran like clockwork". (*Conrad and Marilyn Dehn, and others*)

Open 6 May–15 Oct.
Rooms 15 suites, 110 double – all with bath and/or shower, telephone, refrigerator, baby-listening, air-conditioning, veranda and small garden. All in bungalows.
Facilities Lounge, TV lounge, coffee shop, restaurants, taverna; hairdresser, boutique; disco. 25-acre grounds with 3 tennis courts, swimming pool, children's pool, mini-golf, ping-pong, private sandy beach with restaurant; fishing, bathing, water sports.
Location 2 km (about 15 mins' walk) from Myrina Town. Lemnos is reached by direct flight from Athens, or by boat from Piraeus.
Restriction Not suitable for &.
Credit cards All major cards accepted.
Terms Dinner, B&B: single 12,000–25,000 drs, double 19,500–46,000 drs per person, suite 28,000–50,000 drs. Set lunch/dinner 5,000–7,000 drs; full alc 8,000 drs. Reduced rates and special meals for children.

Italicised entries are for hotels on which we need more feedback – either because we are short of reports or because we have had mixed or inadequate reports.

OLYMPIA Peloponnesus   Map 11

Hotel Amalia
Tel (0624) 22190
Telex 215161 AMAL

On the other side of the modern town from the ancient site of Olympia, a large modern luxury-class hotel amid fields, a bit impersonal, but quiet and comfortable. Garden with swimming pool, international cuisine, good lunchtime buffet. 147 rooms, all with bath and shower. B&B: single 8,300 drs, double 11,800 drs. Set menu 1,600 drs [1989]. No recent reports. More welcome.

PALEA EPIDAVROS Peloponnesus   Map 11

Paola Beach Hotel   Tel (0753) 41397

On the edge of a fishing-village 12 km from the classical theatre at Epidaurus, a modern hotel set quietly by a sandy beach; clean and comfortable, with plumbing that actually works. Open 1 Apr–30 Oct. 27 rooms, all with bath, shower and balcony facing sea or farmland. B&B double 4,200 drs [1989]. No restaurant: tavernas in village. Endorsed this year, but fuller reports welcome.

SIMI Dodecanessus Islands   Map 11

Hotel Aliki   Tel (0241) 71665 / 71655

"For ten years it has been my favourite hotel in Greece," says an ardent philhellene, of this neo-classical mansion on the waterfront of the little port of Simi, capital of the small bare island of that name between Rhodes and the Turkish coast. "Simi used to be a prosperous mercantile centre. Then it declined into a ghost town, but today some of its fine old mansions are being restored. This one has been done up most tastefully by its owner, George Kypreos, who runs it as a very sympathetic little hotel. There is a bar and roof garden, with fine views. Some bedrooms, too, have sea views from their balconies, but others face the back; all have a cool, simple elegance. There are tables with parasols, by the water. No beach, but you can walk straight from the *Aliki*'s front door into the warm, crystal-clear sea. No restaurant: tavernas nearby. Simi today has its share of day-trippers from Rhodes: but in the evening it remains a lovely peaceful unspoilt place."

Open Apr–Oct.
Rooms 2 suites, 11 double, 2 single – 4 with bath, 11 with shower, all with telephone and radio.
Facilities Bar, TV room, breakfast room; roof garden.
Location Simi is about 40 km NW of Rhodes; daily boat services.
Credit cards None accepted.
Terms [1989 rates] B&B: single 4,200–5,000 drs, double 5,400–8,000 drs, suite 10,000–11,800 drs. Breakfast 600 drs. (No restaurant.)

We asked hotels to estimate their 1990 tariffs some time before publication so the rates given are often arbitrary. Please always check terms with hotels when making bookings.

SKOPELOS Sporades   Map 11

Prince Stafylos Hotel   *Tel* (0424) 22775
                                                       Telex 282229 SKOP

Skopelos is the second largest of the Sporades islands, and just outside its main town, also called Skopelos, is this pleasant modern hotel, a long low white construction with verandas and slate roofs, built in local style by its owner, an architect. Clean, well-kept swimming pool amid lawns and flowers; light, attractive bedrooms. Open 1 May–25 Oct. 49 rooms, most with bath or shower, double 6,000–10,000 drs. Breakfast 600–800 drs. Set menus 1,300–1,800 drs. Recent nomination. More reports please, especially on the food.

SPETSES Spetses, Saronic Gulf   Map 11

Hotel Possidonion   *Tel* (0298) 72208 and 72308

This island off the Argolid coast is where John Fowles set *The Magus*, having taught here in the 1950s at a well-known boarding school, founded as a copy of an English public school. Today the English connection continues, in a different manner, for Spetses is given over to the UK package-tour trade. But it also remains a haunt of wealthy Athenians, who have built summer homes along the coast: so, if you wander off into the pinewoods, you might always – who knows? – stumble into the enchanted clutches of some latter-day Conchis. Failing that, you can certainly be beguiled by the 1920s ghosts that haunt the *Possidonion*, described by a recent visitor as "the only surviving historic hotel in all the Greek isles. It was built in 1914 by Sotiros Anagyros, a Spetsian who emigrated to the US, became a rich tobacco baron, then returned to found the boarding school and the hotel. He built it in the grand European manner, with terrace, esplanade and attendant casino, scene of great society parties in the inter-war years. Today it is somewhat down-at-heel, but it remains characterful, and there are plans to refurbish. It keeps away from the package-tour trade and retains a sophisticated clientele – lots of chic French grumbling about 'les Anglais' down in Spetses town." More reports, please, on mundane matters such as food and bedrooms.

Open Apr–Oct.
Rooms 55 – most with bath and/or shower.
Facilities Lounge, restaurant. Beach 300 m.
Location In Spetses town, 30 mins by boat from the mainland.
Terms [1989 rates] Rooms: single 2,220–4,820 drs, double 3,520–7,230 drs. Breakfast 800–850 drs. Set lunch/dinner 1,800–1,850 drs.

THASSOS 64004 Macedonia   Map 11

Hotel Amfipolis   *Tel* (0593) 23101
                                                       Telex 452195 AMF

The sophisticated little town of Thassos, also known as Limenas, is on the island of Thassos in the north Aegean; it has ramparts and an akropolis. The *Amfipolis*, inside the town, is a blue-grey four-storey building, newly nominated: "It was built in the 1920s as a Bulgarian jail and has recently been nicely converted; it is well run by a local family. There is a bar under a tree in the pretty patio, where you can dine outdoors; also a swimming pool (beach about three miles away). Good bedrooms.''

Open 20 Apr–30 Oct.
Rooms 6 suites, 31 double, 5 single – 30 with bath, 12 with shower, all with telephone and radio; some with TV and mini-bar. Some ground-floor rooms.
Facilities Lift. Lounge, TV room, bar, restaurant. Garden with swimming pool. Sand/rock beach nearby.
Location Central. Frequent ferries from Keramoti on the mainland (30 mins).
Credit cards All major cards accepted.
Terms B&B: single 6,000–8,000 drs, double 8,000–10,000 drs. Set lunch/dinner 1,500 drs; full alc 3,600 drs. Children under 10 half price in parents' room; special meals.

TOLO Peloponnesus   Map 11

Hotel Minoa   *Tel* (0752) 59207
56 Aktis Street   *Fax* (0752) 59707
                                                       Telex 298157 MINO

Run by a large family of Cretans, the *Minoa* is one of many modern hotels along the sandy beach of this popular resort, once a simple fishing-village. An inspector in 1989 has summed it up neatly: "Not luxurious or charming in itself, but an OK hotel with pleasant staff in an enchanting *pieds-dans-l'eau* position – you even drive your car onto the sandy beach in front of it, to unload. Apart from the boats putting out for night fishing, it's very peaceful. Essential to ask for a room at the front (moon on sea at night very beautiful): back ones look over a sprawl of houses. Welcome was warm, also brisk and efficient. As in all the hotels we visited in Greece, the bedrooms were no more than basic by British standards, but adequate. The dining-room's marble paved floor and table numbers give a municipal effect – but the full-length windows offer that wonderful view again. The fixed menu has little choice – cheese pie, adequate meat balls, nice oily Greek salad, and just an apple. The waiters had time to be pleasant, everyone speaks English, and there's a pleasant drawing room.'' Other reports this year vary both about the breakfasts and main meals – "better than average Greek fare", says one, "very poor", says another. Clearly it's the location that you come for, not the food. But there are some good tavernas in town, if you are not staying *en pension*. (*JS Jenkinson, Patricia Peterson*) The hotel has two annexes, the *Kronos* nearby and the *Phaistos*, a short way up the hill, with a swimming pool.

Open 15 Mar–7 Nov.
Rooms 75 double, 7 single – all with bath or shower, telephone and radio. 18 in annexe *Kronos*, 20 in annexe *Phaistos*.
Facilities Lift. Lounge with TV, bar, restaurant. Garden. *Phaistos* has a swimming pool. Sandy beach.
Location Near old port; parking. Tolo is 12 km SE of Nafplion.
Restriction Not suitable for &.
Credit cards All major cards accepted.
Terms [1989 rates] Dinner, B&B: single 4.320–5,120 drs, double 6,550–7,460 drs, triple 8,760–9,890 drs. Special meals for children on request.

Many hotels put up their prices in the spring. Tariffs quoted in the text may be more accurate before April/May 1990 than after.

VATHIA Lakonia   Map 11

Kapetanakou Towers   *Tel* (0733) 54244

Not a hotel but a "traditional settlement" – state controlled but locally run. In a fascinating medieval village, not far from Areopoli, by the sea near the tip of the wild and gorgeous Mani peninsula in the southern Peloponnese, some of the ancient grey towers have been converted into well-modernised accommodation – tastefully furnished bedrooms, attractive reception, large restaurant, terraces, lovely views, friendly multi-lingual staff. 44 rooms, all with private facilities. B&B: single 6,273 drs, double 8,159 drs. Meals 1,000 drs [1989]. New nomination. More reports please, especially on the food.

```
**************************************************
*  Traveller's tale The Hôtel Bellevue, which looks upon the sea and  *
*  hears always the waves dashing upon the worn and jagged rocks, was  *
*  overflowed by one of those swarms which are the nuisance of  *
*  independent travellers, known as a "Cooks Party", excellent people  *
*  individually no doubt, but monopolising hotels and steamboats, and  *
*  driving eveybody else into obscurity by reason of their numbers and  *
*  compact organisation. We passed yesterday one of the places on the coast  *
*  where Jonah is said to have left the whale; it is suspected – though  *
*  without any contemporary authority – that he was in a Cooks Party of his  *
*  day, and left it in disgust for this private conveyance.  *
*  Charles Dudley Warner (In the Levant, 1876)  *
**************************************************
```

HOTEL LOGGIATO DEI SERVITI FLORENCE

ACQUAVIVA PICENA 63030 Ascoli Piceno   **Map 10**

Hotel O'Viv   *Tel* (0735) 764649
Via Marziale 43   *Fax* (0735) 83697

In an old hill-village just inland from the Adriatic coast between Pescara and Ancona, this old stone building – once the house of a bishop – is now an oddly named small hotel, delightfully run by its young Anglo-Italian owners. Bedrooms full of character; panoramic terrace; good local cooking. Equestrian centre. 14 rooms, all with shower. B&B double 71,000–80,000 L. Set menus 25,000–28,000 L. New nomination. More reports welcome.

The success of this guide in North America has led to a sister publication on American and Canadian hotels based on the same principles. Readers with recent experience of good hotels in North America are urged to send their nominations to Sandra W Soule, America's Wonderful Little Hotels and Inns, PO Box 150, Riverside Avenue, Riverside, Conn. 06878, USA.

ALPE FAGGETTO 52033 Arezzo Map 10

Fonte della Galletta *Tel* (0575) 793925
Caprese Michelangelo

Secluded amid woodlands in the wild Apennines, this idiosyncratic little restaurant-with-rooms has been described as "quite an experience – as unlike any British hotel as one could imagine". Readers have long enjoyed the robust cooking of its jovial and well-named proprietor, Boncompagni Gheldo, who uses local mushrooms and fungi in various fascinating and unusual ways. "He is intensely energetic and kind", ran a recent report. "Once dinner began the whole place roared into tremendous activity, and it was necessary to eat rapidly (and not to allow attention to wander from one's food) in order to keep up with the vigorous service, led by the Signor himself. After dinner the staff not surprisingly appeared to collapse with exhaustion, and all the clearing up was left till morning. There were big parties for local weddings, evidence of the place's popularity. Above the hotel are some interesting walks and the great monastery of La Verna is not far away." Roads wind down to Michelangelo's birthplace amid lovely flowery countryside. There is no menu but guests are asked for their approval of the night's dinner in advance – this could include mushroom soup and various pastas stuffed with mushrooms and truffles. The local wine is "deep purple and delicious". Clearly the place is more of a "typically Italian experience" than a conventionally dependable hotel – no one speaks English, the local guests make cheerful noise, TV may be on in the restaurant, lighting in the lounge is inadequate for reading, the bedrooms can be rather cold, and a visitor this year found the staff slow. But just think of the compensations. More reports welcome.

Open All year. Closed Wed Feb–May.
Rooms 20 – all with bath, shower and telephone. 6 in bungalows nearby.
Facilities Lounge with TV, bar, restaurant; banqueting facilities. Garden.
Location 5 km SW of Caprese Michelangelo; 50 km NE of Arezzo.
Credit card Amex.
Terms B&B: single 35,000 L, double 50,000 L; dinner, B&B 37,000 L per person; full board 45,000 L. Set meals 15,000–30,000 L; full alc 20,000–30,000 L. Reduced rates and special meals for children.

AMALFI 84011 Salerno Map 10

Hotel Luna Convento *Tel* (089) 871002 and 871050
Via P. Comite 19 *Telex* 770161 LUNAHT

A cool white-walled Byzantine monastery half as old as time (St Francis of Assisi is said to have lived here in 1220), on the dramatically beautiful Amalfi coast. Goethe and Ibsen stayed here too. "The *Luna* is a calming place, and its staff have that grave, serious sweetness that charms and reassures. The hotel is beautifully situated at the sea's edge, looking back over Amalfi, with wonderful views, a lift down to the old tower and private bathing rocks and pool, an old cloister, for breakfast outside, and comfortable though simple accommodation. No air-conditioning, but prompt and friendly room service, and good, simple varied meals (excellent fish). There was a large wedding party going on in the hotel, yet we were not neglected but treated as a welcome audience to a fine free spectacle. A friendly, cheerful hotel with personal attention. And one would never tire of sitting on that balcony." Endorsed this year by an inspector who points out that road-traffic is audible from the dining-terrace, and maybe from some bedrooms.

Open All year.
Rooms 5 suites, 40 double – all with bath, shower, telephone.
Facilities Lift. Lounge, bar, 2 restaurants; banqueting facilities; discothèque. Garden with cloisters, terrace, sea-water swimming pool.
Location 300 metres from centre. Garage and private parking.
Credit cards All major cards accepted.
Terms B&B: single 90,000–100,000 L, double 130,000–170,000 L; dinner B&B 110,000–130,000 L per person. Set meals 50,000 L. Reduced rates and special meals for children.

AMEGLIA 19031 La Spezia   Map 10

Paracucchi-Locanda dell'Angelo   *Tel* (0187) 64391
                                                     Fax (0187) 64393

A sophisticated country hotel in a very modern style, set back from the main road just inland from Lerici and La Spezia. Owner-chef Angelo Paracucchi wins a *Michelin* rosette for his cooking, and readers concur: "Excellent, different food in a lovely dining room with informed, courteous service. Breakfast was lovely too." "A large daily menu based on the best local ingredients. The cooking is adventurous and modern, far removed from the usual idea of Italian cooking. The wine list is superb. Rooms are comfortable and adequately furnished in cool style with well-fitted bathrooms. Each has a small balcony with views to the hills or over the plain. There is a comfortable bar and lounge area, and many interesting paintings hang throughout the building." The hotel's "near-suburban location", just off a busy main road, is compensated by the long sandy beach a mile or so away. More reports please.

Open All year. Restaurant closed 10–12 Jan.
Rooms 1 suite, 26 double, 10 single – all with bath and/or shower, telephone, TV, mini-bar; many with balcony. Some ground-floor rooms.
Facilities Lounge, bar, restaurant; conference facilities. Garden.
Location 3 km SE of Ameglia on Sarzana–Marinella road.
Credit cards All major cards accepted.
Terms Rooms: single 62,000 L, double 125,000 L. Breakfast 16,000 L. Full alc 75,000. Reduced rates and special meals for children.

ASOLO 31011 Treviso   Map 10

Hotel Villa Cipriani   *Tel* (0423) 55444
Via Canova 298   *Fax* (0423) 52095
                                                     Telex 411060 CIPRAS

An old town of arcaded streets and Venetian palaces and villas. One of them is the *Cipriani*, once the home of Robert Browning, and here he wrote the lines, "God's in his heaven, all's right with the world" – sentiments echoed by many of today's visitors to what is now a luxurious hotel, part of the big CIGA chain, but run in personal style. "A magnificent place: we walked straight into paradise," runs one report this year; "the view from our bedroom was breathtaking, the food superb, and all the staff seemed to share the manager's concern for our comfort." A comment last year: "Dinner was delicious (try their grilled vegetables from the garden). Not only did our room look on to the quiet garden and a view of valleys and mountains, but it had a beautiful sitting area with oriental rug, burgundy velvet love-seat, and a marble-topped credenza on which they had placed a basket of fresh fruit and a vase of pink roses." Another visitor found that breakfast on the terrace included wild strawberries and black figs, and called the *Cipriani* "one of those very special hotels that seasoned travellers speak of with nostalgia". "The food and atmosphere are what you dream of when you think of Italy", is a further Browningesque comment. But some rooms are small and some face the street. (*M and D Chambers; Godfrey and Hilary Hodgson, Mary Ann Meanwell*)

Open All year.
Rooms 31 double – all with bath and shower, telephone and TV. 11 in garden annexe.
Facilities Lift. Lounge, bar, TV room, restaurant.Garden.
Location 35 km NW of Treviso. 300 yards from town centre. Parking.
Credit cards All major cards accepted.
Terms [1989 rates] (Excluding taxes) Rooms: single occupancy 190,000–250,000 L, double 210,000–270,000 L. Breakfast 16,500 L. Dinner, B&B 79,500 L added per person; full board 142,500 L added. Alc 90,000 L. Special meals for children.

ASSISI 06081 Perugia   Map 10

Hotel Country House   *Tel* (075) 816363
San Pietro Campagna 178

This Guide newcomer is a *pensione* with a garden, about a mile outside the city walls – "An old house", says its nominator, "with a big chaise-longuey patio, fine views over the valley and pleasant walks around. Italian breakfast is fairly standard. The place doubles up as an antique shop, so if you take a fancy to any of the excellent furniture in your bedroom, you can make an offer for it." This shop is called the "3 Esse" (3 Ss) because "it's kept by three women all of whose names begin with S: I met only one of them, a lady of equal charm and volubility" (probably Silvana Ciammarughi, the owner). (*Jan Morris*)

Open All year.
Rooms 1 apartment with kitchen and private balcony, 10 double, 2 single – all with bath, and/or shower. 2 ground-floor rooms.
Facilities 2 lounges with TV. Garden and terraces.
Location 1½ km from Assisi towards Perugia. Parking.
Credit cards Amex, Visa.
Terms B&B: single 40,000 L, double 75,000 L. Reduced rates for children. (No restaurant.)

Hotel Umbra   *Tel* (075) 812240
Via degli Archi 6

Much renewed praise in 1988/9 for this reasonably priced little family-run hotel down an alley off the main square. It has a touch of Italian elegance about the public rooms, and a pleasant patio at the back where you can eat out under the trees. The food is what counts here, far more than the bedrooms, described as clean but a little basic. "My room was institutional, suitable for earnest young YMCA pilgrims. By contrast, dinner was superb, served in a strikingly beautiful high-ceilinged room: I was given the sweetest prosciutto crudo I've ever tasted, and enough of it to paper my room. The manager insisted on carrying my bags to my car himself." "A delicious veal en croûte with madeira sauce and wild mushrooms. Management friendly." (*PA Bispham, Philippa Herbert, Elizabeth Ring, CLG Worn*)

Open 15 Mar–15 Jan.
Rooms 3 suites, 20 double, 5 single – 17 with bath, 7 with shower, all with telephone; 3 with TV. Some ground-floor rooms.
Facilities 3 lounges, bar with TV, 2 restaurants. Garden with terraces for meals in fine weather.
Location In town centre, near main square.
Credit cards Amex, Diners.
Terms B&B: single 57,000 L, double 90,000 L, suite 120,000 L. Dinner, B&B 75,000–90,000 L per person. Full alc 35,000–45,000 L. Reduced rates for children.

BELLAGIO 22021 Como   **Map 10**

Grand Hotel Villa Serbelloni   *Tel* (031) 950216
Via Roma 1   *Fax* (031) 951529
                                                  Telex 380330 SERBOT

"A superb hotel", says a visitor returning recently to this huge ornate villa beside Lake Como. It enjoys the lake vistas that Stendhal once called "sublime" and is backed by a large park famous for its display of magnolias, camellias and pomegranates. Inside, the palatial public rooms are hung with gold chandeliers and decorated with original frescos; the staircase is flanked by gilt *putti* on giant candelabra, and the spacious bedrooms have wonderful views over lake or gardens. There is a heated swimming pool and a private beach. So far, so good: but whereas the staff are generally found efficient and courteous, both management and cuisine have been criticised this year and last by readers who feel that the hotel does not live up to its sublime appearance – and that it overcharges for extras (e.g. 5,000 lire for orange juice). What's more, rooms facing the road can be noisy. (*Roberta Garza de Elizondo*) More reports please.

Open 15 Apr–20 Oct.
Rooms 6 suites, 71 double, 15 single – all with bath and shower, telephone and mini-bar; radio and TV on request. Some ground-floor rooms.
Facilities Lifts. Lounge, TV room, writing room, games room, bar, breakfast room, restaurant; banqueting and conference facilities; hairdressing salon, boutique; terrace (also for meals), evening orchestra with dancing. Gardens with tennis courts, heated swimming pool with snack bar; private beach with boating, windsurfing, water skiing, boating excursions.
Location Central. Private garage and large parking place.
Credit cards All major cards accepted.
Terms [1989 rates] B&B: single 220,000 L, double 315,000 L, suite 625,000 L; dinner, B&B: single 255,000 L, double 385,000 L, suite 695,000 L. Set lunch/dinner 60,000 L. Reduced rates for children; special meals on request.

The 1991 Guide will appear in the autumn of 1990. Reports are particularly useful in the spring, but need to reach us by May 1990 if they are to help the 1991 edition.

BOLOGNA 40123   Map 10

Hotel Roma   *Tel* (051) 274400
Via Massimo d'Azeglio 9   *Telex* 583270
Bologna

"The best medium-priced hotel in Bologna, and we've tried quite a few", is a comment this year by regular visitors to the biggish *Roma*, centrally located in a narrow street just off the magnificent Piazza Maggiore, heart of the historic core of medieval Bologna. It is fairly quiet, save for a few clock chimes, and even has a roof-garden. The air-conditioning is always appreciated; however, one visitor in July found it turned off from 2 to 8.30 am ("a police regulation", she was told), making her room very hot. She also thought the service unhelpful. The food is "acceptable" though expensive: but there are masses of good cheap places all around in the world capital of good pasta. (*W Ian Stewart, Brian MacArthur*)

Open All year. Restaurant closed 1–23 Aug.
Rooms 80 – most with bath or shower, telephone, TV and air-conditioning (10,000 L).
Facilities Lift. Restaurant; roof-garden.
Location Central: by car, go to the back entrance which is not in pedestrian zone. Garage.
Credit cards All major cards accepted.
Terms [1989 rates] Rooms: single: 77,000 L, double 102,000 L. Breakfast 10,000 L. Full board 121,000–147,000 L per person. Set lunch/dinner 30,000 L.

BORDIGHERA 18012 Imperia   Map 10

Hotel Villa Elisa   *Tel* (0184) 261313
Via Romana 70   *Telex* 272540 ELISA

A handsome white villa with a pretty garden, set quietly on an elegant avenue, ten minutes' walk above the seafront of this busy Riviera resort. Friendly welcome, good service, spotless upkeep, copious meals – "they look boring, but taste good" – in a graceful dining room with outdoor terrace. Many rooms have big balcony facing south; second-floor rooms have sea view. Closed 15 Nov–19 Dec. 32 rooms, all with bath or shower. B&B double 90,000–104,000 L. Set menu 35,000 L. In Aug half or full board only. More reports please.

BRESSANONE 39042 Bolzano   Map 10

Hotel Dominik   *Tel* (0472) 30144
Via Terzo di Sotto 13   *Telex* 401524 DOMNIK

A bright and breezy modern hotel, all orange and yellow colours, set close to the Rienz river on the edge of this busy resort, a good centre for exploring the Dolomites and Tyrol. "Wonderful and good value", says a 1989 visitor; "staff friendly and professional, food excellent – and the indoor swimming pool is marvellous." But another reader found the place somewhat rigid and aloof. The decor is a bit garish, but the gardens are pretty. (*Martin L Dodd*)

> We are particularly keen to have reports on italicised entries.

Open Easter–Nov. Restaurant closed Tue except Jul, Aug, Sept.
Rooms 19 double, 10 single – all with bath and shower, telephone and radio; 15 with TV.
Facilities Lounge, bar, TV room, restaurants. Indoor swimming pool. Garden and terrace.
Location Central, parking. Bressanone is 41 km NE of Bolzano.
Restriction Not suitable for &.
Credit cards Access, Amex, Visa.
Terms [1989 rates] B&B 70,000–120,000 L per person. Dinner, B&B (min 3 days) 90,000–140,000 L. Set lunch/dinner 30,000–40,000 L; full alc 30,000 L. Reduced rates for children; special meals on request.

Hotel Elefante   *Tel* (0472) 32750
Via Rio Bianco 4   *Fax* (0472) 36579

Unlike the modern Dominik, the Elefante is strictly classical – a 16th-century building near the town centre, lavishly furnished with antiques, old paintings and tapestries. Rooms comfortable (some a little dark; back ones quieter and lighter); charming old-fashioned service; food very good. Delightful big garden with curved swimming pool. Open 1 Mar–mid-Nov, 25 Dec–8 Jan, restaurant closed Mon. 44 rooms, all with bath and/or shower. B&B 95,000 L. Full alc 45,000 L. Recent nomination. More reports welcome.

We asked hotels to quote 1990 prices. Not all were able to predict them in the late spring of 1989. Some of our terms will be inaccurate. Do check latest tariffs at the time of booking.

Hotels often book you into their most expensive rooms or suites unless you specify otherwise. Even if all room prices are the same, hotels may give you a less good room in the hope of selling their better rooms to late customers. It always pays to discuss accommodation in detail when making a reservation.

CAPRI 80073 Naples   Map 10

Hotel Luna   *Tel* (081) 8370433
Viale Matteotti 3   *Telex* 721247

A beautiful but expensive hotel in a secluded position above the sea, next to the fashionable Augusto gardens on the southern side of Capri town. Large bedrooms with sea views, attractive public rooms, lovely swimming pool and gardens, good food and impeccable service. Open Apr–Oct. 44 rooms, all with bath or shower. Rooms 110,000–230,000 L. Breakfast 18,000 L; alc meals (excluding wine) 45,000–55,000 L [1989]. Recent nomination. More reports please.

CASALPUSTERLENGO 20071 Milano   Map 10

Hotel Fiesta   *Tel* (0377) 84871, 84945
Viale della Stazione   and 84954

A useful stop-over hotel in a small town just off the Autostrada del Sole, *16 kilometres north-west of Piacenza. Outwardly unpromising, down a back street near the station, and no special chic, but clean, comfortable and modern, run by a most affable family. 40 rooms, all with bath. Double rooms 60,000– 100,000 L [1989]. Set menus 25,000–35,000 L. Recent nomination. More reports please, especially on the restaurant.*

CASTELLINA IN CHIANTI 53011 Siena   Map 10

Pensione Belvedere di San   *Tel* (0577) 740887
Leonino   *Telex* 741034

An old stone farmhouse with outbuildings, all recently and tastefully converted into a bed-and-breakfast pensione, *cleverly combining a rustic ambience with modern comforts. Spacious lounge bar in rural style, pleasant patio for drinks etc; snacks served. Swimming pool. 28 rooms, all with bath and shower. B&B double 85,000 L. Set meals 20,000 L. Recent nomination. More reports welcome.*

Pensione Salivolpi   *Tel* (0577) 740484
Via Fiorentina   *Fax* (0577) 741034

A converted Tuscan farmhouse with beamed ceilings, set on a hill with broad views towards Siena and Volterra; it consists of three buildings in a pretty garden with a sizeable swimming pool. It fell out of last year's Guide through lack of feedback, but is now restored by four reports calling it friendly, modest and agreeable: "Comfortable and good value, very clean, with lovely typical Tuscan rooms; manageress efficient but a bit aloof. Breakfast boring: better to pop down to the main bar in the village." Others have mentioned elegant bathrooms and a family ambience. No restaurant, and the trattoria in the village is not rated highly: but there are others a bit further afield. (*Simon Small, John RL Cook, Michael and Margaret Crick, Richard Osborne*)

Open All year.
Rooms 18 double, 1 single – all with bath, shower and telephone. 7 rooms in 2 annexes.
Facilities Lounge with bar and TV, breakfast room. Garden with swimming pool.
Location 1 km NW of Castellina towards San Donato.
Restrictions Not suitable for &.
Credit cards All major cards accepted.
Terms [1989 rates] Rooms: single 30,000 L, double 60,000 L. Breakfast 7,000 L. (No restaurant.)

Tenuta di Ricavo   *Tel* (0577) 740221
                                                                        Fax (0577) 741014

This much-loved old manor house in rural Tuscany is now back in the hands of the Swiss family Scotoni who originally converted it into a delightfully informal hotel. A report since their return: "It is in 'Chiantishire', the area so beloved of English residents who bought up deserted farm houses. Guests appreciate its classic Quattrocento atmosphere. The central manor contains the dining room, lounges and libraries, plus a few guest rooms; outbuildings around the 'village square' of the old hamlet have been converted into studio rooms and apartments, plus good bathrooms, with Tuscan furniture and Mara Scotoni's luscious flower paintings. The terraces face beautiful views of the hills, with oakwoods, vineyards and distant towns. The food is *alla casalinga*, simple Italian" (one reader felt it lacked variety). "The nice Scotoni family speak all languages; service is excellent, food is good too, and lunch can be taken under trees in the garden, near the two swimming pools. Our room was charming and comfortable." "Beautiful, remote, peaceful and wonderful." Others have enjoyed the Chianti wines from the hotel's own vineyards, and the log fires in winter. Some have found the ambience more international than Italian. Siena, Florence and Volterra are all within easy reach. Guests are expected to dine in the hotel; there is a small à la carte lunch menu.

Open Apr–Nov. Restaurant closed Wed midday.
Rooms 9 suites, 13 double, 2 single – all with bath and shower, and telephone. 3 ground-floor rooms. Some in annexe.
Facilities 3 lounges, TV room, bar, dining room. Garden with 2 swimming pools; table tennis.
Location 22 km NW of Siena, 34 km S of Florence. Leave Siena *superstrada* at San Donato exit.
Restrictions Not suitable for severely &. No smoking in dining room.
Credit cards None accepted.
Terms Dinner, B&B 120,000–168,000 L. Alc lunch 40,000 L; set dinner 42,000–45,000 L. 1-night bookings sometimes refused if made too far in advance. Reduced rates for children sharing parents' room; special meals on request.

CASTIGLIONCELLO 57012 Livorno   **Map 10**

Hotel Villa Godilonda   *Tel* (0586) 752032
Via Biagi 12

This pleasant seaside hotel, making its Guide debut, stands on a rocky promontory with small sandy beaches on either side in a family bathing resort south of Livorno. "All rooms have a sea view. Ours, decorated in glass and plastic, Italian style, was very clean and pleasant. The excellent public rooms are very modern, clean, comfortable, expensively done, with marble floors and chromium. Service impeccable, lots of staff; breakfast room charming with excellent breakfasts – good coffee etc. The attractive swimming pool is not crowded, and has plenty of places to sit and sunbathe. No restaurant, and the ones in town are poor: but the *Antico Moro* in Livorno has marvellous fish stew." (*Gerald Campion*)

Open All year.
Rooms 23 – all with shower, telephone, radio, TV, baby-listening.
Facilities 2 lounges, TV room, bar. Indoor and outdoor swimming pools; direct access to private beach.
Location On edge of village 20 km S of Livorno. Parking.
Terms B&B: single 93,500–108,000 L, double 120,000–254,000 L, suite 226,000–340,000 L. (No restaurant.)

CAVALESE 38033 Trento   Map 10

Mas del Saügo   *Tel* (0462) 30788
Masi

A 17th-century farmhouse, secluded in a forest at the western end of the Dolomites, newly converted with exquisite taste into a fine restaurant with just four guest rooms. It was unearthed for us last year by a well-known British hotelier who has been back this year and found it "better than ever" – and his praise has become more exuberant than ever: "This may be our favourite place in the world, and it's perhaps the best value for money in Europe". Rub your eyes in disbelief, and now read his initial report: "Owned and run by a young couple, Lorenzo Bernardini and Donatella Zampoli. He is an architect (as well as artist and oenophile) and has renovated with great style – stripped wood floors and beams, modern pictures (mostly his own work), bright colours in carpets and fabrics. Window frames and fittings are in bright red which sounds ghastly but looks great. In fact everything delights the eye. They use Ginori china embossed with their own logo. There is a small study with family photographs where they serve breakfast. We drank Müller-Thurgau in the garden, listening to cowbells and admiring the view, then spent three-and-a-half hours over the seven-course set menu that Donatella had composed and cooked. Everything close to perfect: carpaccio, white truffles, freshly-gathered porcini, really good gnocchi, fillet of beef in an intense red wine sauce. Lorenzo is a most professional *sommelier*." (*Paul Henderson*) In 1989 an American couple have assured us that Mr Henderson has not been day-dreaming: "We thoroughly agree. Like visiting in a friend's home. Dinner and wines delicious. Even breakfast was way above Italian standard". (*William and Anita Taylor*) PH tells us that Signor Bernardini, amazingly, is vice-president of a cricket club. Now that explains it all.

Open All year. Restaurant closed Thur.
Rooms 1 suite, 2 double, 1 single – all with shower.
Facilities 2 lounges, bar, restaurant. Large grounds.
Location At Masi, 4 km SW of Cavalese which is 42 km SE of Bolzano.
Restriction No children under 8.
Credit card Visa.
Terms B&B 80,000–100,000 L. Set lunch/dinner 80,000–95,000 L.

CAVASAGRA DI VEDELAGO 31050 Treviso　　　Map 10

Villa Cornèr della Regina　　　　　　　*Tel* (0423) 481.481
Country Hotel　　　　　　　　　　　*Telex* 433391 CORNER

This dazzling new Guide entry (why have we not heard about it before?) is described as "everyone's idea of a Palladian villa": built in c.1500, then rebuilt in *c.*1700 by one of Palladio's pupils, it stands in its own formal park, amid vineyards that provide it with red, white and sparkling wine. Venice is a bare hour's drive away. Two nominating reports this year: "Never before have I come across a hotel of this quality. It has no lifts: but who wants a lift if one can walk up a lovely staircase lined with old prints, to a bedroom the size of a ballroom, decorated in 18th-century Venetian style, with breathtaking views across the Veneto countryside? Beautifully restored in keeping with its illustrious history, the villa has courteous and attentive staff and an excellent restaurant. On our visit, guests were mainly Italian: the hotel doesn't seem to have been much discovered yet by tourists." And this, written *in situ*: "The interior is elegant, more through clever modern design than the use of antiques, though a few of these are sprinkled around. The huge central hall on the *piano nobile* has been decorated in a tent style with pink and white stripes, irresistibly reminiscent of Leander during Henley regatta. In my suite, the luxurious bathroom is housed in a kind of pagoda. The dining room (in what was once the orangerie and keeps that character) aims high, but does not quite get there: my meal last night was mediocre, but tonight's was delicious. The adjacent farm and stable buildings are now an annexe." Large heated swimming pool; bedrooms all different and superbly elegant. (*Robert Ribeiro, ATW Liddell*)

Open All year.
Rooms 7 suites, 14 double – all with bath and shower and telephone. Most double rooms in annexe.
Facilities Hall, lounge, bar, 2 restaurants. Park with tennis court and swimming pool, sauna. Golf nearby.
Location 18 km W of Treviso, near Albaredo.
Terms [1989 rates] B&B: single 180,000 L, double 240,000 L, suite 300,000 L. Set meals 35,000 L.

CEFALÙ 90015 Sicily　　　　　　　　　　　Map 10

Hotel Riva del Sole　　　　　　　　　*Tel* (0921) 21230
Viale Lungomare 25

A very modern, comfortable hotel on the promenade, in a fascinating ancient town on the north Sicilian coast, set below a great Gibraltar-like rock. Cheerful staff, large rooms with balconies, good menu. 28 rooms, all with bath and shower. Full board double 60,000–80,000 L. Set menu 18,000 L. New nomination. More reports welcome.

> Don't keep your favourite hotel to yourself. The Guide supports: it doesn't spoil.

> In your own interest, always check latest tariffs with hotels when you make your bookings.

CETRARO 87022 Cosenza   Map 10

Grand Hotel San Michele   *Tel* (0982) 91012
Loc. Bosco 8/9   *Fax* (0982) 91430

Calabria, Italy's toe, has long been a blank space on our map of good
hotels, so this one on its upper west coast is especially welcome. It's a big
white palace in traditional style, standing alone on a hillside above the
broad blue sea, and *Michelin* gives it three red gables. "After a week's
tiresome touring of Calabria, this was a find and a pleasure. It is very
comfortably furnished, with a huge and splendid lounge. The head waiter
speaks good English and the staff are keen to anticipate your wishes:
miming to the chambermaid regarding pillows, soft bedding and
mosquitoes produced instantly just what we needed. The food is
excellent, with a good choice of local Calabrese dishes. There is a good-
sized pool and excellent sea bathing, with a cabin for every room. The
grounds are large and well kept, with wonderful views of sea and
mountains." A lift leads down a cliffside to the hotel's mile-long private
beach.

Open All year except Nov.
Rooms 6 suites, 52 double, 7 single – all with bath and/or shower, telephone and
TV.
Facilities Lift. Salons, bars, TV room, restaurant; conference facilities. Garden
with terrace, swimming pool, tennis court, 9-hole golf course. Lift down to private
beach.
Location On coast road 6 km NW of Cetraro, 61 km NW of Cosenza.
Restriction Not suitable for &.
Credit cards All major cards accepted.
Terms [1989 rates] Rooms: single 140,000–220,000 L, double 118,000–200,000 L
per person, suite 180,000–260,000 L. Breakfast 15,000 L. Set meals 40,000 L.
Special meals for children.

CHIAVERANO D'IVREA 10010 Torino   Map 10

Castello San Giuseppe   *Tel* (0125) 424370

*Only five miles north-east of industrial Ivrea, where Olivetti produces its
computer-age wizardry, here in utter contrast is an ancient hilltop mansion,
once a monastery, then turned into a fortress by Bonaparte, and now a charming
hotel with large garden and terrace, reached along a narrow winding hill road.
Comfortable bedrooms with modern bathrooms and fine views; dining by
candle-light, with unpretentious home cooking; warm welcome and friendly
service. 16 rooms, all with bath and/or shower. B&B double 110,000–130,000 L.
Set menus 35,000–55,000 L. Endorsed this year, but we'd be glad of reports on
the bedrooms.*

CIOCCARO DI PENANGO 14030 Asti   Map 10

Locanda del Sant'Uffizio   *Tel* (0141) 91271

A graceful old 16th-century monastery, converted into a small, very
attractive hotel in a tiny village set amid peaceful hills in the wine area
north-east of Asti. "A fantastic place, luxurious and comfortable, with

charming rooms", says a reader this year, endorsing last year's nomination: "The owner is also the local estate owner: his family occupy the larger monastery building, and the cloister buildings are now the guest rooms, each with a small terrace overlooking a garden which leads down to a swimming pool. The *Locanda* has views over the village, vineyards and hills. Bicycles are provided for those who wish to explore. Our large room had a small kitchen area with cooker and fridge. Breakfast, taken in the open beside the pool, is a self-service buffet with cheese, meats etc; a buffet lunch is served there too. The food was not cheap, but cooking and ingredients were superb. House wine, served as a matter of course, included a sparkling aperitif, with peach juice and a bottle of their own Barbera. A relaxing, informal, casual place, our only niggle being that housekeeping could have been better." The hotel's restaurant, *Da Beppe* (*Michelin* rosette), serves a nine-course set meal (no menus) that a reader this year found "hedonistic" if expensive, and "totally inappropriate for children". (*Betsy C Maestro*) Half- and full-board rates only.

Open All year except 1–20 Jan, 1–10 Aug. Restaurant closed Tue.
Rooms 3 suites, 26 double, 2 single – all with bath and/or shower, telephone, TV, balcony or terrace. 7 ground-floor rooms.
Facilities 2 salons, bar, restaurant; billiard room, games room. Conference facilities. Small gymnasium. Terrace. Large grounds with unheated swimming pool and tennis court; bicycles available.
Location Village is 20 km NE of Asti, 5 km SE of Moncalvo.
Credit cards All major cards accepted.
Terms Half board 180,000 L, full board 220,000 L. Set meals 90,000 L. Reduced rates and special meals for children.

CISTERNINO 72014 Brindisi	**Map 10**

Country Club Villa Cenci	*Tel* (080) 718208
Via Ceglie Messapico	*Fax* (080) 718208

Our only entry for Apulia lies right in the heart of the region of the *trulli*, those strange little round white stone houses with domed roofs. Nearby are the great caves of Castellana, rich in stalactites and stalagmites. The *Cenci*, on the Semeraro Farm, is rather unusual too, as a recent visitor reports, "Called a 'country club', it consists of an old farmhouse, a collection of *trulli*, and some new self-catering units which blend in well. You can have rooms in the house or, as we did, in one of the *trulli* – simply furnished, lovely tiled floors, comfortable beds. It is a delightfully peaceful place, with a nice swimming pool, charming grounds." Some of the rooms are small apartments with kitchenette, so this could help solve the food problem. The sea is about 12 kilometres away. More reports please.

Open Apr–Oct.
Rooms 17 suites, 3 double – all with shower; some with kitchenette. Many in *trulli* not far from main building.
Facilities 2 lounges, bar, TV room, restaurant. In large farm with garden and swimming pool. Sea with safe bathing 12 km.
Location 48 km W of Brindisi, 1 km from Cisternino.
Restriction Not suitable for &.
Credit cards None accepted.
Terms B&B 35,000–55,000 L. Half board 60,000–86,000 L. Full alc 30,000 L. Reduced rates and special meals for children.

COGNE 11012 Aosta
Map 10

Hôtel Bellevue
Rue Grand Paradis 20

Tel (0165) 74825
Fax (0165) 749192

Renewed praise this year for this solid traditional hotel – a big square block of a building – just outside a summer and skiing resort in a mountain valley south of Aosta, facing the Gran Paradiso massif: "The location is superb, with the elegant dining room seeming to float out over the view. Food and comfort are excellent, and the service is warm and welcoming, maybe because the place has been in the same family for 50 years or more, and many of the staff are old-timers. It has the human qualities of a family place." Others have written in similar vein – "good traditional local food". Fine mountain walks, and good swimming facilities. (*Peter Dingley*)

Open 20 Dec–17 Apr; 1 Jun–30 Sept. Restaurant closed Wed.
Rooms 4 chalets, 3 suites, 32 double, 6 single – all with bath and/or shower, telephone and radio. Chalets have TV and cooking facilities.
Facilities Lift. 3 lounges, TV room, pub with video and music, games room, restaurant; gala dinners once a week; conference room. Indoor swimming pool, whirlpool, sauna, solarium and gymnasium. Garden.
Location 27 km S of Aosta. Hotel is central; parking.
Credit cards None accepted.
Terms B&B: single 130,000 L, double 140,000 L. Dinner, B&B 80,000–120,000 L per person. Set lunch/dinner 30,000–35,000 L. Reduced rates and special meals for children.

COURMAYEUR 11013 Aosta
Map 10

Hotel Bouton d'Or
Strada Statale 26, n.10

Tel (0165) 842380
Fax (0165) 842152

A medium-sized hotel in this big ski-resort: some rooms face Mont Blanc, others look across the valley to lesser peaks. A recent report: "The greeting was friendly, the room modern, clean and comfortable with good-sized bathroom. Breakfast good too." Most rooms are small but tastefully decorated with hessian-lined walls and stylish bedspreads. No dining room, but the owners also have a restaurant in the village, *Le Vieux Pommier*. More reports please.

Open All year except May, June and Nov.
Rooms 21 double, 3 single – 15 with bath, 9 with shower, all with telephone and TV.
Facilities Lift. Salon, bar, TV room, library, games room; sauna and solarium.
Location 100 metres from town centre. Parking.
Restriction Not suitable for &.
Credit cards All major cards accepted.
Terms B&B: single 56,000–62,000 L, double 93,000–103,000 L. Reduced rates for children sharing parents' room. (No restaurant.)

> In all continental European and Scandinavian countries except Denmark, France, Hungary, Malta, Spain and Turkey, the dialling codes begin with a 0. Omit this when dialling from outside the country in question. Spanish codes begin with a 9, which should also be omitted.

ERICE 91016 Sicily Map 10

Hotel Elimo *Tel* (0923) 869377
Via Vittorio Emanuele 75 *Fax* (0923) 869252

An old stone building, fastidiously converted in a whole series of styles, some a bit bizarre, and newly opened as a smart little hotel. Charming owner, helpful staff, nice bedrooms, good pension menu. Roof-terraces. 21 rooms, all with private facilities. B&B double 70,000–88,000 L. Set menus 30,000–35,000 L. New nomination. More reports please.

Hotel Moderno *Tel* (0923) 869300
Via Vittorio Emanuele 63 *Fax* (0923) 869139

Beautiful but tourist-filled Erice has been described as "an atmospheric sun-bleached town at the tip of a high pinnacle of rock, with views of the sea. The medieval atmosphere is stronger than virtually anywhere we've seen. The castle and churches are marvellous." The friendly, family-run *Moderno*, modern indeed but furnished with style and originality, has this year drawn oddly conflicting reports: "Modern fittings squeezed into impossible spaces, lots of stairs and odd-shaped corridors, but warm, clean and welcoming. The food is very good (rare in Sicily), and a large family are all involved in reception, cooking, waiting, and eating with the guests." But: "Service was a bit haphazard, as everything seemed to be done by one girl. Dinner was pretty uninspiring. But the hotel is a wonderful oasis of luxury in parched Sicily." A third new report, between these extremes, found the food "acceptable, with portions not over-generous", the girl at the desk "helpful" and the ambience "welcoming". Driving through the narrow one-way streets is difficult, and visitors are advised to park in the square just inside the town gate. (*Angela and David Stewart, PA Bispham, Philippa Herbert*)

Open All year.
Rooms 6 suites, 28 double, 6 single – all with bath and/or shower, telephone and TV. Some ground-floor rooms.
Facilities Lift. Lounge, bar, dining room; terrace.
Location Central. Parking.
Credit cards All major cards accepted.
Terms B&B: single 55,000–60,000 L, double 85,000–90,000 L, suite 90,000–100,000 L; dinner, B&B 75,000–90,000 L per person; Set lunch/dinner 35,000 L; full alc 40,000 L. Reduced rates and special meals for children.

FASANO DEL GARDA Brescia Map 10

Grand Hotel Fasano *Tel* (0365) 21051
Corso Zanardelli 160, 25083 *Fax* (0365) 21054

A fairly smart and sizeable holiday hotel in traditional rather than modern style, with a fine lakeside setting just outside the busy resort of Gardone Riviera, and liked by several recent visitors: "Lots of wood panelling and comfortable armchairs. Our large and well-furnished room offered a lovely view of the lake. Food was excellent." "The pretty swimming pool among the bougainvillea and cypresses was lovely, with plenty of umbrellas and loungers on the spacious lawns beside the lake.

Dinners are excellent with splendid help-yourself salads; breakfast was also self-service, with scrambled eggs and bacon and much else. Elegant Louis XV chairs. There is ping-pong, tennis and water-skiing." While one reader found the service "fast and friendly", another this year thought it less than courteous. More reports please.

Open May–Sept/Oct.
Rooms 5 suites, 50 double, 20 single – 49 with bath, 26 with shower, all with telephone. Some ground-floor rooms.
Facilities Lift. 2 lounges, bar, 2 dining rooms; conference facilities. Large grounds with garden, terrace overlooking the lake; swimming pool, tennis, private beach, water sports. Yacht marina and golf nearby.
Location 1 km NE of Gardone, on lake shore.
Credit cards None accepted.
Terms [1989 rates] (Excluding 9% tax) Half board 75,000–120,000 L. Full board 20,000–25,000 L added per person. Set lunch/dinner 33,000 L. Reduced rates and special meals for children.

Hotel Villa del Sogno   *Tel* (0365) 20228
Fasano del Garda, 25080   *Fax* (0365) 21145

A magnificent wide flowery terrace with lovely views of Lake Garda is possibly the best feature of this fairly grand but not-too-daunting hotel, a big yellowish villa built in the 1920s. It is perched high above the lake, amid finely landscaped gardens, just north of Gardone Riviera. Biggish rooms, some with balcony; swimming pool; staff helpful; food copious but unremarkable. Open Easter–Oct. 35 rooms, all with bath or shower. B&B: double 200,000–240,000 L. Set menu from 45,000 L [1989]. Endorsed this year but more reports needed.

FIESOLE 50014 Florence   **Map 10**

Hotel Villa Bonelli   *Tel* (055) 59513 and 598941
Via F. Poeti 1/3

Many visitors to Florence prefer to stay up in the peace and quiet of Fiesole, a lovely old town on a cypress-clad hill five miles north of the busy city. Here the *Villa Bonelli*, a modern unpretentious family-run place, partakes of that famous view down to the spires and palaces, and is served by regular buses to the city. "Helpful owners, cheerful young waitresses, well-cooked meals, comfortable bed", is typical of the kind of report that has again been reaching us in 1988/9. Other views: "We were impressed by the sheer professionalism of the owners, the Boninsegni brothers, and by the variety, quantity and quality of the table d'hôte meals"; "The Tuscan cooking was excellent, and the measures of after-dinner sambuca were most generous." Bedrooms vary in size, some being small, some "huge but sparsely furnished", but all are comfortable; those at the back are subject to some traffic noise . The top-floor restaurant (guests share tables) can become overcrowded and a bit noisy, and there's not much in the way of a lounge. (*Alan F Thomas, Mr and Mrs Bernard Dunstan, Ian and Ann Steel, and others*)

> When hotels have failed to return their questionnaire, we have quoted 1989 prices, with a note to that effect.

Open All year. Restaurant closed for dinner Nov–Mar.
Rooms 1 suite, 16 double, 7 single – 1 with bath and shower, 13 with shower, all
with telephone. Some ground-floor rooms.
Facilities Lift. Foyer with TV, restaurant; terrace.
Location Coming from Florence turn right at Piazza Mino da Fiesole; hotel is
300 metres on right. Garage. Regular bus link with Florence.
Restriction Not suitable for &.
Credit cards All major cards accepted.
Terms B&B: single 43,000–52,000 L, double 68,000–86,000 L; dinner, B&B: single
74,000–83,000 L, double 130,000–145,000 L. Set lunch/dinner 35,000 L; full alc
40,000 L. Reduced rates and special meals for children.

FLORENCE   Map 10

Pensione Annalena   *Tel* (055) 222402
Via Romana 34
Florence 50125

*Originally an aristocratic mansion, then successively a convent, a school for
young ladies, a home for the poor, a gambling house, and since 1919 a family
pensione, set on the quieter south side of the Arno. A place of traditional charm
and personality, very hospitable, filled with old furniture and paintings (but
bathrooms are modern and rooms comfortable). Lounge and cocktail bar.
20 rooms, all with bath and shower. B&B: single 77,000–88,000 L, double
120,000–132,000 L. No restaurant. Recent nomination. More reports please.*

Hotel Calzaiuoli   *Tel* (055) 212456
Via Calzaiuoli 6   *Telex* 580589
Florence 50122

*Centrally situated on a pedestrian street leading from the Duomo to the Palazzo
Vecchio, a clean and well-run little hotel, recently modernised, with air-
conditioning and a friendly staff. Back rooms are largest and quietest, front ones
may be noisy. Some upper rooms have views of the Duomo. Street parking
difficult; garage nearby, but expensive. 37 rooms, all with bath and shower,
73,000–109,000 L [1989]. Breakfast 9,000 L. No restaurant. Endorsed this year,
but fuller reports welcome.*

Hotel Loggiato dei Serviti   *Tel* (055) 219165
Piazza SS. Annunziata 3   *Telex* 575808 LOGSER
Florence 50122

Popular with visiting English art lecturers, this lovely building in the
heart of Florence has been described as "probably the city's most elegant
small hotel". It was built in 1527 for a religious order, the Serviti, and has
been newly and sympathetically restored. "We had a light and spacious
two-level room with gorgeous beamed ceiling; breakfast service was
prompt and friendly", runs a 1989 report, and others have agreed. "It
combines the best of old (Renaissance building, antique furnishings) and
new (including the plumbing). The lovely piazza has been mercifully
rescued from its undignified role as a parking lot (but the hotel will park
your car for you)." Air-conditioning is said to have been just installed –
mercifully, for one visitor found the heat stifling. (*Mary Hanson, AF*

Thomas, ML and MM Gravelle) One dissenter this year thought the hotel overrated and criticised staff and beds.

Open All year.
Rooms 4 suites, 19 double, 6 single – all with bath, shower, telephone, radio and TV.
Facilities Lift. Lounges, TV room, bar, breakfast room; air-conditioning. Conferences/functions can be arranged at an adjacent *palazzo*.
Location Central, 200 metres from cathedral in pedestrian zone. Garage service.
Restriction Not suitable for &.
Credit cards All major cards accepted.
Terms B&B: single 90,000 L, double 140,000 L, suite 200,000–350,000 L. (No restaurant.)

Hotel Tornabuoni Beacci
Via Tornabuoni 3
Florence 50123

Tel (055) 268377 and 212645

Centrally situated near the Palazzo Strozzi, this admirable hotel is in a 14th-century palace – and it's on the top floor, so it suffers very little from street noise. "Indeed most pleasant", says a reader this year; "every room is different and all are large and beautifully decorated. The restaurant is nice, the roof-terrace is a lovely oasis after a day in Florence, and the ambience is homey, helped along by the smiling, willing staff and the ever-present whirlwind of Signora Beacci." Others have called the food "satisfactory", and have enjoyed taking breakfast on the roof-garden, amid trees and shrubs, or sitting in the comfortable lounge amid tapestries, plants, bookcases and fine old furniture. (*Roberta Garza de Elizondo*)

Open All year.
Rooms 31 double – all with bath and telephone; TV on request. 5 in annexe.
Facilities Lift. Salon, bar, restaurant; roof-terrace.
Location Central, close to Palazzo Strozzi. Parking.
Credit cards Amex, Diners, Visa.
Terms On application.

Hotel Villa Belvedere
Via Benedetto Castelli 3
Florence 50124

Tel (055) 222501
Fax (055) 223163
Telex 575648 VILBEL

Again commended this year, notably for its thoughtful staff and its swimming pool set in a flowery garden, this modern family-run hotel stands peacefully on Poggio Imperiale hill, removed from the hurly-burly. "We had a large well-furnished room with a huge terrace overlooking the garden and the city below." Another account rhapsodised, "I drove down through a tunnel of trees to the delightful villa, where only the cicadas disturbed the silence. Inside were cool, shiny marble floors, and simply but elegantly furnished rooms. Breakfast is served in a glass-walled veranda which looks down on to the Duomo, the roofs of Florence and the hills beyond. At night you can sip coffee or drinks in the garden, the perfume from the roses scenting the air and the lights of Florence twinkling below." There is no restaurant, but the bar serves snacks and simple dishes such as pasta and omelettes. Some rooms are quite small, and it might be worth asking for one of the larger (and more expensive) upper rooms with big terraces. (*PA Bispham*)

Open 1 Mar–30 Nov.
Rooms 2 suites, 22 double, 3 single – all with bath and/or shower, telephone, TV and baby-listening; some with balcony. Some ground-floor rooms.
Facilities Lift. Lounges, TV room, bar. Garden with swimming pool, tennis, children's play area.
Location 2.5 km S of centre; leave Florence by Porta Romana, turn E off Via Senese.
Credit cards All major cards accepted.
Terms B&B: single 120,000–140,000 L, double 190,000–210,000 L, suite 240,000–250,000 L. Reduced rates for children sharing parents' room. (No restaurant, but light meals available.)

FORTE DEI MARMI 55042 Lucca   Map 10

Hotel Alcione   *Tel* (0584) 89952
Viale Morin 137

Smarter and more expensive than the *Tirreno* (see below), but smaller, this gabled mansion stands in a quiet residential street a mile south of the town centre; the beach is only 150 yards away, but across two main roads. "At the end of September we were virtually the only pebbles on the beach, so abrupt is the end of the Italian holiday season. The hotel is unpretentious, comfortable, clean (our room was adequately furnished); the cuisine is competent, and service pleasant if a bit slow. The owners were friendly." A shady terrace and neat lounge. More reports please.

Open 25 May–end Sept.
Rooms 45 – all with bath and/or shower and telephone.
Facilities Lift. Lounge, bar, restaurant; terrace. Garden with swimming pool.
Location 1.5 km S of resort which is 35 km NW of Pisa.
Credit cards Amex, Diners, Visa.
Terms [1989 rates] Rooms: single 100,000 L, double 130,000 L. Breakfast 12,000 L. Full board 80,000–140,000 L per person. Set lunch/dinner 30,000–45,000 L.

Hotel Tirreno   *Tel* (0584) 83333
Viale Morin 7

One of the most attractive towns on the coast north of Pisa, and very Italian in atmosphere, Forte dei Marmi is a traditional seaside resort of villas with shady gardens, a wide traffic-free promenade, a pier and a long golden beach. Here the family-run *Tirreno* with its "lovely peaceful garden" has again been liked this year, "Warm and homey; generous rooms with balconies, a staff who work hard to please." Previous accounts: "Excellent room, food, service, garden and situation." "Our room afforded a lovely view of both the sea in front and the mountains behind." Another reader had a marble bathroom "as big as a bedroom in some hotels". Most guests receive a complimentary bottle of Italian champagne with dinner on the night before their departure. (*Diane and Joel Morris*) The beach close by is said to be uncrowded and clean.

Open 12 Apr–1 Oct.
Rooms 49 double, 10 single – all with bath and/or shower, and telephone; 20 have balcony with sea views. 21 in villa in garden.

Facilities Lounge, TV room, games room, bar, dining room; dancing. Garden. 50 metres from fine, safe beach with bathing and boat rental.
Location Central; parking. Town is 35 km NW of Pisa.
Restriction Not suitable for &.
Credit cards Amex, Diners, Visa.
Terms [1989 rates] B&B: single 63,400–64,300 L, double 100,600–101.400 L; dinner, B&B 90,000 L per person; full board 98,000–133,000 L. Reduced rates for children sharing parents' room; special meals.

GARDONE RIVIERA 25083 Brescia　　　　　　　　　Map 10

Villa Fiordaliso　　　　　　　　　　　*Tel* (0365) 20158 and 21948
Via Garibaldi 132　　　　　　　　　　　*Telex* 301088 MOLINA

The brochure of this exquisitely beautiful villa on Lake Garda does not balk at reminding its public that this was a favourite residence of Claretta Petacci, Mussolini's consort. But that's past history. And here is an enthusiastic 1989 nomination: "Now a restaurant with seven bedrooms, it's been carefully restored to its former (pre-Petacci) glory – marble and alabaster, tapestries and paintings, blended with modern lighting and high black-lacquer and leather chairs in the dining rooms, to produce a relaxing and attractive atmosphere. The situation is superb – lovely views, its own small pier, waterside gardens and outdoor dining terrace. Our room was lovely, with traditional furniture, and the bathroom was a delight. The excellent cooking is in modern style, but based on traditional and local recipes, with a changing daily menu related to the market; service, a little unsure, was by local girls. Front lake-view rooms are best: back ones could be noisy, for the main road passes there." (*Pat and Jeremy Temple*)

Open Feb–Nov.
Rooms 1 suite, 6 double – 3 with bath, 4 with shower, all with telephone, radio, TV, mini-bar.
Facilities Hall, piano bar, 4 dining rooms. Terrace where meals are served. Garden, private beach. Golf and tennis nearby.
Location 500 metres from centre of Gardone which is 34 km NE of Brescia. Parking.
Restrictions Not suitable for &.
Credit cards Amex, Diners, Visa.
Terms Double room: with breakfast 128,000 L, with half board 254,000 L, with full board 380,000 L. Full alc 70,000 L.

GARGONZA 52048 Arezzo　　　　　　　　　　　　Map 10

Castello di Gargonza　　　　　　　*Tel* (0575) 847021 and 847053
Monte San Savino　　　　　　　　　　　　*Fax* (0575) 847054
　　　　　　　　　　　　　　　　　　　　Telex 571466 REDCO

"A delightful place to stay", "I'll sing its praises to the rafters" are among the superlatives for this unusual paradise which is not exactly a hotel. On a hilltop in the Tuscan woodlands above the Chiana valley, it is an intact 13th-century walled village which Count Roberto Guicciardini's family have owned for centuries and which he has converted into a partly self-catering hotel-cum-conference centre and rural community. Below the *Castello* itself with its tall turreted tower are a score of red-roofed cottages that cluster round it for ramparted protection. The count has turned these village homes into bedrooms and suites, which can be hired either for a week or more on a self-catering basis, or else per night as hotel rooms. He and his wife have done the conversion most elegantly, with true Italian flair – clean stone walls, beamed ceilings, pretty rustic decor, neatly cobbled alleys.

A recent description: "You enter the village through its single great portal, surmounted by a plaque commemorating Dante's stay here in 1302 at the start of his exile from Florence. When the count inherited it, Gargonza was falling into ruin and nearly all the villagers had left. His restoration has been a labour of love, aiming at the recreation of a living community (there are concerts, exhibitions, study-groups, etc). The cottages are furnished in individual style, and there are always flowers when you arrive. Inside the village are two small gardens, one shady under pines, the other an enclosed hanging garden embellished with lemon trees and grapevines. At the foot of the old mule-track down from the village is the restaurant, whose pleasures are country ones. Calves' liver, brains, fillet of beef with green peppercorns, spatchcocked bantam and other meats grilled over charcoal are delicious. They have excellent wines, Chianti and others. In winter you eat indoors with a blazing log fire and the wrought-iron candelabra lit; on warm summer evenings you can sit in the open on the long roofed terrace above the wooded valley, with bats flitting through the rafters." Those booking just for a night or two should be warned that hotel service as such hardly exists. And cars can enter the village only for loading or unloading baggage.

Open All year except 8 Jan–2 Feb. Restaurant closed Mon.
Rooms 37 double – all with bath and/or shower, and telephone; TV on request. 30 in 18 cottages with self-catering facilities, 7 in Guest House.
Facilities Lounge, TV room, restaurant; auditorium, meeting halls, conference rooms. Large grounds with garden, children's play area, woods and farm.
Location 8 km W of Monte San Savino on SS73 towards Siena (35 km). From *autostrada* A1, exit 27, Monte San Savino is 10 km.
Restriction Not suitable for &.
Credit card Amex.
Terms [1989 rates] B&B 63,000–80,000 L, half board 88,000–105,000 L, full board 113,000–130,000 L. Full alc 28,000–35,000 L. 10% discount for children under 10.

GIARDINI NAXOS 98035 Messina, Sicily   Map 10

Hotel Arathena Rocks   *Tel* (0942) 51348
Via Calcide Eubea 55

In a busy seaside resort just below Taormina, this much-admired family-style traditional hotel has a central but quiet location down a private road – "a lovely peaceful place". There is much antique furniture, and doors painted with local scenes, while fresh flowers from the large garden decorate all the rooms – Signora Arcidiacono has an enthusiasm for gardening. The free-form swimming pool hewn out of lava rocks is an extra luxury, but you can also swim in the clear sea a few metres away. Recent visitors have found the place "spotless, bright and cheerful"; some have enjoyed the food, despite the lack of variety on the menus, though others have been critical. Rooms have just been redecorated: ask for one facing the sea and garden. New reports welcome.

> We should be glad to hear of some good hotels in Sardinia.

Open 1 Apr–31 Oct.
Rooms 2 suites, 40 double, 10 single – all with bath and/or shower and telephone. 3 rooms in annexe.
Facilities Lift. Lounge, TV room, 2 bars, restaurant. Gardens with sea-water swimming pool and tennis court.
Location In Naxos, 5 km S of Taormina. Hotel has minibus to take guests to Taormina.
Credit cards Access, Visa.
Terms Dinner, B&B: single 85,000–90,000 L, double 160,000–170,000 L, suite 200,000–220,000 L. Set lunch/dinner 30,000 L. Reduced rates and special meals for children.

LECCE 73100	Map 10

Hotel Risorgimento	*Tel* (0832) 42125
Via Imperatore Augusto 19	*Telex* 860144

The second city of Apulia (Italy's heel) has some glorious Baroque architecture, and one of the fine old buildings in its centre is this old-fashioned, slightly shabby but comfortable three-star albergo. *Rooms air-conditioned, good baths and plumbing, excellent food, anglophone manager. An oasis in a region of few good hotels. 57 rooms, most with bath or shower. B&B double 110,000 L [1989]. Recent nomination. More reports please.*

MANTUA 46100	Map 10

Albergo San Lorenzo	*Tel* (0376) 220500
Piazza Concordia 14	*Fax* (0376) 327194

There is a sombre quality to the flat Mantuan countryside, which may explain the melancholy of Virgil, who was born in a village nearby. Mantua itself, however, is a beautiful city, and has a grand and colourful ducal palace. The *San Lorenzo*, one of its two best hotels, is a modern building with elegant period furnishings. Recent visitors have found it comfortable, cool and very friendly: "Our room with its terracotta floor tiles was a bit austere but well decorated. The quality of the cotton sheets is amazing." "Good breakfast with first-rate coffee." Many rooms have a view of the Piazza delle Erbe and the lovely rotunda church of San Lorenzo. The hotel is quiet (if you don't count the ringing of church bells as noise). Upstairs lounge and well-kept roof-terrace. (*Endorsed this year by Mary Ann Meanwell*)

Open All year.
Rooms 3 suites, 25 double, 10 single – all with bath and/or shower, telephone, radio, TV and baby-listening.
Facilities Lift suitable for &. Lounges, bar, TV room. Rooftop terrace.
Location Central, in pedestrian precinct. Garage 100 metres.
Credit cards All major cards accepted.
Terms [1989 rates] B&B: single 129,000 L, double 200,000 L, suite 179,000–250,000 L. (No restaurant.)

> Important reminder: terms printed must be regarded as a rough guide only to the size of the bill to be expected at the end of your stay. For latest tariffs, check when booking.

MARINA DI CAMPO 57034 Isola d'Elba — Map 10

Hotel Montecristo   *Tel* (0565) 976861
Viale Nomellini 11   *Fax* (0565) 97597
Telex 590220

On the south coast of Elba, a mile outside the fishing port of Marina di Campo, a pleasant and efficient modern seaside hotel with big well-equipped pool and lido, large clean sandy beach, and fine views of sea and hills. Good bedrooms with balconies, superb breakfasts, helpful staff. Open 23 Mar–21 Oct. 43 rooms, all with shower, B&B double 240,000 L [1989]. No restaurant, but plenty in village. Recent nomination. More reports please.

MELE 16010 Genova — Map 10

Hotel Fado 78   *Tel* (010) 631802
Via Fado 82

Recommended as a congenial stopover, we said last year: a small family-run Anglo-Italian hotel on the road that runs up inland from the Riviera at Voltri, west of Genoa. "Worth a detour," adds a correspondent this year, "to enjoy Italian regional cooking at its best. Excellent dinner, a very warm welcome, comfortable beds, fresh mountain air and pleasant views." (*Peter Saynor*) An earlier report: "A gracious old building, with bedrooms in a modern extension, all have stupendous views across the valley. Mine was high and airy, with a marble floor. The owners, Gianni Canepa and his English wife Christine, gave me a courteous welcome, then a first-class dinner of crêpes and rabbit casserole with garden herbs. Lovely secluded garden. The main road is not busy, and trains are infrequent along the line down in the valley."

Open All year. Restaurant closed first 2 weeks in Sept.
Rooms 5 double, 2 single – all with bath and/or shower and telephone.
Facilities Lounge, bar, 2 dining rooms. Garden, terrace.
Location 7 km N of Voltri on SS456 to Ovada. Leave A26 motorway at Masone or Voltri.
Restrictions Not suitable for &.
Credit cards None accepted.
Terms Rooms: single 35,000 L, double 55,000 L. Breakfast 7,000 L. Full alc 25,000 L. Children under 2 free, under 12 half price when sharing parents' room; special meals.

MERANO 39012 Bolzano — Map 10

Hotel Fragsburg (Castel Verruca)   *Tel* (0473) 44071
Via Fragsburg 3 (PO Box 210)

"A beautiful hotel with delightful owner and friendly staff", says a recent visitor to this small but handsome chalet-style hotel with two names. It stands high on a hill overlooking the spa town of Merano in the Alto Adige, and is surrounded by woods, meadows and mountains, as well as its own orchards. It's only a 20-minute walk to the highest waterfall in the country. Most rooms have a balcony and meals are served on an open-air terrace in summer. The owner Hubert Ortner keeps his own bees and has fresh honey on hand. "Our annexe room was small (the only one left), but the front rooms with balcony looked exquisite. Super open-air heated pool." Others have referred to the good food (interesting à la carte), but one visitor found the local red wine poor. "We were the only non-Germans. Everyone was amicable."

Open 10 Apr–5 Nov.
Rooms 2 suites, 14 double, 2 single – all with bath and/or shower, telephone, radio and TV; many with balcony.
Facilities 2 lounges, bar, TV room, dining room; terrace for summer meals. Park with heated swimming pool, children's play area, ping-pong, chess tables.
Location 5 km NE of Merano. From Merano take road to Bolzano (Bozen), turn left towards Schenna; after 2.5 km turn right at Rametz. Hotel is 5.5 km along this road.
Restriction Not suitable for ও.
Credit cards None accepted.
Terms B&B 50,000–60,000 L per person; dinner, B&B 60,000–90,000 L, full board 70,000–100,000 L. Set lunch/dinner 18,000–20,000 L. Reduced rates and special meals for children.

Hotel Villa Mozart   *Tel* (0473) 30630
Via San Marco 26

Black and white is a dominant theme of Emmy and Andreas Hellrigl's much-admired little hotel: it extends to the china and candles on the tables, the chequered marble floors, even the towels and the brochure. The hotel is about ten minutes' walk from the town centre, approached through big iron gates that open electronically to bona fide guests. A visitor this year praised the "unsurpassed personal attention to detail" of Emmy Hellrigl. Others have written: "I cannot think of a hotel that combines luxury, good service and excellent cuisine in such abundance." "Dinner, served at 8 pm to hotel guests only, with printed dated menu cards, offered no choice (even the wines are chosen for you), but all was exquisite. Breakfast on the terrace was also excellent, the indoor pool was refreshing and the staff pleasant and polite." "The building, outside as well as in, is immaculately designed and furnished in the style of the Viennese Secession. This includes everything – carpets, curtains, door fittings, cutlery, crockery, glasses and even the waitresses' uniforms! For architects and interior designers the hotel is worth a detour." Red print and a rosette from *Michelin*, needless to say. (*Dan and Michlyne Thal*) Andreas Hellrigl, who till last year did the cooking himself, remains co-owner, but the chef is now Raimund Frötscher, whose cuisine this year has been found "light and innovative". Two distinguished British restaurateurs, who had come to Merano specially to experience the *Mozart*'s cooking, were bitterly disappointed to discover that as they were the only guests that night, they had been booked into another restaurant for dinner. We should welcome more reports.

Open Easter–2 Nov.
Rooms 8 double, 2 single – 8 with bath, 2 with shower, all with telephone, radio and TV.
Facilities Lift. Lounges, library, bar, restaurant. Large grounds with sun terrace, covered heated swimming pool, sauna, solarium.
Location Coming on main road from Bolzano, via Rome, take third street on right. Private parking.
Restriction Not suitable for ও.
Credit card Access.

Terms B&B 147,000 L; dinner, B&B 195,000 L (excluding beverages). Extra bed in room 81,000 L. Set dinner for non-residents, by arrangement only, 110.000 L.

MILAN   Map 10

Hotel Gran Duca di York   *Tel* (02) 874863 and 874943
Via Moneta 1/a
Milan 20123

Not far from the Duomo this *Duke of York* is not oppressively grand, and medium-range in price. "A gem," says a reader this year; "the atmosphere was calm, quiet and elegant, the staff were competent, the quiet lounge had a lovely desk on which to write. My room was very small, but clean and well decorated." Others have had larger rooms and big bathrooms, and have praised the breakfast coffee, though the room where it is served is said to be no beauty. "A suit of armour outside the lift, but poor reading lights." (*GB Brook, Bettye Chambers*) No restaurant, but the fairly cheap *Al Mercanti* (super fresh fish) is five minutes' walk away. *Warning*: parking in the area is tricky, and the one-way system is such that access by car is a nightmare.

Open All year except Aug.
Rooms 33 – some with bath or shower, all with telephone and TV.
Facilities Lift. Lounge, breakfast room.
Location Central; 500 metres W of Duomo. No private parking.
Credit cards None accepted.
Terms [1989 rates] Rooms: single 80,000 L, double 116,000 L. Breakfast 10,000 L. (No restaurant.)

Hotel Manzoni   *Tel* (02) 76005700
Via Santo Spirito 20   *Fax* (02) 784212
Milan 20121

A modern hotel, well run and fairly cheap by Milan standards, in a small side street near the Via Manzoni which leads to the Piazza della Scala and the cathedral. Difficult to reach by car, and back rooms can be noisy. Accommodation, service and breakfast generally praised. 52 rooms, all with bath and/or shower. Single 90,280 L, double 129,560–178,560 L. Breakfast 12,000 L. No restaurant. Endorsed this year, but further reports welcome.

Hotel Pierre Milano   *Tel* (02) 8056220
Via De Amicis 32   *Fax* (02) 8052157
Milan 20123

Fairly central, about a kilometre west of the Duomo, a newly opened luxury hotel with striking decor, a mix of ancient and modern. Relaxed ambience, good cooking and buffet breakfasts. Most rooms overlook a quiet street or inner courtyard. 47 rooms, all with bath and shower. B&B double 460,000–720,000 L. Meals 60,000–70,000 L [1989]. New nomination. More reports welcome.

Please make a habit of sending in a report as soon as possible after a visit when details are still fresh in your mind.

MONTIGNOSO 54038 Massa-Carrara　　　　　　　　Map 10

Il Bottaccio
　　　　　　　　　　　　　　　Tel (0585) 340031
　　　　　　　　　　　　　　　Fax (0585) 340103
　　　　　　　　　　　　　　　Telex 500283 PPMS

"Tucked away under a ruined castle", between Carrara and Viareggio, here's another startling new Italian discovery: "A beautiful 18th-century olive-oil mill, converted with Italian style and panache into a charming sophisticated restaurant with just five incredible rooms. The spectacular restaurant is beside a cascading fountain with pools: our ten-course *menu degustazione* was fantastic, fully deserving its *Michelin* rosette. Service was by the owner and his wife. The delicious breakfast was equally impressive. And so was our vast room, containing an original mill wheel and a Roman-style sunken bath. The tiled floor had exotic rugs and on the walls were pictures which looked as if they should have been in a museum. Our large modern black steel-framed four-poster had a silk embroidered bedspread; on an antique Arabian chest stood bottles of cognac, grappa, etc. It was all an amazingly successful blending of ancient and modern. The bathroom, covered with tiny mosaic tiles and hand-painted antique tiles, was also fantastic. There's a Roman pavement in the garden, and a beautiful terrace. It was the most expensive night we have ever had anywhere: but worth it." (*Pat and Jeremy Temple*)

Open All year.
Rooms 5 suites – all with bath and telepone.
Facilities Hall, restaurant. Garden; terrace.
Location Montignoso is 5 km SE of Massa: leave Genova-Livorno Autostrada at exit 12.
Credit cards All major cards accepted.
Terms [1989 rates] Suites: 300,000–450,000 L. Breakfast 20,000 L. Set lunch/dinner 60,000–80,000 L.

ORVIETO 05018 Terni　　　　　　　　　　　　　　Map 10

Hotel Virgilio　　　　　　　　　　　　*Tel* (0763) 41882
Piazza del Duomo 5/6

Facing the side of the glorious Duomo, this is "the kind of small city hotel one always hopes to find but rarely does", according to an inspector. "On the outside it is an unspoiled and shuttered old building, inside it is designed and furnished in good modern Italian style – gleaming chrome, white and pink marble. In the reception area, a large piece of Roman sculpture is flanked by good contemporary original drawings; a beautiful old tapestry is hung alongside delightful puppets. Our room had a side view of the Duomo's richly decorated front. The bedroom was not large but attractively furnished, with a big bed, and the bathroom was elegant. Breakfast, as in most Italian hotels, was minimal and expensive. This apart, the hotel is marvellous value. Ask for room 15. Parking under trees across the square." No restaurant, but the *Maurizio*, close by, is recommended. (*Elizabeth Ring*)

Open All year except 20 days in Jan.
Rooms 14 double, 2 single – all with bath, 2 also have shower, all with telephone. 2 doubles in annexe 20 metres away. Some ground-floor rooms.
Facilities Lift. Bar, TV room.

Location Central, near *Duomo*. Parking.
Credit cards None accepted.
Terms B&B: single 60,000 L, double 90,000 L. (No restaurant.)

PALESTRINA 00036 Rome　　　　　　　　　　　　　　　Map 10

Albergo Stella　　　　　　　　　　*Tel* (06) 9558172 and 9558637
Piazzale della Liberazione 3

The 16th-century composer Palestrina was born in this ancient town that bears his name, set in the lovely hills east of Rome: it contains the ruins of a classical Roman temple dedicated to Fortune. A visitor this year returned to the modern and unpretentious *Stella*, found the food as excellent as before ("antipasto a meal in itself, Easter lamb roast to perfection") and confirms his earlier view: "There in the tiny piazza is this delightful hotel, its restaurant very popular with locals. We loved the place. Our room was large and clean, the bathroom modern, and only the church clock disturbed the peace. Ideal as a night stop." (*Paul Palmer*)

Open All year.
Rooms 1 suite, 14 double – all with bath and/or shower, and telephone.
Facilities Lift. Lounges, bar, restaurant. Public park next door.
Location Central. Town is 38 km E of Rome, off S6 to Frosinone. Public parking.
Credit cards Amex, Diners, Visa.
Terms Rooms: single 26,000 L, double 45,000 L, suite 90,000 L. Breakfast 5,000 L. Full board 55,000–65,000 L. Set lunch 18,000–25,000 L, dinner 23,000–30,000 L; full alc 23,000–30,000 L. Reduced rates for children under 7.

PANZANO IN CHIANTI 50020 Florence　　　　　　　　　Map 10

Villa Le Barone　　　　　　　　　　　　　　*Tel* (055) 852215
Via San Leolino 19

A former home of the famous Della Robbia family, this graceful villa stands high on a hilltop between Florence and Siena. It has a swimming pool, and spread out below it is the hilly Tuscan landscape of vineyards, olive groves and cypresses. The Duchessa Visconti is the present owner of what is now a sophisticated *pensione*, retaining the atmosphere of a cared-for private home. Most rooms are elegantly furnished with good antiques, carefully arranged flowers and fine linen sheets. Two reports this year describe the *Villa* as "delightful" and praise the food highly, whereas some earlier visitors have found it too "bland and international" (to suit the mainly Anglo-American and German clientele?). But all agree that the public rooms are charming and the staff discreetly helpful. The "honour system" with the evening drinks is also admired. (*R Andresen, Joan Haslip*)

Open 1 Apr–1 Nov.
Rooms 26 double, 1 single – 21 with bath, 6 with shower; 3 with tea-making facilities. 17 in 3 different garden annexes. Some ground-floor rooms.
Facilities 4 sitting rooms (1 with TV), bar, breakfast room, dining room. 5-acre grounds with swimming pool and table-tennis.
Location Off SS 222 to Siena, 31 km S of Florence. Hotel is SE of Panzano.
Credit card Amex.
Terms On application.

> Give the Guide positive support. Don't just leave feedback to others.

Hotel Villa Sangiovese
Piazza Bucciarelli 5

Tel (055) 852461

Uri and Anna Maria Bleuler, from Switzerland, were till recently managers of the much-admired *Tenuta di Ricavo* in nearby Castellina (q.v.), and now they have opened their own hotel which enters the Guide as our second entry for this little town south of Florence: "The villa lies on the edge of the town, surrounded by the beautiful steep Tuscan hills where cypresses, olives and vines grow. It is an old stone house, remodelled and restored, with terraces offering fine views of countryside which comes right up to the edge of its own grounds. The Bleulers' welcome could not have been kinder, and it is clear that they are aiming to create a homely atmosphere combined with Swiss efficiency. The comfortable public rooms are decorated mainly in soft yellows and fawns to give a cool, cheerful atmosphere. You can dine on the terrace when it's fine. Our bedroom, not large, was simply furnished with meticulous attention to detail – excellent bedside lamps. A Florentine cook produces a limited à la carte menu: the dishes change nightly and all were good. Breakfast with excellent Swiss-style coffee is served in an attractive small room." "Beautiful rooms, food simple and excellent, staff friendly" is another 1989 report. An outdoor unheated pool is planned for 1990. (*Margaret and Charles Baker, Wendy Geiringer*)

Open All year except Feb. Restaurant closed Wed.
Rooms 3 suites, 16 double – all with bath and/or shower, telephone.
Facilities 2 lounges, bar, restaurant; terrace. Garden.
Swimming pool planned for 1990.
Location Parking. Bus to Florence, which is 31 km to N.
Restrictions Not suitable for &.
Credit cards None accepted.
Terms [1989 rates] B&B: double: 95,000–160,000 L, suite 160,000–210,000 L. Alc meals 30,000–35,000 L. Reduced rates and special meals for children.

PERUGIA 06100   **Map 10**

Hotel La Rosetta
Piazza Italia 19

Tel (075) 20841
Telex 563271

A reader this year who spent all August at *La Rosetta* thought the staff friendly and the food excellent, and especially enjoyed eating out in the attractive shady courtyard. Other recent visitors, too, have found it comfortable and efficient and have praised the cooking. "We had a quiet and cool room over the dining courtyard; service was excellent." "The decor is not always alluring – our bathroom in shiny bronze was a bit much – but the bedrooms were large." The hotel enjoys a prime situation at the top of the main street, Corso Vanucci, but this is where Perugia's nightly *passeggiata* takes place – and one reader warns that "this non-stop cocktail party" makes sleep in the front rooms difficult – "bring earplugs, or ask for rooms at the back, which are less attractive". (*David C Craig*)

Open All year.
Rooms 7 suites, 60 double, 32 single – 96 with bath/shower, all with telephone, radio, TV and baby-listening. Some ground-floor rooms.
Facilities Lift. Salons, bar, games room, reading room, restaurant; conference/banqueting facilities. Courtyard where meals are served in fine weather.

Location Central; some traffic noise. Parking and 2 garages (extra charge).
Credit cards Access, Amex, Visa.
Terms [1989 rates] Rooms: single 60,000 L, double 110,000–140,000 L, suite
140,000–190,000 L. Breakfast 8,000 L. Half board 85,000–130,000 L per person.
Set meals 33,000–38,000 L; full alc 38,000–40,000 L. Reduced rates and special
meals for children.

PETTENASCO 28028 Novara
Map 10

Hotel Giardinetto
Via Provinciale 1, Lago d'Orta

Tel (0323)-89118 and 89219
Fax (0323) 89483
Telex 200206 SIMTUR

A sizeable modern white-walled hotel, family-run, in a superb position
on the shore of little Lake Orta, a busy summer resort. "Our room faced
the lake, and we sat on its terrace watching the sunset. Meals were
exceptional." "Friendly informal service, and a fantastic Thursday dinner
buffet." "Excellent breakfast." Those three reports this year back up
earlier praise for the seafood buffet, the swimming pool, and the
watchfulness of the owners, Oreste and Caterina Primatesta. However,
service was sharply criticised by one reader this year. Rooms facing the
road are rather dark and noisy, lake-facing ones are quieter and have a
better view, notably those in a new wing with balconies. (*Brian
MacArthur, Arnold and Joan Wolfe, Barbara Hill*)

Open Easter–end Oct.
Rooms 2 suites, 45 double, 7 single – all with bath and/or shower (2 with
jacuzzi), telephone and baby-listening; 2 with tea-making facilities; TV on request.
Facilities Lift, ramps. Lounge, 2 bars, TV room, restaurant, coffee shop;
conference room; gala evening with dancing Thur in summer; indoor swimming
pool and sauna; terrace on lake. Garden with heated swimming pool, children's
playground; table tennis.
Location 4 km S of Orta San Giulio. Hotel is 500 metres from town centre, on
lake shore. Private parking.
Credit cards Probably Access, Amex, Visa.
Terms B&B: single 53,000–58,000 L, double 168,000–188,000 L, suite 220,000–
240,000 L. Dinner, B&B 44,000–69,000 L per person; full board 54,000–75,000 L.
Set lunch 25,000 L, dinner 30,000 L; full alc 45,000 L. Reduced rates and special
meals for children.

POMPONESCO 46030 Mantova
Map 10

Trattoria Il Leone
Piazza IV Martiri 2

Tel (0375) 86077

An enthusiastic 1989 nomination for this stylish trattoria-with-rooms
beside the river Po, between Parma and Mantua, "In a distinctly
uncharming village of the Po valley we found this hotel of idiosyncratic
charm, with excellent food. It fronts onto the street, giving no outward
clue to its inner delights – antiques and bric-à-brac everywhere,
chaotically organised, and at the back a tiled courtyard with swimming
pool and white garden furniture. In the ornately decorated dining room
(strange blue-tinted frieze of classical scenes just below the beamed
ceiling), we were served by members of the family, charmingly concerned
that we should enjoy our meal. And we did – delicious fish salad with
salmon, trout and octopus; a rich ravioli; wild duck with fruit,

marvellously tender; and a tempting sweet trolley. Oddly, there were no prices on the menu (we were told this was their custom); but we found them to be very fair. The weak spot of the place is the bedrooms, a bit basic, but with modern bathrooms, and comfortable enough for a night stop at what is essentially a restaurant." (*Philippa and Peter Herbert*) More reports eagerly awaited.

Open All year except Jan. Restaurant closed Sun evening and Mon.
Rooms 5 double, 3 single – all with bath/shower, telephone and baby-listening.
Facilities Lounges, bar, restaurant, TV room; conference room. Garden with swimming pool.
Location In village, which is 32 km from Parma, 38 km from Mantova, off S 420.
Credit cards All major cards accepted.
Terms [1989 rates] B&B 40,000 L; dinner, B&B 65,000 L. Full alc 40,000 L. Reduced rates for children.

PORTO ERCOLE 58018 Grosseto · Map 10

Hotel Il Pellicano   *Tel* (0564) 833801
Cala dei Santi   *Fax* (0564) 833418
      Telex 500131 PELICAN

A stylish and very expensive hotel in a lovely rocky coastal setting, unspoilt by mass tourism. "Impossible to find fault after an idyllic week", writes one devotee this year, while another confirms his earlier lyrical words, "Beautiful rooms, furnishings with lots of glamour, classy bar service, but patchy food. Nadia and Ennio Emili, a young couple, bring an Italian warmth to their very personal style of management. Our room, its vast terrace lined with pots of geraniums, looked out across the gardens and up to the mountain on one side, on the other over tiled roofs to the pool and sea. Breakfast included a glass of delicious red orange juice. The hotel is scrupulously maintained in first-class nick. The gardens are similarly immaculate, and the staff efficient and welcoming. The cooking is honest Tuscan, using first-class fresh produce." The cheaper rooms above the garden are said to be less nice than the sea-facing ones. If you want to bathe in the sea be prepared to walk down ninety steps. (*David Wooff, EE Hunt*) One report this year speaks of "friendly efficiency". But one well-known British hotelier found the staff grossly inefficient when adding up the bill, and thought the prices exorbitant, so we'd welcome more reports.

Open 12 Apr–Oct.
Rooms 4 suites, 30 double – all with bath, shower and telephone; TV and radio on request. 9 in annexe, 7 in cottages.
Facilities Lounge, TV room, bar, restaurant; conference facilities; terrace; dinner-dance Fri July and Aug. Large grounds with restaurant, heated swimming pool with bar and barbecue, tennis, rocky beach with safe bathing, water-skiing.
Location 4.5 km S of Porto Ercole on Monte Argentario coast. Parking.
Restrictions Not suitable for &. No children under 12.
Credit cards All major cards accepted.
Terms Double room 180,000–495,000 L, suite 600,000–900,000 L. Breakfast 25,000 L. Dinner, B&B 185,000–545,000 L per person; full board 255.000–615,000 L.

> If you have kept brochures and tariffs for Continental hotels, do please enclose them with your reports.

POSITANO 84017 Salerno   Map 10

Hotel Casa Albertina   *Tel* (089) 875143
Via della Tavolozza 3   *Fax* (089) 811540

"The fabulous view of Positano that you have from every room" is just one of the qualities that draws readers again and again to Michele Cinque's medium-priced hotel in a justly renowned but expensive resort. The lobby and lounges have cool white walls and vaulted ceilings, while the rooms and dining room are decorated in pastels. "We were received with style and warmth, and had one of the best breakfasts ever", is one report this year, while another mentions a very good, simple meal enjoyed on the terrace facing the sea. "Style, intimacy, friendliness, great quality and good value. Grandmother cooks – 'you eat what we eat' – and it is perfect Italian *cuisine paysanne*. Quiet, the rustle of the sea, spotless tiled bedrooms, clean sheets every other day – and cheap, by Positano prices." The best rooms are on the first floor, but the quietest are the smaller top-floor ones. Drinks charges are high, and parking costs 20,000 lire a day extra. (*Tex and Hella Sessoms*)

Open All year.
Rooms 2 suites, 18 double, 1 single – all with bath and/or shower and telephone, 2 with air-conditioning.
Facilities Lift. Sitting room, TV room, bar, dining room, open-air restaurant; terraces. 10 mins' walk to beach.
Location Central, but quietly situated. Parking 300 metres.
Credit cards All major cards accepted.
Terms B&B: single 90,000 L, double 130,000 L, suite 190,000 L; dinner B&B 90,000–125,000 L per person. Reduced rates for children.

PRAIANO 84010 Salerno   Map 10

Hotel Tramonto d'Oro   *Tel* (089) 874008
Via Gennaro Capriglione   *Telex* 720397

In a small resort on the glorious coast between Amalfi and Positano, here's a spruce modern hotel in a splendid setting high above the sea. Most rooms have balconies with sea views. Swimming pool on roof; bus service down to the beach. Friendly staff. 50 rooms, all with bath and shower. B&B single 50,000 L, double 80,000 L. Set menu 20,000 L. New nomination. More reports please.

RANCO 21020 Varese   Map 10

Del Sole   *Tel* (0331) 976507
Piazza Venezia 5   *Fax* (0331) 976620

In a village at the south-east end of Lake Maggiore, the Brovelli family run a well-known stylish restaurant (two *Michelin* rosettes) that has recently added six smart modern bedrooms, and is brought to the Guide this year by two connoisseurs: "One of North Italy's best restaurants. It is charmingly situated by the lake's edge, with views over the harbour and across to the shore opposite. The restaurant is most attractive, with a huge chandelier and fresh flowers; there's a large terrace, too, for summer eating. The food is superb: a small menu with specialities that change daily (including fish from the lake), and an excellent wine list. Breakfast is also very good, served on the terrace in summer. Service was charming and friendly. The bedrooms are split-level, cleverly designed to obtain maximum space, and with good modern furniture. Highly recommended.'' (*Pat and Jeremy Temple*)

Open 10 Feb–1 Jan, closed 25 Dec. Restaurant closed Mon evening and Tue except public holidays.
Rooms 7 suites, 1 double, 1 single – 6 with bath, 3 with shower, all with telephone, TV and mini-bar.
Facilities Lounge, bar, restaurant; functions room. Terrace where meals are served, garden.
Location 67 km NW of Milan. Parking.
Restrictions Not suitable for &.
Credit cards All major cards accepted.
Terms B&B: double 150,000 L, suite 180,000–200,000 L; dinner, B&B 140,000–160,000 L per person. Set lunch/dinner 75,000–90,000 L; full alc 80,000–100,000 L. Reduced rates for children.

RAVELLO 84010 Salerno   Map 10

Hotel Giordano e Villa Maria   *Tel* (089) 857170 and 857255
Via Santa Chiara 2   *Fax* (089) 857071

Two small adjacent hotels, both very attractive, run jointly by the Palumbo family. Villa Maria *is a converted private villa, with large bedrooms, nice terrace.* Giordano *has a swimming pool, and shady garden for summer dining. Elegant furnishings, lovely views. 19 rooms, all with bath and/or shower. B&B double 76,000–90,000 L. Set menus 35,000 L. Recent nomination. More reports welcome.*

Hotel Marmorata   *Tel* (089) 877777
Strada Statale 163   *Telex* 720667 HOTMAR

Again this year judged "very beautiful" and "excellent in every way", the *Marmorata*, which was once a paper mill, is four miles from Ravello itself, nestled in the cliff face beneath the coastal road to Amalfi. "Good varied food, helpful staff, excellent bedrooms"; "the cool, restful interiors designed in the style of a ship, the seafront terraces and the friendly, helpful service are simply superb. The food was well cooked and presented. There is a steep slope from the road down to the hotel and about 30 steps down to sea level, so not suitable for the infirm." "My cabin-like room had a simple stylishness which combined superbly with its fine view of the sea." One recent visitor found the staff and the Signora most helpful, but adds, "It's on the English package-tour circuit, which means they play very safe with the food. Nonetheless, a super place to stay, but the parking is horrific." (*PA Bispham, Mrs MP Richards*) It is essential to ask for a room with a sea view: others have no view at all.

Open All year. Restaurant closed 31 Oct–30 Apr.
Rooms 5 suites, 36 double, 3 single – 3 with bath, 36 with shower, all with telephone, radio, TV, mini-bar and air-conditioning.
Facilities Hall, lounge, 2 bars, restaurant. Small grounds with terraces down to sea, sea-water swimming pool, private rocky beach with safe bathing and fishing.

Location 1 km W of Minori, 3 km E of Amalfi, 300 metres off the road to Ravello. Parking.
Restriction Not suitable for &.
Credit cards All major cards accepted.
Terms B&B: single 103,000–139,000 L, double 165,000–231,000 L; half board 110,000–171,000 L per person; full board 143,000–193,000 L. Set lunch/dinner 45,000 L; full alc 55,000 L. Reduced rates and special meals for children.

Hotel Palumbo   *Tel* (089) 857244
Via S. Giovanni del Toro 28   *Fax* (089) 857347
                            Telex 770101 VUILLE

Pasquale Vuilleumier's startlingly beautiful hotel, much liked again this year for its "old world charm", has a strange story attached to it. In the mid-19th century his grandfather, from Switzerland, bought a 12th-century episcopal palace up the road and on the advice of Wagner (who was writing bits of *Parsifal* in a nearby villa) turned it into a hotel. Over the years his guests there included Longfellow, Grieg, DH Lawrence (he worked on *Lady Chatterley* in one of the rooms), Garbo, Bogart and the Kennedys. But about seven years ago Signor Vuilleumier transferred the hotel to his own residence, the Palazzo Confalone, also 12th-century. The original *Palumbo* is now deserted save for its illustrious ghosts, but the newer *Palumbo* he has converted with exquisite taste. Its high-ceilinged central foyer is a miracle of cool white arches, plants and flowers, and vistas of the azure sea far below. The canopied dining room terrace and the lemon-tree-shaded lounge terrace have the same miraculous view. "The most romantic place I have ever stayed in. The view from our bedroom balcony was breath-taking, literally between sea and sky, and the bedroom itself was stunning with its blue and white tiles. Signor Vuilleumier, now in his seventies, was very amiable although regretting the grandeur of the past." "The food was above average, the staff very courteous, and the Signor ever present", adds a reader this year. (*Miss EH Nicholls*)

Open All year.
Rooms 3 suites, 17 double – all with bath and shower, telephone, TV and baby-listening. 7 in annexe 50 yards from main building.
Facilities Salons, bar, TV lounge, restaurant; sun terrace. Garden; solarium. Beaches 10–15 mins by car.
Location Above the Amalfi Drive, overlooking Ravello. Parking.
Restriction Not suitable for &.
Credit cards Access, Visa.
Terms Dinner, B&B 201,000–319,000 L per person; full board 210,000–350,000 L. Set lunch/dinner 55,000 L; full alc 70,000 L. Reduced rates and special meals for children.

Hotel Parsifal   *Tel* (089) 857144
Via G. d'Anna 5

This delectable hotel is much cheaper than most of our other Ravello choices: "Not grand, but clean, cool, restful and very beautiful. The hotel is built around parts of a 13th-century Augustinian monastery, and has a cloister and flowery garden, with a pool overflowing with fish. Views from our room, from the garden and restaurant were sensational, and the food was almost as good (but breakfast not so hot). The bed was the most comfortable we found in Italy and the towels the thickest." Pastel shades, and a lovely outdoor terrace above the sea. Guests can use the swimming pool at *Le Terrazze* free of charge.

Open 1 Apr–15 Oct. Closed Tue.
Rooms 19 – all with bath and/or shower, and telephone.
Facilities Salon, restaurant. Cloister. Garden.
Location Fairly central. Parking.
Restriction Not suitable for &.
Credit cards All major cards accepted.
Terms [1989 rates] Rooms: single 30,000–37,000 L, double 44,000–56,000 L. Breakfast 7,000 L. Set lunch/dinner 28,000 L; full alc 30,000 L. Reduced rates and special meals for children.

RIVA DI SOLTO 24060 Bergamo   Map 10

Albergo-Ristorante Miranda   *Tel* (035) 986021
  "da Oreste"
Via Cornello 8

The attractive but little-known Lake Iseo lies amid hills and olive groves to the east of Bergamo, and high up on its western shore is this white modern villa: "A family-run hotel with glorious views above the lake. Bedrooms are clean, well lit, with spacious wardrobes, and many have a balcony. The food is simple but well cooked (*Michelin* red *Pas* for good value), and the menu is discussed with guests. Efficient and friendly service. Picnics are readily provided. Pleasant swimming pool down a steep path in the garden." More reports please.

Open All year except 15 Jan–15 Feb. Restaurant closed to non-residents Tue in winter.
Rooms 3 suites, 11 double, 3 single – 6 with bath and shower.
Facilities Lounge with TV, restaurant. Terrace, garden with swimming pool.
Location In centre of village 40 km E of Bergamo.
Credit cards None accepted.
Terms Rooms: single 22,000 L, double 43,450 L. Breakfast 6,000 L. Half board 38,000 L per person, full board 45,000 L. Set lunch 35,000 L, dinner 40,000 L. Full alc 35,000–40,000 L. Reduced rates for children; special meals on request.

ROME   Map 10

Hotel Cesàri   *Tel* (06) 6792386 and 6790882
Via di Pietra 89a, Rome 00186   *Telex* 623300

This "tremendous bargain", just off the strident via del Corso, has been a hotel since the early 18th century, and former guests – says its brochure – have included Stendhal, Mazzini and Garibaldi. But, though it was once a palace, today it is a modest and quite low-priced hotel, rating just one gable in *Michelin*. "This is as near as you will get in central Rome to a *Relais du Silence*: we had a pleasant room overlooking the small street, but as it is a cul-de-sac the curse of the Lambretta is relieved. The phones would have been instantly recognisable to Alexander Graham Bell, and the lift reminded me of Fellini's *Giulietta degli Spiriti*, but it did work. The beds were comfortable and the staff charming. Breakfast was typical of Italy – delicious *hot* coffee with UHT milk pulverised to atoms and reconstituted à la milk-shake, fresh rolls like cannon-balls and revolting soggy buns tasting of some chemical." Visitors this year and last have agreed – about the charming staff, good value, *and* the breakfasts. (*Bettye Chambers*)

Open All year.
Rooms 40 double, 10 single – all with bath and/or shower, and telephone.
Facilities Lift. Lounge, TV room, bar.
Location Central, off via del Corso. Free parking in piazza di Pietra.
Credit cards All major cards accepted.
Terms B&B: single 91,000 L, double 133,000 L. 10% reduction for children under 10. (No restaurant.)

Hotel Forum
Via Tor de' Conti 25–30
Rome 00184

Tel (06) 6792446
Fax (06) 6799337
Telex 622549

A solid classic ochre-coloured building, fairly smart and upper-medium in price. As its name implies, it is very close to the Foro Romano, but tucked away down a small street. And it has an attractive rooftop restaurant and bar. "The ideal place to stay in Rome if you want to explore the pagan monuments and leave the Christian ones alone. The lobby, all polished wood, period furniture, and bits of Roman wall and marble column, offers a welcome respite. There is a clubby, aristocratic, but far from stuffy, atmosphere in the public areas that is appealing. Rooms are on the small side, but ours was clean and comfortable: two sets of shutters and two sets of curtains proved an adequate baffle against the noise of Rome. The service is obliging. But prices are fairly steep." Following that earlier report, a visitor this year thought the service poor and food only average, so we'd welcome other verdicts.

Open All year. Restaurant closed Sun.
Rooms 79 – all with bath or shower, telephone, radio, TV and baby-listening.
Facilities Hall, bar, TV room, panoramic restaurant; meeting rooms; roof-garden.
Restriction Not suitable for &.
Location Central, just E of Via dei Fori Imperiali and Forum. Garage
Credit cards All major cards accepted.
Terms [1989 rates] Rooms: single 140,000–230,000 L, double 230,000–330,000 L. Breakfast 20,000 L. Alc (excluding wine) from 65,000 L. Winter discounts. 20% reduction for children sharing parents' room; special meals.

Hotel Gregoriana
Via Gregoriana 18
Rome 00187

Tel (06) 6794269

A former convent near the top of the Spanish steps has been turned into a clean and sophisticated little hotel with friendly staff and owners; it has unusual decor – a landing with black satin walls and leopard-skin cushions. Despite its location it is fairly quiet, especially rooms at the back (there is some street noise in front); a few upper rooms look out over roof-gardens and orange and lemon trees. Some readers find bedrooms too small and the lack of lounge a drawback, but generally these earlier views are confirmed: "Our room was generous and comfortable in a mixture of Erté and American Chinese, with a big, sunny bathroom in blues and mauves." "No frills offered, but one gets what one pays for: peace and quiet in a prime locality, combined with unpretentious, professional service." Book well ahead. (*Dr DM Keyzer, I Zetterström*)

Open All year.
Rooms 16 double, 3 single – 12 with bath, 7 with shower, all with telephone; TV on request. 4 ground-floor rooms.
Facilities Lift. Hall.
Location Central, above Spanish Steps. Parking.
Credit cards None accepted.
Terms [1989 rates] B&B: single 110,000 L, double 170,000 L. Reduced rates for children. (No restaurant.)

Hotel La Residenza   *Tel* (06) 463271 and 460789
Via Emilia 22   *Fax* (06) 485721
Rome 00187   *Telex* 410423 GIOTEL
                                  attn La Residenza

"A true gem, and excellent value," says an American visitor this year about this small but quite luxurious hotel, nicely located around the corner from the Via Veneto and near the Villa Borghese. Everyone speaks well of the friendly staff, the breakfast buffet, the comfortable rooms and pleasing decor. Some rooms however are quite small, and the hotel faces a night-club which could be noisy; rooms at the back are preferable. No restaurant: but there are good ones in the area, such as the small family-run *Tempio di Bacco*, via Lombardia. (*Arnold H Wolfe, and others*)

Open All year.
Rooms 7 suites, 17 double, 3 single – 24 with bath, 3 with shower, all with telephone, radio, TV and mini-bar.
Facilities 2 lounges, bar, breakfast room; terrace and patio.
Location Central, near the Via Veneto and American Embassy (back rooms quietest). Parking.
Restriction Not suitable for &.
Credit cards None accepted.
Terms [1989 rates] B&B: single 95,000 L, double 170,000 L, suite 190,000 L. (No restaurant.)

SAN GIMIGNANO 53037 Siena   Map 10

Bel Soggiorno   *Tel* (0577) 40375
Via S. Giovanni 91   *Fax* (0577) 940375

A lovely 13th-century building, just inside the ramparts of this splendid little medieval Tuscan town, famous for its 14 slender towers rising above the rooftops. Apart from one complaint of an indifferent meal, again this year every *soggiorno* reported to us has been *bello*, with service, food and fair prices all commended. The top floor of the hotel is to be avoided if possible: hot, and noisy with plumbing. The remaining rooms, though small, are adequate, some with terraces and most with magnificent views. There is a TV salon but no garden, and if hot water is a priority, you had better think twice; otherwise, "a good find"! On the unchanging but "excellent" menu, readers especially admire "a delicious first course called trittico" and "pollo al diavolo which comes aflame". From the wide windows, the views of the Tuscan hills and olive groves are spectacular." (*Richard Osborne, G Evans, RW Baker*)

Open All year. Restaurant closed Mon.
Rooms 25 double, 2 single – all with bath, shower and telephone.
Facilities Lift. Salon with T V, bar, restaurant. Terrace.
Location 30 km from Siena; cars allowed in for loading and unloading only.
Carpark nearby (10,000 L per day).
Restrictions Not suitable for &. No children under 8.
Credit cards All major cards accepted.
Terms [1989 rates] B&B: single occupancy 48,000–55,000 L, double 68,000–73,000 L. Full board 90,000–95,000 L per person.

Hotel La Cisterna *Tel* (0577) 940328
Piazza della Cisterna 23 *Telex* 575152 HOTCIS

"We had to share a bathroom, but waking up to look down into the square of San Gimignano was a real treat", runs one of many favourable 1988/9 reports on this 14th-century ivy-clad *palazzo*. It fronts the animated main piazza, and many rooms have balconies facing either this scene or the wide Tuscan landscape. Rooms are quite large, some simple, some more interesting with painted furniture, and service is mostly friendly. There's a splendid church-like lounge, and a beamed restaurant with stunning panoramic views. The food used to be poor: but a new chef has arrived and the cooking is much improved, say several readers this year. (*Gerald Campion, Daniel and Pamela Waley, ATW Liddell, and others*)

Open 10 Mar–10 Nov. Restaurant closed Tue and Wed midday.
Rooms 50 – all with bath and/or shower and telephone. 4 rooms share a balcony overlooking the town. 9 ground-floor rooms.
Facilities Lift. 14th-century salon, salon with T V, bar, 3 dining rooms. Garden.
Location Central. Cars allowed in for loading and unloading only. Paying car park 400 metres.
Credit cards All major cards accepted.
Terms [1989 rates] B&B: single 54,000–58,000 L, double 86,000–93,000 L; dinner, B&B 72,000–84,000 L per person. Set meals 26,000 L; full alc 38,000–50,000 L.

Le Renaie *Tel* (0577) 955044
Pancole

A quiet rural hotel with lovely views over the Tuscan hills, outside the hamlet of Pancole, just north of San Gimignano. "There's nothing grand about it, but nor is it scruffy or second-rate", runs a 1989 report; "the decor is light and gay, our bedroom was spacious and comfortable. We dined out on the terrace by candle-light: the food was good honest Tuscan, very good value, e.g. wild boar casserole and pork tenderloin in herbs and Chianti. Our only quibble is that the owners, a father and son it seems, do not stamp their personality on the place – it lacks a woman's touch." "Breakfast on the terrace was enjoyable." Many rooms have a balcony, and there's a cool lounge in modern design, also a swimming pool. The cooking is preferred to our other San Gimignano entries. (*Philippa Herbert; Betsy C Maestro*)

Open All year except 10 Nov–2 Dec. Restaurant closed Tue.
Rooms 24 double, 2 single – all with bath/shower and telephone; T V on request.
Facilities Lounge with T V, bar, restaurant. Terrace, garden with swimming pool.
Location 5 km N of San Gimignano towards Certaldo. Parking.
Restriction Not suitable for &.
Credit cards All major cards accepted.

Terms [1989 rates] Rooms: single 48,000 L, double 68,000–74,000 L. Breakfast 6,500 L. Dinner, B&B 64,000 L per person. Full alc 25,000–30,000 L. Reduced rates and special meals for children.

SAN GREGORIO 06081 Perugia   Map 10

Castel San Gregorio   *Tel* (075) 8038009

"Man enters into this magic place with his soul", proclaims the brochure of this Guide newcomer – and also, we suggest, with his sense of humour and conviviality. It's a creeper-covered crenellated neo-Gothic castle, set amid vines and parkland between Assisi and Perugia, overlooking the plain. "Fairly eccentric, but delightfully so", says its nominator; "it's a peaceful, rambling place with varied, well-furnished bedrooms. The dining room has one big table where you all dine together, chatting to your neighbours: food ranges from the very good to the pedestrian, and is washed down by good local cheap wine. We thought the *Castel* bliss and can't wait to get back." (*W Ian Stewart*) Some rooms have antique beds, others have four-posters with medieval-style linen drapes; the bathrooms in the towers are circular. Beamed ceilings, spiral stairways, fancy atmospheric lighting all add to the ambience. More reports, we beg you.

Open All year except 15–30 Jan.
Rooms 12 – all with bath and/or shower and telephone.
Facilities Reading room, dining room. Small garden.
Location 13 km NW of Assisi.
Restrictions Not suitable for &.
Credit cards Access, Amex, Diners.
Terms [1989 rates] Rooms 47,000–66,000 L. Breakfast 6,000 L. Full board 94,000 L per person. Set meals 30,000 L

SAN MAMETE 22010 Como   Map 10

Hotel Stella d'Italia   *Tel* (0344) 68139
Piazza Roma 1   *Fax* (0344) 68729
(postal address: PO Box 46
San Mamete, Valsolda
6976 Castagnola, Switzerland)

Right on Lake Lugano and close to the Swiss border, this "gem of a place" (a report this year) has a very special quality. Its English-speaking owners, the Ortellis, have been running it for decades, and have won a faithful clientele, many of them English. The bedrooms, each with its own balcony on which you can breakfast, have views across the lake to the green slopes and mountains in the distance. There is a garden leading down to a "lido" for swimming or sun-bathing. In good weather, dinner is served on the pretty trellised terrace, with the water at one's feet, but the indoor dining room also has fine views.

Visitors this year have commented especially on the good cooking and very reasonable prices, though one or two have found the upkeep less than perfect (little things like inadequate clothes-hangers). An earlier view, "The un-Italian aura is more than compensated for by the fat delights of the beautiful veranda restaurant, the attentive service, the tranquil lido by the lake and a library which must have the largest collection of Warwick Deeping in north Italy." Some have found the *en pension* food is a little plain and boring. (*Mary and Harold Larsen, Dorys and Murray Bernbaum, BJ Walters*)

Open Apr–Oct.
Rooms 31 double, 5 single – 23 with bath, 13 with shower, all with telephone and balcony.
Facilities 2 lounges, bar, restaurant. Garden with restaurant. Lake bathing, fishing, surfing, boating.
Location 10 km NE of Lugano on Lake Lugano between Gandria and Menaggio. Garage for 14 cars.
Restriction Not suitable for &.
Credit cards All major cards accepted.
Terms B&B: single 57,000 L, double 88,000 L; dinner, B&B 69,000–71,000 L per person; full board 77,000–79,000 L. Set lunch/dinner 27,000 L; full alc 30,000–40,000 L. Reduced rates and special meals for children.

SAN PAOLO 39050 Bolzano   Map 10

Hotel Schloss Korb   *Tel* (0471) 633222
Missiano

West of Bolzano, in a marvellous open setting amid terraced vineyards and fortress-crowned rocky hills, a medieval castle very stylishly converted – beamed ceilings, rough stone walls, strange statuary. Quaint and pretty bedrooms, those in the tower specially recommended. Hearty Tyrolean food. Indoor and outdoor swimming pools, sauna, sun terrace, floodlit tennis courts. Open Apr–5 Nov. 56 rooms, all with bath and shower. B&B 65,000–70,000 L; half board 90,000–95,000 L. Set menu 40,000 L [1989]. Enticing new nomination. More reports eagerly requested.

SANTA MARIA DI CASTELLABATE 84048 Salerno   Map 10

Hotel Sonia   *Tel* (0974) 961172

On the edge of an old fishing-port 45 miles south of Salerno, and only 15 miles from the Greek temples of Paestum, this unpretentious little seaside hotel has been enjoyed by a correspondent who spent a happy beach holiday there with her eight-year-old son: "We went in May, which was lovely as it was not too crowded. The family owners are very kind and Italian in their attitudes to children, and fed my son, who is fussy about food, masses of chips and pasta. The food is very plain, which suited me fine. The rooms, too, are simple but nice, some facing the village square, some the sea. I was able to sit on my balcony and watch my son on the beach. A quiet, civilised place." Deckchairs and umbrellas on the sandy beach, free of charge to guests. More reports please.

Open All year.
Rooms 4 suites, 16 double, 2 single – 20 with bath and/or shower; 2 with telephone. Many with balcony.
Facilities Lounge, TV room, bar, dining room. Hotel is on beach.
Location Castellabate is 71 km S of Salerno.
Credit cards None accepted.
Terms Rooms: single 28,000–30,000 L, double 38,000–45,000 L, suite 74,000–88,000 L. Breakfast 6,000 L. Dinner, B&B 40,000–50,000 L per person. Set meals 18,000 L; alc 22,000 L. Reductions for long stays out of season. Reduced rates for children; special meals on request.

SELVA DI VAL GARDENA 39048 Bolzano   Map 10

Hotel Dorfer   *Tel* (0471) 75204
Via Cir 5

Selva, between Bolzano and Cortina, is a Ladinisch and German-speaking village in the upper Val Gardena, now a popular skiing and summer resort. This is one of its simpler hotels, but homely and comfortable, run with great warmth by Frau Dorfer. An 1989 report, "Selva with its many hotels strikes one as being the Blackpool of the Dolomites, but the *Dorfer* manages to insulate itself from the noise. The view from the front rooms is magnificent, but the back ones are to be avoided. The restaurant manager, a Humphrey Bogart look-alike, is witty and solicitous, breakfast is extensive and the set dinner menu is good." The skiing, too, is good. (*Esler Crawford*)

Open 18 Dec–18 Apr, 16 Jun–30 Sept.
Rooms 21 double, 9 single – all with bath and/or shower and telephone, most with radio and TV; many with balcony.
Facilities Lounge, bar, TV room, restaurant; gym, whirlpool, sauna and solarium. Garden with terrace for alfresco meals and table tennis.
Location 42 km E of Bolzano.
Restriction Not suitable for &.
Credit cards None accepted.
Terms [1989 rates] B&B 55,000–95,000 L. Set lunch 18,000 L; full alc 35,000 L. Reduced rates and special meals for children.

SIENA 53100   Map 10

Hotel Certosa di Maggiano   *Tel* (0577) 288180
Via Certosa 82   *Telex* 574221 CERMAG

Of the oldest Carthusian monastery in Tuscany (built 1314) just the cloister and tower remain, and these now form part of this luxurious and well-converted little hotel, lying a mile outside the city walls in a bucolic setting. It is an unusual place with a powerful personality which may not suit everyone, and some have judged it overpriced. A returning devotee this year thought the food improved but was critical of breakfast. He had written earlier, "Some might find the intimacy, relentless good taste and attention to detail a little precious, but others, myself included, are enchanted by the beautiful old building, the sumptuous bedrooms, the recorded Mozart in the library, the swimming pool looking over the vineyards to the walls of Siena, and the formal but *nice* service. Food is modern Italian: dishes may sound dull (e.g. veal with herbs) but most of them look and taste superb." "The swimming pool is in a natural garden with peach and apricot trees overlooking the vineyard which supplies the excellent house wine. Our room was large, furnished with antiques, chintz curtains and wall coverings. The bathroom was bright and modern with green and white tiles." "We breakfasted and dined in the central courtyard, but could have eaten in a ravishingly pretty dining room. While we were lounging by the pool, a bowl of freshly picked figs and grapes was put in our room; while we dined, a dish of sweets was placed by the bedside. All in all, the manners and civilised charm of an earlier epoch, bolstered by 20th-century plumbing." Several readers have objected to the high prices charged for extras. And one this year received no apology when a booking was not honoured.

Open All year.
Rooms 9 suites, 5 double – all with bath, shower, telephone, radio and TV. Some on ground floor.
Facilities Salon, library, TV room, games room, bar, dining room. Large garden with heated swimming pool and tennis court.
Location 1 km SE of Siena outside Porta Romana. Parking.
Credit cards All major cards accepted.
Terms B&B: single 250,000–290,000 L, double 280,000–320,000 L, suite 430,000–530,000 L; dinner, B&B 215,000–375,000 L per person; full board 280,000–450,000 L. Full alc 90,000 L. Special meals for children.

Park Hotel　　　　　　　　　　　　　　　　　　*Tel* (0577) 44803
Via di Marciano 18　　　　　　　　　　　　　*Telex* 571005 PARKSI

Michelin awards its full range of red print, including four red gables, to this converted 15th-century villa secluded in the north-west outskirts, now a stylish and sizeable hotel. "The rooms recently had a major renovation. Ours was completely upholstered in a beautiful muted blue-pink cloth. All furnishings were ultra-modern, a pleasing respite from Italy's mostly antique-filled hotel rooms. The bathroom had a proper stand-up shower, while its walls and floor were in beautiful blue marble. Some rooms look over to Siena across a wild, flower-filled garden, others face the attractive swimming pool and vine-covered rolling hills beyond. Staff were cordial and professional." "The food is wonderful and the waiters friendly. This is a CIGA hotel, so has a sort of business atmosphere." More reports please.

Open All year.
Rooms 4 suites, 64 double, 1 single – all with bath and shower, telephone, TV and air-conditioning. Some ground-floor rooms. 4 in garden annexe.
Facilities Lift. 3 bars, TV room, 2 restaurants; conference facilities. Gardens with swimming pool, tennis.
Location 2 km NW of city centre. Minibus service into town. Parking.
Credit cards All major cards accepted.
Terms (excluding 19% tax) Rooms: single 150–188,000 L, double 190–250,000 L, suite 450,000 L. Breakfast 18,000 L. Dinner, B&B: single 228,000–258,000 L, double 346,000–406,000 L, suite 606,000 L. Alc meals 80,000 L. Children under 8 free of charge; special meals on request.

Villa Scacciapensieri　　　　　　　　　　　*Tel* (0577) 41441
Via di Scacciapensieri 10　　　　　　　　　*Telex* 573390 VISCA

A Tuscan villa on a hillside, surrounded by vineyards and olive trees (but industrial suburbia is close). Despite some criticisms, it has long been liked for its lovely garden, quiet atmosphere and friendly owners, and is restored to the Guide this year by three positive reports. "We had an excellent large bedroom facing Siena. The service was exemplary, the food first-class, and the grounds are lovely. The weak spots are the bar and lounge." "All very clean. Many dishes quite superb. Service both professional and warm-hearted." (*VN Wright, Mary B Dawson, TCH Macafee*)

We should be glad to hear of some good hotels in Sardinia.

Open Mar–Oct.
Rooms 2 suites, 22 double, 5 single – all with bath and/or shower, telephone and
TV. 10 rooms in annexe.
Facilities Lift. Lounge, bar, TV room, restaurant; terrace. Garden with swimming
pool and tennis.
Location 3 km N of Siena. Regular bus service.
Credit cards All major cards accepted.
Terms B&B: single 160,000 L, double 250,000 L, suite 325,000 L; dinner, B&B:
single 195,000 L, double 329,000 L, suite 395,000 L. Set lunch 35,000 L, dinner
45,000 L; full alc 100,000 L. Reduced rates for children.

SINALUNGA 53048 Siena　　　　　　　　　　　　Map 10

Locanda dell'Amorosa　　　　　　　　　　*Tel* (0577) 679497
　　　　　　　　　　　　　　　　　　　　　Fax (0577) 678216
　　　　　　　　　　　　　　　　　　　　Telex 580047 AMOR

"One of the nicest hotels we have found in Italy" – a cluster of old stone
buildings on the edge of the lovely Sienese hills, transformed from a
private residence into a select and expensive little country inn, had its first
entry last year. Its nominators returned this year and found it unchanged.
They had written, "Converted from an old estate, it is still a working
farm, producing its own wines, jams and honey. The beautiful old
buildings of various shapes and sizes surround a central courtyard with a
huge well. The estate chapel has some superb frescoes. Our room was
really a suite, its beamed rooms comfortably furnished with antiques;
floors were red Tuscan tiles, with rugs. The restaurant, in the old stables,
is a fascinating room in very rustic style. The food is excellent, including
traditional Tuscan dishes and unusual fish from Lake Trasimeno. Service,
by local girls, is quiet and efficient. Breakfast was also excellent, with
lovely hot fresh-baked brioches. There is a comfortable lounge, and chairs
under giant umbrellas in the courtyard. Siena, Arezzo and Perugia are all
within easy reach." (*Pat and Jeremy Temple*) The hotel has this year lost its
Michelin rosette, and we'd be glad to hear from other readers.

Open All year except 20 Jan–28 Feb. Restaurant closed Mon and Tue midday.
Rooms 7 suites, 8 double – all with bath and/or shower, telephone, TV, fridge.
Facilities Lounge, bar, restaurant. Garden and courtyard.
Location 2 km S of Sinalunga which is 45 km E of Siena. Parking.
Credit cards All major cards accepted.
Terms B&B: double 231,000–276,000 L, suite 356,000–536,000 L. Full alc 60,000–
70,000 L.

SIRMIONE 251019 Brescia　　　　　　　　　　　Map 10

Hotel Golf et Suisse　　　　　　　　　　　*Tel* (030) 916176
Via Condominio　　　　　　　　　　　　　　*Fax* (030) 916304
　　　　　　　　　　　　　　　　　　　　Telex 300395

Catullus' *"venusta Sirmio"* is now a delightful medieval walled townlet on
a small peninsula at the south end of Lake Garda. Just outside it is this
clean, modern family-run hotel, set back from the road. "The owner was
charming, and our large rooms had balconies", runs a report this year.
There's a small garden with chairs for drinks and a good swimming pool,
while the hotel also has a nearby jetty and private beach for lake bathing.
No restaurant, but lots in town. (*Wende West*)

Open 1 Mar–31 Oct.
Rooms 14 suites in annexe opposite hotel, 30 double – all with bath and/or shower, telephone and TV; 14 with radio and tea-making facilities. Ground-floor rooms.
Facilities Lounge with TV, bar. Garden with swimming pool. Private beach.
Location 1 km from Sirmione which is 35 km W of Verona.
Credit cards Access, Amex, Visa.
Terms Rooms 65,000–140,000 L. Breakfast 15,000 L. Reduced rates for children. (No restaurant.)

TAORMINA 98039 Messina, Sicily   **Map 10**

San Domenico Palace Hotel   *Tel* (0942) 23701
Piazza San Domenico 5   *Fax* (0942) 25506
                                          Telex 980013 DOMHOT

This famous and palatial hotel on its high promontory began life as a monastery. In 1943 Kesselring used it as his headquarters and much of the original 15th-century building, apart from the cloister, was destroyed by Allied bombs. Today it is rebuilt, and in many ways is very beautiful. The view from its balcony, of Etna and the coast, is sensational; below stretch the palm-studded gardens, ablaze with colour. But there have been tales of dull food, and recently a sharp-eyed British hotelier gave this view: "Lovely cloister and courtyards to which has been added an ill-proportioned, gloomy and ill-furnished Edwardian block. We much preferred the old section, though the rooms lack the large balconies of the Edwardian part. Garden beautifully kept – unusual for Sicily. Housekeeping poor. Would be a wonderful place if properly managed. As it is, passable." So we advised readers to go for the historic splendour but not to expect a "good hotel". This year, a sharp retort to this has come from a leading playwright: "All these comments are ridiculously unfair and almost caused us to pass over what turned out to be the most delightful hotel we've ever stayed at anywhere in the world. 'Don't expect a "good hotel"'. Blimey. Don't expect too much of paradise, either." (*Michael Frayn*) Your views, please, as to which of these controversial noises is 'off', and which is on target.

Open All year.
Rooms 10 suites, 80 double, 28 single – all with bath, telephone, radio, TV and air-conditioning.
Facilities Lift. Hall, 4 lounges, bar, TV room, games room, dining room; conference facilities; mandolin group every night in bar; courtyard terrace. Garden with heated swimming pool and snack bar. Private beach (car service).
Location On promontory on W side of town, but close to centre.
Restriction Not suitable for &.
Credit cards All major cards accepted.
Terms [1989 rates] B&B: single 250,000 L, double 425,000 L, suite 610,000–665,000 L; full board 300,000–330,000 L per person. Set lunch/dinner 90,000 L. Reduced rates for children sharing parents' room.

Villa Belvedere   *Tel* (0942) 23791
Via Bagnoli Croci 79

"A superbly run hotel in a fine situation overlooking the bay. Beautiful garden and swimming pool with a palm growing up through the middle." "Run by a friendly and cultivated Franco-Italian family. The bar by the pool serves delicious snacks." So run two reports, this year and last, on the bed-and-breakfast *Belvedere*. And here, caveats and all, is a third:

"One of the two prettiest places to stay in Taormina. The sea is 800 feet below, palm trees sway and creak, Mount Etna smoulders moodily, the lights of Naxos twinkle in the dark. My room was unique. It was cool and shaded, with a little garden of its own; the bathroom was cramped but functioning, though prone to ant invasions. The garden rambles as much as steep terracing will allow, with little hidden places for a quiet read or writing a report to the Guide. The pool is not for Olympic swimmers, nor for those muscular Germans who tense their pectorals and breasts at each other; it is a pool for a quick cooling dip. Beside it one can have a tolerable and cheapish lunch." Since last year, air-conditioning has been installed in the top-floor rooms (which have balconies) and in the rooms facing the street which can be noisy. (*Christina Bewley*)

Open 15 March–31 Oct.
Rooms 38 double, 3 single – 13 with bath, 28 with shower, all with telephone. Some with air-conditioning. Ground-floor rooms.
Facilities Lift. Lounge, 2 sitting rooms (1 with TV), lounge bar, breakfast room. Garden with terrace, swimming pool and snack bar. Sea 3 km away.
Location Central, near public gardens and tennis court. Parking.
Credit cards Access, Visa.
Terms B&B: single 60,000–65,000 L, double 106,500–116,500 L. Reduced rates for children. (No restaurant.)

Villa Fiorita   *Tel* (0942) 24122
Via L. Pirandello 39

A villa that clings to the hillside, amid paved patios filled with flowers and foliage, right next to the cable car station that takes you down to the beach. Honeymooners this year much enjoyed their private terrace and fine views over the coast. Others have written: "It's on the busiest stretch of the approach road to Taormina yet manages to be cool and quiet. Our room was large and comfortable with french windows opening onto a large terrace, where breakfast amid the flowers was the high spot of our stay. But the lounges are somewhat gloomy." "We missed the sense of being in the hub of things: but for those who want solitude and quiet this place is excellent; there are plenty of nooks and crannies to sit inside, and the staff are charming." No restaurant: lots in town. (*Andrew Meyn, Philippa Herbert, Angela and David Stewart, and others*)

Open All year.
Rooms 2 suites, 22 double – 21 with bath and shower, 3 with shower, all with telephone, radio, TV, mini-bar and air-conditioning; some doubles have terrace or balcony.
Facilities Hall, 2 lounges, bar, restaurant (for breakfast and snacks), games room. Large garden with terraces and swimming pool. 50 metres to sandy beach (cable car down).
Location Central, near Greek theatre, but quiet. Garage (5,000 L).
Restrictions Not suitable for &. No children under 10.
Credit cards Amex, Visa.
Terms [1989 rates] Rooms 74,000 L. Breakfast 6,500 L. Reduced rates for children sharing parents' room. (No restaurant.)

Please write and confirm an entry when it is deserved. If you think that a hotel is not as good as we say, write and tell us.

TELLARO DI LERICI 19030 La Spezia   Map 10

Il Nido di Fiascherino   *Tel* (0187) 967426
Via Fiascherino 75

A bright and airy modern hotel in a splendid location: set above a cove in a village near Lerici, on the Gulf of Spezia, it has fine views over beach, rocks and pine trees. Our readers are appreciative, "A tremendous welcome from the staff, and excellent food, with fish better than meat," say recently returning devotees. Others have written: "The coast is as idyllic now as it must have been when Shelley drowned here. The beach facilities have room for improvement, but the dining room is cool, white and spacious with lovely views of the bay, and food was good and plentiful – salads from a self-service buffet. Breakfast is also self-service, with cheese and ham: sybarites who opt for breakfast in bed do less well on packaged toast." "Our room with balcony overlooked the bay where waves crashed thrillingly day and night over the rocks below." *Warning*: there are 140 steps down to the small private beach which is crowded in high summer. Air-conditioning has just been added to almost all bedrooms. More reports please.

Open Mar–Nov and Christmas and New Year.
Rooms 1 suite, 34 double, 4 single – 2 with bath, 35 with shower, all with telephone, TV and baby-listening; some with balcony. 30 with air-conditioning. 22 in annexe across road.
Facilities TV room, bar, 2 dining rooms; terraces. Garden. Small private beach.
Location 2 km SE of Lerici; follow signs for Lerici and Tellaro. Parking.
Restriction Not suitable for &.
Credit cards All major cards accepted.
Terms B&B: single 66,000–73,000 L, double 113,000–124,000 L. Dinner, B&B 92,000–115,000 L per person. Set lunch/dinner 38,000 L; full alc 49,000 L. Reduced rates for children; special meals.

TORGIANO 06089 Perugia   Map 10

Le Tre Vaselle   *Tel* (075) 982447
Via Garibaldi 48   *Fax* (075) 985214
                    Telex 564028 TREVAS

This "elegant country residence" is set quietly in a side street of a charming Umbrian village south of Perugia; it is owned by the ambitious Lungarotti wine firm, which also runs a wine museum in Torgiano. More praise this year: "We enjoyed the undeniable style, the refined yet honest food, the attentive and friendly staff. The interior has thick white walls, archways, wooden beams, terracotta tiles, comfortable sofas. Rooms are tranquil and simple, in very good Italian pared-down style (but bathrooms are small: heaven help the obese). Cooking is regional, gently modernised, using first-rate local ingredients, and flavours are fresh and uncluttered – try insalata di rucola (rocket with sliced mushrooms and cheese), home-made papardelle with truffles, pink filet of beef or sturgeon from nearby Lake Trasimeno. Breakfast is buffet-style, with fruit, ham, sausages. The admirable Lungarotti firm, much concerned with self-promotion, runs wine courses locally, and their hotel gets much custom from groups." (*David Wooff*)

Report forms (Freepost in UK) will be found at the end of the Guide.

Open 15 Jan–15 Nov.
Rooms 1 suite, 47 double – all with bath and/or shower and telephone.
Facilities Reading room, piano bar (music every evening), TV room, breakfast room, restaurant; conference facilities. Terrace where meals are served.
Location 15 km S of Perugia, just E of *autostrada*.
Restriction Not suitable for &.
Credit cards All major cards accepted.
Terms B&B: single 180,000 L, double 260,000 L, suite 360,000 L. Full alc 60,000 L. Children under 8 free of charge; special meals on request.

TORNO 22020 Como   Map 10

Villa Flora   *Tel* (031) 419222

Superbly located on a stone platform sticking out into Lake Como, this big pink villa is now a lively but modest hotel, again admired by several readers this year – especially for its cuisine, so good that many locals use the place for wedding parties. "Food wonderful, location terrific, rooms small." "An attractive terrace ablaze with flowers; the best rooms have balconies and all are quiet, save for the sound of lapping water." Breakfast is remarkable. However, some visitors have found the beds too soft, and the rooms are really quite basic: one reader this year thought them downright dreary, and considered the food no more than "OK". Another complained of inadequate heating during a cold spell in April. The hotel is run by an engaging male duo: one cooks, the other does the waiting in a multitude of languages, English included. (*Ellen and John Buchanan, H and B Shames, Stefan and Cosima Sethe, and others*)

Open Mar–Oct. Restaurant closed Tue.
Rooms 20 double – all with shower, and telephone.
Facilities Lounge with TV, bar, restaurant; conference facilities; terrace, where meals are served. Garden with private beach on lake, bathing.
Location 6 km N of Como. Take road to Bellagio: hotel is down road on left just past centre of Torno. Private parking.
Restriction Not suitable for &.
Credit cards Access, Visa.
Terms Rooms: single 45,000 L, double 70,000 L. Breakfast 8,000 L. Full alc 25,000–30,000 L. Children sharing parents' room free of charge; special meals.

TORRI DEL BENACO 37010 Verona   Map 10

Hotel Gardesana   *Tel* (045) 7225005
Piazza Calderini 20   *Fax* (045) 7225771

A small resort with a 14th-century castle on the eastern shore of Lake Garda, crowded in summer, especially with German tourists. The *Gardesana* faces the little harbour, a traditional hotel with arcades and orange-brown stucco walls, but modernised inside; many rooms have a balcony with views across the lake. "A delightful hotel," runs a recent report; "the beds are comfortable, the welcome friendly, the staff courteous; hors d'oeuvre buffet every night, and excellent buffet breakfast." An earlier view: "An ideal honeymoon-style hotel. We spent a delightful week, enjoying the very comfortable rooms, above-average food and friendly service." The dining room has an outdoor terrace facing the harbour. Some rooms are small and simple, and noise can be a hazard: one reader this year complained of thin party walls, while another has written that the groups of musicians who play outside in the evenings till 11.30 may well consist of "a loud band with a Frank Sinatra impersonator singing Italian favourites such as *My Old Kentucky Home*" – perhaps not be quite what honeymooners would want.

Open 26 Dec–10 Nov. Restaurant closed lunch and 10 Oct–28 Apr.
Rooms 31 double, 3 single – 4 with bath and shower, 30 with shower, all with telephone and air-conditioning; some with balcony.
Facilities Lift. TV lounge, bar, dining room with outdoor terrace; conference room; portico with dancing in summer. Private cabins at lido 150 metres from hotel.
Location In traffic-free centre of Torri del Benaco which is 47 km NW of Verona. Private parking.
Credit cards All major cards accepted.
Terms B&B: single 50,000–65,000 L, double 80,000–140,000 L. Dinner, B&B: single 65,000–85,000 L, double 110,000–170,000 L. Set meals 35,000 L; full alc 45,000 L. Reduced rates and special meals for children.

TRICESIMO 33019 Udine   Map 10

Hotel Ristorante Boschetti   *Tel* (0432) 851230 and 851531
Piazza Mazzini 10

In a small town just north of delightful Udine, this old inn has been much enlarged and modernised, with a new wing, and is now a smart hotel well known for its food (*Michelin* rosette). It is family-owned and run, and well kept. Lack of up-to-date reports pushed it out of the 1989 Guide, but one admirer has now returned: "The staff were kind and thoughtful, my room was comfortable, and the food and wine are fantastic, a combination of regional and traditional recipes with a modern approach." This reader found the place much quieter, now that a newly opened motorway is diverting much heavy traffic: but another visitor still found the rooms noisy (as well as small). We'd be glad of further reports. (*Jeremy Temple*)

Open All year except 5–20 Aug. Restaurant closed Mon.
Rooms 32 double – all with bath or shower and telephone; 16 with TV.
Facilities Lift. 3 salons, bar, restaurant.
Location 12 km N of Udine.
Credit cards Amex, Diners, Visa.
Terms [1989 rates] (Excluding 12% tax) Rooms 70,000–100,000 L. Breakfast 10,000 L. Full board 120,000 L per person. Alc meals 42,000–61,000 L.

TRIESTE   Map 10

Hotel Riviera e Maximilian's   *Tel* (040) 224136 and 224300
Strada Costiera 22   *Telex* 460297
34014 Trieste

Our only entry for the Trieste area, again approved in 1989 by its nominator last year: "It is on an attractive stretch of the coast road running north-west from Trieste along a wooded hillside, with fine views of the sea. It is in two buildings on either side of the road, close to the castle of Miramare in its romantic park and the busy little fishing and pleasure port of Grignano. A lift goes down to its seaside bar and bathing places. The rooms are furnished differently in the two buildings: ours was in the *Riviera*, and had elegant comfortable modern furnishings and a good bathroom. The outstanding experience is to dine on the flowery terrace as the sun sets over the sea and the lights come up around the bay. The food is simple, with much emphasis on local fish and pasta dishes, but carefully cooked and well served. The house wines are notable. One hazard: the main road has a high accident rate. Another: large and lengthy wedding parties at weekends." (*Prof. Sir Alan and Lady Cook*)

Open All year.
Rooms 57 – all with bath and/or shower. Rooms in two separate buildings.
Facilities Lift. Salon, restaurant; conference facilities; terrace. Garden with swimming pool. Lift to seaside bar and bathing.
Location NW of Trieste on coastal road S14.
Terms On application.

TURIN   Map 10

Hotel Conte Biancamano   *Tel* (011) 546058 and 513281
73 Corso Vittorio Emanuele II
Turin 10128

A small family-owned hotel in an arcaded *corso*, five minutes' stroll from the 17th-century Piazza San Carlo. "Unlike many of Turin's 'best' hotels," says its inspector, "it does preserve something of the atmosphere of faded grandeur that is so much part of the city. The narrow and quaint lift to the entrance on the second floor, and the elegant sitting room, give it something of the ambience of a private residence. Bedrooms are unexciting but comfortable and well equipped (those at the front are noisy). The cheerful breakfast room with its white bentwood chairs is a brave attempt to compete with the fine old *Café Platti* opposite. The hotel's owners favour a literary and artistic clientele. No restaurant, but I recommend the expensive *Vecchia Lanterna* round the corner."

Open All year except Aug.
Rooms 3 suites, 15 double, 7 single – 2 with bath, 23 with shower, all with telephone, radio and TV; 3 with tea-making facilities.
Facilities Lift. Lounge, bar, breakfast room; meeting room.
Location Near main station (windows double-glazed). Garage nearby.
Credit cards All major cards accepted.
Terms [1989 rates] Rooms: single 66,000 L, double 95,000 L, suite 110,000 L. Breakfast 10,000 L. Reduced rates for children. (No restaurant.)

VAGGIO-REGGELLO 50066 Firenze   Map 10

Villa Rigacci   *Tel* (055) 865.67.18 and 865.65.62
                                                  Fax (055) 8656537

A graceful 15th-century villa-farmhouse in the mellow Tuscan countryside, "What a find! A farmhouse in the hills half-an-hour's drive from Florence, full of character and warmth, run with style by a French-Italian family, the Pierazzi. Lots of antiques. Our room was enormous, overlooking the picturesque pool. Horse riding is available. The food was excellent and copious, and fresh flowers were on each table." A large shady garden, a library, beautiful country furniture; excellent Tuscan and French cuisine and reasonable prices for the area. (*Mrs JA Patterson*) More feedback welcome.

Open All year. Restaurant closed to non residents Tue.
Rooms 1 suite, 13 double, 4 single – all with bath and/or shower, telephone, radio, TV.
Facilities Bar/lounge, library, 4 salons, 2 dining rooms. Garden with swimming pool and golf practice.
Location 1 km N of Viaggio which is 30 km SE of Florence. Take exit Incisa off Autostrada del Sole.
Restriction Not suitable for &.
Credit cards All major cards accepted.
Terms B&B: single 85,000–110,000 L, double 133,000–210,000 L. Dinner, B&B 105,000–150,000 L per person; full board 130,000–195,000 L. Full alc 50,000 L. Reduced rates and special meals for children.

VARENNA 22050 Como	Map 10

Hotel du Lac	*Tel* (0341) 830238
Via del Prestino 4	*Fax* (0341) 801081

Set charmingly by the water's edge in an unspoilt fishing-village on the east side of Lake Como, a clean and pleasant holiday hotel with good food, helpful signora and fine views. Some rooms are small. Open 1 Mar–15 Dec. 19 rooms, all with bath and/or shower. B&B double 139,000–149,000 L. Set menu 38,000 L. Re-nominated. More reports please.

VENICE	Map 10

Pensione Accademia	*Tel* (041) 5237846 and 5210188
Fondamenta Maravegie	
Dorsoduro 1058-1060	
Venice 30123	

An admired bed-and-breakfast *pensione*, housed in a delightful 17th-century villa facing a side canal (sometimes a bit noisy) only a few yards from the Grand Canal at the Accademia bridge. In its patio garden you can take breakfast, tea or drinks, or even bring your snacks and picnics for which they will supply plates and cutlery at no charge. Rooms vary in size, some being fairly small, and in past years we have had complaints about poor housekeeping. More recently, however, the comfort and cleanliness are stressed; and most readers, but not all, find the staff helpful. You do need to book well ahead. (*Patricia Corbett*)

Open All year.
Rooms 20 double, 6 single – 8 with bath, 13 with shower, all with telephone.
Facilities 2 lounges, TV room, breakfast room; terrace. Garden.
Location Central, near Grand Canal.
Restriction Not suitable for &.
Credit cards All major cards accepted.
Terms [1989 rates] B&B: single 40,000–83,000 L, double 74,000–145,000 L. Reduced rates for children. (No restaurant.)

> Hotels often book you into their most expensive rooms or suites unless you specify otherwise. Even if all room prices are the same, hotels may give you a less good room in the hope of selling their better rooms to late customers. It always pays to discuss accommodation in detail when making a reservation.

Hotel Flora

Calle larga 22 Marzo 2283/a
Venice 30124

Tel (041) 5205844
Fax (041) 5228217
Telex 410401 FLORA

A quiet and friendly little hotel just west of St Mark's, "full of baroque mahogany and blue velvet" and laurelled with red print by *Michelin* for special charm and quality. It remains as popular as ever with readers: "We had a lovely large room with baroque decor, overlooking the courtyard/garden, blissfully quiet. Obliging staff, charming management." "Our spacious room was nicely decorated with antiques and Venetian glass, and had a fine view of the walled garden, beautifully landscaped with vines and flowers, an oasis amid the bustle of the big city. Service was the best we had in Italy." Bedrooms vary, some large and sumptuous, others much smaller and simpler. Most rooms face the garden; those that overlook the front can be noisy. Air-conditioning costs extra and one reader found that noisy. The Art Buchwald of regular Guide correspondents chips in, "The beds are the sort that Habitat sold for £39.95 before it owned Mothercare, but they are comfortable and do not squeak. The bathroom proves that Italian plumbing has long defied the laws of physics, but is beautifully appointed. In sum, a delightful place, where the laughing, smiling desk staff are a scream. The rolls are fresh and the coffee divine." (*Paul Palmer; NM Mackintosh, Mary Hanson and others*)

Open 1 Feb–20 Nov.
Rooms 38 double, 6 single – all with bath or shower and telephone. 2 on ground floor.
Facilities Lift. Lounge, TV room, bar, small breakfast room; air-conditioning. Courtyard/garden where breakfast and drinks are served.
Location Central, near St Mark's Square.
Credit cards All major cards accepted.
Terms B&B: single 118,000 L, double 180,000 L. (No restaurant.)

Hotel Gritti Palace

Campo Santa Maria del Giglio
2467
Venice 30124

Tel (041) 794611
Telex 410125 GRITTI

This famous *palazzo* on the Grand Canal is one of the great hotels of Venice. Some readers feel that it rests too readily on its laurels and that its quality does not match its prices. But recent visitors have mainly enjoyed it: "The food is delicious and the service perfection. We had a side room, which was beautiful and later a huge corner room which was marred by a lumpy mattress." "On the plus side, a superb position, exquisite lounge, breakfast on the terrace by the canal a joy, staff aesthetically efficient [*sic*], lovely luxurious bathroom. The minuses: dreary bedroom decor, and an atmosphere of mass-produced impersonal conveyor-belt luxury (it's a CIGA hotel)" – perhaps the mood was different in the good old days, when Somerset Maugham and his ilk were regulars. The quietest rooms are said to be the side ones, and the small attic rooms with four-posters.

Open All year.
Rooms 9 suites, 66 double, 13 single – all with bath and shower, telephone, radio and TV. Some ground-floor rooms.

Facilities Lift. 3 salons, TV room, bar, restaurants; terrace-restaurant overlooking the Grand Canal; conference facilities; beauty parlour. Free shuttle to Lido in summer.
Location On Grand Canal, 500 metres W of St Mark's.
Credit cards All major cards accepted.
Terms B&B: single 375,000 L, double 450,000–550,000 L, suite 950,000–1,350,000 L. Full alc 100,000 L. Children under 6 free; special meals.

Hotel Monaco & Grand Canal	*Tel* (041) 5200211
Calle Vallaresso, 1325 San Marco	*Fax* (041) 5200501
Venice 30124	*Telex* 410450 MONACO

This elegant hotel on the Grand Canal, near San Marco, would make a slightly cheaper (but still expensive) alternative to the *Gritti*. It has a leafy courtyard, the public rooms are impeccable and the staff friendly. "A thrilling restaurant on the waterfront, with almost *too* much bustle and activity," says one recent visitor, who thought the food "average", whereas another spoke of "best food we had in Venice, with some local dishes". Breakfasts are only so-so, says a reader this year. (*Diane and Keith Moss*)

Open All year.
Rooms 3 suites, 53 double, 19 single – all with bath and shower, telephone, radio.
Facilities Lift. Lounges, piano bar, restaurant; conference room; terrace. Garden.
Location Central, near Piazza San Marco. Quietest rooms overlook garden.
Credit cards Access, Amex, Visa.
Terms B&B: single 140,000–220,000 L, double 185,000–330,000 L, suite 550,000–750,000 L. Dinner, B&B 70.000 L per person. Alc meals 70,000–100,000 L. Reduced rates and special meals for children on request.

Hotel Saturnia e International	*Tel* (041) 5208377
Calle larga 22 Marzo 2398	*Fax* (041) 5207131
Venice 30124	*Telex* 410355 SATURN

"A cool haven after hot sightseeing. We had a huge room with huge bed and attractive carved and gilded ceiling. Staff helpful and courteous" – a recent plaudit for this comfortable and unpretentious 14th-century *palazzo*-cum-hotel about three minutes' walk from St Mark's. The reception area makes quite an impact: a Gothic patio with an elaborate inlaid ceiling. "We liked the ambience, the friendly staff and, in particular, our room – on a back canal with two large windows and a huge Venetian glass chandelier." "Our room was smallish but adequate, and the bathroom's modern decor a bit alarming at first", says a reader this year. The hotel has two restaurants: the *Michelin*-rosetted *Caravella*, described this year as "excellent", though sometimes criticised in the past, and the slightly cheaper, but still expensive, *Cortile* (much liked by readers) where you can eat outdoors in summer. (*David and Patricia Hawkins*)

Open All year. Restaurants closed Wed.
Rooms 79 double, 16 single – 87 with bath, 8 with shower, all with telephone and TV; baby-listening on request.
Facilities Lifts. 2 lounges, bar, TV room, 2 restaurants; conference facilities.
Location Central, W of Piazza San Marco.
Restriction Not suitable for &.
Credit cards All major cards accepted.

Terms B&B: single 150,000–220,000 L, double 200,000–350,000 L; dinner, B&B 60,000 L added per person. Full alc 70,000–85,000 L. Special meals for children on request.

Pensione Seguso   *Tel* (041) 5222340
Dorsoduro, Zattere 779
Venice 30123

The superb view of the Giudecca canal from front-facing windows is one main attraction of this modest and amiable *pensione* on the Zattere; side rooms overlook a small canal. It's a refined, old-fashioned establishment, somewhat shabby, with fine old Venetian furniture, and embroidered silk wall-coverings in the dining room. "It's the imperfections of the place that make it so charming," writes one reader this year; "our room was clean and peaceful. The decor throughout is quietly elegant and the dining-room has a relaxed, refined air. But meals are served at rigidly set times, and the food is no more than adequate, with poor breakfasts." Others have relished "Madame's gracious welcome"; one found the place "comfortable and quaint, full of character and of characters. I enjoyed the quiet, the Venetian glass windows and chandeliers, the heating, the service, and the position." (*Francis Durham*)

Open 1 Mar–30 Nov. Restaurant closed Wed.
Rooms 31 double, 5 single – 9 with bath, 9 with shower, all with telephone.
Facilities Lift. Lounge, restaurant; breakfast terrace.
Location 15 mins from the centre, overlooking the Giudecca canal.
Credit cards Access, Amex, Visa.
Terms On application.

VERONA 37121   **Map 10**

Hotel Colomba d'Oro   *Tel* (045) 595300
Via Cattaneo 10   *Telex* 480872 COLOMB

A dignified and serviceable hostelry, very central, on a side street near the Arena in a traffic-restricted zone. The interior has a club-like atmosphere with lots of polished wood and comfortable armchairs. A reader this year had a large room and found the staff pleasant and helpful, while others recently have enjoyed the quiet, comfort and good service: some rooms, however, are small. (*Mary Ann Meanwell*)

Open All year.
Rooms 2 suites, 30 double, 17 single – 36 with bath, 13 with shower, all with telephone and TV.
Facilities 3 lounges, bar; conference room.
Location Central, in pedestrian zone near Arena. Garage nearby.
Credit cards All major cards accepted.
Terms [1989 rates] Rooms: single 101,000 L, double 137,000 L. Breakfast 14,500 L. No restaurant.

Hotel Torcolo   *Tel* (045) 8007512
Vicolo Listone 3

A small bed-and-breakfast hotel in a side street near the Arena, very centrally located but not noisy by Italian standards – and rooms are air-conditioned. Readers this year have again commented on the good breakfasts, and on the charm of Signora Pomari and her staff. Some rooms are large, and furnished with antiques: but others are more modern, and some have been judged a little basic, with pillows too hard. (*Anita Taylor, Michael and Margaret Crick*)

Open All year except 10 days in Jan. Restaurant closed Mon.
Rooms 15 double, 4 single – all with bath and shower, telephone and TV.
Facilities Lift. Breakfast room, TV room; terrace.
Location Central, off Piazza Bra, near Arena. Parking for 10 cars.
Credit cards None accepted.
Terms B&B: single 47,000–67,000 L, double 74,000–93,500 L. (No restaurant.)

VICENZA 36100 Map 10

Hotel Campo Marzio *Tel* (0444) 545700
Viale Roma 21 *Fax* (0444) 320495
Telex 341138 EUROHOT

A good practical modern hotel, very spruce, and usefully situated between the station and the wonderful centre of this old city, beside a canal and facing a park. Small but comfortable modern-style, air-conditioned rooms with excellent bathrooms. Good service and quite good food: for a superb meal, try the Cinzia e Valerio. *35 rooms, all with bath and shower. B&B double 132,000 L. Full alc 25,000–41,000 L [1989]. Endorsed this year, but further reports welcome.*

ZERMAN 31020 Treviso Map 10

Villa Condulmer *Tel* (041) 457100
Zerman, Mogliano Veneto

A beautiful 18th-century Venetian villa, in a pleasant rural setting on the misty plain between Venice and Treviso. Ronald and Nancy Reagan chose to stay here during the 1987 Venice summit; their autographed photo is displayed in the foyer. The hotel is much approved again this year, especially for its palatial public rooms in rococo style: "A lovely old building, elegantly furnished, with a dining terrace overlooking the attractive grounds where comfortable loungers surround the swimming pool. We had a delightful large room in the new wing, which has been skilfully integrated into the old part. The restaurant nicely presents good food at fair prices." "Food a bit on the *nouvelle* side in portions. All staff helpful save the receptionist." The rooms in the old part are not yet air-conditioned: but the newer ones are, and this year were called "the only truly cool and comfortable rooms we found in all Italy". (*Betsy C Maestro*)

Open 15 Mar–15 Nov.
Rooms 45 – all with bath and/or shower; most with telephone; 8 with radio.
Some in annexe. Some ground-floor rooms.
Facilities Salon, reading room, TV room, bar (with piano), 3 restaurants;
conference room. Park with unheated swimming pool, tennis court, 18-hole golf
course and riding.
Location Outside village; 4 km NE of Mogliano Veneto and 22 km N of Venice.
Credit cards All major cards accepted.
Terms [1989 rates] Rooms: single 70,000 L, double 200,000 L. Breakfast 14,000 L.
Full board 160,000–200,000 L. Alc meals 40,000–60,000 L plus 10% service.

Luxembourg

HÔTEL BEL-AIR, ECHTERNACH

ECHTERNACH 6409   **Map 3**

Hôtel Bel-Air   *Tel* 729383
Route de Berdorf 1   *Telex* 2640 BELAIR

A rather grand country house hotel, newly renovated, on the edge of the
attractive and popular resort town of Echternach, in the wooded and hilly
"Luxembourg Suisse" near the German frontier. It is a palatial kind of
place, with extensive and imposing gardens full of pools, flowering
shrubs and Doric columns: pity that the facade facing the gardens is so
ugly, in such a jumble of styles. Most of the bedrooms are in the modern
part, each with a balcony where you can take breakfast: here Americans
this year enjoyed their spacious room and also liked the food in the
panoramic dining-room (*Michelin* rosette for such dishes as loup de mer
en croûte). (*Geo F Outland*)

Open All year except 4 Jan–10 Feb.
Rooms 10 suites, 21 double, 2 single – all with bath and shower, telephone, radio
and TV.

Facilities Bar, 2 salons, TV room, 2 dining rooms; conference facilities. 1½-acre grounds with tennis court and children's playground. Fishing nearby.
Location On W side of Echternach, off Diekirch road; follow river Sure to Berdorf turn-off. 35 km NE of Luxembourg city. Parking.
Credit cards All major cards accepted.
Terms [1989 rates] B&B: single 2,200–2,900 Lfrs, double 3,000–4,000 Lfrs, suite 4,000–5,000 Lfrs; dinner, B&B 3,100–3,700 Lfrs per person; full board 3,300–4,000 Lfrs. Set lunch/dinner 1,350–2,300 Lfrs; full alc 1,500–3,000 Lfrs. Reduced rates and special meals for children.

EHNEN 5416   Map 3

Hôtel Bamberg   *Tel* 76022 and 76717
131 Route du Vin

Formerly known as the Hôtel de la Moselle but still owned and run by the Bamberg family, this neat modern hostelry lies across a busy road from the Moselle river. Hospitable owners, comfortable rooms (some with balconies), and excellent food in the restaurant with its river views. Some night noises from traffic and striking clocks. Closed 1 Dec–mid-Jan and Tuesday. 15 rooms, all with bath and shower. B&B double 1,800–2,200 Lfrs. Set meals 1,500–1,900 Lfrs. More reports welcome.

Hôtel Simmer   *Tel* 76030
117 route du Vin

The quality of the bedrooms, also the excellent food (*Michelin* rosette) and the friendly welcome, have again this year been commended at the venerable little family-run hotel facing the river. It has a 15th-century dining room (with soft lighting and quiet recorded music), much frequented by locals and by EC officials. "Wonderfully fresh asparagus and fish, and a superb rhubarb tart." "Our comfortable room was sombrely furnished but met our needs: there was even a chamber-pot. A homely atmosphere and good local wines." "Our room at the back was very quiet." (*Diana Cooper, Stephen Ruell*)

Open 12 Mar–31 Dec. Closed Tue in low season.
Rooms 19 double, 4 single – 18 with bath (14 also have shower), all with telephone.
Facilities Salon with TV, bar, dining room, banqueting facilities; terrace. Garden.
Location 10 km N of Remich. Central, parking.
Restrictions Not suitable for &.
Credit cards Access, Amex, Visa.
Terms B&B: single 1,650 Lfrs, double 2,300 Lfrs; dinner, B&B 2,150–2,300 Lfrs per person; full board 2,350–2,500 Lfrs. *Menu de Dégustation* 1,950 Lfrs. Reduced rates for children under 8.

ETTELBRÜCK 9010   Map 3

Hôtel Central et Restaurant   *Tel* 82116
Taste-Vin
25 rue de Bastogne

In a small town where two rivers meet, the Central is no beauty from the outside but has inner virtues, such as pleasant owners, faultless service, large

German-style breakfasts, and an elegant dining room with food fully worthy of its Michelin rosette. Comfortable rooms – upper ones have the best views and are quietest (some noise on the street side). Closed 31 July–31 Aug, 24 Dec–4 Jan. 16 rooms, all with bath or shower. B&B double 1,900–2,600 Lfrs. Set menus 950–1,400 Lfrs. No recent reports. More please.

LUXEMBOURG 1453   Map 3

Hostellerie du Grünewald   *Tel* 431882
10–16 Route d'Echternach   *Telex* 60543 HGRWD
Luxembourg–Dommeldange

The Queen of Sweden is said to have stayed at this sedate country hostelry in the northern outskirts; it is stronger on comfort and opulence than on personal charm, but staff are helpful. Elegant dining room with very good food (Michelin rosette); pleasant garden. Restaurant closed 1–23 Jan, Sat midday and Sun. 28 rooms, all with bath or shower. B&B double 2,900–3,900 Lfrs. Full alc 2,000–2,500 Lfrs. Endorsed this year but further reports welcome.

****
Traveller's tale *Among the brilliant throng that frequented the Savoy were some – not so brilliant. Ritz had induced the best society to dine there, but if these others, chiefly ladies of doubtful reputation and uncertain revenue, were allowed to frequent the place too much, what then? Yet how to avoid offending some of these "ladies" who brought along their princely partners of the moment? They were too ornamental, too influential, to turn away. But the others! Decidedly, something must be done!*

Ritz ordained that evening dress was de rigueur in the dining rooms. Ladies without hats or ladies unaccompanied by gentlemen could not be admitted (another Ritz precedent that has since been always followed). The effect was magical.

"You can lay down the law now," said Liane de Pougy, laughing airily. "For you have reached the height of your career in your profession – as I have in mine!"

"Alas," said Ritz, "I am afraid with far less pleasure and far more trouble than you have experienced, mademoiselle."

Mari Louise Ritz (César Ritz, 1938)
****

CORNUCOPIA HOTEL, XAGHRA

SANNAT Gozo   **Map 10**

Hotel Ta' Cenc   *Tel* (00356) 55.68.19 and 55.68.30
                                            Telex 1479 REFINZ

Beautifully located on a high promontory, on a little island off the north-east coast of Malta, this long-admired single-storey hotel is cunningly terraced to blend into the hillside, and is built in the local honey-coloured limestone. Some rooms are bungalows, most with their own small patio. They are ranged round a central pool, with plenty of space between for oleanders, fig trees and cacti. The pool itself offers a breath-taking view of the sea and Malta beyond, and many guests are content to brown and browse there all day. There is also plenty of good rock bathing all round the island (but only one first-class sandy beach, ten kilometres away). The hotel has been criticised in recent years, but it now has an efficient new manager who is busily refurbishing the hitherto drab decor, and 1988/9 reports are nearly all favourable. "So much better than the average modern hotel. The staff were faultless and the food delicious." "Food and amenities are first-class and the staff all friendly." One reader this year thought the food erratic – some dinners superb, but breakfasts and pool-side lunches disappointing. Lack of air-conditioning is a drawback, in torrid Malta. (*Michael Rubinstein, P Russell, Martin A Batteslieu, Alasdair and Moira Brown*)

Open 1 Mar–30 Nov.
Rooms 10 suites, 34 double (also let as singles) – all with bath and shower, telephone, radio, TV and patio or garden. All on ground floor. Some self-contained family bungalows.
Facilities Lounge, TV lounge, bar, snack bar, games room, restaurant; conference facilities. 3-acre garden with terraces, heated swimming pool, bar, 2 tennis courts (small charge). Disco; music in bar in season. Chauffeur service, car and motorbike hire. Hotel's rock beach with bar 2½ km (free transport by hotel bus 3 times a day), water-skiing, boats for hire, boat excursions.
Location 5 mins' walk from village (hotel provides free transport), on southern part of Gozo island, near Ta' Cenc cliffs.
Credit cards All major cards accepted.
Terms B&B £M14–£M32; dinner, B&B £M17–£M35. Set lunch/dinner £M7; full alc £M12. 1-night bookings may be refused in high season. Reduced rates and special meals for children.

XAGHRA Gozo   Map 10

Cornucopia Hotel   *Tel* (0356) 55.64.86 and 55.38.66
10 Gnien Imrik Street   *Telex* 1467 VJB

This cheerful family-run hotel, two miles inland, is a converted farmhouse with modern extensions in white stone, set attractively beside its swimming pool. It has again been liked this year: "Relaxed and informal, with plentiful, well cooked and imaginative food (poolside barbecues most enjoyable). Well-run, without being regimented; staff all friendly." A report last year was on similar lines, adding: "The new bedrooms, all well appointed and maintained, either overlook the pool or have a stunning view over the valley. A splendid honeymoon suite with jacuzzi is being completed." (*Fiona Mutch*)

Open All year.
Rooms 5 suites, 35 double – all with bath and shower, telephone; baby-listening on request. Some (with self-catering facilities) in annexe. Some ground-floor rooms.
Facilities Lounge, bar, TV room, restaurant. Garden. 2 swimming pools; 1 children's pool.
Location Outside village of Xaghra: follow signs to Xerri's Grotto.
Credit cards All major cards accepted.
Terms [1989 rates] B&B £M6–£M11.50; dinner, B&B £M7.25–£M13.50; full board £M8.75–£M14.75 per person. Set lunch/dinner £M2.75; full alc £M6.00. Reduced rates and special meals for children.

Morocco

LA ROSERAIE, OUIRGANE

FES | **Map 13**

Hôtel Palais Jamai | *Tel* (06) 343.31
Bab El Guissa | *Telex* 51974

The spiritual capital of Morocco, which was founded in 808, lies in a bowl north of the Middle Atlas; in summer the lower part of the city is oppressively hot. Its grandest buildings are in Fes el-Jedid (new Fes), above Fes el-Bali (old Fes); one of these is the *Palais Jamai*, built in the 18th century by Sidi Mohamed Ben Arib El Jami, Grand Vizier to the Sultan. It now is a large and luxurious hotel in a magnificent Andalusian garden with panoramic views of the city. The bedrooms are decorated in traditional Moroccan style; the most luxurious are in the old building. "Most attractively furnished. Rooms in the new wing have breath-taking views of the old town. It is efficiently run, but a little cold and impersonal. It has an international restaurant and a traditional Moroccan one; the food is entirely satisfactory, but not memorable – the Moroccan restaurant is worth visiting for the decor, but the food and atmosphere in similar restaurants in the old town are to be preferred." "Lovely breakfasts with fresh orange juice. Good service in the Moroccan restaurant." (*PR Glazebrook, Joan Williamson*) More reports please.

Open All year.
Rooms 12 suites, 120 rooms, all with bath, telephone, radio, TV. Some on ground floor.
Facilities Lift, bar, 2 restaurants, night-club. Garden with swimming pool and tennis court.
Location North of Fes el-Bali.
Credit cards All major cards accepted.
Terms Rooms: single 650–900 Dhs, double 800–1,050 Dhs, suite 2,400 Dhs.

MARRAKECH   Map 13

Es Saadi   *Tel* (4) 488.11
Avenue Quadissia   *Telex* 72042

This old-established privately-owned hotel, built in the 1960s, set in attractive gardens with good views to the Atlas mountains and less than ten minutes' walk from the old town, has pleased readers this year: "We were made very welcome on arrival. Our bedroom had all the facilities you would expect of a five-star hotel; all rooms have a small balcony with table and seating arrangements. There is a beautiful large swimming pool with a small island; lunch by the pool offered a choice of simple and more elaborate dishes. We breakfasted outside (in March). Evening meals excellent; service efficient. Nothing Moroccan about the decor, just typical large hotel arrangements." "We could find no fault; extremely well run, with very friendly staff. Food is quite simple, but beautifully cooked and presented." (*B Ollendorff, PR Glazebrook*) The rooms in the main block are preferable to the poolside rooms. As we go to press we learn that the hotel may be up for sale.

Open All year.
Rooms 147 – all with bath and/or shower and balcony.
Facilities Salon, restaurant; boutique, hairdresser. Garden with terrace and swimming pool.
Location Central.
Credit cards All major cards accepted.
Terms [1989 rates] Rooms: single £55, double £80–£85. Breakfast from £3.50. Set meals from £5.

Hôtel Tichka   *Tel* (4) 48710
Route de Casablanca, Semlalia BP 894   *Telex* 74855

Although *La Mamounia* (see p. 634), with its 180 rooms, 50 suites, six bars and six restaurants, remains *hors de concours* Marrakech's grandest hotel, with prices to match, and the *Es Saadi* (above) is a reasonable luxury alternative, the recently opened *Tichka* is also highly recommendable – and its tariff is a quarter that of the former. Its one shortcoming is that it is in the new city, a mile or two from the Medina and the amazing souk, in an area full of look-alike multi-storey package hotels. But the *Tichka* eschews group tourism, and is an architectural and designer's treat. Dusky rose from the outside, like most buildings in the city, its windows and balconies are chocolate-brown and turquoise; and the interior decor (by the American designer Bill Willis) is equally striking in its colour contrasts, as well as in the quality of the materials; the rooms are a pleasure to behold, besides being as comfortable as one could wish – no sign of cheese-paring anywhere. There is a large pool surrounded by palms, willows and orange trees and a well-kept substantial garden. "Best rooms are those with a pool view. Breakfast, lunches and evening drinks are taken poolside. The hotel is run with *brio* and charm. The buffet lunch was excellent." The hotel recently built a Moroccan restaurant, on which we'd be glad to have reports. Alternatively you can dine at *Stilia* or the *Yacout* in the old city – expensive but outstanding introductions to Morocco's distinctive *haute cuisine*.

Open All year.
Rooms 140 – all with bath, telephone and air-conditioning.
Facilities Lounges, bar, restaurant; night-club; health centre. Garden with swimming pool.
Location In new part of city, 3 km from the Medina.
Credit cards All major cards accepted.
Terms [1989 rates] (Excluding 5% tax) Rooms: single 280 Dhs, double 358 Dhs. Breakfast 31 Dhs. Set meals 109 Dhs.

OUIRGANE   Map 13

La Roseraie   *Tel* Ouirgane 4 and 5
Val d'Ouirgane   (via Marrakech)
BP 769 Marrakech

A charming small hotel outside a very simple mountain village, with bedrooms in rustic-style bungalows, each with a private bathroom and individual patio, set in a fragrant rose garden, with the High Atlas Mountains as a backdrop. It is fairly remote, being an hour or more by car from Marrakech, and the latter part of the drive is on fairly primitive mountain roads, so it is not a good base for touring. But there is plenty to do at *La Roseraie* – it has two immaculately maintained tennis courts, a large swimming pool, a newly built health centre with saunas, hammam, exercise room, and salt-water baths, and an equestrian centre where you can ride by the hour or from which you can go on treks of several days into the mountains, staying with Berber families. There are lovely walks in the grounds and in the surrounding mountains. Coach parties may stop for lunch, but are accommodated out of ear and eyeshot of the residents. Staff are friendly, the atmosphere is relaxed and peaceful. Breakfast is somewhat variable, lunch and dinner are cheerful occasions though the menu, with few options on each course, changes little from day to day, and the cooking is adequate rather than inspired. But the lunch-time table of hors d'oeuvre make an excellent meal and there are good grilled dishes. A more interesting alternative (but not recommended to those allergic to cats) is to eat at the *Auberge au Sanglier Qui Fume* in the nearby village. If you go in winter ask for a central-heated room; although the sun is bright by day, the nights can be very cold; and be warned – the water is not hot throughout the day and housekeeping can be somewhat erratic. (*CR, Joan Williamson*)

Open All year.
Rooms 15 suites (5 2-bedroomed, 10 1-bedroomed), 6 double, 3 single – all with bath and/or shower, telephone and patio. All in bungalows.
Facilities 4 salons, TV room, 2 bars, 3 restaurants. Health centre; terraces. 25-acre grounds with garden, swimming pool, 2 tennis courts, riding centre.
Location 10 mins' walk from village which is 60 km S of Marrakech.

Restrictions Not suitable for &.
Credit cards All major cards accepted.
Terms Rooms: single 280 Dhs, double 358 Dhs, Breakfast 31 Dhs. Set meals
109 Dhs.

TANGIER   Map 13

Hôtel El Minzah   *Tel* 358.85
85 rue de la Liberté   *Fax* 345.46
                                                               Telex 33775

A long-established and luxurious hotel, built by the Marquess of Bute in
the centre of the cosmopolitan port (it is essential to ask for "superior"
rooms, those on the road are noisy), set in exotic gardens, with extensive
views of the harbour and the Straits of Gibraltar. "One of the best hotels
we have ever visited. Splendid Moorish decor, with a feeling of space.
Pleasant, friendly staff. Front room a bit noisy but spacious, with
international standard of fittings combined with genuine local style. Nice
choice of restaurants, though food in the main European one was rather
ordinary and the Moroccan one was rather touristy (a contrast to the
elegance elsewhere). We liked the small bar/restaurant best. The garden,
its seating and pool were also good of their sort." (*R and J Freeman*)

Open All year.
Rooms 8 suites, 83 doubles – all with bath and shower, telephone, radio, TV and
mini-bar.
Facilities 4 lounges, 2 bars, 2 restaurants, snack bar, tea-room. Courtyard. Large
garden with swimming pool.
Location Central, near French consulate.
Credit cards All major cards accepted.
Terms [1989 rates] Rooms: single 460–640 Dhs, double 600–820 Dhs, suite 1,200–
2,400 Dhs. Set meals 210 Dhs; full alc 260 Dhs. Special meals for children on
request.

TAROUDANT   Map 13

La Gazelle d'Or   *Tel* Taroudant 20.39 and 20.48
BP 260 Taroudant   *Telex* 81902 GAZELOR

Readers often ask us to recommend a small hotel of character, well away
from the bustle of a city or tourist crowds, where they can be shamelessly
pampered and recuperate from the frenzy of their working lives. *La
Gazelle d'Or* fulfils these needs. Classed as a 5-star establishment, it is
expensive for Morocco, but not at all by the standards of Western Europe.
Two kilometres from the ancient walled city of Taroudant, and an hour
by a fast road from Agadir, *La Gazelle d'Or* is in a different world from
either. It was once the home of a French baron, who built handsome
bungalows in the grounds for his guests. There are now 30 of these small
individual villas scattered round a large garden, with the High Atlas
Mountains framing the horizon. Each has its own private terrace where
they bring you breakfast. There are first-class tennis courts and riding
stables, but life at the hotel tends to centre round the large pool, heated in
the winter, where a decent buffet lunch is served. The evening meal takes
place in an elegant tented dining-room. The hotel is managed with
relaxed professional assurance by Bruno Hill, late of the *Savoy*. A high

proportion of the clientele is English-speaking. Rooms are often booked months ahead. It is in no sense a Moroccan experience, but for those who want to get away from it all in sybaritic comfort and can afford its prices, the *Gazelle d'Or* offers a taste of one sort of earthly paradise; but be warned, the location is remote, and there are no distractions apart from what the hotel has to offer.

Open All year except August.
Rooms 2 suites, 28 double, all with bath (1 also has shower), telephone, TV, baby-listening and terrace. All in cottages.
Facilities Lounge, TV room, bar, 2 restaurants; conference facilities. Gardens with heated swimming pool, tennis and stables.
Location 2 km from Taroudant.
Credit cards All major cards accepted.
Terms Half board rates only: single occupancy 1,253 Dhs, double 1,708 Dhs, suite 3,076 Dhs. Full alc 250 Dhs.

Hôtel Palais Salam   *Tel* (085) 21.30 and 25.01

A romantic palace built into the impressive red-earth walls of the city, now converted into a well-run hotel, with rooms scattered higgledy-piggledy around the premises. "The ones to ask for", we said last year, "are in the original palace facing banana groves, or the more modern suites and duplexes – designed and furnished in simple good taste, spacious and comfortable. The ones to avoid are the twin rooms on the first floor largely used for the in-and-out coach parties." But a regular visitor says: "We always *choose* the twin rooms on the first floor; in winter they are sunnier and warmer than the more sumptuous ones in the new wing – and excellent value". Another had a "charming, quiet room on an old courtyard, split level, with a sort of minstrels' gallery, nice bathroom and sitting room below; comfortable beds, best pillows yet." There is a key-shaped pool on the ground-floor, enclosed by great palms and the city walls, and a smaller rectangular one on a higher level for residents only. There are two restaurants as well – one serving bland international fare, often crowded with tourists, and another, in Moroccan style with low banquettes instead of chairs, serving specialities of the national cuisine – "very good food and lovely pâtisserie; excellent and witty head waiter. The hotel is a popular lunch or drinks stop for coach-parties from Agadir, but the coaching crowds are contained in the public rooms and swimming pool on the ground floor. Upstairs, the hotel is a peaceful and sympathetic haven. Taroudant has a good souk, with prices cheaper than in the great Marrakech one, but is not otherwise of much touristic interest. The *Palais Salam* makes an agreeable base for a stay of a night or two, but its attractions might pall on a longer visit. (*Lesley Goodden, Joan Williamson*)

Open All year.
Rooms 38 suites, 95 double – all with bath and/or shower, and telephone.
Facilities Lounge, 2 bars, TV room, 2 restaurants; conference facilities; health centre. Garden with 2 swimming pools; tennis nearby; bicycles available.
Location In town centre, within the old walls. Parking.
Credit cards All major cards accepted.
Terms [1989 rates] (Excluding 5% tax) Rooms: single 280 Dhs, double 358 Dhs. Breakfast 31 Dhs. Meals 109 Dhs.

We depend on detailed fresh reports to keep our entries up-to-date.

This selection of short listings is generously contributed by Annie Austin of Creative Leisure Management in London. We should be glad to get feedback from readers who have visited any of these hotels recently, or who can add fresh deserving names.

CASABLANCA **Hôtel Riad Salam Meridien** (5-star) *Tel* 363535 and 367922 *Telex* 24692. On beachside corniche of Casablanca. 100 rooms, 12 superb suites and 50 bungalows. Also an excellent and unique (to Morocco) Health Institute of Sea-water Therapy. Recommended for those who wish to avoid a nervous breakdown.

EL JADIDA **Club Salam des Doukkala** (4-star B) Avenue El Jamaiaa Al Arabia. *Tel* (34) 3622 and 2575 *Telex* 78014. Well-equipped club hotel with many sporting facilities and 82 rooms. Right on beach; about ten minutes' walk from centre of town. Ideal in summer for those who want a social sporting holiday on the beach in an unspoilt Moroccan town.

EL JADIDA **Hôtel de Provence** (1-star) 42 Avenue Fkih Rafy *Tel* (34) 2347. In centre of El Jadida with its own restaurant. 16 rooms, 14 with bath – good food and excellent value.

ESSAOUIRA **Hôtel des Iles** (4-star A) *Tel* (47) 2329 *Telex* 31907. Essaouira is a charming unspoilt fishing village. The *Hôtel des Iles*, with 77 rooms, belongs to the ONCF chain. Well-run and popular with British tourists.

IMMOUZER, Nr Agadir **Hôtel des Cascades** (3-star B) *Tel* 14. A lovely small (14-room) hotel recently refurbished. Next to the eponymous cascades and with superb views – a perfect place for a break. An hour's picturesque drive up from Agadir.

LAYOUNE **Hôtel Parador** *Tel* 2245 and 2200 *Telex* 28800. A beautifully decorated 31-room modern hotel in the far south run by Club Méditerranée. New on the Morocco tourist map and well worth a visit.

MARRAKECH **Hôtel Semiramis Meridien** (5-star) Route de Casablanca *Tel* (4) 313.77 *Telex* 72906. Attractive and well-run hotel in the new part of town. 186 rooms and a spectacular swimming pool – the best we have seen anywhere – set in spacious gardens.

MARRAKECH **Hôtel la Mamounia** (5-star) Avenue Bab J'did. *Tel* (4) 489.81 *Telex* 72018. Marrakech's most luxurious hotel – Winston Churchill's favourite – recently restored in lavish style. 180 rooms and 50 suites, a far cry from the original old pasha's palace. Service is excellent – and the gardens with their views towards the snow-capped Atlas Mountains superb. Accommodation and meals very expensive, even by European standards.

MARRAKECH **Hôtel Tafilalet** (4-star) Route de Casablanca. *Tel* (4) 345.18 *Telex* 72955. Immaculately run hotel with 84 rooms personally supervised by its owner, Madame Lamon.

MARRAKECH **Hôtel Imilchil** (3-star) Avenue Echouhada. *Tel* (4) 476.53 *Telex* 72018. A relatively small hotel – 86 rooms – with charming Moroccan decor but no bar serving alcohol. Well-run and excellent value.

MIDELT **Hôtel Ayachi** (3-star A) Route d'Agadir. *Tel* 21.61. 28-room *pension* hotel, owned and run by a resident family, useful as a stop-over.

MIDELT **Dayet Aoua** (2-star) Route de Fes, Ifrane. *Tel* 0. A simple small hotel with 26 rooms but one of the best French restaurants in Morocco. Set on a lovely lake with good fishing and shooting. Hotel has boats for hire.

OUALIDIA **Hôtel Hippocamp** (2-star A) *Tel* 111. On road from El Jadida to Safi overlooking the lagoon. A simple establishment, with 20 rooms. Excellent fish meals at reasonable cost.

RABAT **La Tour Hassan** (5-star) *Tel* (7) 21401 and 33814 *Telex* 31914. First opened its doors to guests in 1914 and can be considered one of the best traditional hotels in Morocco. 150 bedrooms, decorated in the latest modern pastel shades. Facilities include an authentic Chinese restaurant and an excellent Moroccan room. Centrally situated and built around a pretty Andalusian garden.

TAFRAOUT **Hôtel Les Amandiers** (4-star B) *Tel* 8. A rather run-down 60-room hotel (the pool has not been filled for years), but friendly and a good base for anyone wishing to visit this spectacularly picturesque area.

ZAGORA **Hôtel Tinsouline** (3-star A) *Tel* 22 An unpretentious pleasant 90-room hotel at the edge of the desert in exotic, rugged surroundings. Plain but comfortable rooms and a swimming pool. Very French – many French tourists including children – and interesting food in restaurant.

Traveller's tale *It is the boast of* Barribault's Hotel, *which caters principally to American millionaires and visiting maharajahs, that it can make the wrong sort of client feel more like a piece of cheese – and a cheap yellow piece of cheese at that – than any other similar establishment in the world. The personnel of its staff are selected primarily for their ability to curl the upper lip and raise the eyebrows just that extra quarter of an inch which makes all the difference.*
PG Wodehouse (*Full Moon, 1947*)

The Netherlands

HOTEL-RESTAURANT DE SWAEN, OISTERWIJK

ALMEN 7218 AH Gelderland   **Map 3**

De Hoofdige Boer   *Tel* (05751) 1744
Dorpsstraat 38

Almen is a village in eastern Holland, close to the charming old town of Zutphen and not far from Arnhem and the Kröller-Müller museum (splendid Van Goghs). Here this old-established hotel, with tea-garden, comfortable lounge and unusual beamed decor, has again been liked in 1989: "An excellent place. The bedrooms are quite modern in decor, spacious and well lit, with lots of attention to homey detail – in our room, sewing and shoe-shine kit, and fresh fruit. The food is good substantial Dutch fare, and the ever-present staff are full of good cheer." Others have also enjoyed the cooking and the "friendly informality". At the back is a pleasant garden giving on to open fields. (*Lynne and David Allen*)

Open All year except New Year's Day.
Rooms 18 double, 2 single – all with bath and/or shower, and TV; 12 with telephone; baby-listening arranged. 2 ground-floor rooms.

Facilities Bar, lounge, TV room, restaurants; functions room; table tennis. Garden with tea-garden and dinner terrace. 5 mins' walk to heated swimming pool.
Location Central, near the church. Parking.
Credit cards Access, Amex, Diners.
Terms B&B: single 75 glds, double 115 glds; full board: single 115 glds, double 195 glds. Full alc 55 glds. Off-season and Christmas packages. Reduced rates for children sharing parents' room; special meals.

AMSTERDAM Noord-Holland   Map 3

Hotel Ambassade	*Tel* (020) 262333
Herengracht 341	*Fax* (020) 245321
Amsterdam 1016 AZ	*Telex* 10158 AMBAS

No other hotel on the Continent receives more reports, and more enthusiastic ones, than the bed-and-breakfast *Ambassade* – and that's truer than ever in 1988/89: "A treasure", "we were thrilled to bits", "the best small hotel in Amsterdam", "a wonderful greeting", are some of the enthusiastic reports we have received on this elegant bed and breakfast hotel. The secret of this success lies above all with Mr van der Velden, the manager, "always there, courteous, friendly, running the whole show without effort or tension", and with his team – "the most charming and polite hotel staff I've ever come across" and "extremely good-looking". But much depends, too, on the building and its location: seven adjoining 17th-century patrician houses on the Herengracht, Amsterdam's grandest canal. Rooms, varying in size according to their altitude in these tall buildings, are furnished in period or modern Dutch style and each has a bathroom. The public rooms have many items from the owner's personal collection of antiques – old china, clocks, paintings. Room service is amazing: "No charge for baby-sitting – one night the bell-boy rocked our son back to sleep." A feature of the hotel is the very steep steps to upper floors (normal in these old Amsterdam houses) and the spiral staircases, "hard to climb if you've been knocking back the Heineken". One reader saw all this as "an integral part of the charm". Now a lift has just been installed in a newly acquired house which connects with two of the others; there are seven rooms on the ground floor. (*John Clabaugh Leitch, Susan Chait, Patrick MacNamee, David Wurtzel, Georgene Smith, and many others*)

Open All year.
Rooms 5 suites, 39 double, 3 single – all with bath and/or shower, telephone, radio and TV; baby-sitters available. 15 in annexe. 7 ground-floor rooms.
Facilities Lift. 2 lounges, breakfast room. 24 hour room service.
Location Central, but quietly situated on Herengracht canal. Meter parking; public garage 5 mins' walk.
Credit cards All major cards accepted.
Terms B&B: single 170 glds, double 195 glds, suite 245–350 glds. Reduced rates for children sharing parents' room. (No restaurant, but drinks and light refreshments available 24 hours a day.)

In all continental European and Scandinavian countries except Denmark, France, Hungary, Malta, Spain and Turkey, the dialling codes begin with a 0. Omit this when dialling from outside the country in question. Spanish codes begin with a 9, which should also be omitted.

Hotel Bodeman *Tel* (20) 201558
Rokin 154–6
Amsterdam 1012 LE

Centrally situated near the Rembrandtsplein, a recently opened B&B hotel in an
old building, with antique furniture and a bar. Friendly owners; some rooms are
large and overlook a canal. Open 1 Mar–10 Jan. 17 rooms, all with shower. B&B
double 125–175 glds. New nomination. More reports welcome.

Het Canal House *Tel* (020) 225182
Keizersgracht 148 *Fax* (020) 241317
Amsterdam 1015 CX *Telex* 10412

This 17th-century merchant's house, rather elegant, stands quietly on a
canal close to the Anne Frank House and five minutes' walk from the city
centre. It has an attractive enclosed garden, illuminated at night. Visitors
this year have again warmed to its American owners, Jane and Len Irwin,
and their friendly staff; they have also liked the cosy bar, and the other
public rooms. These, furnished with antiques, "have an air of faded
elegance that we enjoyed". "The hall opens onto a high-ceilinged
breakfast room with huge mirrors, a grand piano and white lilies
everywhere. But the bedroom furnishings are ordinary." However, all
rooms are comfortable and some double ones overlook the canal: the
small single attic rooms are less admired. Stairs are steep, as in most canal
houses of this type, but a lift has just been installed. Not all visitors
admire the breakfasts. (*Dr Madeleine Montefiore, WR Halstead, Michael and
Eloise Hulse, and others*) No restaurant: lots nearby.

Open All year.
Rooms 24 double, 3 single – all with bath and/or shower and telephone.
Facilities Lift. Lounge, bar, breakfast room. Garden.
Location Central. Street parking.
Restriction Not suitable for ප. No children under 12.
Credit cards All major cards accepted.
Terms B&B: single 110–125 glds, double 145–200 glds. (No restaurant.)

Hotel de l'Europe *Tel* (020) 234836
Nieuwe Doelenstraat 2-8 *Fax* (020) 242962
Amsterdam 1012 CP *Telex* 12081

Built on the Amstel in 1895, this is one of the city's grander hotels. It has
beautiful rooms and pleasant service, and this year was liked as much as
ever by visitors endorsing their earlier account: "Our room was not so
very spacious, but prettily decorated in cream and blue. All the public
rooms are attractive, but breakfast for 15 florins is very basic." However,
an inspector enjoyed a New Year's brunch that was anything but basic,
"A huge variety of spectacular seafoods, and many delicious desserts.
This was served in a restaurant of the highest elegance, overlooking the
Amstel. The whole place had an air of ineffable grand-hotel superiority
without being disdainful or snobbish." Bedrooms at the back, facing the
river, are quietest. (*Kate and Stephan Murray-Sykes,*)

All inspections are carried out anonymously.

Open All year. Restaurant closed Sat midday.
Rooms 12 suites, 62 double, 40 single – 103 with bath and shower, 11 with shower, all with telephone, radio and TV. Baby-listening on request. 24-hour room service.
Facilities Lift. Lounge, bar, 2 restaurants; banqueting and conference facilities; indoor heated swimming pool, sauna, solarium; terrace overlooking Amstel where meals and drinks are served in summer.
Location Central, opposite the Mint Tower and Flowermarket (rooms double-glazed: quietest ones at back). Parking, public garage nearby.
Credit cards All major cards accepted.
Terms Rooms: single 305–405 glds, double 405–505 glds, suite 955 glds. Breakfast 20 and 30 glds. Set lunch from 52.50 glds, dinner from 65 glds; full alc 100 glds. Reduced rates for children; special meals on request.

Hotel Pulitzer
Prinsengracht 315-331
Amsterdam 1016 GZ

Tel (020) 228333
Telex 16508

One of the largest hotels in our book, a sophisticated place that straddles a terrace of nine 17th-century houses, some facing the Prinsengracht and some the neighbouring canal, the Keizersgracht. "Despite its size (over 200 rooms), it feels intimate and friendly rather than impersonal. The rooms are a decent blend of old and new – original beams, exposed brickwork, slightly rustic furnishings. There is a pleasant glass-covered walkway through the gardens, with modern pictures on its walls and sculptures in the courtyards." Garden-facing rooms are quieter. The others enjoy the prospect over the canal.

Open All year. Restaurant closed in Aug.
Rooms 7 suites, 178 double, 44 single – all with bath and shower, telephone, radio, TV and mini-bar; baby-listening arranged. 25 ground-floor rooms.
Facilities Lifts. 2 lounges, bar, 2 restaurants; conference facilities; art gallery; gift shop; terrace for light meals, drinks, concerts in summer. Large garden. Private landing stage and canal boat.
Location Central, near Wester Church; garden rooms best for light sleepers. Garage 8 mins' walk; valet parking.
Credit cards All major cards accepted.
Terms Rooms: single 290–340 glds, double 340–390 glds, suite 775 glds. Breakfast 25 glds. Set lunch/dinner 35–60 glds; full alc 100 glds. Reduced rates for children; special meals for children on request.

BLOKZIJL 8356 DV Overijssel   **Map 3**

Kaatje bij de Sluis
Brouwerstraat 20

Tel (05272) 833
Fax (05272) 836

Blokzijl used to be a prosperous Hanseatic port on the Zuiderzee and has many fine 17th-century houses; today it's an attractive yachting centre. This restaurant-with-rooms, "Katie by the canal lock", is named after a local 17th-century heroine who became an expert cook – and today the cooking is still stylish enough to earn a *Michelin* rosette, as our nominator attests: "The food is exceptional, far removed from the deservedly stodgy image that Dutch food has. The style is French-influenced, but Dutch ingredients are used intelligently, and the dishes are beautifully presented. The staff are helpful and attentive. The bedrooms, created more recently, are in a building across the bridge: our large double room was elegantly furnished and had a profusion of potted plants, typically Dutch.

Breakfast – also typically Dutch, with five types of bread – is served on the terrace or in the garden room, with a good view of the small but pretty garden and the boating manoeuvres." (*Diana Cooper*) The hotel and restaurant are in two separate buildings, one on either side of a drawbridge.

Open All year except Feb. Closed Mon and Tue. Restaurant closed for lunch on Sat.
Rooms 8 double – all with bath and shower, telephone, radio, TV and tea-making facilities. 4 ground-floor rooms. All in separate building from restaurant.
Facilities Lounge, restaurant, breakfast room. Garden, 2 terraces.
Location Blokzijl is 33 km N of Zwolle. Hotel is central (rooms double-glazed). Parking.
Credit cards All major cards accepted.
Terms B&B: single 160 glds, double 250–300 glds; dinner B&B: single 235 glds, double 400 glds. Set lunch 55 glds, dinner 75 glds; full alc 90 glds.

DELFT 2611 EE Zuid-Holland	**Map 3**

Hotel Leeuwenbrug   *Tel* (015) 147741
Koornmarkt 16   *Fax* (015) 159759
Delft 2611 EE   *Telex* 33756 ref no 013

A visitor this year found the buffet breakfast "sumptuous" and enjoyed his front room facing the canal, at this reasonably priced and friendly little B&B hotel in one of the best parts of Delft. Opposite, across the canal, are a picturesque foot-bridge and gabled houses – "the loveliest view from a hotel bedroom that I've ever had" (and at least one room has a flower-decked balcony). Some rooms are small. Only limited space in the lounge but a pleasant little bar. (*Geo F Outland*)

Open 1 Jan–25 Dec.
Rooms 30 double, 8 single – all with bath and/or shower, telephone, radio and TV. 6 ground-floor rooms.
Facilities Lift. Lounge, bar, TV room, conference facilities.
Location Take Delft Zuid turning off Rotterdam–Amsterdam highway, and follow signs to Centre West. Paid parking next to hotel.
Credit cards All major cards accepted.
Terms B&B: single 95 glds, double 135-175 glds. Reduced rates for children. (No restaurant.)

Museumhotel   *Tel* (015) 140930
Oude Delft 189   *Fax* (015) 140935
Delft 2611 HD   *Telex* 38026 MUSHL

Two 17th-century canal houses have recently been converted into a friendly and well-modernised hotel, set in the heart of Delft's old quarter, next to the Prinsenhofmuseum and opposite the Oude Jan church tower. Visitors this year found the staff courteous, and breakfast quite good. An earlier view: "It is run by an enthusiastic and efficient young team. The bedrooms have all amenities." Recently the hotel opened a restaurant, but we have no reports on this. (*Kathleen and Jack Beal*)

Open All year except Christmas and New Year. Restaurant closed to non-residents.
Rooms 2 suites, 26 double, 2 single – all with bath and/or shower, telephone, radio, TV and mini-bar. 4 ground-floor rooms.

Facilities Lift. Lounge, breakfast room, bar, restaurant; conference/functions room. Car and bicycle hire.
Location Next to Prinsenhofmuseum and opposite Oude Jan church. Parking.
Credit cards All major cards accepted.
Terms [1989 rates] B&B: single 118–178 glds, double 162–198 glds. Full alc 35–50 glds. Reduced rates for children sharing parents' room.

THE HAGUE (DEN HAAG) 2514 EG Zuid-Holland   Map 3

Hotel des Indes
Lange Voorhout 54-56

Tel (070) 632932
Fax (070) 451721
Telex 31196

Situated opposite the Lange Voorhout Palace in the city centre, and facing a large tree-lined square, the elegant and expensive *Indes* was built in 1856 as a baron's residence and is now British-owned (Crest). "An excellent hotel where old-fashioned values of courtesy and good service are allied with efficiency and good food (presented prettily in the modern manner)." "The more sumptuous ground and first-floor bedrooms are better than the smaller ones higher up. But all are well equipped, with extras such as potions and fluffy bathrobes. Twin beds were narrow. Impressive flower-filled public rooms and pretty furniture. Service willing, but sometimes slow. Excellent breakfast, wonderful afternoon tea." (*Endorsed this year by Kate and Stephan Murray-Sykes*)

Open All year.
Rooms 5 suites, 55 double, 20 single – all with bath and shower, telephone, radio and TV. 24-hour room service. Ground-floor rooms.
Facilities Lift. Lounge, bar, restaurant; conference facilities. Park opposite.
Location Central, near palace. Private parking.
Credit cards All major cards accepted.
Terms B&B: single 369.50 glds, double 499 glds, suite 871 glds. Dinner, B&B: single 424,50 glds, double 609 glds, suite 981 glds. Set lunch/dinner 55–89 glds; full alc 70 glds. Reduced rates and special meals for children.

HEEZE 5591 HE Noord-Brabant   Map 3

Hostellerie du Château
Kapelstraat 48

Tel (04907) 3515
Fax (04907) 3876)
Telex 59355

This ambitious restaurant-with-rooms (one rosette in *Michelin*) is in a pretty little town with an impressive castle in pleasant wooded country to the south-east of the big, ugly industrial town of Eindhoven, headquarters of Philips, "an attractive long two-storey yellow building with a Mediterranean touch: dark green shutters, flower-boxes, and lots of tables for outside eating and drinking". It was redecorated in 1987 and two visitors in 1989 have pronounced the accommodation quite as good as the food: "Decor and furnishings excellent and housekeeping perfect. Suite in 'attic' well worth the extra money. Dinner superb – *nouvelle* but with a local touch. Service excellent throughout." "Food and bedrooms both of a very high standard. Our double room was very attractive and large with lobby, large modern bathroom, separate loo, comfortable sleeping area divided from the sitting area by the fitted wardrobes and TV table (rotating TV so that it could be watched from the bed or the sofa). The colour scheme was pastel and soothing. Lots of windows and mirrors added to the light spacious feel. Dinner was excellent and the staff helpful and unpretentious despite the *Michelin* rosette. All in all a very pleasant experience." (*Cyril and Joyce Baily, Kate and Stephan Murray-Sykes*) One warning: "The steep stairs to the bedrooms make them inaccessible to anyone with a walking problem."

Open All year except New Year. Restaurant closed Sat midday.
Rooms 4 suites, 8 double, 2 single – all with bath and shower, telephone, radio, TV, mini-bar and baby-listening.
Facilities Lounge, bar, 2 restaurants; conference/functions facilities; covered terrace. Large garden. Golf, tennis, riding, walking and cycling nearby.
Location 10 km SE of Eindhoven, between E34 and E25 motorways.
Restriction Not suitable for &.
Credit cards All major cards accepted.
Terms [1989 rates] B&B: single 160–190 glds, double 210–240 glds, suite 280 glds. Set meals 52.50–115 glds; full alc 75 glds. Reduced rates and special meals for children.

HILVERSUM 1200 AP Noord-Holland   Map 3

Hotel Lapershoek   *Tel* (035) 231341
Utrechtseweg 16, Postbus 609   *Fax* (035) 284360
                                                      Telex 73068 LAPH

Near the Amsterdam-Utrecht motorway, on the edge of a city that houses the main Dutch TV and radio stations, a newly opened modern hotel, quite smart, with attentive and enthusiastic staff. Rooms vary in size but all are well furnished, some have water-beds. Very good nouvelle-ish *food. 39 rooms, all with bath and/or shower. B&B double 195 glds. Set menus 37–55 glds. New nomination. More reports please.*

LAGE VUURSCHE 3749 AJ Utrecht   Map 3

De Kastanjehof   *Tel* (02156) 248
Kloosterlaan 1   *Fax* (02156) 444

In a village north-east of Utrecht, near Baarn, a delightful white-walled restaurant-with-rooms in a large garden beside a stream, amid wooded countryside. Bright and airy rooms, a warm welcome, good sophisticated cooking. Closed 31 Dec–5 Jan. 12 rooms, all with bath or shower. B&B: single 130 glds, double 160 glds. New nomination. More reports welcome.

LEEUWARDEN 8911 AG Friesland   Map 3

Oranje Hotel   *Tel* (058) 126241
Stationsweg 4   *Fax* (058) 121441
                                                      Telex 46528

Our only entry for northern Holland is in that region's second largest city, an attractive place of canals and gabled houses. Here the *Oranje* is a sizeable and very spruce modern hotel, across a busy road from the station: rooms, however, are quiet, as well as spacious and well equipped.

"Benign owner, friendly and relaxed atmosphere, an outstanding restaurant with *nouvelle*-ish dishes, and breakfast the best I've had in Holland", says a reader this year. (*Imogen Cooper*)

Open All year except Christmas.
Rooms 78 – all with bath and shower, telephone and radio; some with TV. 1 room suitable for &.
Facilities Lift. Lounge, bar, 2 restaurants; conference facilities.
Location Opposite central station. Parking.
Credit cards All major cards accepted.
Terms B&B: single 140 glds, double 180 glds, suite 220–295 glds. Dinner B&B: single 165 glds, double 250 glds. Set lunch 30–45 glds, dinner 30–75 glds; full alc 40–70 glds. Reduced rates for children sharing parents' room; special meals.

LEUSDEN 3832 RS Utrecht   Map 3

Hotel Huize den Treek   *Tel* (03498) 1425
Trekerweg 23

A 17th-century mansion in a lovely wooded lakeside setting near Amersfoort, a good base for cyclists. Elegant public rooms; some bedrooms have antiques and gold brocade bedspreads and face the lake. French cuisine, possibly too ambitious; breakfast in the library. Closed 20 Dec–2 Jan. 18 rooms, all with bath and/or shower. B&B double 115–145 glds. Set menus 39–90 glds. Some criticisms of room upkeep this year. More reports welcome.

OISTERWIJK 5061 HT Noord-Brabant   Map 3

Hotel-Restaurant De Swaen   *Tel* (04242) 19006
De Lind 47   *Telex* 52617

A very elegant and sophisticated little hostelry on the tree-lined main street of the pleasant shady town of Oisterwijk. "Superb accommodation and a wonderful meal", runs a report this year (in *Michelin*, this is one of the three restaurants in the whole country with as many as two rosettes). Other delights include a terrace in the front and a beautiful formal garden at the back; bedrooms are modern and comfortable, each with a small balcony. One reader, on her sixth visit, praised especially the breakfasts and maid service, and the availability of free bicycles. "Recently converted by a local furniture-maker, from the outside it looks like many other pleasant Dutch provincial hotels. But inside it's a veritable Aladdin's cave." "The bathrooms have gold-plated fittings!" "An exquisite and memorable meal, and the staff were most solicitous and efficient." (*Mrs V Walker-Dendle, and others*)

Open All year except 10–15 June.
Rooms 1 suite, 17 double – all with bath, shower, telephone, radio and TV.
Facilities Lift. Bar, lounge, restaurant; 2 conference rooms. Garden, terrace.
Location Central. Oisterwijk is 10 km NE of Tilberg. Parking.
Credit cards All major cards accepted.
Terms B&B: single 225 glds, double 275 glds, suite 345 glds. Set lunch 50–100 glds, dinner 110–165 glds; full alc 150 glds. Weekend rates. Special meals for children.

We are particularly keen to have reports on italicised entries.

OOTMARSUM 7631 HX Overijssel   Map 3

De Wiemsel
Winhofflaan 2

Tel (05419) 2155
Fax (05419) 3295
Telex 44667

Leading Dutch politicians and businessmen often come to relax at this spacious and sophisticated ranch-style hotel, which lies in gentle pastoral country near the German border, just east of the pretty little town of Ootmarsum. Set quietly in its own grounds, it is a number of low bungalow-style apartments attached to the main block which houses the restaurant; the modern decor is light and attractive. "Superbly luxurious, with excellent food and impeccable service", is a comment this year. Others have written: "Our room was lovely with a view over fields, and its bathroom luxurious." (*Dr GM Chapman*) One correspondent considers the food to be even better at *De Wanne* which is down in the town and under the same management. The hotel has a stable of horses for the use of guests, as well as a floodlit tennis court and a big indoor pool. It is 20 minutes' drive to the German casino across the border at Bad Bentheim.

Open All year.
Rooms 42 suites, 5 double (all also let as single) – all with bath, shower, telephone, radio, TV, tea-making facilities and baby-listening; many with terrace. 3 in villa, 50 metres from main building. Some ground-floor rooms with bathrooms equipped for &.
Facilities Hall, lounge, bar, restaurant; conference facilities; indoor heated swimming pool, sauna, solarium, billiard room. Large garden with terrace, tennis court and stables. Bicycles for hire.
Location 1 km E of Ootmarsum, which is 28 km N of Enschede.
Credit cards All major cards accepted.
Terms B&B 176 glds, suite 264.50 glds. Set lunch 52.50 glds, dinner 75 glds. Christmas, New Year, Easter, Whitsun packages. Reduced rates and special meals for children.

ROOSTEREN 6116 AW Limburg   Map 3

Hotel De Roosterhoeve
Hoekstraat 29

Tel (04499) 3131
Fax (04499) 4400

On the edge of a quiet village beside the Belgian border, north of Maastricht, a nicely converted farmhouse with plenty of rustic touches (beamed ceilings, log fire, painted furniture) but large modern bedrooms. Indoor and outdoor swimming pools, sauna; garden, patio; friendly staff, quite good simple food. 44 rooms (10 in annexe), most with bath and shower. B&B double 110–135 glds. Alc meals (excluding wine) 40–72 glds. New nomination. More reports welcome.

We asked hotels to quote 1990 prices. Not all were able to predict them in the late spring of 1989. Some of our terms will be inaccurate. Do check latest tariffs at the time of booking.

We get less feedback from smaller and more remote hotels. But we need feedback on all hotels: big and small, far and near, famous and first-timers.

VALKENBURG 6301 HV Limburg   Map 3

Hotel Prinses Juliana   *Tel* (04406) 12244
Broekhem 11   *Fax* (04406) 14405
                                                   Telex 56351 JULIA

Set in pretty countryside east of Maastricht, the charming and historic old
town of Valkenburg has a ruined castle, Roman catacombs and countless
grottoes, and is now a flourishing summer resort. Its best hotel, though
not its largest, is the very superior *Prinses Juliana*, with cool modern decor.
It has a garden, and a delightful shady terrace for summer eating, and the
food, mainly traditional, wins two rosettes in *Michelin*. Recent visitors
were impressed: "In the big restaurant with its well-spaced tables and
silver candelabra, we tried the *menu gastronomique*, including smoked
duck with foie gras, grilled fish with a herb sauce, and lamb with spinach
and truffles – all excellent. Service was friendly and unstuffy. The hotel is
nicely decorated in soft colours, with subdued lighting, and an open fire
in the lounge. Our room also had pleasing colours, and was provided
with trouser-press, hair-drier and fresh fruit. Good breakfast." Annexe
rooms are cheaper, but this year one reader found them "uninspiring".
We'd welcome more reports.

Open All year. Restaurant closed Sat midday.
Rooms 24 double, 3 single – all with bath, shower, telephone, radio, TV and
baby-listening. 10 in annexe across road.
Facilities Lounge, TV room in annexe, bar, 2 restaurants; conference facilities.
Garden, terrace.
Location Central. Garage and open parking.
Restriction Not suitable for &.
Credit cards All major cards accepted.
Terms Rooms: single 100–175 glds, double 120–210 glds. Breakfast 20 glds.
Dinner, B&B 110–200 glds per person. Set lunch 55 glds, dinner 75 glds; full alc
75 glds. Special meals for children.

VLIJMEN 5251 EC Noord-Brabant   Map 3

Hotel Prinsen   *Tel* (04108) 9131
Julianastraat 21

Down a quiet road in a small town just west of 's-Hertogenbosch, and
convenient for the motorway, an old family-run inn has been given a new wing
of comfortable bedrooms overlooking an enclosed garden, where tables, chairs
and pink parasols are set neatly on the lawn. Top-quality design and
maintenance; friendly ambience; good cooking, well patronised locally.
29 rooms, all with bath and/or shower. B&B double 120 glds. Set meals 15–
30 glds [1989]. Recent nomination. More reports please.

WELLERLOOI 5856 CL Limburg   Map 3

Hostellerie de Hamert   *Tel* (04703) 1260
                                                   Fax (04703) 2503

A fairly expensive restaurant-with-rooms (*Michelin* rosette), well suited
for a self-indulgent stopover: it stands pleasantly amid lawns and tall

trees by the banks of the wide Meuse (Maas), near the German frontier in northern Limburg. "It's in the middle of nowhere, between the river and a nature reserve, and close to a busy main road (but the traffic did not bother us at night, as the bedrooms do not face the road). The people of this little-known part of the Netherlands are more voluble and convivial than most Dutch, and perhaps this contributes to the dining-room's relaxed and pleasant atmosphere and its excellent service from owner and staff. People come here to eat, preferably on a fine day when you can dine on the terrace and watch the river flow past. The food is very rich, and I found it good but not exceptional – lots of high-quality expense-account ingredients such as salmon, quail, and the local asparagus for which they are famous. The cooking is old-fashioned, with lots of creamy vague-tasting sauces: none of your *nouvelle* plating in the kitchen, but carving at table. Wine list stuffy on the whole, but with a few local wines. The place does not have the feel or amenities of a hotel (no lounge) and is deserted in the morning: breakfast was poor and its service brusque. The bedrooms are comfortable, clean and neat, with some nice furniture, but have an air of faded gentility." A reader this year had no complaints: "Excellent hotel, magnificent staff, a beautifully served menu."

Open All year, but closed Tue and Wed 1 Nov–31 Mar.
Rooms 4 double – 2 with bath, all with radio.
Facilities Lounge, restaurant; 2 conference/function rooms; 2 terraces (meals served outdoors in fine weather). Garden leading to river.
Location 15 km N of Venlo on road to Nijmegen. Parking.
Credit cards All major cards accepted.
Terms B&B [1989 rates] single 70–90 glds, double 115–150 glds. Alc meals (excluding wine) 89–123 glds. Reduced rates and special meals for children.

DE WIJK 7957 NV Drenthe Map 3

Havesathe de Havixhorst *Tel* (05224) 1487
Schiphorsterweg 34–36 *Fax* (05224) 1489

In a little-known part of the Netherlands, De Wijk is a village north-east of Zwolle, just off the motorway to Groningen – and here a reader this year has discovered this small 18th-century moated castle: "The red carpet leading to the front door gives way to marble inside. High ceilings, large windows - pity about the musak. Our room was clean and comfortable but not remarkable: the rooms are due to be refurbished within the next two years. The staff are young, friendly and very professional. We opted for no-meat meals and enjoyed fried quail egg, red pepper soup, herb soufflé, amid much else: all was thoughtfully conceived, and breakfast was the usual robust Dutch affair. I would recommend *Havesathe* for the food and welcome." (*Diana Cooper*) More reports welcome.

Open All year.
Rooms 8 double, 1 single – all with bath and/or shower, telephone, radio and mono TV.
Facilities Lounge, 2 bars, restaurant; conference/functions facilities. Garden; terrace. Golf nearby.
Location 6 km SE of Meppel and 25 km NE of Zwolle. Parking.
Restrictions Not suitable for &.
Credit cards All major cards accepted.

Terms [1989 rates] B&B 72, 50–95 glds. Dinner B&B 110–137.50 glds. Set lunch/dinner 45.50–111 glds; full alc 65 glds. Reduced rates and special meals for children.

WITTEM 6286 AA Limburg   Map 3

Kasteel Wittem   *Tel* (04450) 1208
Wittemerallee 3   *Fax* (04450) 1260
                                                        Telex 56287 KAWIT

This grey-walled 15th-century castle east of Maastricht was renovated in the 19th century in neo-Gothic style, and is now an elegant restaurant-with-rooms, surrounded by a flower garden and ancient trees, and a pond with black swans. In 1988/9, praise has again poured in, led by this report: "A real treat. The welcome was friendly and genuine. The bar area is cosy and intimate, the dining-room more grand. Here the food is superlative (*Michelin* rosette), especially ravioli filled with scallops, duck with honey, and grilled goats' cheese with quince sauce. Breakfast comes with strawberries, cherries, pumpernickel, three fruit breads, eggs, tomatoes, 'a real castle breakfast' said my daughter. A royal red carpet leads to the rooms: we had a round one, with suitably heavy furniture, wallpaper that can best be described as 'very busy'. But the bath-taps dripped, and one shelf was made of acrid yellow plastic 'enhanced' with cigarette burns. Apart from these small faults, the place is perfection." "Utterly charming." "Europe's best breakfast. Superb food, excellent service, and the twinkling eyes of the cordial owner always in evidence." One reader took the turret suite, with window seats overlooking the moat, and found the sitting-room and the grounds all "gorgeous". (*Diana Cooper; also John W Behle, Bettye Chambers, Geo Outland and others*)

Open All year.
Rooms 12 double – all with bath and shower, telephone, radio and TV.
Facilities Lounge, bar, breakfast room, restaurant; conference/banqueting facilities; terrace. Park with garden, river. Golf, cycling, walking, tennis and trout-fishing nearby.
Location Between Maastricht (17 km) and Aachen (15 km). 2 km SW of Gulpen on Maastricht road.
Restriction Not suitable for &.
Credit cards All major cards accepted.
Terms Rooms double 175,00 glds. Breakfast 20 glds. Set lunch 52.50–75 glds, dinner 75–110 glds; full alc 90–110 glds. Reduced rates and special meals for children.

Norway

HOTEL MUNDAL, FJÆRLAND

Grand Hotel Bellevue   *Tel* (072) 21 011
PO Box 184

Mountain walking, rowing, and sea, lake and river fishing (trout and salmon, etc) are among the attractions of this resort at the head of the Romsdal fjord, south-west of Trondheim. The *Bellevue* is outwardly a rather graceless white block, but inside bright and cheerful: "A superbly friendly hotel with attentive and very obliging staff. Large modern rooms (ours overlooked the mountains) and an excellent bar and restaurant: superb local specialities such as reindeer prepared several ways, and good wine list." (*James M Lamont*)

Open All year except Christmas, New Year and Easter.
Rooms 42 double, 4 single – some with bath and/or shower, all with telephone; 22 with radio and TV. 2 ground-floor rooms.
Facilities Salon, TV room, bar, dining-room, bistro; disco. Grounds with tennis court; bicycles available; fishing nearby.
Location Central. Town is 160 km SW of Trondheim.

Credit cards All major cards accepted.
Terms [1989 rates] B&B: single 380–630 Nkr, double 500–785 Nkr. Set lunch
115 Nkr, dinner 140 Nkr. Reduced rates and special meals for children.

ASKIM 1800   Map 1

Granheim Hotell   *Tel* (02) 88.15.30
Vammaveien 6

*Attractive small inn, recently renovated, with new bedroom wing, in town
50 kilometres east of Oslo, near Swedish border, on road to Stockholm.
Recommended as good overnight stop. Comfortable bedrooms with modern
decor, relaxing and enjoyable atmosphere, good à la carte meals. Gentle hills,
meadows, forests and inland lakes nearby; good cycling country. 25 rooms, all
with private facilities. B&B double 560 Nkr. New nomination. More reports
please.*

BERGEN   Map 1

Augustin Hotel   *Tel* (05) 23.00.25
C. Sundtsgt. 24   *Fax* (05) 23.31.30
5004 Bergen   *Telex* 40923 AUGUS

A dapper small hotel centrally located near the harbour in a busy fjord-
girt city. "The bedrooms are small but clean and neat, and the additional
facilities – large parlour and TV room, delightfully decorated breakfast
room, and adjoining restaurant owned by the same management – make
the hotel feel spacious. The staff are pleasant and helpful. The central
location, minutes from the wharf and popular old Bryggen, made it easy
to explore the city on foot." (*JT Simon; also Lizbeth and Craig Anderson*)

Open All year except Christmas.
Rooms 28 double, 10 single – all with shower, telephone, radio, and TV. 2 rooms
suitable for &.
Facilities Lounge, TV room, breakfast room, café.
Location Central, near harbour. Public parking.
Credit cards All major cards accepted.
Terms B&B: single 395–575 Nkr, double 540–720 Nkr; Dinner, B&B: single 475–
655 Nkr, double 700–880 Nkr. Set lunch/dinner 90 Nkr, full alc 175 Nkr.
Reduced rates for children under 12; special meals.

Myklebust Pensjonat   *Tel* (05) 31.13.28
Rosenbergsgt. 19
5015 Bergen

"Deserves as many stars as possible," says a recent visitor of the
unpretentious *Myklebust*, which occupies the upper floor of a block of
flats, in a quiet but very steep street fairly near the centre. Another view,
"Friendly and efficient family owners, who speak excellent English.
Large, airy, comfortable, clean rooms and a good location, not too noisy."
And a third, "Wonderful breakfast – every item one could think of from a
Norwegian selection, brought to our room. Excellent value at half the
price of some Bergen hotels." (*Rev. AG Mursell, DR Ritchie, and others*)

Open All year except Christmas, New Year and Easter.
Rooms 1 family, 4 double, 2 single – 2 with bath and shower; all with TV.
Facilities No public rooms or restaurant.
Location Central. Street parking.
Restriction Not suitable for &.
Credit cards None accepted.
Terms [1989 rates] B&B: single 295–480 Nkr, double 500–635 Nkr.

Hotell Neptun
Walckendorffsgt. 8
5012 Bergen

Tel (05) 32.60.00
Fax (05) 23.32.02
Telex 40040

Modern hotel, centrally situated overlooking harbour and old market, well equipped, quiet at night. Attractive restaurant offers some of the best food in Bergen – "elegant and delicious". Generous buffet breakfasts. 122 rooms, most with private facilities. B&B double 1,150 Nkr [1989]. Was in earlier editions of the Guide, but dropped for lack of feedback. Re-nominated this year. More reports please.

Park Pensjonat
Harald Hårfagresgt. 35
5007 Bergen

Tel (05) 32 09 60
Fax (05) 31 03 34
Telex 40365

Established as a bed-and-breakfast hotel for over 25 years, the *Park Pensjonat* comprises two old houses two minutes' walk apart, in a quiet residential district near the university and an attractive park. 15 minutes' walk *down* to the centre of the city (but considerably *more* to climb the steep hill back. Public rooms are slightly fussily furnished, but with some pleasant antiques. Our inspector's bedroom on the top of four floors was small, but comfortable; rooms on the lower floors, including two on the ground floor, are more spacious. Reception was friendly and helpful. Breakfast was the customary Norwegian self-help cold buffet, with good coffee and bread. The hotel caters primarily for foreign tourists and one-nighters joining or returning from cruises. Verdict: a reasonably priced, family-run, unpretentious hotel, acceptable for a two-or-three day stay.

Open All year except Easter and Christmas.
Rooms 14 double, 6 single – all with shower, telephone, radio and TV.
Facilities Breakfast room, meeting room.
Location 10–15 mins' walk from station. Parking.
Restrictions Not suitable for &. No smoking in breakfast room.
Credit cards Access, Visa.
Terms B&B single 360–450 Nkr, double 470–550 Nkr. Reduced rates for children.

Hotel Victoria
Kong Oscarsgt. 29
5017 Bergen

Tel (05) 31.50.30
Fax (05) 32.81.78
Telex 42190

Attractive white bow-windowed building, central and extremely comfortable. Bedrooms "with everything one could desire including umbrella (necessary) and mini-bar; conventional bedding available as alternative to duvets. Splendid buffet breakfast. Friendly, helpful staff speak excellent English." 43 rooms, all with bath/shower. B&B: single 690–740 Nkr, double 840–890 Nkr. New nomination. More reports please.

EIDFJORD 5783   Map 1

Vøringfoss Hotel   *Tel* (054) 65184

Comfortable and welcoming white-washed hotel in lovely position at water's edge, in small village at head of Eidfjord, a branch of the great Hardangerfjord. Well situated for exploring Hardangervidda national park. Warm welcome from owner. Pleasant sitting room and bar, with old photographs, interesting pictures. Bedrooms in modern block at rear. Pretty, well-appointed dining-room overlooking water; evening meals available until 10 o'clock (unlike many Norwegian hotels, which serve promptly at 7). Recommended for a brief visit, but unexciting menu and criticisms of the cooking. 57 rooms, most with bath and shower. Dinner, B&B double 580–780 Nkr. New nomination. More reports welcome.

FJÆRLAND 5855   Map 1

Hotel Mundal   *Tel* (056) 93101
                                       Telex 74745 POLAR attn ORHEIM

Fjærland lies at the head of an arm of Sognefjord, Norway's longest and deepest fjord. The trim white clapboard-fronted *Mundal* sits by the water, in the shadow of Norway's largest glacier, the Jostedalsbreen. It has been run by the same family since it was built in 1891. The present owner's wife is English. A regular returning this year found the owners as kind and charming as ever, and says that the hotel is even better, thanks to continuing improvements. "The bedrooms are all different and all Norwegian in atmosphere. There is a library with English books, a billiard room and a music room with a piano. The food is plentiful and very good – for example fjord trout with butter sauce and cucumber salad – and served punctually at 7 pm. Many of the old traditions are carried on here – even breakfast butter balls fashioned by the kitchen ladies. There are antiques and beautiful furnishings made by past members of the family. Even the stair carpet is hand-woven." An inspector this year found the hotel "thoroughly congenial, and would happily return", but warned that service from some of the older staff was "kindly but slow", and that a request for a double bed resulted in "two wooden-sided beds placed next to each other". He appreciated the friendly information about nearby walks, and the electric driers for walking boots (for which no extra charge is made). Olav Orheim, a grandson of the hotel's founder and a glaciologist who has led three Norwegian expeditions to Antarctica, will take guests to visit the glacier at some 5,000 feet. (*Elizabeth Sandham, and others*)

Open Apr–end Nov.
Rooms 2 suites, 24 double, 11 single – 31 with bath and shower, 4 with shower, all with telephone.

Facilities Hall, lounge, TV room, music room, library/billiard room, bar, 2 restaurants. Garden on fjord; rowing boat free of charge; fishing (equipment can be borrowed); swimming possible, but very cold.
Location 180 km NE of Bergen. Reached by express boat service, ferry and bus.
Restriction Not suitable for &.
Credit cards None accepted.
Terms B&B 335–550 Nkr; dinner, B&B 510–725 Nkr. Set dinner 175 Nkr; full alc 250 Nkr. Reduced rates on special meals for children.

LOEN 6878   **Map 1**

Alexandra Hotel   *Tel* (057) 77 660
                                                  Fax (057) 77 770
                                       Telex 42665 ALEX

A luxurious large modern six-storey hotel "with a touch of luxury", in a valley surrounded by majestic mountains and fjords, waterfalls and glaciers, in an area good for summer skiing, mountain climbing and fishing. Not a typical Guide hotel, but readers have appreciated the beautiful situation, spacious and well-equipped bedrooms and public rooms, the friendly and helpful staff, the facilities offered for both parents and children including "endless activities" (see below), and the good food. More reports please.

Open All year.
Rooms 210 – all with bath and shower, telephone and radio.
Facilities Lift. 3 bars, 4 lounges, children's playroom, café, restaurant; conference facilities; hairdresser; indoor heated swimming pool, sun terrace, saunas, solarium, gym; dancing nightly in bar. Garden with tennis and mini-golf. Near sea with fishing and water sports.
Location 10 km E of Olden. Nearest station at Otta (200 km); bus connection.
Credit cards All major cards accepted.
Terms [1989 rates] B&B: single 540–1,190 Nkr, double 640–1,880 Nkr. Set lunch 115 Nkr, dinner 200 Nkr. Reduced rates and special meals for children.

LOM 2686   **Map 1**

Røisheim Hotell   *Tel* (062) 12031
Bøverdalen

High above sea-level on the ancient Sognefjell road, a cluster of picturesque turf-roofed 18th-century farm buildings, a hotel since 1858. Bedrooms in romantic old annexes, some with private bath. Nominators' room was old-Norwegian in appearance, with painted wooden walls, wooden floor with a rug and little furniture apart from beds. Recommended for warmth, comfort, charming decor, good food, attractive public rooms, welcoming hosts. Open Apr–Oct. 25 rooms, 9 with bath and/or shower. B&B double 441–725 Nkr. Set dinner 200 Nkr. New nomination. More reports please.

Hotels often book you into their most expensive rooms or suites unless you specify otherwise. Even if all room prices are the same, hotels may give you a less good room in the hope of selling their better rooms to late customers. It always pays to discuss accommodation in detail when making a reservation.

NORDFJORDEID 6771 Map 1

Nordfjord Hotell Tel (057) 60 433
POB 144 Fax (057) 60 680
 Telex 42971 EIDRB N

Near fjord and not far from west coast and mountains, well-placed for tours of the region. Modern Scandinavian in style with sleek, warm furnishings; open plan sitting rooms, spacious dining-room; discos, billiards, sauna, large garden with tennis; fishing, excellent walks nearby. Recommended for friendly staff, well-equipped bedrooms, unexpectedly high standard of cooking. Closed 22 Dec–4 Jan. 55 rooms, all with bath and/or shower. B&B 350–670 Nkr. Set dinner 170 Nkr. New nomination. More reports please.

OSLO Map 1

Hotel Continental Tel (02) 41.90.60
Stortingsgt. 24-26 Fax (02) 42.96.89
0161 Oslo 1 Telex 71012 CONTI

Opposite the National Theatre, this large solid building, dated *c.* 1900, has been in the same family for four generations and is in the grand old style. Over 100 of its bedrooms have recently been renovated and the windows are now triple-glazed against street noise. But the dining-room remains classically formal, with chandeliers and serious waiters. "Oslo has, more than any other European capital, preserved the traditions and atmosphere of the 19th century. The *Continental* retains the grave dignity, courtesy and friendly warmth which visitors to Norway so much appreciate. I could wax even more lyrical over the breakfast's cold table." And of the hotel's famous *Theatercaféen*, another correspondent writes, "The last really Viennese-style restaurant in Scandinavia – a large room, with stained wood, mirrors and a stuccoed ceiling supported by tall white columns with decorated capitals. Food was super and people were having a good time, including us." We would welcome more reports.

Open All year except Easter.
Rooms 12 suites, 124 double, 43 single – all with bath, shower, telephone, radio, TV with video.
Facilities 2 lifts. Lounge, bar, restaurant, grill, café; conference/banqueting facilities; discothèque daily except Sun and Mon; terrace.
Location Central, between Royal Palace and National Theatre. Underground carpark.
Restriction Not suitable for &.
Credit cards All major cards accepted.
Terms B&B weekday rates: single 1,190 Nkr, double 1,450–1,530 Nkr, suite 2,100–3,400 Nkr; weekend rates: single 515 Nkr, double 830 Nkr. Extra bed 100 Nkr (cots free).

Gabelshus Hotell Tel (02) 55.22.60
Gabelsgt. 16 Telex 74073 GABEL
0272 Oslo 2

A quiet, comfortable and friendly hotel on a tree-lined residential street not far from the centre of Oslo, with the city's excellent public transport only three minutes' walk away. Considerably cheaper than the large city-centre hotels – booking is usually essential. The lobby, decorated in dark wood, is reminiscent of a hunting lodge in the country. Bedrooms are clean and comfortable with an "understated and very restful decor. We had an early train to catch so the staff prepared a continental breakfast for us at 6.30 am." The restaurant offers good (but not gourmet) reasonably priced meals. (*Lizbeth and Craig Anderson, Martha Swartz*)

Open All year except July.
Rooms 32 double, 14 single – all with bath and shower, telephone, radio and TV.
Facilities Lift. Lounge, TV room, bar, dining-room; conference facilities. Garden.
Location Between Bygdøy alle and Drammensv. 15 mins' walk from city centre; bus and tram nearby. Parking.
Restriction Not suitable for &.
Credit cards All major cards accepted.
Terms [1989 rates] B&B: single 750 Nkr, double 950 Nkr. Full alc from 250 Nkr. Special meals for children.

ØVRE EIDFJORD 5754   Map 1

Besså Touristhytta   *Tel* Hardangervidda west 88938
                                             (via operator – 0104)
                                          Off season (054) 65927

By a substantial margin, our most way-out entry! The Hardangervidda is a vast high plateau east of Bergen, dotted with lakes; vast herds of reindeer graze on its pastures. There are no roads, or settlements of any size. It is "a walkers' paradise", with an extensive system of paths usually running from one lake to another and linking the mountain huts, one of which is nominated this year by intrepid walkers: "Besså is a single-storey wooden building 29 kilometres from the nearest road; walking boots are necessary for crossing the rough terrain. There are only 30 beds, but all who turn up are guaranteed accommodation. The reception was homely and efficient. Our twin-bedded room (others have four to six beds) had pine walls and furniture, table, mirror, chair, jug and bowl for washing – hot water came from an urn near the kitchen. The lights above the firm and comfortable beds were adequate for reading and we were given candles for when the generator stopped working at 9.15 pm. There was floor space for luggage. Take your own sheets or sleeping bag; pillows, blankets and duvets are supplied. There is a large cold shower room, the earth closet, clean and throne-like, is a short walk across the yard. The sitting-room is well furnished with comfortable chairs, tables for route-planning and open fires. The dining room is light and airy, waitress service prompt and efficient. The three-course meal was excellent, everything home-made – soup, beef stew, three vegetables – and served very hot; pudding was fruit salad with huge helpings of fresh cream. The breakfast was the best we had in Norway: home-smoked salmon, fresh salmon, huge plate of home-made butter, cheeses and ham all served with good hot coffee. (*Susan and John Aglionby*)

Open Easter and April, 1 July–10 Sept.
Rooms 7 double, 5 4-bedded; 3 in annexe.
Facilities Lounge, dining room. Lake with fishing and swimming 15 metres.
Location In the Hardangervidda, S of Eidfjord, 5 hrs' walk from nearest road.
Terms [1989 rates] Per person: In 4-bedded room 75 Nkr, in double 110 Nkr. 55 Nkr for bedlinen. Breakfast 48 Nkr. Set dinner 90 Nkr.

SKJOLDEN 5833 Map 1

Skjolden Hotel
Tel (056) 86 606
Fax (056) 86 720
Telex 40654 SOGTU

Situated at the end of the Lusterfjord (a branch of the long Sognefjord), this square flat-roofed hotel, owned by the Galde family for 75 years, is popular as a base for hiking, fishing and other sports. The surrounding countryside is magnificent for touring as well. The hotel offers large sitting-rooms furnished in a modern style, an open terrace, a fairly big garden, and a "very large and light restaurant serving plain but adequate food, well cooked, in substantial portions". Bedrooms are simply but comfortably furnished with light wood furniture and feathered duvets, though with poor insulation. Recommended for its beautiful situation and good value, acceptable for a three-to-four day stay. More reports welcome.

Open May–Sept.
Rooms 38 double, 16 single – 50 with bath and shower.
Facilities Lift. Lounges, restaurant. Large garden, badminton. Fjord 20 metres, free rowing boats.
Location In the western fjords north-east of Bergen, 75 km from Sogndal airport.
Credit cards Visa.
Terms B&B 255–360 Nkr. Set meals 130 Nkr. 50% reduction for children up to 15.

TRONDHEIM 7011 Map 1

Neptun Hotel and Bistro
Ths Angellsgt. 12b
Tel (07) 51.21.33

Newly renovated, a modern hotel centrally situated in the historic cathedral city, on the site of a seamen's hostel, rebuilt in the early 1980s to a high standard. "Our spacious bedroom was remarkable. It had four windows facing the street; the double bed which had a firm and comfortable mattress in a creaking old bedframe, was in a curtained alcove. The furniture had been rescued from a Norwegian cruise ship built in 1908. More modern facilities included TV, mini-bar and telephone. The bath was deep and there was a good supply of towels. Most of the double rooms look over the street which is noisy; singles face the rear. The reception area is part of the bistro/restaurant and there is a lounge. We did not dine in the hotel but the à la carte meals appeared to be reasonably priced and adequate. The breakfast buffet offered a good choice including fresh fruit. Our fellow guests were mainly Norwegian." (*Susan, Francis and John Aglionby*) More reports please. Visitors in search of more luxurious accommodation could try the nearby 177-roomed *Britannia*, Dronningensgt. 5, *Tel* (07) 53.00.40, *Fax* (07) 51.09.00, *Telex* 55451.

Open All year. Bistro/restaurant closed Sun evening.
Rooms 36 – all with bath/shower, telephone, radio, mini-bar.
Facilities Lounge, bistro/restaurant; banqueting room.
Location Central.
Credit cards Probably some accepted.
Terms [1989 rates] B&B: single 365–665 Nkr, double 540–825 Nkr.

ULVIK 5730   Map 1

Ulvik Fjord Pensjonat   *Tel* (05) 526170
Fax (05) 526170

A small guest house, new to the Guide this year, on the edge of an attractive village, now a popular resort, in western Norway on an arm of the Hardangerfjord, sheltered on three sides by impressive mountains. It has been run by for the past 16 years by Lilly and Odd Hammer, who speak excellent English. It has a white weatherboarded exterior and is separated from the road by a small garden. Lounges are pleasantly furnished, there is a spacious dining-room; dinner, announced by a bell, is served punctually at 7 pm – "beautifully cooked by Odd Hammer, and served by Lilly with the help of a young girl, in a friendly unhurried manner. No choice but it included fresh sea trout, and second helpings were offered. Breakfast was the usual generous self-help buffet. Our bedroom was small but adequate, though lighting, except for the bedside lights rather poor. Comfortable bed. The private shower/loo had been cut out of the long side of the room and was really too small, but the baths for general use were excellent. All the other guests were British; it is well situated for walking holidays." (*Francis and Susan Aglionby*) More reports please.

Open 1 May–20 Sept.
Rooms 18 double, 2 single – 17 with shower. 7 in annexe.
Facilities 3 sitting/ TV rooms, dining-room. Garden.
Location 500 metres from centre. 44 km E of Voss.
Restriction Not suitable for &.
Credit card Visa.
Terms B&B 225–375 Nkr. Set meals 135 Nkr. 5-day rates.

UTNE 5797   Map 1

Romantik Utne Hotel   *Tel* (054) 66 983

Warmly admired for many years, this delightful little hotel on the Hardangerfjord, east of Bergen, is Norway's oldest (founded 1722) and has been run by the same family since 1787. It is a white clapboard building, lovingly maintained, with flowers in all the public rooms, embroidered cushions, lace curtains, and lots of old painted Norwegian furniture. "Its setting is splendid, at the foot of a steep promontory where the Hardanger branches into two small fjords; high blue mountains across the water; sheer cliffs above it; a waterfall plunging down the cliff face and rushing through the village; apple orchards on each side. There are fine walks along the fjord in both directions or you can climb paths to the high pastures. The village is small and tranquil; the *Utne* stands in its centre opposite the boat landing. Behind it, on the hillside, is a small modern annexe. Meals (taken communally) are hearty and excellent. Fru Aga Blokhus and her staff, wearing the Hardanger costume, look after you with grace and enthusiasm." "We were made to feel as house guests in a gracious and charming country house." An inspector this year confirmed these accounts, "A comfortable, charmingly furnished room. The food was delicious and there was an interesting wine list with prices moderate by Norwegian standards." (*Elizabeth Sandham, Mrs J Gould, and others*)

Open All year except Christmas and New Year.
Rooms 20 double, 4 single – 4 with bath, 15 with shower. 7 in nearby annexe.
Facilities 3 sitting-rooms, basement café, dining-room; some off-season conference facilities; games room, badminton. Garden and terrace; sailing, fishing, boating, cycling and good walks.
Location At tip of Folgefonn Peninsula; at Odda cross bridge on to peninsula, or take ferry from Kvanndal or Kinsarvik.
Restriction Not suitable for &.
Credit cards All major cards accepted.
Terms B&B 275–460 Nkr. Set lunch 125 Nkr, dinner 170 Nkr. Reductions for long stays. 50%–70% reduction for children under 12 in parents' room.

VOSS 5700   Map 1

Park Hotell Voss   *Tel* (05) 51.13.22
Boks 190   *Fax* (05) 51.00.39
                                                         Telex 42587

Voss is a well-known resort at east end of the Vangsvatn, in the heart of beautiful fjord country – Sognefjord to the north, Hardangerfjord to the south – a region of orchards, waterfalls, glaciers, winter sports. The Park is central; well run, with attractive public rooms and bedrooms, "magnificent" buffet dinner including four hot dishes, good breakfasts. Coffee bar always open. Bedrooms "nice but small". 106 beds. B&B double 850–2,100 Nkr. Set meals 175 Nkr. New nomination. More reports please.

> There is inevitably less feedback from Scandinavia than from other more touristy parts of Europe. If you have been to Scandinavia and stayed in a good hotel, whether in the present Guide or not, please write and tell us.

ESTALAGEM QUINTA DA CAPELA, SINTRA

AMARANTE 4600 Porto   Map 6

Zé de Calçada   *Tel* (055) 42.20.23
Rue 31 de Janeiro

Amarante is a picturesque small town, its 16th-, 17th- and 18th-century
houses with wooden balconies and wrought-iron grilles are built in tiers
up a hillside overlooking the river Tâmega. It is well-known for its
pastries and its vinho verde, and now appears in the Guide for the first
time with this nomination: "Just by the old bridge in the centre stands the
Zé de Calçada restaurant with a rustic decor, where you eat well and
prettily on the riverside terrace. It has a house across the narrow cobbled
street containing seven bedrooms, each with a bath, one with a kitchen
too. All are refurbished, with a touch of the Laura Ashleys. Mount, if you
can, the four flights of gleaming wooden steps to the topmost room which
has a tiny terrace and a three-star view of the Italianate front of the
church of San Gonçalo, the patron of conjugal love – on his day the town

celebrates by baking properly priapic pastries. Amarante's finest residence is being converted into a spectacular *pousada*, but we shall return to the *Zé de Calçada*.'' (*Christine and Stephen Wright*)

Open Probably all year.
Rooms 7 double – all with bath, 1 with kitchen. All in building opposite restaurant.
Facilities Restaurant; terrace.
Location In centre of town 64 km E of Oporto.
Credit cards Possibly some accepted.
Terms Double room 6,150 esc. Set dinner 1,500 esc.

ARMAÇÃO DE PERA 8365 Faro   Map 6

Hotel do Levante   *Tel* (082) 323.22
                                                        Telex 57478 LEVANT

Eight miles west of Albufeira, on the Algarve coast, a modern family-run holiday hotel, functional but attractively so, set on a cliff above a lovely sandy beach. Large swimming pool, lido and garden; fine views. Service good and cooking well above average, especially fish. 41 rooms, all with bath and shower. B&B: single 4,300–11,500 esc, double 6,050–16,500 esc. Set menu 2,500 esc [1989]. Recent nomination. More reports please.

AZEITÃO 2925 Setúbal   Map 6

Estalagem da Quinta das Torres   *Tel* (065) 208.00.01

Azeitão, on the old Lisbon–Setubal road, consists of two small adjacent villages set amid vineyards and olive orchards. It is a good base for touring the Arrabida peninsula with its beautiful coastline and fine beaches. The *Quinta das Torres* – "a poetic retreat" – is a beautiful rather shabby old house, said to have been an elegant social venue for the wealthy residents of Lisbon before the 1974 Revolution, in its own grounds, with a small ornamental lake. It is finely furnished with family antiques, portraits and prints (including, oddly, some of Scotland). Readers enjoy its "old-world charm, tinged with gentle melancholy" and the high-ceilinged bedrooms. One is in a tower wing overlooking the courtyard with its Renaissance fountain and orange trees, and has a four-poster bed "worthy of Catherine of Braganza". "Dinner was excellent and exquisitely served; breakfast is taken in the bedroom." "Wholeheartedly endorse your report. It is one of the most atmospheric places to stay in Portugal." (*ATW Liddell*)

Open All year.
Rooms 2 suites, 6 double, 2 single – all with bath, shower and tea-making facilities. 2 bungalows in grounds with kitchenette and lounge. Some ground-floor rooms.
Facilities Lounge, bar, restaurant; terrace. 30-acre grounds. Sandy beaches 15 km.
Location 27 km W of Setúbal off N10; in village centre. Parking.
Credit cards None accepted.
Terms On application.

Report forms (Freepost in UK) will be found at the end of the Guide.

BOM JESUS DO MONTE 4700 Braga   Map 6

Hotel do Elevador   *Tel* (053) 250.11
Parque do Bom Jesus do Monte

Bom Jesus is a 19th-century religious shrine on a mountain-top just outside the old town of Braga, in the "tender green vinho-verde country of the Minho, glorious to drive through, with some interesting old towns and villages". The old-style *Elevador* is inside the park surrounding the shrine. It is a small hotel, "the best at Bom Jesus, with an old-fashioned elegance and fantastic views, more a place for the Portuguese than foreign tourists, so it has not been gussied up and spoiled". A recent visitor praised her large and comfortable room with lovely views and found the staff very friendly. The food has been described as "standard hotel type", but there's a good selection of local wines. More reports please, especially on the food.

Open All year.
Rooms 25 double – all with bath.
Facilities Salon, restaurant. Garden.
Location 50 km NE of Oporto, 6 km SE of Braga.
Credit cards All major cards accepted.
Terms [1989 rates] B&B double 8,500 esc. Full board 7,450–10,700 esc. Set meals 1,700 esc.

BUÇACO 3050 Aveiro   Map 6

Palace Hotel do Buçaco   *Tel* (031) 931.01
Floresta do Buçaco   *Fax* (031) 936.09
                                                     Telex 53049 BUCACO

Readers continue to disagree about the merits of this 19th-century royal hunting lodge situated in the middle of the ancient oak and cypress forest on the ridge of Buçaco, described by Wellington as "a damned long hill". Wellington prepared for battle against Masséna in the Carmelite convent next to the hotel. The *Palace Hotel* itself is decorated with faience and paintings illustrating both the battle and Portuguese maritime journeys. "It's difficult not to succumb to its cake-frosting architecture – like a wealthy dowager, who has piled on the rouge and ruffles and yet is fun to be around. I highly recommend this hotel. Even with its rough edges and excesses, it is a wonderful stop." (*Suzanne Carmichael*) But also, "Wins the prize of the decade as the hotel we least wish to return to." Or, "The charm of the place is its run-down old maple furniture, its quaint plumbing, and its period atmosphere – a bit like a Portuguese version of *Raffles* in Singapore"; and, "Bathrooms are ghastly – worn enamel, stained loos, and tatty decoration – untouched for thirty or forty years." Now much frequented by coach parties, it is praised for its good wine list. The owners tell us that the hotel is being completely renovated this year. More contributions to the debate welcome.

Open All year.
Rooms 4 suites, 56 double – all with bath and telephone. Some ground-floor rooms.
Facilities Lifts. Salon, TV room, bar, restaurant; conference facilities. Garden and large park; tennis courts.
Location 22 km N of Coimbra on N234.

Credit cards All major cards accepted.
Terms B&B: single 17,300 esc, double 18,150 esc. Set lunch/dinner 3,100 esc.
Reduced rates and special meals for children.

CASCAIS 2750 Lisbon   Map 6

Hotel Albatroz   *Tel* (01) 28.28.21
Rua Frederico Arouca 100   *Fax* 284.48.27
                                            Telex 16052 ALTROZ

A trim classical villa, built for the Portuguese royal family in the mid-19th
century, now a hotel with a modern wing, and "highly recommended for
understated luxury". It is set on a rocky headland by the sea, in a
relatively unspoiled fishing-port west of Lisbon; most rooms have
panoramic views over the Bay of Cascais and the adjacent coastline.
Recent reports praise the locally popular restaurant, the immaculate linen
and towels, the comfortable beds, and the service; a writer who has
known the hotel for years now finds it "quite restored to its former
excellence". (*Suzanne Carmichael, Ralph Dubery, and others*) Some readers,
however, have had reservations: poor reading lights in the bedroom,
variable housekeeping, and discourtesy from the staff at reception.

Open All year.
Rooms 3 suites, 36 double, 1 single – all with bath and shower, telephone, radio
and TV; most with air-conditioning and balcony. 2 ground-floor rooms.
Facilities Lift. Salon, bar, TV room, dining room; conference facilities; terrace.
Music evenings. Unheated saltwater swimming pool.
Location On bay, near station. Parking.
Restriction Not suitable for &.
Credit cards All major cards accepted.
Terms B&B: single 13,000–26,500 esc, double 15,000–31,000 esc, suite 21,000–
45,000 esc. Full alc 5,500 esc. Reduced rates for children; special meals on request.

Estalagem Senhora da Guia   *Tel* (01) 28.92.39 and 28.97.85
Estrado do Guincho   *Telex* 42111 GUIA

"Two families – two adults and two children each – were made to feel *so*
welcome. Every request was answered and the children were treated like
royalty. Breakfasts out of this world, including fresh fruit, as much as we
wanted to eat, and we were never hurried. Our bedrooms were spotless,
clean towels all the time, beds turned down at night." "Food good and
clientele civilised." "Pleasant atmosphere, still something of a private
house." This enticing white-walled holiday hotel on a promontory amid
trees, about ten minutes' drive from Cascais, was once a villa built by a
brewer. Some of the rooms have been converted from the stables, others
have terracotta-tiled balconies with coastal views, where one can
breakfast or have drinks. The large, comfortable lounge/bar and
restaurant are "beautifully kept"; drinks and meals are also served on the
terraces in the garden by the ample but unheated sea-water swimming
pool. (*Susan Haskell, HR, and others*) A drawback is the hotel's position –
"it is on the main road, with the constant noise of traffic passing along the
coast, and is in a very windy spot". And one reader this year considered
the meals "not wonderful, and rather pricey", but concluded, "we would
certainly recommend this hotel to our friends".

Open All year.
Rooms 4 suites, 24 double – all with bath and shower, telephone, baby-listening; TV on request. 12 in 2 annexes. Some ground-floor rooms.
Facilities Lounge/bar with fireplace and balcony, restaurant. *Fado* singers once a week. Garden with swimming pool, children's pool, bar/restaurant. Beach 3 km (bus from hotel). Golf, tennis and riding nearby.
Location 2 km W of Cascais on road to Guincho.
Restriction Not suitable for &.
Credit cards All major cards accepted.
Terms B&B: single 6,500–20,500 esc, double 7,000–21,000 esc, suite 12,000–25,000 esc; dinner, B&B: single 9,000–23,000 esc, double 12,000–26,000 esc, suite 17,000–30,000 esc. Set lunch/dinner 2,500 esc. Children under 8 half price; special meals on request.

ESTOI 8000 Faro   Map 6

Monte do Casal   *Tel* (089) 91503 and 91341
Cerro do Lobo   *Telex* 56682 MONTCA
Estoi, Nr Faro

Converted farmhouse with swimming pool, and one-acre garden, run by English couple, Bill and Carol Hawkins. Twenty minutes by car from Algarve coast. Recommended – "if you have to be near this overdeveloped area" – for tranquil setting, informal atmosphere, simple, clean bedrooms, reasonable food. No children under 16. Open 2 Mar–4 Jan. Limited menu on Mon. 3 suites, 4 double rooms, all with bath and shower; 4 more planned for 1990. Double room £30–£53, suite £39–£70. Set lunch £8.75, dinner £12.75. New nomination. More reports please.

FUNCHAL 9000 Madeira   Map 6

Quinta Penha de França   *Tel* (091) 290.87
Rua da Penha de França 2

This small hotel of real character, "an astonishing green oasis, not far from the centre of busy Funchal" is exceptional in Madeira's sadly overdeveloped capital, now crammed with many large and impersonal hotels. It is an old building in a charming garden and several readers have written this year in praise of "the peace and comfort among the high-rise horrors", the friendly, hard-working staff, the "very leisurely, elegant" breakfasts on the terrace, and the "nicely furnished, very comfortable" bedrooms, particularly the studios in the grounds, and the rooms in the handsome new annexe. "The sea-water swimming pool is spotless; there are several restaurants within walking distance, but if you are unambitious you can survive pleasantly on the *quinta*'s simple but tasty and nicely presented meals – soups, salads, omelettes, dish of the day and fruit – served on the terrace. Recent visitors have not been bothered by evidence of package trade; the building works in the neighbourhood are now completed, but during the day there can be some noise from the harbour below. (*Mrs A Colbatch Clark, Isabel and John Brasier, Dr and Mrs IM Ingram, and others*)

Open All year.
Rooms 35 double – all with bath and/or shower, and telephone. Some in annexe, some in garden studios.

Facilities Lounge, snack bar, terrace. Large garden with sea-water swimming pool; near sea and rock beach.
Location Central.
Restriction Not suitable for &.
Credit cards All major cards accepted.
Terms [1989 rates] B&B double 12,000 esc. (No restaurant, but light meals served.)

Reid's Hotel   *Tel* (091) 230.01
Estrada Monumental 139   *Fax* (091) 304.99
                                                             Telex 72139

A large, grand and very famous 19th-century hotel on the outskirts of Madeira's capital, set gracefully apart on a cliff above Funchal Bay with magnificent semi-tropical gardens and numerous impressive and high-ceilinged public rooms, including a "superb pre-war style billiard room". There are two swimming pools on the level of the hotel, where a buffet lunch is served, and you can walk down through the gardens to swim in the sea or in a rock pool. *Reid's* has over the last few years been extensively renovated, and all the sea-facing rooms now have a balcony, but it keeps up the old traditions such as afternoon tea on a terrace and formal dress at dinner, where a pianist plays "the tunes of yesteryear". It has many devotees who return year after year. "After a break of three years, nothing seemed to have changed – that is why so many visitors go back. We recognised many old faces, both staff and guests. An ideal place for total rest. We had a quiet, spacious bedroom in the main building; rooms are not luxurious but very clean and comfortable, with excellent housekeeping and the most charming and discreet chambermaids. Service could not be faulted. In the dining-room there is a set menu with a reasonable amount of choice; the Grill Room has more choice, on an à la carte menu; it is more expensive, but not necessarily better. *Reid's* reminds me of one of those traditional hotels in India, but with the the benefit of Madeira's equable climate, high standards of cleanliness and expertise of service and management." (*Alan Greenwood; also Isabel and John Brasier*) The hotel tells us that a new road will take much transit traffic away from the rear of the building. A new manager arrived early in 1989 so we'd be glad of more reports.

Open All year.
Rooms 15 suites, 145 double, 21 single – all with bath and/or shower, telephone, radio and baby-listening. Suites have TV. Room service.
Facilities Lifts. 3 lounges, 2 bars, TV room, card room, restaurant, grill room; tea terrace. Large garden with 2 heated swimming pools, 2 tennis courts; lift and 3 flights of stairs down to sea with swimming pool, changing rooms and bathing platform; windsurfing, sailing, fishing etc.
Location 1 km from town centre.
Restriction Not suitable for severely &.
Credit cards Access, Amex.
Terms [1989 rates] B&B: single £61–£91, double £88–£141, suite £140–£500. Half board £19 added to room rate, full board £34 added. 1-night bookings sometimes refused over Christmas/New Year. Reduced rates and special meals for children.

In Portugal, reservations for pousadas can be made direct or through Enatur, Avenida Santa Joana Princesa, 10-A, 1700 Lisbon.Tel (01) 88.12.21. Telex 63475.

GUIMARÃES 4800 Braga

Map 6

Pousada da Santa Marinha   *Tel* (053) 41.84.53
Estrada da Penha   *Telex* 32686

This ancient town at the foot of the mountains north-east of Oporto was the birthplace in 1109 of Portugal's first king, Alfonso Henriques, and is now a prosperous commercial city. It has two *pousadas*, the centrally situated *Santa Maria da Oliveira*, a quite small, remodelled 17th-century castle, which is omitted this year for lack of feedback, and the *Santa Marinha*, newly opened and luxurious, and recommended to the Guide this year. It is a former monastery, set above Guimarães, overlooking the surrounding hills, with beautiful cloisters with fountains, formal gardens "and lots of fascinating nooks and crannies". The original church next door still operates. Some bedrooms are in a lower wing, modern, luxurious, but impersonal; the most attractive ones are in the former cells. "This was one of the most spacious, well-furnished *pousadas* we visited. It is discreetly grand, with enormous reception rooms filled with antiques, oil paintings, luxurious carpets, hand-painted wall tiles. The cells are off a vast hall, and are comfortably furnished, each with private bath; ours had an unusual small double window with a prayer stool. They look over the garden or the town (we recommend the town view)." "The dining room is a somewhat cavernous refectory with high ceilings, many archways. Food typically *pousada*, i.e. acceptable but not noteworthy. Probably the best *pousada* in Portugal; prices are high as it is in the de luxe range." "Service efficient and unobtrusive, room quiet and comfortable, gardens and woods to wander in. Peace and tranquillity." (*Nigel and Sarah Walker, Suzanne Carmichael, ATW Liddell, RM Rowan*)

Open All year.
Rooms 51 – all with bath and shower.
Facilities Lift, salons, bars, dining-room; conference facilities; courtyard, terrace, garden.
Location 2.5 km E of Guimarães on road to Penha.
Credit cards All major cards accepted.
Terms [1989 rates] B&B: single 7,500–12,600 esc, double 10,000–14,400 esc. Set meals 2,500 esc.

LAMEGO 5100 Viseu

Map 6

Villa Hostilina   *Tel* (054) 623.94

A former farmhouse on a hill overlooking the attractive old town of Lamego, in a wine-growing area near the Douro Valley. "A beautiful location. There always seems to be a festival going on. From the little tiled terrace that leads off your bedroom, gentle vine-covered hills roll into the blue distance. Immediately below is the house's own vineyard where, if you're up early enough, you can watch the workers tend the vines. It is the most peaceful prospect imaginable. Downstairs a breakfast awaits you, both generous and gorgeous to behold – figs, peaches, quince jelly." Other readers add: "Breakfast was the best we had in Portugal, especially the caramelised plums and freshly made pineapple cake." "The service was cheerful." The villa is comfortable and up-to-date, with its own health centre and gym, and the welcome is warm. Guests may find themselves invited to eat with the Senhor in his private dining-room.

"Happily I was able to praise all the food – which *was* delicious. Our host was delightful, but conversation (in my laborious pidgin Portuguese and English) was a bit of a strain." Others have found communication easiest in French. There is no restaurant, but there are places to eat nearby. Don't miss the amazing staircase of over 600 steps leading up to the shrine of Our Lady of the Cures, a flowering of the Baroque concept, surrounded by lush woodland. (*Deborah Loveluck, and others*) A July 1989 report tells of major building work close by seriously impairing "the beautiful location".

Open All year.
Rooms 7 double – all with bath, shower, telephone, radio; TV on request.
Facilities Lounge, TV room, bar, dining room; health centre with gymnasium, massage, sauna etc. Garden with swimming pool (unheated) and tennis courts. River with fishing rights nearby.
Location 1,000 metres from war memorial; private parking.
Credit cards None accepted.
Restriction Not suitable for &.
Terms [1989 rates] B&B: single 6,000 esc, double 8,500 esc. Extra bed 3,000 esc. Meals by arrangement.

LISBON   Map 6

Hotel Príncipe Real   *Tel* (01) 346.01.16
Rua da Alegria 53, Lisbon 1200   *Telex* 44571 PREAL

Clean and comfortable, centrally located near Botanical Gardens, Avenida da Liberdade and the Bairro Alto, known for its restaurants and casas de fado. *Comfortable lounge. Rooms vary: some have balcony, about half are air-conditioned, but some are said to be small and dull. Staff friendly. Top-floor breakfast room with panoramic views over Lisbon. 24 rooms, all with private facilities. B&B: single 8,000–13,000 esc, double 10,000–16,500 esc. Set menu 1,200–1,500 esc. More reports please.*

Albergaria da Senhora do Monte   *Tel* (01) 86.28.46
Calcada do Monte 39
Lisbon 1100

In residential area with colourful tile-faced houses, small shops and cafés, few tourists. Slightly awkward to find, the exterior is more like a house than a hotel. Inexpensive simple accommodation – clean, comfortable bedrooms with modern bathrooms; some, on ground floor, have terrace, others have marvellous views over Lisbon. "We felt someone had placed the city at our feet." Basement bar, continental breakfasts, no restaurant. 27 rooms, all with bath and shower. B&B single 6,000–6,500 esc, double 7,000–7,800 esc, suite 8,500–9,500 esc. More reports please.

Hotel Tivoli Jardim   *Tel* (01) 53.99.71
Rua Julio Cesar Machado 7   *Telex* 12172 JARDIM
Lisbon 1200

A useful modern establishment, centrally located just off the city's main avenue, and catering for the business and package trade as well as the individual traveller. Readers enjoy the comfort, good food, quiet location down a side street, and general value for money. "Nothing fancy, but adequate facilities, friendly staff and pleasant atmosphere". It should not be confused with its sister hotel, the *Tivoli*, next door, with which it shares "a very pleasant swimming pool surrounded by a lawn". More reports please.

Open All year.
Rooms 69 double, 50 single – all with bath and shower, telephone, radio, TV, air-conditioning and mini-bar.
Facilities Lift. Hall, bar, restaurant. Gardens with Tivoli club, heated swimming pool, tennis.
Location 10 mins from town centre, off Avenida da Liberdade, NE of Botanical Gardens. Garage and carpark.
Restriction Not suitable for &.
Credit cards All major cards accepted.
Terms [1988 rates] B&B: single 9,000–10,000 esc, double 11,000–12,500 esc. Full alc 1,550–2,780 esc. Reduced rates for children sharing parents' room.

York House (Residencia Inglesia)
Rua das Janelas Verdes 32
Lisbon 1200

Tel (01) 66.24.35
Telex 16791

In a somewhat inconvenient location two kilometres from the city centre, but near the National Art Museum, embassies, and the Tower of Belem, a converted 17th-century convent with an annexe across the street (the latter recently redecorated in contemporary style). Its great attraction is its shady courtyard for drinks and snacks – "an oasis of calm". Front rooms overlooking a tram route are noisy; courtyard ones are quieter. Staff friendly. Meals in a charmingly tiled old refectory are not recommended. 48 rooms, all with bath or shower. B&B: single 13,500 esc, double 15,700 esc. Set meals 2,500 esc. More reports please.

MANTEIGAS 6260 Guarda　　　　　　　　　　　　　　**Map 6**

Pousada de São Lourenço
Tel (075) 981.50 and 981.73
Telex 53992 PSLOUR

"The views are splendid, the surrounding scenery is spectacular, the location very peaceful." High on the Serra da Estrela, this pousada is 13 kilometres up the mountain from the old town of Manteigas. It is well placed for exploring this highest part of Portugal. "We were made very welcome", runs one recent report. "The hotel has a family feel and the cooking is homely and generous to match." "The charming and locally costumed restaurant staff could not have been nicer. After finishing a gargantuan dinner (we had forgotten that the fish and meat courses would both come with substantial vegetable accompaniment), we were presented with *pousada* port 'on the house'. The breakfast included fruit juice, fresh fruit, local mountain cheese, ham, rolls, toast, madeira cake, butter, jams and good coffee and tea." (*WK Reid*) Rooms are pleasantly furnished, and there's a terrace where you can sit gazing down over the valley. Best for a summer visit: it can be bleak in winter and the snow can be nine feet deep. The local lake, near Penhas Douadas, has a small beach surrounded by wooded slopes, "and the water is clear and like warm milk to bathe in". (*J Hillas, and others*)

359

Open All year.
Rooms 23 double – all with bath and shower; some with balcony. 7 ground-floor rooms.
Facilities Bar, TV room, restaurant. Garden. Lake with beach and safe bathing 4 km.
Location 13 km N of Manteigas on estrada de Gouveia.
Credit cards All major cards accepted.
Terms B&B: single 4,000–7,700 esc, double 5,300–8,800 esc. Set lunch/dinner 2,250–2,400 esc. Reduced rates for children sharing parents' room.

MARVÃO 7330 Portalegre   Map 6

Pousada de Santa Maria   *Tel* (045) 932.01
                                                  Telex 42360 PMARIA

A simple, small and charming *pousada*, built of stone with tile floors, in an equally small and charming village on a rocky escarpment near the Spanish border, four miles north of the main Lisbon–Madrid road, thus useful for a stopover. The white houses and narrow cobbled streets are entirely inside the walls of a castle over which the keep stands guard. You can walk round the ramparts, looking within at the roofs, gardens, chicken runs, kitchens and television sets, or without over the Sierra de Torrico in Spain and the valleys below in Portugal. Its entry is warmly endorsed again this year: "A wonderful place to stay, and very accommodating. When we checked in they showed us to one of their newer rooms – perhaps assuming that being American we would prefer it; it was nice but not special. We asked if there was anything in the older section and were given a small but pretty room with a balcony from which you could see hills, farms, and Spain." Other readers, however, have been enthusiastic about the "very attractive new rooms, with air-conditioning". "The staff are young, enthusiastic and eager to help." "Bedrooms comfortable, public rooms well-furnished, good local food and vinho verde at dinner; breakfast excellent." (*Suzanne Carmichael, Mrs JE Lyes, and others*) One reader, while agreeing about the breakfast is less enthusiastic about the dinner.

Open All year.
Rooms 1 suite, 12 double – all with bath and telephone, baby-listening on request. Some ground-floor rooms.
Facilities Lounge, bar, TV room, restaurant. Garden.
Location 27 km N of Portalegre on N521.
Credit cards All major cards accepted.
Terms [1989 rates] B&B: single 5,000–9,400 esc, double 6,500–10,600 esc, suite 9,000–14,300 esc. Set lunch/dinner from 2,100 esc. Reduced rates for children under 10 sharing parents' room; special meals on request.

MIRANDA DO DOURO 5210 Bragança   Map 6

Pousada de Santa Catarina   *Tel* (073 422.55
                                                      Telex 22388

Miranda do Douro is a small town in north-east Portugal, dramatically perched above the Douro valley where it divides Portugal from Spain. It is a timeless place, with its own special dialect, rather similar to low Latin; on special holidays the local men, wearing white kilts and black, colourfully embroidered shirts, perform the Pauliteiros Dance, a rhythmic stick dance, reminiscent of sword-fighting. The *pousada*, new to the Guide this year, is small, purpose-built, not aesthetically pleasing, but bright and airy. The bedrooms, with balcony, and the "very pleasant dining-room and lounge" overlook the splendid view. "Our room was well-furnished and had plenty of drawers and wardrobe space, the bathroom, also spacious, was one of the best we had in three weeks in Portugal. The staff were welcoming and meals *much* better than those we had in higher-priced *pousadas* elsewhere." "Upholstery in the lounge needed repair, rugs needed cleaning, but we learned that money was not forthcoming owing to the *pousada*'s out-of-the way situation. However, the charming and friendly manager and dramatic setting made this a pleasant place to stay." (*John Hillas, Suzanne Carmichael*)

Open All year.
Rooms 12 – all with bath/shower, telephone.
Facilities Lounge, dining room.
Location 83 km SE of Bragança, near Spanish border.
Credit cards All major cards accepted.
Terms [1989 rates] B&B: single 4,000–7,000 esc, double 5,300–8,100 esc. Set meals 1,950 esc.

MONCHIQUE 8550 Faro	Map 6

Estalagem Abrigo da Montanha	*Tel* (082) 921.31

Corte Pereira/Estrada de Foia

"The warmth of welcome was most endearing, they are all so anxious to please", writes a visitor this year to this small family-owned restaurant-with-rooms, a pretty building in a flower-filled garden. The surrounding forests of cork, chestnut and eucalyptus trees are lovely, and the inn, which is halfway between the Algarve hill-town of Monchique and the peak of Foia, has fine views over green hills, lush valleys and the coastline. There is a main building and, at the other end of a pretty garden, a tier of separate apartments which readers have approved. "Breakfasts are memorable, with freshly squeezed orange juice, and local honey; given notice they are willing to arrange any requested dish for dinner." Lunch on the terrace under the chestnut trees with the sweeping view of the valley below is also described as "memorable". The peacefulness of the surroundings is only slightly marred by the rock quarry down the hillside. Prices are very modest. (*Mrs RB Richards*)
Warning: It can be cold and wet in Monchique even when blazing on the coast, and the peace can be shattered when coach parties arrive for lunch.

Open All year.
Rooms 3 suites, 5 double – all with bath, shower and telephone. 2 suites in annexe.
Facilities Lounge, bar with TV, dining room; terrace. Garden.
Location About 25 km inland from Portimão. Hotel is 2 km from Monchique on road to Foia.
Restriction Not suitable for &.
Credit cards All major cards accepted.
Terms B&B: single 7,700 esc, double 8,000 esc. Alc meals (excluding wine) 1,500–2,400 esc.

When hotels have failed to return their questionnaire, we have quoted 1989 prices, with a note to that effect.

MONSARAZ 7200 Évora   Map 6

Estalagem de Monsaraz   *Tel* (066) 551.12
Largo de S. Bartolomeu

Modest little inn, charming in a simple, rural way, in old fortified town on a hilltop near the Guadiana Valley on the border with Spain, much visited by tours by day, but totally quiet at night. Overhanging beams, tiny stairs, rooms and bathrooms at different levels. Tiny dining-room serving acceptable fare, handkerchief-size garden with mini swimming pool. Very cheap – rates on application. New nomination. More reports please.

ÓBIDOS 2510 Leiria   Map 6

Pousada do Castelo   *Tel* (062) 951.05
Paço Real   *Telex* 15540 POSOBI

A 15th-century castle, now a small, fairly expensive pousada, *above little walled medieval hilltop town, rather spoiled by tourism, near coast north of Lisbon. Well-restored "maintaining the ambience of an old castle without too many of the discomforts", but little in the way of public rooms. Most bedrooms overlook the delightful courtyard, not the view; the tower bedroom, supposedly the best, is poorly ventilated. "Good regional food at dinner, staff pleasant and helpful, but breakfast variable." 9 rooms, all with bath and shower, and air-conditioning. B&B double 10,000–14,400 esc. Alc meals (excluding wine) 2,300–3,100 esc. More reports please.*

Estalagem do Convento   *Tel* (062) 952.17 and 952.14
Rua Dom João de Ornelas   *Telex* 44906

Part ancient, part modern, this hotel lies just outside the walls of a medieval town full of cobbled alleys and flower-girt piazzas. Readers last year took a room in the new annexe: "Beautifully designed to blend with the older existing house and the garden. We had a very pretty room with balcony looking over to the countryside and city walls. Nice staff, and the best hotel food we had in Portugal." A frequent visitor this year concurs: "I have always found the rooms comfortable (if somewhat tiny), the decor stylish, and the food very good indeed. The building has a lot of character, and I'd be surprised if anyone failed to be enchanted." (*ATW Liddell, also Julia Mallach, and others*)

Open All year.
Rooms 6 suites, 21 double – all with bath and shower, telephone and radio; suites have TV.
Facilities 2 lounges, 2 bars (1 with TV), dining room. Garden.
Location In town centre. Parking.
Restriction Not suitable for &.
Credit cards Access, Visa.
Terms [1989 rates] B&B 3,000–8,000 esc. Half board 1,900–1,950 per person added.

Don't keep your favourite hotel to yourself. The Guide supports: it doesn't spoil.

OPORTO   Map 6

Hotel Infante de Sagres   *Tel* (02) 281.01
Praça D. Filipa de Lencastre 62   *Fax* (02) 31.49.37
Oporto 4000   *Telex* 26880 SAGRES

"A splendid old-style Anglo-Portuguese hotel", the grandest in town,
"where the British connection is still appreciated, and where you can find
superb ports and the best vinho verde outside the Tras es Montes". Many
visitors this year have confirmed this previous verdict. "We endorse all
praise for this most serious of hotels. Service is extraordinarily attentive,
both indoors and out; and you can forget all parking problems (how
Oporto has them!) once the doorman has taken over your car keys. The
rooms, public and private, are luxuriously furnished in keeping with
another era. Dornford Yates would have loved it." (*Christine and Stephen
Wright; Roger Bennett, Brian L Davis*) The hotel was originally built by a
textile magnate to accommodate his clients. The restaurant specialises in
French and Portuguese dishes, but also grilled salmon and roast beef
"English style".

Open All year.
Rooms 4 suites, 70 double, 10 single – all with bath and shower, telephone, radio
and TV.
Facilities Lift. Lounges, bar, restaurant. Garden. Sandy beach with safe bathing
15 km.
Location In city centre, near Avenida dos Aliados. Parking arranged.
Credit cards All major cards accepted.
Terms B&B: single 16,500–20,000 esc, double 19,000–25,000 esc, suite 40,000–
50,000 esc. Set lunch/dinner 3,900 esc; full alc 7,500 esc. 50% reduction for
children under 8 sharing parents' room; special meals.

Hotel Malaposta   *Tel* (02) 262.78
Rua da Conceição 80,   *Telex* 20898
Oporto 4000

*Modest hotel, central, near main station, but very quiet, simple but comfortable,
staff friendly and helpful. No restaurant, but there are plenty a short walk away.
37 rooms, some with bath. B&B single 4,300 esc, double 5,300 esc. No recent
feedback. More reports please.*

PALMELA 2950 Setúbal   Map 6

Pousada do Castelo de Palmela   *Tel* (01) 235.12.26
                                                Telex 42290

This small and pretty white-walled town stands in tiers on the northern
slopes of a hillside, 43 kilometres south of Lisbon. Here a convent, built in
1423, has been transformed into a state-run *pousada*, liked by readers
especially for its setting and its location. "High above the beautiful town
with its houses cascading down the slopes, surrounded by the plains and
olive groves, and in the distance the coastline in clear view. Our room
afforded splendid views over the plains towards Évora. The standard of
furnishings and comfort was about the best we encountered. The
swimming pool, open during the summer months, is in a delightful

location, in a low walled courtyard. The cloisters are wonderful, full of the most exotic and vivid array of plants." This year two readers report happy visits: "Beautifully maintained, marvellous flowers, very clean, unbelievable view! Excellent food (all eight of our meals very tasty), helpful and friendly waiter, large elegant room (we had four people in ours). A wonderful experience." "Breakfast (in our room) almost the best anywhere ever – offering the choice of two honeys, one mild and runny, the other dark and aromatic. Food average, with a representative selection of local dishes such as cabbage soup and ocean fish dishes, but not the hotel's strong point. But worth its entry for the position alone." (*Susan Haskell, Charles A Quest-Ritson*)

Open All year.
Rooms 2 suites, 25 double – all with bath, telephone, radio and TV. Some ground-floor rooms.
Facilities Lift. Lounge, bar, TV room, dining-room; conference room; art gallery. Large grounds with unheated swimming pool and children's play area. Sandy beaches with safe bathing and life-guard nearby.
Location 7 km from Setúbal in centre of village; signposted. Parking for 40 cars.
Credit cards All major cards accepted.
Terms [1989 rates] B&B: single 10,800–13,900 esc, double 12,500–15,600 esc. Set lunch/dinner 2,300 esc; full alc 3,350 esc. Reduced rates for children.

PONTA DELGADA Azores   Map 6

Hotel de São Pedro   *Tel* (096) 22223
Ponta Delgada, São Miguel   *Telex* 82602 BENS

Our first hotel in the Azores, on the island of São Miguel "which is like a lush, giant garden. Rows of hydrangeas separate the fields, blue-green lakes dot the volcanic countryside; there are mineral-spring spas, pineapple and tea plantations. The pavements of Ponta Delgada are made from squares of white marble and black lava arranged in artistic patterns. The hotel, a 19th-century building, is set across the street from the inner harbour; like so many others in town it is white with black volcanic stones on the edges, around windows and doors. Originally the town house of a wealthy orange importer, it is filled with antiques, comfortable furniture and warm wood tones. Our bedroom was comfortable, but not special, with a nice view to the quay. The dining room had white-clothed tables, each with a fresh bird of paradise centre-piece. Service was excellent, the food fair, the fresh pineapple for dessert exquisite. The staff was friendly; we communicated in a smattering of English and French." (*Suzanne Carmichael*) More reports please.

Open All year.
Rooms 6 suites, 17 double, 3 single – all with bath or shower, telephone and TV.
Facilities Lounge, bar, 2 restaurants. Garden. Beach 10 mins by car.
Location 5 mins from centre, opposite inner harbour.
Credit cards Probably all major cards accepted.
Terms [1989 rates] B&B: single 5,700–7,250 esc, double 6,900–11,500 esc, suite 14,000–17,500 esc. Extra bed 1,500 esc. Set lunch/dinner 1,500–2,000 esc. No charge for children under 3.

In Portugal, reservations for pousadas can be made direct or through Enatur, Avenida Santa Joana Princesa, 10-A, 1700 Lisbon.Tel (01) 88.12.21. Telex 63475.

SAGRES 8650 Faro   **Map 6**

Pousada do Infante   *Tel* (082) 642.22
                                                        Telex 57491 PINFA

"What a joy it is to be in a civilised place like this! The meals are not at all bad, and are served to perfection. We were struck by the quality of the staff." "Ideal for rest and relaxation. Hotel very clean, staff very pleasant and helpful." With those endorsements this modern purpose-built *pousada*, a short walk from the centre of a small village, returns to the Guide, having been absent only for lack of feedback. It is on the south-western tip of Europe, the point from which the great Portuguese navigators set sail in the 15th century. There are long sandy beaches nearby, though "a car is needed as the *pousada* is isolated". An earlier report described "the stunning views" and recommended Sagres as a good base from which to explore the Algarve, "though the early or late season could be chilly with strong Atlantic winds." Fish is landed daily at the port of Sagres, and *À Tasca* and *Mar à Vista* are recommended as good seafood restaurants nearby. (*HR, NR Measey*)

Open All year.
Rooms 2 suites, 21 double – all with bath and shower, telephone, radio, TV and balcony.
Facilities Lounge, bar, restaurant. Garden with terrace and swimming pool. Sandy beach 100 metres, safe bathing and fishing.
Location 35 km W of Lagos. Follow *pousada* signs in Sagres.
Credit cards All major cards accepted.
Terms B&B: single 10,800–13,900 esc, double 12,500–15,600 esc, suite 16,400–20,700 esc. Set meals 2,550–3,500 esc; full alc 5,300 esc. Reduced rates for children; special meals by arrangement.

SÃO BRÁS DE ALPORTEL 8150 Faro   **Map 6**

Pousada de São Brás   *Tel* (089) 423.05
                                                        Telex 56945

About 12 miles north of the coast town of Faro in the Algarve, this *pousada*, in a small town of Moorish origin, is on a hill with beautiful views all round. Some rooms are large, with a balcony. Readers praise "the comfort, warmth, superb service, smiling friendliness and attention, and the simple food done in the regional style, their local fish dishes are excellent." The entry is endorsed this year by *JA Matheson*: "Excellently situated. Reception was cheerful and efficient. Our room was very small, but adequate, and had been recently decorated. But it had no view, being on the ground floor. The dinner was very good and I sympathise with *Drew Smith* who complained last year that he missed the caldeirada de borrego (stewed lamb) – it was delicious. Breakfast was good value." Other readers are equally positive about the cooking: "Breakfasts probably the best we had in three weeks' touring. Delicious bread soup at dinner." (*P and M Horswell*) One correspondent, however, while liking the quiet situation and swimming pool and agreeing about good value for money, writes: "Typical *pousada* restricted menu and poor preparation and presentation." More reports please.

Open All year.
Rooms 23 – most with bath/shower and telephone.

Facilities Salon, restaurant. Garden with swimming pool.
Location 2 km N of São Brás de Alportel on the Lisbon road.
Credit cards All major cards accepted.
Terms [1989 rates] B&B: single 4,000–7,000 esc, double 5,300–8,100 esc. Set lunch/dinner 1,950 esc.

SÃO TIAGO DA GEMIEIRA 4990 Ponte de Lima   Map 6

Casa do Barreiro   *Tel* (058) 941937

A new nomination, one of the Turismo de Habitação (tourism in private homes) group. "A guest house on a gentle slope, looking down over its own vineyards to the Lima valley. It is a rectangular building surrounding a central court. Painted tiles abound, including a tiled description of the history going back to 1643 and erected when it was restored in 1928. Furnishings are rustic and antique and the house has a delightfully rural character with a very agreeable swimming pool next to the hen-run. The front rooms overlooking the vines are the nicest, though they have basins and loos, but not bath or shower – but there is a large and well-equipped bathroom serving them; they also overlook the road, but it is not busy. The back rooms are self-catering duplexes, which might be a godsend for a young family, but to my mind are lacking in atmosphere. No restaurant, but snacks are available." (*AWT Liddell*)

Open All year.
Rooms 1 suite, 6 double, 2 single – 6 with bath and shower. 2 with WC.
Facilities Salon, TV room, bar, games room. Garden with unheated swimming pool.
Location 4.5 km from Ponte de Lima.
Credit cards None accepted.
Terms B&B: single 6,100 esc, double 7,200 esc. (No restaurant.)

SINTRA 2710 Lisbon   Map 6

Estalagem Quinta dos Lobos   *Tel* (01) 923.0210
Estalagem Quinta da Capela   *Tel* (01) 929.01.70
Monserrate

Both the *Quinta dos Lobos* and its sister the *Quinta da Capela* (four kilometres down the road to Colares, past Monserrate), manor houses rebuilt after the 1755 earthquake, have been tastefully restored. An inspector last year liked them both, "At the *Lobos* I had a large bedroom with antique furniture and paintings. It was very quiet. You help yourself to drinks in the bar and sign for them. A big log fire in the candle-lit lounge, with peaceful classical music and big comfy armchairs. The *Capela*, too, is lovely – light and airy public rooms, very clean, pretty little pink breakfast room, smallish bedrooms (but not poky), and fantail doves in a garden with a pond and orange grove. Friendly staff in both places." We asked for more reports, and have two this year on the *Capela*: "Superlative, and good value. On the edge of a wooded hill, with lovely views. Magical peace: breakfast from 8 am up to noon, and it's the only hotel I've ever been in without a single admonitory notice. A big and beautiful garden and the absence of formality make one feel one is staying in a friendly Cotswold manor house." "The decor is a judicious mixture of ancient and modern, done with unerring taste. There is no restaurant, but omelettes and sandwiches are readily produced. Impeccably clean and civilised; I would rather stay here than at the *Palacio de Seteais* (q.v.) at twice the price. It's a real find." (*Ben Whitaker, ATW Liddell*). We would welcome reports on the *Lobos*.

Estalagem Quinta dos Lobos

Open All year.
Rooms 8 double – all with bath and shower, telephone and baby-listening.
Facilities 2 lounges, bar. 8-acre grounds with woods, gardens, small unheated swimming pool; near sandy beaches with fishing.
Location From National Palace of Sintra take road to Seteais, *Quinta* is on right.
Credit cards None accepted.
Terms On application. (No restaurant but use of kitchen.)

Estalagem Quinta da Capela

Open All year except Christmas.
Rooms 3 suites, 10 double – all with bath and/or shower (not all *en suite*) and telephone. 3 cottages in the garden. Some ground-floor rooms.
Facilities 2 lounges, bar; gym and sauna. Large garden with small unheated swimming pool; sandy beaches, fishing nearby.
Location 3 km W of Sintra on Colares road, next to Palace of Monserrate.
Credit card Visa.
Terms [1989 rates] B&B: single 9,000 esc, double 11,000–13,000 esc, suite 15,000 esc. Reduced rates for children sharing parents' room. (No restaurant.)

Quinta São Thiago   *Tel* (01) 923.29.23

"Not for the faint-hearted," writes a recent visitor, describing both the long rough private access road and also the *en famille* dinner arrangements and other characteristics of this 16th-century manor guest house. The *quinta* is owned and run by Tereza Braddell – Portuguese, Spanish and American by birth and English by marriage. Her establishment is mildly eccentric – utterly acceptable, indeed wonderful to some, a bit over the top to others. "The approach road is horrendous to the newcomer, but supremely worth traversing. Hospitality is generous and imaginative, and Mrs Braddell's enthusiasm for her guests' comfort is remarkable." "Once or twice a week Mrs Braddell organises a home-cooked dinner, which often ends with music and dancing. At other times she advises on restaurants in the area." "Evening meals are like successful dinner parties, eaten at a huge refectory table loaded with candles and flowers. Music figures largely." "Whether a snack or a full blown dinner, the food is superb." Bedrooms are individually furnished with antiques, and the bathrooms are decorated with hand-painted tiles. Nearby are lovely walks with plenty of bird life and wild-flowers. "Most beautiful house and setting." (*Mark Gerson, Mrs P Rowe-Evans, WA Howard, A Wheeler*) Criticisms have included an arbitrary style requiring that everyone participate in after-dinner entertainments (charades, dancing etc), an unfilled swimming pool, a poorly maintained tennis court, fitful and uneven housekeeping. The "ayes" have it, just. More reports please.

Open All year.
Rooms 1 suite, 8 double – 7 with bath, 1 with shower. 2 ground-floor rooms.
Facilities Drawing rooms, library, music room, bar. Patio, garden with swimming pool and tennis court. Sea and sandy beaches nearby.

PORTUGAL

Location 4 km W of Sintra, off road to Colares. Watch for green sign on right after *Hotel Seteais*.
Credit cards None accepted.
Terms [1989 rates] B&B double 10,000–12,000 esc. Set dinner 3,500 esc. Special meals for children.

Hotel Palácio de Seteais *Tel* (01) 923.32.00
Rua Barbosa do Bocage 8   *Fax* (01) 923.42.77
           Telex 14410 HOPASE

Immortalised by Byron in *Childe Harold*, this famous hill town is set dramatically against the north face of the *serra*. The *Palace of Seteais*, built a year before the poet's birth, sits regally about a mile away up the Colares road. It is one of the few de luxe country houses in Portugal – "a beautifully proportioned classical mansion with an elegant formal garden on one side and a series of terraces, lemon groves and wilder gardens spilling down the hillside on the other. Everything is spotless. The staff are friendly and considerate, yet discreet. The salons have fine tapestries and exceptional murals and, like the bedrooms, are carefully furnished with antiques." A report in 1989 praised the well-equipped bedrooms ("big bowls of fresh fruit, towelling gowns, even a safe") and the food – international hotel fare, but – "particularly good soups, a traditional Portuguese dish in each course, delicious Portuguese white wine, and excellent pastries. The swimming pool is heated all year and there are fine walks, to the Monserrate gardens, and in the hills around. Views from the front of the hotel up to the Pena Palace, "flood-lit at night, very romantic"; from the back, down over farmland and little hamlets to the sea. (*HMW, Alisdair Aird*)

Open All year.
Rooms 1 suite, 17 double – all with bath and shower, and telephone. Some ground-floor rooms.
Facilities Lift. Salons, bar, TV room, restaurant; terrace. Garden. Heated swimming pool, tennis courts and riding centre. Beach 10 km.
Location 1 km W of Sintra on Colares road. Parking.
Credit cards All major cards accepted.
Terms [1989 rates] B&B: single 20,500 esc, double 22,000 esc. Set lunch/dinner 4,100 esc. Special meals for children on request.

Vila das Rosas *Tel* (01) 923.42.16
Rua António Cunha, 2-4

19th-century architecturally interesting guest-house a kilometre from centre on road to Ericeira. Recommended for beautifully furnished bedrooms – "period furniture yet modern as well" – and "excellent, friendly service". Pleasant garden, tennis court. Breakfasts taken communally with other guests. Owners enjoy helping guests plan visits to nearby beaches, villages, restaurants, and will serve dinner given one day's notice. 7 rooms, all with bath or shower, 3 in garden apartment with kitchen. B&B double 7,500–10,000 esc. Set meals 3,000 esc. New nomination. More reports please.

> Italicised entries are for hotels on which we need more feedback – either because we are short of reports or because we have had mixed or inadequate reports.

VALENÇA DO MINHO 4930 Viana do Castelo   Map 6

Pousada de São Teotónio   *Tel* (051) 222.52 and 222.42
Telex 32837 PSTEOT

This welcoming *pousada* is built on the 17th-century ramparts of a Vaubanesque frontier fortress; it commands a fine view of the Minho river border with Spain and the Spanish cathedral citadel of Tuy. The pleasant modern bedrooms, the airy and comfortable lounge and restaurant all share this view. "Comfortable and clean public rooms. Great views", wrote a reader this year. Another, writing several years ago, caught the flavour: "In the Portuguese tradition, everything starts late in the morning – the hot water as well as the 8 o'clock breakfast – but we can heartily recommend this beautifully located and well-managed *pousada*. I especially recommend the Minho river salmon, and broa, the local bread made with cornmeal." Valença itself (the *pousada* lies within its walls) is trippery, but the Minho valley offers gentle classical landscapes. Readers continue to recommend the inn, even though meals have disappointed, and one reader mentions "amateurish service, e.g. wrong wine presented already opened".

Open All year.
Rooms 15 double – all with bath and shower, and telephone. 3 in nearby annexe.
Facilities Lounge, TV room, bar, restaurant. Garden. River 1 km; fishing. Sea 30 km.
Location On Portuguese/Spanish frontier, 37 km NE of Viana do Castelo, on E50.
Restriction Not suitable for &.
Credit cards All major cards accepted.
Terms [1989 rates] B&B: single 5,000–10,300 esc, double 6,500–11,500 esc. Set lunch and/or dinner 1,950 esc; full alc 5,600 esc. Reduced rates and special meals for children.

VILA NOVA DE CERVEIRA Vian do Castelo   Map 6

Estalagem da Boega   *Tel* (051) 952.31
Quinta do Outeiral, Gondarem
Vila Nova de Cerveira 4920

Four kilometres south-west of Vila Nova de Cerveira, near the Spanish border, overlooking the river Minho. Purpose-built bedrooms in bungalows, basic but clean, surrounding old quinta with reception/lounge area. Interesting, generally very good Portuguese food. Portuguese, not international clientele; staff very helpful and friendly. Swimming pool, tennis. "Amazingly cheap; not without fault, but interesting." 30 rooms, most with private facilities. B&B double 6,000 esc. Set meals 1,500 esc [1989]. New nomination. More reports please.

Pousada de Dom Diniz   *Tel* (051) 956.01
Praça da Liberdade   *Telex* 32821
Vila Nova de Cerveira 4920

An unusually atmospheric *pousada* is brought to the Guide by an enthusiastic recommendation from an American travel writer: "Vila Nova de Cerveira, at the foot of a mountain, on the bank of the Rio Minho which divides Portugal from Spain, and not far from the sea, is a quiet little town centred on a small square. We registered at a small office facing the square then walked up a cobbled path through a double walled gate to the interior of the walled city which, except for the church, is entirely owned by the *pousada*. Our bedroom, No 6, was part of a series of rooms built directly out from the ancient fortress wall. It was large, with a bathroom, separate sitting room, well-stocked refrigerator and private courtyard. The dining area was in a large modern building with views of the river, the sea, and Spain; other public rooms are in a converted old building. On Christmas Day we were the only couple in the *pousada* and it was perfect. We walked along the top of the wall and wandered the narrow streets. We were served dinner by a waiter and waitress who doubtless would rather have been elsewhere, but were charming and friendly, and the food was grand. The waiter invited us to join the staff Christmas party, but we declined, feeling this might put a damper on their fun." (*Suzanne Carmichael*)

Open All year.
Rooms 3 suites, 26 double – all with bath/shower and telephone.
Facilities Lounge, 2 bars, library, dining room, banqueting room; terraces, patios.
Location In town centre.
Credit cards Probably all major cards accepted.
Terms [1989 rates] B&B: single 7,500–12,600 esc, double 10,000–14,400 esc. Set meals 3,100 esc.

****
Traveller's tale *This small country hotel deserved all the accolades your entry accorded it. A sumptuously furnished room, an imaginative dinner with service which even the Ritz in Paris would have found hard to match. Refreshed after a night of great tranquillity, we breakfasted quietly and then sauntered out across the new-mown lawn towards the park beyond. Turning a corner, we espied a small boy instantly recognised as the proprietor's youngest son. The lad looked up at us glumly. "What have all you people come here for? I don't want you here. Why don't you all bugger off?"*
****

Spain

HOTEL LA BOBADILLA, LOJA

ALCALÁ DE GUADAIRA 41500 Seville   Map 6

Hotel Oromana   *Tel* (954) 70.08.04
Avenida de Portugal

Plenty of red print in *Michelin*, including three red gables for attractiveness and a red rocking-chair for peaceful seclusion, endorses our own
nominator's liking for this small hotel south-east of Seville, by the main
N334 road to Granada: "It is situated above the town of Alcalá de
Guadaira, by a pine forest where you can take lovely walks down to and
along the river below it. The verandas give a fine view, and the outdoor
pool is set in pleasant gardens. Privately owned by Sr Ramirez, who
carefully renovated the original building some five years ago, it's a hotel
with a very traditional Spanish feel. All rooms are large, clean and well
furnished and have balconies with views. A comfortable lounge and bar,
and simple but good food (best gazpacho ever). Management helpful and
service good." (*Angela Langdon*) Recent visitors were less enchanted with
the food and management and tell of creeping industrialisation spoiling
the views. We'd welcome more reports.

Open All year.
Rooms 30 – all with bath and/or shower, telephone and air-conditioning.
Facilities Lounge, bar, restaurant; conference facilities. Garden with swimming pool.
Location Town is 14 km SE of Seville, on N 334.
Credit cards All major cards accepted.
Terms [1989 rates] (Excluding tax) Double room 6,000–7,000 pts. Breakfast 500 pts, set lunch/dinner 2,000 pts.

ALCÁZAR DE SAN JUAN 13600 Ciudad Real　　　　　　Map 6

Hotel Don Quijote y　　　　　　　　　　　　*Tel* (926) 54.38.00
Restaurante Sancho
Av. de Criptana 5

This clean modern hotel is in a market town south-east of Toledo on the wide plain of La Mancha (hence its Cervantesian name). Though no beauty, it has large airy rooms with good bathrooms, an amiable and efficient staff, and serves excellent food. A useful stopover travelling south from Madrid. Restaurant closed Sun and holiday nights. 44 rooms, all with bath and shower. Rooms double 5,000–6,500 pts. Breakfast 350 pts. Set lunch 1,000 pts; alc dinner 3,000 pts. Recent nomination. More reports please.

ALMAGRO 13270 Ciudad Real　　　　　　　　　　　Map 6

Parador de Almagro　　　　　　　　　　　*Tel* (926) 86.01.00
Ronda de San Francisco　　　　　　　　　　　*Fax* (926) 86.01.50

A converted 16th-century convent in a small town on the open plain of *La Mancha* 190 kilometres south of Madrid – a short detour off the main road south to Granada, and an important milestone on the route taken by Don Quixote in Cervantes' epic. Readers continue to endorse the entry: "The town has many fine 16th-century buildings in a heavenly reddish stone, and a splendid main square. The *parador* is a delightful calm oasis, beautifully furnished in the public areas with handsome dark chests and tables, lots of attractive pottery about, and pleasing pictures and tapestries on the walls. Our room was large, extremely comfortable and well equipped. We chose regional specialities for dinner, enjoying a vivid roast sweet red pepper salad and roast (baby) lamb Manchego style. Breakfast was an excellent buffet – tortillas, bacon, chorizos, eggs, cold meats and toast." (*Mrs KE Rawes; Martin L Dodd*)

Open All year.
Rooms 1 suite, 48 double, 6 single – all with bath and/or shower and telephone; some with air-conditioning. 5 ground-floor rooms.
Facilities Bar, salon with TV, 2 restaurants; conference rooms. Garden with swimming pool.
Location Central (*parador* is sign-posted). Parking.
Credit cards All major cards accepted.
Terms [1989 rates] (Excluding 12% tax) Rooms: single 4,435–6,800 pts, double 7,000–8,500 pts, suite 10,500–12,855 pts. Breakfast 800 pts, lunch/dinner 2,500 pts, full pension 4,930 pts. Special meals for children.

> We are particularly keen to have reports on italicised entries.

ANTEQUERA 29200 Málaga

Map 6

Parador de Antequera
Paseo Garcia del Olmo

Tel (952) 84.02.61
Fax (952) 84.09.91

A little more than an hour by car from Málaga airport, this modern *parador*, somewhat unprepossessing in appearance, is on the outskirts of an old white-walled town – "a living, noisy place, but genuine Andalusia" – up in the hills behind Málaga and useful for exploring the Andalusian countryside away from the frenzy of the coast. It is designed rather in Swedish style with split-level reception areas and first-class furnishings; the bedrooms are large, even by *parador* standards; the interior courtyards and public rooms have decent modern furniture and antiques. "The dining room is beautiful, with flowers and well-spaced tables. The breakfast buffet was a work of art." "All the staff delightful – I couldn't believe I wasn't staying in a de luxe hotel at double or treble the price." (*Charles A Quest-Ritson, David and Angela Stewart, A and J Sennet, M and R Milner, Mrs EH Prodgers*) Some readers, while praising the rooms, report unkempt grounds, impersonal service and disappointing food. We'd welcome more reports.

Open All year.
Rooms 55 double – all with bath, shower, telephone and air-conditioning.
Facilities 3 lounges, T V room, bar, dining room; conference room. Garden with swimming pool.
Location Off N342 between Granada and Jerez de la Frontera. Hotel is on the outskirts of town. Parking.
Credit cards All major cards accepted.
Terms [1989 rates] (Excluding tax) Rooms: single 5,200–6,400 pts, double 6,500–8,000 pts. Breakfast 800 pts, set lunch/dinner 2,500 pts.

ARCOS DE LA FRONTERA Cádiz

Map 6

Parador Casa del Corregidor
Plaza del Cabildo

Tel (956) 70.05.00

A welcome return to the Guide of a *parador* that was in earlier editions until it closed some years back for extensive redecoration. "The town of Arcos is perched on a vertical outcrop of rock overlooking the Guadalete river with spectacular Andalucian views of castles and rolling country-side. The *parador* is a former magistrate's mansion in the Renaissance style, its front facing the plaza and the rear the edge of the cliff face. The interiors have been restored and, in typical Moorish style, there is a central open patio surrounded by public rooms. Ask for bedrooms overlooking the cliff – they have private patios with magnificent views. Service was especially good at reception, but only average in the restaurant, as was the food, which was expensive. Overall the setting and the hotel interiors are outstanding. It was one of the few *paradors* which were full during our trip." (*David Ball*)

Open All year.
Rooms 20 double, 4 single – all with bath and shower.
Facilities Salon with T V, bar, restaurant.
Location Central.
Credit cards All major cards accepted.
Terms B&B: single 7,450 pts, double 11,100 pts. Set meals 2,800 pts; full alc 3,100 pts.

BAGUR 17255 Gerona   Map 6

Hotel Aigua Blava   *Tel* (972) 62.20.58
Playa de Fornells, Aigua Blava   *Telex* 56000 HABIT

Built in the style of a typical Catalan village round a small fishing beach
and harbour, *Aigua Blava* has delighted readers since it first appeared in
the Guide in l979. "The best hotel on the Costa Brava", "one of the best-
run hotels in Spain". Its charm is due partly to its setting, amid trees and
rocks, on various levels, on a specially lovely stretch of coast. "It has been
extended in such a way that you never see the whole place at one go –
and everything is in the best design and possible taste. Nothing kitsch –
all fresh, spotless and loved." But the "excellent" food and "friendly and
helpful" staff also play a big role in its success story – "the waiters and
waitresses are obviously paid well and seem extremely happy in their job;
most have been working here for years." A report written some years ago
still holds good, "The *Aigua Blava* (which is Catalan for Blue Water) has
literally grown from a fisherman's hut. Xiquet (pronounced Chickee)
Sabater, who owns it, is quarter-Japanese, quarter-French, half-Spanish,
and married to a local woman. He is a great charmer. Some of his first
guests are still coming back after more than 30 years." (*AS*) Sr Sabater is
an anglophile and his hotel is something of a traditional British
stronghold, but "less encroachingly anglophilic" than one recent visitor
had feared. "The wine list is well worth exploring – there are some
wonderful, good-value Riojas." (*Minda Alexander, Dave Watts*)

Open 1 Apr–22 Oct.
Rooms 14 suites, 67 double, 8 single – all with bath and/or shower, telephone
and air-conditioning; 4 with TV; some with balcony. All in 5 different buildings.
Facilities 4 lounges, 2 bars, 4 restaurants, TV room; conference and banquet
rooms; boutique, hairdresser. Gardens with tennis (floodlit after dark), volleyball,
paddling pool, swimming pool (disco by pool every night); children's play area.
Sand and rock beach with safe bathing and water sports. Golf 7 km.
Location 4 km SE of Bagur, 8 km E of Palafrugell. Garage and parking.
Restriction Not suitable for &.
Credit cards Access, Amex, Visa.
Terms (Excluding 12% tax) B&B: single 5,100–6,500 pts, double 7,400–10,900 pts,
suite 9,700–14,900 pts; half board: single 6,400–7,900 pts, double 10,800–
15,800 pts, suite 15,600–19,600 pts. Set lunch/dinner 2,500 pts; full alc 4,000 pts.
Reduced rates for children under 7; special meals.

Parador Costa Brava   *Tel* (972) 62.21.62
Aigua Blava   *Fax* (972) 62.21.66

Nominations from two regular Guide correspondents introduce Bagur's
parador: "Aigua Blava is one of the gems of the Costa Brava, and we spent
a long weekend here in warm November sunshine. It must run the *Aigua
Blava*, which is closed in the winter, a very close second. It is a large, ugly
flat-roofed white concrete building in a fabulous setting opposite the tiny
harbour, with trees, surf, sea and sky all around you. A smiling welcome
was combined with an irresistible offer of an exceptional room with a
circular whirlpool bath big enough for 12, separate sunken shower room,
two wash basins – all in pale coffee-coloured marble. Acres of space,
enough wardrobes for a small army, large balcony." "Every outlook is
entrancing. There's a walk down through pine-woods to a sandy cove for
sea bathing. Rather cosmopolitan – no GB cars parked in rows outside the

hotel (British visitors mustn't expect fluent English at reception or in the dining room). Bedrooms are elegant. Huge squidgy chairs in the lounge. Ferocious modern paintings in soft lime greens, lemon yellow and terra cotta. The breakfast buffet is stupendous: champagne, of course, at no extra charge. Chilled melon, cherries, strawberries, grapes and plums, six different kind of juice. Baskets piled high with sugared fairy sponge cakes – croissants and bread which you toast at a revolving grill. Cold table of cheese, hams, salami, hot tray with eggs. Dinner doesn't quite match this perfection, but the fish is fresh and the meat very good." (*Angela and David Stewart, Eileen Broadbent*)

Open All year.
Rooms 72 double, 8 single – all with bath and shower, telephone, air-conditioning, balcony.
Facilities Lift. Lounge, bar, restaurant; conference facilities. Garden, swimming pool; cove for sea bathing.
Location In Aigua Blava, 3½ km from Bagur.
Credit cards All major cards accepted.
Terms [1989 rates] (Excluding 12% tax) B&B double 8,000–11,000 pts. Breakfast 800 pts. Set lunch/dinner 2,700 pts.

BAÑALBUFAR Mallorca   **Map 6**

Hotel Mar I Vent   *Tel* (971) 61.00.25 and 61.80.00
José Antonio 47-49

New plaudits for this small, inexpensive hotel in a fishing village on the rugged west coast of Mallorca, popular with readers since our first edition. There are fine views of the sea and cliffs from the hotel and its swimming pool. You can also bathe from a tiny cove about 15 minutes' stroll away by taking the winding paths through the terraced tomato fields; the hills behind the hotel offer exhilarating walking, too. Run by a brother and sister, Tony and Juanita Vives, it has been in the same family for four generations. It still retains some older features, in spite of considerable modernisation. There is antique furniture; the comfortable lounges have English books (the Vives speak excellent English) and many of the guests are British. Bedrooms are furnished in local style: some are small, but all are bright and airy. "The balconies are delightful and the bathing cove uncrowded and beautiful. We enjoyed a very good breakfast, with juicy sweet melon, served on the terrace – and dinner was a pleasant experience with good wine and straightforward home-cooking." "Don't expect luxury – but the hospitality is great and the ambience enchanting." "The two Vives work very hard and were much in evidence in the dining room in the evening. There is no beach to speak of, but the sea was beautifully warm, warmer in autumn than the swimming pool which is unheated and gets little sun owing to the hotel's north-facing position." (*A and C Herxheimer, Gabriele Berneck, and others*) One guest comments on our mention last year of the Vives' house rule of up-to-bed-by-11.30, "Some friends who were there in April report Juanita firmly urging them bedwards at *10:30*, and when Juanita urges – you go!" The dining room is closed for lunch except on Sunday, but there is a nice café down the road.

Open 1 Feb–end Nov. Restaurant closed for lunch except Sun.
Rooms 16 double, 3 single – all with bath, telephone and balcony. 8 in adjoining annexe. Some ground-floor rooms.

Facilities 2 salons (1 with TV), bar/restaurant. Terrace with swimming pool. Sea bathing.
Location 24 km NW of Palma, at entrance to village. Parking.
Restriction Not really suitable for &.
Credit cards None accepted.
Terms B&B: single 3,830 pts, double 5,170 pts; dinner, B&B: single 5,440 pts, double 8,390 pts. Set lunch/dinner 1,650 pts. 10% reduction for children sharing parents' room.

BAYONA 36300 Pontevedra   Map 6

Parador Conde de Gondomar   *Tel* (986) 35.50.00
Carretera de Bayona   *Fax* (986) 35.50.76
                                                 Telex 83424 RRPP

Bayona is famous as the Atlantic port, south of Vigo, that first received, in 1493, the news of Columbus' discovery of the New World. The white-walled *Conde de Gondomar* stands in a splendid setting high above the sea, a mock *pazo* in the public grounds of the old Monte Real fortress and governor's palace; the old walls and tower remain, but the hotel itself is thoroughly modern. A report last year: "Beautiful pool, service friendly, rooms good (you must ask for one with a view)." This year the *parador* wins praise for its food: "The most imaginative of the holiday"; "Breakfast of a high standard and dinners magnificent, with a daily change of menu – Paella Valenciana, broad beans and clams, and crêpes with cream recommended." The hotel is large, on two floors only, necessitating a lot of walking along corridors. Huge tapestries and suits of armour adorn the main staircase. The bedrooms have traditional furnishings, good lighting, comfortable beds, and well-equipped bath-rooms, though hot water isn't quite constant. "The romantic sandy beach viewed from our bedroom on closer acquaintance turned out to be shingle covered with tar and infested seaweed – but the sound of the waves breaking on the rocks more than compensated for the reality". (*C and M Dehn; M and R Milne-Day, and others*)

Open All year.
Rooms 2 suites, 106 double, 20 single – all with bath and shower, telephone, radio and baby-listening. 20 with TV. Some ground-floor rooms.
Facilities 4 salons, TV room, bar, 2 restaurants; conference facilities. Park with swimming pool, tennis court and children's play area. Beach nearby with bathing and fishing.
Location On coast, 18 km SW of Vigo by C550. Garage and parking.
Credit cards All major cards accepted.
Terms [1989 rates] (Excluding 12% tax) Rooms: single 5,800–6,850 pts, double 8,000–11,000 pts. Breakfast 800 pts; set lunch/dinner 2,700 pts. Reduced rates and special meals for children.

BENAOJAN 29370 Málaga   Map 6

Molino del Santo   *Tel* (952) 167151
Bda. Estacion s/n.   *In UK* Bury St Edmunds
                                                 (0284) 750512

British-owned and managed small hotel high in mountains two hours from coast. Old watermill set in flower-filled gardens beside mountain stream. Recommended for "breath-taking scenery, interesting excursions, warm and friendly welcome". Bird-watching, walks along river or on goat and mule tracks, cycling. "Excellent, imaginative" local and regional cooking. Three minutes' walk from Benaojan railway station. Open 17 Mar–17 Nov. 10 rooms – all with shower. B&B double 3,500–7,000 pts, family suite 4,500–9,000 pts. Set lunch 1,200 pts, dinner 1,500 pts. New nomination. More reports please.

CALA RATJADA 07590 Mallorca   Map 6

Hotel Ses Rotges   *Tel* (971) 56.31.08 and 56.43.45
Calle Rafael Blanes 21

A newcomer to the Guide last year, and now warmly endorsed, this hotel is in a small fishing resort on the north-east coast of Mallorca, near the mighty Artá caves and adjoining clean sandy beaches. It is an old stone mansion of some character, gracefully converted with attention to detail. The *patron*, Gérard Tétard, is French and his food has earned a *Michelin* rosette. "We can truthfully say that we could find no fault. Arriving at 1 am, we found the tone was set by Madame Tétard's being there to greet us and a cold meal being served in our room. The bedroom was spacious and furnished in the Spanish style; the bathroom had been equipped to a very high standard, the heating/air-conditioning unit was a welcome addition on cool April evenings. The food, as expected, was of the highest standard. In the summer one eats out in a lovely courtyard. A highly efficient small hotel run by a hard-working dedicated and delightful young couple." (*Alasdair and Moira Brown, also Ann and Sidney Carpenter*)

Open 1 Apr–30 Oct. Restaurant closed Wed morning in Oct.
Rooms 2 suites, 20 double, 2 single – all with bath and shower, and telephone.
Facilities 2 salons (1 with TV), bar, restaurant. Terrace for summer meals.
Location Fourth street to the right after the sign "Calaratjada".
Restrictions Not suitable for &.
Credit cards All major cards accepted.
Terms B&B: single 6,020 pts, double 7,490 pts, suite 10,465 pts, dinner, B&B: single 7,775 pts, double 11,000 pts, suite 13,975 pts. Set menu 2,035 pts. Full alc 3,500–5,000 pts.

CAMBADOS 36630 Pontevedra   Map 6

Parador del Albariño   *Tel* (986) 54.22.50
Paseo de Cervantes   *Fax* (986) 54.20.68

On the indented west coast of Galicia, not far from Pontevedra and the white sandy beaches of La Toja, here in the small modern port of Cambados is an attractive *parador*: "It has been converted from a beautiful aristocratic manor house set within a large walled and tree-shaded garden, and has been furnished with taste: the bedrooms have polished pine floors and luxurious bathrooms. The central courtyard with its sunshades captures the cooling breezes off the sea. Service is good, and so is the seafood. Some traffic noise at night." Endorsed recently by two readers, but more reports welcome.

Open All year.
Rooms 51 double, 12 single – all with bath and shower, and telephone; some with TV. Ground-floor rooms.

Facilities Lift. 2 salons with T V, bar, restaurant, games room. Garden.
Location Central; parking. Town is 53 km S of Santiago.
Credit cards All major cards accepted.
Terms [1989 rates] (Excluding 6% tax) B&B: single 4,800–6,800 pts, double 6,000-8,500 pts. Breakfast 800 pts; set lunch/dinner 2,500 pts. Special meals for children.

CARMONA 41410 Seville — Map 6

Parador Alcázar del Rey   *Tel* (954) 14.10.10
  Don Pedro   *Fax* (954) 14.17.12
           Telex 72992

"Here's a *parador* about which I can't eulogise enough," writes one correspondent, and he speaks for nearly all our readers. Opened by the King and Queen of Spain in 1976, it is built inside the massive walls of the ancient Moorish *alcázar* on the top of a hill, from which there are marvellous views over the wide green plain of the Guadalquivir valley, with mountains on the horizon. Moorish influences prevail in the decor – pierced wooden shutters and doors in the public rooms, a patio with a fountain in the middle. The interior walls, white-washed or of honey-coloured brick, are complemented by black or brown wooden-and-leather furniture. The swimming pool is "a model of good taste, with natural brick and grass surrounds, arcades to protect you from the sun, white-painted garden furniture and colourful flowers". In the baronial dining hall with its high beams, the food generally receives good reports – as does the service. But only the top-floor rooms have a balcony with views; there is some traffic noise if windows are opened; poor insulation between rooms and between floors continues to be mentioned this year, and one reader thought his bathroom "showed distinct signs of wear and tear". (*David Ball, and many others*) *A helpful tip*: Driving in Seville is difficult. Stay here and use the good bus service instead.

Open All year.
Rooms 51 double, 8 single – all with bath and/or shower, and telephone; 25 with radio and T V; some with balcony. 6 ground-floor rooms.
Facilities Lifts. Hall, sitting room with T V, bar, dining room; room for functions and banquets; air-conditioning. Patio and garden with swimming pool.
Location In town centre (hotel is signposted). Parking.
Credit cards All major cards accepted.
Terms [1989 rates] (Excluding 12% tax) Rooms: single 7,600–8,400 pts, double 9,500 pts–10,500 pts. Breakfast 800 pts, set lunch/dinner 2,700 pts. Reduced rates and special meals for children.

CAZORLA Jaén — Map 6

Parador El Adelantado   *Tel* (953) 72.10.75 and 72.13.03
Cazorla 23470   *Fax* (953) 72.10.75

New to the Guide this year, a *parador* built 25 years ago, 27 kilometres from the pretty village of Cazorla (shady squares, winding narrow streets, balconies cascading with flowers, towering mountains all around). "The distance seems much more because the road through the glorious national park winds up and up, and the *parador* is sited at around 4,000 feet with mountains still climbing up behind it." It has a rather austere monastic feel about it. There is a large lounge with a huge wood fire and a pleasant dining room serving excellent cold soups and traditional main courses. Our bedroom was spacious and adequate, but a little dark. It is worth asking for one with a view. The place would be heaven for the serious walker – wild goats with huge curly horns reputed to be nearby." (*Ray and Angela Evans*)

Open All year except Feb.
Rooms 33 double – all with bath and shower, telephone and TV.
12 in annexe. 4 on ground floor.
Facilities Bar, lounge with TV, restaurant. Garden, children's play area.
Location 27 km from Cazorla, in the mountains.
Credit cards All major cards accepted.
Terms [1989 rates] (Excluding 6% tax) B&B single 6,400–7,600 pts. Double 8,600–10,100 pts. Half board 2,500 pts added, full board 4,930 pts per person. No charge for child in cot.

Hotel Sierra de Cazorla   *Tel* (953) 72.00.15
Carretera de la Sierra
La Iruela 23476

A modern box-like hotel, far from expensive, and popular with Spanish families, set in lovely open country just outside the town of Cazorla. It entered the Guide last year: "It's in a fine position at the foot of the mountains of two of Spain's most dramatic National Parks, the Sierra de Cazorla and the Guadalquivir. It faces into the sun, all rooms have terraces with sweeping views. Because the ground is so steep, in the pool one has the pleasant feeling of swimming beside the treetops. The large bar – facing the view and furnished with old-fashioned armchairs with thick, thick cushions – is nice to relax in over a drink and watch the sun go down. The rooms are spacious, with a third bed in each for a child. The food, well cooked, slants towards the Spanish: local salmon and fat rainbow trout at prices that will bring a smile." "The staff are all helpful, though few speak English. The food only fair, but good for the price." (*Madeleine Polland; JR Lloyd*) A dissenter, while agreeing about the lovely setting, comments: "Service so-so, much used by coach parties, very thin walls and fittings are cheap and rather dilapidated." More reports please.

Open All year.
Rooms 30 rooms – most with bath and shower, all with balcony, telephone.
Facilities Lounge, bar, TV room, restaurant, café; solarium. Garden with swimming pool.
Location 2 km W of Cazorla, 101 km E of Jaén, in La Iruela. Parking.
Credit card All major cards accepted.
Terms B&B: [1989 rates] (Excluding tax) single 2,950 pts, double 4,700 pts.
Breakfast 300 pts; set lunch/dinner 1,100 pts. Reduced rates and special meals for children.

COSGAYA 39539 Cantabria   **Map 6**

Hotel Del Oso   *Tel* (942) 73.04.18

In the Picos de Europa National Park in northern Spain, an area renowned for winter sports, mountaineering, horseback riding, trout and salmon fishing. Handsome stone hotel in spectacular setting, with inviting public rooms, lovely swimming pool, good tennis court, spotlessly clean modern bedrooms (some with balcony). Helpful and attentive staff. Recommended "for lovers of mountain scenery, bird-watching, and comfort in out of the way places". Closed 1 week Christmas. 36 rooms, all with bath and shower. B&B double 5,550– 6,550 pts. Alc dinner 3,000 pts (1989 rates, excluding 6% tax). New nomination. More reports please.

DEYÁ Mallorca   Map 6

Hotel Es Molí   *Tel* (971) 63.90.00 and 63.90.50
Carretera de Valldemossa   *Fax* (971) 63.93.33
                                                    Telex 69007 SMOLI

This village, at the foot of the Teix mountains on the rugged coast of north-west Mallorca, has one of the loveliest settings in the Mediterranean, close to a beautiful coastline, with sunny valleys of oranges and lemons. And it is this setting above all that draws many readers back again and again to the *Es Molí.* "Luxurious. The gardens, dazzling with blossom and fruit, fragrant with scents galore, huge colourful butterflies, and the cheerful gossipy frogs shouting across the lily ponds. The stunning views to the sea and the marvellous meandering walk through olive, orange and lemon groves down to the rocky cove of Port Deyá." "For people who enjoy shade, as well as sun, the gardens are superb." Meals in summer are served on the terrace overlooking the gardens. The swimming pool is "bedazzling in its beauty"; the hotel also provides a mini-bus to its small private beach at Muleta, 20 minutes' drive away, for deep-water bathing from a rocky platform, rather than for sunbathing. (There is no nearby sandy beach.) Another reader delighted in a morning walk led by "Pepe, the mainstay at reception: he takes guests over the mountains or along the coast. We had a memorable day that ended at 5.30 pm with lunch under the trees." Other readers have referred to "the courtesy of Mr and Mrs Peters and their staff" – everyone "friendly and helpful". The hotel has been fully redecorated recently; a reader reports that the lighter, more modern rooms in the annexe "have the highest and therefore the best view of the sea". A weak point in recent years has been the food, "made of fresh and plentiful ingredients", but often unimaginative. There are still gripes, but also compliments. Service is speedier, twice a week there are numerous "delectable" hors d'oeuvre, once a week there's a "Mallorcan evening", and the menu is altogether "more adventuresome". (*Alice and John Sennett, Tim Brown; also Dr R Wise, and others*)

Open 6 Apr–29 Oct.
Rooms 1 suite, 61 double, 11 single – all with bath and shower, telephone, radio and air-conditioning; most with terrace (300 pts supplement). Annexe with 15 additional rooms 50 metres from main buildings.
Facilities Lift. 2 lounges, TV room, 2 bars, card and writing room; dining terrace, dancing by the pool weekly in summer. Large gardens with swimming pool, tennis court, pétanque. Free mini-bus to rock beach with bar; restaurant (not hotel's) 6 km away.
Location ½ km from Deyá; Palma 29 km.
Credit cards All major cards accepted.
Terms B&B: single 7,500–10,000 pts, double 13,800–18,000 pts, suite 24,000– 30,000 pts; dinner, B&B: single 9,000–11,500 pts, double 16,000–21,000 pts, suite 27,000–33,000 pts. Set lunch/dinner 3,000 pts; full alc 4,500 pts. Reduced rates for children sharing parents' room; special meals on request.

La Residencia *Tel* (34.71) 63.90.11
Telex 69570 DEYA

Smaller, more exclusive, and pricier than the *Es Moli* above, *La Residencia* also causes its admirers to reach for their superlatives: "Absolute magic – just what we needed. Peace, tranquillity, and beautiful surroundings." "Without a doubt the best hotel on the island." "Lovely place. Can't wait to get back." Two adjacent manor houses in the heart of the village have been converted most elegantly, and this setting plus the "welcoming staff" and "surprisingly good restaurant" have again pleased visitors to this visually stunning hotel, "It is in the style of a Spanish grandee's house, cool, spacious and a bit dark, the swimming pool lined with elegant cypresses and silver birches, against a magnificent backdrop of mountains and forests, and grounds of orange and lemon trees, lawns and bright flowers. Our room was a charming mixture of elegance and austerity, with antique furniture including a four-poster bed, and original modern paintings. A superb breakfast was brought punctually by smiling waiters; luxurious towels and bed-linen were changed daily. The restaurant was a beautiful evocation of a stately banqueting hall, with its minstrels' galleries and intimate alcoves, lit by white candles in silver and wrought-iron sticks and candelabra. The *nouvelle cuisine* was delicious." "Fantastic wines are delightfully served by a marvellous team of girls who have been superbly trained." (*Brian and Jan Goodenough, L Morley, and others*) There are now 15 new bedrooms in an extension by the swimming pool.

Open Easter–6 Jan.
Rooms 14 suites, 26 double, 9 single – all with bath and/or shower and telephone; baby-listening on request. 15 in new extension by pool.
Facilities 5 salons, 3 bars, 2 restaurants (1 by pool); conference room; concerts, poetry readings, fashion shows etc. in summer. 32-acre grounds with gardens, tennis court, swimming pool 15 mins from sea – private beach, snack bar, sailing, windsurfing.
Location On edge of village, on road to Sóller.
Restriction Not suitable for &.
Credit cards None accepted.
Terms (Excluding 12% tax) B&B: single 8,000–12,000 pts, double 14,000–20,000 pts, suite 23,000–25,000 pts. Set meals 4,000 pts; full alc 5,000 pts. Reduced rates for children; special meals on request.

FORMENTOR 07470 Mallorca Map 6

Formentor *Tel* (971) 53.13.00
Playa de Formentor *Fax* (971) 53.11.55
Telex 68523

"A dream spot – swimming first-class, about the best on the island – and so also the service and food. More expensive than the Es Moli, *(q.v.), but there is no comparison." In splendid setting amidst pine trees and flowers, large established hotel with air-conditioned public rooms and bedrooms, two restaurants (terrace and beach), heated swimming pool, children's pool and play area, tennis, riding and miniature golf. 127 rooms – all with bath, some suites. Single room 14,250 pts, double 22,000 pts. Breakfast 1,500 pts. Set lunch/dinner 4,950 pts [1989]. (Tax added.) New nomination. More reports please.*

GIBRALTAR

Map 6

The Rock Hotel
3 Europa Road

Tel (350) 73000
Fax (350) 73513
Telex 2238

Our first in Gibraltar. Large, old-fashioned British hotel in terraced gardens with fine views across bay to Algeciras. Sea-water swimming pool, open-air grill in summer, afternoon teas. "Like a Trust House hotel of ten years ago – a mixture of English custom and a Spanish setting, familiar yet strange. Superb lounge where most locals seem to meet; dining-room serving traditional British food rarely found now in the UK. Useful stop between the Costa del Sol and Cadiz, now that the frontier with Spain is open." 8 suites, 120 double, 32 single – all with bath and shower. B&B single £45; double £75–£85, suite £160–£210. Set dinner £15, full alc £20–£25. New nomination. More reports please.

GOMERA 38800 Canary Islands

Map 6

Parador Conde de la Gomera
Orilla del Llano de la Villa 5
San Sebastián de la Gomera

Tel (922) 87.11.00
Fax (922) 87.11.16

"If you have come this far, go just a bit further, an hour and a half by ferry, to the tiny island of Gomera." So begin, in one way or another, virtually all of our reports on this aristocratic island *parador*. The island of Gomera, neglected by the tourist hordes, is a far cry from its extrovert sister, Tenerife. It has a mountain, valleys and forests, and hidden beaches along the coast. In the capital port of San Sebastián, Christopher Columbus prepared his ships to sail for the New World (arrival nowadays is by roll-on–roll-off ferry). On a cliff above the town sits the *parador*, a long, low-built stone-and-tile mansion surrounded by a garden of date palms. "A splendid situation overlooking the harbour with attractive scented gardens." "Our main memory is of abundant birdsong and tropical trees." "It's hard to believe it's a new building. Utterly timeless and harmonious, with cool leafy courtyards and lots of lovely places to sit indoors and in the garden. The pool is sparkling. The staff, especially the receptionists, are pleasant and helpful." "Bedrooms are beautifully appointed and furnished (even the reading lamps are good) and the public rooms are magnificent." "Our bedroom was lofty and spacious; the bathroom had two large wash-basins and good plumbing." "Excellent breakfasts, efficient laundry service, and the unheated swimming pool – in a magnificent setting – was clean." (*Wendy Whelan; JS and F Waters, and others*) Only flaw in this paradise is the food: portions are "enormous" but the set menu "is uninspiring – based on tinned tuna, tinned asparagus, tinned sweetcorn. The à la carte menu (local specialities) was a much better bet, and little more expensive."

Open All year.
Rooms 1 suite, 40 double, 1 single – all with bath, shower, telephone, radio and TV.
Facilities 3 salons (1 with TV), bar, restaurant (air-conditioned). Large garden with unheated swimming pool, bar. Black sand beach 15 mins' walk.
Location 700 metres from centre of San Sebastián, overlooking the port. Parking.
Restriction Not suitable for &.

Credit cards All major cards accepted.
Terms (Excluding 4% tax) Rooms: single 8,800 pts, double 11,000 pts, suite 13,200 pts. Breakfast 800 pts. Set lunch/dinner 2,700 pts. Full alc 3,600 pts. Children under 2 free; special meals on request.

GRANADA 18009   Map 6

Hostal América   *Tel* (958) 22.74.71
Real de la Alhambra 53

More praise again for this civilised small hotel of character, splendidly situated on the hill of the Alhambra, right next to the palace. "It is in an enviable location from which you can take evening strolls around the Alhambra grounds after the tourists have left. The colourful architecture immediately attracted us. Geraniums drip from glazed pots around the windows and doors; dinner was served in an *al fresco* setting in the central courtyard." "Solid comfort amidst a treasury of art; the food isn't all that bad either, and the wines are fairly priced." "The staff were friendly and the convivial atmosphere encouraged conversations between the guests. The food was plain, but substantial and good – our vegetarian tastes catered for at a moment's notice. Our room was tiny, but this was more than compensated for by being the only one with a balcony overlooking the gardens of the *Generalife*. It was simply furnished with Moorish curtains and bedspreads and lemon-scented sheets." (*Mark and Sue Rubinstein, J Michael Morrison, Clayton Blackburn, and others*) The hotel insists on half board terms; one reader found the food too lacking in choice for other than a short stay.

Open Mar–9 Nov.
Rooms 1 suite, 8 double, 4 single – all with bath and/or shower, and telephone.
Facilities Lounge, dining room. Patio.
Location On Alhambra hill. Parking, guarded by day.
Restriction Not suitable for &.
Credit cards None accepted.
Terms Dinner, B&B: single 5,355 pts, double 9,000 pts.

Parador de San Francisco   *Tel* (958) 22.14.40
Alhambra   *Fax* (958) 22.22.64
                                                     Telex 78792

Often regarded as a flagship among *paradors*, and certainly one of the most expensive, the *San Francisco* is splendidly situated on the Alhambra hill. It has modern extensions, and has been much renovated, but its core is an old Franciscan monastery. "Such a marvellous setting," wrote an inspector last year; "the delights of sitting in the lovely patio, and walking round the garden and exquisite Moorish courtyard, outweigh most failings." Readers last year criticised front desk "hostility", but this year "our welcome was cordial and our car safely parked". "Reception was courteous and helpful despite being very busy." Bedrooms are comfortable and well furnished, with good lights. The rooms to go for are in the 200s and 300s (the 400s are downstairs and lack a view). Food continues to be a cause for grumbles – "unadventurous" – and service can be slow when the *parador* is full (which is most of the time). (*M and R Milner, A and J Sennett, Nancy Raphael, JA Matheson, and others*)

Open All year.
Rooms 39 – all with bath and/or shower, telephone and TV; air-conditioning.
Facilities Salons, bar, breakfast room, restaurant; patio, garden.
Location On Alhambra hill, 3 km from city centre. Parking.
Credit cards All major cards accepted.
Terms [1989 rates] (Excluding 12% tax) Rooms: single 10,400–11,600 pts, double 13,000–14,500 pts. Breakfast 800 pts, set lunch/dinner 2,700 pts.

GUADALUPE 10140 Cáceres   Map 6

Parador Zurbarán   *Tel* (927) 36.70.75
Marqués de la Romana 10   *Fax* (927) 36.70.76

Named after famous 17th-century artist, some of whose paintings can be seen at nearby monastery, beautiful restored convent with courtyards full of orange trees. Many bedrooms are luxurious and have good bathroom and balcony. Lavish breakfasts, with cakes and biscuits; staff friendly. A recent visitor reports the swimming pool out of commission in June, and poor insulation between rooms, but hotel otherwise satisfactory. 40 rooms, most with bath, double 6,000–8,000 pts. Breakfast 800 pts. Set lunch/dinner 2,500 pts [1989]. (Tax added.) More reports please.

GUALCHOS 18614 Granada   Map 6

La Posada   *Tel* (958) 64.60.34
Plaza Constitucion 9   *Reservations* in UK (0223) 323618

Just out of reach of the madding crowds of the Costa del Sol, Gualchos is a still unexploited inland village in the foothills of the Sierra de Lujar, in a region of almond groves. Here two adjacent 18th-century houses in the main square have been restored to create this "absolute gem" of a *posada* (inn), with terraced gardens and a minute swimming pool. Gualchos is unspoilt Spain – the square outside the hotel (almost inaccessible by car) is alive with children playing, old men talking, others drinking at the bar till 1 am. Yet the coast and Granada are only short drives away. "We endorse all aspects of your 1989 entry", wrote a reader who spent ten days at *La Posada* this year. "We must add the heavenly perfume of jasmine filling our room at night. An idyllic haven in the Spanish hills." "The restoration of the old houses is exemplary – a maze of inner courtyards and gardens on many levels provides enchanting private rooms: ours had its own large balcony/terrace and a view of mountains and Med from the bed." The owner-chef José Gonzalez trained in France and Switzerland and spent 20 years in London. His cooking is warmly commended in all our reports; many dishes have a Spanish accent, but the cuisine is essentially French. (*Lesley Heal, Kenneth Richards, and others*) But a few readers have not been so happy: "We had an inner room which was dark and airless; the small garden was pleasant but infested with flies so I had nowhere to sit and read; the food was good, but ruined by electronic music." "Extremely well restored and the food excellent, but the menu was exactly the same for lunch and dinner the whole seven days we were there – and we were not made to feel welcome."

Open All year except June, July and Aug. Closed 28–30 Sept. Restaurant closed Mon.
Rooms 8 double, 1 single – all with bath and shower.
Facilities Lounge, bar, restaurant; patio. Small garden with pergola, tiny swimming pool. Pebble beach 20 mins' drive.
Location 9 km inland from coast at Castell de Ferro which is E of Motril. Hotel is in village centre; leave your car at edge of village and walk; hotel will collect and park it.
Restrictions Not suitable for &. No children under 12.
Credit cards None accepted.
Terms Dinner, B&B 7,500 pts. Full alc 7,250 pts.

JAÉN 23000   Map 6

Parador Castillo   *Tel* (953) 26.44.11
  de Santa Catalina   *Fax* (953) 26.44.11
Carretera del Castillo

Many readers continue to praise the *Santa Catalina*: "An exquisite *parador*, the interior a fine example of creative architecture, stylish and at times breathtaking." It is a colossal eagle's nest of a castle perched precariously on a mountain above the town of Jaén, with dizzying views. Only south-facing rooms have a balcony, but all have remarkable vistas. "Lovely large rooms, cool tiled interiors, new swimming pool, good food," wrote a visitor last year. Most have been equally enthusiastic: "The ante-room to the dining room has an arch springing from each of the four corners of the room to meet 60 or 70 feet above your head, and is worthy of a cathedral. The dining room itself, with its priceless tapestries, is only slightly less grand." Since that report, dining-room and ante-room have been transposed: but no one has tinkered with the "friendly ambience" and "well-appointed rooms", nor with the "wide range of local specialities and international cuisine". (*JA Matheson, A and J Sennett*) But one reader had a different impression: the public rooms with small barred windows recalled dungeons, he found the food unimaginative or unsuccessful, the prevailing mood one of gloom. . .

Open All year.
Rooms 45 rooms – all with bath and shower, and telephone; some with balcony. 11 ground-floor rooms.
Facilities Lift. 2 lounges, chess and card room, TV room, bar, 2 restaurants; air-conditioning. Large garden with trees; swimming pool.
Location 3 km SW of Jaén.
Credit cards All major cards accepted.
Terms [1989 rates] (Excluding 12% tax) Rooms: single 6,800–7,200 pts, double 8,500–9,000 pts. Breakfast 800 pts, set lunch/dinner 2,500 pts.

LAGUARDIA 01300 Álava   Map 6

Marixa   *Tel* (94) 10.01.65
Sáncho Abarca 8

High on a hill, overlooking Riojan plain, restaurant with "truly breathtaking views" and bedrooms "well furnished with lots of cupboard space and nice bathrooms". Bar, terrace. Recommended for good food and friendly staff: "they were especially kind to my bicycle, bringing it into the entrance hall at night, after the last guest had retired." Closed 23 Dec–Jan. 10 rooms – all with bath, telephone, TV: single 2,900 pts, double 3,950 pts. Breakfast 490 pts. Alc meals (excluding wine) 1,825–2,950 pts [1989]. (Tax added.) New nomination. More reports please.

LEÓN 24001 Map 6

Parador Hostal de San Marcos *Tel* (987) 23.73.00
Plaza de San Marcos 7 *Telex* 89809 HSML

The glory of the proud city of León is its huge Gothic cathedral, one of Europe's finest. Its second glory is the former 16th-century monastery of San Marcos, with a splendid Renaissance facade: today part of it is an archaeological museum, and part is a very grand hotel (five red *Michelin* gables), recently nationalised and now a *parador*, and again admired this year. There are three-quarters of a mile of carpeted corridors, lined on both sides with exquisite reproductions of Spanish furniture through the ages. Large paintings and tapestries soften the cool stone walls; the furnishings are understated, restrained, elegant. Stone staircases are carpeted; there are fast, efficient lifts. The restaurant – "surprisingly modern in style" gives on to a summer terrace, with the river beyond; "the entrance provides guests with reassuring glimpses of chefs at work in a sparklingly clean kitchen." One recent visitor preferred the *San Marcos* to other *paradores*, "As you know, they mostly lack the personal touch, whereas this is a proper hotel and its staff are prepared to put themselves out for guests." Another, however, disagreed: "The service was offhand and the food indifferent." Another criticism: the rooms in the modern extension, while "still on the grand scale", enabled "our neighbours' (regrettably uninteresting) conversation in their bathroom to be audible in our own."

Open All year.
Rooms 13 suites, 245 double – all with bath, shower, telephone, radio, TV.
Facilities Lift. Salons, TV room, bar, restaurant, breakfast room; conference facilities; hairdresser, beauty parlour. Archaeological museum. Garden.
Location On river. Parking.
Credit cards All major cards accepted.
Terms [1989 rates] (Excluding 12% tax) Rooms: double 10,000–11,500 pts, suites 16,000–33,000 pts. Breakfast 800 pts. Set lunch/dinner 2,700 pts.

LOJA 18300 Granada Map 6

Hotel La Bobadilla *Tel* (958) 32.18.61
Finca la Bobadilla, Apartado 52 *Fax* (58) 32.18.10
  Telex 78732 BOBA

"It must be one of the great hotels of Europe" writes a reader this year of *La Bobadilla*, a modern Swiss-owned luxury hotel of striking originality and character. Set in open rolling country just off the Granada–Málaga road, it entered our pages a year ago after an inspector's report: "We were enchanted. It is not so much a building as an assembly of 35 suites, brilliantly designed; the building style is *cortijo* – that of an old country

---

Please make a habit of sending a report if you stay at a Guide hotel.

house. Once past a foyer of breathtaking beauty, you enter a quiet, almost austere world: the finest traditional materials have been used, and it is hard to believe it is all new. There is much carved wood and tile, and small patios where fountains bubble. The furniture in the suites is plain and exquisite – heavy silk curtains, dark carved woodwork, bathroom walls of plain red brick. The five-star luxury here is very subtle. Sherry greets you at lunchtime, and champagne before dinner, where the food in the charming *La Finca* restaurant is memorable (*Michelin* rosette e.g. for duck with truffles). Another correspondent adds a few more awesome details: "There is a fully equipped 'gym' for men and women, two large saunas, the most up-to-date exercise equipment, an indoor pool and a beauty salon for all treatments – with good operators. Outdoors is an enormous pool, horse riding from their own stables, and tennis courts. The cost of the suite includes riding." The grounds are extensive and "there are splendid walks in the surrounding area". It is possible to have a room, but "the suites cost only 30% more, and not to have one is to escape the special flavour and atmosphere of the hotel" – including "an open fire which was lit every evening". (*Paul M Jackson*)

Open All year.
Rooms 7 suites, 24 double, 4 single – all with bath and shower, telephone and TV.
Facilities Salons, TV room, bar, 2 restaurants; conference rooms; terraces. Garden. Indoor and outdoor swimming pool. Tennis, sauna, jacuzzi, fitness centre. Concerts weekends.
Location At Km 502 marker on N342 Granada–Málaga road, turn off towards Rute: hotel, down its own 3 km drive, is signposted.
Restriction Not suitable for &.
Credit cards All major cards accepted.
Terms [1989 rates] (Excluding tax) B&B: single 19,000–20,300 pts, double 26,000–28,700 pts, suite 36,300–38,900 pts. Set lunch/dinner 6,500 pts. Reduced rates for children.

MÁLAGA 29016   Map 6

Parador de Gibralfaro   *Tel* (925) 22.19.03
Apartado de Correos 274   *Fax* (952) 22.19.02

A *parador* of stone arcades and terraces on a hill above Málaga, with magnificent views of city, coast and mountains from bedroom balconies and public rooms. "As a blood-red sun sinks behind the Sierra Mijas, the city turns pink and the lights twinkle on – magical. Even the hideous high-rise modern blocks acquire a certain grandeur at this distance." The bedrooms (only 12, so it is essential to book) are in predictable Spanish style, with heavy carved wooden furniture and large bathrooms. A regular visitor last year noted a great improvement in the cooking. This year his report is highly critical: "Alas, little remains to be said in favour of this once outstanding *parador*, other than its magnificent views. The food very indifferent, the service poor and unfriendly, the whole place noisy, with festoons of loudspeakers in the public rooms and restaurant. A year or two ago it was difficult to get a table; now we had the place almost to ourselves." Could we have more reports, please?

Open All year.
Rooms 12 double – all with bath and/or shower, and telephone.
Facilities Lounge, bar with TV, restaurant. Terrace.
Location 3 km from town centre, on Almeria side of city, in large park.

Credit cards All major cards accepted.
Terms [1989 rates] (Excluding 12% tax) Rooms: single 6,800–7,200 pts, double 8,500–9,000 pts. Breakfast 800 pts, set lunch/dinner 2,500 pts.

MOJÁCAR 04638 Almería   Map 6

Parador Reyes   *Tel* (951) 47.82.50
  Católicos   *Fax* (951) 47.81.83
Playa de Mojácar

A modern white-walled *parador*, just outside a small ancient town on a rocky hill, above the coast and plain between Almería and Murcia. "From the road the building looks rather like a sanatorium, but inside it proves a peaceful haven from the once lovely, but now increasingly garish and touristy Mojácar. The reception area is spacious, and there are many lounges with soft leather sofas, lovely pottery, and good modern prints on the walls. Everything is built for coolness – corridors to the bedrooms are open to the sky and the bedrooms are large, forty feet from the door to the terrace. Below are terraces on different levels, a good-sized pool with palm trees, and the sea beyond. Breakfast is a vast array of meats, cheese, bacon, eggs, cakes, buns, croissants, toast, yoghurt, fruit etc. Room service is quick and efficient. This would be a good place for a complete rest or as a base to visit the many pleasant and interesting small villages nearby." (*Ray and Angela Evans; Lesley Heal*) One reader found the welcome at the *parador* "efficient, but not particularly friendly", and another mentioned "horrid muzak".

Open All year.
Rooms 98 double – all with bath and shower, telephone, and TV; some with balcony. Some ground-floor rooms.
Facilities 2 salons, bar, TV room, restaurant; terrace. Garden with swimming pool.
Location 2.5 km SE of Mojácar on N340 coastal road. Parking.
Credit cards All major cards accepted.
Terms [1989 rates] (Excluding 12% tax) Single 5,200–7,200 pts, double 6,500–9,000 pts. Breakfast 800 pts. Set lunch/dinner 2,500 pts.

MONZÓN DE CAMPOS 34410 Palencia   Map 6

Hotel Castillo de Mónzon   *Tel* (988) 80.80.75

On road to Santander, good overnight stop en route to ferry. Comfortable modern hotel inside restored 10th-century castle on a hill. Medieval, but light in feeling; rooms pleasantly furnished, opening onto central courtyard. Quiet setting, acceptable food. Closed Nov. 10 rooms, all with bath and shower, telephone. B&B double 6,500–12,000 pts. Set lunch/dinner 2,000 pts (excluding tax). New nomination. More reports please.

In Spain, reservations for state-run establishments can be made direct or through their central booking office: Central de Reservas de los Paradores de España,Calle Velazquez 25, Madrid 28001. Tel (91) 435.97.00.

NERJA 29780 Málaga   Map 6

Parador de Nerja   *Tel* (952) 52.00.50
Playa de Burriana   *Fax* (952) 52.19.97

A modern parador splendidly situated high on a cliff above the beach, at the eastern edge of one of the largest resorts on the Costa del Sol. Large well-furnished rooms with good bathrooms and sea or mountain views from their balconies. Swimming pool in a shady garden. Average parador food in a restaurant with sea views. 73 rooms, all with bath and shower, double 9,500–11,000 pts. Breakfast 800 pts. Set lunch/dinner 2,700 pts [1989]. (Tax added) Reinstated in Guide after period of rebuilding: recent visitor reports new garden, and interior looking beautiful. More reports please.

NUÉVALOS 50210 Zaragoza   Map 6

Hotel Monasterio de Piedra   *Tel* (976) 84.90.11 and 84.90.42
                                      Fax (976) 84.90.54

This "unique" hotel between Madrid and Zaragoza, dropped last year for lack of feedback, returns to the Guide with recommendations from two readers. It began life in the 12th century as a Cistercian monastery; part of it is open to the public as an ancient monument, the other part is a hotel. Surrounding the monastery are "magnificent gardens full of waterfalls – some very dramatic, and all amazing considering the miles of arid countryside around". The hotel is also impressive – the vestibule has a beautiful romanesque ceiling with paintings and gilded rib-vaulting. "There are large grand hallways and staircases and an enormous dining room, but the general atmosphere is relatively informal rather than luxurious." Bedrooms vary – "the best are roomy with a sitting-room and balcony"; others are in the former monks' cells, "most with balcony, but the rooms themselves are fairly small and plain (our bath could have done with some retiling, but the shower packed a lot of power)". An à la carte dinner was "very fresh, well prepared and enormous". Readers are cautioned that the park is a major tourist attraction; while the hotel itself remains tranquil, there are full parking lots, souvenir stands and cafés nearby. (*Stephan and Kate Murray-Sykes, Myrna Malec*)

Open All year.
Rooms 7 suites, 45 double, 9 single – all with bath, shower, and telephone. Ground floor rooms.
Facilities 2 lounges with TV, 2 cafeterias, 2 restaurants. Large park with gardens, swimming pool, tennis court. Fishing and shooting nearby.
Location Turn off main Zaragoza–Madrid road at Catalayud; hotel is 28 km S.
Credit cards All major cards accepted.
Terms [1989 rates] (Excluding tax) Rooms: single 2,700–4,500 pts, double 3,400–6,500 pts. Breakfast 375 pts. Set lunch/dinner 1,500 pts.

Many hotels put up their prices in the spring. Tariffs quoted in the text may be more accurate before April/May 1990 than after.

We need feedback on all entries. Often people fail to report on the best-known hotels, assuming that "someone else is sure to".

OJEN 29610 Málaga   Map 6

Refugio de Juanar   *Tel* (952) 88.10.00
Sierra Blanca   *Fax* (952) 88.10.00

In a state nature reserve in the foothills of the Sierra Blanca, just inland
from Marbella, this attractive little white-walled hotel is a converted
hunting-lodge, new to the Guide last year, "This is where the Spanish
come. When it's busy, you can only stay two nights. Our bedroom was
small but adequate, with a large bathroom. Comfortable public areas with
sofas and a log fire. You can find yourself legless over the generous gins
in the bar. Specialities are the superb game casseroles – we watched wild
deer on the lawn eating chestnuts. Walk up to the viewpoint for sunsets
over Marbella." This year another reader reports, "The atmosphere is
relaxing and friendly, the staff are local young ladies, the lack of skill
made up for by their charm. The food is uncomplicated but freshly
cooked and hot. The surroundings are pine forests, away from the
cosmopolitan coast line. The bedrooms are rustic, but with all amenities;
everything works, very cosy." (*David Ball*)

Open All year.
Rooms 1 suite for 6–8, 4 smaller suites, 14 double, 1 single – all with bath,
shower, telephone and TV. Ground-floor rooms.
Facilities 3 salons, 2 bars, TV room, restaurant; functions room. Garden with
swimming pool and table tennis.
Location 20 km N of Marbella, 10 km W of Ojen. Hotel is signposted.
Credit cards All major cards accepted.
Terms (Excluding 6% tax) Rooms: single 5,100 pts, double 6,200 pts, suite 8,600–
13,200 pts. Breakfast 600 pts. Set lunch/dinner 1,980 pts. Full alc 2,500 pts.
Reduced rates for stays of 3 or more nights.

ORIENT 07110 Mallorca   Map 6

Hotel L'Hermitage   *Tel* (971) 61.33.00
Carretera de Alaró

Orient is "a Shangri-La hidden valley of orchards hemmed in by
mountains, and for that reason alone lovely to stay in." Up in the wooded
hills near the rugged north-west coast of Mallorca, and just outside the
old village of Orient, *L'Hermitage* has been converted from a 17th-century
country mansion whose former guests included King Farouk of Egypt and
the King of Bulgaria. There is a swimming pool amongst pine trees, and
two tennis courts. Our nominator found an enormous range of delights,
including "the main house with a reading room and games room, a small
bar with interesting Mallorcan watercolours, plenty of German and
UK/US magazines, and large bowls of splendid fresh flowers. The dining-
room, in the old olive mill, has an olive press as its focal point, and the
grinding-stone is now used as a table where a lavish breakfast buffet is
laid out, including the island's delicious specialty, ensaimadas. Bedroom
comfortable, with European cable TV programmes, and modern bathroom. Four rooms are in the older building, the rest in a chalet-like block;
ours had easy chairs, a wall safe, a large balcony." This year readers
report "adventurous food – fresh, and soundly cooked" – "the consistently best hotel food we experienced anywhere in Spain." One reader warns
that there is no public transport in Orient, so a car is essential: "the scenic,

climbing shorter route to Palma is 28 kilometres; the faster, 35 kilometres, is via Alaró and Consell." (*LH, JR Lloyd, David Ball*)

Open All year.
Rooms 20 double – all with bath, telephone, TV and terrace. 4 in annexe.
Facilities Lounge, salons, bar, TV room, games room, restaurant. Garden with 2 tennis courts, swimming pool, sauna.
Location 1.3 km NE of village of Orient, 25 km N of Palma.
Credit cards Access, Diners, Visa.
Terms [1989 rates] (Excluding 12% tax) Double room 15,800 pts. Breakfast 1,075 pts. Alc meals (excluding wine) 2,500 pts.

PORT MAHÓN 07700 Menorca   Map 6

Hotel Port Mahón   *Tel* (971) 36.26.00
Avenida Fort de l'Eau, 12   *Fax* (971) 36.43.62
                                                       Telex 69473 PORME

Our first entry for the smaller, less touristy Balearic island of Menorca: "A comfortable, old-fashioned four-star hotel in best position in Mahón, near harbour. Bedrooms overlooking water recommended for view; breakfast served on balconies. Excellent service from maids and waiters (staff in reception and bar less welcoming). Average food, well cooked, with good buffet of desserts. Swimming pool and terrace. Close to harbour walk, where there are lots of little cafés." 74 rooms – all with bath or shower, single 4,900–7,100 pts, double 6,050–10,000 pts. Breakfast 750 pts. Set lunch/dinner 2,300 pts [1989]. (Tax added.) More reports please.

RIBADEO 27700 Lugo   Map 6

Parador de Ribadeo   *Tel* (982) 11.08.25

A relatively modern *parador*, overlooking a magnificent deep inlet on the Galician coast, just outside Ribadeo, a town of faded elegance. There's an unusual feature: you go down by lift from the ground floor to the bedrooms below – the most expensive have fine views over the estuary. "From the outside this is a small and unimpressive building, though with obvious charm and a pretty garden. Inside all is clean and comfortable. Our bedroom was well appointed and adequate in size; it had a big bathroom and large walled balcony overlooking the water and the little town beyond." (*C and M Dehn*) Other visitors were equally pleased: "Lovely position, extremely comfortable, with good food and helpful staff. It was our first visit to Galicia, where there are miles of empty beaches, lots of ancient churches, and friendly people. We certainly recommend this *parador*." (*M and R Milne-Day*) The Bay of Ribadeo and the magnificent river valley make this an attractive stop on the long north coast.

Open All year.
Rooms 41 double, 6 single, all with bath and shower, and TV.
Facilities Lift. 2 salons, restaurant, bar, terrace. Beach 200 metres.
Location On outskirts of town. Parking.
Credit cards All major cards accepted.
Terms (Excluding 6% tax) B&B 4,050–7,600 pts. Set lunch/dinner 2,500 pts. Full alc 2,000–3,000 pts.

SANTIAGO DE COMPOSTELA La Coruña   Map 6

Hotel de los Reyes Católicos   *Tel* (981) 58.22.00 and 58.23.00
Plaza de España 1   *Fax* (981) 56.30.94
Santiago de Compostela 15705   *Telex* 86004 HRCS

This *very* large, grand and famous hotel stands in the heart of medieval Santiago and was built by Ferdinand and Isabella in the 15th century as a hostel for pilgrims to the shrine of St-James. ("Imagine staying at a cross between Hampton Court and All Souls, furnished with the best pieces from the Victoria and Albert Museum", wrote one reader.) It forms one side of the *plaza* on which the cathedral sits. Some reports this year: "We were escorted to our room through a series of small, cloistered courtyards, containing either a fountain, ornamental flower beds, or miniature topiary. During our journey we heard evocative music which – blended with the romanesque arches and stone staircases – was reminiscent of a scene from *Brideshead*." "We had a four-poster, and I wrote my postcards in a huge armchair overlooking a beautiful courtyard, with a piano playing in the background." Rooms vary greatly in size and style, but at least some have canopied beds, very high ceilings and period Spanish furniture. "Expensive but worth it", has been one recent comment, although another reader suggests that if you eat in the elegant cafeteria, and take a room with a shower, not a bath, the expense need not be so great. The dining room is an enormous gracefully vaulted crypt, but the food – and the room's decor – get mixed reports: "The cod with almonds on Saturday was particularly good, but on Sunday it was reheated." "The banquette seats in the dining room were remarkably uncomfortable – but the food quite good." "Breakfast was superb, both for choice and presentation – set out like a harvest festival." Don't expect impeccable room maintenance; the plumbing is "noisy and not always efficient". But readers still support an earlier report: "For a knock-out hotel experience (honeymoon or something), you really couldn't do much better in Spain."

Open All year.
Rooms 3 suites, 114 double, 13 single – all with bath and/or shower, telephone, radio, TV, and baby-listening. Some ground-floor rooms.
Facilities Lifts. Reception hall, salons, TV room, bars, dining-room, cafeteria; conference facilities; hairdressing salon, boutiques; Chapel Royal with occasional concerts. Gardens.
Location In town centre, by cathedral. Garage parking nearby. Special bus to station.
Credit cards All major cards accepted.
Terms (Excluding 12% tax) Rooms: single 9,600–12,000 pts, double 12,000–15,000 pts, suite 27,000–31,200 pts. Breakfast 800 pts. Set lunch/dinner 2,700 pts; full alc 4,000–5,000 pts. Reduced rates and special meals for children.

Hostal Windsor   *Tel* (981) 59.29.39
República de El Salvador 16
Santiago de Compostela 15701

Useful for short stay; half the price of Reyes Católicos, *above. B&B in newer part of town, five minutes' walk from historic quarter. Recent visitors found rooms clean, and Italian manager and staff helpful; though one complained of plumbing and other noises at night. "Though modern, it has been attractively decorated in traditional Spanish style, using wood, glass and brasswork to great effect. Our bedroom was attractive, quiet and comfortable, though the bathroom was tiny." 50 rooms, all with bath and/or shower, double 3,700–4,700 pts. Breakfast 350 pts [1989]. (Tax added.) No recent reports. More needed.*

SANTO DOMINGO DE LA CALZADA 26250 La Rioja   Map 6

Parador Santo Domingo   *Tel* (941) 34.03.00
de la Calzada   *Fax* (941) 34.03.25
Plaza del Santo 3

In heart of the Rioja wine country, a "serviceable" parador, converted from what was once a hostel for pilgrims en route for Santiago – though little now remains of the old building but the facade and an imposing main hall. Commended in the past for its food, service, and its 27 smallish but clean and comfortable rooms, all with bath and shower. B&B 4,300–7,600 pts. Set meals 2,500 pts [1989]. Little recent feedback. More reports please.

SEGOVIA 40001   Map 6

Parador de Segovia   *Tel* (911) 43.04.62 and 43.07.50
Apartado de Correos 106   *Fax* (911) 43.73.62
Carretera de Valladolid   *Telex* 47913 RRPP

An elegant, modern hotel perched on a hill above the town, with fine views of the golden cathedral and the romantic *alcázar*. Praise in earlier editions has been endorsed again: "With its two pools and grassy lawn, this is a great place to relax in. Every room has a view, the lobby is vast with glass from floor to ceiling; the food is very good." "It should be ugly since it is only concrete beams and brick walls. But lines in every direction give pleasure to the eye, and the place is full of small gardens." "It is palatial, stylishly designed and sumptuously furnished. Bedrooms are ultra-modern, excellently equipped." A reader this year adds, "The large comfortable bedrooms have refrigerators and balconies, and the garden/pool area is lovely. The handsomely decorated public rooms are cavernous, however, and the general tone is impersonal." Some readers have found the food uninspiring, and have recommended venturing into the more atmospheric restaurants in the town.

Open All year.
Rooms 5 suites, 70 double, 5 single – all with bath and shower, telephone, radio and TV; air-conditioning. Some ground-floor rooms.
Facilities Salons, library, TV room, bar, restaurant; conference facilities; indoor swimming pool, sauna. Garden with swimming pool.
Restriction Not suitable for &
Location 2 km N of Segovia on N601.
Credit cards All major cards accepted.
Terms [1989 rates] (Excluding 12% tax) Rooms: single 7,200–8,000 pts, double 9,000–10,000 pts, suite 12,150–13,500 pts; dinner, B&B: single 10,700–11,500 pts, double 16,000–17,000 pts. Breakfast 800 pts. Set lunch/dinner 2,700 pts; full alc 4,000 pts. Special meals for children.

Hotels are dropped if we lack positive feedback. If you can endorse an entry, please do so.

LA SEU D'URGELL 25700 Lerida   Map 6

Hotel El Castell   *Tel* (973) 35.07.04 and 35.10.41
Apt. Correos 53   *Telex* 93610 cseu

20 kilometres south of Andorra, a modern single-storey luxury hotel on a hillside with beautiful views over the valley below, well situated for exploring the Pyrenees, with fishing, river canoeing and golf nearby. It enters the Guide this year with the following report: "In a very pleasant small town, *El Castell* has previously been classified as a motel, but is now 'three-turret red' in *Michelin*, with a rosette. It lies one kilometre south of the town on the side of a ruined castle. Towards the castle, and surrounded by a rose garden, is an attractive swimming pool. All the bedrooms are off a long corridor, well appointed with private bathrooms, small fridge and T V. Balconies have pleasant views. The dining-room is restful and pleasant, and the owners (or managers) very much in evidence (also at breakfast!) speak excellent English. Food superb as one might expect from the *Michelin* rosette. I had a perfectly cooked roast kid and my wife an equally perfect duck. Hot puff pastry sweets – which I can still taste! Presentation modern without being excessively *nouvelle*. (*Dr Ian Anderson*)

Open All year. Restaurant closed Christmas.
Rooms 2 suites, 38 double – all with bath and shower, telephone, T V, mini-bar, baby-listening by arrangement. Ground floor rooms.
Facilities Salon, T V room, reading room, bar, 2 dining rooms; conference/functions rooms. Garden with unheated swimming pool, badminton. Fishing (permits arranged); Nordic and Alpine skiing nearby.
Location On edge of village 20 km S of Andorra la Vella, on Lerida road.
Credit cards All major cards accepted.
Terms (Excluding 12% tax) Room: single 8,500 pts, double 11,000 pts, suite 21,000 pts. Breakfast 1,200 pts. Lunch and dinner alc 3,500–5,000 pts.

SIGÜENZA 19250 Guadalajara   Map 6

Parador Castillo de Sigüenza   *Tel* (911) 39.01.00
Plaza del Castillo   *Fax* (911) 39.13.64
                                                Telex 22517

130 kilometres north-east of Madrid, Sigüenza is a historic old town, with a castle and a fine cathedral. The *parador* is set in a medieval fortress, with splendid views from the ramparts. "Well worth a journey just for the opulence of the setting," writes a correspondent this year, who also appreciated its warmth when it was snowing outside. Usual "traditional" *parador* furnishings (e.g. suits of armour in the lounge), plus well-furnished bedrooms and "quite good" cooking. (*Martin L Dodd*)

Open All year.
Rooms 5 suites, 68 double, 3 single – all with bath and shower, telephone and T V.
Facilities Lifts. Restaurant, bar, T V room. Small gardens.
Location 200 metres from town.
Credit cards All major cards accepted.
Terms (Excluding tax) Rooms: single 6,000–6,800 pts, double 7,500–8,500 pts, suite 9,500–10,500 pts. Breakfast 800 pts. Set lunch/dinner 2,500 pts.

We depend on detailed fresh reports to keep our entries up-to-date.

SOLDEU Andorra   Map 6

Hostal Sant Pere   *Tel* (9738) 510.87
El Tarter   *Telex* 234

One of our two entries for the principality of Andorra, this restaurant-with-rooms on the main road from the capital to the French border was nominated last year by a distinguished British restaurateur, now retired: "I must have had between 50 and 100 dinners here over the past two years and stayed on several occasions, and in my experience it is by far the best hotel and restaurant in Andorra, where nearly all the others are either cheap for skiers or overdone Pyrenean style. The restaurant, not expensive, is very professionally staffed in the Spanish manner and has a limited menu of good quality." (*Kenneth Bell*) Endorsed this year: "Location – excellent! At the foot of a ski trail, ten miles from very noisy downtown Andorra. Room very nice, appropriately alpine, but not rustic. A wonderful shower room. Only the skiers were noisy and awoke before I did – soundproofing was sparse. Food – excellent! Catalan-inspired and very expertly presented. Service was equal to the food. One of my all time top dozen meals." (*Paul A Hoffstein*)

Open All year.
Rooms 6 double – all with shower and telephone. Also 11 studio apartments nearby.
Facilities 2 salons with TV, restaurant; terrace.
Location At El Tarter, 3 km W of Soldeu on main road to Andorra la Vieja. Parking.
Credit cards All major cards accepted.
Terms [1989 rates] B&B double 7,500–9,000 pts. Full alc 3,500–4,500 pts. Special menus for children.

TOLEDO   Map 6

Hostal del Cardenal   *Tel* (925) 22.49.00
Paseo de Recaredo 24   *Fax* (925) 22.29.91
Toledo 45004

This "true Toledan palace", home of the local archbishop in the 18th century, adjoins the city walls. It is well known for its excellent restaurant, and offers good hotel accommodation as well; some of its rooms overlook the terraced garden which extends to the city gates. A report last year, "A magical setting and a lovely hotel. Bedroom *very* adequate with a fab view of the gardens. Public rooms furnished with Spanish antiques. Ate well at dinner, with heavenly view of floodlit city gates. Service was both polite and patient. Bottled orange juice at breakfast was the only jarring note." "The distinguished furnishings are in total keeping with the surroundings. The walk through the gardens and along the inner walls is a delight – a haven from the crowded streets outside." Endorsed again this year: "Memorable. Proof that excellence doesn't have to cost a fortune. (Minor grievance: Why, in a palace with so many spectacular rooms, must breakfast be offered in a cramped and sunless chamber?)" (*J Michael Morrison; also Ray and Angela Evans*)

Open All year.
Rooms 2 suites, 22 double, 3 single – all with bath and shower, and telephone.
Facilities Lounges, TV room, dining room. Garden, patios and courtyards.

Location 10–15 mins' walk from centre; by the old walls at Puerta de Bisagra.
Parking.
Restriction Not suitable for &.
Credit cards All major cards accepted.
Terms [1989 rates] (Excluding 6% tax) Rooms: single 4,200 pts, double 6,900 pts,
suite 10,000 pts. Breakfast 400 pts. Set meals 1,800 pts.

Parador Conde de Orgaz
Paseo de los Cigarrales
Toledo 45002

Tel (925) 22.18.50
Fax (925) 22.51.66
Telex 47998 RRPT

"For the view alone, this is *the* place to stay in Toledo," wrote a visitor
last year of this showpiece *parador*, often crowded with coach parties.
First impressions are of 16th-century Spain at its most baronial – coats of
arms, shields and antique weapons forged from Toledo steel in the halls
and corridors, and banners and portraits of grave-faced bearded grandees.
In fact the hotel was built in 1968, and the rooms, although furnished in
the old style, have every modern amenity including a fridge. It is on the
site where El Greco executed his famous painting of Toledo, high on a hill
to the north. A room with a view of the city is well worth the extra
money. "Ours was in the most expensive range, but worth it for the
stupendous sight of the floodlit cathedral at night and the sandy pinks of
the buildings contrasting with dark cypresses by day. Splendid furnishings – heavily fringed woollen curtains and bed covers to match. Plentiful
lighting. Pretty rugs on the tiled floor: 45 feet from the door to the
balcony." Alas, other aspects of the hotel are less satisfactory: "Breakfast
excellent, but dinner almost inedible: half-emptied plates collected by
waiters, and strong complaints from fellow guests. We had flavourless
soup, bitter-tasting scrambled eggs with shrimp, dry fresh tuna with
undercooked boiled potatoes. Luckily there are good restaurants in
Toledo, but what a pity the *paradores* don't take more pride in their food."
Another reader found reception unhelpful, and the service indifferent.
More reports welcome.

Open All year.
Rooms 71 double, 6 single – all with bath and shower, telephone, radio and TV.
Facilities Lift. 3 salons, TV room, bar, restaurant – all with air-conditioning.
Extensive landscaped grounds with terraces and unheated swimming pool.
Hunting and fishing nearby.
Location 3 km S of town centre; well signposted.
Restriction Not suitable for &.
Credit cards All major cards accepted.
Terms (Excluding 12% tax) B&B: single 10,500 pts, double 13,800 pts. Set
lunch/dinner 2,900 pts.

Hotel Maria Cristina
Marqués de Mendigorria 1
Toledo 45003

Tel (925) 21.32.02
Telex 42827 HMCT

Just outside city walls 100 metres from Puerta de Bisagra, modern hotel with
traditional Spanish interior. Spacious cool dining-room with blue painted
ceiling, red tiled floors, soft muslin curtains. Recommended for well-appointed
bedrooms, comfortable beds, spotless bathrooms, friendly staff. "Service in
dining room impeccable – though food not spectacular." Air-conditioned. Used
by tour groups, it has extensive business and conference facilities. 66 rooms, all

with bath and shower; single 3,900–4,125 pts, double 5,800–6,250 pts. Breakfast 395 pts, lunch/dinner 1,800 pts [1989]. New nomination. More reports please.

TORTOSA 43500 Tarragona   **Map 6**

Parador Castillo de la Zuda   *Tel* (977) 44.44.50
                                      Fax (977) 44.44.58

On a hilltop dominating this historic town on the banks of the Ebro, a massive feudal castle dating from Moorish times, now much restored in true *parador* style, and warmly endorsed by several readers: "An attractive building in a lovely setting overlooking Tortosa; the views from all sides are interesting (river, mountains, rooftops, the cathedral, the old town), and it is well worth wandering round the perimeter walls and looking out from each vantage point. The public rooms are well kept and attractive (except the bar) and there are three fireplaces preserved from the 13th century. The bedrooms (twin beds only) are pleasantly furnished in traditional Spanish style – terracotta tiled floors with patterned cotton rugs, dark wooden furniture, iron lamps, heavy wooden doors, shutters. Good lighting, modern and clean bathroom, good plumbing and ventilation. All the staff were pleasant and hardworking." "The hotel has been renovated from a ruin with much care and feeling. Everything sparkles with polish and love. All the staff are fantastic." "The restaurant is a baronial hall, with a tiled ceiling between wooden beams. Helpful staff, and good, simple authentic local food: the fried fish platter was particularly tasty." (*JK Baker, S Croft, and others*) Not everyone agrees about the food, except for the "excellent" breakfast. "Avoid the set menu," was the advice of one reader.

Open All year.
Rooms 3 suites, 71 double, 8 single – all with bath and shower, telephone and T V.
Facilities Lift. Salon, bar, restaurant. Garden with swimming pool.
Location 500 metres from centre, sign-posted.
Restrictions Not suitable for &.
Credit cards All major cards accepted.
Terms [1989 rates] Dinner, B&B: single 6,375 pts, double 9,800 pts.

TRUJILLO 10200 Cáceres   **Map 6**

Parador de Trujillo   *Tel* (927) 32.13.50
Plaza de Santa Clara   *Fax* (927) 32.13.66

Trujillo is the birthplace of Pizarro, whose magnificent statue stands in the town square. On a hilltop in its ancient citadel is this new *parador* (opened 1985), built within the ancient convent of Santa Clara. Rooms in the old part have been tastefully modernised and have good bathrooms, but remain in keeping with the character of the rambling old building with courtyards; there is also a modern annexe. Recent comments: "A very pleasant hotel with a tranquil atmosphere. The staff were helpful; the dinner menu was interesting and the food most attractively presented." "We happened to arrive on a day of fiesta when 90,000 people from all over Extremadura descended on the small town, and the fireworks and bands in the streets made us dubious about our location.

We need not have worried: the bedrooms were peaceful, the swimming pool clean, and the bar gave good service despite the influx of local politicians. The food was superb. The selection of cold fish for starters included a generous serving of smoked salmon on a bed of red cabbage, decorated with radishes *en rosette*, and hot aubergines with ham and salami. The main course included roast suckling pig and half a cold partridge. The puddings were less exciting, but very good. An '81 Extremaduran red wine at 850 pesetas was excellent in value and flavour." (*WK Reid; Diane Sumner*)

Open All year.
Rooms 1 suite, 41 double, 4 single – all with bath, telephone and mini-bar. Some in annexe.
Facilities T V room, bar, dining room; conference facilities. Garden with swimming pool.
Location 47 km E of Cáceres. Hotel is central. Garage.
Restrictions Not suitable for &.
Credit cards All major cards accepted.
Terms [1989 rates] (Excluding 12% tax) Rooms: single 6,400–6,800 pts, double 8,000–8,500 pts. Breakfast 800 pts; set lunch/dinner 2,500 pts.

UBEDA 23400 Jaén   **Map 6**

Parador Condestable Dávalos   *Tel* (953) 75.03.45
Plaza Vazquez de Molina 1   *Fax* (953) 75.12.59

Ubeda, in north-eastern Andalusia, is an exceptionally beautiful old town with some fine churches (notably San Pablo and El Salvador), and many Renaissance buildings. In its historic main square is this "lovely 16th-century stone palace with a wonderful internal patio, surrounded by tiled corridors leading to cool rooms; the best ones look onto the square or small courtyards." "Antiques add to a sense of nobility, though our room was not entirely in keeping with this style, having bright and modern furnishings. It was, however, spacious, and had a cavernous bathroom." Readers this year have been enthusiastic about the food, especially the *tapas*, and "the most delicious olives – Ubeda is surrounded by miles of olive groves". Service is by "rather taciturn ladies, attired in national costume". (*Marion and David Fanthorpe, A and J Sennett, and others*) One warning: "there is no public room other than the rather gloomy and uncomfortable bar; with dinner not served until 9.30 pm, the wait during darker months of the year can be a trial."

Open All year.
Rooms 1 suite, 25 double – all with bath and shower, telephone, radio and T V.
Facilities Bar, T V room, restaurant; air-conditioning. Garden.
Location Central. Ubeda is 57 km NE of Jaén.
Restriction Not suitable for &.
Credit cards All major cards accepted.
Terms [1989 rates] (Excluding 6% tax) Rooms: single 7,200–8,000 pts, double 9,000–10,000 pts. Breakfast 800 pts; set lunch/dinner 2,500 pts.

Our italicised entries indicate hotels which are worth considering, but which, for various reasons – inadequate information, lack of feedback, ambivalent reports – do not at the moment warrant a full entry. We should particularly welcome comments on these hotels.

VALENCIA DE DON JUAN 24200 León Map 6

Hotel Villegas II *Tel* (987) 75.01.61
Calle el Palacio 21

Small hotel in small market town 38 kilometres south of León, "quiet, cheap, unpretentious, agreeably managed, comfortable and charmingly decorated", with garden and, in season, swimming pool. The rather simpler 24-roomed Villegas *nearby is under the same management. 12 rooms, all with bath, single 2,000–2,500 pts, double 3,500–4,500 pts. Breakfast 250 pts; set lunch/dinner 1,200 pts [1989]. (Tax added.) New nomination. More reports please.*

VALVERDE 38900 Hierro, Canary Islands Map 6

Parador de El Hierro *Tel* (922) 55.80.86 and 55.80.36
Las Playas

A pleasant modern parador in quiet and beautiful countryside on the east coast of the small island of Hierro, the smallest and most remote of the Canaries. 20 km from Valverde and 15 from the airport. Attractive rooms, each with balcony, overlook the garden and the sea. Large well-kept pool; friendly service; food above parador average; excellent breakfasts. Open all year. 47 rooms, all with bath and shower. B&B double 8,960–9,600 pts. Set menu 2,500 pts [1989]. Recent nomination. More reports please.

VERÍN 32600 Orense Map 6

Parador de Monterrey *Tel* (988) 41.00.75
Fax (988) 41.20.17

Verín lies just a few kilometres north of the Portuguese border. It is a well-preserved medieval town, with narrow streets and attractive old houses, and fine views of burnt Castilian countryside all around – "the most perfect site for a hotel we have ever seen". There is a pear-shaped swimming pool, surrounded by lawn and variegated trees, which must be welcome on hot days. The hotel is modern, with two storeys, clean and light outside, in the style of an old Spanish manor house, cool and dark inside. The staircase is wide and shallow and the corridors long; the bedroom was well appointed. The food was good, with plenty of choice, though the menu did not change. The place was, however, less efficient than other *paradores*; no one spoke English, no forms were signed on arrival, and the system of charging for extras was casual and led to duplication and disquiet." (*LH, Conrad and Marilyn Dehn*)

Open All year.
Rooms 1 suite, 22 double – all with bath, and telephone. 8 in annexe.
Facilities Lounge with TV, bar, dining room. Garden with swimming pool.
Location 71 km SE of Orense on N525. *Parador* is 4 km NW of Verín.
Restrictions Not suitable for &.
Credit cards All major cards accepted.
Terms [1989 rates] (Excluding tax) Rooms: single 4,800–6,000 pts, double 6,000–7,500 pts. Breakfast 800 pts; set lunch/dinner 2,500 pts.

VICH 08500 Barcelona   Map 6

Parador de Vich   *Tel* (93) 888.72.11
                                                              Fax (93) 888.73.77

Off the Barcelona-Andorra road, 14 kilometres north-east of Vich, an
austere stone Catalan *parador* with views over the lake and distant
Pyrenees. "As in other *paradores*, the room was large and clean, the beds
large and comfortable, the furniture generally large and ornate, the
bathroom large and the managers nicely assuming you will need at least
ten towels. The water was abundant and always hot. The mini-bar was
overpriced. Dinner was acceptable and very reasonably priced: artichokes
stuffed with cod, and quail and bean casseroles followed by lamb cutlets.
After dinner came the first highlight of our stay – we drank wine on the
balcony until about midnight. It was peaceful and our conversation was
accompanied by the croaking of what sounded like thousands of frogs,
calling and answering back and forth down the valley. In the morning we
saw our view – we overlooked the swimming pool, which in turn
overlooked a lake which stretched away into the distance between the
hills. We ate breakfast on the balcony accompanied by our second
highlight – our first cuckoos of the year, not just one or two, but maybe
ten or twenty calling down the valley in the same manner as the frogs the
night before. This *parador* was not the prettiest we have stayed in, but it
was certainly in an extremely attractive setting. There are plenty of public
rooms laid out for billiards, cards, television or just conversation. The bar
was large and well stocked." (*Elizabeth Jones*)

Open All year.
Rooms 1 suite, 31 double, 4 single – all with bath and shower, telephone and TV.
Facilities Lift. 3 lounges, bar, TV salon, restaurant. Garden with swimming pool,
tennis court. Large artificial lake nearby, accessible on foot.
Location 14 km NE of Vich, well signposted.
Credit cards All major cards accepted.
Terms [1989 rates] (Excluding 12% tax) B&B: single 6,000–8,000 pts, double
8,100–10,600 pts. Set meals 2,500 pts. Full alc 2,000–6,500 pts. Special meals for
children on request.

VILLALBA 27800 Lugo   Map 6

Parador Condes de Villalba   *Tel* (982) 51.00.11
Valeriano Valdesuso   *Fax* (982) 51.00.90

In a town on the Galician plain in north-west Spain, and a possible
staging post between Gijon and Santiago, this small *parador* is a converted
medieval bastion with a drawbridge and an octagonal tower – "a delight,
and quite astonishing", a reader wrote this year. "We had a huge room,
with magnificent antique furniture, a vast bathroom, and a curtained
alcove with loopholes for shooting at pedestrians below." Traditional
high-quality furnishings, comfortable beds, "service nice, but amateur".
There is no bar and few interesting drinks – e.g. "no dry Amontillado or
Oloroso (unheard of)". The restaurant is in the dungeon: the food is good
according to one report, "pretty ordinary" according to another. More
reports welcome.

Open All year.
Rooms 6 double – all with bath and shower, telephone and TV.

Facilities Lift. Salon with TV, cafeteria, dining room. Garden.
Location 36 Km N of Lugo. Hotel is central. Parking.
Restrictions Not suitable for &.
Credit cards All major cards accepted.
Terms [1989 rates] (Excluding 6% tax) Rooms: single 7,200–8,000 pts, double 9,000–10,000 pts. Breakfast 800 pts; set lunch/dinner 2,500 pts.

VITORIA-GASTEIZ 01192 Álava   Map 6

Parador de Argomániz   *Tel* (945) 28.22.00
Apartado 601 Vitoria   *Fax* (945) 28.22.00

A converted 18th-century country mansion in a peaceful setting amid the Navarre hills of the Basque country, just off the Pamplona–Vitoria road. Vitoria, capital of the largest of the Basque provinces, lies 12 kilometres to the west. The *parador* is comfortable, clean and attractive, with many public rooms, ancient stone floors, modern wooden floors, and a raftered, barn-like restaurant, where "good wine and *very* good food" are served. "Friendly service" is reported by one reader, "little personal charm" by another. Recommended as a useful overnight stop. (*Elizabeth Jones, PW Arnold*)

Open All year.
Rooms 54 double – all with bath and shower, telephone.
Facilities Lift. Salon, TV room, bar, restaurant. Garden.
Location 12 km E of Vitoria by N1 to Irun.
Restrictions Not suitable for &.
Credit cards All major cards accepted.
Terms [1989 rates] (Excluding 6% tax) Double room 6,000–7,000 pts. Breakfast 800 pts; set lunch/dinner 2,500 pts.

ZAFRA 06300 Badajoz   Map 6

Parador Hernán Cortés   *Tel* (924) 55.02.00
Plaza Corazón María 7   *Fax* (924) 55.10.18

In a small town just off the Badajoz–Seville road, this *parador*, like so many others, is a converted castle. It has massive grey walls and is austere from the outside, but cool and inviting inside: "An inspired conversion, modern enough for convenience but retaining the best of the period (tapestries everywhere)", wrote a reader last year. This year a regular correspondent writes: "The only *parador* I have encountered which I think is splendid. Distinguished architecture, a humane and well-furnished interior, exceptionally well-furnished bedroom and the best-appointed bathroom I have found in Spain. My one reservation: the food is mediocre, in the standard *parador* way." (*ATW Liddell*) One reader this year found the pool closed in June, and didn't like his bottled water *sin gaz* arriving *sin stopper* too. Poor insulation between rooms has also been mentioned; upper rooms or those not facing the town square are quietest.

Open All year.
Rooms 22 double, 6 single – most with bath or shower, all with telephone.
Facilities Salon, bar, dining room. Garden with swimming pool.
Location Central; parking. Town is 76 km SE of Badajoz.
Credit cards All major cards accepted.
Terms [1989 rates] (Excluding 6% tax) Rooms: single 5,200–6,400 pts, double 6,500–8,000 pts. Breakfast 800 pts; set lunch/dinner 2,500 pts.

ZAMORA 49001 — Map 6

**Parador Condes de
  Alba y Aliste**
Plaza de Viriato 5

Tel (988) 51.44.97
Fax (988) 53.00.63

By the banks of the upper Duero, in the heart of an old city north of Salamanca, this beautiful 15th-century palace with an inner court has been carefully restored. Recommended for friendly service and its fine restaurant: "the best food we have had at a parador – cuisine bourgeoise with a strong regional accent, and interesting puddings." Large bedrooms, antiques, modern well-lit bathrooms. Swimming pool with fine view. 27 rooms, all with bath and shower. B&B double 8,600–10,600 pts. Set lunch/dinner 2,500 pts (Excluding 12% tax). A recent visitor encountered "unhoovered carpets, waterstained table, less than splendidly clean bedspreads". Just an off-day? More reports please.

****

Traveller's tale *The brochure stipulates 'No dogs'. This augurs well for those who object to animals in public rooms. But the proprietors have two dogs and at least three cats. These are allowed access to all the public rooms and have occasionally to be ejected from the bedrooms if doors are left open. In the lounges, cats' claws have caused some damage to clothing, but more serious is their presence in the dining room and – unbelievably – the kitchen. In the bar one of the dogs was seen to be eating crisps out of a bowl and attempting to drink the beer of one of the guests; and we were cheerfully informed one evening that there was a shortage of cheese biscuits because one of the dogs had eaten them in the kitchen.*

****

TIDBLOMS HOTEL, GOTHENBURG

BORGHOLM 387 00 Öland   Map 1

Hotell Guntorps Herrgård   *Tel* (0485) 13 000
Guntorpsgatan

A four-mile bridge, Europe's longest, links the mainland to Öland,
Sweden's second largest island (87 miles by 10 miles). Rich in wildlife, it
is a breeding ground for many different varieties of land and sea birds,
and has an abundance of protected wildflowers (30 species of orchid,
15 of violet); there are also Viking rune-stones and prehistoric burial
chambers. Our previous entry for Borgholm was *Halltorps Gästgiveri*, a
17th-century royal stables, now dropped for want of feedback. We'd
welcome more reports. *Guntorps Herrgård* is a picturesque manor house,
converted from a family home six years ago, with self-contained suites in
one wing, ten-minutes' walk from the village centre. "We found this hotel
was sheer paradise. We had only planned to stay a day or two but
enjoyed it so much we spent the rest of our vacation here. It was
wonderfully peaceful and relaxing. We chose one of the suites, furnished
in warm light pinks and creams with typically Scandinavian furniture.

403

Breakfast was a pure delight. The owner and manager treated us like family rather than guests." (*Capt Richard M Seitz*) The hotel serves only breakfast, but has an arrangement with restaurants in the area and will reserve tables and sometimes drive guests in the hotel's car. More reports please.

Open All year.
Rooms 14 suites, 6 double, 1 single – all with bath and shower, telephone, radio and TV. Suites, in separate wing, have fridge and kitchenette.
Facilities Ramps to suites. Salon, breakfast room; conference room. Garden with heated swimming pool, children's pool, croquet. Sandy beaches 1 km.
Location 800 metres from centre; 50 metres N of traffic lights.
Credit cards All major cards accepted.
Terms B&B: single 400–450 Skr, double 470–550 Skr, suite 570–650 Skr. (No restaurant but snacks available).

GOTHENBURG 416 66   Map 1

Tidbloms Hotel   *Tel* (031) 19.20.70
Olskroksgt. 23   *Fax* (031) 19.78.35
        Telex 27369 TIDBLO

"We were pleasantly surprised by Gothenburg, a pretty, walled city with an interesting waterfront and a fabulous new amusement park, Liseborg, which our children thoroughly enjoyed. We did notice, however, that most of the hotels looked pretty institutional, and were glad we were at *Tidbloms*. It was extremely comfortable. We had two adjoining rooms, one of them under the turret, very pretty, especially the 'master' which was decorated in lovely soft colours." "We were charmed by the very helpful staff in both the hotel and the restaurant. The place felt Swedish rather than international, but our strangeness as foreigners was swept away by the staff who made us feel at home." *Tidbloms* is a turn-of-the-century, turreted, red-brick house, close to the centre of Sweden's second city, well situated, with bedrooms comfortably furnished in modern contract style. The restaurant and bar, "dark and cosy", are built into the rocky hillside and have a cavernous feel, softened by hand-woven rugs, real oil lamps and rustic furniture. There is a good selection of Swedish specialities (including snow goose and reindeer fillet) with carefully prepared sauces. "The food was outstanding; we had an excellent dinner and wonderful buffet breakfasts." (*Mary Hanson, AP Baxter*)

Open All year except 23 Dec–2 Jan.
Rooms 28 double, 14 single – all with bath and shower, telephone, radio and TV.
Facilities Lift. Cocktail bar, restaurant; conference facilities. Rock and sand beach 20 mins.
Location In E part of Gothenburg, within a pedestrian housing area (take small access road behind filling station). Parking.
Credit cards All major cards accepted.
Terms [1989 rates] B&B: single 350–660 Skr, double 480–785 Skr. Dinner, B&B 550–785 Skr per person.

We get little feedback from Scandinavia. Please help if you can.

Don't let old favourites down. Entries are dropped when there is no endorsement.

GRYTHYTTAN 710 60 Västmanland — Map 1

Grythyttans Gästgivaregård
Prästgt. 2

Tel (0591) 147.00
Fax (0591) 141.24

The village of Grythyttan is in "a peaceful corner of old Sweden", off the beaten track some 270 kilometres west of Stockholm, in a region of small lakes just north of huge Lake Vanern. This unusual and sophisticated hotel is run with showmanlike *brio* by Carl-Jan Granqvist who restored the 17th-century house and converted the surrounding old shops and cottages to give additional bedrooms – many are "lavish and furnished with the Swedish sense of colour"; others are much simpler – and cheaper. The popular restaurant, a series of connecting rooms, is well known in Sweden for its French-influenced cuisine. Breakfast is generous and "impeccable"; "service by the dedicated young staff is outstanding, wines marvellous". Some of the plumbing is said to be idiosyncratic. We'd be glad of more reports.

Open All year.
Rooms 9 suites, 53 double, 18 single – 26 with bath, 52 with shower, all with telephone and radio. 52 in cottages and houses in grounds; 18 in annexe *Saxa Mansion* (15 mins' drive away). Some ground-floor rooms.
Facilities Lounges, bars, T V room, restaurant; conference facilities. Dancing on Sat. 2-acre grounds with tennis, children's playground. 150 lakes in area; boating, bathing, fishing and golf nearby.
Location 70 km W of Orebro. In centre of village. Parking.
Restriction Not suitable for &.
Credit cards All major cards accepted.
Terms [1989 rates] B&B: single 590–690 Skr, double 690–1,070 Skr; dinner, B&B 630 Skr per person. Budget rooms: single 475 Skr, double 600 Skr. Reduced rates and special meals for children.

LUND Skåne 221 04 — Map 1

Hotel Lundia
Knut den Stores Gata 2

Tel (046) 12.41.40
Fax (046) 14.19.95
Telex 32761

Comfortable modern hotel in centre of old university town 20 km north of the large port of Malmö, with fine Romanesque cathedral. Attractive, well-provided bedrooms with desk space and good lighting. Excellent Swedish buffet breakfast and popular, reasonably priced self-service lunch. Closed 24–26 Dec. 97 rooms, all with bath/shower. B&B double 990 Skr. An alternative is the Lundia's sister hotel, the much older, aptly named Grand. New nomination. More reports please.

SIGTUNA 193 00 Uppland — Map 1

Stadshotellet-Mälarens Pärla
Stora Nygt. 3

Tel (0760) 501.00
Fax (0760) 51.587

Sigtuna, between Stockholm and Uppsala, is a picturesque little town, one of the oldest in Sweden, on Lake Skarven. It has wooden 18th-century houses and the ruins of very early Christian churches. The *Stadshotellet-Mälarens Pärla* stands on an embankment at the end of the main street, with phenomenal views from the restaurant and upper back rooms. Bedrooms, in pastel shades, are very pleasant; some have an adjoining sitting room. The attractive restaurant, separately managed, is very well known and people drive out to it from Stockholm. The food is "very good, with spectacular sweets. Breakfast adequate. Everyone speaks good English." More reports please.

Open All year.
Rooms 4 suites, 13 double, 9 single – 25 with bath and shower, all with telephone, radio and TV.
Facilities Bar, restaurant; sauna, solarium.
Location About 45 km NW of Stockholm. Parking.
Credit cards All major cards accepted.
Terms [1989 rates] B&B: single 470–825 Skr, double 560–980 Skr, suite 750–1,150 Skr (lowest prices at weekend). Alc meals 80–200 Skr.

SIMRISHAMN Skåne 272 31 Map 1

Hotell Svea *Tel* (0414) 117.20
Strandv. 3 *Fax* (0414) 143 41
Telex 33473

A new nomination in a quiet seaside town east of Malmö in Skåne, an area of gently rolling countryside with sandy beaches and wooded dunes. "Built in 1936, and overlooking the Baltic Sea, it has the charm of an old hotel, with the advantage of having recently been completely renovated. Every inch is new, fresh and very Swedish – contemporary, but not stark. Nice prints on draperies and bedspreads. Spotless hardwood floors, lots of white and lots of light. The dining room was large, comfortable and restful; Wonderful meals and good breakfasts. Staff extremely friendly and helpful. (*Lizbeth and Craig Anderson*) More reports please.

Open All year.
Rooms 38 double, 23 single – all with bath/shower.
Facilities Lounge, bar, dining room. Garden.
Location On seafront.
Credit cards All major cards accepted.
Terms [1989 rates] B&B: single 440–630 Skr, double 540–740 Skr. Set lunch 43 Skr, dinner 90 Skr.

STOCKHOLM Map 1

Clas på Hörnet *Tel* (08) 16.51.30
Surbrunnsgatan 20 *Fax* (08) 33.53.15
Stockholm 113 48 *Telex* 14619 CPH

This elegant little restaurant-with-rooms was first opened as an inn in 1731, then became successively a smart ballroom, hospital, apartment block and garage, but has now reverted to its original vocation. 15 minutes walk' from the centre of Stockholm, it is known more by locals for its excellent restaurant – but there are lovely bedrooms on the upper floor. 18th-century furnishings, modern office conveniences (telex, etc). Open all year, except Christmas, New Year, mid-summer. 10 rooms – all with shower. B&B double 695–1,400 Skr. Set menus 210 Skr. Recent nomination. More reports please.

Hotel Diplomat	*Tel* (08) 663.58.00
Strandvägen 7C	*Fax* (08) 783.66.34
Stockholm 104 40	*Telex* 17119

The Diplomat is an expensive, fashionable and comfortable hotel which enjoys a fine central position by the waterfront. Its attractive ground-floor tea-house, with potted plants, white chairs and check tablecloths, is a smart local rendezvous, as well as serving lavish buffet breakfasts, and is praised this year, as is the "unusually attractive and helpful staff". Bedrooms vary in price; the better ones face the harbour, front ones can be noisy in warm weather. "The pleasantest Stockholm hotel we have yet stayed in," writes *John Woolsey* this year. More reports please.

Open All year except Christmas.
Rooms 5 suites, 70 double, 55 single – 98 with bath, 34 with shower, all with telephone, radio, TV.
Facilities Lounges, TV room, bar, tea room, restaurant, open-air café, sauna; conference facilities.
Location 5 mins' walk from centre. Parking.
Credit cards All major cards accepted.
Terms [1989 rates] B&B: single 750–1,300 Skr, double 1,200–2,200 Skr. Full alc 280 Skr.

Lady Hamilton Hotel	*Tel* (08) 23.46.80
Storkyrkobrinken 5	
Stockholm 111 28	

Lord Nelson Hotel	*Tel* (08) 23.23.90
Västerlånggt. 22	*Telex* 10434 NELSHAM
Stockholm 111 29	*(for both hotels)*

Readers continue to be pleased with this "two hotels in one" enterprise in the old-town area of Stockholm. "My first stay, although I've stayed in Stockholm previously. Will definitely use the hotel again. Excellent housekeeping, friendly helpful staff, simple but more than adequate Swedish breakfast." Each hotel carefully portrays its historical theme: there are models of ships, nautical pictures and items taken from boats, such as figure-heads and brass rails. The bedrooms are modern and attractive, but not large; some are positively poky. "If you can pretend that the very small rooms are cabins, it helps." Other parts of the hotel reflect the older origins of the buildings: the basement plunge pool at the *Lady Hamilton* was a well in the 15th century. The *Lord Nelson* is on a pedestrian street that can be lively until the small hours; but despite the possibility of noise, some readers prefer its location to that of the *Lady Hamilton*: "It's in an area of fascinating cobbled streets and little shops – with an open-air rooftop for a drink while viewing the city skyline." (*Mrs A Rooker*)

Lady Hamilton Hotel
Open All year.
Rooms 3 triple, 18 double, 13 single – all with bath and/or shower, telephone, radio and TV.
Facilities Bar/breakfast room/tea-room; conference facilities; sauna, plunge pool.
Location Central, in pedestrian zone, near royal palace. (Front rooms might be noisy.) Street parking.
Credit cards All major cards accepted.

Terms [1989 rates] B&B: single 1,090–1,200 Skr, double 1,100–1,400 Skr. (Light meals only, no restaurant.)

Lord Nelson Hotel
Open All year.
Rooms 9 double, 22 single – all with shower, telephone, radio and TV.
Facilities Small lift. Bar/breakfast-room/tea-room; conference facilities; rooftop terrace; sauna.
Location Central, in pedestrian zone, near royal palace. Street parking.
Credit cards All major cards accepted.
Terms [1989 rates] B&B: single 825–910 Skr, double 1,050–1,200 Skr. (Light meals only, no restaurant.)

TÄLLBERG 793 03 Dalarna   Map 1

Hotell Åkerblads   *Tel* (0247) 508.00
                                                         Fax (0247) 506.52

"A remarkable place for a rural holiday", praised for many years by our readers. Halfway between Leksand and Rättvik on Lake Siljan, the hotel, the oldest part of which is a 17th-century farmhouse, is comfortable and spacious in the old style. Bedrooms are pleasantly furnished, hardly any two being alike. "A first-class hotel, classically Swedish in style, warmth and comfort. Our suite had views over the beautiful lake and forests. Staff friendly and efficient." This supports an earlier report, "We had a delightful bedroom with verandas. It felt very Swedish, painted in different shades of green and orange. The atmosphere in the hotel is easy and informal. We loved the meals too. Lunch seemed to be the main one – often with several kinds of fish and potatoes with dill. It always ended with cake and excellent coffee in the upper hall. Local parties coming for meals often included men and women in national costume." Christina and Arne Åkerblad, the owners, and their sons are the 19th and 20th generations of the founders – probably the oldest reigning hotel family in Europe. Few recent reports, more welcome.

Open All year except Christmas.
Rooms 15 suites, 29 double, 15 single – all with bath and/or shower, telephone, radio, TV. 39 in 3 annexes in garden, some on ground floor (4 steps to main building).
Facilities 2 sitting rooms, bar, 2 TV rooms, coffee/dancing room, restaurant; functions facilities; sauna, whirlpool. Large garden with tennis, badminton, table tennis, skating rink; bicycles; Winter sports; lake with beach, bathing, fishing, boating nearby.
Location 12 km from Leksand; on road between Leksand and Rättvik. Parking.
Credit cards All major cards accepted.
Terms [1989 rates] B&B 320–460 Skr; dinner, B&B 470–630 Skr. Set lunch 135 Skr, dinner 145 Skr. 1-night bookings sometimes refused. Reduced weekend rates in low season. Reduced rates and special meals for children.

TROLLHÄTTAN 461 27 Västergötland   Map 1

Hotel Swania   *Tel* (0520) 125.70
Storgatan 47   *Fax* (0520) 397.02
                                                        Telex 42225

Some 80 kilometres north of Gothenburg, this industrial town on the Götaälv, has Saab and Volvo connections, but areas by the river are idyllic and here the

Swania *has pleasant views. It's a sizeable and urbane hotel in international style, with rather over-insistent decor (lots of potted palms). Breakfast copious, staff friendly. 143 very pleasant and well-equipped bedrooms, all with bath/shower. B&B double 885–915 Skr [1989]. Recent nomination. More reports welcome.*

****

Traveller's tale *John and Amanda Booth found something unexpected in their hotel bed on the first night of their honeymoon. . .the manager. Blushing bride Amanda, 23, said: "We were given the key to the suite but when we opened the door a man rushed to block us from coming in." The newlyweds stormed out of the country hotel and went back to the reception where they had said goodbye to relatives and friends a few minutes earlier. A guest said: "The party was going with a swing but we were surprised to see the couple back so soon. It must have been one of the quickest honeymoons on record." The apologetic manager of the hotel said later that there had been "a terrible mix-up". He explained: "I was taking my rest in the hotel room when the couple, covered in confetti, came in. I said the honeymoon suite was the room below but they said they had booked Number 14. They were immediately offered another room but they refused it and left." The Daily Mirror*

****

Switzerland

HOSTELLERIE BON ACCUEIL
CHÂTEAU-D'OEX

AMSTEG AM GOTTHARD 6474 Uri   **Map 8**

Romantik Hotel Stern und Post   *Tel* (044) 6.44.40
Fax (044) 6.32.61
Telex 866 385 STEPO

An old coaching inn, useful as a stopover, in a village south of Altdorf on
the way to the St-Gotthard pass: "A charming place. The village has been
by-passed by the motorway and the principal noise is the rushing torrent
right by the hotel. Mr Tresch and all his staff gave us warm and friendly
service. We had the choice between enchantingly atmospheric period
rooms with no bathroom and much more expensive modern ones. All
was spotlessly clean. Food was well cooked and copious (excellent trout);
breakfast, served in the old pine-panelled dining room, was a very good
buffet. There are two small and picturesque lounges, straight out of a
romantic novel."

Open All year. Closed Tue and Wed in winter.
Rooms 25 double, 15 single – 20 with bath and shower, all with telephone.

Facilities Lift. 2 lounges, bar, 3 restaurants; conference room. Garden with direct access to two rivers; fishing.
Location In centre of village, 14 km S of Altdorf, off N2 motorway. Parking.
Restriction Not suitable for &.
Credit cards All major cards accepted.
Terms [1989 rates] B&B 27.50–80 Sfrs. Dinner, B&B 57.50–110 Sfrs. Set lunch/dinner 30–50 Sfrs; full alc 50–70 Sfrs. Reduced rates and special meals for children.

APPENZELL 9050 Appenzell   Map 8

Romantik Hotel Säntis   *Tel* (071) 87.87.22
Landsgemeindeplatz   *Fax* (071) 87.48.42
                                                             Telex 883733

In an attractive little mountain town south of Lake Constance, not far from Austria, the Säntis, owned and run by the Heeb family, is a highly traditional chalet-style inn, with painted facade and antique wood furnishings. Recently renovated, the light and airy rooms are a blend of the old and the high-tech new, with lots of mirrors. A warm welcome, and very good food including buffet breakfast. 35 rooms, all with bath or shower, some equipped for the disabled. B&B: double 130–180 Sfrs. Set menus 30–48 Sfrs. Complaints this year of noise from nocturnal gatherings such as wedding parties. More reports welcome.

AROSA 7050 Graubünden   Map 8

Hotel Hof Maran   *Tel* (01) 31.01.85
                                                             Telex 851629

"Superb hospitality", say devotees revisiting this fairly large and very well-equipped modern hotel that has been grafted on to an old chalet: it has a fine mountain setting, high above Arosa, beside the golf cum cross-country ski course. Other regular fans report it better than ever – especially the food, both in the main restaurant and in the atmospheric little *Stübl*. "Half board is almost inevitable," they wrote earlier, "as it is a long way down to the town. The bedroom door was nearly a foot thick and totally soundproof; the bedroom furniture in honey-gold wood veneer was superbly finished. The beds were wonderfully hard, the bathroom fitted with all the latest gadgets. Dinner at 7 pm – ushered in and out with Swiss efficiency – did mean rather a long evening, but on some nights the lounge fairly rocked with music and dancing. Surprisingly, the only thing missing was a swimming pool."

Open Mid-Jun–mid-Oct, mid-Dec–mid-Apr.
Rooms 44 double, 15 single – 50 with bath, 9 with shower, all with telephone, radio, TV and baby-listening.
Facilities Lift. Lounge, TV room, bar (dancing), 3 restaurants; conference room; games room with ping-pong; sun terrace on roof. Large grounds with 2 tennis courts (pro available), children's play area; skating rink in winter, 4 curling rinks. Sauna, solarium, fitness-room. Ski-lift and ski school behind hotel; 9-hole golf course nearby.
Location 1 km from Arosa near Maran golf course. Bus service every 20 mins. Parking.
Restriction Not suitable for &.
Credit cards All major cards accepted.

Terms Dinner, B&B: single 80–190 Sfrs, double 160–400 Sfrs; full board 20 Sfrs per person added. Reduced rates and special meals for children.

ASCONA 6612 Ticino   Map 8

Hotel Casa Berno   *Tel* (093) 35.32.32
                                                  Telex 846167

This modern four-star hotel stands on a hillside above Lago Maggiore, between Monte Verità and Ronco: it's about 30 minutes' walk up a steep winding road from the centre of smart, animated Ascona, so a car is an asset. The views from its terraces and heated swimming-pool are stunning; all rooms face south over the lake and have a balcony. Readers again have especially praised the charming managers, the Goetschis, and their staff. "A very well-run hotel, full of courtesy, with breath-taking vistas of the lake from the beautiful rooms. The food is excellent. But we cared less for the hotel's utter formality – guests dress for dinner." Another reader, too, has found the style "rather tired 'sixties'". But others continue to extol the bedrooms, breakfast buffet, and "delicious" Franco-Helvetico-Ticinese cuisine, including the pension meals. (*H and B Shames, Ellen and John Buchanan*)

Open Mar–Oct inclusive.
Rooms 11 suites, 43 double, 7 single – all with telephone, radio, balcony/terrace.
Facilities Lift. Lounges (1 with TV), bar on roof-garden, grill room, restaurant with terrace; sauna, massage, solarium, fitness room, ladies' hairdresser. Garden with heated swimming pool. Golf, tennis nearby.
Location Between Monte Verità and Ronco; about 20–30 minutes' walk from Ascona. Parking.
Credit cards Access, Amex, Visa.
Terms B&B 125–155 Sfrs; half board 145–185 Sfrs; full board 165–195 Sfrs. Reduced rates for children sharing parents' room; special meals. Weekly package in spring.

BASLE 4001   Map 8

Hotel Drei Könige   *Tel* (061) 25.52.52
Blumenrain 8   *Fax* (061) 25.21.53
                                                  Telex 962937

Basle's grandest hotel, and one of Europe's oldest (royalty have stayed often). A bit old-fashioned, but comfortable, with a fine Rhineside position: some room balconies face the river, as does the dining-room terrace (food is good). 90 rooms, all with bath and shower. B&B double 275–405 Sfrs. Meals 17–92 Sfrs [1989]. Restored to Guide. More reports please.

BERN 3001   Map 8

Hotel Bären   *Tel* (031) 22.33.67
Schauplatzgasse 4   *Fax* (031) 22.01.01
                                                  Telex 912819

The hotel is named after the city's mascot, and it is full of emblems of the black teddy rampant; but the service, happily, is more bullish than Bär-ish. This, our first-ever entry for Switzerland's charming capital, is four-star and usefully central, very near the station and main square; but also quiet (rooms are double-glazed, most face the inner courtyard). A modern interior, and plenty of modern facilities. Excellent food in a stylish restaurant. 91 beds, all with bath and shower. B&B double 145–185 Sfrs. Meals 20–45 Sfrs [1989]. Endorsed this year. Further reports welcome.

BRAUNWALD 8784 Glarus   Map 8

Hotel Bellevue   *Tel* (058) 84.38.43

Ideal for families with children, and the kind of classic holiday hotel that the Swiss do so very well. It is a big white turn-of-the-century building, no great beauty but with many other virtues, and peacefully set amid meadows and woodlands at the top of a mountain railway above Linthal, between the Klausenpass and Glarus. "The large rooms and high ceilings give a feeling of spaciousness, and the views are stunning. The hotel is superbly well run by its ubiquitous young owners, the Vogels – she charming her guests in her many stunning fashionable outfits, and he every evening before dinner telling fairy-tales to the children grouped around him, as he sits in a high-backed cane armchair. Children are especially welcome and have their own dining room and playroom. Our large and comfortable bedroom had a wrought-iron balcony facing the superb view. The food is always good. The sitting-room is a real one, and the large indoor pool looks out on the view. The staff are a happy selection; and one token of the hotel's good value is that it changes travellers' cheques at the same rate as a bank." More reports would be welcome.

Open Jun–Oct, Dec–Apr.
Rooms 100 beds – most rooms with bath and/or shower, telephone and balcony.
Facilities Lift. Lounge, sitting room, T V/video room, children's playroom, bar (with dancing), restaurant; conference facilities; indoor swimming pool, whirlpool, fitness room, sauna, solarium; table tennis. Garden with terrace, 2 tennis courts. Winter sports nearby.
Location 4 km by railway from Linthal which is 17 km S of Glarus. No access by car.
Credit cards None accepted.
Terms [1989 rates] Dinner, B&B: single 55–137 Sfrs, double 110–274 Sfrs; full board 15 Sfrs added per person. Reduced rates and special meals for children.

CHÂTEAU-D'OEX 1837 Vaud   Map 8

Hostellerie Bon Accueil   *Tel* (029) 4.63.20

A converted 18th-century chalet, up a steep road from the wide and sunny Alpine village of Château-d'Oex, ten minutes west of Gstaad. Regulars in 1989 liked it as much as ever. Last year they attended a New Year's Eve dinner that was "more like a private house party than being in a hotel" and they got on well with the "hard-working and friendly" English manager. "Our bedroom was wood-panelled, with rustic but comfortable furnishings and a glorious view over meadows and snowy peaks. The public rooms are attractive, and tables and chairs were set out in the pleasant gardens. Dinner in another wood-panelled room with a log fire was very enjoyable."

Open Dec–Apr.
Rooms 1 suite, 16 double, 2 single – 19 with bath, 1 with shower, all with telephone. 8 in annexe.
Facilities Lounge, cellar bar, dining room. Garden. Winter sports.
Location 1 km from centre of village which is 15 km SW of Gstaad.
Credit cards Amex, Diners, Visa.
Terms [1989 rates] B&B: single 65–90 Sfrs, double 100–160 Sfrs; half board 30 Sfrs added per person; full board 40 Sfrs added. Reduced rates and special meals for children.

DAVOS DORF 7260 Graubünden   Map 8

Hotel Flüela   *Tel* (083) 6.12.21
Bahnhofstrasse 5   *Fax* (083) 5.44.01
                                                      Telex 853100 FLUA

"Outstanding food and service", "exceptional value for money", run two recent reports on this sizeable ski-hotel, owned and managed by the Gredig family for over a century, and now much modernised. Open only in the winter, it is close to the Parsenn Bahn, the largest ski-lift in this big and bustling resort. "Five- or six-course dinners, a mixture of *nouvelle* and traditional cuisine, with second helpings encouraged." "Super lounges, with pianist every evening, open log fire, indoor swimming pool, sauna, solarium; and quite outstanding breakfast and dinner." The staff tidy the bedrooms twice a day, and will even clean your boots. This year, a reader admired the food, but criticised the decor and "boring" ambience.

Open 25 Nov–18 Apr.
Rooms 10 suites, 55 double, 25 single – 75 with bath and shower, 5 with shower, all with telephone, radio and TV.
Facilities Bar lounge (with pianist), sitting rooms, restaurants; function rooms; games room. Indoor swimming pool, sauna, solarium, massage, fitness-room; ski boutique, barber, hairdresser; bank.
Location In town centre. A few roadside rooms may be noisy. Parking.
Restriction Not suitable for &.
Credit cards All major cards accepted.
Terms B&B 115–405 Sfrs; dinner, B&B 160–450 Sfrs; full board 185–475 Sfrs. Set lunch 35 Sfrs, dinner 50–70 Sfrs; full alc 70–100 Sfrs. Reduced rates and special meals for children.

DAVOS PLATZ 7270 Graubünden   Map 8

Hotel National   *Tel* (083) 3.60.46
Obere Strasse 31   *Fax* (083) 3.86.50
                                                      Telex 853103

On the edge of Davos Platz, the lower part of this straggling resort, this great white modern cube of a hotel might not be to every taste, but its nominator this year was well pleased, "Isolated from all but the noise of church bells, it has rooms with balconies that look along the valley, while others look back along the the town. The staff all seemed enthusiastic and interested. Over ten days we had the best half-board evening food I've ever encountered, generally in the *minceur* style, invariably interesting, and attractively served. Wines are moderately priced. Occasionally a piano player entertained – preferable to the Swiss night when a poor accordionist did his worst and an alpenhorn blasted nearby. Breakfast was the usual spread. A small games room with table tennis, and a lounge with a fire. Warmly recommended." (*TH Nash*)

Open 2 Dec–17 Apr, 2 Jun–30 Sept
Rooms 4 suites, 40 double, 24 single – all with bath and/or shower, telephone and radio; TV on request.
Facilities Lift. Lounge, 2 bars, TV room, 2 restaurants; Piano player, dancing, entertainment. 2 games rooms for children. Garden.
Location 400 metres from town centre.
Credit cards All major cards accepted.
Terms B&B: summer 52–108 Sfrs per person, winter 137–192 Sfrs. Dinner, B&B 60–200 Sfrs, full board 75–215 Sfrs. Set lunch 15–30 Sfrs, dinner 25–45 Sfrs; full alc 35 Sfrs. Reduced rates for children; special meals on request.

LES DIABLERETS 1865 Vaud   Map 8

Hôtel Les Lilas   *Tel* (025) 53.11.34

"Our children were sure that Heidi would appear at any minute and must live somewhere in the village" – that new report sets the tone for this "charming and homely" little chalet-like roadside hotel, run by Jean-Pierre Matti and his "delightful" wife, in an unspoilt village between Aigle and Gstaad. "Our room was small and rustic, and its balcony gave a marvellous view of the mountains", runs another letter this year, "in the candlelit restaurant the food was excellent, if expensive; the breakfast rolls were delicious." Specialities include such dishes as poulet à la bière and filet de boeuf aux morilles. One possible snag: a new hotel is being built opposite. (*R Maxwell-Gumbleton, H and B Shames, Stephen Ruell*)

Open All year.
Rooms 10 double, 5 single – 11 with bath and/or shower.
Facilities Bar, TV room, 2 restaurants. Garden.
Location In village 20 km E of Aigle on road to Gstaad.
Credit cards Access, Amex, Visa.
Terms B&B: single 50–60 Sfrs, double 90–100 Sfrs; dinner, B&B: single 75–90 Sfrs, double 140–160 Sfrs. Set lunch 15–25 Sfrs, dinner 35–60 Sfrs; full alc 35–65 Sfrs. Reduced rates and special meals for children.

ENGELBERG 6390 Unterwalden   Map 8

Hotel Eden   *Tel* (041) 94.32.94

Just rebuilt and modernised, this friendly little *restaurant-mit-Zimmer* stands in a well-known resort high up in a lovely isolated mountain valley south of Lucerne. "Our lasting memory is of the superb food and warm hospitality provided by Sybille and Thomas Reinhardt-Waser", runs one report this year; "our bathroom was small, but everything functioned perfectly". Others have enjoyed the mountain views from those rooms that have a balcony, and the good food, such as vegetable mousse with basil sauce and fresh lake perch. "The homely gentle ambience created by Sibylle in the restaurant is so fitting for the food that Thomas prepares. Both find time to spend talking with their guests." "Yes, a real Eden, this *Eden* – delightful public rooms, atmosphere, rocking-chairs, a nursery which would keep any child quiet on a wet day." (*GL Turner, Leonard and Lora Moss*) One reader this year regretted the lack of choice on the menus. More to the point, the hotel has just added a lift and other facilities, so that all rooms now have bath or shower: prices have risen somewhat, but we are reassured by recent visitors that the improvements have not been to the detriment of the hotel's simple friendly charm.

Open Dec–Oct.
Rooms 3 suites, 7 double, 2 single – 9 with bath, 3 with shower, all with telephone, radio and TV, some with balcony.
Facilities Lift, bar, TV room, library, bistro, restaurant, conference room, children's games room, sauna, solarium. Garden, terrace for meals in summer.
Location Central, near station. Garage and outdoor parking.
Restriction Not suitable for &.
Credit cards All major cards accepted.
Terms B&B: single 80–100 Sfrs, double 130–180 Sfrs, suite 170–210 Sfrs; dinner, B&B: single 110–130 Sfrs, double 190–270 Sfrs. Set lunch/dinner 18–60 Sfrs; full alc 45–65 Sfrs. Reduced rates and special meals for children.

FLIMS-WALDHAUS 7018 Graubünden   Map 8

Hotel Adula   *Tel* (081) 39.01.61
Fax (081) 39.43.15
Telex 851960 ADUL

Flims is a popular medium-height (1,100 metre) summer and winter resort in the Grisons, west of Chur. The pinewoods of the Waldhaus offer miles of easy walking, and there are plenty of mountain hiking-paths for the more energetic. The large chalet-style *Adula* has this recent adula-tor: "The service, quality of food, and the friendly spirit of owners and staff have, if anything, improved. A new extension, *Soldanella*, has very comfortable rooms." The hotel has a huge range of facilities; in summer it also organises conducted walks, and has barbecues outside the large indoor pool. But one guest was depressed to find that dinner started at 6.45 and the place was dead quiet by 9.30. It might be best suited to older citizens.

Open All year except mid-Oct–mid-Dec.
Rooms 10 suites, 67 double, 22 single – most with bath and/or shower, all with telephone and radio, some with TV. 39 in new annexe with underground connection to main building.
Facilities Lift. Salon, TV room, bar with pianist, 3 restaurants; children's playroom; conference facilities; indoor swimming pool, sauna, steam bath. Garden with terrace, 3 tennis courts.
Location Flims-Waldhaus is about 15 km W of Chur. Follow main road to Laax; hotel is signposted. Parking.
Credit cards All major cards accepted.
Terms B&B: single 115–175 Sfrs, double 190–310 Sfrs, suite 270–390 Sfrs. Dinner, B&B 20 Sfrs added per person. Set lunch 25 Sfrs, dinner 40–55 Sfrs. Reduced rates for children sharing parents' room; special meals. Walking tours in summer, ski packages in winter.

> Set dinner refers to a fixed price meal (which may have ample, limited or no choice on the menu). Full alc is the hotel's own estimated price per person of a three-course meal taken à la carte, with a half-bottle of house wine.

FTAN 7551 Graubünden   Map 8

Hotel Haus Paradies   *Tel* (084) 9.13.25
                                            Telex 854154

Most Alpine hotels, even the new smart ones, tend to be in the traditional chalet style. This one, extremely elegant and far from cheap, was built in the 1920s in a mode closer to Le Corbusier, and its decor is original and pleasing, with Scandinavian touches. It is in the lovely country of the Upper Engadin just west of Scuol (Schuls), with views towards the Lischana peaks and the hilltop castle of Tarasp, "The setting is maybe the most spectacular of any hotel we know. All the rooms, spacious and luxuriously furnished, have large picture windows and balconies looking across this dramatic valley, and it is a lovely base for walking or skiing. Managers are Brigitte and Roland Jöhri: she is very sweet and runs the service team efficiently, he is one of the rising young chefs of Switzerland. His menu is perhaps too complicated, but his local dishes are excellent." Very *soigné* dining room and salons; sleek, well-stocked classical library; lovely panoramic terrace. The hotel's brochure is one of the most civilised we have ever seen. More reports please.

Open 15 Jun–15 Oct, 22 Dec–17 Apr.
Rooms 8 suites, 13 double – all with bath, telephone, radio, mini-bar, and balcony or terrace; T V on request.
Facilities Lounge, library, bridge room, dining-room, restaurant. Sauna, solarium, massage.
Location 3 km W of Scuol.
Credit cards None accepted.
Terms B&B: single 160–180 Sfrs, double 320–350 Sfrs, suite 390–440 Sfrs. Dinner, B&B: single 200–220 Sfrs, double 360–420 Sfrs, suite 490–520 Sfrs. Reduced rates and special meals for children.

GENEVA 1204   Map 8

Hôtel L'Arbalète   *Tel* (022) 28.41.55
3 rue de la Tour Maîtresse   *Telex* 427293 ARBA

Well located near the lake, museums and best shops, a small de luxe hotel that this year has again won approval: "Reception charming and helpful, food and service very good. A spacious, comfortable room, but decor a bit heavy ('arbalète' means crossbow)." Earlier comments: "The staff were marvellous, serving us a special breakfast when we overslept." "A homely feel, and quiet, because windows are double-glazed; good food." "Nice touches like an umbrella in the bedroom to help with Geneva rain." The ground-floor brasserie is cheaper than the main first-floor restaurant. (*NPD & J Levine*)

Open All year.
Rooms 20 double, 12 single – all with bath and shower, telephone, radio, T V, mini-bar and baby-listening.
Facilities Lift. Hall, 2 bars, pub with pianist, 3 restaurants. Lake Geneva 2 mins' walk, with sandy beach, safe bathing, fishing.
Location Central; near Mont Blanc bridge. Windows double-glazed. Garage and parking.
Credit cards All major cards accepted.

Terms B&B: single 210–240 Sfrs, double 270–300 Sfrs. Set lunch 25 Sfrs, dinner 40 Sfrs; full alc 40–50 Sfrs. Reduced rates for children sharing parents' room; special meals on request.

Hôtel Les Armures   *Tel* (022) 28.91.72
1 rue du Puits St-Pierre   *Telex* 421129

In a small square near the cathedral, up in the old town, this elegant small hotel makes a pleasant contrast to the grand, impersonal places down by the lake; like them it is not cheap – but in Geneva, what is? It is an old stone building dating mainly from the 17th century, when it was extended to accommodate Huguenots fleeing from France. A recent visitor enjoyed the hotel and the location, but thought the prices charged for breakfast extras were excessive. The quietest rooms are on the interior court, where one reader had one "beautifully furnished, with a small roof-garden outside its window". The cosy *stüberl* restaurant is noted for its local dishes, including raclette.

Open All year. Restaurant closed Easter, Christmas and New Year.
Rooms 4 suites, 20 double, 4 single – all with bath and shower, telephone, radio, TV, tea-making facilities and baby-listening.
Facilities Lift. Lobby, salon, breakfast room, bar, lounge, restaurant, *Stüberl* (rustic bar/restaurant).
Location Central, near St-Pierre Cathedral. No special parking facilities.
Restriction Not suitable for &.
Credit cards All major cards accepted.
Terms B&B: single 195–230 Sfrs, double 315 Sfrs, suite 305–390 Sfrs. Full alc 50–60 Sfrs.

GSTAAD 3780 Bern   **Map 8**

Hotel Christiania   *Tel* (030) 4.51.21
Hauptstrasse   *Fax* (030) 4.71.09
                                                             Telex 922250

In the main street of fashionable Gstaad, a small, spruce hotel with a four-star rating. Dropped from last year's Guide for lack of new reports, it is now re-nominated by two readers: "A warm greeting, wonderful breakfasts, and good food in their cosy restaurant. Our bedroom had a balcony, writing desk, easy chairs. Very quiet"; "The public rooms are small and cosy, and have a lived-in feel. In the rustic-style restaurant we had a good lunch. Many bedrooms overlook a pleasant garden." The owner's daughter is chef and her son-in-law head waiter – a true family affair. (*Ellen and John Buchanan, Kate and Stephan Murray-Sykes*)

Open All year.
Rooms 3 suites for 4 to 6 people with bath and shower, salon, dining-room; 15 double with bath – all with telephone, radio, TV; most with balcony.
Facilities Lift. Salon with TV, bar, restaurant (pianist in high season). Garden with restaurant. Free use of outdoor swimming pool at nearby *Palace Hotel* in summer.
Location Central, near station; street-facing rooms can be noisy. Garage (16 Sfrs).
Credit cards Diners, Visa.
Terms [1989 rates] B&B: (low season) single 60–150 Sfrs, double 120–220 Sfrs; (high season) single 90–200 Sfrs, double 230–350 Sfrs. Dinner, B&B 45 Sfrs per person added. Special meals for children.

ISELTWALD 3807 Bern   Map 8

Hotel Bellevue   *Tel* (036) 45.11.10
                                                      Fax (036) 45.12.77

Iseltwald is a picturesque hamlet and summer resort on a peninsula
beside the lake of Brienz, east of Interlaken. You can sail or water-ski, or
go for mountain walks or climbs; the beautiful Giessback falls are worth a
visit. The chalet-style *Bellevue* has a good position close to the lake, with
two terraced gardens for drinks and light meals: but woods rise steeply
just behind and some visitors have found this setting sombre, especially if
you have a back room (front ones with a balcony are best). The food
served in its two restaurants is the hotel's strongest feature, especially
local fish, but it's not cheap: fish soup, salmon trout in pernod, pike
charcoal-grilled or poached, have all been enjoyed this year, but one
visitor found the service very slow. The breakfast buffet is lavish. The
design of the hotel is "typically Swiss", with much use of wood and
folkweave fabrics; bedrooms are not large, but they have been provided
with new, improved lighting (this was formerly criticised by readers). A
motorway has just been completed high behind the hotel, but its status as
a *Relais du Silence* is unaffected, for the traffic is out of earshot. (*Eileen
Broadbent, Mike and Judi Taylor-Evans, Padi and John Howard, and others*)

Open 15 Feb–4 Jan. Closed Tue.
Rooms 9 double, 2 single – all with bath and/or shower; telephone, radio and T V,
many with balcony.
Facilities Salon, bar, restaurant. Terrace garden. On lake shore with beach and
sailing.
Location On S shore of Lake Brienz, 10 km E of Interlaken.
Restriction Not suitable for &.
Terms B&B 40–60 Sfrs. Half board 22 Sfrs added. Full alc 19–28 Sfrs. Special
meals for children.

Hotel Chalet du Lac   *Tel* (036) 45.11.12

*Our second entry for this pretty fishing village is an authentic lakeside chalet
remodelled as a spotless small hotel, with modern wood furnishings and good
but informal service. Some rooms face the mountain, others have a balcony
above the lake. Meals on a lakeside terrace or indoors; food and service
commended this year. Closed Nov. 12 rooms, all with shower (2 also have bath).
B&B: double 80–134 Sfrs. Set menu 20 Sfrs [1988 rates]. Recent nomination.
More reports please.*

KANDERSTEG 3718 Bern   Map 8

Hotel Ermitage   *Tel* (033) 75.15.12

Run by the friendly Hirschi family, the *Ermitage* stands amid meadows
and trees on the edge of this big resort, near to a chairlift and a carpark. It
has just installed a lounge for guests, and several readers this year speak
well of this, also of the cheerful service, relaxed atmosphere and good
food: "The evening meal was a delight, but it took a long time because
each dish is specially prepared"; "the food was delicious, astonishingly
sophisticated, but with rather too much cream"; "good buffet breakfast".

Rooms vary: those at the front have balconies, but rear ones can be cramped. A returning devotee confirms earlier praise, "If you love the sound of rushing water to go to sleep by, several waterfalls and a steep brook provide that. Rooms are beautifully furnished, and some have a fully equipped kitchenette. Lovely garden restaurant." (*Mr and Mrs BW Boyd, E Goldby, Richard Pinner*)

Open 22 Dec–15 Apr, 26 May–28 Oct. Restaurant closed Mon in low season.
Rooms 2 suites, 11 double – 9 with bath and shower, 4 with shower, all with telephone, radio, TV and mini-bar; many with balcony; 6 with kitchenette.
Facilities Lounge with TV, restaurant, grill room, breakfast room; sun terrace. Garden with restaurant and children's play area. Winter sports, heated swimming pool, tennis, walking, climbing, fishing nearby.
Location Turn left off road from Spiez and Thun, near the Oeschinensee chairlift. Hotel is quietly situated. Parking.
Restriction Not suitable for &.
Credit cards Access, Diners, Visa.
Terms B&B 55–85 Sfrs; dinner, B&B 75–105 Sfrs. Set lunch 10–30 Sfrs, dinner 20–40 Sfrs; full alc 40 Sfrs. Reduced rates and special meals for children.

KLOSTERS 7250 Graubünden   Map 8

Romantik Hotel Chesa	*Tel* (083) 4.22.22
Grischuna	*Fax* (083) 4.16.82
Bahnhofstrasse 9	*Telex* 853348 CHESA

In the centre of this busy resort, a very *gemütlich* traditional hotel with flowery balconies and lots of character, but also well modernised. "Very friendly staff, food and service excellent" is this year's endorsement of previous panegyrics: "Lots of antiques, pretty dining room (excellent fresh vegetables), front desk kind and pleasant. We had a nice large room with pretty balcony in the chalet-annexe." "An ancient timber door unlatches into a bright interior modernised with honey-coloured wood, set off with furnishings in the traditional Swiss green, white and scarlet. The bright reception area is new, but the rest of the hotel is delightfully old and mellow, made of wood dark with age. Our room on the fourth floor of the main building (no lift) was not large, but had bright rugs on the polished floor and hand-woven bedspreads. Everything was shiningly clean. The food is good, pleasantly served by girls in Klosters costume. The cellar-bar is where the young locals and the après-skiers meet: wonderful lively friendly atmosphere." (*David Thibodeau*)

Open Early Jun–mid-Apr.
Rooms 16 double, 10 single – 17 with bath and/or shower, all with telephone and radio. 11 in annexe opposite.
Facilities Lounge with TV, restaurant; cellar bar with pianist in high season; bowling. Sun terrace, small garden.
Location In centre of Klosters Platz, near the station.
Restriction Not suitable for &.
Credit cards All major cards accepted.
Terms Dinner, B&B: single 90–190 Sfrs, double 160–380 Sfrs; full board 20 Sfrs per person added. Set lunch 15–28 Sfrs, dinner 41–61 Sfrs; full alc 79 Sfrs. Special meals for children on request.

We asked hotels to estimate their 1990 tariffs some time before publication so the rates given are often arbitrary. Please always check terms with hotels when making bookings.

LAUSANNE 1006 Vaud   Map 8

Hôtel Le Château d'Ouchy   *Tel* (021) 26.74.51
2 place du Port, Ouchy   *Telex* 455402
Lausanne 6   *Fax* (021) 275137

Two kilometres from the city centre, an old castle in a splendid lakeside setting at Ouchy, converted into an expensive classic hotel. Furnishings, many in period style, are somewhat heavy, but rooms are comfortable and spacious, with fine views of the Alps. Helpful staff; good food, served on a terrace above the lake. 44 rooms (some subject to traffic noise), all with bath and/or shower. B&B double 160–210 Sfrs [1989]. Recent nomination. More reports please.

LENK 3775 Bern   Map 8

Hotel Wildstrubel   *Tel* (030) 6.31.11
                                                            Telex 922258

A sizeable modern chalet-style hotel, opposite the railway station (but quiet), in a mountain resort (walking and skiing) up a valley in the Bernese Oberland. Large comfortable rooms with balconies and views, big heated swimming pool, food good and varied. Open June–mid-Oct, mid-Dec–mid-Apr. 45 rooms, all with bath and shower. B&B: single 74–95 Sfrs, double 143–189 Sfrs. Full alc 60–80 Sfrs. Recent nomination. More reports please.

MEGGEN 6045 Lucerne   Map 8

Hotel Sonnegg   *Tel* (041) 37.21.64
Hauptstrasse 37

A popular family hotel just east of Lucerne, up a hill above its lovely lake. "Simple, unpretentious and comfortable, with meticulous housekeeping", runs a report this year; "the seafood restaurant is superlative, with a friendly, informal ambience." Others agree that the fish and seafood dishes are excellent, if expensive (but there's also a cheaper coffee-shop, serving pizzas, etc). "A good hotel, with good service and modern comfort combined with Swiss rustic touches. The helpful staff will baby-listen and even supervised our teenage sons. There is a small park on the lake's edge." (*H and B Shames, J Michael Morrison*) However, some bedrooms have this year been found noisy, either from traffic or owing to thin party-walls. And a muddle has been reported over a room booking.

Open All year. Restaurant closed Sun, and Mon lunch.
Rooms 18 double – 9 with bath and shower, all with TV.
Facilities Lift. Bar, restaurant.
Location On lake Lucerne, 5 km E of Lucerne towards Rigi, Gotthard on old road.
Credit cards All major cards accepted.
Terms [1989 rates] B&B: single 55–60 Sfrs, double 85–90 Sfrs; half board 30 Sfrs per person added.

If you think we have over-praised a hotel or done it an injustice, please let us know.

MONTREUX 1820 Vaud   Map 8

Hôtel Eden au Lac	*Tel* (021) 963.55.51
11 rue du Théâtre	*Fax* (021) 963.18.13
	Telex 453151

Montreux, with its backcloth of Lac Léman and mountains, its beautifully manicured flower walk by the waterfront, and its many elegant Edwardian Victorian villas, is a delightful town. The *Eden*, one of its larger hotels, is set right by the lake and has recently been restored to its turn-of-the-century glory. "The glorious pink-and-white first-floor dining-room makes a romantic setting for dinner, looking out on the lake. The food is excellent (there is an à la carte restaurant downstairs and another in the garden in the summer) and breakfasts are buffet affairs, with wonderful muesli. Service combines style with friendliness. Bedrooms well equipped, bathrooms large but old-fashioned." All lake-facing rooms have a balcony with awning.

Open All year except Jan.
Rooms 10 suites, 76 double, 18 single – all with bath, shower, telephone and TV. Baby-sitting on request.
Facilities Hall, 2 salons, TV room, bar, 2 restaurants; 3 conference rooms. Garden; terrace for meals. Swimming pool nearby.
Location Central, on lake. Parking.
Credit cards All major cards accepted.
Terms [1988 rates] B&B: single 150–200 Sfrs, double 200–250 Sfrs, suite 350–480 Sfrs; dinner, B&B 35 Sfrs added.

MÖREL 3893 Valais   Map 8

Hôtel Relais Walker	*Tel* (028) 27.24.45
	Fax (028) 27.17.16
	Telex 473355

Just east of Brig up the Rhône valley, Walter Walker's modern hotel makes a good base for climbers and skiers as well as for his more eponymous guests. "Mörel used to be familiar to many of the British upper classes as the starting point for the 4,000-ft climb to the Villa Cassel, the surprising mock-Tudor mansion built for Sir Ernest Cassel, the father of Lady Edwina Mountbatten; today nearly all that climb can be done in a cable car. The *Relais* has comfortable rooms, but no real lounge, though the bar provides a meeting and eating place for locals. The grill room serves excellent meat and fish dishes, and in autumn some delicious game specialities such as back of roe deer served with cooked fruits. Drawing sheets and colouring pencils are provided to keep younger guests happy. Good local wines. Herr Walker trained in Cornwall and speaks good English." More reports please.

Open All year.
Rooms 22 – all with shower, telephone and radio.
Facilities Lift. Bar, grill room, restaurant.
Location Village is 7 km E of Brig. Parking.
Credit cards All major cards accepted.
Terms [1989 rates] B&B 45–68 Sfrs; dinner, B&B 20 Sfrs per person added.

> Report forms (Freepost in UK) will be found at the end of the Guide.

MURTEN 3280 Fribourg   Map 8

Le Vieux Manoir Au Lac   *Tel* (037) 71.12.83
Meyriez   *Fax* (037) 71.31.88
                                                    Telex 942026

Murten (Morat in French) is an attractive medieval ramparted city built by
the Zähringers. In its outskirts, by the shores of Lac Morat, the stylish
Vieux Manoir – "expensive but worth it" – has pleasant views across the
lake to the vineyards opposite. The rooms, most overlooking the lake, are
large and tastefully decorated, well furnished in period style. The staff are
pleasant, friendly and professional. The good Swiss breakfasts include
freshly squeezed and peeled fruit, proper muesli, real jams and excellent
coffee served in a nicely decorated room overlooking the lake. Cooking,
presentation and service at dinner have all been commended. But we'd
welcome further reports.

Open Mid-Feb–mid-Dec.
Rooms 5 suites, 15 double, 4 single – all with bath and/or shower, telephone,
radio and TV.
Facilities Lift. 2 lounges, restaurant, veranda, terrace restaurant; conference
facilities. Lakeside garden, beach, swimming, sailing and fishing. Public indoor
and outdoor swimming pool 200 metres.
Location 1 km SE of Murten right on road to Lausanne.
Credit cards All major cards accepted.
Terms B&B single from 100 Sfrs, double from 180 Sfrs, suite 380 Sfrs. Full alc
75 Sfrs. Reduced rates for children sharing parents' room; special meals.

NEUHAUSEN 8212 Schaffhausen   Map 8

Hotel Bellevue   *Tel* (053) 22.21.21
Bad Bahnhofstrasse 17

Just two kilometres from the attractive medieval town of Schaffhausen
are the Rhine Falls, not the highest waterfalls in Europe but the most
powerful, and 500 feet wide. Here the *Bellevue*, aptly named, has a
breath-taking situation: most bedrooms, and some bathrooms, overlook
the falls. "From my bed, I had a fine view of the falls, in my splendid
double room," says a reader this year; "the food was excellent, especially
the game (huge helpings), and the service was *svelte*." Another visitor
had "an interesting room with the structural beams appearing out of the
floor". The spectacular views extend also to the "splendid lofty dining-
room" where there is lots of choice and breakfast includes cooked dishes.
Hotel staff pleasant. "The hotel's exterior is ordinary; without the Guide
we'd have passed it by." (*Trevor Lockwood*)

Open All year, except 24 Dec–26 Jan.
Rooms 24 double, 3 single – 13 with bath, 7 with shower, all with telephone,
radio and mini-bar.
Facilities Lift. Lounge, restaurants; functions room. Large garden with terrace.
Location By the Rhine on outskirts of Neuhausen, 2 km SW of Schaffhausen.
Parking.
Credit cards All major cards accepted.
Terms [1989 rates] B&B: single 42–98 Sfrs, double 80–170 Sfrs.

Give the Guide positive support. Don't just leave feedback to others.

NYON 1260 Vaud

Map 8

Hôtel du Clos de Sadex   *Tel* (022) 61.28.31

A dignified creeper-covered house on Lac Léman, formerly the home of Major and Madame Louis de Tscharner. They now run it as a hotel, seeking to preserve its patrician atmosphere as well as its elegant furnishings. And they appear to succeed. "What a delight", runs a recent report, "to be welcomed as if to a private house. Our beautiful bedroom had pretty butterfly wallpaper and a view on to the delightful gardens which run down to the lake. Our meal was reasonable but not remarkable." A visitor this year thought highly of the staff, but was less impressed by the food – "The plat du jour did not change during the three days of my visit." In fine weather, breakfast and lunch are served on the terrace overlooking the lake and mountains. One reader stayed in the annexe, on the ground floor, "I lived like a princess, in a huge beautifully furnished room with its own entrance hall. First-floor rooms are smaller." Bedrooms are expensive – but less so than in exorbitant Geneva, not far away.

Open All year except mid-Jan–mid-Feb.
Rooms 13 double, 5 single – 12 with bath and shower, 2 with shower, all with telephone and baby-listening. 5 in annexe 10 metres away. 2 ground-floor rooms.
Facilities Hall, salon with TV, restaurant; conference room. Gardens with terrace for meals, leading directly to lake (hotel has small harbour); swimming, boating, water-skiing.
Location 1 km from Nyon towards Lausanne on lake road; hotel is on right. Parking.
Credit cards All major cards accepted.
Terms B&B: single 65–160 Sfrs, double 110–230 Sfrs. Set lunch 40 Sfrs, dinner 60 Sfrs; full alc 60 Sfrs. Reduced rates for children sharing parents' room; special meals on request.

PONTRESINA 7504 Graubünden

Map 8

Hotel Garni Chesa Mulin   *Tel* (082) 6.75.75
Via Mulin   *Fax* (082) 6.70.40

Pontresina is an anagram of "inane sport", non-skiers may be relieved to hear. This is a smaller and quieter resort than its flashy neighbour, St-Moritz, but it still gets its fill of athletes. Here the modern white-walled *Chesa Mulin* has its admirers. "A warm personal welcome from the Schmid family, who work hard. Rooms are attractively furnished, and the excellent and varied buffet breakfast is served in a bright Alpine-style room." "Bedrooms have comfortable beds and armchairs. Lights are sensibly arranged and you can read in bed. There is a lovely garden with a fine view. Led by Mr and Mrs Schmid, the staff are most polite, friendly and helpful." In summer there are walks in woods and across meadows and glaciers. No restaurant, but good ones nearby. (*R Pinner*)

Open Dec–Apr, June–Oct.
Rooms 23 double, 4 single – all with bath and/or shower, telephone, radio, mini-bar and TV. 1 specially designed for ♿.
Facilities Lift. Lounge, bar, TV room, breakfast room; sauna; solarium; terrace. Garden.
Location Central; turn off main road towards station. Garage and parking.
Credit cards All major cards accepted.

Terms [1989 rates] B&B: single 72–98 Sfrs, double 124–176 Sfrs. 1-week bookings (Sat–Sun) preferred in winter; ski packages in winter low season. Reduced rates for children sharing parents' room; special meals on request. (No restaurant, but snacks available.)

ROUGEMONT 1838 Vaud   Map 8

Hôtel Valrose   *Tel* (029) 48146
                                                       Fax (029) 48854

Set on the edge of a pretty village west of Gstaad, here is a simple modern chalet-style hotel without frills or graces: but it is clean and welcoming, and offers good value to those on a budget holiday in an expensive country. "The owner is pleasant and humorous, the food is plentiful, and nearly every room has a view of the mountains. The railway station is close by, but Swiss trains are quiet, and after 10 pm the only sound was the tinkling of cow bells." (*Esler Crawford; Stephan and Kate Murray-Sykes*)

Open All year except Nov. Restaurant closed Tue.
Rooms 12 double, 3 single – 7 with shower, all with mini-bar; TV on request.
Facilities Salon with TV, bar/cafe, 2 dining-rooms. Terrace, garden.
Location Rougemont is 4 km W of Saanen. Parking.
Restriction Not suitable for &.
Credit cards All major cards accepted.
Terms [1989 rates] B&B 33–46 Sfrs; dinner B&B 16 Sfrs added per person; full board 28 Sfrs added. Set lunch/dinner 18–20 Sfrs; full alc 40–45 Sfrs. Reduced rates for children; special meals on request.

SAANENMÖSER 3777 Bern   Map 8

Hotel Hornberg   *Tel* (030) 4.44.40
                                                       Fax (030) 4.62.79

"Situation lovely, food excellent, owners and staff warm and genuine" – a new plaudit for a typical family-run chalet-style hotel which stands alone at the foot of the Hornberg and looks out over the valley near Gstaad. "The bedrooms are extremely comfortable and well equipped. The food is imaginative, artistically presented and *hausgemacht*. The breakfast buffet is the best I've ever seen. Children are made welcome and are well provided for. The owners, the von Siebenthals, run excursions at no extra charge: the trip may be to the family cheese-making hut high up in the mountains, a mountain lake or some remote local beauty spot." (*Confirmed this year by K and SM-S*)

Open Jun–Oct, Dec–Apr.
Rooms 7 suites, 20 double, 6 single – 27 with bath, 6 with shower, all with telephone and radio; some with balcony.
Facilities Lounge, bar with TV, children's playroom, restaurant, dining-room; terrace. Large garden, indoor and outdoor swimming pool, sauna. Winter sports. Trips, barbecues, picnics organised for guests.
Location 20 km N of Gstaad.
Restriction Not suitable for &.
Credit cards All major cards accepted (but only in restaurant).
Terms Half board: single 80–135 Sfrs, double 148–320 Sfrs. Set lunch 20–25 Sfrs, dinner 40–60 Sfrs; full alc 40 Sfrs. Reduced rates for children; special meals.

Please make a habit of sending a report if you stay at a Guide hotel.

ST MORITZ 7500 Graubünden

Map 8

Hotel Chesa sur l'En

Tel (082) 3.31.44
Fax (082) 3.64.74

A romantic and unusual hotel, probably not to all tastes, and very different from most others in swanky St-Moritz. It is a huge 19th-century chalet, set amid pines on a hillside just outside the town, and its old-style decor is lavish: the massive front door opens onto a richly panelled and ornately carved main hall. The warm personal touch of the ever-present owners, the Schwarzenbachs, is admired: but the rooms are defiantly old-fashioned (few have private baths), and it was this above all that took the *Chesa* out of last year's Guide. But it has many devotees who return affectionately year after year – such as the American couple who sent this year's report: "A jewel of Swiss belle époque architecture, with an enveloping ambience – a wonderful experience. The Schwarzenbachs have been running the inn for 30 years. Eliane is in front organising glühwein parties and making little favours for the ladies; Dieter is preparing delicious four-course meals. This is not a place for those who want mod cons. Many of the rooms would be ruined if *en suite* bathrooms were installed. In fact, with a little imagination one can imagine oneself back in the 1880s: to get a bath you ring a bell, soon there's a soft knock on the door and clean towels are presented. But it's a very dreary bathroom." Upper rooms have fine views over the mountains. The central heating has been described as "of venerable age and infirmity". Four rooms *do* now have baths *en suite*. (*Lynne and David Allen*) More reports would be appreciated.

Open 15 Dec–30 Apr, 10 Jul–6 Nov.
Rooms 12 double, 2 single – 4 with bath and shower, 3 with shower; 5 with radio, 7 with TV.
Facilities Hall, salon with TV, dining-room, functions room. Sun terraces.
Location In St Moritz Bad, 5 mins by bus to St Moritz. Parking.
Restrictions Not suitable for &.
Credit cards All major cards accepted.
Terms B&B 35–99 Sfrs; dinner B&B 58–127 Sfrs. Set dinner 32 Sfrs; full alc 42–49 Sfrs. 50% reduction for children sharing parents' room.

SCHAFFHAUSEN 8200

Map 8

Rheinhotel Fischerzunft
Rheinquai 8

Tel (053) 25.32.81
Fax (053) 24.32.85
Telex 897162 FZFT

A very picturesque medieval town on the upper Rhine, close to Europe's most powerful waterfall, the Rhine Falls – that is the suitable setting for this former fishermen's guild house, now converted into an exceptionally brilliant and stylish restaurant (three red *Gault Millau toques*), with glorious bedrooms and bathrooms to match. The owner-chef André Jaeger met his Chinese wife Doreen in Hong Kong, and their inspired partnership continues to draw superlatives from readers. "Cooking with a decidedly oriental accent, served with great style by the glamorous Doreen and her team in a beautiful dining-room; she runs her busy restaurant with discipline *and* style. The food is served on clear glass plates which are placed on black lacquer trays decorated with flower petals. My favourite dishes were sautéed foie gras coated with sesame, and crisply fried duck breast with shitake mushrooms in oyster sauce. There are spectacular large flower arrangements in the restaurant and in the bedrooms. Our room had every mod con imaginable, including beds which adjust so that either your head or your feet can be elevated." Most reports also comment on the Closomat machines attached to the loos, with "a warm water jet if you press one lever, a warm air jet if you press another". "Dinner was one of the best we have ever had; I am told that the dishes have a 'Celestial Empire' taste. Breakfast was a buffet affair. We felt the hotel fell apart a bit in the morning, as the owners were not there and the whole place was being hoovered and polished – it is a restaurant-with-rooms, rather than a hotel." (*Minda Alexander*)

Open All year, except last week Jan, first 2 weeks Feb, 23/24 Dec.
Rooms 3 suites, 8 double – all with bath and/or shower, telephone, radio, TV and mini-bar.
Facilities 2 lounges, card room, restaurant; conference facilities. Terrace for alfresco dining in summer.
Location On banks of Rhine, 5 mins' walk from centre (all windows triple-glazed). Parking.
Restriction Not suitable for &.
Credit cards All major cards accepted.
Terms [1989 rates] B&B: single occupancy 110–160 Sfrs, double 150–220 Sfrs, suite 260–305 Sfrs. Children under 6 sharing parents' room free; special meals on request.

SCHÖNRIED-GSTAAD 3778 Bern   Map 8

Hotel Ermitage-Golf
Tel (030) 4.27.27
Fax (030) 4.71.95
Telex 922213

Surrounded by pinewoods and upland meadows, smooth with snow in winter, the village of Schönried stands 180 metres higher than Gstaad and is now a reputed resort with superb skiing facilities. The smartest and largest of its hotels is the *Ermitage-Golf*, two big connecting chalets, magnificently equipped, recently refurbished and enlarged. "The new rooms are of high quality," says a reader this year; "the young staff are pleasant and attentive, and the food is interesting, varied and plentiful, much of it buffet style. The breakfast buffet is enormous, and can be taken out on the terrace facing the pretty garden." Others have written: "There are now four restaurants – a charcoal grill, two French restaurants, and an intimate *Stübli* for modest fare. Dishes are finely prepared and elegantly served. Tucked well away in the basement is a disco, and a 'sauna park' with steam baths and bio-sauna. The garden provides beautiful views." A prime attraction is the *Solbad*, a large indoor swimming pool fitted with briny water heated to 35°C. This indoor pool opens to an outdoor one heated similarly: "It was a sensational experience in December to swim outside, the body most comfortably warmed, but the head in the nippy night air of -10°C, the steam of the water rising to reveal the high surrounding snow banks." (*Kenneth Bishop*)

Open Mid-Dec–Easter; mid-May–end Oct.
Rooms 28 suites, 28 double, 15 single – all with bath and/or shower, telephone, radio and TV.

Facilities Lift. Hall, salon, TV room, 2 bars, snack bar, 2 restaurants, café, terrace restaurant; conference facilities. Billiards, table tennis, squash, indoor and outdoor swimming pool, sauna, fitness room. Garden with tennis, squash. Ski lifts, cable cars opposite hotel.
Location On N11, 8 km E of Gstaad. Underground parking.
Credit cards All major cards accepted.
Terms [1989 rates] Dinner, B&B: single 105–2,420 Sfrs, double 190–560 Sfrs. Full board 20 Sfrs per person added. Reduced rates and special meals for children.

SCHWANDEN 3657 Bern   Map 8

Gasthof-Restaurant Rothorn   *Tel* (033) 51.11.86

This "authentic Swiss mountain village", full of yodelling and creamy milk, stands high above Gunten, facing across the lovely lake of Thun to the Bernese Alps. Here the *Rothorn*, a big brown chalet amid meadows, backed by pinewoods, has evoked four new plaudits this year for its genuine local character and rural charm – and for the "friendly and gracious hospitality" of the owners, Werner and Trudi Amstutz-Rentsch. "The place is a social centre for the village – pensioners sit smoking, gossiping, playing cards, and spontaneous singing comes and goes. And the warmth and professionalism of the whole operation are augmented by the breathtaking views. Our room was simple but tasteful and spacious." "The food was wholesome, plentiful, local in style: fresh wild fruit (bilberries, etc) were often the basis of delicious puddings. An outstandingly pleasant hotel." Others, too, have admired the "delightful" Amstutzes, the friendly staff, the rooms, the good and copious food – and the yodelling in the bar. Rooms at the back look out onto the hillside and are very quiet. Those at the front are larger and have balconies, but suffer from some noise from traffic and from the bar around midnight. (*David and Hanna Rampton, AD and JE Stokes, Ellen Buchanan, R Barratt*) One reader filed a disgruntled minority report, complaining of poor room and bathroom maintenance, and a spartan breakfast.

Open All year except 3 weeks in Nov and 3 weeks after Easter. Restaurant closed Mon.
Rooms 13 double – 10 with bath and/or shower; some with balcony. 4 in annexe.
Facilities Lounge, TV room, dining-room, restaurant with occasional folk music.
Location 30 mins' drive NW of Interlaken, 15 mins NE of Thun.
Credit cards None accepted.
Terms B&B: single 38–50 Sfrs, double 64–94 Sfrs; dinner, B&B: single 55–67 Sfrs, double 98–128 Sfrs; full board: single 67–78 Sfrs, double 120–150 Sfrs. Set lunch/dinner 12–26 Sfrs. Children under 6 sharing parents' room half price, 6–12 30% reduction.

SILS-MARIA 7514 Graubünden   Map 8

Edelweiss Hotel   *Tel* (082) 4.55.51
Dorfstrasse   *Fax* (082) 4.55.22
                                                         Telex 852235

In a smart village resort of the upper Engadin valley, between two lakes, this sedate hotel dating from 1875 has been properly modernised and is well run, with friendly staff and good food. But it's a bit impersonal and lacks cosiness. 74 rooms, all with bath and shower. B&B double 180–320 Sfrs. Set menus 25–40 Sfrs. Little recent feedback. More reports welcome.

SOGLIO 7610 Graubünden   Map 8

Pension La Soglina   *Tel* (082) 4.16.08

Hitherto in the Guide under the name of *Stüa Granda*, this hotel has now rechristened itself *La Soglina*, the name of its main annexe. It's an unpretentious, appealing and very well-run place, in a high mountain village above the main valley highway from St-Moritz to Chiavenna in Italy. It continues to be popular, "We were met off the bus by the courteous owner, Roland Nass, and taken to a lovely room with a balcony and fine view down the valley. The food was delicious, and though the set menus offered little choice, they varied daily. Staff were efficient, serving breakfast at 6.30 am when we needed it." An earlier view, "Chestnut trees surround the village and the air is unusually crisp. The sunny terrace restaurant is a favourite meeting place for hikers and the fare is hearty and fresh. Guest rooms (some small) have high-beamed ceilings and lace curtains. The aroma of fresh bread and local specialities such as bundner gerstensuppe fill the air. A romantic hotel for those who love out-of-the-way places in beautiful settings." More reports would be welcome.

Open All year. Restaurant closed in Nov.
Rooms 31 double – all with bath, shower, telephone and radio; some with balcony. Ground-floor rooms.
Facilities 2 sitting rooms, restaurant. Garden terrace. Sauna, turkish bath, whirl-pool, solarium and fitness room.
Location On edge of village, just N of route N3 between Chiavenna (to W) and Maloja pass (to E). Nearby parking.
Credit cards None accepted.
Terms [1989 rates] B&B 43–50 Sfrs per person; dinner, B&B 68–73 Sfrs. Special meals for children on request.

SPORZ 7078 Graubünden   Map 8

Hotel Guarda Val   *Tel* (081) 34.22.14
                                                 Fax (081) 34.46.45
                                                 Telex 851776

Near Lenzerheide on the Chur–St-Moritz road, the alpine village of Sporz offers indeed plenty of sports (skiing, tennis, golf), as well as this stylish, very attractive and somewhat unusual holiday hotel, its bedrooms in eight old wooden buildings scattered on a hillside: "A 'picture postcard' hotel, the rooms being converted from original barns and cowsheds in a most tasteful manner. Ours also had a lounge and settee, thus providing a room for our teenage son, separated from the main bedroom by a small kitchenette. The view from the window took in mountain streams, alpine meadows and Swiss cows with bells. Lunch was an excellent buffet affair, with mountain cured ham. Not a cheap place, but idyllic." Plenty of old beams, and a handsome candle-lit dining-room.

Open 15 Dec–15 Apr, 10 June–30 Oct.
Rooms 12 suites, 21 double, 2 single – 25 with bath, 10 with shower, all with telephone and radio. Some with kitchenette. Rooms in 8 different buildings.
Facilities TV room, bar, 2 restaurants; functions room. Sauna.
Location 2 km from Lenzerheide, 16 km S of Chur.
Restriction Not suitable for &.
Credit cards All major cards accepted.

Terms B&B: single 100–155 Sfrs, double 180–270 Sfrs, suite 270–380 Sfrs; dinner, B&B: single 130–185 Sfrs, double 240–330 Sfrs, suite 330–440 Sfrs. Reduced rates for children; special meals on request.

VADUZ 9490 Liechtenstein   Map 8

Park-Hotel Sonnenhof   *Tel* (075) 21192
Mareestrasse 29,   *Telex* 889329 soho fl

In a glorious mountain-backed parkland setting just outside Liechtenstein's tiny capital, a luxurious and elegant villa-style hotel, run by the warmly welcoming Real family. Large, well-fitted bedrooms, spacious gardens and lounges, indoor heated pool, excellent food. Closed 23–27 Dec. 29 rooms, all with bath and shower. B&B double 240–330 Sfrs. Set menu 45 Sfrs. New nomination. More reports welcome.

VEVEY 1800 Vaud   Map 8

Les Trois Couronnes   *Tel* (021) 921.30.05
49 rue d'Italie   *Fax* (021) 922.72.80
                                                          Telex 4511489

A five-star late-Victorian hotel in the grand tradition, right on the lakeside promenade in one of the smartest of Lac Léman resorts, well known for its exclusive girls' finishing-schools. Rooms have large french windows and balconies facing the lake. Dropped from the 1989 Guide for lack of reports, it is restored by a visitor this year: "Indeed a great hotel! Our 4th-floor room had a wonderful lake view and its embroidered bed-linens were wonderful. Breakfast the best on our tour." Others have praised the efficient and courteous service, and the food in the beautiful Louis XV-style dining room. Public rooms have an abundance of carved, gilded and marbled decor, with much fine furniture. There are fountains and flowers on the terrace. (*NPD and J Levine*)

Open All year.
Rooms 7 suites, 41 double, 27 single – all with bath and shower, telephone, radio and TV; baby-listening on request.
Facilities Lift. Salons, TV room, bar, restaurant; conference facilities; large terrace with open restaurant. Pianist several evenings a week.
Location Central, but quietly situated. Parking in courtyard.
Restrictions Not suitable for &.
Credit cards All major cards accepted.
Terms [1989 rates] B&B: single 150–250 Sfrs, double 250–350 Sfrs; dinner, B&B: 45 Sfrs added per person; full board 90 Sfrs added. Set lunch/dinner 50–60 Sfrs. Reduced rates and special meals for children.

VITZNAU 6354 Lucerne   Map 8

Hotel Floralpina   *Tel* (041) 83.13.86
PO Box 77

For a really stunning view, take Europe's oldest mountain rack-railway (1871) up to the Rigi-Kulm, which towers above Vitznau, one of the more elegant resorts on Lake Lucerne. Just outside the village, in a glorious lakeside setting backed by steep wooded hills, is this handsome modern hotel, praised again this year for its comfort, fine views and "simple but tasty" meals (good solid Swiss fare from a limited menu). It has huge grounds, direct access to swimming in the lake (private beach), and unbeatable views from the dining terrace. "Some of the largest double bedrooms one can find these days in Europe, and it's well worth paying extra for a lakeview room. Good cheese-board." (*WG Francis*) One reader criticised the food and its presentation and felt the hotel was too closely geared to package holidays and conferences.

Open 12 Apr–19 Oct.
Rooms 6 suites, 49 double, 9 single – all with shower, telephone, radio; TV on request.
Facilities Lift, ramps. Lounge, TV room, bar, restaurant, room; whirlpool, sauna, solarium. Terrace, park with children's playground, private beach.
Location 2 km S of Vitznau on Brunnen road.
Credit cards All major cards accepted.
Terms B&B 48–60 Sfrs. Set lunch/dinner 16 Sfrs; full alc 30 Sfrs. Reduced rates and special meals for children.

WEGGIS 6353 Lucerne   Map 8

Hotel Beau Rivage

Tel (041) 93.14.22
Fax (041) 93.19.81
Telex 862982

Weggis is a delightful resort some 30 minutes by road or 45 by steamer from Lucerne; other lake pleasures are easily accessible, as are the heights of Rigi, served by Weggis's funicular. The ever-popular *Beau Rivage* has a choice position right by the water, a few minutes' walk from the quay, with its own garden and swimming pool. "Charming and well appointed," runs a report this year; "food good, but not extraordinary." Previous verdicts: "The delightful hard-working Geering family make this an outstanding hotel, and it keeps on improving. The bedrooms are now superb and we can never fault the food." "The rooms are lovely with pleasant lake views and the staff were friendly and very helpful." (*Aaron W Esman, RS McNeill*) Some package tours, out of season only.

Open Early Apr–mid-Oct.
Rooms 4 suites, 31 double, 9 single – all with bath and/or shower, telephone, radio and TV.
Facilities Lift. Hall, lounges, TV room, bar, garden room, restaurant; lakeside terrace; band twice a week. Garden with swimming pool, beach, fishing.
Location 20 km E of Lucerne; on lake, near quay. Garages and parking.
Credit cards All major cards accepted.
Terms B&B: single 80–130 Sfrs, double 136–234 Sfrs, suite 240–270 Sfrs; half board: single 110–160 Sfrs, double 196–294 Sfrs, suite 300–330 Sfrs. Set lunch/dinner 40–45 Sfrs; full alc 60 Sfrs. Reduced rates for children sharing parents' room; special meals.

There are many expensive hotels in the Guide. We are keen to increase our coverage at the other end of the scale. If you know of a simple place giving simple satisfaction, please write and tell us.

Always let a hotel know if you have to cancel a booking, whether you have paid a deposit or not. Hotels lose thousands of pounds and dollars from "no-shows".

WENGEN 3823 Bern

Map 8

Hotel Eiger

Tel (036) 55.11.31
Fax (036) 55.10.30
Telex 923296

Family-run by the Fuchses for generations, but rebuilt in 1980 in traditional style (neat balconies, masses of stripped pine), here's a typical ski-hotel in a leading resort of the Bernese Oberland. Two nominations this year: "Very comfortable. The rooms are large, and the beds, duvets, etc, are pushed away each morning to create a sitting room, reinstated as a bedroom at 7 pm. The well-designed balconies look onto a marvellous view of the Jungfrau. Breakfast buffets were excellent (muesli with blackcurrants and bilberries); dinner was not so good, but adequate." "Warm and welcoming. Next door to station, so convenient for skiers. The charming staff join in the fun of your being on holiday. The small Eiger bar is the focal point of Wengen après-ski." (*M Scott Russell, and others*)

Open All year except 29 Apr–17 June. Grill Room closed Mon.
Rooms 9 suites, 20 double, 4 single – 31 with bath, 2 with shower – all with telephone and radio; TV on request.
Facilities Lift. Lounge, TV room, 2 restaurants, bar (in winter).
Location Central. No cars in Wengen. Park in Lauterbrunnen and take train.
Credit cards All major cards accepted.
Terms B&B: single 60–98 Sfrs, double 60–108 Sfrs, suite 75–118 Sfrs. Set lunch 13–22 Sfrs; dinner 35 Sfrs; full alc 35–65 Sfrs. Reduced rates and special meals for children.

WORB 3076 Bern

Map 8

Romantik Hotel Löwen
Enggisteinstrasse 3

Tel (031) 83.23.03
Fax (031) 83.58.77

In a village four miles from Bern, this small traditional hotel of character has been run by the same family for over 300 years,and has a solid local reputation for its good food. Lack of news forced it out of last year's Guide, but Americans now restore it: "A fine, elegant hostelry whose staff are courteous beyond courtesy, helpful to a fault. The rooms are spacious: ours had an armoire whose door hinges and locks were sensuously magnificent. Dinner was beautifully served and the atmosphere was relaxed." (*H and B Shames*)

Open All year. Restaurant closed Wed, Thur midday, 4 weeks Jul/Aug.
Rooms 14 – all with bath, shower, telephone and radio; 7 with TV.
Facilities Lounge, bar, TV room, restaurant, functions room. Garden with restaurant, children's playground, bowling alleys. Tennis, swimming nearby in summer, skating in winter.
Location Central, by church; parking. Worb is 10 km E of Bern on Lucerne road.
Restriction Not suitable for &.
Credit cards All major cards accepted.
Terms [1989 rates] B&B: single 70–85 Sfrs, double 130–145 Sfrs. Set lunch/dinner 10 and 30 Sfrs; full alc 55 Sfrs. Reduced rates and special meals for children.

Please make a habit of sending in a report as soon as possible after a visit when details are still fresh in your mind.

ZERMATT 3920 Valais   Map 8

Hôtel-Garni Metropol   *Tel* (028) 67.32.31
                                               Fax (028) 67.23.42
                                               Telex 472137

More affectionate plaudits in 1988/9 for this unpretentious little hotel
beside a river in the town centre, run tirelessly by the friendly
Taugwalder family. The views of the Matterhorn, from the bedrooms
with balconies on the south side, are a star feature: "The sight of this peak
from your window each morning, so close you could almost touch it, is an
exhilarating experience. Wonderful little hotel, reasonably priced."
Another new report: "Good and clean as ever, everyone so friendly, Frau
Taugwalder's cooking is really good and the helpings enormous, while
the buffet breakfast seems to improve each year." One devotee, after a
new two-week stay, regards it as "still my favourite hotel anywhere, and
I'd like to take it with me on my travels". He wrote earlier: "Zermatt with
its 107 hotels has developed in such an ugly way that almost every bit of
green is replaced by grey concrete. But the Taugwalders bought a
meadow in front of their hotel, so you have a clear view to the south. The
rooms have sensible beds, spacious cupboards and well-equipped
bathrooms. The constant rush of the river is soothing at night." There is
no full-scale restaurant, but snacks are available in the evening, and more
substantial dishes can be ordered specially in advance. (*Karen and David
Bashkin, Alex and Beryl Boyd, D and J Morris, Richard Pinner*)

Open 1 Dec–10 May, 10 June–20 Oct.
Rooms 20 double, 4 single – 16 with bath and shower, 4 with shower, all with
telephone, radio, TV and baby-listening.
Facilities Lift. Lounge, bar, TV room, dining-room. Garden and terrace.
Location Central; near station. Hotel porter will fetch you (no cars in Zermatt).
Credit cards All major cards accepted.
Terms B&B: single 55–94 Sfrs, double 100–188 Sfrs. Reduced rates for children.

ZÜRICH   Map 8

Hotel Florhof   *Tel* (01) 47.44.70
Florhofgasse 4, Zurich 8001   *Telex* 817364

A converted 16th-century patrician house with a small garden, in a
residential street near the *Kunsthaus* and university, and next to the music
conservatoire. This year, praise has flowed in more than ever – above all
for the friendly staff, also for the pleasant rooms and good food. "If you
don't turn up by the time breakfast ends, you get a call asking if they may
bring it up to you (free of charge). Most hotels don't care a bit whether
you have had your breakfast. We also had an oustandingly good lunch in
the garden." The restaurant is closed at weekends. (*Dr TJ David; also
Shelley B Andrews, Mrs PA Godden, EM Jacob, and others*)

Open All year. Restaurant closed Sat and Sun.
Rooms 23 double, 10 single – 22 with bath, 11 with shower, all with telephone,
radio, TV and mini-bar.
Facilities Lift. Salon, restaurant. Garden with restaurant.
Location Near *Kunsthaus* and university. Parking.
Restriction Not suitable for &.
Credit cards All major cards accepted.

Terms B&B: single 115–155 Sfrs, double 160–220 Sfrs. Set lunch 25–35 Sfrs, dinner 30–50 Sfrs; full alc 55–70 Sfrs. Reduced rates/special meals for children.

Hotel zum Storchen	*Tel* (01) 211.55.10
Am Weinplatz, Zurich 22	*Fax* (01) 211.64.51
Zürich 8001	*Telex* 813354

A pleasant riverside hotel, in the heart of old Zürich. Half the bedrooms, also the restaurant and terrace, face the river Limmat and have the classic view of the cathedral and the Baroque town hall. Those not facing the river overlook the charming Weinplatz, now a pedestrian precinct. The hotel is in a fairly new building, but its history dates back 600 years: past guests have included Paracelsus and Richard Wagner. "Really civilised", says one old admirer. "The cuisine is distinguished, international with a Swiss touch, service is courteous and regulars are greeted like old friends." "The panelled restaurant, with the atmosphere of one of Zurich's old guild-halls, is good", runs one report this year; "in summer drinks and light meals are served on the lovely canopied terrace facing the river. My room was simple but cosy." Another 1989 visitor commended the "reliable, efficient" staff, but a third thought the place rather characterless and found his riverside room a bit noisy and his breakfast uninspiring. (*Dr AJ Pearce, FR; also Arnold Horwell*)

Open All year.
Rooms 37 double, 40 single – all with bath and shower, telephone, radio and TV; baby-listening on request.
Facilities Lift. Bar, restaurant. Conference and banqueting facilities. Terrace.
Location Central, on river; no private parking.
Restriction Not suitable for &.
Credit cards All major cards accepted.
Terms B&B: single 160–240 Sfrs, double 240–360 Sfrs. Set lunch /dinner 50 Sfrs; full alc 75 Sfrs. Reduced rates for children; special meals on request.

Hotel Tiefenau	*Tel* (01) 251.24.09
Steinwiesstrasse 8–10	*Fax* (01) 251.24.76
Zürich 8032	*Telex* 816395

This well-located family-run hotel, gracefully furnished in period style, makes a useful addition this year to our still modest selection for Switzerland's largest city. "Cosy without being Swiss-stuffy. It's in a tiny quiet street very close to the Kunsthaus (with its wonderful Munchs, Impressionist and post-Impressionist collections) and the tram terminus which will get you in ten minutes to the Bahnhofstrasse. There's a terrace where you can eat or drink under huge shady trees and the food is quite good. You can walk to any number of good restaurants, including the *Krönenhalle*, James Joyce's favourite. The rooms are very comfortable, prettily furnished, and the service friendly." (*Nadine Gordimer, KA*)

Open All year except 2 or 3 weeks over Christmas/New Year.
Rooms 5 suites, 14 double, 11 single – all with bath, shower, telephone, radio, TV.
Facilities Lift. Salon, restaurant; conference facilities. Garden; terrace.
Location Fairly central, by Schauspielhaus. Free parking.
Credit cards All major cards accepted.
Terms [1989 rates] B&B: single 145–190 Sfrs, double 220–290 Sfrs, suite 340–410 Sfrs. Set lunch 25 Sfrs, dinner 30 Sfr; full alc 47.50 Sfrs. Reduced rates and special meals for children.

Turkey

TURBAN ADALYA OTELI, ANTALYA

ANAMUR Akdeniž   Map 12

Otel Anahan   *Tel* (7571) 3511
Tahsin Soylu Cad. 109   *Fax* (0751) 1005

*On the long beach outside this south coast town, a newly opened hotel with
clean, simple rooms, eager service and a large restaurant. 30 rooms, all with
bath and shower. B&B double US$47. Set menus US$8. No recent reports. More
welcome.*

ANKARA   Map 12

Bulvar Palas Oteli   *Tel* (4) 117.50.20
Atatürk Bulvari 141   *Telex* 42613 BLVD

"Good value: the rooms are airy, and though the plumbing creaks, it
works," says a recent visitor. An earlier comment: "The rest of Ankara
may try to impress with its modernity, but the *Bulvar Palas* sails through

still in the fifties, with its big bedrooms, solid plumbing and comfortable beds. Staff are efficient and abundant, meals are reasonably priced and of fair quality, but it is the atmosphere that is the thing: a 'B' movie remake of Istanbul's *Pera Palas*."

Open All year.
Rooms 177 – 167 with bath or shower, all with telephone, radio, TV, mini-bar and air-conditioning.
Facilities Lift. Lounge, restaurant; conference facilities; hairdressing salon.
Location Central. Next door to Belgian Ministry in area called "Ministries". Parking.
Credit cards All major cards accepted.
Terms On application.

ANTALYA   Map 12

Turban Adalya Oteli   *Tel* (31) 11.80.66 and 17.69.05
Kaleiçi Yat Limani   *Fax* (31) 123679
                                                     Telex 56241 TBA

Antalya's famous harbour has recently been much restored, and it is now a showplace resort. "Sleek yachts", we are told, "are moored alongside beautifully preserved Turkish houses with their dark wooden balconies and colourful tiled roofs. The *Turban Adalya*, originally a bank and then a warehouse, has been converted into a most individual small luxury hotel. The refreshing sound of running water from the fountains in the atrium-patio greets you as you walk into its welcome coolness; the charmingly decorated bedrooms lead off from upstairs galleries. There is a small bar-terrace at the back overlooking the harbour, with another bar and an excellent restaurant on the top floor." Endorsing that account, one visitor this year had a spacious, clean and quiet room with efficient air-conditioning, and found breakfast "a feast". Others agree that the rooms are charming, but point out that they have no view and there is no lounge; the hotel might be better for a stopover than for a long stay. A new "Presidential Suite" has just been opened in an old house nearby, with all modern facilities, balconies and harbour views. (*Mr and Mrs SC Jones-Parry*)

Open All year.
Rooms 2 suites, 26 double – all with shower, telephone, radio, TV, air-conditioning and mini-bar. "Presidential Suite", in building 15 metres away.
Facilities Lounge, 2 bars, restaurant; terrace. Garden. Swimming pool nearby.
Location Central, near citadel and harbour; parking.
Credit cards Possibly some accepted.
Terms [1989 rates] B&B: single US$49–US$66.50, double US$63–US$85.50, suite US$91–US$170. Reduced rates for children sharing parents' room.

ARSUZ Hatay   Map 12

Arsuz Turistik Oteli   *Tel* (881) 217.82 and (8873) 1444
Uluçinar,   *Telex* 68676 SEDT
Arsuz-Iskenderun

"Certainly the best resort-hotel on the eastern Mediterranean coast of Turkey. Its clean white block sits like a docked liner on the shore of this tiny fishing village, now officially renamed Uluçinar. The Mistikoglu family have made it the weekend seaside retreat of wealthy Alexandretta (Iskenderun) and Antioch (Antakya). Bedrooms are sparsely furnished but well maintained; public rooms have a relaxed Mediterranean style; the broad paved terrace – with its palms, flower-beds, globe lanterns, white wrought-iron balustrades and well-upholstered garden furniture – is worth the front cover of any tourist office hand-out. The brothers who host the operation are unforced charm itself and speak excellent English. Other staff are obliging and professional. Food in the restaurant is fine and unfussy. High season high jinks extend to an open-air disco – Turkish hotel discos are relatively dressy and sedate affairs. Potential hazards are the local mosquitoes and the village itself which has little to offer apart from a good back-drop of distant mountains." More reports please.

Open 15 Mar–31 Oct.
Rooms 20 suites, 74 double – all with bath or shower, telephone and radio.
Facilities Lift, ramps. 2 lounges, T V room, 2 bars, restaurant; banqueting room; Terrace with snack bar. Private beach.
Location 32 km S of Iskenderun.
Credit cards Diners, Visa.
Terms B&B: single US$31, double US$39, suite US$78; dinner, B&B: single US$38, double US$52, suite US$104. Set lunch/dinner US$9. Children under 5 free; special meals.

BODRUM Muğla   Map 12

Manzara Oteli   *Tel* (6141) 1719
Kumbahçe Mah, Meteoroloji Yani

A small hilltop hotel, some five minutes' walk from the seafront of an attractive resort town opposite the Greek island of Kos. Its position gives a stunning view of the bay and of the 'crusader castle', especially when illuminated at night. Rooms are in the style of small apartments, each with a terrace for outdoor eating, small sink unit and refrigerator. Enthusiasm again this year: "The most delightful discovery of our trip. Staff are very welcoming. We took dinner at sunset on the flower-decked poolside terrace, overlooking the castle and twin harbours: food was delicious, imaginative, served with friendly care. The bedrooms are small suites, artfully strewn down a steepish hill, linked by meandering whitewashed steps lined with pots of brilliant flowers. There are great swatches of bougainvillea, trumpet vine, morning glory, and other lovely climbing plants, creating privacy, providing shade, and framing spectacular views. I felt that I could understand at last what the Hanging Gardens of Babylon must have been like. We loved the hotel and the charming though touristy atmosphere of the busy yacht harbour. Only two small niggles: some mosquitoes, and an uncomfortable bed." There is a small heated swimming pool with an adjoining bar and small restaurant, with service throughout the day. (*Dr Suzanne L Martin*) The *Manzara* may now be insisting on half-board terms despite the self-catering facilities.

Open All year.
Rooms 20 double, including some suites – all with bath or shower, arranged in small apartments with living room, with sink unit and refrigerator, and terrace.
Facilities Restaurant. Terrace with swimming pool and bar.
Location On hill overlooking Bodrum.
Terms On application.

| **Hotel Myndos** | *Tel* (6141) 2591 and 3080 |
| Eski Çeşme Cafer Paşa Caddesi 68 | *Telex* 52802 AGSO |

Brand new: 6 attractive white 2-storey villa-style blocks, set round a lovely central pool with loungers and chairs, all floodlit at night. 62 rooms, cool, elegantly simple, with marble floors, all with modern shower. Restaurant poor, but lots in town. Some teething troubles: e.g. hot water erratic. Double room with breakfast US$55, with half board US$75. Recent nomination. More reports please.

BURSA

Map 12

| **Çelik Palas Oteli** | *Tel* (24) 361900 |
| Çekirge Caddesi 79 | *Telex* 32121 CEPA |

A large pre-war "grand hotel" in a smart suburb, overlooking the old town. Recently renovated and enlarged, it has large, clean comfortable rooms, some with balconies facing the mountains and valley. Marble hammam, indoor pool, disco; copious breakfasts, decent international restaurant with violinists and dance floor. 173 rooms, all with bath and shower. B&B double 150,000 Tl. Breakfast 10,000 Tl [1989]. No recent reports. More welcome.

ÇAVUŞIN Nevşehir

Map 12

Turbel Pansion Restaurant   *Tel* (4861) 14.27

"Definitely the best place to stay in Cappadocia", writes this year's enthusiastic nominator; "Çavuşin is a village in the heart of the Göreme region with its 'fairy chimneys' of lava and ancient churches cut in the soft rock, many with fine frescos. Hence every tour seems to pass through here and every town boasts a host of tacky hotels. Çavuşin is the only unspoilt place in Göreme, and this small *pension* is its only hotel, set at the mouth of a beautiful valley where the locals grow grapes and vegetables between the strange rock chimneys. The pale rock cliffs lining the valley are a lovely pink which deepens beautifully at sunset. The *pension* itself is a fine converted farm, with an open-air restaurant in its ample courtyard. The lower bedrooms, once the stables, are cut in the rock; cool at all times of the day, they are downright musty at night. Upper rooms have lovely views and are less musty, but warm during the day. Each room has pretty blue striped sheets. The loos and showers, located across the courtyard, were clean. The best thing about the *pension* is the owner/manager Mustala Kaygisiz, extremely kind and pleasant, who worked in France for many years and is intent on making his hotel comfortable and attractive. He will take you for tours round the valley in his van. As for his food, the chicken and lamb are good, but the local fish is bony and tasteless. The local rosé wine is excellent." (*Claire Enders*) More reports eagerly awaited.

Open 1 Apr–15 Nov.
Rooms 3 double, 7 triple – some ground-floor rooms.
Facilities Salon, 2 bars, TV room; restaurant. Garden with children's play area. Occasional traditional music and dance evenings.
Location Çavuşin is 15 km E of Nevşehir, 3 km N of Göreme. Parking.

Restrictions Not suitable for &.
Credit cards Access, Visa.
Terms B&B: single 15,000 Tl, double 30,000 Tl; dinner, B&B: single 22,000 Tl, double 45,000 Tl; full-board single 28,000 Tl, double 55,000 Tl. Set dinner 10,000 Tl; full alc 13,000 Tl. Reduced rates and special meals for children.

ÇEŞME 35930 İzmir   Map 12

Kanuni Kervansaray Oteli   *Tel* (549) 26490
Çeşme Kalesi Yani   *Telex* 51902 GOLD

This attractive Guide newcomer is a converted caravanserai (inn for travellers), with a massive arcaded courtyard and rooms of real Turkish character, set in a small town on the coast west of Izmir: "Çeşme is said to be destined to be *the* major Turkish resort and big hotels are shooting up outside it: but as yet it retains a lovely quiet village ambience. This atmospheric hotel looks up to the superb 15th-century walled castle, lit up at night. The garden courtyard itself is a wonderful place to sit of an evening. Rooms are fair sized with good bathrooms, and cool because of the thickness of the walls. The staff are charming and attentive. Food is twice the price of a Turkish restaurant but nicely prepared and less bland and 'international' than in many hotels: we enjoyed our meals by the beautiful old fountain in the courtyard. There's no pool, but guests can go 3 kilometres to the pool and beach of the *Golden Dolphin*, part of the same chain. Nearby beaches are sandy and pleasant." (*C and N Brooks-Matthew*)

Open Apr–Oct.
Rooms 2 suites, 30 double – 30 with bath, 2 with shower, all with telephone and radio. 9 ground-floor rooms.
Facilities Lounge, TV room, bar, restaurant. Garden, courtyard. Swimming pools 3 km.
Location Central, parking. Çeşme is 70 km W of İzmir.
Credit cards All major cards accepted.
Terms [1989 rates] B&B: US$22–US$39, suite US$81–US$100. Set lunch/dinner US$12,50, full alc US$15. Reduced rates and special meals for children.

DATÇA Muğla   Map 12

Perili Köşk   *Tel* (081) 44027
PO Box 46   *Fax* Istanbul (1) 345.36.25
                                                    Telex 29279 MRCC

Few hotels in this book are more beguilingly idiosyncratic than this "Fairies' Castle" (literal translation) on the coast opposite Rhodes. "From Marmaris after a tortuous 60-kilometre drive through the mountains, a neat sign on the left directs you along a rough track that you'd think only fit for a donkey. After about 700 metres, a lovely tiled roof and chimneys come into view, peering over cascades of oleander and bougainvillea. The hotel faces a beautiful crescent bay with no other building in sight (Datça village is 18 kilometres away). The design is impressive – a wealth of lovely natural pine, with balconies and latticed windows, and the rooms have stunning traditional framed panelled ceilings. We had a good-sized room – some are cramped, but all have bathrooms." That nominator's report has since been qualified by an inspector who was at once dazzled and infuriated: "That tortuous drive is spectacular, hair-raising, stunningly beautiful, past vistas of islands and bays. This part of Turkey is blessedly green. The *Köşk* is the fantasy of a rich Turk (seldom there) who regards it as his toy, which he delights to embellish. Tiled terraces at different levels, a blue-tiled fountained courtyard, a wrought-iron gateway leading to the beach, and a white wrought-iron pavilion like a Victorian bandstand. The interior is even more Turkish, its core being a windowless mosque-like dome. My husband thought it all a bit over-the-top, but I swallowed it delightedly, partly because it's the only hotel in Turkey outside Istanbul that we found to have any personal eccentricity. However, there are drawbacks. While most rooms have a balcony, those at the rear must be dark (though cool). It's a summer place, and in mid-October it was all a bit *triste*. Though breakfast was good, the main meals were poor. And the place is expensive, and remote from anywhere of interest." *Since receiving that report, we learn this year that the hotel has a new manager, and has added 17 bedrooms in pavilions in the grounds, almost doubling its size. Have these changes spoilt the wayward charm, or do they mean that bed and board are now improved? More reports badly needed.*

Open Apr–end Oct.
Rooms 37 double – all with shower. 23 in pavilions in grounds. Ground-floor rooms.
Facilities Lounge, bar, dining room; terrace. Garden with tennis court; beach with water sports.
Location 18 km E of Datça towards Marmaris.
Restriction Not suitable for &.
Credit card Visa.
Terms Dinner, B&B: double US$54–US$90. Full alc US$10–US$15. Reduced rates and special meals for children.

INCEKUM Antalya   Map 12

Alara Oteli   *Tel* (3237) 1146 and 1153
Yeşilköy, Bay of Incekum   *Telex* 56613 ALRA

Enjoyed for its tranquil setting and unspoilt beach, the *Alara* is 23 kilometres from the big popular resort of Alanya, but it runs a twice daily mini-bus service into town. "It is in a prime position high up at one end of the bay giving wide vistas over the surrounding area. Built in the Moorish style, it is made up of five separate buildings. The main one houses reception, lounge, bar and open-air dining-room and is ringed by a pleasant patio and pool overlooking the cliffs. The four bedroom blocks are set amid the well-tended gardens which run down to the sea. The rooms all have a sea view and are clean and fresh, though rather unsophisticated. All the staff are helpful, though only the manager spoke English. The food was palatable, if hardly a gastronomic experience. A pleasant and relaxing base for a most enjoyable holiday." More reports please.

Open 1 Apr–31 Oct.
Rooms 6 suites, 119 double – all with bath and shower and telephone; many with balcony. All in 4 separate buildings in grounds.
Facilities 2 bars, breakfast room, snack bar, restaurant; shops; belly dancing once a week. Garden with table tennis and swimming pool. Private beach, with water sports.
Location 23 km W of Alanya; mini-bus service twice a day.

Credit cards Amex, Visa.
Terms Dinner, B&B: single 50–88 DM, double 100–200 DM. Set meals 11 DM; full alc 15 DM. Reduced rates for children.

ISTANBUL   Map 12

Ayasofya Pansiyonlari   *Tel* (1) 513.36.60
Soğukçeşme Sokaği   *Telex* 23841 TSAP
Sultanahmet

An admirable work of restoration by the Touring Club of Turkey (see also *Hidiv Kasri* and *Yeşil Ev*, below): it is a terrace of nine historic houses, with attractive pastel-coloured wooden exteriors, down a narrow lane between Topkapi Palace and Hagia Sophia. Two houses have ground-floor breakfast and tea rooms, one has been converted into a library, strong on books about Old Constantinople. The old Roman cistern in the same road has recently been converted into a good restaurant, whose food, service and atmosphere have all again been found "delightful" this year. Earlier accounts: "The location is amazing. Try to get front rooms with the view of Hagia Sophia, for back ones face a wall. The omnipresent musak of a good sort (such as Chopin) seems to symbolise the yearning to make westerners feel at home." "The buildings are modernised yet have kept the charm of the period; their decor is lovely, with Turkish rugs on every floor." "Rooms comfortable, but plumbing could be better." The sluggish service, it is suggested, might not appeal to businessmen in a hurry. (*Mrs JA Patterson, Claire W Enders, Dr Suzanne L Martin*)

Open All year.
Rooms 5 suites, 6 triple, 34 double, 12 single – all with bath and/or shower, telephone and radio. All in 9 different houses.
Facilities Library, breakfast room, tea-room, two restaurants. Garden where breakfast and snacks are served.
Location Central, near Hagia Sophia.
Credit cards Access, Amex, Visa.
Terms On application.

Hidiv Kasri   *Tel* (1) 331.26.51
Çubuklu-Kanlica   *Fax* (1) 32.34.34
                                                   Telex 23346

Of the three Istanbul hotels converted from Ottoman mansions (see also *Ayasofya Pansiyonlari* and *Yeşil Ev*), this is by far the most bizarre and spectacular – the old summer palace of the last Viceroy of Egypt, set on a wooded hill on the Asian side of the city above the Bosphorus-shore villages of Çubuklu and Kanlica (famed for its yoghurt). The palace was built and originally furnished in a fabulous mixture of styles – stolid Middle-Eastern opulent, Tuscan villa and Belgian *Art Nouveau*. The restoration and refurbishment have kept many of the fittings, including regal mahogany-surrounded loos from a works in Lambeth, bronze cage-lifts from Munich and baths as big as boats with elaborate *fin-de-siècle* shower attachments surmounted by chrome crescent moons and stars. All the present furniture is fetchingly clumsy reproduction *Art Nouveau*. The master-mind of this enterprise, Çelik Gülersoy, decides on and designs everything according to how he sees the buildings in his dreams. His fantasy here includes features such as a vast marble fountain in the central hall, a wood-panelled salon hung with a riot of crystal and gilt chandeliers, a field of roses growing through grass outside a marble-floored tea-room lit by pastel-coloured blown glass flowers. A piano trio plays in the banana-shaped dining room at night – Mozart, Schubert, then *The Blue Danube*. Most rooms have views that it would be hard to better anywhere in the city. The superb Viceroy's suite has a long, wide terrace looking out over the trees to a sumptuous bend in the Bosphorus. On the same floor at the back, where the Tuscan eaves are most harmonious, the bedrooms overlook a rose field framed by cypresses. The cheaper rooms on the second floor are on a more human scale, but have no terrace. In order not to destroy the room plan of the palace, bathrooms and loos have not been knocked into the bedrooms – they are shared between two or three rooms but have the advantage of retaining their original impressive proportions. The grounds, with their wooden viewing-pavilions and a glass house selling local honey and preserves, are popular with day-trippers from all around. Getting to the hotel is not so easy. The infrequent boat all the way from the city centre to Kanlīca takes up to two hours – although this is a trip worth taking on its own account; or take the ferry to Uskudar, then bus, dolmuş (shared taxi) or taxi along the Asian shore of the Bosphorus to Kanlīca. We are still hoping for new reports, please.

Open All year.
Rooms About 30 including 2 suites – all with telephone and radio.
Facilities 3 restaurants, tea-room; tavern, beer garden; terrace. Wooded grounds.
Location On Asian shore of the Bosphorus, 2 hours by boat from the city centre (45 mins by ferry and land transport).
Terms [1989 rates] B&B double US$143.

Kalyon Hotel   *Tel* (1) 511.44.00
Sahil Yolu   *Fax* (1) 526.62.51
Sultanahmet   *Telex* 23364 K L Y N

A modern hotel on the edge of the Bosphorus, away from the crowds yet only ten minutes' walk from the Blue Mosque, Hagia Sophia and Topkapi Palace. A reader this year was delighted, "Our room looked out over the hotel lawn, past the fishermen who sit by the water to the constant, silent fascinating stream of ships moving through the Bosphorus: I was enchanted by the combination of the hotel's peaceful setting and the swirl of activity in the crowded, ancient streets just behind. Our rooms, though clean and pleasant, were nondescript: but the staff were pleasant, and we enjoyed our Turkish buffet breakfasts (with yoghurt, honey, fresh fruit, herb-scented breads, etc), taken facing the water." Others have reported that rooms at the back can be small; front ones are larger, with sea views, but lower floors would hear traffic noise. (*Dr Suzanne L Martin*) The hotel this year has been hugely enlarged, moving from 38 rooms to 110, and we'd be glad of reports on the impact of these changes.

Open All year.
Rooms 8 suites, 100 double, 2 single – all with bath and shower, telephone, radio and TV; many with balcony.
Facilities Lift. Lounges, bar, restaurant, cafeteria; conference room, meeting room.
Location Central; on the waterfront; near Blue Mosque. Parking.
Terms B&B: single US$71–US$89, double US$93–US$115, suite US$140–US$176. Set lunch US$12, dinner US$15; full alc US$18. Reduced rates and special meals for children.

Hotel Sokullu Paşa Tel (1) 512.37.53
Ishakpaşa Mah. Mehmetpaяsa
Sokak 10
Sultanahmet

Another splendid Ottoman conversion of a wooden house in the Old City, just round the corner from the superb Sokullu Paşa mosque, below the south end of the Hippodrome. Attractively decorated – small lobby with fountain; Turkish bath; garden at back, "a haven of peace". Staff exceptionally helpful and friendly. But some bedrooms very small, with awkwardly installed plumbing, and buffet breakfast, though generous, criticised for too many packaged items. 35 rooms, all with private facilities. B&B: single US$65, double US$85 [1989]. New nomination. More reports please.

Yeşil Ev Oteli Tel (1) 528.67.64
Kabasakal Sok 5, Sultanahmet Telex 30470

Located high up in the oldest part of the Old City, in an area of carpet shops between Hagia Sophia and the Blue Mosque, this charming hotel of character is a large wooden Ottoman mansion, painted a fresh apple green and white. Till recently it was derelict, but the Touring Club of Turkey has now restored it lovingly. An expert on Turkey gives his reactions: "The interiors are now in highest 19th-century Victorian-Ottoman taste, with velveteen chaises-longues, loving-bird table lamps, heavy flock drapes, ornate wooden pelmets and the like. The wooden floors creak; the light bulbs' wattage is low; a pianist at an upright accompanies afternoon tea in the cramped lobby; out back is a sheltered courtyard with marble fountain – the idea is that one should feel like a guest in an Ottoman household. It all worked perfectly for me, but I could understand some finding it precious and vulgar. The food is unimaginative, clumsy attempts at Turkish international. The dining rooms are small and low-ceilinged (the back one is best)." An earlier view: "Our ground-floor bedroom was almost more bed than room: the huge and well-sprung bed left just enough room to squeeze past an armchair, a polished mahogany wardrobe and a chest of drawers. The room was high and had tall sash windows hung with lace and brocade curtains, and fitted with latticed shutters giving what were basically light rooms a pleasantly secretive, Ottoman feeling. Communication with the outside world – and the present century – was via a brass 'candlestick' telephone made in Coventry in 1930. The walled, paved garden is the hotel's happiest asset. Water splashes down from a porphyry fountain; fig and plane trees are edged with pansies and stocks, wallflowers and marigolds; roses and vines climb the walls. On one side stands a pelargonium-filled conservatory, for cool evenings. The food is good, typically Turkish, with enough variety for a week's stay. And where better than here to take the last Turkish coffee of the day, turning one's gaze from the great dome of

---

Detailed information about many Turkish hotels was not available in mid-1989 when we went to press.

Our feedback on Turkish hotels is patchy. Please help if you can.

Hagia Sophia to the six slender minarets of the Blue Mosque?'' But be prepared also for the muezzin at 5 am. A reader this year enjoyed the food and comfort, but found the Turkish ambience spoilt by the large numbers of tourists. (*Claire Enders*)

Open All year.
Rooms 1 suite, 19 double – 1 with bath, 18 with shower, all with telephone and radio; suite has TV and Turkish bath. Some ground-floor rooms.
Facilities Salon, coffee shop, bar, restaurant. Garden with restaurant.
Location In Old City, mid-way between Hagia Sophia and the Blue Mosque.
Credit card Access, Amex, Visa.
Terms On application.

KALKAN Antalya   Map 12

Kalkan Han Hotel   *Tel* (3215) 1151
                                                         Telex 56524 KLKH

In a fishing-village in a deep bay backed by mountains, on Turkey's south-west coast, a pleasant small hotel with good views. Friendly staff, simple but nicely furnished rooms, buffet breakfasts; terrace for meals. Open 1 May–31 Oct. 16 rooms, all with shower. B&B double US$ 39–49. Set menus US$ 10. Children discouraged. New nomination. More reports please.

KONYA   Map 12

Başak Palas Oteli   *Tel* (331) 111.338
Hükümet Meydani 3

In the centre of an ancient city between Ankara and the Taurus mountains, a clean and characterful hotel with outstanding service (e.g. breakfast with boiled eggs served at 5 am for an early start). No restaurant, but the staff will advise on good ones near by. 2-star. 40 rooms, some with bath. Prices on application. More reports please.

KÖYCEĞIZ Muğla   Map 12

Hotel Özay   *Tel* (6114) 1300 and 1361
Kordon Boyu 11

In a small town on the north side of Köyceğiz lake, just off the Izmir–Antalya main road, a family-run 2-star lakeside hotel on the promenade, with efficient plumbing, clean and airy bedrooms all with balcony and fine views. Attentive service, pleasant pool, food so-so. 22 rooms, all with shower. B&B double US$26–30. Full alc US$10. New nomination. More reports please.

We asked hotels to estimate their 1990 tariffs some time before publication so the rates given are often arbitrary. Please always check terms with hotels when making bookings.

KUŞADASI Aydin — Map 12

Hotel Kismet
Akyar Mevkii

Tel (636) 12005
Telex 58556

This pleasant resort not too far from Ephesus has a fashionable marina; and high on a small peninsula just above it stands the white modern *Kismet*, surrounded by its pleasant palm and pine-shaded gardens. A recent report: "Quiet, relaxing and well run, in an understated way. All the staff were industrious and keen to help you enjoy yourself. Food was reliable and plentiful." Others have relished the sea breezes and the wide views (many rooms have a balcony). "The *Kismet* is far from the tavernas and carpet shops which make the evenings agreeable with colour, and loud with amiable huckstering. Its small paradise of a garden is liberally set with lounging chairs and with a tennis court for the energetic, niched above the Aegean into which you can plunge from a private, rocky 'beach'. The bedrooms are well maintained and offer remarkable value. The dining room is adequate, but we would not recommend full *pension*. However, the breakfast is self-service and there is a full vat of yoghurt on which to start the day. Nicely served afternoon teas remind one of what one is not missing in Britain, so to speak." Some noise from a disco round the bay; and a huge new hotel is being completed nearby. The *Kismet* itself has recently been enlarged. We'd welcome more reports.

Open 15 Mar–31 Oct.
Rooms 2 suites, 90 double, 6 single – 29 with bath, 69 with shower, all with telephone and radio; suites with TV. 10 in garden annexe.
Facilities Lift. Hall, salon, TV room, bars, restaurant. Garden with restaurant and tennis court. Private beach.
Location On peninsula in Kuşadasi bay.
Restriction Not suitable for &.
Credit cards Access, Amex, Visa.
Terms B&B: single US$66, double US$88, suite US$154; half board: single US$82.50, double US$121, suite US$187. Set lunch/dinner US$16.50; full alc US$20. Reduced rates for children.

OF Trabzon — Map 12

Hotel-Restaurant Çaykent
Cumhuriyet Cad.

Tel (0441) 2424 and 1230

In a town east of Trabzon on the Black Sea coast, at the mouth of a lovely valley with luxuriant vegetation and curious covered footbridges, a modern concrete hotel, no beauty, but clean, comfortable and efficient, with good plumbing and sea views; excellent if expensive restaurant, best for fish. 27 rooms, all with shower. B&B double 30,000 Tl [1989]. New nomination. More reports please.

PAMUKKALE Denizli — Map 12

Tusan Oteli

Tel (621) 1010

Set in a weird landscape high above the broad Meander valley, Pamukkale has been called "one of the seven wonders of Turkey", with its hot springs constantly adding to the petrified cascades of gleaming white marble. It is also the site of ancient Hierapolis, whose ruins are scattered over the hillside. Admired again recently, the "clean and well-kept" *Tusan* is the best hotel in the area: it has a helpful management, its own thermal pools on the lip of the escarpment, pleasant if fairly basic rooms in single-storey motel style, and cooking similarly adequate. We'd be glad of more reports.

Open All year.
Rooms 47 – all with bath or shower, and telephone.
Facilities Restaurant. Thermal pools.
Location 14 km N of Denizli.
Terms On application.

ÜRGÜP Nevşehir   Map 12

Hotel Eyvan   *Tel* (4868) 2424
Karagendere Mah.   *Telex* 49686 EVYA

The surrealistic scenery of Cappadocia, with its caves and its strange white hills rising out of the plain, is one of the main attractions of southern inland Turkey. This new hotel offers a chance to savour it, with modern comforts too: it is in traditional stone style, literally carved out of a rock cliff near the centre of a town that makes a good base for exploring such cave cities as Göreme. "English-speaking staff offering good service and good breakfasts, plus that rarity in Turkey – hot water. We had dinner in town." More reports please, especially on the food.

Open Apr–Oct.
Rooms 1 suite, 26 double – all with shower and telephone.
Facilities Bar, TV room, restaurant. Swimming pool.
Location 5 mins' walk from centre. Ürgüp is about 50 km W of Kayseri.
Terms On application.

VAN Van   Map 12

Hotel Akdamar   *Tel* (061) 18100
Kâzimkarabekir Cad. 56   *Telex* 73164 ATOY

In the far east of Turkey, on the main street of a town near the shores of the beautiful mountain-girt Lake Van, "a last outpost of civilization between Trabzon on the Black Sea and Diyarbakir in the south". An outwardly characterless three-star hotel with somewhat cheerless 'East European' ambience and decor, but clean and quite comfortable, with plumbing that works. Good Turkish cooking, helpful staff. Back rooms are quietest. 75 rooms, all with bath. Single 25,000 Tl, double 36,900 Tl. New nomination. More reports please.

Yugoslavia

GRAND HOTEL TOPLICE, BLED

BLED 64260   **Map 11**

Grand Hotel Toplice   *Tel* (064) 77.222
Telex 34588 TOPLIC

Set beside Yugoslavia's loveliest lake, in its smartest inland resort, this traditional 'grand hotel' was built soon after 1918 but has now been brought up to date, and is well run by a charming and efficient management who speak good English. Lots of praise this year and last: "We had a beautiful room facing the lake. The breakfasts were huge and sumptuous and the service exemplary." "Old-fashioned rooms with curtained sleeping alcoves. Food excellent for Yugoslavia, service friendly. The classic 'grand hotel' atmosphere is barely affected by the large number of English group tours." "Our quiet room on the third floor had excellent beds, comfortable furniture upholstered in gold velvet (with curtains to match) and a terrace with a splendid view. The chef creates magnificent things à la carte (e.g. roast sucking pig, rašniči, good soups). We admired the way the staff coped with the Great British Public, always smiling and anxious to please even though the Brits never said thank you, never gave any praise." Back rooms mostly lack views and can be small. (*S and E Holman, H and B Shames*) The covered colonnaded swimming pool has its own thermal spring.

Open All year.
Rooms 10 suites, 121 double or single – all with bath, telephone and balcony. Also 194 beds in 3 annexes.
Facilities Lift. Salon, reading room, TV room, bar, restaurant; conference facilities, reading room. Indoor swimming pool, sauna, solarium, fitness room. Lakeside terrace and bathing beach; boats, fishing available.
Location Central. Bled is 55 km NW of Ljubljana.
Credit cards Access, Amex, Diners.
Terms [1989 rates] B&B: single 68–115 DM, double 115–250 DM, suite 250–380 DM. Half board 20 DM per person added, full board 40 DM added. Reduced rates for children sharing parents' room.

Hotel Vila Bled
Cesta Svobode 26

Tel (064) 77.436
Telex 34515 VILABL

This white palace above Lake Bled, Yugoslavia's most sumptuous hotel, was remodelled by President Tito after World War II and was used as his official summer residence: here he entertained Eden, Nehru, Brandt, and many other world leaders. The government in 1984 turned it into a luxury hotel, which stands in its own 13-acre park, overlooking Yugoslavia's leading inland resort: views of the lake and the Alps are spectacular. Prices for so much pampered splendour are amazingly low by Western standards, but quality is not skimped, as a recent visitor discovered: "A wonderful display of flowers just inside the big gates. Our taxi deposited us on to the red carpet (yes, a real red carpet), where the commissionaire greeted us warmly. The receptionist rushes to meet you, then you are handed over lovingly to under-manager, then to cocktail-lounge waiter. There's an awful lot of marble, white and black, and lots of chandeliers – all very thirties. A pianist tinkles. The dining room has wonderful white linen, good modern prints, good silver and candles – everything glistens. Large menu, too large (most of it must be frozen): but dinner was good (wonderful veal escalope and banana soufflé, good salad, which is unusual in Yugoslavia, but bad coffee, as it imports inferior stuff). The bedrooms are well modernised, with bathrooms of gleaming white marble. Flower arrangements dreadful. The rooms don't really have a lake view, I suppose for security reasons. On the top floor is a small concert hall, which Tito used for receptions." This year, three other readers were equally impressed by the gardens, the views and the general splendour; two thought that the food and service fully lived up to the setting ("refined taste...courteous and efficient staff...best dinner we had in Yugoslavia...food excellently presented"), but a third judged the food poor and the service "virtually non-existent". A fourth, visiting out of season, saw no red carpet, no rushing receptionist, no flowers; service was haphazard, the rooms with the lake view were closed for the winter and her husband's mattress had "little plastic needle-shaped things sticking out so that he had to wrap a towel round himself to try to sleep". (*Aileen Stone, Joe van der Sneppen*)

Open All year.
Rooms 21 suites, 10 double – all with bath and/or shower, telephone and radio; 21 with TV.

Facilities 3 lifts. Lounge, TV lounge, bar with piano music, 2 breakfast rooms, restaurant; concert hall, conference facilities; terrace. Garden with tennis, private beach on lake with café in summer, rowing boats. Golf, riding, hunting, fishing, gliding nearby.
Location 1 mile along the lake from Bled, towards Bohinj.
Restriction Not suitable for &.
Credit cards All major cards accepted.
Terms B&B: single US$71–US$91, double US$92–US$122. Dinner, B&B US$66–US$151 per person; full board US$86–US$171. Set lunch/dinner US$20; full alc US$35. Special meals for children on request.

DUBROVNIK 50000   Map 11

Villa Dubrovnik
Tel (050) 22.933
Telex 27503

This is the smallest of the three smart hotels on the south side of Dubrovnik, and the one that readers continue to prefer ("I've seen only happy faces", says one this year). It is a modern building, terraced into a cliff, with lovely views of the old walled town and harbour, and the island of Lokrum opposite. Pine trees, flowers and blue awnings give a Riviera flavour. The bar and dining room both have superb views, and you can eat outdoors in fine weather. Most bedrooms face the front with a small balcony, and are well furnished; it's worth paying extra for a sea-facing room. The hotel has its own concrete "beach" with rock bathing in unpolluted water. A report this year: "A beautifully run hotel, with neat, clean rooms: ours had a lovely view from its private balcony. The food was ordinary, but the staff are exceptionally courteous and helpful." Others agree that the food is only average – but very cheap. "Our room was beautifully quiet save for the lapping of the waves below." A few minor gripes, such as bed-lights too dim, furnishings not perfect. There is no nightlife on the spot, but you can wander down to the city in about 20 minutes or take the hotel's own motor-boat, and it is easy to get a taxi back. A hotel not recommended for the elderly or infirm, as there are 66 steep steps up from the hotel to the road above. (*H and B Shames, Joe van der Sneppen*)

Open All year.
Rooms 54 – most with bath or shower, all with telephone; many with sea-facing balcony.
Facilities Lifts. Lounge, bar, restaurant. Sub-tropical gardens;
Location On S side of Dubrovnik. Garage parking.
Restriction Not suitable for &.
Credit card Amex.
Terms [1989 rates] Rooms: single US$32–US$100, double US$44–US$131.

HVAR 58450   Map 11

Palace Hotel
Tel (058) 74.966
Telex 26235 HVAR

About an hour by hydrofoil from Split, this charming little port on Hvar island has a gentle winter climate, and is backed by pines, olives and vines. You can visit the remains of a Greek colony and a neolithic cave. Devotees this year have again enjoyed the *Palace*, a classic white-fronted hotel, centrally located just above the busy quay: "Another lovely holiday at a lovely hotel, Hvar's best. Rooms were clean, the food excellent, and service efficient and courteous, while the weekly cocktail party was enjoyed by everyone. Entertainment was provided several evenings." Front rooms are more attractive and have a view; back ones are duller but quieter. Best avoid high summer and its package tours. (*Noreen Redfern*)

Open All year.
Rooms 76 double – all with bath and shower, and telephone; some with TV.
Facilities Lifts. Lounge, salon, TV room, bar, restaurant; indoor swimming pool. Sun terrace overlooking harbour with music and dancing every night during summer.
Location Central.
Credit cards Access, Diners, Visa.
Terms [1989 rates] Rooms: single 35–72 DM, double 57–120 DM, Half board 36–90 DM per person.

LOVRAN 51415   **Map 11**

Hotel Beograd   *Tel* (051) 731.022

A large *fin-de-siècle* hotel "with a calm 1920s flavour", in a quiet Slovene seaside resort just west of Opatija. "The rooms with bath and balcony are clean and spacious", says its nominator, "and some have superb views of the bay. Helpful staff. The large restaurant resembled a typical package-tour eatery and we did not try it: but we ate very well at the small *Hotel Belvedere* next door". (*Tony and Kathy Gillett*) Endorsed this year: "It was built in about 1900 for the Austrian aristocracy and still has a strong Hapsburg flavour (the Grand Duchess Stephanie did a lot along this coast). Friends who went recently said it was 'like staying in Buckingham Palace'. Our rooms were furnished in rich Venetian style, with beautiful woods all upholstered in gold velvet. Set in a pleasant garden facing the sea, the hotel has discreet creeper-covered booths where you can sit in the evenings listening. On our visit a three-piece Viennese-type orchestra played Strauss. There's no beach, but to swim you go down an iron ladder into a roped-off bit of sea, full of fish and very clear. The food was as good as any we have eaten in Yugoslavia, with the names of various Austrian royals used for puddings. The day we left, the other packagers had to vacate their rooms by noon, but our chambermaid let us remain until we had to leave for the airport at five. Could it have been because of my Christian name?" (*Stephanie Sowerby*)

Open 1 May–31 Oct.
Rooms 102 – all with bath and/or shower; many with balcony. Ground-floor rooms.
Facilities Lounge, restaurant; terrace. Garden with tables and chairs. Sea bathing.
Location Lovran is 16 km W of Rijeka. Parking.
Credit cards None accepted.
Terms [1989 rates] Dinner, B&B: single 41–74 DM, double 31–64 DM per person. Reduced rates for children sharing parents' room.

> In all continental European and Scandinavian countries except Denmark, France, Hungary, Malta, Spain and Turkey, the dialling codes begin with a 0. Omit this when dialling from outside the country in question. Spanish codes begin with a 9, which should also be omitted.

PLITVIČKA JEZERA 48231 Map 11

Hotel Jezero

Tel (048) 76.526
Fax (048) 76.310
Telex 23817 PLITVICE

The Plitvice National Park, in the wooded hills of western Croatia, is a place of "serene beauty", and its focal point is this huge and unusual holiday complex, again enjoyed this year for its pleasant staff, good food, comfort, and "wonderful ambience". An earlier account set the scene: "Sixteen lakes, linked by streams and waterfalls, are surrounded by lovely maple trees, firs and beeches which range in colour from blazing autumn crimson to a breathtaking variety of greens. A well-contrived system of paths, often built on stilts, makes walking easy. The forest is so tranquil that even chamois, deer and bear live at ease with the visitors. A few boats commute to hamlets on the largest lake: there is no machinery and no pollution.

Here the *Jezero* is a huge well-planned wooden chalet-type hotel, and no one looking at it would guess that it held 247 bedrooms, a big lounge with snug bar area, an attractive restaurant, and indoor swimming pool, ladies' hairdresser and souvenir shop. Plus a nightbar with dancing during the high season, and facilities for many sports. The hotel is mainly concealed by the forest, but there are glimpses of lakes from some bedrooms. On one day every year many young couples, usually wearing national dress, come to the hotel in preparation for their wedding, which is celebrated beside the highest of the many waterfalls. Staff are efficient; food is good, with lake trout among the specialities. Prices are moderate and cleanliness ideal." "Rooms are clean, quiet and spartan." (*H and B Shames*)

Open All year except 1 Feb–9 Mar.
Rooms 7 suites, 240 double or triple – all with bath and shower, telephone and radio; many with balcony. Some ground-floor rooms.
Facilities Large lounge with bar (dancing in high season), 2 bars, 3 restaurants; cinema and conference hall; heated indoor swimming pool, sauna, ladies' hairdresser. Adjoins sports and recreation centre with automatic 4-lane bowling alley. Near lake with safe bathing.
Location In National Park, 140 km SW of Zagreb.
Credit cards Access, Diners, Visa.
Terms [1989 rates] Rooms: single 36–86 DM, double 50–128 DM. Half board 30–103 DM per person, full board 35–111 DM.

SVETI STEFAN 85315 Map 10

Hotel Miločer
Hotel Maestral
Vila Miločer

Tel (all hotels) (086) 41.333
and 41.411
Telex 61188 SV STF

This is not one hotel but four, all state-run and close together on the lovely Montenegrin coast just south of the old walled city of Budva. The *Miločer* was built as a summer palace by Alexander I for his wife, and still retains an air of opulence. It is much smaller than the other hotels in the complex. The central block has a handsome vine-shaded terrace where meals are served. Most of the rooms are in annexes set discreetly in the grounds. Readers enjoy the *Miločer* for its privacy, its big gardens, and its fine, if pebbly, beach. One recent verdict: "Food good by Yugoslav standards. Breakfast under the vines, with toast, toast and more toast, and anything cooked that you want. Bedroom like a suite, with damask linen, fresh flowers, a fireplace." However, some have thought the main lounge unattractive and institutional in appearance, the food mediocre, and the service at meals rather sluggish. The second hotel, on the coast near the *Miločer*, is the *Maestral*, considerably larger and with a lot of group clients. A devotee this year enjoyed it as much as ever and confirms her earlier praise: "From the outside it is hideous, but inside it is beautifully furnished, with good-sized bedrooms, all now with TV and mini-bar, excellent reception rooms and restaurant, cool marble floors. It has a good private beach with a water-skiing school and a superb swimming pool. The food is a lot better than at the other hotels and the service much superior too." (*Stephanie Sowerby*) More recently opened is the *Vila Miločer*, between the *Miločer* and the *Maestral*, with its own beach. The fourth and much the most expensive hotel in the complex, *Sveti Stefan*, is on a small island joined to the mainland by a causeway. It has been liked in the past, but food and service have again been sharply criticised this year, and we are dropping it from the Guide ("It's fit only for oil kings and ageing film stars", says a reader this year). Even with the other three recommended hotels, there have been murmurs of discontent about food and service, and about dishonoured bookings, indicating that the centralised state management may be in need of some *perestroika*. So, please, send us more reports.

Hotel Miločer
Open May–end Oct.
Rooms 27 – most with bath or shower. Also cottages in grounds.
Facilities Bar, large terrace for meals. Large secluded wooded grounds and gardens; private beach; tennis.
Terms [1989 rates] Rooms: single 110–157 DM, double 120–220 DM.

Hotel Maestral
Open May–end Oct.
Rooms 156 – all with bath or shower, telephone, TV and mini-bar, most with terrace.
Facilities Lift. Bar, café, restaurant; indoor swimming pool, sauna. Grounds with swimming pool, tennis, private beach.
Terms [1989 rates] Rooms: single 75–149 DM, double 92–264 DM. Half board: single 85–149 DM, double 112–304 DM.

Vila Miločer
Open May–end Oct.
Rooms 4 villas, 55 double rooms – most with bath or shower and telephone.
Facilities Café, restaurant. Indoor swimming pool, sauna. Private beach.
Terms [1989 rates] Rooms: single 70–143 DM, double 86–350 DM.

Alphabetical list of hotels

Austria

Alexandra Lech am Arlberg 10
Alpbacherhof Alpbach 1
Amadeus Vienna 17
Astoria Igls 8
Böglerhof Alpbach 2
Elefant Salzburg 13
Elisabeth Mayrhofen 11
Erika Kitzbühel 9
Friesacher Anif 2
Gasthof Deim zum Goldenen Hirschen Freistadt 5
Gasthof Gams Bezau 3
Gasthof Salome Lech am Arlberg 11
Gasthof Weisses Rössl Innsbruck 9
Gasthof Zur Traube Lans 10
Hahnenhof Kitzbühel 10
Hanneshof Filzmoos 4
Haus Senger Heiligenblut 7
Kaiserin Elisabeth Vienna 17
Krone Schruns 16
König von Ungarn Vienna 18
Lärchenhof Mösern Bei Seefeld 12
Madrisa Gargellen 5
Moawirt Wagrain 20
Museumsverein Schloss Rosenau Schloss Rosenau 15
Muttererhof Mutters 12
Nonntal Salzburg 14
Nossek Vienna 18
Pörtschacherhof Pörtschach 13
Post Lech am Arlberg 10
Romantik Hotel Post Villach 20
Römischer Kaiser Vienna 19
Rupertihof Fuschl-am-See 5
Sacher Vienna 19
Schloss Dürnstein Dürnstein 4
Schloss Fuschl Hof Bei Salzburg 7
Schloss Mönchstein Salzburg 14

Schlossberg Graz 6
Seehotel Grüner Baum Hallstatt 6
Singer Sporthotel Berwang 3
Strasserwirt Strassen 16
Suzanne Vienna 19
Walkner Seeham 16
Weinhaus Happ Innsbruck 8
Zistelalm Salzburg 15

Belgium

Adornes Bruges 21
Agenda Brussels 24
Amigo Brussels 25
Anselmus Bruges 22
Auberge du Moulin Hideux Noirefontaine 29
Bryghia Bruges 22
Casino Tilff-sur-Ourthe 31
Convent Reninge 30
Hostellerie du Prieuré de Conques Herbeumont 27
Hostellerie Le Fox De Panne 30
Hostellerie le Sanglier des Ardennes Durbuy 26
Hostellerie Shamrock Ronse 31
Hostellerie Trôs Marets et Résidence Malmédy 28
Kasteel van Neerijse Neerijse Leuven 29
Orangerie Bruges 22
Petit Chef Couvin 25
Ramiers Crupet 26
Le Roly du Seigneur Maissin 28
St Jorishof Gent 27
Die Swaene Bruges 23
Ter Duinen Bruges 24
Wilgenhof Bruges 24

Denmark

d'Angleterre Copenhagen 33

France

Germany

Greece

Italy

463

Spain

Exchange rates

These rates for buying currency are correct at time of printing but in some cases may be wildly awry at the time of publication. It is essential to check with banks or newspapers for up-to-date rates.

	$1US
Austria (Schillings)	13.83
Belgium (Belgian francs)	41.40
Denmark (Danish kroner)	7.70
France (French francs)	6.73
Germany (Deutschmarks)	1.98
Gibraltar (pounds sterling)	1.58
Greece (drachmae)	168
Ireland (punts)	1.34
Italy (lire)	1,433
Luxembourg (Luxembourg francs)	41.40
Morocco (dirhams)	8.69
Malta (Maltese cents)	0.32
The Netherlands (guilders)	2.23
Norway (Norwegian kroner)	7.10
Portugal, Madeira (escudos)	163.45
Spain, Andorra, Balearics, Canaries (pesetas)	124.20
Sweden (Swedish kronor)	6.60
Switzerland (Swiss francs)	1.73
Turkey (lira)	1,571
Yugoslavia (dinars)	15,000

Maps

Map 1 Southern Scandinavia

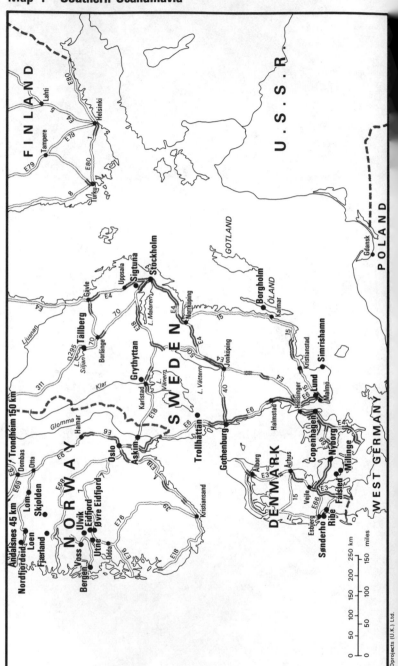

© GEOprojects (U.K.) Ltd.

Map 2 North–West France

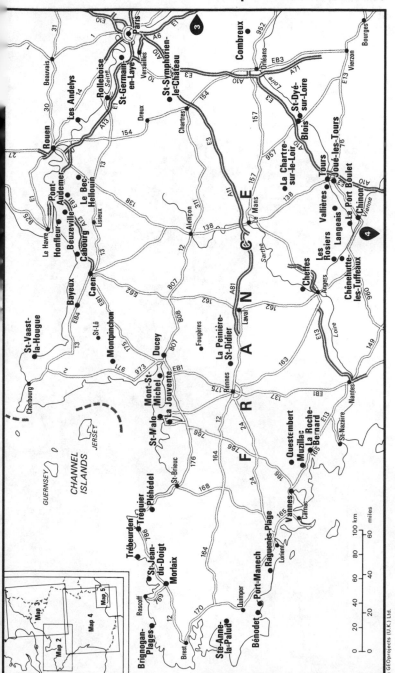

© GEOprojects (U.K.) Ltd.

Map 3   Benelux and North-East France

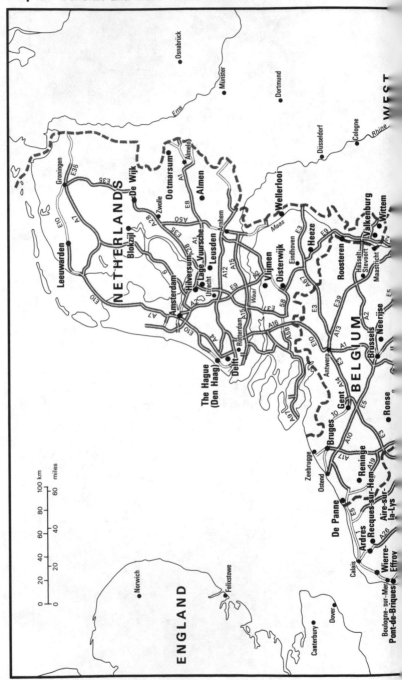

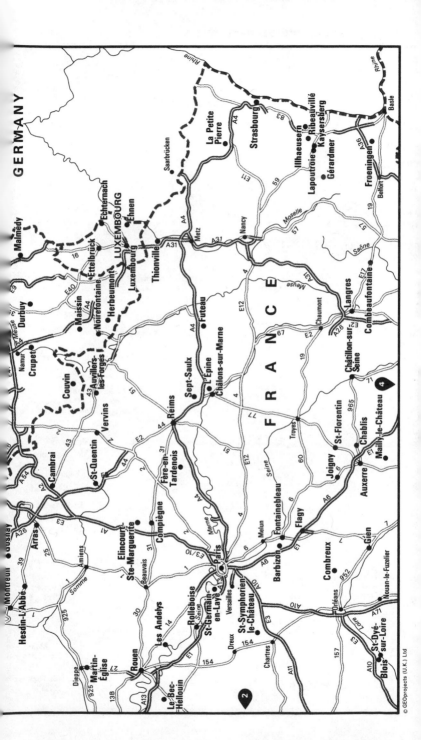

Map 4 Central and Southern France

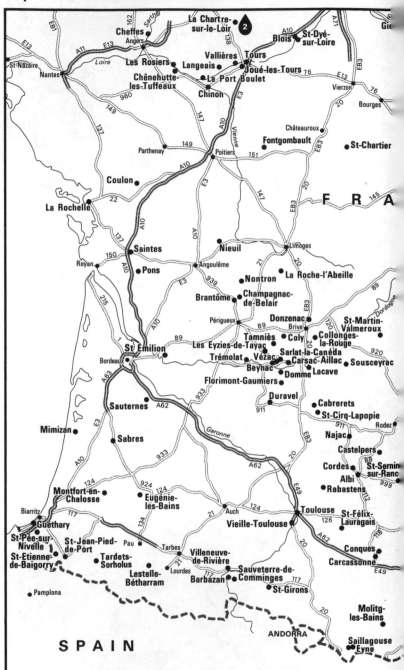

© GEOprojects (U.K.) Ltd.

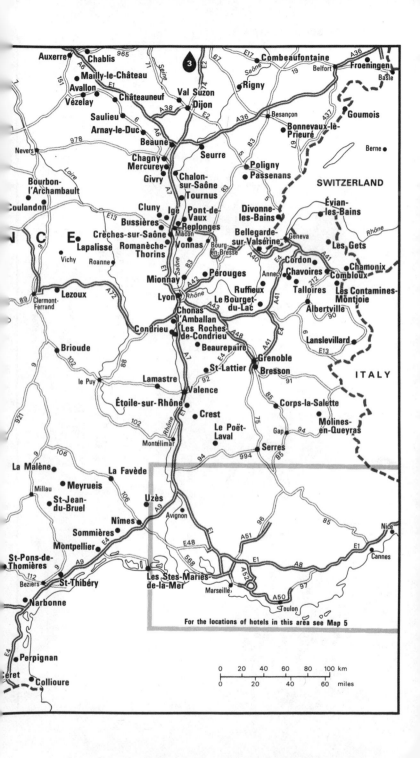

For the locations of hotels in this area see Map 5

| 0 | 20 | 40 | 60 | 80 | 100 km |
| 0 | 20 | 40 | | 60 miles |

Map 5 The South of France

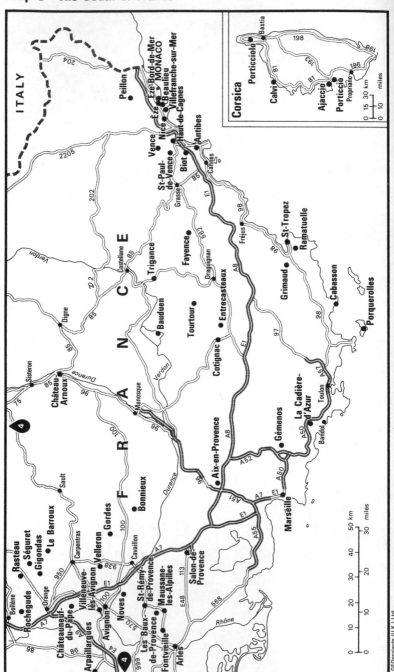

Map 6   Spain and Portugal

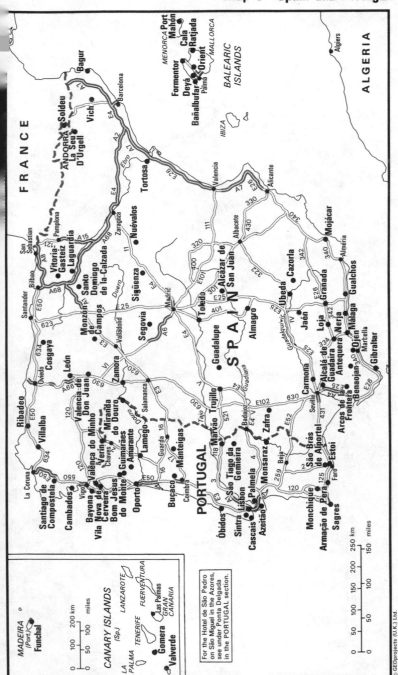

Map 7   Germany

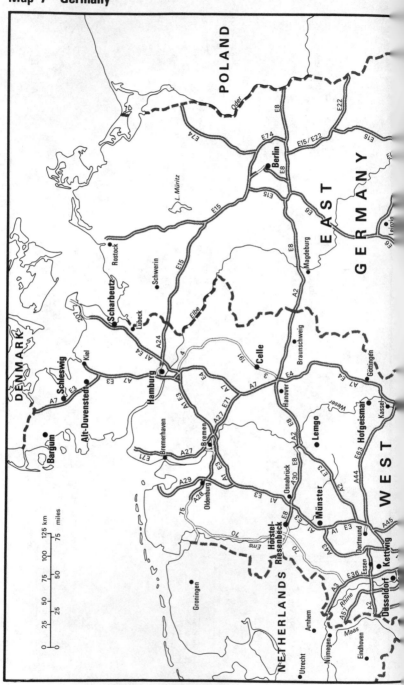

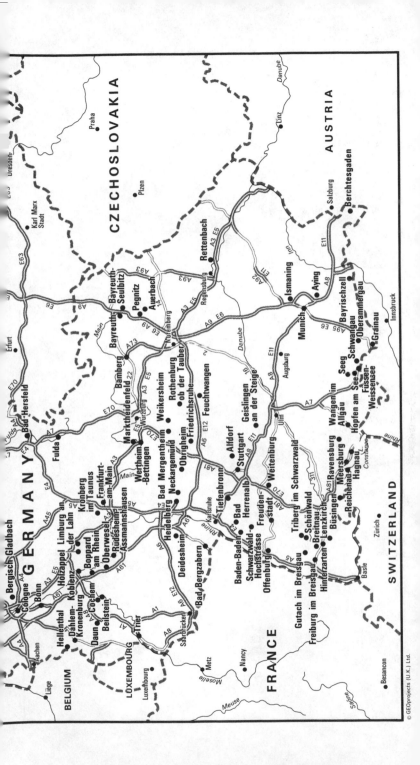

© GEOprojects (U.K.) Ltd.

Map 8 Switzerland

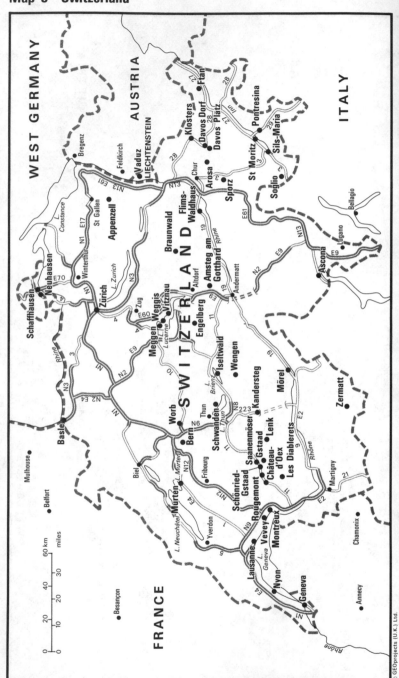

© GEOprojects (U.K.) Ltd.

Map 9   Austria

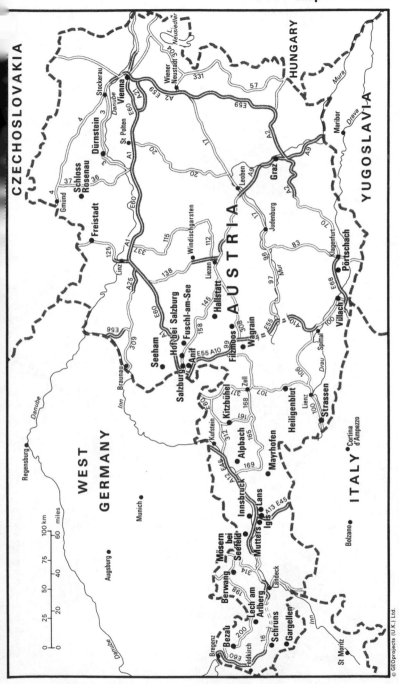

© GEOprojects (U.K.) Ltd.

Map 10 Italy and Malta

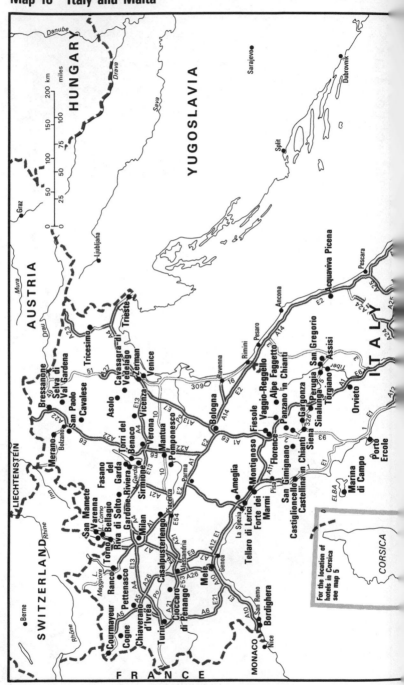

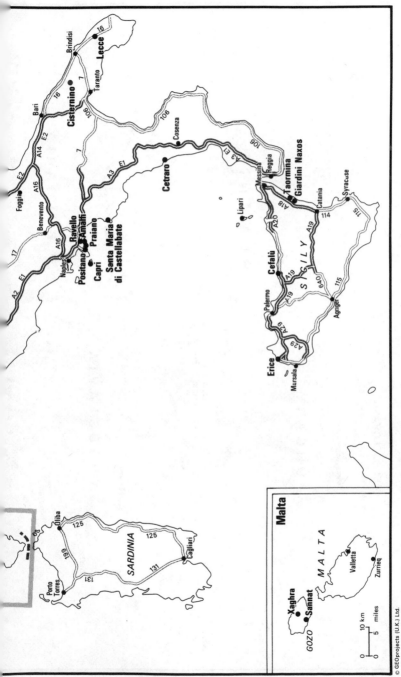

Brindisi

16

Lecce

Taranto

7

Cisternino

100

Bari

16

7

106

Cosenza

Foggia

A14 E2

E2

A16

Benevento

A3 E1

Cetraro

17

A16

E1

Ravello Amalfi

Positana Praiano

Naples Capri Santa Maria
di Castellabate

A2

A3 E1

106

Reggia

Messina Taormina

Giardini Naxos

Lipari

Catania

Syracuse

A18

A18

A19

114

115

A20

S I C I L Y

Cefalù

A19

A19

A19

Palermo

A29

A19

6A0

115

Agrigur

A29

Erice

Marsala

Oliba

125

199

125

SARDINIA

131

Porto
Torres

Cagliari

© GEOprojects (U.K.) Ltd.

Malta

Xaghra

GOZO Sannat

M A L T A

Valletta

Zurrieq

10 km

5 miles

0

0

Map 11 Greece and Yugoslavia

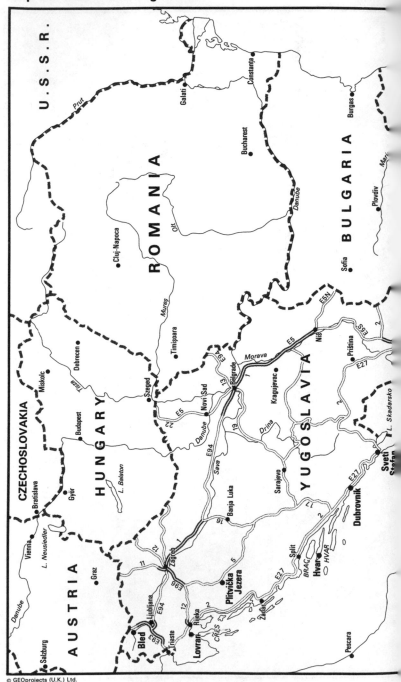

© GEOprojects (U.K.) Ltd.

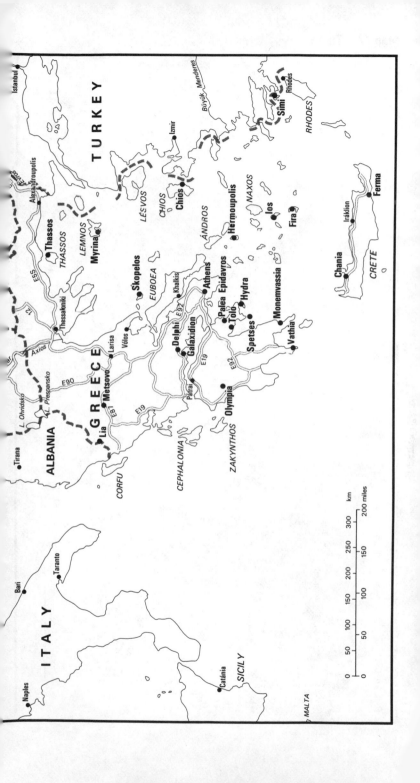

Map 12 Turkey

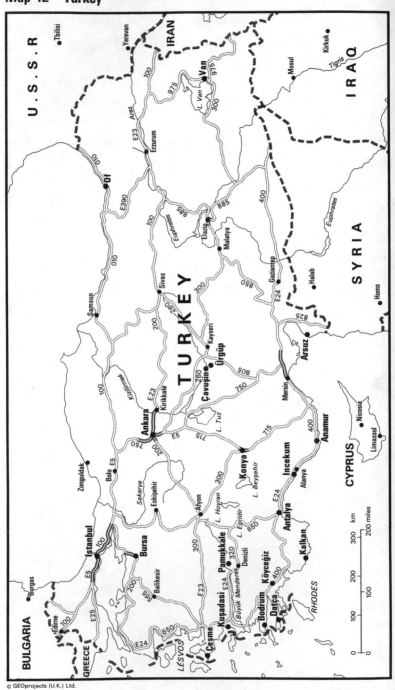

© GEOprojects (U.K.) Ltd.

Map 13 Morocco

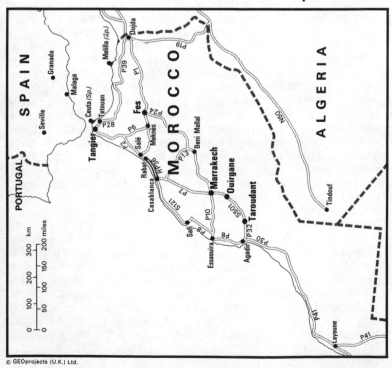

© GEOprojects (U.K.) Ltd.

Hotel reports

The report forms on the following pages may be used to endorse or criticise an existing entry or to nominate a hotel that you feel deserves inclusion in next year's guide. Either way, there is no need to use our forms, or, if you do, to restrict yourself to the space available. All nominations (each on a separate piece of paper, please) should include your name and address, the name and location of the hotel, when you stayed there and for how long. Please nominate only hotels you have visited in the past 12 months unless you are sure from friends that standards have not fallen off since your stay. And please be as specific as possible, and critical where appropriate, about the character of the building, the public rooms and bedrooms, the meals, the service, the night-life, the grounds. We should be glad if you would give some impression of the location as well as of the hotel itself, particularly in less familiar regions.

You should not feel embarrassed about writing at length. More than anything else, we want the guide to convey the special flavour of its hotels; so the more time and trouble you can take in providing those small details which will help to make a description come alive, the more valuable to others will be the final published result. Many nominations just don't tell us enough. We mind having to pass up a potentially attractive hotel because the report is inadequate. There is no need to bother with prices or with routine information about number of rooms and facilities. We obtain such details direct from the hotels selected. What we are anxious to get from readers is information that is not accessible elsewhere. And we should be extremely grateful to be sent brochures if you have them available. Nominations for the 1991 edition should reach us not later than 1 May 1990. The latest date for comments on existing entries is 1 June 1990. Our address is Europe's Wonderful Little Hotels and Inns, 61 Clarendon Road, London W11 4JE, England.

We would ask you please never to let on to a hotel your intention to file a report. Anonymity is essential to objectivity. We would not have thought it necessary to say this, but we have heard that some readers have made a habit of telling hotel managers or owners that they would be reporting to us.

Please let us know if you would like more report forms, which may also be used, if you wish, to recommend good hotels in North America to our equivalent publication in the US, America's Wonderful Little Hotels and Inns. Its address is PO Box 150, Riverside, Conn. 06878, USA.

[1990]

To: *Europe's Wonderful Little Hotels and Inns*, 61 Clarendon Road,
London W11 4JE, England

NOTE: Unless asked not to, we shall assume that we may publish your name if
you are recommending a new hotel or supporting an existing entry. If you
would like more report forms please check ☐

Name of Hotel _____

Address _____

_____

Date of most recent visit   Duration of visit
☐ New recommendation   ☐ Comment on existing entry
Report:

I am not connected directly or indirectly with the management or proprietors
(Continue overleaf if you wish or use separate sheet)

Signed _____

Name and address (capitals please) _____

_____

To: *Europe's Wonderful Little Hotels and Inns*, 61 Clarendon Road, London W11 4JE, England

NOTE: Unless asked not to, we shall assume that we may publish your name if you are recommending a new hotel or supporting an existing entry. If you would like more report forms please check ☐

Name of Hotel _____

Address _____

_____

Date of most recent visit   Duration of visit
☐ New recommendation   ☐ Comment on existing entry
Report:

I am not connected directly or indirectly with the management or proprietors
(Continue overleaf if you wish or use separate sheet)

Signed _____

Name and address (capitals please) _____

_____

THE INNGOER'S

Europe's Wonderful Little Hotels and Inns, 1990, *Great Britain and Ireland* ◀

Europe's Wonderful Little Hotels and Inns, 1990, *The Continent* ▶

America's Wonderful Little Hotels and Inns, 1990, *U.S.A. and Canada* ◀

America's Wonderful Little Hotels and Inns, 1990, *New England* ▶

America's Wonderful Little Hotels and Inns, 1990, *The Middle Atlantic* ◀

America's Wonderful Little Hotels and Inns, 1990, *The South* ▶

America's Wonderful Little Hotels and Inns, 1990, *The West Coast* ◀